PATTERNS OF REFORM

PATTERNS OF REFORM

Continuity and Change in the Reformation Kirk

JAMES KIRK

T & T CLARK
EDINBURGH

T & T CLARK LTD.
59 GEORGE STREET
EDINBURGH EH2 2LQ
SCOTLAND

© T & T Clark Ltd., 1989

First Published 1989

British Library Cataloguing in Publication Data

Kirk, James
    Patterns of reform.
    1. Church of Scotland, history
    I. Title
    285'.2411'09
ISBN 0 567 095053

Typeset by Buccleuch Printers Ltd., Hawick
Printed and bound by Page Bros (Norwich) Ltd

for A. B. K.

Acknowledgments

I place on record my gratitude to the Rev. Professor James K. Cameron and the Rev. Professor A. C. Cheyne for their unfailing assistance and encouragement over many years. A particular debt, greater perhaps than is at first apparent in the following pages, is owed to the teaching and writing of Professor Gordon Donaldson. Over the decades, I have profited from conversation with friends and colleagues: here I thank Professor Ian Cowan, Dr Jenny Wormald and Dr John Durkan. I also owe much to my good friend Dr Donald Meek, with whose collaboration, I once embarked on a study of Carswell: in the fourteen years which have elapsed since that text was published, I have uncovered further insights into Carswell's career which it seems appropriate, at this opportunity, to bring together.

Grateful acknowledgment is made to the Ecclesiastical History Society for permission to utilise material from *Studies in Church History* vol. 23, in chapter 1; to the Librarian of Edinburgh University Library for material from *Edinburgh University Library, 1580–1980* in chapter 2; the Scottish Church History Society for material from its *Records* vols. 18–19, in chapters 3 and 7; the Inverness Field Society for material from *The Seventeenth Century in the Highlands*, in chapter 12; the Editor of *Northern Scotland* for material from vol. 7, in chapter 8; the Editor of *Scottish Historical Review* for material from vol. 59, in chapter 9; the Scottish Academic Press and John Donald Publishers for material from *The Renaissance and Reformation in Scotland* and *Church, Politics and Society* in chapter 10; and the Society of Friends of Glasgow Cathedral for chapter 11, the substance of which formed part of its lecture series.

JAMES KIRK
Innocents' Day, 1988

Contents

Introduction

Protestantism had secured a firm foundation in the politically assertive and progressive areas of Scotland for over a generation before the Reformation parliament in 1560 finally acknowledged the nature of the religious upheaval by intervening to abrogate papal authority, prohibit the mass and recognise a reformed Confession of Faith. Succeeding waves of Lutheran, Zwinglian and Calvinist literature and preaching,[1] fortified by English propaganda and intervention, had struck a responsive chord over the decades not merely among intellectual élites of clerics, scholars and the literate but among a remarkable section of the population in town and countryside: nobles, lairds, lawyers, merchants, craftsmen and tenant farmers were attracted by the evangelical message propagated by the printed, spoken and sung word: by reading and discussing, by the power of preaching and psalm singing, by public disputation and private conference and by acts of defiance, iconoclasm and self-sacrifice. Discussion of the message of the Reformation occurred not just in isolated house 'cells' by families and friends or in the numerous conventicles in the fields, formed for worship and Bible-study, but increasingly, in the market place (where preachers often found a captive or curious audience), at fairs and festivals where ideas could be exchanged as readily as any other commodity, in taverns and at work: the activism displayed by the craftsmen in Perth in support of the Reformation and even the decision by the Hammermen in Edinburgh to appoint their own protestant minister in 1559 seem to indicate that religious issues were aired within the context of the workplace and in gilds and incorpor-

---

[1] J. K. Cameron, 'Aspects of the Lutheran Contribution to the Scottish Reformation', *Records of the Scottish Church History Society [RSCHS]*, xxii, pt. 1 (1984), 1–12; D. Shaw, 'Zwinglian Influences on the Scottish Reformation', *RSCHS*, xxii, pt. 2 (1985), 119–39; for Calvinism, see below, 70ff.

ations; and the shock-tactics of disrupting religious services and processions, as happened in Ayr, Perth, Dundee, Edinburgh and elsewhere, were designed to provoke consternation, ferment and reappraisal. Accepted beliefs were critically challenged as new ideas freely circulated.[2]

Catholics and protestants in Scotland were, of course, all but unanimous in recognising and proclaiming the necessity of renewal and reform; disgreement centred only on the remedies to cure the affliction. The programme of Catholic reform initiated by Archbishop Hamilton and the provincial councils, augmented by Cardinal Sermoneta's sombre appraisal of Scottish clerical shortcomings, prepared for the papacy in 1556 at Mary of Guise's request, came late in the day; it all resulted in half-hearted tinkering with structures, the remedying of some wrongs at the periphery, and an apparent desire, through a measure of doctrinal modification, to achieve accord with the disaffected who had succumbed to evangelical protestantism: there was silence, too, on the rôle of the papacy, and an apparent acceptance by Hamilton of accommodation with Luther's doctrine of salvation. Yet, no wholesale reform resulted; the provincial council of 1559, whose tone was decidedly defeatist, was reminded of how, despite earlier resolutions, 'thar hes folowit nan or litill fruict as yitt bot rathare the said Estate is deteriorate'. Fundamental problems were not addressed, and the urgent need for a redistribution of ecclesiastical finances in favour of the parishes went unheeded.[3]

Protestant reformers, by placing their emphasis on the preaching of the Word, rendered in the vernacular, itself a novel emphasis in services, concentrated on the supremacy of the Bible's teaching and the sole mediation of Christ. Churchgoers, hitherto depicted as 'the laity', were no longer expected to measure up to clerical ideals of the religious life; religion and devotion were to be freed from many of the burdens and demands of the later middle ages, and from the clutter of inessentials. Part of the religious appeal of protestantism was precisely its ability to provide a clear and direct answer to those troubled by the seemingly inability of the established church (at least before Trent had finalised its pronouncements) to speak with an authoritative and consistent voice on central aspects of the faith.

[2] See below, 1–15, 134, 152, 154ff., 283.
[3] *Statutes of the Scottish Church*, ed. D. Patrick (Edinburgh, 1907), 82–191; *Papal Negotiations with Mary, Queen of Scots*, ed. J. H. Pollen (Edinburgh, 1901), 528–30; *The Catechism of John Hamilton*, ed. T. G. Law (Oxford, 1884); *Statutes*, 188–90; 156; J. K. Cameron, '"Catholic Reform" in Germany and in the Pre-1560 Church in Scotland', *RSCHS*, xx (1979), 105–17.

No longer was it the prerogative of the clergy to read and write theology. The complex cultural context which enabled a layman like Clement Little, with his massive collection of theological works, Catholic and reformed, to move from Erasmian humanism and Catholic reform to espouse enthusiastically a radical reform in root and branch, effected in defiance of the higher powers, deserves more attention than it has usually received.[4] And much earlier, of course, informed laymen like Henry Balnaves, the distinguished lawyer, wrote eloquently and cogently (and for some persuasively) on the subject of salvation from a protestant perspective.[5] For protestants as a whole, the problem of salvation was solved not by affirming the merits arising from man's good works or by securing the intercession of saints, endowed with superabundant merit, but by recognising that the justice of God was redemptive not punitive, that sinners, unworthy of salvation, were forgiven and saved by placing their faith wholly in the redeeming work of Christ, who had paid the debt in full for the sins of mankind. Added to this theology of liberation (from the thraldom of a sense of all-pervading sin), with all its evident appeal to widespread popular piety, the protestant programme for ecclesiastical reform and educational renewal focused on essentials by devising new mechanisms for expressing the Gospel in the context of daily work, for revitalising the religious life of communities and congregations, and for caring for the impotent poor, the oppressed and underprivileged, whose social injustices the reformers sought to rectify.

The path to the kingdom of heaven, which protestantism offered, placed a special emphasis on the need to secure 'true preachers of the Word', 'ministers of the pure Word of God', faithful expositors of the Bible's message. Long before official action came in 1560 reform-minded communities had taken the initiative in securing the services of godly preachers, sometimes in direct defiance of the established church; and when widespread change was signalled by nobles, lairds and magistrates, and countenanced by parliament in 1560, many more communities readily acquired reformed staff for their churches, men who were sometimes paid from their parishioners' own resources, in place of the parsons and vicars who continued to be sustained, for the best part, from existing benefices.[6]

In its final form, the Scottish Reformation was carried through in defiance of the wishes of the crown; it came about as a revolt

---

[4] See below, 16–69.
[5] See below, 232–4.
[6] See below, 96–153.

against constituted authority, a rebellion undertaken by the protestant Lords of the Congregation against the higher powers. In challenging the existing order, protestants resorted to political action, first, by creating a collective identity and objective, then, by deposing Mary of Guise as regent and, with Mary's death, by transferring effective power to a provisional government, the godly 'great council of the realm'. At best, politics only help explain the timing of the Reformation, and its successful outcome, not its *raison d'être*, which has to be found elsewhere. In any event, longstanding religious discontent and agitation rather than extensive political unrest had been consistently the prelude to attempts at radical reform initiated, somewhat prematurely, in 1546, 1557 and, to greater effect, in 1559. And if the Reformation were genuinely a 'movement', whose adherents were conscious of a common purpose and whose antecedents are to be traced over four decades, it is less than convincing to portray the crisis of 1560 merely as the antics of a numerically insignificant pressure group devoid of popular support, the mere coincidence, that is, of political dissatisfaction expressed by a few nobles and the religious radicalism of a handful of preachers which achieved so remarkable a *coup*.

The revolutionaries, by contrast, who accorded such prominence in their manifestoes to religious reform clearly considered their tactics were good strategy in securing a powerful body of opinion to their cause. They succeeded in rallying popular support in a way in which their opponents did not; and as soon as they had attained an end to the domination of France and Rome, many of the insurgents actively canvassed the marriage of the Earl of Arran, son of the heir presumptive to the Scottish throne, to Queen Elizabeth of England, a scheme which carried the prospect of replacing Scotland's former reliance on France by Scottish dependence on England. To those who pursued such a policy (beyond mere familial ambition), the religious issue of securing protestantism, it almost seems, took precedence over safeguarding national integrity; it counted for rather more than the appeal to patriotic independence.

In advocating revolution, by justifying the duty to resist a tyrannous or idolatrous monarch, Knox and his associates had certainly departed from earlier Scottish examples of Lutheran piety set by John Johnsone whose *Exhortation* in the 1530s had commended no more than passive resistance to persecution, and by Henry Balnaves, in 1548, who still reaffirmed Paul's doctrine of non-resistance.[7] Elsewhere, however, Lutherans had moved toward a defence of active resistance, reiterated in the Magdeburg Confession of 1550 (which both Knox and Beza cited approvingly), as had Martin Bucer by 1530, Pierre Viret by 1547, Theodore Beza by 1554, and Peter Martyr by 1558; Calvin himself, who by the 1530s had cautiously considered the possibility of resistance by lesser magistrates had come by 1559 to explore the case for active resistance, and by 1562 had recognised the rôle of the inferior magistrates in coercing tyrants.[8] There were clearly ample precedents for Calvinist revolutionaries in Scotland when they came to advocate what, in effect, was rebellion by 1559.

With startling success the revolution of 1560 had challenged and overthrown the church which once had commanded the devotion of the nation but which, when faced with collapse, had shown so little inclination or resolution in mustering the faithful to recover the lost ground. The work of the Reformation parliament, though denied royal sanction, was short and swift: in three principal, decisive measures, it cut the ground beneath the old order by abolishing the mass and papal jurisdiction and substituting a protestant Confession. This done, parliament assigned to others the details of working out the nature of the settlement. In all, the Scots found no need for the ponderous and protracted deliberations which had characterised the Henrician 'Reformation' parliament from 1529 to 1536, which severed the English church from the papacy by subjecting it to the control of the crown in parliament.

In Scotland, whose Catholic queen was still in France, the new kirk was accorded that rare and exhilarating experience, denied to most churches, of determining its own programme and constitution; and its cherished independence in governing its affairs, which political circumstances permitted it to achieve, was

---

[7] J. K. Cameron, 'John Johnsone's *An Confortable Exhortation of Our Mooste Holy Christen Faith and Her Frutes*: An Early Example of Scots Lutheran Piety', *Reform and Reformation: England and the Continent c.1500–c.1750*, ed. D. Baker (Oxford, 1979), 133–47, at 147; *The Works of John Knox*, ed. D. Laing, 6 vols (Edinburgh, 1846–64), iii, 539–40.

[8] Knox, *Works*, ii, 453; W. D. J. Cargill Thompson, 'Luther and the Right of Resistance to the Emperor', *Studies in the Reformation*, ed. C. W. Dugmore (London, 1980), 3–41; R. D. Linder, *The Political Ideas of Pierre Viret* (Geneva, 1964), 127–42; T. Maruyama, *The Ecclesiology of Theodore Beza* (Geneva, 1978), 35–6, 60; *The Political Thought of Peter Martyr Vermigli: Selected Texts and Commentary*, ed. R. M. Kingdon (Geneva, 1980); *John Calvin on God and Political Duty*, ed. J. T. McNeill (New York, 1956); Calvin, *Institution de la religion chrestienne*, ed. J.-D. Benoit, 5 vols (Paris, 1957–63), IV, xx, 31; J. W. Allen, *A History of Political Thought in the Sixteenth Century* (London, 1967), 103ff; Q. Skinner, *The Foundations of Modern Political Thought*, 2 vols (Cambridge, 1978), ii, 206ff.; see below, 78, 246.

not to be lightly cast aside. The radical and innovative approach adopted by the reformed kirk marked a decisive break with the immediate past. In doctrine, the characteristic protestant emphasis on original sin, atonement, unmerited grace, justification by faith alone, predestination and the verbal inspiration of scripture found homely expression in the Confession of 1560 which, with the Book of Discipline, prepared in 1560, rejected transubstantiation, denounced the mass and replaced the seven sacraments of the old church by the two dominical sacraments, baptism and the Lord's Supper. In worship, out went Latinity, sacerdotalism, altars and unleavened wafers, auricular confession, the cult of Mary and the saints, the celebration of holy days and feast days, prayers for the dead, belief in purgatory, the sign of the cross, crucifixes, images and elaborate ritual, surplices (or choir dress) and eucharistic vestments, organs and choristers, the plainsong of great churches and the silence of poor churches. In came a simple service based on preaching, Bible study, prayers and the metrical psalms sung to popular tunes, and with this active participation by the people, who, no longer passive spectators, were encouraged to sing God's praise and, seated corporately at tables, to receive both wine and bread at communion.

The new responsibility assumed by reformed congregations was channelled in other directions, too, not least in the rôle assigned to representatives of the Christian community on the reformed courts of the kirk, and, again, in the recognition that the congregation's consent was necessary in hiring and firing a minister, and in appointing from the community elders and deacons to assist in running the kirk's affairs. In discipline, the penitential system of the medieval church was jettisoned, as were its judicial courts and legislative councils, and, with their disappearance, the displacement of the corpus of canon law. In their place, the new church set up its own concentric series of courts, linking the parishes to the general assembly at the centre in a manner unprecedented in secular society.

In establishing its own reformed ministry and distinctive system of government, the kirk with equal resolution in 1560 rejected the ancient system of benefices and, with it, all hierarchical titles from acolyte to archbishop. Here was no attempt at rehabilitating the familiar ecclesiastical edifice. Besides, the concept of 'holy orders', as traditionally conceived, was decisively repudiated and replaced, in reformed thinking, by the 'inauguration' of ministers to particular charges; the disappearance of the tonsure, the obligation of clerical celibacy, clerical dress, clerical privilege (including immunity from the secular courts)

and even clerical life-styles was accompanied by the disappearance
of the clerical 'estate' itself (which, in turn, raised the issue of
ecclesiastical representation in parliament), and the anticipated
elimination of clergy from the king's government. The solution
was radical and primitivist.

In reformed Scotland, there was neither 'clergy' nor 'laity'.
The new learning and the new doctrines had gone far in effacing
the old theological, educational and cultural division between
clergy and laity. No longer consigned to the ranks of the
illiterate, laymen had demonstrated an eagerness, as seldom
before, to participate in, and even to initiate, theological debate.
The substitution of 'minister' for 'priest' involved far more than
mere tinkering with terminology. The priest who offered the
sacrifice of the mass, at the centre of the church's worship, was
hitherto seen as the essential link between God and man; he acted
as intermediary; he administered five of the seven sacraments
through which those who received them in faith were infused
with fresh grace; he held the key to the kingdom of heaven. By
rejecting the mass and the papacy, the reformers, at a stroke, had
challenged the whole medieval system. In distinguishing no
special priesthood beyond the universal priesthood of all
Christians, the reformers conceived the minister as a servant to
God and to his brethren; as pastor, he had a particular
relationship to his flock, by living in their midst, offering care,
guidance, instruction, edification, even discipline, in accordance
with the Word; through preaching, he opened up the mysteries
of scripture, and pointed the way to salvation; he also administered
the two sacraments; but he did not possess the same key to
unlock the door to the kingdom of heaven. Here was no trace of
a clerically dominated church. The whole theology had changed.

The acceptance of a pastoral concept of ministry entailed a
drastic diminution in the size of what may be termed the
professional ministry. The church had no longer a need, or a
place, for the assorted services of monks, nuns, friars and canons
regular, archbishops, cathedral dignitaries, archdeacons, rural
deans, canon lawyers, vicars choral, prebendaries, chaplains, and
the colleges of priests employed to repeat masses for the souls
of the departed in the richly endowed collegiate kirks. In all,
a clerical establishment of what conceivably amounted to over
3,000 staff, sustained (though not in equal measure) by a financial
structure with resources ten times those of the crown, serving
(directly or indirectly) a population of perhaps 800,000, was
replaced by a parish ministry never designed to exceed 1,000,
augmented by no more than a handful of supervisors. The old

top-heavy structure was replaced by a leaner, fitter, better-educated ministry, dedicated to caring for the souls of the living in the parishes.

The disappearance of so many clerics may have made the ministry numerically less conspicuous, especially in the towns, but it assuredly had the effect, by eliminating a clutter of competitors, of enhancing the minister's rôle and status within the community by focusing attention on his indispensable work in the parishes. The higher standards demanded of ministers and the modest competence offered in stipend may have had a combined effect on levels of recruitment; the ministry no longer offered lucrative advancement for careerists; and opportunity for ministers (or even assistant readers) to indulge in secular occupations, perhaps by acting as schoolmasters or notaries, was severely curtailed and discouraged; all of which fostered a more earnest, vocational outlook among aspiring recruits, who were expected to be university-trained or otherwise schooled in theology, and not as hitherto for so many in canon law. Despite the inevitable shortage of recruits, more parishes at the Reformation had the services of protestant preachers than has generally been appreciated; indeed, most lowland parishes had become accustomed to reformed service in the 1560s; even in outlying areas, where communications were poorer, the kirk succeeded in establishing its presence in many highland parishes during the 1570s. The harvest was not unrewarding. The protracted Reformation was also very largely a peaceful Reformation.[9]

There was throughout a curious combination, on the one hand, of radicalism and revolution, so evident in doctrine, in defiance of authority, and in the new patterns of worship and church government, and, on the other hand, of continuity, so marked in the recruitment of personnel from the old to the new kirk, in the survival of the old financial machinery (which the new kirk wanted to dismantle), and even of comparative moderation, exemplified in the virtual absence of executions in or after 1560 or, indeed (until 1573), of the dispossession of benefice holders for declining to accept the Reformation. Again, the religious houses survived as legal entities and as financial corporations; admittedly they were no more than relics of the past, but the monks and nuns for the most part continued to live within the precincts as before, supported by their 'portions' (and the friars likewise received their 'wages') as retirement pensions;

[9] See below, 152–3.

the monasteries were not dissolved, as in England; only the religious observances had ceased or were suppressed. Regardless of the Reformation, Catholic prelates retained their right to sit in parliament and vote as the ecclesiastical estate, at a point when the reformers declined to make new arrangements for the ministry to assume to this lordly rôle. All this may hold the key to the Reformation's success in Scotland. Decisive change was effected not in any one year, but over more than a decade, from 1557 to 1573; the impact was cumulative, yet profound; and much which happened gradually, even unobtrusively, proved all the harder, in the end, for conservatives to reverse or overturn.

Once the parishes were staffed with ministers, exhorters, readers and (in more cases than may be imagined) with schoolmasters, protestantism became difficult to avoid; few dissidents, at any rate, had the resources or ingenuity of·some recusant nobles who, by moving from one of their properties to another, had the option of changing parishes, thereby keeping the kirk at bay that little longer. And where lingering attachment to conservative practices or a fondness for old forms could not at once be eradicated, the kirk in a remarkable gesture 'for the reconsiliatioun of breder and uthair affaris' fully expected 'ony persone or personeis, papest or protestantis' with criticism of a minister's doctrine or behaviour to report the matter to the kirk session for determination.[10] In assuming its rôle of communicating with the whole people of Scotland, the new kirk intended to subject its ministry to the entire community for appraisal. Anticlericalism could scarcely have been taken further.

In devising patterns for government, Scottish reformers instinctively chose to follow the examples of the 'best reformed churches' on the continent. In this, they pointed a way ahead which some more radical reformers in England would readily have followed. Lordship, hierarchy and the old distinction between the 'higher' and 'inferior' clergy were replaced by brotherhood, collegiality and conciliar government.[11] The contrast could scarcely have been more pronounced. At every level, individual action and initiative was made accountable to a concentric series of courts from kirk session to general assembly. The introduction of superintendent ministers, as a replacement for bishops, is again to be seen within the framework of radical efforts to remodel traditional concepts of oversight by experimenting with new modes of supervision. In doing so, the

[10] *The Buik of the Kirk of the Canagait, 1564–1567*, ed. A. B. Calderwood (Edinburgh, 1961), 32.
[11] See below, 164ff., 186ff., 194ff., 341ff.

reformers succeeded in retaining the unity of the pastoral ministry. The superintendent's office conferred none of the accustomed perquisites of property or benefices on its holders, who remained salaried servants devoid of episcopal privilege. As preaching supervisors or as supervising preachers, the superintendents were also denied any rôle in parliament or council; they lacked, in short, the social and political authority traditionally exercised by bishops. But their purely ecclesiastical duties were consistent with a reformed conception of ministry. They remained brothers among brethren.[12]

The Reformation therefore, in a very real sense, was understood to mark a victory for the Christian community, and its representatives, in governing the new church at the expense of pope, prelate and prince. In advancing the cause of reformation, the wider community had struggled for ascendancy. As Knox had reminded people in his 'Letter to the Commonalty of Scotland', the care of religion was the responsibility of more than prelates and princes: the people had an obligation to defend their preachers against opponents. For Scottish reformers, ministers and magistrates had their distinctive and separate duties to perform. Papal headship of the church was not to be readily replaced by royal supremacy.[13] The powers which the community had vested in the general assembly were not to be easily abrogated. The elimination of bishops merely increased the crown's difficulties in influencing the kirk's policies, formulated in its self-governing courts, where fresh emphasis was placed on reaching decisions by 'plurality of votes'. Only through finance and patronage did the crown finally secure a lever for gaining a say in ecclesiastical affairs.

The survival of the ancient financial framework of benefices, which the reformers did not so readily overturn, ultimately invited the possibility of assigning this entire structure (apart from monastic properties) as endowment to the new kirk. This compromise between the interests of the crown and the needs of the kirk, achieved by 1572, prepared the way for the reappearance of bishops, so essential for the crown's success in exercising at least a measure of control over the kirk. Yet the prospect of achieving episcopal subordination to the crown proved elusive so long as the general assembly required bishops to acknowledge their subjection to the assembly *in spiritualibus* and to the crown merely *in temporalibus*. And the more the crown sought to strengthen the social and political standing of bishops, the harder

[12] See below, 154–231.
[13] See below, 232–79.

it became to reconcile episcopal pretensions with a reformed conception of ministry eschewing traditional patterns of lordship and dominion.[14]

If finance and patronage proved something of a stumbling-block for the kirk, it can too readily be assumed by writers unfamiliar with financial records that on these two issues the Scottish reformers moved less quickly than the English. Such a claim[15] ignores more than just the different starting points of the Reformation within the two countries. It fails to recognise that out of almost 9,000 English livings, half were worth less than £10 sterling in annual income, and of these 1,000 livings yielded less than £2 sterling, a figure which, if anything, compares unfavourably with ministers' stipends in Scotland (modest though they often were) in 1574, when due allowance is made for converting pounds Scots, valued at a fifth of the English pound. Besides, although the ancient system of patronage survived (and was not dissolved, as Scottish reformers contended it should be), the exercise of ecclesiastical patronage for a generation after the Reformation was substantially concentrated in the hands of the crown, which for the most part, conscientiously discharged its duties in fostering a preaching ministry. All this was at variance with much English practice where the fragmentation of patronage in the hands of others often frustrated efforts at securing a godly ministry. There again, ecclesiastical patronage formed part of the wider network of patronage in society; it need not always serve a reforming cause.[16]

The inadequacies of the men advanced as bishops in 1572 and the exploitation of the system by nobles who stood to benefit financially went far, in the eyes of the general assembly, to discredit the process of identifying the old structure of patronage with a reformed polity, pledged as it was to uphold congregational rights and to remedy the far from satisfactory legacy in ecclesiastical finance. By the late 1580s, the rôle of presbyteries in supervising admissions to benefices helped strengthen the church's hand in checking abuses of patronage; and the general assembly continued its campaign for a redistribution of ecclesiastical revenues on a model more consistent with the example of the early church. In the end, only the exceptional determination of King James VI made bishops a reality in Scotland, and through

---

[14] See below, 426–48.

[15] Cf., M. Lynch, 'From privy kirk to burgh church', in *Church, Politics and Society*, ed. N. Macdougal (Edinburgh, 1983), 92.

[16] See below, 368–425; M. R. O'Day, 'Clerical Patronage and Recruitment in England in the Elizabethan and early Stuart periods, with special reference to the Diocese of Coventry and Lichfield' (London Ph.D. thesis, 1972).

episcopal government James was the better able to advance his own claims as supreme governor of the church.[17] The tensions between the adoption of a reformed church order and the continued adherence, at the crown's insistence, to earlier practices reminiscent of the unreformed regime were not to be readily resolved by peaceful compromise. The campaign for further change, by sacrificing continuity and stability for far-reaching reform, ultimately proved irresistible in the Covenanting revolution of the 1640s.

[17] See below, 255, 433.

I

The 'Privy Kirks' and their antecedents: The Hidden Face of Scottish Protestantism

The history of Scottish protestantism as a clandestine, underground movement can be traced, albeit unevenly, over three decades from parliament's early ban on Lutheran literature in 1525 to the protestant victory of 1560 when, in disregard of the wishes of its absent queen then resident in France, parliament finally proscribed the Roman mass and the whole apparatus of papal jurisdiction in Scotland and adopted instead a protestant Confession of Faith.[1] Out of a loosely-defined body of beliefs in the 1530s, ranging from a profound dissatisfaction at ecclesiastical abuse (shared by those who remained Catholic), to a recognition of the need for a reformation in doctrine (less readily conceded by orthodox Catholics), Scottish protestantism by the 1550s had developed a cellular organisation, enabling it to survive periodic persecution. Early protestants, themselves brought up within the Catholic church as baptised and communicating members, by the 1550s had taken the agonising and momentous step of separating themselves from the fellowship of the established church by forming their own separate communities of believers, worshipping in secret and centred on the privy kirks which arose in the years immediately preceding the Reformation.

Such was the assurance of salvation which one individual, Elizabeth Adamson, experienced from participating in these secret protestant assemblies for scripture study and prayer, fostered in Edinburgh by Knox and others, that on her deathbed

[1] *Acts of the Parliaments of Scotland* [hereafter *APS*], ed. T. Thomson (London, 1814–75), ii, 295, 341–2, 526–34; iii, 14.

this wife of a prominent merchant and magistrate (himself in touch with Knox from Genevan days) rejected all offers of priestly ministration and intercession. 'Depart from me, ye sergeantis of Sathan', she is reported to have uttered, 'for I have refused, and in your awin presence do refuise, all your abominationis. That which ye call your Sacrament and Christes body (as ye have deceaved us to beleve in tymes past) is nothing but ane idole, and hes nothing to do with the rycht institutioun of Jesus Christ; and thairfor, in Goddis name, I command yow nott to truble me'. Extreme unction and the services of a church which hitherto was seen to hold the key to unlock the doors to the kingdom of Heaven were despised by Elizabeth Adamson in Edinburgh. Instead, with simple evangelical piety, she asked those around her to sing the 103rd psalm, because, as she explained, 'at the teaching of this Psalme, begane my trubled soule first effectually to taist of the mercy of my God, which now to me is more sweat and precious then all the kingdomes of the earth war gevin to me to possesse thame a thowsand yearis'.[2]

For Elizabeth Adamson, protestantism, with its emphasis on individual personal faith, had taught her to find a confirmation of her faith in the Bible with a clarity and intensity which the established church seemed less able to provide. Her story also says something about the convictions of those protestants who dissociated themselves from the existing ecclesiastical structure and who sought spiritual nourishment in the company of others who shared their religious preferences in the shadowy underground world of the privy kirks.

The emergence of this tightly-knit cellular structure, in which familial ties afforded both contact and protection, assisted the development of a network of protestant communities, no longer isolated and dispersed, but increasingly organised and militant, so that when the revolution against France and Rome got underway by 1559, protestantism, which had gradually infiltrated local communities for over thirty years, was at last sufficiently responsive to seizing the initiative presented. This it did by wresting control of parish kirks from priests and patrons to ministers and kirk sessions, that is, reformed consistories of elders and deacons, whose immediate antecedents are, again, to be found in the organisation of the privy kirks.

---

[2] *The Works of John Knox*, ed. D. Laing (Edinburgh, 1846–64), i, 246–7.

The phenomenon of the privy kirk, therefore, marks an intermediate stage between an earlier phase of inchoate, unorganised protestantism and the reformers' concerted bid for power in the revolution of 1559–60 which brought them victory. Although so very little is known about its history, the privy kirk does seem to possess a significance not always adequately appreciated by historians who, by concentrating on the political aspects of the Reformation, have sometimes been insufficiently attentive to the dimension which the religious movement contributed in the highly complex situation which developed at the Reformation-rebellion, and so they have underestimated the strength of attachment to the reformed cause.

That Scottish protestantism acquired and exhibited many of the characteristics of a popular movement, of which the privy kirks were to form only one element, need hardly be doubted. Initially, of course, protestant sympathisers had been found confined to articulate and educated but disputatious divines. The first Scottish casualty of the Reformation had been Patrick Hamilton, titular abbot of Fearn, student of Paris, Louvain, St Andrews and Marburg, burned at St Andrews in 1528 for espousing Lutheran heresies. Yet his evangelical theology continued to circulate in the little compilation known as 'Patrick's Places'. Thereafter, Henry Forres, in minor orders, from Linlithgow met a similar fate after conviction for possessing an English New Testament and for approving Hamilton's doctrine.[3]

Others, threatened for their heterodox opinions, chose exile rather than the prospect of the scaffold. Alexander Alane, Augustinian canon of St Andrews and convert to Lutheran doctrines, escaped in 1532 to the safety of Malmö and eventually to Wittenberg where, as an adherent of Melanchthon, he was recommended to Cromwell and Cranmer and lectured in theology at Cambridge, then at Frankfurt on Oder and finally at Leipzig.[4] Another exile from St Andrews, John Fethie, studied at Wittenberg and also taught at Frankfurt.[5] By 1534, two friars, John Macalpine and John Macdowell, priors at Perth and Wigtown and graduates of Cologne, had fled to England where they preached for Bishop Shaxton in Salisbury. But whereas

[3] P. Lorimer, *Patrick Hamilton* (Edinburgh, 1857); Knox, *Works*, i, 13–35, 52–3; J. Foxe, *Acts and Monuments*, ed. J. Cumming (London, 1875), ii, 248–63.

[4] J. T. McNeill, 'Alexander Alesius, Scottish Lutheran (1500–1565)', *Archiv für Reformationsgeschichte*, iv (1964), 161–91.

[5] *Album academiae Vitebergensis*, ed. C. E. Foerstemann (Leipzig, 1841), 213; *Die Matrikel der Universität Frankfurt an der Oder* (1506–1648), edd. G. Liebe and E. Theuner (Leipzig, 1887), 99.

Macdowell continued to serve in the English church in Dorset and Lincoln for over twenty years, Macalpine by 1540 had left for Wittenberg and then for Copenhagen as theology professor in 1542.[6] Even King James V's confessor, Alexander Seton, prior of the Dominican friary in St Andrews, was suspected of Lutheran heresies and so escaped to Berwick and found service as chaplain to the Duke of Suffolk.[7] A further Dominican friar, John Willock, fled about 1535 from Ayr, where Lutheran doctrines were expounded 'both in private and public', together with other 'blasphemies' against the eucharist. There, too, the English New Testament and other reformed works circulated; instances of iconoclasm occurred in the parish kirk in 1534 and again at the Franciscan friary, where a statue of the Virgin Mary was decapitated. After pursuing a career in the English church which had taken him to Emden as a Marian exile in 1554, Willock returned to Scotland to help organise the privy kirks and establish a Calvinist discipline.[8] To this catalogue of clerical converts in the 1530s, who escaped abroad, may be added Robert Richardson, Augustinian canon of Cambuskenneth, who sought Cromwell's patronage in England.[9]

What all this amounted to in practice may not be readily determined; but it does suggest that Scottish protestantism was already at work making significant converts among the clergy, even though its exponents found it safer to enunciate their beliefs beyond the realm. What is not so readily disclosed is the number of protestant sympathisers who concealed their views from the authorities, the sort of people who might be expected to resort to the privy kirks at a later stage. Yet an indication of the firm foothold which protestantism had gained in certain towns, later to have implications for the nascent privy kirks, is the series of prosecutions for heresy among laymen in the late 1530s and early '40s.

Nothing like a complete record of these heresy trials has survived; for a start, the proceedings in the ecclesiastical courts are now missing; and evidence is usually forthcoming only in

---

[6] M. A. F. Bredahl Petersen, 'Dr Johannes Macchabeus: Scotland's contribution to the Reformation in Denmark' (Edinburgh Ph.D. thesis, 1935); J. Durkan, 'Some Local Heretics', *Transactions of the Dumfriesshire & Galloway Natural History & Antiquarian Society*, xxxvi (1959), 66–77.

[7] Knox, *Works*, i, 45–52; Foxe, *Acts*, ii, 593–5.

[8] D. Shaw, 'John Willock', *Reformation and Revolution*, ed. D. Shaw (Edinburgh, 1967), 42–69; *St Andrews Formulare, 1514–1546*, ed. G. Donaldson (Edinburgh, 1944), ii, no. 367; D. Calderwood, *History of the Kirk of Scotland*, ed. T. Thomson (Edinburgh, 1842–9), i, 286.

[9] J. Durkan 'Scottish "Evangelicals" in the Patronage of Thomas Cromwell', *Records of the Scottish Church History Society*, xxi (1982), 127–56, at 134.

instances where the crown had an interest in disposing of the escheated goods of convicted heretics or in granting heretics remissions for their crimes. Nonetheless, it emerges that, at this date, three inhabitants of Edinburgh, including the schoolmaster, and three more from Leith were convicted of heresy and had their property confiscated;[10] five more were detected in Stirling; some merely had suspect literature, others were more severely punished with forfeiture and at least one was sent to the stake;[11] in Perth, at least seven heretics were convicted at that stage, four of whom were hanged and a fifth drowned; but besides this group, other inhabitants of the burgh including a priest and notary are on record as having fled on account of their heretical inclinations when the periodic searches took place for 'Christers' or protestants.[12] In Dundee, sentences of forfeiture or even death were pronounced in cases involving no fewer than twenty heretics in the burgh; and eighteen more Dundonians were charged with image-breaking and oppressing the friars in the burgh, at a point when Arran as governor of the realm had inclined towards protestantism.[13] Similar prosecutions are known to have taken place in the west country, particularly in Ayr; and if the details remain partly obscured, it was Archbishop Hamilton, as primate, who impressed on the pope in 1554 how 'a great part of the diocese of Glasgow' was 'infected with heresies' in the 1540s and how thereafter 'the greatest scandals were perpetrated against the Catholic faith'.[14]

To the problems affecting the south-west may be added those of the north-east. In Angus, the Mearns and Aberdeenshire, thirty members of noble or lairdly families, including the Earl

[10] *Registrum Secreti Sigilli Regum Scotorum* [hereafter *RSS*], edd. D. H. Fleming, *et al.* (Edinburgh, 1908 – in progress), ii, nos. 2915, 2946, 2988; *Registrum Magni Sigilli Regum Scotorum* [hereafter *RMS*], edd. J. M. Thomson, *et al.* (Edinburgh, 1882–1914), iii, no. 2179; *Accounts of the Lord High Treasurer of Scotland* [hereafter *TA*], edd. T. Dickson, *et al.* (Edinburgh, 1877 – in progress), vi, 175; vii, 67, 77, 79, 233–4; Knox, *Works*, i, 57; *A Diurnal of Remarkable Occurrents in Scotland*, ed. T. Thomson (Edinburgh, 1833), 18; *Acts of the Lords of Council in Public Affairs, 1501–1554*, ed. R. K. Hannay (Edinburgh, 1932), 486. See also Scottish Record Office, JC1/5, Justiciary Court Book, 21 Feb., 28 Feb., 7 March, 1539 where another individual faced charges of possessing suspect and prohibited literature.

[11] *RMS*, iii, no. 1955; *RSS*, ii, nos. 2923, 2975; *TA*, vii, 77, 79; Knox, *Works*, i, 62; *Criminal Trials in Scotland*, ed. R. Pitcairn (Edinburgh, 1829–33), i, 216.

[12] *RSS*, ii, no. 3033; iii, nos. 609, 611–13; *TA*, viii, 215, 219; Knox, *Works*, i, 117–18; Calderwood, *History*, i, 171–5; Foxe, *Acts*, ii, 708–9.

[13] *RSS*, ii, nos. 2644, 2648, 2686, 2704, 2733, 2742, 2962, 3016; iii, no. 1635; iv, no. 2580; *TA*, vi, 307, 376–7; vii, 79, 153; x, 369–70; A. Maxwell, *Old Dundee* (Edinburgh, 1891), appendix B; *The Hamilton Papers*, ed. J. Bain (Edinburgh, 1890–2), ii, no. 30.

[14] *TA*, vi, 313; *Liber Officialis Sancte Andree*, ed. C. Innes (Edinburgh, 1845), 167.

Marischal, the provost of Aberdeen and the parson of Aberdour, were pardoned by the crown in 1544 for activities which included reading suspect books, disputing on scripture and holding opinions forbidden by act of parliament; and by 1547, the bishop of Aberdeen himself acknowledged that heresy was then 'thriving greatly' within his diocese. Elsewhere, details of at least a further sixteen convictions among laymen for heresy have survived for these years.[15]

The incidence of heresy was no longer confined to quiescent family cells of believers. Circumspection, of course, was still essential for survival and few protestants willingly advertised their presence to the authorities. Yet, in Perth, a rather remarkable foursome – a 'merchant', maltman, flesher [butcher] and skinner – were convicted in 1544 for holding a conventicle, 'an assemblie and conventioun', in St Anne's chapel where they, and no doubt others, conferred and disputed on texts of holy scripture, in defiance of the acts of parliament, to the 'dishonouring of the glorious Virgin Mary and the communioun of sanctis in hevin'. One member of this little company was said merely to have been 'a simple man, and without learning . . . with no great knowledge in doctrine; yitt because he often used the suspect companie of the rest, he was accused'. The others presumably knew what they were about; the man in the group depicted as a merchant (but who may have been a maltman) was sufficiently literate, at any rate, to have his copy of the English Bible. What is more, two of the disputants, one with his English Bible in his hand, also had the courage or rashness of their convictions later to interrupt a friar, as he preached from the pulpit, by denouncing his doctrine as false and contrary to scripture. Retaliation, however, was swift; and the heretics were hanged. But greater leniency appears to have been shown to another burgess of Perth, a relative of the burgh's fugitive priest, who received a remission from the crown in 1544 for his crime of holding 'quiet conventions in secret places', disputing on sacred scripture and dishonouring the Virgin Mary.[16]

The problem of conventicles was serious enough to have warranted parliament's attention in 1541 when, in an effort 'to stop the privat congregatioun and conventiculis of heretikis quhair thair erroris ar spred', a reward was offered to any with

[15] *RSS*, iii, no. 820; *Registrum Episcopatus Aberdonensis*, ed. C. Innes (Aberdeen, 1845), ii, 317; *TA*, vi, 8, 176; vii, 78–9; viii, 219; *RSS*, ii, nos. 1302, 1583, 1585, 1611, 1736, 2420, 2797, 2936, 2952, 2976, 2987, 3396; v, no. 1267; *Diurnal of Occurrents*, 19; *Criminal Trials*, i, 297; *Acts of the Lords of Council*, 446.
[16] Calderwood, *History*, i, 171–5; *RSS*, iii, nos. 609, 611–13.

knowledge of these secret associations; informants who had
attended such a gathering, no more than once, were to be free
from prosecution; outsiders with information incriminating
heretics holding conventicles were to receive a share in the
property of the convicted heretic. This act, passed together with
a series of statutes requiring the sacraments to be honoured, the
Virgin Mary to be worshipped, the statues of saints to be revered,
the pope's authority upheld, ecclesiastical abuses reformed, and
heretics incapacitated from holding public office, helps to convey
an impression of the magnitude of the problem which the
ecclesiastical authorities faced. Even two years later, during
Arran's governorship, when parliament authorised laymen to
read the Bible 'in Inglis or Scottis of ane gude and trew
translatioun', disputations on scripture were expressly forbidden
by law.[17]

Despite the existence and, in some cases, detection of
clandestine gatherings, where literate laymen might read passages
from the vernacular Bible to those in their company and discuss
controverted texts, there was still a conspicuous absence of
protestant-inclined preachers to provide the necessary guidance
and leadership. Some sympathetic clerics, of course, had been
detected – men like the provost of Roslin, the vicar of Dollar, the
priest in Perth, the curates of Lunan and Tullibody, a chaplain in
Kirkwall, another in Dunfermline and a third in Stirling, two
Franciscans from Aberdeen and Dumfries, two Dominican friars
burned at Stirling, a third who preached in Angus and was
murdered at St Andrews, and the wayward chaplain from
Brechin diocese whose bishop was instructed to have him
punished for heresy. The list is not unimpressive; even more
significant is the geographical spread from Kirkwall in the
Orkneys to Dumfries in the extreme south west. Even parts of
the Highlands were not immune from heresy: the bishop of Ross
was empowered by the cardinal to proceed against heretics from
his far-distant diocese to be found in the archdiocese of
St Andrews.[18]

At the same time, the distribution of devotional literature in
protestant circles helped to compensate for the shortage of

[17] APS, ii, 370–1, 415.
[18] RSS, ii, nos. 2858, 2903, 3612; iv, no. 916; Calendar of State Papers relating
to Scotland and Mary, Queen of Scots, edd. J. Bain, et al. 13 vols (Edinburgh,
1898–1969), i, no. 206; TA, vii, 77, 79–80; Diurnal of Occurrents, 18; Regality of
Dunfermline Court Book, 1531–1538, edd. J. M. Webster and A. A. M. Duncan
(Dunfermline, 1953), 143–4; Knox, Works, i, 56–7, 62–5, 118–19; Criminal
Trials, i, 209–16; Acts of the Lords in Council, 427, 437, 482; St Andrews
Formulare, ii, no. 416.

preachers by providing a clear evangelical message.[19] Besides, apart from the personal contact of individual Scots with protestant Europe, the new doctrines were spread at home, as Knox appreciated, 'partlie by reading, partlie by brotherlye conferance, which in those dangerous dayis was used to the comforte of many'.[20] The conventicles thus afforded an element of protection while providing a focus for fellowship and for imparting religious knowledge among the faithful.

A sudden stimulus to protestant preaching came in 1543 from an unexpected quarter with the temporary defection to protestantism, effective for no more than a few months, of the Earl of Arran, then governor during Queen Mary's minority. Not only did he sponsor the heretical preaching at court of a Dominican friar, Thomas Gwilliam, but he also supported as his family's chaplain another unorthodox Dominican, John Rough, from Stirling who also preached in places as far apart as St Andrews and Dumfries and later was burned for heresy at Smithfield in 1557. As governor, Arran supported the heterodox preaching of Robert Richardson, and even asked the magistrates in Aberdeen to appoint two friars as official preachers of 'the trew Word of God'. One of these friars, the Dominican John Roger, is said by Knox to have 'fructfully preached Christ Jesus to the conforte of many in Anguss and Mearnes'. Yet this 'godly' experiment, promoted as part of the government's programme, proved short-lived. Within three months of their appointment, the two preachers at court had been inhibited from preaching: one left for England, the other for Kyle in Ayrshire, 'a receptakle of Goddis servandis of old'. The renewed repression of heresy ensued; the movement resumed its underground activities; and an act of council in June 1543 depicted heretics as 'Sacramentaris' (or sacramentarians) who held disputations on the effect and essence of the sacraments to the detriment and 'enervatioun of the faith Catholik'.[21]

---

[19] J. Gau, *The Richt Vay to the Kingdom of Heuine*, ed. A. F. Mitchell (Edinburgh, 1888); *A Compendius Book of Godly and Spiritual Songs*, ed. A. F. Mitchell (Edinburgh, 1897); J. K. Cameron, 'John Johnsone's *An Confortable Exhortation of our mooste Holy Christen Faith and her Frutes*: an early example of Scots Lutheran Piety', *Studies in Church History*, Subsidia 2, (Oxford, 1979), 133–47; cf., *Devotional Pieces in Verse and Prose*, ed. J. A. W. Bennet (Edinburgh, 1955).

[20] Knox, *Works*, i, 61.

[21] Ibid., i, 95–7, 105, 184; *TA*, viii, 168, 170, 183; *Extracts from the Council Register of the Burgh of Aberdeen*, ed. J. Stuart (Aberdeen, 1844), i, 189; *Calendar of Letters and Papers*, Foreign and Domestic, Henry VIII [henceforth, *Cal. LP*], edd. J. S. Brewer, *et al.* (London, 1864–1932), pt. i, no. 448; Foxe, *Acts*, iii, 957–61; *Concilia Scotiae: Ecclesiae Scoticanae Statuta . . .*, ed. J. Robertson (Edinburgh, 1846), 294; see further, *Register of the Privy Council of Scotland*, 1st ser. edd. J. H. Burton, *et al.* (Edinburgh, 1877–98), i, 28–9, 61, 63, 65.

If the disputations and conventicling activities of protestants in burghs such as Perth are clear enough in outline, it is harder to say with certainty what was happening in the countryside behind the closed doors of a noble's castle or laird's keep, isolated from the prying eyes and ears of informants in the towns. There are indications, however, that private meetings for Bible study and conference similar to those in the towns were features of rural society too. The thirty landowners in the north-east pardoned in 1544 for disputing on scripture and reading forbidden books clearly illustrate the broad tendencies at work; but an earlier episode, narrated by Knox, illuminates the spiritual searching of one laird in Angus who 'delyted in nothing but in reading (albeit him self could not reid)'. His immediate problem was surmounted by having his son read him the English New Testament 'in ane certane qwyet place in the feildis'; and frequently he sought the company of that proto-protestant, Erskine of Dun, near Montrose. Other lairds, too, were thumbing through the pages of their copies of the English Bible in their homes or in small groups, if an expositor like Erskine of Dun could be found. James Kirkcaldy of Grange, later taken prisoner with his son, William, for their part in Cardinal Beaton's assassination in 1546, was reputed to have been a heretic during his service as treasurer to James V, when, it was noted, 'he had always a New Testament in English in his pouch'; and Sir John Borthwick, well-travelled in England and France and later a visitor to Geneva, was declared a heretic in 1540 not only for denouncing papal authority, the canon law, indulgences, the church's wealth and the religious orders but also for possessing a New Testament in English as well as the works of Oecolampadius, Melanchthon and Erasmus.[22]

Even so, it is really with the preaching mission in 1545 of George Wishart, who helped popularise the views of the Swiss reformers, that the secret network of protestant associations among the lairds begins to be uncovered. A student in Arts at Louvain and later at Cambridge, Wishart was the 'stiff-necked Scot' who had stirred up trouble in Bristol and was obliged to recant some of his more radical tenets. Returning to Edinburgh in 1543, Wishart began to preach in 1545, 'nott in secreat but in the audience of many', first at Montrose and then from the pulpit in Dundee on the Epistle to the Romans before the Earl Marischal and other nobles. His progress to the west country

[22] Knox, *Works*, i, 58–60; *Memoirs of Sir James Melville of Halhill*, ed. A. F. Steuart (London, 1929), 15; Foxe, *Acts*, ii, 695–706; *Register of the Minister, Elders and Deacons of the Christian Congregation of St Andrews* [henceforth *RStAKS*], ed. D. H. Fleming (Edinburgh, 1889–90), ii, 89–104; *Acts of the Lords of Council*, 504.

took him to Ayr, where he preached at the market cross after dissuading his followers, the Earl of Glencairn and lairds in Kyle, from taking the kirk by force; so, too, in Mauchline where he resisted Campbell of Kinyeancleuch's offer to storm the church which the sheriff had barricaded. Yet, he did preach in Galston kirk and at the home of the laird of Bar before returning to plague-ridden Dundee, where he visited the sick, preaching from the 107th psalm; and so to Montrose again 'to salute the Kirk thare' in preaching and 'secreat meditatioun'. Thereafter, he left for Edinburgh, lodging near Dundee at the home of 'a faythfull brother', James Watson in Invergowrie, earlier convicted of Lutheran heresies in 1532, then on to Perth, through Fife to Leith where he remained in secret before preaching; but when it proved too dangerous to remain there, Wishart was taken to the homes of East Lothian lairds at Brunstane, Longniddry and Ormiston, and preached in Tranent and in the kirks of Inveresk and Haddington, where he was sheltered by David Forres, later master of the mint and who undertook to 'exhort' the brethren in the privy kirk by 1558. Yet Wishart also found refuge at the home of Maitland of Lethington, who was 'ever civile, albeit not persuaded in religioun'. Captured at Ormiston and condemned to be burned as a heretic, Wishart, in his last prayer 'to conserve, defend and help thy Congregatioun, which thow hast chosen befoir the begynning of the world', helped make more explicit than ever before the belief among Scottish protestants who began to see themselves as forming a congregation of believers, a definition which ultimately led to the gathered church of the radical reformers.[23]

Wishart's translation of the first Swiss Confession of Faith, published in 1548, may also have contributed towards a clearer understanding of church fellowship; but the first attempt to organise a recognisably reformed congregation as such, of which we have direct knowledge, arose as a sequel to Wishart's martyrdom when a group of protestants who occupied St Andrews castle after the cardinal's murder in 1546 invited Knox to become their preacher. After a sermon preached by John Rough on the election of ministers and the power of the congregation to call its minister, Knox was charged to receive the call. At this stage, too, in disputations with Catholic opponents, Knox affirmed: 'we must defyne the Church by the rycht notes gevin to us in Goddis Scriptures of the trew Church'. For Knox, the church malignant must be distinguished from the true church: 'I wilbe of none

[23] Foxe, Acts, ii, 709–17; The Maire of Bristowe is Kalendar by Robert Ricart, ed. L. T. Smith (London, 1872), 55; Knox, Works, i, 125–71.

other church, except of that which hath Christ Jesus to be pastor, which hearis his voce, and will nott hear a strangeir'. In administering the Lord's Supper, Knox extended an invitation to those within the town, as well as the castle, who were willing openly to profess their faith. Yet this attempt at setting up the open face of a reformed church was cut short when French reinforcements stormed the castle and shipped off to France the members of this revolutionary group.[24]

Even so, as a counterpoise to French influence, English intervention in south-east Scotland from 1547 to 1549 helped sustain the hopes of a party in Scotland anglophile in its outlook and sympathetic to the cause of reform. The destruction caused by English occupying forces may have alienated many; the timid and uncertain may have waited on events; but not only did the provost and bailies of Dundee promise 'to be faithful setters forth of God's word', after which it was said that, in the town, 'most of the honest and substantial men favour the Word of God', but several earls like Glencairn and Lennox also undertook 'to cause the Word of God to be taught and preached'. The inhabitants of Leith were considered 'all good Christians'; and 'Angus and Fife', it was noted, 'greatly desire a good preacher, bibles and testaments and other good English books of Tyndale and Frithe's translation'. The cause of reform, through English aegis, was clearly making further headway. Yet the departure of the English and ascendancy of Mary of Guise meant that Scottish protestantism was again reduced to secret meetings behind closed doors.[25]

Arrested in 1550 at Winton castle, Lord Seton's home, in East Lothian, Adam Wallace, a native of Ayrshire and tutor to Cockburn of Ormiston's children, admitted that 'sometymes at the table and sometymes in other prevey places, he wald reid and had red the Scriptures and had gevin such exhortatioun as God pleaseth to geve to him and to such as pleased to hear him'. He also affirmed that he could find no scriptural warrant for purgatory and prayers to the saints, and appeared to condemn the mass as blasphemy, for which he was burned on castlehill in Edinburgh, despite the Earl of Glencairn's protests.[26]

Nevertheless, from 1555 onwards, freshly recruited preachers 'did sometymes, in severall cumpanyes, assemble the brethrein, who by thare exhortationis begane greatlie to be encouraged, and

[24] *Miscellany of the Wodrow Society*, ed. D. Laing (Edinburgh, 1844), i, 1–23; Knox, *Works*, i, 184–202.
[25] *CSP Scot.*, i, nos.71, 74, 107, 129; *Cal. LP*, xviii, pt.i, no.974; xix, pt.i, no.522.
[26] Knox, *Works*, i, 237–41; Foxe, *Acts*, ii, 717–20.

did schaw that thei had ane earnest thrist of godlines'. In 'privy conferance as in doctrin', Knox and others helped impress on protestant sympathisers the need to refrain from the sacraments of the established church and to organise themselves effectively in their own secret communities; and in his preaching tour in the Mearns, Knox detected a readiness among most of the lairds to refuse 'all societie with idolatrie'. By then, however, the protestants, it was said, 'keapt thare conventionis and held counsallis with such gravitie and closnes that the ennemyes trembled', or so Knox claimed; but the Catholic John Leslie also noted how protestant preaching took place 'in chimlay nuikis, secreit holes and sik priuat places, to truble the hail cuntrie, quench al quyetnes, banise al pease out of the land'. Both seem agreed that the underground organisation among protestants was becoming more effective and that protestants were more defiant and assertive.[27]

Certainly, by December 1557, the Lords of the Congregation had bound themselves to renounce the congregation of Satan and to establish the Word of God and his congregation and to sustain faithful ministers. They also committed themselves to provide in every parish each Sunday the reading of scripture and passages from the English prayer book either by the curates, if considered qualified, or by other more suitable parishioners. On the more contentious issues of preaching and interpreting scripture, however, they still planned to meet 'privatlie in qwyet houssis, without great conventionis of the people' until such time as protestant preaching in public was permitted by the prince. Their main aim, however, was for 'Christes religioun to be restored to the originall puritie' by following the example of 'the grave and godlie face of the primitive Churche'.[28]

If protestant prayer-meetings, held intermittently over two decades, were to become authentic churches, they required an authentic structure; hence resort to the congregational eldership, especially so when the church lay under the cross and was subject to persecution. Only evidence for the structure of the privy kirk in Edinburgh has been preserved. There protestants gathered in 'secreit and privie conventiounis' in the large houses of faithful merchants during winter or in the fields by summer. Some were elected 'to occupie the supreame place of exhortatioun and reading'; others were called as elders to exercise a godly

[27] Knox, *Works*, i, 245–57; J. Leslie, *The Historie of Scotland*, ed. J. Dalrymple (Edinburgh, 1895), ii, 397; *Statutes of the Scottish Church*, ed. D. Patrick (Edinburgh, 1907), 186.
[28] Knox, *Works*, i, 273–6, 299–307.

discipline, or as deacons to collect and distribute alms for the poor within the group. The similarities in polity with French protestantism or with the Marian exiles or even the strangers' churches in London are not coincidental: circumstances dictated a primitive government consistent with the example of the early church.[29]

As well as Edinburgh, the towns of Dundee, Perth, Stirling, Ayr, Brechin and Montrose all had reformed congregations with established ministers by 1559; and if, as was claimed at the Reformation, Fife, Angus, Argyll, Strathearn and the Mearns were already largely protestant, it is hard to resist the conclusion that innumerable clusters of privy kirks had taken root in countryside and town alike. But although they might breed a sense of purpose, self-reliance and esteem among the converted, the privy kirks alone could not hope to change society or bring about widespread revolution. The townspeople and country-dwellers who attended their meetings were still accustomed to looking above and beyond their own religious communities for direction and leadership – to preachers and magistrates, to lairds and nobles. Political action was imperative for sustained religious change. Certainly, support for the Reformation from Haliburton, as provost of Dundee, or from Lord Ruthven in Perth helped smooth the transition from privy kirk to parish church. Even an absence of local sanctions could prove helpful: in Dumfries, the magistrates refused the official of Nith's request to have a protestant preacher arrested in 1558.[30] In the end, however, only the aristocratic revolt and the physical presence in leading burghs of the para-military Lords of the Congregation signalled decisive change and entrusted the reformers with local power.

In Dundee, the town council in August 1559 assigned the town's preacher a stipend as minister and recognised the work of the kirk session already operating.[31] Perth, too, was reported in June 1559 to have received the 'Order of the Commoun Prayers';[32] and thereafter, in April 1560, William Harlaw, a

[29] Beza, Histoire ecclésiastique des églises réformées au royaume de France, edd. G. Baum and E. Cunitz (Paris, 1883–9), i, 120ff.; A. N. Galpern, The Religions of the People in Sixteenth-Century Champagne (London, 1976), 134–5, 150, 152, 166–7; F. A. Norwood, 'The Stranger's "Model Churches" in Sixteenth-Century England', Reformation Studies, ed. F. H. Littell (Richmond, 1962), 181–96; P. Collinson, Godly People (London, 1983), 213–44.
[30] Knox, Works, vi, 78; Hamilton Papers, ii, 749; cf., Wodrow Society Miscellany, i, 54; R. Keith, History of the Affairs of Church and State in Scotland, ed. J. P. Lawson (Edinburgh, 1835–50), i, 495–6.
[31] I. E. F. Flett, 'The Conflict of the Reformation and Democracy in the Geneva of Scotland, 1443–1610' (St Andrews M.Phil. thesis, 1981), 68.
[32] Knox, Works, vi, 22.

former Canongate tailor turned protestant preacher with a record of service in the Edwardine Church of England, was already installed as 'minister for the tyme', preaching in the parish kirk of St John 'in presens of nobill and rycht honourable men and the haill congregatioun of the burgh' assembled on the 'Sabbith day callit Sounday to the heiryng of Goddis name'. There, too, the reforming Alexander Gordon, bishop elect of Galloway and commendator of Inchaffray priory, confessed before the same congregation that he was 'na bischop preist' and had been a marrried man for 'fourtene yeiris'.[33] Indeed, a measure of the reformation achieved in Perth is again apparent in a petition from the craftsmen to parliament and to the 'haill Congregatioun of this realme' in 1560, remarkable not least for its claim how the merchants and craftsmen, 'sen God sperit up our haill communite of merchandis and craftis be assistance of his Holy Spreit to be jonit in ane congregatioun of Crist being memborris of his misticall body, ressavit his Holy Word and promis amangis us, for the quhilk our persecutioun is notorius. . . .'[34] The authorities in Ayr dispensed with the services of chaplains in May 1559 and appointed Christopher Goodman as minister and their schoolmaster as assistant minister.[35] Nearby Dalmellington had its own minister in 1559;[36] and in the east, the magistrates in Crail instructed their chaplains 'to apply thameselfis to Goddis Word and lyf godly, conforme to the congregatioun', and specifically ordered one of them to 'renuns the papis lawis and all uther abominatiounis'.[37] Besides, the primatial city of St Andrews, Scotland's ecclesiastical capital, had its reformed congregation and kirk session operating in public by October 1559.[38] The privy kirks had surfaced to assume the rôle of parish churches. Clearly, all this activity was taking place in the localities well before the work of the Reformation parliament got underway in August 1560. Even in a rural parish like Glenholm, near Peebles, the parishioners were accustomed to attending the 'preching and commoun prayaris' in their parish kirk; and they therefore took legal action before the Lords of Council in February 1560/1 to recover their stolen church bell, 'quhilk daile rang and warnit the perrochinneris of

---

[33] SRO, B59/1/1, Protocol Book of Henry Elder, fo. 184.
[34] Perth Museum, MS Original papers and letters of the Convener Court of the Incorporated Trades of Perth, no. 34.
[35] SRO, B6/12/3, Ayr Burgh Court Book, 22 May, 6 Nov., 20 Nov., 1559.
[36] Ibid., 29 Nov. 1559.
[37] SRO, Crail Town Clerk's Scroll Book, 4 Dec. 1559.
[38] RStAKS, i, 5.

the said perochin to preching and commoun prayaris'.[39]

Yet to magnify the rôle of the privy kirks, which appeared with deceptive suddenness in the late 1550s, is possibly to underestimate the importance of the earlier conventicling phase in the 1540s, when protestantism was perceived by the authorities as a widespread and formidable problem to combat. The main distinguishing feature of the privy kirks, however, was the emphasis on Calvinist discipline, determination and dedication instilled through the eldership and diaconate. If conventicles were gatherings of the converted, the privy kirks became churches with a mission to convert. All in all, the formation of privy kirks did not by themselves produce the Reformation victory of 1560 but, in the pursuit of that victory, they did provide the mechanism for transferring religious authority from voluntary communities of believers to a Calvinist church, equipped with a congregational structure and intent on becoming the church of a nation.

[39] SRO, CS7/20, Register of Acts and Decreets of the Court of Session, xx, fos. 330v–331r.

2

Clement Little's Edinburgh

By the sixteenth century, Edinburgh had become the acknowledged and undisputed capital of Scotland. Yet before the late fifteenth century, it would have been hard to say how far, if at all, Edinburgh predominated among the Scottish burghs. It is true that as early as the reign of David II the French chronicler Froissart had designated Edinburgh as the 'capital of Scotland', presumably because it then tended to be 'the residence of the king',[1] but a later monarch, James I, made Perth his preferred place of residence, so that by the early fifteenth century Edinburgh was not the recognised seat of government, the place where the king's business was transacted; it possessed no centralised law courts; it was not an episcopal seat or 'city' (and indeed was denied this status until the reign of Charles I); and partly as a consequence, unlike St Andrews, Glasgow and Aberdeen whose bishops had acted as founders and chancellors, it had no university of its own. In short, it lacked all the attributes associated with a capital city.

Periodic English invasions across the border into the Merse and Lothians – not least during the 'rough wooing' of 1544 – had left Edinburgh vulnerable as a town, though the castle remained a fortified and strategic standpoint. In other ways, however, Anglo-Scottish strife helped ultimately to enhance Edinburgh's economic status. The final cession to England in 1482 of Berwick, the port where much of Scotland's wool exports had once been channelled, facilitated the development of Edinburgh and its port of Leith, granted to the burgh by King Robert I in

[1] *Early Travellers in Scotland*, ed. P. H. Brown (Edinburgh, 1891), 9–10.

1329, as a leading centre for trade and commerce. Its steady urban growth, far outstripping all other Scottish burghs, despite plague or pestilence and periods of dearth, was sustained by the rich granaries of its 'extremely fertile' hinterland, an area noted by George Buchanan for its 'abundance of the necessaries of life'.[2]

Alexander Alane, or Alesius, the Lutheran heretic who had travelled extensively on the continent, compared Edinburgh's elevated situation with that of Prague in his contribution to Sebastian Münster's *Cosmographiae*, published at Basle in 1550; but in truth Edinburgh's outstanding feature was not its elegance: Glasgow, by all accounts, was then the burgh which most impressed contemporaries as a 'noble toune', a 'goodly cytee and universitee', with its handsome cathedral acclaimed by an English visitor as 'the fairest and stateliest in Scotland'.[3] By contrast, what caught the visitor's eye in Edinburgh was the concentration of its expanding population in so restricted an area along the ridge from the castle down the High Street, with its array of narrow 'closes' and wynds branching off at right-angles, past the collegiate Kirk of St Giles to the Netherbow and Cowgate, and to the adjacent abbatial burgh of Canongate, with its Abbey of Holyrood, founded by 1136, where James IV chose to build a royal palace which his son, James V, duly enlarged. The narrow confines of the burgh dictated that further expansion should take place vertically rather than horizontally in the form of tall tenements sometimes rising ten storeys high. 'Such a multitude of people in so small a space'[4] had led William Dunbar, the poet of James IV's reign, to upbraid Edinburgh for its apparent indifference to dirt and foul smells by asking:[5]

> 'Quhy will ye, Merchantis of renoun,
> Lat Edinburgh, your nobill toun,
> For laik of reformatioun,
> The commone proffeitt tyne and fame?
> Think ye nocht schame
> That ony uther regioun
> Sall with dishonour hurt your Name?

[2] A. Alesius, 'Edinburgi Regiae Scotorum urbis descriptio', *Bannatyne Miscellany* (Edinburgh, 1827–55), i, 185; *Scotland before 1700*, ed. P. H. Brown (Edinburgh, 1893), 106, 220.
[3] *Bannatyne Miscellany*, i, 186; *Scotland before 1700*, 106, 120; *Early Travellers in Scotland*, 23, 150; R. Holinshed, *Chronicles of England, Scotland and Ireland* (London, 1807–8), v, 11.
[4] *Early Travellers in Scotland*, 82–4, 92–3; *Scotland before 1700*, 314.
[5] *Scotland before 1700*, 109–11.

May nane pas throw your principall Gaittis,
For stink of haddockis and of scaitis;
For cryis of carlingis and debaittis;
For fensum flyttingis of defame:
      Think ye nocht schame,
Befoir strangeris of all estaittis
That sic dishonour hurt your Name?

. . .

Tailyouris, Soutteris, and craftis vyll,
The fairest of your streittis dois fyll;
And merchandis at the stinkand styll
As hamperit in ane hony-came:
      Think ye nocht schame,
That ye have nether witt nor wyll
To win your selff ane bettir Name?'

Cramped and crowded conditions inevitably led to outbreaks of disease: the plagues of 1568, 1574 and 1585 were particulary severe; and Calderwood's exaggerated figure of 20,000 deaths in Edinburgh from the pestilence of 1585 underlines the effect which the disaster had on one who, as a boy of ten in a nearby town, had managed to survive its visitation.[6] Estimates of Edinburgh's population in the mid-sixteenth century have proceeded on little more than guesswork, ranging from a mere 9,000 to an exceedingly high 30,000. Even with a population of perhaps around 12,000, Edinburgh still vied with the larger cities of England, apart from London, and it was comparable in size with the Swiss republican cities of Geneva and Zürich, though it clearly could not compete with towns on the Rhine like Strasbourg around the 40,000 mark, and it was indeed small in relation to the gigantic Italian or imperial cities or to Paris with 200,000 citizens or Amsterdam, Antwerp and London with some 100,000 inhabitants.[7]

[6] *Extracts from the Records of the Burgh of Edinburgh, 1403–1589*, ed. J. D. Marwick, vols. ii–vi (Edinburgh, 1869–92), iii, 256, 259; iv, 28, 29, 30, 35, 413–14, 416–18, 421; R. H. Stevenson, *The Chronicles of Edinburgh* (Edinburgh, 1851), 101; D. Calderwood, *The History of the Kirk of Scotland*, ed. T. Thomson, 8 vols. (Edinburgh, 1842–9), iv, 377; S. G. E. Lythe, *The Economy of Scotland in its European Setting, 1550–1625* (Edinburgh, 1960), 18.

[7] I. F. Grant, *The Economic History of Scotland* (London, 1934), 86 (9,000); P. H. Brown, *Scotland in the Time of Queen Mary* (London, 1904), 52; Lythe, *Economy of Scotland*, 117 (30,000); W. E. Monter, *Calvin's Geneva* (New York, 1967), 2 (Geneva; 10,000); G. R. Potter, *Zwingli* (Cambridge, 1976), 53 and n. 1 (Zürich; 6,000); H. G. Koenigsberger and G. L. Mosse, *Europe in the Sixteenth Century* (London, 1968), 29; *Fontana Economic History of Europe*, ed. C. M. Cipolla (Glasgow, 1974), 42. When Edinburgh was divided into parishes in 1592, it was recorded that the burgh contained 2,239 households with 8,000 persons 'counted to discretion'; City of Edinburgh District Archives [ECA], Moses bundle 195, no. 7029. I am grateful to Dr Walter Makey, then City of Edinburgh District Archivist, for drawing this source to my attention.

Even so, a supplication to the papacy in 1438 noted that Edinburgh was 'the most populous of all' the towns of Scotland; in 1444 it was said that many magnates and nobles attending parliament in Edinburgh were entertained at the hospital of St Anthony near Leith, 'the common port of the kingdom', frequented by many foreign sailors; and in 1468 the town council claimed that Edinburgh was 'among the most populous, famous and splendid towns of the realm' where 'a great multitude of people' resorted and where the king and many prelates were accustomed to reside.[8] The tendency for kings to prefer Edinburgh to Perth or Stirling as their usual place of residence, so marked under James II and James III, had all the semblance of an established tradition by the reigns of James IV and James V.

When not on circuit, James II (who was born, crowned, married and buried in Holyrood) made Edinburgh his chief place of residence and therefore the seat of administration. Consequently, under James, the estates in parliament or general council met more frequently in Edinburgh than in either Stirling or Perth;[9] and in the reigns of his three immediate successors Edinburgh all but invariably became the venue for parliament, and it also became the usual meeting place for the exchequer.[10] In the administration of civil justice, too, James III, who acknowledged Edinburgh in 1482 as the 'principal burgh of our kingdom',[11] encouraged litigants to secure redress at the centre where Lords of Council meeting normally in Edinburgh took over the work of the 'session', designed by James I to help to relieve the burden of judicial cases on parliament and council. Thereafter 'Lords of Council and Session' were accustomed to meet in Edinburgh and the idea of a central civil court firmly took root. Yet the creation of a full-time salaried judicial bench looked like being achieved only by the 1530s when James V announced his proposal to endow the Court of Session by establishing a College of Justice, financed from ecclesiastical resources and composed of seven churchmen, seven laymen and a president who was an ecclesiastic, but even here James' scheme scarcely concealed his underlying intention of securing for the crown additional revenue from

[8] Vatican Archives, Register of Supplications, 348, fo. 28v; 394, fos. 184v, 231; 621, fo. 229.

[9] Acts of the Parliaments of Scotland [APS], edd. T. Thomson and C. Innes, 12 vols. (Edinburgh, 1814–75), ii, 6–32.

[10] The Exchequer Rolls of Scotland, edd. J. Stuart, et al., 23 vols. (Edinburgh, 1878–1908), ix, 1, 63, 92, 144, 163, 197, 209.

[11] Charters and other documents relating to the City of Edinburgh, A.D. 1143–1540, ed. J. D. Marwick (Edinburgh, 1871), 162.

clerical taxation.[12]

The emergence of a secular legal profession centred at the higher levels on Edinburgh may be said to date from the early sixteenth century. It was then, too, that a printing press was introduced to Edinburgh when Walter Chepman and Andrew Myllar, who had gained experience in printing at Rouen, obtained by royal licence in 1507 a monopoly to print 'the buikis of our lawis, actis of parliament, cronicles, mess bukis' and all other necessary works.[13] The emphasis on printing legal texts was consistent with the act of 1496 designed to foster an 'understanding of the lawis' so that local justice could be strengthened by providing the sons of substantial landholders with a legal training in 'sculis of art and jure'.[14] Much work of a legal nature, however, was undertaken not by the secular courts but by the church courts where the ecclesiastical judge, trained in canon law and frequently in both laws (canon and civil), could claim, certainly before 1532, to possess a greater professional expertise than the hitherto unpaid and somewhat amateurish group of 'Lords of Council and Session' appointed to give judgment in civil actions. The extensive ecclesiastical jurisdiction – in actions relating to morals, slander, marriage, separation and legitimacy, questions of dowry, benefices and their revenues, the failure to fulfil contracts, the confirmation of testaments and the administration of the moveable goods of persons dying intestate – plainly included categories which could be recognised to fall properly within the competence of the secular courts. Such cases, however, were heard in the episcopal courts by the officials and commissaries who exercised the judicial duties delegated to them by the bishops. The archdiocese of St Andrews, to which Edinburgh belonged, was divided into two officialates with the court of the official principal or general in St Andrews itself and that of the subordinate official *foraneus* for Lothian in Edinburgh. The oversight of notaries public appointed by papal authority also pertained to the official's court, and as notaries performed much of the work of solicitors (notably in conveyancing, the transfer of lands and houses, in drawing up instruments of sasine necessary for the completion of titles, and in authenticating contracts and deeds) the church courts, either directly or

[12] A. A. M. Duncan, 'The central courts before 1532', in *An Introduction to Scottish Legal History*, ed. G. C. H. Paton (Edinburgh, 1958), 321–40; R. K. Hannay, *The College of Justice* (Edinburgh, 1933), *passim*.

[13] *Register of the Privy Seal of Scotland* [*RSS*], edd. M. Livingstone *et al.*, 8 vols. (Edinburgh, 1908–82), i, no. 1546; *Essays on the Scottish Reformation, 1513–1625*, ed. D. McRoberts (Glasgow, 1962), 275, 317–18.

[14] *APS*, ii, 238.

indirectly, had an interest in many branches of the law which were not primarily, or even strictly, ecclesiastical.[15]

As a centre for ecclesiastical law, however, Edinburgh was overshadowed by St Andrews, where Archbishop Hamilton as papal legate established what has been termed a 'little Vatican', and as the primatial and metropolitan seat St Andrews remained the ecclesiastical capital 'the cheif and mother citie of the Realme'[16] – until the Reformation in 1560, when its former pre-eminence was allowed to lapse, for a spell at least. Even so, Edinburgh's importance in St Andrews diocese was recognised not only as being a seat for the official's court but also as an appropriate meeting place for provincial synods and diocesan synods, the church's legislative councils as distinct from its judicial courts. In the years immediately preceding the Reformation, the three reforming provincial councils of 1549, 1552 and 1559, over which Archbishop Hamilton presided, were all held, significantly enough, in Edinburgh and not in the archbishop's own headquarters of St Andrews.[17] Besides, Edinburgh could boast a variety of ecclesiastical institutions which few towns could match. The burgh itself possessed no monastery, though the adjacent Canongate had its house of Augustinian canons, not cloistered monks but active preachers, at Holyrood Abbey; but, in any event, changing fashions had led to a greater emphasis, first, in the thirteenth and fourteenth centuries, in favour of the friars, who, again, were active as preachers, theologians and evangelists in the towns, and who were represented in Edinburgh in the houses of the Carmelite, Dominican and Franciscan orders; and secondly, in favour of the foundation, in the fifteenth and early sixteenth centuries, of collegiate kirks, secular colleges, such as St Giles, the parish church raised to collegiate status, or Trinity College and Kirk o' Field (the future site of the university), served by a college or group of priests who said mass and offered prayers for the souls of the founder and his family, and quite distinct from the communities of the religious orders. A late religious foundation, however, was the nunnery of the Sciennes, the nuns of St Catherine of Siena, a Dominican house established in 1517, the year of Luther's revolt, whose exceptional reputation among nunneries – commended by

---

[15] *An Introductory Survey of the Sources and Literature of Scots Law*, ed. H. McKechnie (Edinburgh, 1936), 133–53; *An Introduction to Scottish Legal History*, 363–73; D. Murray, *Legal Practice in Ayr and the West of Scotland in the 15th and 16th Centuries* (Glasgow, 1910), 7–21.

[16] *Scotland before 1700*, 137.

[17] *Statutes of the Scottish Church, 1225–1559*, ed. D. Patrick (Edinburgh, 1907), 84, 135, 149, 261, 281.

Bishop Leslie as 'that pure and cleine clostir' – was maintained up till the Reformation.[18] Apart from its parish church of St Giles, Edinburgh had numerous churches and chapels attached to hospital foundations and to the religious houses, such as Greyfriars, while at the foot of castle rock outside the burgh lay St Cuthbert's, annexed to Holyrood Abbey.

The care of the poor was also the church's concern, and Edinburgh, with so relatively large a population, had its share of hospitals: the hospitals of St Leonard, St Mary and St Paul, St Mary Magdalene in the Cowgate, the almshouse of St Mary for poor women, the hospitals attached to the collegiate kirks of St Giles, St Mary in the Fields (Kirk o' Field) and Trinity College, the last founded by James II's widow for thirteen poor people; besides these were the leperhouse at the north port near Trinity College and the maison dieu of St Thomas Martyr in the Watergate within the burgh of Canongate; and in the port of Leith were to be found the Hospital of St Anthony, where foreign sailors were said to lodge,[19] and the more recent foundation in 1555 of Holy Trinity as a hospital for seamen by the shipmasters and mariners of Leith.[20] Yet, despite the church's work, Dunbar observed at the turn of the sixteenth century (before the burgh had its full complement of hospitals) that:[21]

'Your Burgh of beggaris is ane nest,
To schout thai swenyouris will nocht rest;
All honest folk they do molest,
Sa piteouslie thai cry and rame:
    Think ye nocht schame,
That for the poor hes no thing drest,
In hurt and sclander of your Name?

Your proffeitt daylie dois incress,
Your godlie workis less and less;
Through streittis nane may mak progress,
For cry of cruikit, blind, and lame:
    Think ye nocht schame,
That ye sic substance dois possess,
And will nocht win ane bettir Name?'

Such an array of ecclesiastical establishments befitted a large and prosperous burgh which, in economic terms, was assessed for taxation at a far higher level than that of its nearest competitors – Dundee, Aberdeen and Perth: indeed, by the mid-

[18] *Scotland before 1700*, 126.
[19] Vatican Archives, Reg. Supp., 349, fo. 231.
[20] *Medieval Religious Houses, Scotland*, edd. I. B. Cowan and D. E. Easson (London, 1976), 175–8, 184–5.
[21] *Scotland before 1700*, 111.

sixteenth century, its assessment came close to equalling the combined contributions from these three rival burghs.[22] Much of the burden incurred by taxation was borne by the merchant community, sustained largely by Edinburgh's increasingly dominant position, recognised by 1526 as one of the 'principale townis of merchandice' and by 1600 as 'by far the busiest commercial town in the country', with its overseas trading outlets through Leith, reckoned by Major to be 'the most populous seaport of Scotland'.[23] As a consequence, Edinburgh became the natural meeting place for the Convention of Royal Burghs, which regulated economic affairs; and by 1578 parliament accorded Edinburgh the privilege of sending two commissioners, instead of one, to the Convention.[24] All in all, Edinburgh's economic pre-eminence among the burghs could scarcely be contested.

Economic activity whetted, rather than diminished, an appetite for learning; the provision of schooling, not just for aspiring clerics but for the sons of merchants, craftsmen and neighbouring lairds, as well as for a small but growing professional circle of lawyers, was a prized achievement; and although it lacked a university, Edinburgh was not ill-equipped with schools. Teaching at almost every level was still very much the preserve of the church whose responsibility extended to supervising education, for the schools and colleges, in origin at least, formed an integral part of a complex ecclesiastical structure. The universities, which all had bishops as their chancellors, were largely staffed by clerics; and the schools, initially attached to a larger ecclesiastical foundation, such as a cathedral, monastery, collegiate church or even a university college, were subject to similar influences. The master of the song school was usually a chaplain, and it was by no means unknown for teachers in the grammar schools, even where the burgh had acquired control, also to hold office in the church, perhaps as a stipendiary chaplain, sometimes even as a vicar. David Vocat, master of Edinburgh grammar school in 1519, had associations with Holyrood, whose abbot possessed the right of presenting to the mastership of Edinburgh grammar school; his successor Henry Henryson, Vocat's 'freind and discipill' formerly master of Canongate grammar school, was obliged at 'hie solempne festuale tymes' to attend divine service in the abbey 'at hie mess and evinsang with his surples apon him'; but by 1534 Henryson was convicted of heresy and stood

[22] *Records of the Convention of the Royal Burghs of Scotland . . . 1295–1597*, ed. J. D. Marwick (Edinburgh, 1866), 47–8, 514–15, 518–19, 526, 530.
[23] *APS*, ii, 305; *Early Travellers in Scotland*, 93; *Scotland before 1700*, 42.
[24] *APS*, iii, 102.

condemned along with James Hamilton of Kincavill.[25] Even so,
by 1531, Edinburgh had succeeded in attracting as grammar
schoolmaster Adam Mure from Glasgow diocese, who had just
returned from Paris where John Douglas, the future provost of
St Mary's College in St Andrews, had sponsored him for his
degree in 1530.[26] Yet Mure, who agreed 'to mak the bairnys
perfyte grammariarris within three yeris', was only assigned a
stipend by the town council 'quhill he be provydit to ane
benefice'.[27] He had earlier held the united vicarages of Gartly and
Drumdelgie, but then had resigned them in 1531 to enable
Robert Reid, the future bishop of Orkney and benefactor of
Edinburgh University, to exchange them, when abbot of
Kinloss, for the commend of Beauly.[28] Mure's tenure of these
northern vicarages is, however, a reminder of his associations
with the north-east. Before his Paris days, he had studied at
King's College, Aberdeen, then the foremost centre of humanism
in Scotland, where he would have been familiar with the new
teaching methods pioneered by John Vaus, the grammarian,
which he may have adopted in Edinburgh.[29] But his stay, in any
event, was short-lived; and by 1539 he had found alternative
employment as pedagogue to Cardinal Beaton's nephews, who
were studying at Crail grammar school.[30]

The links with the ecclesiastical structure of benefices were no
less evident in the case of the master of the song school,
responsible for training choristers and for teaching the 'grace
buke prymar and plane donatt'.[31] The incumbent master of
Edinburgh's song school in 1553 was Edward Henryson, a
chaplain and prebendary of St Giles, who in accordance with the
foundation was required 'to furneis walx to the hie altar and lamp
as he aucht to do and nocht to procur with the Lady bred in the
kirk be him self'.[32] Even after the Reformation, Henryson

[25] Register of the Great Seal of Scotland [RMS], edd. J. B. Paul et al., 11 vols.
(Edinburgh, 1882–1914), ii, no. 918; A Diurnal of Remarkable Occurrents, ed.
T. Thomson (Edinburgh, 1833), 19; RMS, iii, no. 2179. Henryson may have been
the student of that name who studied at Aberdeen about 1512: Rentale
Dunkeldense, ed. R. K. Hannay (Edinburgh, 1915), 226. He appears to have been
a married clerk.
[26] W. A. McNeill, 'Scottish entries in the Acta Rectoria Universitatis Parisiensis
1519 to c. 1633', Scottish Historical Review [SHR], xliii (1964), 66–86, at 79.
[27] Extracts from Edinburgh Burgh Records, ii, 48, 85.
[28] L. N. Nowosilski, 'Robert Reid and his time', Th. (Rome, 1965), 265–6.
[29] J. Durkan and W. S. Watt, 'Adam Mure's Laudes Gulielmi Elphinstoni',
Humanistica Lovaniensia, xxviii (1979), 199–233.
[30] Rentale Sancti Andree, ed. R. K. Hannay (Edinburgh, 1913), 95, 107, 121,
140, 199.
[31] Extracts from Edinburgh Burgh Records, i, 194.
[32] Ibid., ii, 185–6, 223–4.

retained his chaplainries, conformed to the new regime, became precentor of the psalms in St Giles, as well as master of work,[33] and the report that he was still a 'papist' in 1570, the accuracy of which may be doubted, is hard to reconcile with his duties in the reformed church, which he continued to perform till his death in 1579.[34]

The existence of a variety of schools helped to foster the growth of a more literate society in the burgh and surrounding countryside. The curriculum in the elementary schools offered at least a training in reading, writing and arithmetic, subjects useful to merchants and craftsmen alike; even the song school taught the alphabet and rudiments of Latin grammar; and at a higher level grammar-school pupils were able to acquire a knowledge of rhetoric, logic and the languages of classical antiquity, especially Latin, a pre-requisite for university entrance and a passport to the world of learning, and so to a career in the church, law, medicine or even politics. Yet in pursuit of a university training, students were forced to leave Edinburgh, usually for St Andrews or Glasgow, and often for a university abroad to complete their professional training.

Episcopal patronage which facilitated the proliferation of university colleges in fifteenth-century Europe had left Edinburgh untouched. No archbishop of St Andrews was prepared to champion within the same diocese a rival college in Edinburgh; and by the sixteenth century successive archbishops had sought to enhance the status and prestige of the colleges in their primatial city, not least by securing the foundation of St Mary's as a new college for training candidates to the priesthood. But if the archbishops were preoccupied with advancing higher studies in St Andrews, the needs of the capital were not neglected by another episcopal patron, Robert Reid, bishop of the little northern diocese of Orkney, who finally set aside the necessary finance in 1558 for founding in Edinburgh a college devoted primarily to the study of law, so important a component in the equipment of aspiring churchmen at a time when law, and not theology, was a recognised avenue to promotion in the church. Reid's own advancement had been rapid: on graduating in Arts from St Andrews in 1515, where his uncle Robert Shanwell, vicar of Kirkcaldy and commissary of St Andrews, had been dean of the Faculty of Arts, Reid acted as a notary public in Moray and

[33] Ibid., iii, 147; iv, 60.
[34] *Calendar of the State Papers relating to Scotland and Mary, Queen of Scots* [*CSP Scot.*], edd. J. Bain *et al.*, 13 vols. (Edinburgh, 1898–1969), iii, no. 601; ECA, MS. Edinburgh Town Council Records, v, fo. 180v, 27 Nov. 1579.

as procurator in the Fife courts; he then became subdean and official of Moray, acquired the vicarage of Kirkcaldy and several other parochial benefices before his promotion to the abbacy of Kinloss, the commendatorship of Beauly and, finally, to the bishopric of Orkney by 1541.[35]

His interest in Renaissance scholarship was sustained through his association with the Piedmontese scholar Giovanni Ferrerio whom Reid, on returning from Rome, had first met in Paris in 1528 through an introduction by Robert Richardson, a canon regular of Cambuskenneth. Through Reid's patronage, Ferrerio left his university studies in Paris (where he had become acquainted with Hector Boece, George Buchanan and William Gordon, later bishop of Aberdeen), attended the court of James V in Edinburgh and, finally, settled at Kinloss, where he lectured for several years to the monks on philosophy, classical literature and a little theology – on Aristotle and Cicero, on Sacrobosco's sphere and the *Sententiarum* of Peter Lombard – but he incorporated, too, the humanist scholarship of Jacques Lefèvre, Rudolph Agricola, Erasmus and Melanchthon, though there was no word of Hebrew, and understandably the Greek authors were taught from Latin translations and not from the original Greek text.[36]

Reid's own belief in the twin Renaissance ideals of ecclesiastical renewal and educational progress was also applied in his own diocese of Orkney. There Reid's new constitution for the cathedral chapter in 1544 required the provost, who was to be a Doctor or at least a Bachelor of Divinity, to preach in the vernacular in the cathedral four times a year; the archdeacon, who like the treasurer had to be at least a Master of Arts, had to preach in the vernacular four times a year; the chancellor, preferably a Doctor of both laws or at least a Bachelor of Canon Law trained in a 'flourishing university' was to be judge, as the bishop's delegate, in the ecclesiastical courts, and to lecture publicly on canon law each week to the chapter; the chaplain of St Peter, as a Master of Arts and an expert in grammar, was to be master of the grammar school; and the chaplain of St Augustine, as one skilled in both chants, was placed in charge of the song school. Such an ambitious programme, however, was to be financed only by the diversion of further revenues from the

[35] 'Robert Reid and his time', 259ff.
[36] Ibid., 267; *Records of the Monastery of Kinloss*, ed. J. Stuart (Edinburgh, 1872), 53–5; J. Durkan, 'Giovanni Ferrerio, Humanist: his influence in sixteenth-century Scotland', *Religion and Humanism*, ed. K. Robbins (Oxford, 1981), 181–94.

parishes, revenues which might have been devoted more profitably to the service of the parish ministry.[37] Reid's insistence that a legal training should be sought only at a 'flourishing university' rather suggests that some universities had a less than flourishing tradition in legal teaching. Certainly, Glasgow had ceased to teach law by the early sixteenth century; Aberdeen and St Andrews, at best, each possessed a civilist and a canonist, though in the former both lawyers were found to be absent during a visitation of King's College in 1549, and in the latter the delayed appointment in 1556 of William Skene, 'licentiate in both laws' as canonist at St Mary's College was possibly prompted by the rival lectureships in law initiated in Edinburgh by the crown in 1556. In any event, the limited legal training provided by the Scottish universities was clearly no substitute for the specialised teaching offered in continental centres; and there was substance in the criticism advanced by the Edinburgh advocates in the 1590s that 'the erectioun of ane man onlie in quhatsoevir sort or professioun can import na commoditie mekill less in the professioun of the law, the studie quharof is sa great and infinite that without plouralieter of techeris emulacioun als weill of professouris as auditouris contenuall disputacionis and utheris scholastik exerceissis na fruit can fallow'.[38]

Even where legal instruction was provided, the emphasis all along, until the Reformation, had been on training canonists – men, skilled in the vast corpus of canon law, who would take their place in the ecclesiastical courts as judges and as procurators. Besides, what still remained the essentially clerical nature of the universities meant that there was comparatively little provision either for lay teachers or for training laymen in civil law – men who would pursue careers as civilists in the secular courts. The clergy, after all, were primarily interested in canon, not civil, law. It is true that hitherto the relative dearth of lay legal practitioners had been largely offset by a multitude of ecclesiastical lawyers and notaries public appointed by papal authority; but by the sixteenth century there was increasingly a need for lay judges,

[37] *RMS*, iii, no. 3102; 'Robert Reid and his time', 513–21.

[38] J. Durkan and J. Kirk, *The University of Glasgow, 1451–1577* (Glasgow, 1977), 129–33; *Fasti Aberdonenses*, ed. C. Innes (Aberdeen, 1854), 259; *Early Records of the University of St Andrews, 1413–1579*, ed. J. M. Anderson (Edinburgh, 1926), 264. After the Reformation, it was envisaged that Skene should undertake teaching in theology, but he continued to teach and practise law as a commissary to St Andrews: Scottish Record Office [SRO], PA10/1, Papers relating to the Visitation of St Andrews University (unfoliated). *The Autobiography and Diary of Mr James Melvill*, ed. R. Pitcairn (Edinburgh, 1842), 26, 28–9; W. C. Dickinson, 'The Advocates' protest against the institution of a Chair of Law in the University of Edinburgh', *SHR*, xxiii (1926), 205–12, at 209.

men who were not ecclesiastics and who possessed a training in civil law. As it was, almost half the places on the bench of the College of Justice were reserved for lay judges, and at the bar there was further scope for civilists to act as advocates or procurators in the central court for civil justice.[39] The regular meetings in Edinburgh of the Court of Session, parliament, privy council and exchequer, not to mention the official's court and justiciary, sheriff and burgh courts, all strengthened the claims of the capital to become a centre for legal training and not just for legal practice.

As a senator, and then as president, of the College of Justice, Bishop Reid was well aware of the practical difficulties within the existing structure in providing a thorough legal training for laymen. Not every student intent on pursuing a legal career in civil law had the means or inclination to embark on a further period of study at the great legal schools of Orléans, Bourges, Paris, Poitiers or Louvain. The only alternative lay in serving an apprenticeship thereby enabling students to observe the practitioners at work in the courts.[40] But in seeking to establish in Edinburgh a college of Arts and Law, Reid offered a fresh solution to the problem of providing a legal education for laymen. His plan was to erect three schools within one college: the first a grammar school for 'bairnis', similar to the schools attached to university colleges; then, an Arts school 'for thame that leirnis poetre and oratore'; and, thirdly, a Law school 'for the techeing of the civile and canon lawis'; with chambers for the regents, a hall and other necessary accommodation.[41]

Reid's college looked rather as if it would be freed from the conventional university structure with all its clerical emphasis, and while canon law was by no means neglected, civil law was accorded a greater prominence. His proposed Arts course on rhetoric and poetry was aimed at providing a moral training for aspiring scholars who might then proceed to a study of the law; the emphasis was evidently on expounding the value of the literary text, grammar being reduced to due proportions; and Reid notably refrained from adopting the philosophy-based curriculum of the existing university Arts courses. At the same time, the intended foundation of a new grammar school as part of Reid's college posed a possible threat to the existing

[39] *College of Justice*, 63; G. Donaldson, 'The Legal Profession in Scottish Society in the Sixteenth and Seventeenth Centuries', *Juridical Review*, new ser., xxi (1976), 1–19.

[40] See below, 31–2, 38, 58.

[41] *Register of the Privy Council of Scotland* [*RPC*], edd. J. H. Burton *et al.*, 1st ser. 14 vols. (Edinburgh, 1877–98), ii, 528–9; iii, 472–4.

grammar school, whose patronage belonged to the Abbot of Holyroodhouse; and it is curious that an advocate should appear as teacher in the established grammar school during the winter of 1559–60, at a point when Reid's plans were intended to have effect. The teacher was Alexander Mauchane, a lawyer of some distinction, who had been admitted advocate by the Lords of Council in 1554.[42] Such an appointment to the grammar school may of course reflect no more than the dislocation caused by the Reformation. William Robertoun, the grammar master appointed in January 1546/7, was described in 1562, as 'ane obstinat papeist', and he seems to have deemed it prudent to depart for a spell 'with his bukis and utheris his guddis be the space of twa yeris' during the upheaval of the Reformation.[43] Nonetheless, it might just emerge that John Letham, on record as teacher in the grammar school in 1556, was none other than John Letham, the advocate.[44] Were this so, then it would almost seem as if a deliberate effort was made to attract teachers who were also lawyers, perhaps in a bid to undermine Reid's project. Even after the Reformation, the tendency to appoint masters who had also an interest in law was apparent, first, in the attempts to secure the services in 1563 of James White, 'Scottisman in Londone', a Paris scholar, and 'ane man of excellent lernyng bayth in Lating and Greik toung', who as well as running his school in England was also qualified as a notary public;[45] then, in the appointment by 1568 of Thomas Buchanan (nephew of George) who later appeared on record as an advocate, as well as Keeper of the Privy Seal;[46] and thirdly, in the election in 1584 of Hercules Rollock (kinsman of the university's principal) who had earlier practised as commissary and notary public.[47]

[42] *Extracts from Edinburgh Burgh Records*, iii, 98; SRO, CS1/1, Books of Sederunt of the Court of Session, fo. 30v.
[43] *Extracts from Edinburgh Burgh Records*, iii, 131–3, 141–2.
[44] Ibid., ii, 255; cf., SRO, RH2/1/9, where Lethame was on the bench in 1542. The identification is at best tentative.
[45] *Extracts from Edinburgh Burgh Records*, iii, 157, 209. When studying at the University of Paris, James Quhyte, 'notary public of the realm of Scotland' and domestic servant of James Stewart, commendator of Kelso and Melrose, was received by the curé of St Nicolas du Chardonnet in Paris: *Histoire générale du Paris: Recueil des actes notariés relatifs à l'histoire de Paris et ses environs au XVIe siècle*, ed. E. Coyecque (Paris, 1905), ii, no.6088. I am grateful to Dr John Durkan for this reference.
[46] *Extracts from Edinburgh Burgh Records*, iii, 250–2, 259; iv, 559–60; RPC, vi, no.589; SRO, GD122, Craigmillar Writs, Liberton Papers and Correspondence, no.2.
[47] *Extracts from Edinburgh Burgh Records*, iv, 340, 346–7; SRO, CS1/3/1, Books of Sederunt of the Court of Session, fo. 128r.

Apart from his projected grammar school, Reid's college did not seriously conflict or compete directly with existing Arts teaching elsewhere. All this, perhaps designedly so, lessened the prospect of any intervention by the Archbishop of St Andrews as chancellor of his own university. In any case, Bishop Reid, who had taken part in numerous diplomatic missions, plainly enjoyed the patronage of the queen-regent, Mary of Lorraine, who had already sought to encourage the teaching of legal and classical studies in the capital by establishing royal lecturers in law and Greek. The model for this experiment was evidently borrowed from France where Francis I had appointed royal professors to lecture in his Trilingual College established in 1530. The *Collège royal*, or *Collège de France*, so conceived, originally possessed no buildings of its own and consisted of professors, drawn from colleges in the University of Paris, who gave formal, public lectures on Greek, Hebrew, law, medicine and mathematics, and whose salaries were paid by the crown and not by fees from students. It was there, too, that the educational reformer, Peter Ramus, principal of the *Collège des Presles*, was currently lecturing as a royal professor, through the influence and patronage of Charles, Cardinal of Lorraine, the brother of the queen-regent in Scotland who more modestly appointed the advocate Alexander Sym in February 1555/6 as 'hir lectoure and reidar in the lawis or ony uthiris sciences at oure burgh of Edinburgh or quhair he salbe requirit', with an annual stipend of £100.[48] Sym had been admitted by the Lords of Council to practise as an advocate in the central civil court in the preceding November;[49] and the expectation was now that Sym's public lectures on the laws, to be held in the Magdalen Chapel, would 'gife all utheris young men of fresche and queik ingynis occasioun to apply thair hale myndis to studie for like reward'.[50] The intention was plainly to appoint further royal lecturers in Edinburgh, and Reid himself must have lent the project his support, for the next royal appointment, it seems, was that of Reid's own candidate, Edward Henryson, Doctor of Civil Law, who had studied and taught at Bourges.[51] Henryson was also acquainted with Henry Sinclair, then dean of Glasgow and a

[48] A. Lefranc, *Histoire du Collège de France* (Paris, 1893), 101ff; F. P. Graves, *Peter Ramus and the Educational Reformation of the Sixteenth Century* (New York, 1912), 48ff; J. J. Guillemin, *Le Cardinal de Lorraine* (Paris, 1847), 445–68; *RSS*, iv, no.3144.

[49] SRO, CS6/29, Acta Dominorum Concilii et Sessionis, fo. 4v, 13 Nov. 1555.

[50] *RSS*, iv, no. 3144; *Extracts from Edinburgh Burgh Records*, ii, 251, 319.

[51] *RSS*, iv, no.3268; T. Dempster, *Historia Ecclesiastica Gentis Scotorum*, ed. D. Irving, 2 vols. (Edinburgh, 1829), ii, 349–50.

senator of the College of Justice, and was said by his son to have received Sinclair's patronage in 1552 when he planned a Latin translation of the *Enchiridion* of Epictetus by Arrianus, which failed to materialise owing to printing difficulties, the appearance of other editions by Schegk and Wolf, and finally the death of his patron in 1565.[52]

It was probably as the friend of Henry Scrimgeour, who had studied at Paris and Bourges before professing civil law at Geneva, that Henryson had acted as a Greek tutor to Ulrich Fugger when studying at Bourges.[53] His reputation abroad had led to competition for his services at home from Archbishop Hamilton and from Bishop Reid. As early as December 1553, efforts had been made to attract Henryson, along with John Rutherford from Paris, to Hamilton's College of St Mary in St Andrews; Rutherford finally came, but Henryson, commended to Reid by Ferrerio as a Greek and Latin scholar, preferred to practise as an advocate in Edinburgh, and to accept an appointment in June 1556 as royal lecturer in the capital, there to 'profess teiche and reid' for three years 'ane publict lessoun in the Lawis and ane uthir in Greik' three times a week for a stipend of £100.[54] The creation of royal lectureships in 1556 was certainly modest in scale, but even the Trilingual College at Louvain began in 1517 with no buildings of its own and with only three lectors or professors, and much the same was true for the *Collège royal* in Paris, which initially after its foundation in 1530 had merely lecturers in Greek, Hebrew and mathematics.[55]

In the absence of Inns of Court on the English model, the intention was to provide advanced legal instruction through a course of public lectures for aspiring advocates. Indeed, Henryson's series of lectures on Greek and law was to cease during the 'vacance fra Lammes to Martymes' which largely coincided with the recess of the Court of Session.[56] Nor was it purely coincidence that the public lectures should be followed by an increase in the admission of advocates to practise before the

[52] Edinburgh University Library [EUL], N.15/1.84. This copy of Epictetus' *Enchiridion* by Arrianus (1535) contains a prefatory manuscript note by Henryson's son, Thomas.

[53] J. Durkan, 'Henry Scrimgeour, Renaissance Bookman', *Transactions of the Edinburgh Bibliographical Society*, v, pt. 1 (1978), 1–32, at 2.

[54] EUL, MS. La.III.321, Collection of instruments by George Makeson, notary, 1554, fo. 188v, 12 Dec. 1553; *Papal Negotiations with Mary, Queen of Scots*, ed. J. H. Pollen (Edinburgh, 1901), 416; *RSS*, iv, no. 3268.

[55] H. de Vocht, *History of the Collegium Trilingue Lovaniense 1517–1550* (Louvain, 1951–55), i, 238ff, 250–1, 283ff, 360ff; *Histoire du Collège de France*, 101ff.

[56] *RSS*, iv, no. 3268.

Lords of Council: Alexander Skene in April 1557, John Dunbar in July, George Creichton in November, Adam Foules as a probationer to hear disputations so that 'he may be able to procur' in such actions 'as he may get to do', in January 1557/8, and Thomas Scott in December; all were graduates, probably with experience of continental universities.[57]

Reid's efforts, in turn, were intended to supplement and to embody in more permanent form the experiment in royal lectureships. The scheme for founding the college outlined in Reid's testament, made shortly before he died unexpectedly on a diplomatic mission to France in 1558, was to proceed with the counsel of three eminent lawyers – James McGill of Rankeillor-Nether, clerk register and senator of the College of Justice, Thomas Macalzean, an advocate and later provost of Edinburgh, and Abraham Creichton, provost of the collegiate kirk of Dunglass and senator of the College of Justice, who, as official of Lothian, was particularly well qualified to advise on the teaching of canon law.[58] Reid's bequest provided as endowment for the college 8,000 merks, half to be uplifted from a wadset on the lands of Strathnaver, and half from 'his awin proper guidis and geir'[59] for the purchase of a site from property belonging to the late Sir James Ramsay of Balmane in the southside of the Cowgate,[60] not far from the Magdalen Chapel where Sym's royal lectures on law had been held. Reid's instructions, however, were not immediately effected, partly as a consequence of the confusion arising from the Reformation crisis of 1559–60 and partly as a consequence of the disinclination of the executors, notably his nephew Walter Reid, abbot of Kinloss, to fulfil the terms of the will. The executors were named as John Reid of Aikenhead, Walter Reid, Sir Robert Carnegie of Kinnaird, Thomas Tulloch, William Forsyth, sub-prior of Kinloss, and John Anderson, a canon of Orkney; several died shortly after the Reformation; and it was not until 1593, five years after Walter Reid's own death and thirty-five years after Robert Reid had died that 2,500 merks from the bishop's legacy were finally recovered by the town from Walter Reid's estate.[61]

The impact of the Reformation on the church was clearly bound to affect both the development of the law and the future

---

[57] SRO, CS6/29, Acta Dominorum Concilii et Sessionis, fos.43v, 49r, 56v, 74v.
[58] *RPC*, ii, 528; iii, 472.
[59] Ibid., iii, 472.
[60] Ibid.; cf., SRO, B22/1/18, Protocol Book of Alexander King, 28 June 1555.
[61] SRO, CC8/2/1, Decreets of Edinburgh Commissary Court, fo.53r; ECA, MS. Edinburgh Town Council Records, vi, 8 June 1582; *Extracts from Edinburgh Burgh Records*, v, 90–1.

of education, two areas closely linked to the church; and all this, in turn, had implications for the burgh. For one thing, the Reformation limited the extent of ecclesiastical jurisdiction, thus checking the tendency for ecclesiastical lawyers to engross to themselves work which was purely civil in scope. The abrogation of papal jurisdiction by act of parliament in 1560 created a vacuum which was filled by several competitors – not least the Court of Session and Privy Council – of which the courts of the reformed church formed only one element. The reformers' distaste for clerical participation in affairs of state – for ministers holding public office – and their preference for separating the jurisdictions of church and state contained an obvious appeal to the laity in the elimination of clerical bureaucrats, so permitting added scope to laymen in royal service. The decline of canon law after 1560 marked a triumph for civil law, and likewise benefited the civilist, or secular practitioner, though the forensic skills of men formerly trained in canon law were still required in the commissary courts which were secularised as a consequence of reorganisation in 1564.[62]

As the seat of the central civil court, Edinburgh profited from the ascendancy of civil law over canon law, unlike St Andrews and Glasgow which lost their former episcopal status and prestige. With its own kirk session and superintendent's court for Lothian, the burgh was no longer dependent on St Andrews, as an ecclesiastical centre, which instead was reduced like Glasgow to a similar provincial status. Again, Edinburgh gained by becoming the usual meeting place for the earlier general assemblies of the reformed church, and ministers of the capital had special power to convene assemblies in emergencies. In education, too, the reformers' intention was to improve schooling by founding in Edinburgh and other main towns colleges of Arts on the model of the protestant academies on the continent, endowed with adequate finances, which, it was hoped, would be forthcoming from an ambitious programme to reorganise the chaotic state of ecclesiastical finances.[63]

These major developments affecting the church, law and education which Edinburgh witnessed by the middle of the sixteenth century were all mirrored in quite exceptional fashion in the career of Clement Little, the Edinburgh advocate and benefactor of the university library, who as a child of the Renaissance and Reformation was deeply affected by the

---

[62] *The Records of the Synod of Lothian and Tweeddale, 1589–1596, 1640–1649*, ed. J. Kirk (Edinburgh, 1977), i–viii.
[63] *The First Book of Discipline*, ed. J. K. Cameron (Edinburgh, 1972), 120, 131.

humanist reappraisal of religion and learning. During the Reformation struggle, he was converted to protestantism, became an elder of the kirk, showed a singular solicitude for the plight of the poor in the burgh and was active in the campaign to establish Edinburgh as a centre of higher education through the creation of a college of Arts organised on the humanist model of the continental academies.[64]

One of several sons of an Edinburgh burgess, Clement Little was christened after his father, who traded in such assorted merchandise as Scots cloth, wool, skins, felt hats, velvet bonnets, black velvet and reams of paper.[65] With his father's death by the early 1550s, his mother, Elizabeth Fisher, took over the family booth or shop in the burgh, and his brother, William, soon established himself as a prosperous merchant burgess, who stood for the council by 1567 and later rose to become lord provost of the burgh by 1591.[66] Clement Little was born about 1530 and received his education, it would seem, in the burgh's grammar school, which was only just recovering from the scandal of its former schoolmaster's conviction for heresy in 1534.[67] The training which he received in rhetoric, Latin grammar and classical literature equipped him to enter St Andrews University where he matriculated at St Leonard's College by December 1543, along with three others assigned to the Lothian 'nation', including Adam Heriot from East Lothian who entered the Augustinian house at St Andrews and later became minister in St Andrews and in Aberdeen.[68]

[64] *Extracts from Edinburgh Burgh Records*, iii, 256; iv, 105. See further below, 42–4, 48.

[65] SRO, GD122/3, Craigmillar Writs, Bundle I, no. 865; 'Inventory of goods of Clement Litill, burgess of Edinburgh', 10 July 1551. Clement Little, the advocate, had at least two brothers, Edward and William, who both became town councillors: in 1567, Edward Little was described as 'eldest sone of umquhile Clement Little, quha was maid burges and gyld brother the xix day of September be ressoun of his fatheris privelege', and 'William Littill, alsua sone to the said umquhill Clement . . . was maid burges and gild brother the xxvj day of September 1567, be the ressoun of the privilege of his said father . . .' (*Edinburgh Records, Dean of Guild's Accounts, 1552–1567*, ed. R. Adam (Edinburgh, 1899), 232).

[66] ECA, MS. Edinburgh Town Council Records, iv, 65, 19 June 1562; SRO, B22/1/15–18, Protocol Book of Alexander King, iii, 28 Jan. 1551; v, 26 Sept. 1555; SRO, B22/1/19 Protocol Book of John Guthrie, 17 Sept. 1558; *Extracts from Edinburgh Burgh Records*, iii, 247; v, 48. Clement Little senior left an estate of £726: SRO, GD122/3, no. 865. In 1641, the family house was described as a 'great lodging in the close called Clement Little's and then John Little's on the south side of the High Street below the weighhouse at present possessed by Sir Thomas Nicholson, advocate': ECA, MS. Moses' Bundle 22, no. 904.

[67] See above, 25.

[68] *Early Records of St Andrews University*, 250; *Register of the Minister, Elders and Deacons of the Christian Congregation of St Andrews* [RStAKS], ed. D. H. Fleming, 2 vols. (Edinburgh, 1889–90), i, 3 and n. 1.

Clement Little's student days at St Andrews coincided with a sudden change in the fortunes of Scottish protestantism following the death of James V and the ascendancy of the Earl of Arran who, as Governor, had briefly imprisoned Cardinal Beaton, had permitted an act of parliament in 1543 legalising the reading of the Bible in the vernacular, and as protector of Scottish protestantism had taken as his own chaplain a renegade friar, Thomas Gwilliam, from Inverness. As Clement Little left Edinburgh a crowd had burned the new English Bibles in protest at the Governor's pro-English protestant policies, but on his arrival in St Andrews to begin his studies the news from Dundee was rather different: there the crowd had taken to looting the friaries and destroying images. The stability of town and countryside seemed under threat.[69]

Although Arran's protestant policy proved short-lived, St Leonard's College was already noted for its heterodox opinions. Two of its former teachers, Alesius and John Fethie, had left for Lutheran centres abroad; so too had two of its students, the Wedderburn brothers, the probable authors of *The gude and godlie ballatis*; and by 1541 another teacher, David Guild, 'professor of the liberal arts, regent of St Leonard's College and bachelor of divinity' was suspected of venting unorthodox ideas on the Trinity at the quodlibet disputations on the feast of St Thomas the Apostle, which resulted in an investigation by the Faculty of Divinity in which John Major, as dean, and other members of the faculty accepted Guild's petition that he had not intended to depart from Catholic doctrine. Other regents in the college during Clement Little's period of study – John Shiel, David Garden, James Wilkie, John Lermonth and Thomas Fyffe – avoided controversy; but the times were not particularly conducive to sound scholarship.[70] The town, threatened by an English invasion, witnessed the martyrdom of the protestant preacher, George Wishart, in March 1546, and thereafter hostilites broke out when a band of protestants seized the castle and murdered the cardinal in revenge for Wishart's burning as a heretic.[71]

[69] *APS*, ii, 415; *The Works of John Knox*, ed. D. Laing, 6 vols. (Edinburgh, 1846–64), i, 95–105; *The Hamilton Papers*, ed. J. Bain, 2 vols. (Edinburgh, 1890–2), i, 477; ii, 15, 20–21; *The State Papers of Sir Ralph Sadler*, ed. A. Clifford (Edinburgh, 1809), i, 216; *Two Missions of Jacques de la Brosse*, ed. G. Dickinson (Edinburgh, 1942), 20.

[70] *Acta Facultatis Artium Universitatis Sanctiandree, 1413–1588*, ed. A. I. Dunlop, 2 vols. (Edinburgh, 1964), i, p. lx; ii, 316, 340, 346; St Andrews University Archives, MS. SS110.AE14; J. Herkless and R. K. Hannay, *The College of Saint Leonard* (Edinburgh, 1905), 220–3.

[71] Knox, *Works*, i, 149ff.

Despite the upheavals, efforts were nonetheless made during the 1540s to establish in St Andrews a trilingual college modelled on Louvain and Paris. As a teacher at the College of Montaigu in Paris, Archibald Hay had argued the case between 1538 and 1540 for introducing to St Andrews the teaching of Greek and Hebrew, and even of Chaldaic and Arabic if such were feasible, as well as a training in medicine and the laws, while in Arts Hay recommended the study of poetry, rhetoric and history. The humanist arguments advanced by Hay in his *Panegyricus* looked almost like being effected when Beaton appointed Hay, his cousin, to the provostry of St Mary's College in 1546. But with the death of the cardinal, who was the university's chancellor, followed by Hay's death within fifteen months of his appointment, the ambitious plans were not at once fulfilled and the university in a petition to the governor depicted its plight as 'sa desolate and destitute bayth of rederris, techarris, and auditours that it is neir perist and meretis nocht to be callit ane universitie'.[72]

Amidst this disruption and dislocation, it looks rather as if Clement Little left St Andrews without completing his course for the Master's degree. This was not altogether unusual: somewhat later James McGill, after matriculating in 1562, decided to leave St Andrews in 1565 on being incorporated as a Bachelor to pursue legal studies on the continent. No graduation records exist for 1546 and by 1547 only five of the fifteen students who matriculated at St Leonard's in 1543 are entered as 'intrant' Masters. Instead, Clement Little decided to abandon St Andrews, perhaps after the burning of Wishart in March, to pursue his studies overseas at Louvain, where he matriculated in July 1546 followed by William Harvey in August, who also became an advocate in later life. Unlike Harvey, however, who is described as 'Magister Guilhelmus Herwe, Scotus' in the Louvain register, Clement Little, having still to acquire the Master's insignia, simply styled himself 'Clemens Parvus, Scotus'.[73]

---

[72] *Ad reverendissimum in Christo patrem D. Iacobum Betoun . . . pro Collegii erectione, Archibaldi Hayi*, oratio (Paris, 1538), fos. 1–22v; A. Hay, *Ad illustriss . . . cardinalem D. Davidem Betonum . . . gratulatorius panegyricus* (Paris, 1540); R. G. Cant, *The University of St Andrews* (Edinburgh, 1970), 35–6.

[73] *Early Records of St Andrews University*, 269; 149, 159, 249–50; *CSP Scot.*, ii, no. 182; *Matricule de l'Université de Louvain*, ed. A. Schillings (Brussels, 1961), iv, 322, 326. The printed record gives the date of Little's matriculation as June but Dr John Durkan who examined the original MS. points out that the correct reading is July. Little probably studied at one of the legal colleges – St Yves, Saint Donatien or Winchel. Certainly, his name does not occur in the lists of promotions in Arts. I am grateful to M. Andrée Schufflaire, Archives Générales du Royaume, Brussels, for this information. The title of 'master' was probably assumed once Little's Arts training had been supplemented by legal studies.

His choice of Louvain is not difficult to explain. Unlike St Andrews, it was already a thriving centre of humanist studies where Rudolph Agricola had once studied and where Erasmus had lectured, with its famous Trilingual College founded by Busleyden in 1517, which acted as a model for Oxford's bilingual Corpus Christi, established in the same year, and for the *Collège royal* in Paris. More importantly for Clement Little, Louvain also possessed an established tradition in the laws, which evidently attracted both Little and Harvey to Brabant.

It is quite possible that John Annand, the Principal of St Leonard's, may have guided Clement Little in the direction of Louvain. Annand, it is true, was a theologian, not a canon lawyer, but he was also a 'disciple'[74] of Jean Standonck, the Dutch mystic who was influenced by the Brethren of the Common Life, and who not only recognised the College of Montaigu in Paris, on which St Leonard's was modelled, but had also established at Louvain the *domus pauperum* which emerged with the *paedagogium Porci* to form the *paedagogium Standonck* where a number of Scots had studied.[75] As well as the university's Faculty of Law, the Trilingual College, which had attracted François Baudouin as an aspiring law student, offered free public lectures on jurisprudence conducted by Gabriel van der Muyden, or Mudaeus, himself a product of the college, who concentrated on the exact text of the laws, eschewing all unprofitable commentaries. Clement Little was also likely to attend the *collegium baccalaureorum juris utriusque*, which had originated as a meeting of the law students in the university.[76] It was possibly during his studies there that he acquired copies, published at Lyons in 1520 and 1533 respectively, of Accoltis' *Commentarii de constitutionibus* and Socinus' *Super decretales*, two legal text-books.[77]

Despite Erasmian influences, Louvain remained staunchly orthodox in the religious quarrel; Luther stood condemned; and the writings of Erasmus increasingly came under the scrutiny of Louvain theologians distrustful of the effect which his philological studies had on the biblical text, and in Francis Titelmans, a Louvain Franciscan, they found a scholar ready to attack Erasmus on his own territory. In April 1528, Louvain had congratulated the Archbishop of St Andrews for executing Patrick Hamilton for heresy. Yet George Wishart had studied

---

[74] *Essays on the Scottish Reformation*, 195.

[75] *History of the Collegium Trilingue Lovaniense*, ii, 209–18, 418; iii, 264ff, 517ff.

[76] Ibid., ii, 418; iii, 517ff.

[77] J. Durkan and A. Ross, *Early Scottish Libraries* (Glasgow, 1961), 123.

there in 1529 and even later a protestant like Robert Bruce chose to pursue law at Louvain before finally entering the ministry in Edinburgh.[78]

Fortified with a knowledge of the laws, Clement Little returned home by 1550 ready to practise as a lawyer. His father's final illness may even have hastened his return. As a graduate, signing himself 'Mr. Clement Littill', he witnessed a document in April 1550 in favour of James Marjoribanks, a notary public and clerk of the official's court of St Andrews within the archdeaconry of Lothian; by September 1552 he was party to a transaction in favour of Abraham Creichton, official of Lothian; and it is more than a guess that he was already serving his legal apprenticeship in the official's court, though his presence recorded in the fragmentary extant register of the official's court in March 1552 was a party summoned to compear and not as a procurator for a client.[79]

The sheriff and burgh courts offered further scope. Promotion came rapidly: he was acting as sheriff by 1556, when the Lords of Council observed that a case had already been 'persewit of befoir Maisteris Robert Hereot, Alexander Sym, Robert Creichtoun, Thomas Kincragy and Clement Litill, sheriffis of the sherifdome of Edinbrucht'.[80] Between 1558 and 1560, he appeared as procurator for parties before the Admiralty Court,[81] and frequently served as 'prelocutour for the pannell' in the Court of Justiciary.[82] By 1557, he was already practising as an advocate entitled to plead before the Court of Session; and somewhat later, in 1557, he received a commission from the Regent Morton to become one of several 'advocat deputis etc., constitut in the kingis persewit be the said advocat aganis certane men of

---

[78] History of the Collegium Trilingue Lovaniense, ii, 80ff; iii, 144; Knox, Works, i, 512–14; Matricule de l'Université de Louvain, iv, 27: 'Georgius Wischert de Sancto Andrea in Scotia', 30 Aug. 1529; The Sermons of Robert Bruce, ed. W. Cunningham (Edinburgh, 1843), 5.

[79] SRO, B22/1/15, Protocol Book of Alexander King, 28 April 1550, 7 Sept. 1552; SRO, CH5/3/3, Liber Actorum Officialis S. Andree infra Laudoniam, fo. 281r, 27 Mar. 1552. For further entries, see SRO, B22/1/15–18, Protocol Book of Alexander King, 17 Sept. 1550, 3 April 1551, 28 Jan. 1551/2, 2 Aug., 6 Oct. 1552, 31 July 1553, 24 Jan. 1554/5, 26 Sept. 1555, 8 Aug. 1556, 4 Feb. 1556/7, 23 June 1557; SRO, B22/1/19 Protocol Book of John Guthrie, 17 Sept. 1558; Calendar of the Laing Charters, ed. J. Anderson (Edinburgh, 1899), no. 630.

[80] SRO, CS7/13, Register of Acts and Decreets of the Court of Session, fo. 197r, 27 March 1556.

[81] Acta Curiae Admirallatus Scotiae, ed. T. C. Wade (Edinburgh, 1937), 50, 66, 68–70, 121, 180–1.

[82] SRO, JC1/11, Justiciary Court Book (unfoliated), e.g. 6 June 1559, 8 Oct. 1560 (also 18 Feb. 1560/1 as prelocutor for accused).

Edinburgh and certane utheris'.[83] He formed part of a tightly-knit group of lawyers at work in the capital, a privileged circle of advocates, whose ranks included Alexander Sym, Thomas Macalzean, James MacCartney, John Moscrop and Richard Strang, and senators such as Bishop Robert Reid, president of the College of Justice, and his successor, Henry Sinclair, dean of Glasgow and later bishop of Ross.

It looks rather as if both Henry Sinclair and Abraham Creichton were influential in commending Little as an aspiring advocate to Bishop Reid as president. His admission as an advocate by the late 1550s was certainly more rapid than that of his colleague at Louvain, who – if this is indeed the same William Harvey – secured admission only in 1576 after having served as a notary, apparently in the west of Scotland.[84] Little's contacts with Bishop Reid and his family were evidently close: not only did he come to possess Reid's copy of Herold's *Orthodoxographa*, published at Basle in 1555, later donated to the university library,[85] but he was also appointed in 1561 as a curator for John Reid of Aikenhead (for whom the bishop had once been tutor) 'in absens of Walter, abbot of Kinlos now being in France'.[86] His associations with Henry Sinclair's circle are equally evident in his witnessing a charter ratified by Henry Sinclair in 1563, secondly, in his acting as executor, with William Sinclair of Roslin and James Balfour, dean of Glasgow, for the estate of Henry Sinclair, who died in 1565, and, thirdly, in his acquisition of a substantial part of Henry Sinclair's library.[87] No doubt, his contacts with Sinclair help to explain why another Sinclair, the Earl of Caithness, frequently chose Little as his procurator in the Court of Session and Privy Council.[88]

Clement Little acted in a variety of legal capacities for a number of substantial clients. In 1555, he received a commission from the crown for executing brieves of service in favour of Grant of Freuchie; he was procurator for the Earl of Crawford in

---

[83] SRO, CS7/14, Register of Acts and Decreets, fo.205, 22 March 1556/7; SRO, CS1/3/1, Books of Sederunt of the Court of Session, fo.39v, 29 March 1577.

[84] SRO, CS1/3/1, Books of Sederunt of the Court of Session, fos.31v, 40r, 14 Nov. 1576, 15 April 1577.

[85] EUL, Dd.3.24.

[86] SRO, CS1/1, Books of Sederunt of the Court of Session, fo.24v, 14 June 1561.

[87] *RMS*, v, no.201; SRO, RD1/8, Register of Deeds, fos.441v–442v, 29 Nov. 1566; *Early Scottish Libraries*, 49–60.

[88] SRO, CS6/29, Acta Dominorum Concilii et Sessionis, fo.86v, 14 June 1559; *RPC*, ii, 37, 437; SRO, RD1/17, Register of Deeds, fos.98r–99r; cf., *RMS*, iv, no.2783.

1559, for Kennedy of Bargany in 1561, for Lord Boyd in 1562, Melville of Raith in 1563, Lord Fleming in 1565 and for Lachlan McIntosh of Dunnachtoun, chief of Clan Chattan in 1568.[89] The barons of the Mearns employed him as their lawyer in 1569 when they banded together for defence against the Earl of Huntly; Maitland of Lethington made him his bailie for granting sasine in 1570; and during the 1570s he acted as advocate for Lord Seton, for Robert Stewart feuar of Orkney and Shetland, and for Alexander, commendator of Kilwinning, while his servitor, John Brown, witnessed a charter granted by Lord Oliphant to George Sinclair, son of the Earl of Caithness.[90] As a successful lawyer, Little lent money, as was customary,[91] acted as cautioner,[92] and invested some of his earnings in acquiring some land at Liberton, where Henry Sinclair and Edward Henryson also had property.[93] Through his wife, Elizabeth Fawside, an Edinburgh burgess's daughter, whom he contracted to marry in 1563, Clement Little also came to hold, in joint fee, part of the Burgh Muir.[94] As was to be expected from a man of his standing in the community, he contributed £60 in 1562 in response to the kirk session's appeal for donations to build a new poor's hospital in the burgh; he was placed fifth for assessment at £60 in a list of sixteen advocates in 1565; for the support of the ministry in 1573, he contributed £4, the third highest sum forthcoming from the advocates; in the following year, he lent the town council £20; and in 1576 his contribution to the ministry amounted to 10 merks, the top figure donated by any of the advocates.[95] With his death in April 1580, his goods were valued at just under £4,000, a figure comparable with that of Thomas Macalzean, a senator of the

[89] W. Fraser, *The Chiefs of Grant* (Edinburgh, 1883), iii, 117–18, no. 115; SRO, CS6/29, fo. 86v; *RPC*, ii, 166–7, 180; SRO, CS1/1, Books of Sederunt of the Court of Session, fo. 53r, 25 May 1562; W. Fraser, *The Melvilles* (Edinburgh, 1890), iii, 105, no. 91; cf. 108–9, no. 92; *The Mackintosh Muniments, 1442–1820*, ed. H. Paton (Edinburgh, 1903), 29, no. 90.

[90] W. Fraser, *The Douglas Book* (Edinburgh, 1885), iii, 265–6, no. 212; *RMS*, iv, no. 1927; *RPC*, ii, 424 (Seton); ii, 332, 341, 414, 518 (Stewart); iii, 11 (Kilwinning); SRO, GD96/140, May Papers, 1 April 1574 (Sinclair).

[91] SRO, GD122, Craigmillar Writs, Bundle III, nos. 911, 913.

[92] SRO, RD1/6, Register of Deeds, fo. 177.

[93] SRO, GD122, Craigmillar Writs, Additional Charters, cccxxi–cccxxxviii, cccxliii–cccxlv, ccclxv; *RMS*, iv, no. 2914.

[94] SRO, GD122, Craigmillar Writs, Bundle II, Marriage Contracts, no. 879; W. M. Bryce, 'The Burgh Muir of Edinburgh', *Book of the Old Edinburgh Club*, x (1918), 2–263, at 156; ECA, Edinburgh Town Council Records, iv, 18 Sept. 1566.

[95] M. Lynch, 'The "Faithful brethren" of Edinburgh: the acceptable face of Protestantism', *Bulletin of the Institute of Historical Research*, li, no. 124 (1978), 194–9, at 199; ECA, MS. Edinburgh Town Council Records, iv, fo. 274; SRO, GD122, Craigmillar Writs, Liberton Papers and Correspondence, nos. 2–3; SRO, CS7/66, Register of the Acts and Decreets, fos. 344v–347v.

College of Justice, who died in June 1581, leaving assets of less than £4,500; and it was considerably higher than that of his colleague Alexander Sym, who left less than £2,500 on his death in December 1584; but it plainly was still much lower than the estate of Edward Henryson who died in September 1585 leaving assets worth £6,700.[96] As a group, the advocates possessed material resources greater than many farmers and smaller lairds, and were matched only by the wealthier burgesses.

To a lawyer educated at the orthodox University of Louvain and familiar with the work of the ecclesiastical courts, the Reformation raised particular problems, especially so since it had taken the form of a rebellion effected in defiance of the crown. It swept aside the existing ecclesiastical structure, displaced canon law and overthrew the whole system of church courts, while a parliament, of irregular composition and of dubious legality, meeting in Edinburgh in August 1560 had abrogated papal authority in Scotland, had forbidden the celebration of mass and had approved a reformed Confession of Faith.[97] All this must have had an unsettling effect on Little as a lawyer, for his circle had included at least two prelates – Bishop Reid and Henry Sinclair, who were themselves lawyers.

The existence of heresy in the burgh can be traced back at least as far as the 1530s; and as a lawyer with a knowledge of the ecclesiastical courts, Clement Little might be expected to have been aware of the case history of the earlier heresy trials which had taken place during his boyhood in Edinburgh in 1534 and in 1539.[98] Protestant sympathisers, of course, did not seek to advertise their presence to the authorities; to do so merely invited forfeiture and death. Instead, the movement remained underground, confined to small cells of practising protestants, meeting by the mid-1550s in their 'privy kirks'. Consequently, their detection is far from easy; but even the emergence of organised protestantism by 1557, the names of more than two dozen protestants in Edinburgh reveal a remarkable cross-section of the population attracted to the reformed faith. Though they were numerically still small, their ranks included influential merchants trading with the Low Countries, some craftsmen (a goldsmith, a tailor, a saddler and a mason), a friar, a schoolmaster,

[96] SRO, GD122/3, Craigmillar Writs, Bundle I, Wills, no. 867; SRO, CC8/8/11, Register of Edinburgh Testaments, fos. 365v–367v (recorded 20 Feb. 1582/3); CC8/8/17, fos. 239v–345v (recorded 5 July 1587) [Syme]; CC8/8/21, fos. 334r–335v (recorded 24 July 1590) [Henryson].

[97] APS, ii, 534–5.

[98] Knox, Works, i, 56ff; Criminal Trials in Scotland . . . AD. 1488 to AD. 1624, ed. R. Pitcairn, 3 vols. (Edinburgh, 1829–33), i, 216ff.

two apothecaries, a doctor of medicine, and a small legal circle
consisting of two advocates, the wives of two common clerks of
the burgh, the brother-in-law of one clerk register and the wife
of another clerk register.[99] All this is suggestive of the degree to ·
which protestantism had infiltrated the structure of Edinburgh
society.

As the seat of the queen-regent's government and garrisoned
by French troops, Edinburgh was also a rallying point for the
forces of Catholicism, but whatever the growth of protestantism
in the capital, the three provincial councils meeting in Edinburgh
in 1549, 1552 and 1559 were unanimous in lamenting 'how many
heresies cruelly assail the Lord's flocks' at such a 'turbulent time
when Lutheranism, Calvinism and very many other nefarious
heresies are being propagated everywhere in this realm'.[100]
Protestantism, in fact, had become ineradicable. There are a few
indications of Clement Little's own reaction to the growth of
protestantism in the burgh, to Knox's preaching mission to
Edinburgh in 1556, the thefts of the image of St Francis from
St Giles, the arrival of the protestant Lords of the Congregation,
the riots, the attacks on the friaries, the jostling for position by
the two rival town councils of 1559, or the inflammatory
preaching of Knox and Willock in St Giles as mass was
celebrated in Holyrood and Leith. It is evident, however, that a
majority of the bar, including Clement Little, conformed at the
Reformation; and Clement Little may have taken his cue from
James McGill, the clerk register, who joined the reformers late
in 1559. Some senators, including Henry Balnaves and the Earl
Marischal, also supported the reformers; but in becoming a
convert Clement Little chose to adopt a divergent path from that
of the president of the College of Justice, Henry Sinclair, who
still remained his good friend and colleague, and from the
conservative ecclesiastical element on the bench which withheld
active support from the new regime. Nonetheless, he would be
well aware that among those who threw in their lot with the
protestant cause were Abbot Walter Reid of Kinloss and Edward
Henryson who had been associated with the circles of Robert
Reid and Henry Sinclair.[101]

Yet, as his subsequent career so clearly shows, Clement Little
possessed a religious commitment beyond the merely conventional
and there is no need to doubt the sincerity of his conversion by

[99] Knox, *Works*, i, 57, 97, 106, 246–7, 268; iv, 245, 247; Calderwood, *History*, i,
108, 134, 303–4, 320.
[100] *Statutes of the Scottish Church*, 84, 95, 103, 122–3, 150, 161.
[101] G. Brunton and D. Haig, *An Historical Account of the Senators of the
College of Justice* (Edinburgh, 1832), 60, 65, 99; *CSP Scot.*, iii, no. 601.

1560. He seems to have arrived finally at protestantism through Erasmian humanism and reformist Catholicism. Certainly, his devotion to theology and to the kirk is demonstrated not least by his remarkable theological library of over two hundred and seventy books in which virtually all the leading protestant theologians figure prominently. His 'luiffing affectioun and grit zeale borne be him to the kirk of God and to the advancement of his word'[102] inevitably led to his involvement in ecclesiastical affairs, both locally and nationally. The Reformation, after all, had given laymen as never before a say in the running of the kirk.

The structure of the new church, with its emphasis above all else on the parish ministry, to be supervised by superintendents and governed by a series of church courts from kirk session to general assembly, deeply engaged Clement Little's attention. His annotated copy of John à Lasco's *Forma ac ratio*, published in 1550, for use by the exiled strangers' church in London illustrates his particular interest in the superintendent's office, introduced to the Scottish church by 1561.[103] Although Knox, with all his distaste for 'lord-like bishops' and his emphasis on an energetic pastoral ministry, had declined to become superintendent, his colleague John Spottiswoode accepted the office for Lothian in 1561 and John Willock, who had formerly preached in Edinburgh, became superintendent of Glasgow and the west. Whatever the arguments on whether Scotland derived the superintendent's office from Denmark or from Cologne, or indeed from elsewhere, Clement Little evidently believed that à Lasco's superintendent had a relevance for Scottish practice; and his copy contained the marginal note for ready reference 'superintendentis officium'.[104]

Little's practical support for the kirk is also well-attested. In response to the kirk session's appeal in November 1562 for funds for the new hospital, Clement Little was among one hundred and sixty 'faythful bretherin of Edinburgh' who contributed to the project.[105] In later life, as well as serving as an elder on the kirk session for the north-west 'quarter' of the burgh,[106] he was frequently appointed commissioner from the burgh to the general assembly. At a point when the town council was anxious

---

[102] *Extracts from Edinburgh Burgh Records*, iv, 182.

[103] EUL, Dd.6.6.

[104] G. Donaldson, '"The Example of Denmark" in the Scottish Reformation', *SHR*, xxvii (1948), 57–64; J. K. Cameron, 'The Cologne Reformation and the Church of Scotland', *Journal of Ecclesiastical History*, xxx (1979), 39–64; EUL, Dd.6.6, *Forma ac Ratio*, sig. C, verso.

[105] M. Lynch, 'The "Faithful Brethren" of Edinburgh', 194–9.

[106] Little came first in the leet of elders proposed in October 1575: SRO, CH2/450/1, Edinburgh General Session Records, 13 Oct., [20] Oct., 3 Nov. 1575. He also occurs as elder in 1562: see below, 110 n. 56.

to secure an effective voice in electing commissioners (often from within its own ranks) to the general assembly, it is a significant reflection of Clement Little's standing in the community that he should be returned as commissioner, though not himself a councillor; and there is more than a hint that the kirk session also had its say in the choice of commissioners to the assembly. He was certainly chosen to represent the burgh in the assemblies of December 1563, June and July 1567, July and December 1568, August 1574 and October 1578.[107] In the assemblies of the earlier 1560s, he witnessed the kirk's attempts to come to terms, as best it could, with a sovereign unsympathetic to the reformed faith but not altogether unheedful of the church's claims. But, with Queen Mary's deposition in 1567 and the triumph of King James' party in the aftermath of the civil war, Clement Little increasingly came to be identified with the presbyterian cause, championed by Andrew Melville and led in Edinburgh by the town's ministers James Lawson, John Durie and Robert Pont. He was active in negotiations between church and state on the limits of ecclesiastical jurisdiction, was present in the assembly of October 1578 which criticised the rôle of bishops in the kirk, and he took part in the drafting of the Second Book of Discipline and in examining its contents and claims as part of the discussions arranged by parliament at Stirling in 1578.[108]

His commitment to the kirk and his legal expertise led to his selection in 1563 to an assembly committee for hearing an appeal in a divorce case; and by 1567 the assembly had chosen him as one of the recognised advocates for the kirk.[109] In the 1560s, too, his legal career expanded with his appointment by the crown in March 1563/4 as one of the four commissaries of the reorganised and secularised commissary court of Edinburgh. This was one area, at least, where a knowledge of canon law was still considered to be advantageous; and Little probably owed his appointment to the Earl of Moray and Maitland of Lethington who headed Mary's government. His three colleagues on the commissary court were all skilled in canon law: Sir James Balfour of Pittendreich was formerly official of St Andrews; Edward Henryson was Doctor in both laws; and Robert Maitland was

---

[107] Extracts from Edinburgh Burgh Records, iii, 175; ECA, MS Edinburgh Town Council Records, iv, 2 July, 24 Dec. 1568; v, 4 Aug. 1574, 17 Oct. 1578.
[108] Acts and Proceedings of the General Assemblies of the Kirk of Scotland [BUK], ed. T. Thomson, 3 vols. and appendix vol. (Edinburgh, 1839–45), i, 262, 271, 352, 362, 365; Calderwood, History, iii, 416.
[109] BUK, i, 35, 113; cf. 118.

dean of Aberdeen.[110] Their duties consisted largely of executory and testamentary work, as well as determining causes involving divorce, adherence, legitimacy and defamation, for Edinburgh had an exclusive jurisdiction in matrimonial cases denied to local commissaries, and a general jurisdiction for recording testaments from any part of the country.[111] Clement Little, therefore, could scarcely afford to throw away his copy of the decretals, and his acquisition of Theodore Beza's treatise on polygamy, divorce and separation, published at Geneva in 1568–9 (complimentary copies of which Beza had sent to Knox and George Buchanan in 1569) had a practical application in Clement Little's work as commissary.[112] Although Luther had attacked the Catholic belief in marriage as one of seven sacraments in his *De captivitate Babylonica ecclesiae*, and Martin Bucer had also written on marriage in his *De regno Christi Jesu* copies of both of which works Clement Little possessed on the shelves of his library,[113] Theodore Beza was really the first reformed theologian to provide a systematic exposition of the subject in the light of post-Tridentine Catholic teaching, for the Council of Trent had formulated the official Catholic doctrine as late as 1563. Beza's *Tractatio de polygamia* (1568–9) and his *Tractatus de repudiis et divortiis* (1569) sought to refute, on the one hand, the arguments of Trent on clerical celibacy, on the sacramental concept of marriage and on its indissolubility, and, on the other hand, the views of Bernardino Ochino, the Italian reformer who understood polygamy to be more a matter of custom than of ethical concern.[114] The reformed belief in matrimonial dissolution, and in divorce *a vinculo*, which Beza defended, had been accepted after the Reformation in Scotland, where Clement Little and his colleagues gave judgment in divorce hearings in the commissary court.[115] Throughout his career, indeed, Clement Little succeeded in combining his duties as commissary with those of advocate, and it was only in April 1580, three weeks after his death, that the Lords of Council and Session forbade commissaries from

[110] *The Practicks of Sir James Balfour of Pittendreich*, ed. P. G. B. McNeill (Edinburgh, 1962–3), ii, 671.
[111] Ibid., ii, 655ff; *An Introduction to Scottish Legal History*, 368–71.
[112] *Early Scottish Libraries*, 123; EUL, Dd.6.11; Knox, *Works*, vi, 564.
[113] 'Catalogus librorum . . . Clemens Litill', *Miscellany of the Maitland Club*, i, pt. 2 (Edinburgh, 1834), 285–301, at 293–4.
[114] T. Maruyama, 'The Reform of the True Church: the Ecclesiology of Theodore Beza', *Th.* (Princeton, 1973), 116ff.
[115] Cf., *The Records of the Synod of Lothian*, ii–iv. For Little's activities as commissary, see SRO, CC8/2/1, Decreets of Edinburgh Commissary Court, fo. 52v and *passim*; CC8/2/2, fos. 7r, 9v, 18r, 24r.

undertaking cases as advocates or as procurators before any judges.[116]

For one steeped in the traditions of canon and civil law, Clement Little displayed a surprising radicalism in his attitudes towards religion and politics. He instinctively chose protestantism and supported the revolution-rebellion of 1560; and seven years later he again was ready to lend his approval to Mary's enforced abdication and to her replacement by James VI, an infant only thirteen months old. He accordingly witnessed the general assembly's insistence in 1567 that all future monarchs 'befor they be crownit and inaugurit sall make ther faithfull league and promise to the true kirk of God' and that they acknowledge the mutual contact and band between 'the prince and God and also betuixt the prince and faithfull peiple according to the word of God'. The legal basis of kingship in the constitution, in effect, was being redefined by a group of revolutionaries, to which Clement Little was a party, who after deposing one monarch were intent on prescribing the terms of his rule to the next.[117] Whatever his lawyerly instincts, Clement Little formally subscribed to the assembly's statement, and with 'the erles, lords, barrones and uthers commissioners present' bound himself 'to ruit out, destroy and alluterlie subvert all monuments of idolatrie, and namely, the odious, blasphemous messe', to punish such recusants 'quhilk Gods law and the civill law of this realme commands to be punished', and to 'reforme schooles, colledges, and universities throughout the whole realme . . . to the effect that youth be not infectit be poysonable doctrine at the beginning, quhilk afterward cannot be well removeit away'.[118]

All the evidence of Clement Little's subsequent career suggests that he sought to honour this pledge of 1567; and he may have found it reassuring that among the subscribers were fellow lawyers and politicians like James McGill, William Maitland of Lethington, and Sir James Balfour, his former colleague as principal commissary of Edinburgh and senator of the College of Justice. Even so, he still seemed in dubious company for by then McGill had been forfeited by Mary for his part in Rizzio's murder and Balfour himself was implicated in Darnley's murder, which the same assembly had denounced as 'so odious not only before God but also the whole world'.[119] During the ensuing

[116] He died on 1 April 1580; SRO, CC8/8/11, Register of Edinburgh Testaments, fo. 365v; *The Acts and Sederunts of the Lords of Council and Session* (Edinburgh, 1790–1813), 12, 23 April 1580.
[117] *BUK*, i, 109; *APS*, iii, 39, cf. 23–4.
[118] *BUK*, i, 109–10.
[119] *RSS*, v, no. 2725; Brunton and Haig, *Senators of the College of Justice*, 110, 111; *BUK*, i, 108.

civil war, however, when Edinburgh was captured by the Queen's party in the summer of 1571, the town council was dismissed, many inhabitants, including the town's ministers, sought refuge in Leith, and Knox found it prudent to retreat to St Andrews; but Clement Little seemingly trimmed his sails and continued to act as commissary in Edinburgh, despite the departure of his colleagues, until as late as June, when he finally left for the safety of Leith where he and his fellow commissaries resumed their duties in November 1571.[120]

Little's prominence in the life of the burgh had been recognised by the town council as early as 1561 when he participated in the town council's election in October; and he was appointed by the council, in the following year, as one of several 'cunning and leirnit men of understanding' to examine the aptitude of William Robertoun, the grammar school master, who, in spite of the Reformation, still remained 'ane obstinat papeist'. The council appealed to Lord James Stewart, the protestant leader of Mary's government, to persuade his brother Robert Stewart, the commendator of Holyrood, in whose patronage the office of grammar schoolmaster resided, to dismiss Robertoun, who claimed to have a sound title in law and to be properly qualified in both Greek and Latin grammar. The schoolmaster accordingly sought legal advice from a Catholic advocate, Edmund Hay, who acted as prelocutor in his defence. One technicality was whether Robertoun's admission in January 1546/7 had been strictly legal, since the commendator was then a minor and the presentation had proceeded on the advice of the Abbot of Cambuskenneth acting as Stewart's coadjutor and administrator. In the end, however, the Council obtained Stewart's consent to proceed with the case, and it dismissed Robertoun from teaching, for a term at least, on finding that he had 'nane or littill eruditioun in grammar greik or latene', was ignorant of 'all letteris humane and divine' and, worst of all, was 'ane inimie to Godis word and contemnar thairof'. With more than a little civic pride, the town council concluded that as 'this burgh is the maist nobill and famous burgh and murrour of gude maneris and civilitie within this realme, sua the same aucht to have the maist famois and literat pedagogis for instructing of the youthheid of the samin, and to gif utheris wis and nobill men

---

[120] Calderwood, *History*, iii, 72ff; R. Bannatyne, *Journal of the Transactions in Scotland* (Edinburgh, 1806), 139ff; *Diurnal of Occurrents*, 295. The decreets of Edinburgh Commissary Court, SRO, CC8/2/5, ended on 2 May and began again at Leith on 2 November 1571. The Commissary Court's Register of Deeds and Protests, SRO, CC8/17/1 ended on 11 June, with Little still in control, and resumed at Leith on 5 December 1571.

occasioun, as had the said Cicero, to send their bairnis to be instructit thairin, to the greit increse of science and augmenting of the commoun weill thairof'.[121]

Beyond the grammar school, Little was anxious to see 'ane universitie' established in the burgh. The idea was by no means new. As a curator of John Reid of Aikenhead, who was an executor of Bishop Reid's testament,[122] Clement Little was well aware of Reid's plans for a college. He was also in frequent contact with the three lawyers whose assistance Reid had sought in establishing his college.[123] In addition, he was present as one of the judges in the commissary court in June 1564 when Walter Reid, abbot of Kinloss, and John Reid compeared as executors, and in name of the remaining executors, of Bishop Reid's testament 'allegit that the said umquhile bischop befoir his deceis maid his testament and nominat thame his executouris testamentaris thairin and that thairfoir na dativis aucht to be gevin'.[124] He was therefore familiar with the terms of Reid's will. Moreover, in his capacity as an elder of the kirk as well as kirk lawyer and commissioner to the assembly, he would appreciate the reformers' intentions in the First Book of Discipline of 1560 to establish colleges in principal towns such as Edinburgh on the model of the protestant academies on the continent.[125] The Jesuits were also active in this field. The papal emissary, Nicholas de Gouda, even suggested to Queen Mary in 1562 that she should 'establish a college where she could always have pious and learned men at hand who might instruct in Catholicism and piety both the people and the young who were the hope of the commonwealth'; but Mary, more realistically, considered such a project to be 'impracticable just then'.[126]

As early as 1562, the town council, then pondering on the problem of its recusant schoolmaster, raised the wider issue of adequate finance to maintain the school, to erect a college in the burgh and to establish hospitals for the poor. The claim was made at a point when Queen Mary showed a willingness to assign to burghs for the use of the schools and the poor the friaries and chaplainries of the pre-Reformation church. The council's intention was to utilise the Blackfriars as a hospital and Kirk o' Field as a site for 'ane scule', possibly in the sense of a

---

[121] *Extracts from Edinburgh Burgh Records*, iii, 127, 142–3; 131, 133, 135, 139, 141–5, 149, 150, 190, 193, 196–7, 215, 227; iv, 104–5, 330, 342, 346–7, 517.
[122] See above, 32.
[123] *RPC*, iii, 472.
[124] SRO, CC8/2/1, Decreets of the Edinburgh Commissary Court, fo. 53r.
[125] See above, 43–4.
[126] *Papal Negotiatons*, 133.

college. The original distinction between a collegiate kirk (like Kirk o' Field) and a university college, in any event, had become somewhat blurred, for collegiate kirks usually provided some educational instruction, at least for choristers, and the clerical emphasis in university colleges before 1560 is evident in the ecclesiastical provisions for maintaining service at the altar. Efforts to acquire the Kirk o' Field site for an educational establishment were not, however, immediately effective, and when renewed attempts were made to found a 'university' by 1579, another collegiate kirk, Trinity College, was chosen for the project. The prospects for success certainly looked brighter, for the town council had acquired Trinity College and its hospital in 1567 and the provost of the college was Robert Pont, an associate of Andrew Melville who, as principal, had already effected far-reaching reforms at Glasgow University.[127] In February 1578/9, Clement Little's brother, William, was one of the councillors deputed to discuss the scheme with Pont 'and entir in further resonyng with him tuiching the erectioun and fundatioun of the universeteis in the Trinitie college'. The ambitious idea may even have been to establish schools of Grammar, Arts, Divinity and possibly Law. Thereafter, both Clement and William Little undertook further negotiations in April 1579 'in the ministeris luging' for 'founding of ane universitie'. That they should convene in the manse is significant for James Lawson, who succeeded Knox as minister in 1572, had earlier served as sub-principal of King's College in Aberdeen, and was active, with Andrew Melville and Thomas Smeaton from Glasgow, in the reorganisation of St Mary's College in St Andrews as a school of divinity.[128]

As his colleague in the kirk session and general assembly, Clement Little fully shared Lawson's enthusiasm for extending provision for university education. The town council was also impressed by the part which Lawson had played, by royal invitation, in erecting a college of theology in St Andrews and agreed even to pay all his expenses, as he had been 'sent thair be

---

[127] *Extracts from Edinburgh Burgh Records*, iii, 132, 146; *RPC*, i, 202; *Charters and Documents relating to the Collegiate Church and Hospital of the Holy Trinity . . . Edinburgh*, AD. *1460–1661* (Edinburgh, 1871), 67–72; *Extracts from Edinburgh Burgh Records*, iv, 103, 105; Durkan and Kirk, *University of Glasgow*, 262ff.

[128] *Extracts from Edinburgh Burgh Records*, iv, 103, 105, 136; *RSS*, vi, no. 663; Melville, *Diary*, 76, Lawson had been a student with Andrew Melville at St Mary's and after further study on the continent received a royal gift of a place in St Mary's college in February 1568/9 (*Early Records of St Andrews University*, 267; *RSS*, vi, no. 518).

the kingis maiestie'.[129] Nor is it surprising that the town council should seek to imitate the St Andrews project. By December 1579, the town council's modified aim was clearly to found in the capital, with the advice of Pont and Lawson, 'ane college of theologe'. Bishop Reid's earlier emphasis on the laws had now been superseded by a concern for theology. Melville and Smeaton had conceived St Mary's as an 'anti-seminary' to the Jesuit colleges established on the continent for training seminary priests: they are credited with being 'the first motioners of an Anti-Seminarie to be erected in St Androis, to the Jesuit Seminaries, for the course of Theologie; and cessit never, at Assemblies and Court, till that wark was begoun and sett fordwart'. Indeed, Melville himself became first principal of the reconstituted divinity college in St Andrews; and the establishment of a further college of protestant theology in the capital was designed to keep at bay the forces of the counter-Reformation at a time when Esmé Stewart, newly arrived from France, had won the king's affection and looked like acting as a focus for papalist interests.[130]

Amidst these preparations, Clement Little, who died on 1 April 1580, bequeathed in his testament to 'his native town of Edinburgh and to the kirk of God thairin' his whole theological library, valued at 1,000 merks.[131] The precise terms of the bequest vary slightly from one account to another. In his testament, the original of which still survives as well as the copy recorded in the register of testaments and confirmed by all three commissaries of Edinburgh, Clement Little left his theological works 'in legacie to the toun of Edinburgh to be usit be the ministeris thairof', and, more exactly, 'to the kirk of Edinburgh to be usit and kepit be the said kirk to the use of ministeris, elders and deacones thairof'.[132] Yet according to the town council's interpretation of the bequest, as explained by William Little, as sole executor of his brother's estate in October 1580, it was Clement Little's intention 'that the buikis and workis off Halie Scripturis in gret nummer conquiest be him in his tyme suld nocht perische or be separatet' and that they should be donated as a collection to the town and kirk 'to the effect and purpois that

[129] *Extracts from Edinburgh Burgh Records*, iv, 131 (11 Dec. 1579); ECA, MS. Edinburgh Town Council Records, vi, fo. 1r (13 Jan. 1579/80).
[130] *Extracts from Edinburgh Burgh Records*, iv, 136; Melville, *Diary*, 76; Calderwood, *History*, iii, 457.
[131] *Extracts from Edinburgh Burgh Records*, iv, 182; SRO, GD122, Craigmillar Writs, Liberton Papers and Correspondence, no. 6.
[132] SRO, CC8/8/11, Register of Edinburgh Testaments, fos. 366r, 367v; SRO, GD122/3, Craigmillar Writs, Bundle I, Wills, no. 867.

sic personis knawin off honest conversatioun and guid lyff (and
na utheris) quhilkis ar and salbe willing to travell and be exercesit
in the service and vocatioun of ministrie or utherwayis of dewetie
desyrous, and in especiall to sic personis as ar or salbe of bluide
to the said umquhill Maister Clement' should have free access to
the library, which was to be administered by James Lawson and
his successors in the ministry, 'for reding and collecting the
frutefull knawledge be the said buikis as it sall pleis God to
distribut his graces to the reidaris'.[133]

The library was clearly intended to serve the needs of divinity
students and other scholars, as well as the ministers, elders and
deacons of the burgh. The provision that access to the library
should be available especially to Clement Little's kinsmen was
not without effect, for although Clement Little had no children
himself, two of his nephews, William and John Little, apparently
graduated from Edinburgh University in 1559 and 1604 respectively, and as students they were able to profit from their uncle's
library which, by then, had formed the nucleus of the university
library. Stimulated by his uncle's collection, John Little, in
particular, was intent on studying theology. After graduating
from Edinburgh, both pursued further studies on the continent;
William was in Paris in 1613 when he wrote home to his brother,
Edward, and John, as a student of theology, died in July 1622 at
Geneva, where an autopsy was carried out and a certificate of
death issued in November 1623.[134]

Now is it plain that the 'buiks of the common librarie' (as the
town council somewhat loosely described the collection) would
be of strictly limited value even to divinity students from
Edinburgh who were still obliged to pursue their university
studies at St Andrews, Glasgow or elsewhere; and Clement
Little's expectation may well have been that his collection would
ultimately serve as the basis of the library for the planned college
of theology, which James Lawson had advocated and which
Clement Little and his brother were anxious to see established in
Trinity College or elsewhere. It is, at any rate, indicative of his
intentions that Clement Little should make provision only for
the donation of his theological books; his 'haill law bukes and
uther bukes for scollaris' valued at over £140 were specifically
excluded from the collection, presumably because they were

---

[133] Extracts from Edinburgh Burgh Records, iv, 182; SRO, GD122, Craigmillar
Writs, Liberton Papers and Correspondence, no. 6.

[134] A Catalogue of the Graduates . . . of the University of Edinburgh since its
foundation (Edinburgh, 1858), 16, 21; SRO, GD122/3, Craigmillar Writs,
nos. 820, 822–3, John Little, on his death at Geneva, left an estate of £4,600 (Ibid.,
Bundle III, Wills, no. 873).

considered to be of less relevance to students of theology.[135] Not
only was Trinity College regarded as a suitable site for the
divinity school, but it had also been earmarked since 1567 as the
site for the town's new hospital; and fully aware of both these
projects, Clement Little shortly before his death assigned a
legacy of 300 merks (£200 Scots) 'to be employit to the
sustentatioun of the puris of the new hospital of the said burgh
and thair successouris perpetualie'.[136]

William Little, as executor, handed over to James Lawson and
the kirk session, in May 1580, his brother's legacy for the new
poor's hospital 'to be wairit upoun land or anuelrent yeirlie', and
by October he had formally presented to the town his brother's
theological library of two hundred and sixty-eight volumes, each
to be stamped with 'the armes off the said umquhill maister
Clement with thir wordis: I am givin to Edinburgh and kirk of
God be maister Clement Litill thair to remaine, 1580'. The town
council assigned the collection to the safe keeping of James
Lawson, as minister, so the books initially came to be housed in
the manse of St Giles. Restrictions were placed on lending, and a
quarterly inspection was to be held so that the books 'may and
sall remane together in the said place . . . in perpetuall memorie
of the guid affectioned mynde of the said umquhill maister
Clement to the singular confort of the kirk of God and to all his
faythfull servandis'. A special library in the loft of the manse was
constructed to contain the collection, and the minister became
keeper of the library.[137]

In the circumstances, the device adopted was probably the
most readily available solution to fulfilling the terms of the will,
but in the absence at the higher levels of any academic theological
education in the capital, it is evident that a strictly theological
library donated with the specific intention of helping divinity
students in their studies was bound to remain of limited use, so
long, that is, as Edinburgh was denied its college. At best, the
library could really hope only to be of service to probationary
ministers who had completed their university courses and who,
as they awaited licence, were attending the 'exercise' in Edinburgh,
the regular meeting of ministers and elders from the surrounding
district for interpreting scripture, which became merged with the

---

[135] *Extracts from Edinburgh Burgh Records*, iv, 175, 382; SRO, CC8/8/11,
fo. 366r; *Miscellany of the Maitland Club*, i, pt. 2, 287.
    [136] SRO, CC8/8/11, Register of Edinburgh Testaments, fo. 367r.
    [137] SRO, GD122, Craigmillar Writs, Liberton Papers and Correspondence,
nos. 5–6; *Extracts from Edinburgh Burgh Records*, iv, 175, 181–3; ECA, MS.
Edinburgh Town Council Records, vi, 16 May, 20 May 1580.

new court of the presbytery between 1579 and 1581.[138]

Clement Little's collection looked almost like becoming the ministers' library or, at best, the 'common librarie', as the town council sometimes termed it. Yet, within four years, it became the college library, with the foundation of the town's college by 1583. Renewed efforts to find a site for the projected, and long deferred, college had resulted in the acquisition by 1582 not of Trinity College as had been planned but of the property of another collegiate kirk, St Mary's in the Fields or Kirk o' Field, whose buildings lay in a somewhat ruinous conditions after partial demolition carried out by a former provost of the college.[139]

The town's loan to the king of 10,000 merks in 1581 (to which William Little among others contributed) helped to facilitate the royal grant of April 1582 whereby the king confirmed his mother's earlier gift to the town in 1567 of the chaplainries and friaries in the burgh for the support of the ministry and hospitals, and extended the scope of the gift to include the repairing of schools and promotion of letters and science. The charter, moreover, expressly recognised that the property of Kirk o' Field undoubtedly belonged to the burgh, and it permitted the town council to utilise any of the collegiate kirks or friaries, now 'waste and vacant places', as suitable accommodation for 'professors of the schools of grammar, humanity and the languages, philosophy, theology, medicine and law, or any other liberal sciences'. This royal gift allowed the council to found a college or colleges of several faculties which could compete directly with the courses taught in the established universities.[140] No financial provision for the college was forthcoming from a king already in debt, and so the council, resorting to Reid's elusive bequest of 1558, renewed its efforts to compel Walter Reid, as a principal executor, to hand over the 8,000 merks of Reid's legacy for the college; but in the end only 2,500 merks were recovered.[141]

---

[138] *Miscellany of the Wodrow Society* (Edinburgh, 1844), 407–8; *BUK*, ii, 439, 465–8.

[139] For details, see D. B. Horn, 'The origins of the University of Edinburgh', *University of Edinburgh Journal*, xxii (1966), 213–25, 297–312, at 303; *History of the University of Edinburgh*, ed A. L. Turner (Edinburgh, 1933), 10–13.

[140] *Extracts from Edinburgh Burgh Records*, iv, 200; ECA, MS. Edinburgh Town Council Records, vi, fo.126, 15 March 1580/1 (Little); *University of Edinburgh: Charters, Statutes and Acts . . . 1583–1858*, ed. A. Morgan (Edinburgh, 1937), 12–16.

[141] *Extracts from Edinburgh Burgh Records*, iv, 236, 563; v, 90; ECA, MS. Edinburgh Town Council Records, vi, 8 June 1852.

More immediately, funds were raised through taxation for establishing the college; in April 1583 two masters of work were appointed to supervise building 'the wallis of the colleges to be maid at the Kirk of Feild'; by September Robert Rollock was appointed as master and regent of the college; in October the students matriculated for the first session; and shortly thereafter William Little and another bailie convened a meeting of expert advisers 'to sett downe and devyse the ordour of teacheing with the discypline to be keipit in the College now erectit'.[142] As first principal, Rollock had been recruited from St Andrews where he had matriculated in St Salvator's College in 1574, had attained the baccalaureate in 1576, and gained the Master's insignia by 1578.[143] He probably graduated in 1577 when as parson of Forteviot, a prebend of St Salvator's, he is described as 'maister and ane of the studentis in Sanct Salvatouris college'.[144] He evidently combined teaching as a regent in St Andrews with further studies in theology, at a point immediately preceding the new foundation of St Mary's as a college of divinity in 1579 with Andrew Melville as its principal from 1580, and thereafter he attended divinity classes in St Mary's where James Melville, the principal's nephew, taught Rollock 'the Hebrew toung' in his 'lessone and chalmer to that effect'.[145] Rollock was therefore equipped to teach theology, and indeed later acted as minister of Greyfriars Kirk in Edinburgh; but, initially at least, the emphasis in the newly created College of Edinburgh was neither on theology nor on law but on providing instruction in Arts; and Clement Little's collection still remained in the minister's custody and housed in the loft of the manse.

As master of the college, Rollock was assigned the duty of instructing 'the youth and professing of guid leirning' according to 'the reules and injunctiounes quhilk salbe gevin unto him be the provest, baillies and council'. He was soon joined in November by a 'secund maister', Duncan Nairn, a product of the Andrew Melville regime at Glasgow, where he had won first place in the academic disputations for graduation in 1580. The curriculum, later defined in the *Disciplina Academiae Edinburgense* of 1628 which preserved elements dating from the college's early years, consisted for first-year students of Latin and Greek grammar, and Ramist logic; further grounding in the classical authors, in Talon's and Cassander's rhetoric, in Aristotle's

---

[142] *Extracts from Edinburgh Burgh Records*, iv, 571; 289, 298, 300.
[143] *Early Records of St Andrews University*, 175, 179, 285.
[144] St Andrews University Archives, MS. SS110.E4.7.
[145] Melville, *Diary*, 86.

philosophical treatises and also in arithmetic formed the work of the second year; Hebrew grammar, logical analyses and the works of Aristotle were studied in the third year, with disputations in logic, ethics and physics, and Sunday lectures on the commonplaces of theology; and, finally, the fourth year was reserved for further instruction in logic, physics, geography and theology. The course resembled teaching patterns elsewhere; the introduction of Ramist logic and Talon's rhetoric certainly followed Melville's example at Glasgow, but Rollock's pioneering class in human anatomy was clearly novel.[146] Of Rollock's own adherence to Ramist principles, there is, of course, ample testimony, and one regent in the college, who had been a student during Rollock's principalship, confirmed how Rollock 'attached the greatest value' to the *Dialecticae* of Ramus, which he taught 'as an instrument so admirably adapted to the study of logic', together with the *Rhetorica* of Ramus' disciple, Omer Talon (to which Ramus himself had contributed).[147] All this, it would seem, directly contradicts a recent attempt to portray Rollock as an anti-Ramist.[148]

As teaching proceeded, further work was undertaken on the college buildings, on 'sclaitting of the studeis' and 'inclosing of the said college and other wark thairof', which necessitated raising further finance from additional taxation. A college library had still to be assembled; and with the flight to London, where he died in October 1584, of James Lawson and other leading presbyterian ministers during the 'anti-presbyterian dictatorship' of Arran's government in Scotland, the town council, in September 1584, decided to take possession of the keys to the manse and library. This was done on the 'understanding that the spous of maister James Lowsoun is chairget to devoyde and remove fra the lugeing' for her steadfast opposition to the Archbishop of St Andrews. An inventory was ordered of the 'tymmer wark and buiks', which William Little was to keep 'quhill forther ordour be tane thairwith'. The report which William Little and two others submitted to the council showed that they had found 'the touns librarie in place according to the inventour assigned thairwith, togidder with the haill skelffs,

[146] *E. U. Charters, Statutes and Acts*, 90; *Extracts from Edinburgh Burgh Records*, iv, 305; Durkan and Kirk, *University of Glasgow*, 359; 291–2; *E.U. Charters, Statutes and Acts*, 60ff.
[147] *A Logical Analysis of the Epistle of Paul to the Romans*, by Charles Ferme, ed. W. L. Alexander (Edinburgh, 1850), 25; W. J. Ong, *Ramus and Talon Inventory* (Harvard, 1958), 2.
[148] M. Lynch, 'The Origins of Edinburgh's "Toun College": a revision article', *Innes Review*, xxxiii (1982), 3–14, at 7–8.

buirds, futegangs, pres and tymmer wark, with the loks, keyis and bandis'. The council then declared Lawson's custody of the library to be terminated, and assigned to William Little 'the keyis and custodie of the said lugeing and librarie'. Shortly thereafter, the council decided to transfer 'the townis librarie, shelffis and buirds thairof' from the manse to 'the townis college in a hous convenient at the sicht of William Littill' to be placed under Rollock's supervision.[149]

Clement Little's theological library thus became the nucleus of the college library, but it was not until August 1587 that the study of theology, as such, was introduced into the curriculum, when the town council finally recognised that Rollock had:[150]

> 'now completitt ane cours of philosophie in the said College, and inrespect of his lang travells tayne thairinto of before, and that he is thocht to be qualefeit for the professioun of theologie, thairfore and for uther caussis moving thame, they fand it expedient that the said maister Robert sall begyn and teache theologie in the said College, and ordanet the sam to be proponet to the presbitery that thair consultatioun and avyse micht be had heirinto'.

The presbytery, in turn, agreed that Rollock should also undertake 'to teich every Sounday in the morning in the new kirk'; and in November the town council assigned to Rollock a stipend of 400 merks 'for his service as principall of the townis College and teacheing of ane class of theologie and of publict lessouns in the said College, and for his teacheing upoun the Sondayes in the morning in the Eister Kirk'.[151] Among Rollock's forty-seven students who had entered the college after it opened in 1583 and who proceeded to graduation in 1587, at least fifteen decided to pursue careers in the church, and with Rollock's new course on theology begun in 1587, Clement Little's theological collection, housed in the college, at last looked like satisfying its donor's wishes by being available for training candidates for the ministry.[152]

Yet these developments were achieved not without setback. An outbreak of plague forced the college to close in May 1585, when the two masters reported to the council that 'the haill students, throw the feir and bruit of the pestilence, hes left the scholes and thairby thai haif nathing to do', and so Rollock and Nairn were given leave 'to depairt and visy thair freinds for a

[149] Extracts from Edinburgh Burgh Records, iv, 318, 329–30, 349–50; Calderwood, History, iv, 65, 73–8, 126–41.
[150] Extracts from Edinburgh Burgh Records, iv, 499.
[151] SRO, CH2/121/1, MS. Edinburgh Presbytery Records, 5 Sept. 1587; Extracts from Edinburgh Burgh Records, iv, 508.
[152] Catalogue of Graduates, 7–8.

seasoun' until classes resumed in February 1585/6 when Rollock was appointed 'first and principall maister of the Townis College'.[153] Doubts were also expressed on the permanency of the transference of the town's library to the town's college. In January 1584/5, the council had insisted that 'the buikis of the commoun librarie aucht nocht to be lent furth to ony maner of persoun, bot grantis and permitts that maister James Hammiltoun, minister, sall haif access thairto in the place appoyntet for custodie of the samyn'; and although Rollock continued to act as custodian of the collection, the council intervened again in April 1588 when it ordered the treasurer 'to prepair, dres and sett up skelffis in the over study of the ministers lugeing for putting the townis library thair quhen it sall be fund expedient'.[154] The intention was clearly to remove Clement Little's books from the college and to return them to the minister's study; but the plan was not effected, and it was appropriate that the collection should remain with the university library at a point when theological teaching, conducted by the principal himself, had just got under way.

The 'Tounis College' was now equipped to provide instruction in both Arts and Divinity, with a library to match; graduation figures remained strong, without rivalling the record for 1587;[155] and it was only a matter of time before Law was added to the curriculum. Already, some Edinburgh graduates in Arts were forced to pursue legal studies elsewhere: Robert Johnstone, a graduate of 1587, became Doctor in both laws; James Bannatyne, who graduated in 1587, and Alexander Gibson, in 1588, became judges in the Court of Session; James Sandilandis, who left Edinburgh in 1588, became an advocate and commissary of Aberdeen; and John Shairp, younger of Houstoun, a graduate of 1590, also became an advocate, continuing the legal traditions of his family which also had close links with Clement Little's family, for two daughters of Shairp of Houstoun married members of the Little family.[156] A need for legal training in the capital undoubtedly existed, as Bishop Reid had perceived in 1558, and as the Lords of Council and Session later observed in 1580 when they claimed that not all advocates were 'lernit bayth in the law and practiques'.[157] Certainly, some who sought admission to plead as advocates already possessed appropriate

[153] *Extracts from Edinburgh Burgh Records*, iv, 421, 448–9.
[154] Ibid., 382, 518.
[155] *Catalogue of Graduates*, 8ff.
[156] Ibid., 7–9; SRO, GD122/3, Craigmillar Writs, Bundle I, Wills, no. 871; Bundle II, Marriage Contracts, nos. 880–1.
[157] SRO, CS1/3/1, Books of Sederunt of the Court of Session, fo. 116r.

academic qualifications, often acquired after a period of further study on the continent; but others who lacked a formal or systematic training in the laws sought to gain a practical knowledge by being admitted to the tolbooth as observers to hear cases in the Court of Session and also to receive some theoretical instruction from any advocate prepared to undertake some teaching. Before their admission as advocates, expectants submitted to the Lords of Council and Session an account of their legal training, and often gave a 'specimen doctrine' to demonstrate their qualifications, even to the extent of undertaking 'publict teiching in the Tolbuith as is accustommat be lawaris befoir thair admissioun'.[158]

James Foulis, seeking admission in 1576, claimed that he had been an 'auditor' before the Lords of Session 'this lang tyme bigane' and had 'experiencit my self in practise of the lawis befor the commissaris, sheriff, provest and ballies of this burgh and utheris juges, quhairthrow I am now of sufficient habilitie to procure' before the Lords of Session. Alexander Guthrie and John Lermonth, who advanced similar claims, were also admitted as advocates in 1576.[159] Robert Lumsden, admitted in 1577, was already a licentiate in the laws, and had for 'divers yeris continewit in studie of the lawis and teching thairof publict in famous universities within the realm of France', and now wished to 'deduce in practik'. William Harvey, who sought licence in April 1577, had already been admitted by the Lords to 'heir causis resonit' in the tolbooth; and before then had for 'ten or twelft yeris bigane exercesit my self in studeing of the lawis within the cuntrie of France and uthir forein cuntries'. Much the same was true of Alexander Cheyne, who was admitted in July 1577, after observing procedure in the Session; and he had earlier 'studeit in the civile and canoun lawis in Levane divers yeris'.[160] Again, Robert Linton, admitted in 1577, had studied the laws in France and Italy; and William Oliphant and Thomas Gilbert had both studied in France before becoming advocates in October 1577.[161] All in all, relatively little legal teaching, at the higher levels, seems to have been undertaken, at this point, by the Scottish universities; and at his admission in 1580, John Arthur related that 'haifing completit my cours of philosophie and techit the same publictlie divers yeirs in the universitie of Sanct Androis, thairefter I past to the partis of France and thair in the

---

[158] Ibid., fos. 137–9.
[159] Ibid., fos. 27r–v, 29r.
[160] Ibid., fos. 36v, 40r, 49v.
[161] Ibid., fo. 52r–v.

universitie of Poitiors and Tulloyis and utheris' had studied 'gud lettres and namelie of the lawis' for seven years or so, before returning home where he had given proof of his diligence for two years to the Lords of Council.[162] It almost seemed as if the tolbooth rather than the town's college would emerge as the recognised centre for legal training and teaching, where applicants, with or without appropriate academic qualifications, would receive instruction through private lessons, attendance at court as auditors, through practice in the inferior courts, and by giving 'specimen doctrine' as proof of their attainments and of their fitness to plead before the Lords of Session. Aware of the disparity in standards among applicants, and of the need to develop legal training in the capital, the Lords of Council and Session in January 1589/90 offered to advance £1,000 for 'the intertenement of ane teacher and professour in the lawis' to be appointed in the town's college if the town council and advocates each contributed a similar figure; and by 1590 the Fleming, Adrian Damman, had been chosen to lecture on the laws or, at least, to act as 'ane publict professour in the lawis or humanitie'. With his resignation in 1594, Damman was succeeded, after a contested election, by Adam Newton, a Glasgow graduate and advocate, in 1595; but two years later provision for legal teaching was abandoned, and the funds were reallocated to sustain a regent of 'humanitie in authouris Greek and Latene' and six bursars, as a result of opposition by a group of advocates, who protested that they should be 'nawayis burdenit' with supporting 'ane professor in the law', and they resisted any scheme which might increase their numbers at a time when there already was 'als mekle law in Edinburgh as thar is sillver to pay for it'. The advocates therefore 'demandit quha salbe auditouris of this new professour nane as apperis except sum exspectantis in the tolbuith quha may weill for the fassioun heir thre lessonis', and they argued that there were already teachers in St Andrews and Aberdeen who were paid to provide legal instruction but who had made little impact. Moreover, it was revealed that 'na man almaist hes bene refusid upoun ane supplicacioun to be admittit advocat albeit he haid nevir red nor studiet law quharof this confused multitude of threscoir and ten advocattis hes arissin'.[163]

[162] Ibid., fo. 115r.
[163] Extracts from Edinburgh Burgh Records, v, 10, 15, 115–16, 131, 134, 202, 206; W. C. Dickinson, 'The Advocates' Protest against the Institution of a Chair of Law in the University of Edinburgh', SHR, xxiii (1926), 205–12.

Efforts to advance legal studies in Edinburgh on the pattern set by Bishop Reid's example had failed to make headway, and for the immediate future Edinburgh remained a college of Arts and Divinity, where Clement Little's library proved singularly useful in equipping students 'willing to travell and be exercesit in the service and vocatioun off ministrie'.[164] The collection itself contained many theological works which Clement Little had acquired from earlier owners. Some works, for example, came from the library of the Friars Minor in Edinburgh, presumably as a result of the 'dissolution' of the friaries, at least as religious communities, after the Reformation. His copy of Antonius Broeckwey's *Concordantiae maiores* (Lyons, 1529) had formerly belonged to Alexander Arbuckle, Provincial of the Franciscans, with whom Knox had once crossed swords, and also to William Symson of the Friars Minor. Little also obtained Arbuckle's copy of St Bonaventure, *Super libros sententiarum*, a work by the thirteenth-century Italian Franciscan who produced commentaries on Peter Lombard's *Sententiarum,* yet came to prefer mysticism to philosophical speculation, and his writings were later esteemed by Luther. Other copies of Arbuckle's books belonging to Clement Little include certain volumes of the works of the Latin father, St Jerome (Paris, 1533); the four-volume *Summa* of the thirteenth-century English Franciscan, Alexander of Hales (Lyons, 1515–17); and Driedo's, *De ecclesiasticis scripturis . . . libri quatuor,* written by a Catholic opponent of Luther and published at Louvain in 1550. Clement Little's philological interest in the sacred languages is apparent, too, in his acquisition of a work by the Italian Dominican friar and classical and oriental scholar. Sante Pagnino, whose *Isagogae ad sacras literas* was published at Cologne in 1542, a volume formerly owned by the Edinburgh Franciscans and in which Arbuckle was named as 'gardianus'.[165]

Further books from the Edinburgh Franciscans' library came into Clement Little's possession: certain volumes of the works of St Victor, a twelfth-century Flemish mystic, published at Paris in 1526, and a volume by the Greek father Epiphanius, *Contra octoaginta haereses* (Basle, 1543) were formerly owned by John Scott, a Franciscan, and by the Friars Minor of Edinburgh, though Scott's copy of the Louvain theologian Francis Titelmans' *Elucidatio in omnes epistolas apostolicas* (Lyons, 1546) first

---

[164] *Extracts from Edinburgh Burgh Records,* v, 4, 182.
[165] EUL, Dd.5.43; Dd.4.5; Dd.1.20; Dd.3.25–8, Dd.4.2; Dd.3.11; *Early Scottish Libraries,* 71. I am grateful to Dr J. T. D. Hall and Miss M. H. Robertson of Edinburgh University Library for their help in producing many of the books in the Clement Little collection for my inspection.

passed into the possession of Henry Sinclair, dean of Glasgow and then bishop of Ross, before ending up in Clement Little's library.[166] He also collected works previously belonging to the Dominicans in Edinburgh. In this category were Giovanni Marchesini, *Incipit vocabularius in Mamotrectum* (Venice, 1478) and Giovanni Annio, *Glossa super Apocalypsim* (Louvain, 1481), earlier owned by John Adamson, Provincial of the Dominicans who died in 1523; Pierre de Palu, *Exactissimi . . . quartus sententiarum* (Paris, 1518), formerly possessed by James Crichton, an Edinburgh Dominican; Cardinal Cajetan's *De peccatis summula* (Paris, 1530), owned by John Towers, another Edinburgh Dominican and by the common library of the friars preachers in Edinburgh. Similarly, the copy of Raymundus Jordanus, *Contemplationes idiotae* (Paris, 1519), belonging to Andrew MacNeill, Dominican prior in Stirling at the Reformation, passed into Clement Little's collection.[167]

From the Cistercian abbey at Coupar Angus came a copy of the *Summa theologica* (Lyons, *c.* 1507) of St Antonius, the thirteenth-century Spanish Franciscan who taught theology at Bologna and Padua; and from Glasgow, Little acquired the Hebrew *Biblia Bombergiana* in five volumes, owned by John Davidson, the principal of Glasgow University after the Reformation and minister at Hamilton.[168] Other acquisitions from the west of Scotland included a copy of John Huss, *De causa Boemica*, published at Prague and owned by George Lockhart, dean of Glasgow. Several medieval works by William of Ockham, Michael de Cesena and Paulus de Sancta Maria were also obtained from the same library, and that of the dean's kinsman Andrew Lockhart, but again they became the property of Clement Little only after they had come into the possession of Henry Sinclair.[169] Two volumes of the *Conciliorum quatuor generalium* (Paris, 1535), owned by Martin Balfour, who was professor of theology at St Andrews, provost of St Salvator's College and official of St Andrews till his death in 1553, also gained a place on the shelves of Clement Little's library. A printed copy of a breviary according to Sarum use also came into Clement Little's possession; it had been owned by John Crawford, a prebendary of St Giles, who had erected on the Burgh Muir (where Clement Little later acquired a holding), to

[166] EUL, Dd.3.13–15; Dd.1.21; Dd.6.2; *Early Scottish Libraries*, 141–2; 56.
[167] EUL, Dd.5.11; Dd.5.21; Dd.2.12; Dd.2.27; *Early Scottish Libraries*, 66, 86, 154; 127.
[168] EUL, Dd.4.29; Dd.1.1–5; *Early Scottish Libraries*, 165; 89; Durkan and Kirk, *University of Glasgow*, 217, 242, 248.
[169] EUL, Dd.5.42; Dd.5.18; *Early Scottish Libraries*, 124; 50.

the west of Causewayside, a chapel or hermitage, dedicated to St John the Baptist (and later acquired by the Sciennes nunnery), to which he presented his *Breviarium secundum ad usum Sarum* (Rouen, 1496).[170]

A copy of Guillaume d'Auxerre's *In sententias* (Paris, *c.* 1518) was earlier owned by Alexander Mylne, abbot of Cambuskenneth and first president of the College of Justice. Three works by Denys the Carthusian came from the collection of Andrew Durie, abbot of Melrose and then bishop of Galloway, who died in 1558.[171] Other episcopal libraries yielded further books: another set of works by Denys the Carthusian, in three volumes, published at Cologne in 1535, formerly belonged to William Gordon, bishop of Aberdeen, who died three years before Clement Little in 1577; and Bishop Robert Reid of Orkney, who succeeded Mylne as president of the College of Justice, formerly possessed Little's copy of Herold's *Orthodoxographa* (Basle, 1555).[172] But the largest number of books which Clement Little acquired from any single collection were the works from the library of Henry Sinclair, bishop of Ross, a 'cunning letterit' man of 'singular erudition', who appointed Clement Little as one of the executors of his estate shortly before his death in 1565.[173]

Some forty works were forthcoming from this source: they ranged from the patristic writings of St Justin Martyr, St Cyprian, St Basil and St Epiphanius, to the works by St John Damascene, the seventh-century theologian of the eastern church, Theophylact, the eleventh-century Greek exegete, who wrote commentaries on much of the Bible, and the writings of such medieval commentators as Peter Lombard, Vincent of

---

[170] EUL, Dd.2.15; Dd.1.24; *Early Scottish Libraries*, 74; 85; W. M. Bryce, 'The Burgh Muir of Edinburgh', *Book of the Old Edinburgh Club*, x (1918), 2–263, at 102–3.

[171] EUL, Dd.5.17; Dd.4.23; Dd.3.33; *Early Scottish Libraries*, 132; 31.

[172] EUL, Dd.4.24–26; Dd.3.24; *Early Scottish Libraries*, 37; 46.

[173] *Early Scottish Libraries*, 49–60, 171; *Diurnal of Occurrents*, 98; see also above, 39. From the library of John Sinclair, bishop of Brechin, who succeeded his brother, Henry, as president of the College of Justice, Clement Little obtained a copy of Ruard Tapper, *Explicationis Articulorum Venerandae Facultatis Sacrae Theologiae Generalis Studii Louvaniensis* (Antwerp, 1555–7), vol. i (Dd.4.17); *Early Scottish Libraries*, 63. Volume ii was donated to the Library by David Colt in 1612 (Dd.4.18).

Beauvais, Alexander of Hales, Hugh of St Victor, Petrus de Aquila, Nicholas Denyse and Bonaventure.[174] The Italian Renaissance was represented by Gianfrancesco Pico della Mirandola's *De animae immortalitate* (Paris, 1541). This copy had been presented to Henry Sinclair by Giovanni Ferrerio, who was greatly influenced by Pico's treatise on immortality, an edition of which he had not only brought back to Paris from Piedmont but offered it to the press of Jean Roigny in 1541.[175] The northern Renaissance, too, was exemplified in Sinclair's copy, which Little acquired, of Erasmus' *Declarationes . . . ad Censuras Lutetiæ vulgatas sub nomine Facultatis Theologiae Parisiensis* (Basle, 1532), the Dutchman's guarded reply to the Sorbonne's condemnation in 1526 of the *Colloquies* and certain other writings.[176]

An interest in the conciliarist movement is evident in the acquisition of a copy of Monserrat's work on the Pragmatic Sanction of Bourges (1438), whereby the French crown and church acknowledged conciliar supremacy over the pope. Sinclair also possessed copies of the reforming enactments of the Council of Constance (1414–18), which sought to end papal autocracy and initiate a reform of the church in head and members. The text of the Constitutions of the Provincial Council of Mainz, held in 1549 with the aim of further Catholic reform, likewise passed from Henry Sinclair's library into Clement Little's collection; so too (though not from Sinclair) did a copy of the *Antididagma*, published at Louvain in 1544.[177] This was a catechism authorised by the canons of Cologne, where Archbishop Hermann von Wied had embarked on a policy of Catholic reform in his

---

[174] EUL, Dd.3.34; Dd.3.1; Dd.4.16; Dd.3.29; Dd.6.57; Dd.6.62; Dd.5.13; Dd.4.3; Dd.1.22; Dd.3.13; Dd.5.4; Dd.6.53; Dd.4.1; *Early Scottish Libraries*, 49ff. From sources other than Sinclair's library, Clement Little collected the patristic writings of Tertullian (Dd.3.23), Hegesippus (Dd.4.1), Chrysostom (Dd.1.6–9), Augustine (Dd.1.10–17) and Hieronymus or Jerome (Dd.1.18–20) and the later scholastic works of Thomas Aquinas (Dd.3.2) and Duns Scotus (*Miscellany of the Maitland Club*, i, pt. 2, 296). From the library of John Stewart, prior of Coldingham and a natural son of James V, Little obtained Antonius Corvinus' edition of *Augustini et Chrysotomi Theologia* (1539), Dd.6.61; *Early Scottish Libraries*, 150.

[175] EUL, Dd.5.12; *Early Scottish Libraries*, 176; J. Durkan, 'Giovanni Ferrerio', 188. Another product of the Italian Renaissance (though not from Sinclair's library) was Clement Little's copy of Laurentius Valla's *. . . In Novum Testamentum Annotationes* (Basle, 1526) (Dd.6.64).

[176] EUL, Dd.5.6; *Early Scottish Libraries*, 53.

[177] EUL, Dd.2.25; Dd.2.6; Dd.2.47; *Early Scottish Libraries*, 50, 57. Little also owned a copy of the canons of the Council of Trent published at Antwerp, 1564 (Dd.6.38).

provincial council of 1536,[178] and which possibly was used in the drafting of the Scottish catechism issued in Archbishop Hamilton's name in 1552, a copy of which Clement Little also possessed, acquired from a source other than Sinclair's library.[179]

Other reformist literature inherited from Sinclair is exemplified in the *Quaestiones in quartum sententiarum* (Paris, 1530) by Adrian VI, the Dutch reforming pope of the early sixteenth century; Michael Lochmaier's *Parrochiale curatorum* (Rouen, c. 1510) was a popular guide to the liturgy and sacraments; and there were copies, too, of Lutzenburg's *Catalogus haereticorum* (Cologne, 1523), the *Opuscula theologica* of Josse Clichtove, the Flemish humanist and Paris theologian, published at Paris in 1523, and a Paris edition of the Vulgate printed in 1541.[180] The writings of Jacques Almain (c. 1480–1515), the French conciliarist and disciple of Ockham, who expounded his belief in popular sovereignty, were also present; and Almain's Scottish teacher in Paris, John Major, was represented in his *In quatuor evangelia* (Paris, 1529). Also acquired was Sinclair's copy of the Canon of the Mass by Gabriel Biel, the last great exponent of the Occamist *via moderna*, who emphasised the miraculous ministry of the priest in consecrating the elements at communion, and of the necessity for complete observance of every aspect of the liturgy; and it was against Biel's nominalist theology that Luther had reacted so vigorously.[181] Further Catholic works in the list of volumes formerly owned by Sinclair are apparent in the writings of Titelmans, Royard, Coussord and Eck, the great opponent of Luther; but Sinclair also had Calvin's *Defensio orthodoxae fidei de sacra Trinitate contra . . . Serveti* (Geneva, 1554), issued in reply to Sebastian Castellion's plea for toleration, and in defence of the Augustinian principle of repressing heresy by the secular sword and of Geneva's treatment of Servetus.[182]

From sources other than Henry Sinclair's library, Clement Little collected a series of volumes by prominent anti-Lutherans: the list includes Johannes Cochlaeus, the German Catholic who moved from supporting Luther to become his bitter critic; Albert Pighius, another German Catholic, who published his

---

[178] J. K. Cameron, 'The Cologne Reformation and the Church of Scotland', *J. Eccl. H.*, xxx (1979), 39–64; J. K. Cameron, '"Catholic Reform" in Germany and in the pre-1560 Church in Scotland', *Records of the Scottish Church History Society*, xx (1979), 105–17.
[179] EUL, Dd.2.33.
[180] EUL, Dd.6.8; Dd.6.31; Dd.5.9; *Early Scottish Libraries*, 51.
[181] EUL, Dd.4.34; Dd.3.12; Dd.5.26; *Early Scottish Libraries*, 52; 50.
[182] EUL, Dd.6.2; Dd.2.7; Dd.2.48; Dd.2.4–5; Dd.2.19; *Early Scottish Libraries*, 56, 59; 57; 55, 59.

material at Cologne; the Dominican controversialist from Piedmont, Sylvester Prierias (Mazzolini) who began a Thomist revival and promoted papal absolutism; as well as a number of Louvain theologians – Tapper, Driedo, Hessels and Latomus.[183]

This tradition, however, was more than balanced by the numerous Lutheran treatises in Clement Little's collection. Luther himself was well represented; so too was Melanchthon, the friend of Reuchlin and Luther, and Greek professor at Wittenberg, who took part with Luther in the disputations with Eck. Clement Little, for example, possessed a copy of his famous *Loci communes,* as well as other Melanchthonian material.[184] Other Lutheran authors included Bugenhagen, the Pomeranian who settled at Wittenberg as theology professor and helped Luther not only in his translation of the Bible but took part in organising the churches in Saxony and elsewhere in Germany; Andreas Knopken, the reformer in Riga and disciple of Bugenhagen; Niels Hemmingen, student of Maccabaeus, who ultimately lost his theology chair at Copenhagen for his tendency towards Calvinism; Georg Meier (or Major), the Melanchthonian teacher at Wittenberg and superintendent at Eisleben; Bartholomew Camerarius, humanist friend of Melanchthon and teacher at several Lutheran universities; Johann Brentz, the Swabian reformer of Württemberg, who was associated with Luther in the Catechism of Tübingen, a copy of which belonged to Clement Little's collection; and Pellicanus (Conrad Kürsner), an Alsatian Hebrew scholar and former Franciscan friar, who became a reformer at Basle and supported Luther before Zwingli brought him to teach Greek and Hebrew at Zürich.[185]

The Dalmatian Flacius Illyricus (Matthias Vlachich) was a champion of Lutheran orthodoxy and an anti-Philippist on the issue of good works, who taught the Old Testament at Wittenberg: at Magdeburg, he became associated with the *Centuriatores,* a comprehensive history of the Christian church, century by century, and, in effect, the first modern work on universal history, written from a Lutheran standpoint to illustrate the decline of the church under the papacy. A copy of the first Basle edition of 1560 containing Clement Little's

[183] EUL, Dd.2.35; Dd.4.19; Dd.2.32; Dd.4.17; Dd.4.2; Dd.6.17; Dd.2.26; Dd.2.35.
[184] EUL, Dd.2.51; Dd.2.52; Dd.2.56; Dd.6.10; Dd.6.29; Dd.6.39; Dd.6.66; Dd.2.41; Dd.6.23; Dd.6.37.
[185] Dd.6.27; Dd.6.18; Dd.6.40; Dd.2.54; Dd.6.50; Dd.3.30; Dd.5.14; Dd.5.31; Dd.2.51; Dd.4.7.

autograph was included in the theological donations of 1580.[186] Tilemann Hesshus, with whom Calvin had crossed swords in his *Defensio*, was another ultra-Lutheran theologian, who as a student of Melanchthon at Wittenberg was appointed professor at Heidelberg on Melanchthon's recommendation.[187]

By the 1560s, however, opponents of the Reformation in Scotland were agreed that the leading Scottish reformers had become 'Calvinians',[188] and the earlier Lutheran phase was superseded by a more distinctively Reformed tradition associated with the Swiss school of reformers, who, in turn, figured prominently in Clement Little's theological collection. The writings of Calvin were certainly much in evidence, not only his influential *Institutio, Commentarii* and *Harmonia in evangelia*, but other works including his *Epistolae* and his *Defensio orthodoxe fidei de sacra Trinitate*, discussed above.[189] The more important works of Theodore Beza, the French theologian and Calvin's colleague in Geneva, were also at hand, notably his famous *Annotations on the New Testament*, his *Confessio Christianae fidei*, his treatise on divorce, and his volume on the civil magistrate's duty to punish heresy.[190] Nor was Zürich ignored: the works of Zwingli and Bullinger were prominent; Theodore Bibliander, the orientalist and Zürich reformer, and Caspar Megander (or Grossman), the reformer at Zürich and Berne, were also represented.[191] The commentaries of Musculus, the Augsburg reformer, and those of Lambert Daneau, the prolific French Calvinist theologian, were evidently favoured; and there were treatises, too, by Pierre Viret, the reformer of Lausanne and the Pays de Vaud, and by the ecumenical Martin Bucer, the former Dominican who settled at Strasbourg and tried to reconcile Luther and Zwingli, including a copy of Bucer's influential *De regno Christi Jesu*, a work dedicated to Edward VI of England.[192] Peter Martyr (Vermigli), the former Augustinian from Lucca, who taught in Strasbourg and Zürich, and the

---

[186] EUL, Dd.4.22; *Miscellany of the Maitland Club.*, i, pt.2, 293, 294; cf., D. Hay, *Annalists and Historians* (London, 1977), 123–5.

[187] EUL, Dd.2.38.

[188] See below, 76.

[189] EUL, Dd.1.23–28; Dd.2.9; Dd.2.19–20; Dd.4.6; Dd.5.15; Dd.6.63; see above, 64.

[190] *Miscellany of the Maitland Club*, i, pt.2, 292; EUL, Dd.2.9; Dd.2.11; Dd.2.17; Dd.5.1; Dd.6.11; Dd.62.0.

[191] EUL, Dd.4.9–10; *Miscellany of the Maitland Club*, i, pt.2, 293 (Bullinger, *Decades*); EUL, Dd.2.13; Dd.2.50; Dd.2.54; Dd.2.56; Dd.3.4; Dd.3.20; Dd.5.46; Dd.6.14; Dd.6.21; Dd.6.46–7; Dd.6.58; Dd.2.17; Dd.5.46; Dd.6.18.

[192] EUL, Dd.3.5–10; Dd.3.22; Dd.2.14; Dd.3.21; Dd.6.52; Dd.2.23–4; Dd.3.30; Dd.5.44.

German reformer Oecolampadius, who assisted Erasmus in his edition of the Greek New Testament and settled at Basle where he produced commentaries on the Bible and translations from the fathers, were two further authors whose works Clement Little evidently valued.[193] Besides the leading continental reformers, Clement Little had the works of several English protestant divines: these included Archbishop Cranmer, Bishop Ridley and Thomas Becon on the eucharist; Robert Barnes, who as chaplain to Henry VIII had once been imprisoned for Lutheranism, on the lives of the popes; Robert Watson, a Marian exile; and Bishop Jewel's *A replie unto M. Hardinges answear* and his famous *Apologia ecclesiae Anglicanae*, a copy of which Clement Little acquired from the library of Lord James Stewart, Earl of Moray, who had received it as a present from the English ambassador.[194] By contrast, the only Scots writers featured were all Catholics: John Major, Archbishop Hamilton, who promoted the Catechism of 1552, and Ninian Winzet, Linlithgow schoolmaster, literary disputant with Knox and later abbot of Ratisbon, whose *The buke of the four scoir-thre questions*, which Clement Little possessed, is a terse assault on the validity of the Reformed ministry.[195]

Several of these works – Major's . . . *Sententiarum*, Hamilton's Catechism, Winzet and Jewel's *A replie* – were not included in the original collection handed over to the town in August 1580. They formed part of a supplementary list of ten titles added to the earlier donation by William Little 'in name of the executouris of umquhile M. Clement Litill'. These additional volumes were duly received by James Lawson and were 'eikit to the rest of the buikis left be the said umquhile Mr. Clement to the commoun Librarie'.[196]

With such a catholicity of taste in theological treatises, and with a lawyer's eye for what was permissible, it was not inappropriate that Clement Little should have taken part in the general assembly's scrutiny of forthcoming religious publications: in March 1573/4 he was asked 'to revise and consider' the reply made by a minister, John Duncanson, to the latest work by the Scots Jesuit, James Tyrie, and to report on another entitled 'Of God's Providence'.[197]

[193] EUL, Dd.2.18; Dd.3.3; Dd.5.2; Dd.5.16; Dd.5.41; Dd.2.40; Dd.3.35; Dd.5.7; Dd.6.49.
[194] EUL, Dd.6.12; Dd.6.44; Dd.6.60; Dd.6.30; Dd.6.7; Dd.2.49; Dd.5.32; *Early Scottish Libraries*, 149. Bishop Ponet was also represented in the collection (Dd.6.32).
[195] EUL, Dd.3.12; Dd.5.19; Dd.5.22; Dd.2.33; Dd.6.9.
[196] EUL, *Miscellany of the Maitland Club*, i, pt.2, 300–1.
[197] *BUK*, i, 289.

Yet not all books in the collection were strictly theological. Some volumes dealt with aspects of ecclesiastical law, despite the exclusion of 'his haill law bukis' from the donation of 1580: there were treatises on the church's jurisdiction, on matrimony and divorce, on ordination and on matters relating to benefices; there was even a guide to canon law; several were medieval treatises, but some were contemporary, notably the work of the German Franciscan Ferus (or Wild) on ordination, and *De Sacris ecclesiae ministeriis ac beneficiis* (Paris, 1551) by François Duaren, the civil lawyer at Bourges who had been the colleague of Edward Henryson.[198] These volumes all had a relevance to Little's work as commissary; but there was no trace of any works on civil law. His books on civil law evidently became dispersed, as they formed no part of the donation of 1580, and only four titles have been traced to Worcester College, Oxford.[199]

One literary work, owned by Clement Little, which was excluded from the theological collection of 1580, later found its way into the university library: this was Johannes Ravisius, *Epitheta studiosis omnibus poeticae artis maxime utilia* (Paris, 1524), formerly belonging to Henry Sinclair, and later donated to the library by mastership candidates in 1643.[200] William Little (either Clement's brother or his brother's son) also donated to the library in 1599 a copy of Horantius, *Locorum catholicorum . . . libri vii* (Paris, 1565), with the inscription: 'Ego donatus sum academia Edinburgensi a Guilielmo Littillo, Guiliemus Littillus, 1599'. This work had been previously owned by James Lawson, who as minister was first keeper of the theological library, and it was then bought for 16s. by Robert Rollock, the first principal and keeper of the college library.[201] This volume is of particular interest, for it links the names of Lawson, Rollock and William Little; and according to Henry Charteris, who succeeded Rollock as principal in 1599, both Lawson and William Little were the leading spokesmen for founding the town's college, Lawson, in particular, being credited with recommending to the council the choice of Rollock as principal.[202]

---

[198] EUL, Dd.2.22; Dd.2.39; Dd.2.10; Dd.5.45; Dd.6.11; Dd.2.36; Dd.5.10; Dd.3.18–19; Dd.6.4; Dd.2.22.

[199] *Early Scottish Libraries*, 123–4.

[200] EUL, S*18.24; *Early Scottish Libraries*, 51.

[201] EUL, Dd.7.121. William Little's son, William, graduated from Edinburgh in 1599 and may have presented a copy of Horantius to the Library at his graduation (*A catalogue of graduates*, 16).

[202] *Select Works of Robert Rollock*, ed. W. M. Gunn, 2 vols. (Edinburgh, 1844–9), i, lxii–lxiii.

Clement Little's richly assorted collection was highly esteemed and much prized, not least, by Rollock as custodian and reader, for the university's first principal was himself a theologian of considerable distinction, and he published numerous theological works whose fame spread well beyond Scotland, winning solid praise from Beza in Geneva.[203] Other books were purchased for the library, and students on graduating presented further volumes which helped to enhance the ever-growing collection. Although the library grew apace with subsequent acquisitions, the most substantial section long remained Clement Little's collection until overshadowed by further gifts in the course of the seventeenth century. The university and its library had been born but they had still to come of age; and Edinburgh had yet to achieve a wider acclaim as a distinguished centre not only of courtly culture but of scholarship and learning.

[203] Ibid., i, lxx–lxxiii.

3

The Calvinist Contribution to the Scottish Reformation

The comparatively late arrival of the Reformation in Scotland provided Scots with ample opportunity to assimilate the theological standpoints of most influential continental reformers. Through first-hand experience and personal contact, through correspondence and the printed word, Scottish reformers were able to keep abreast with the latest developments in Europe. In church government, as in doctrine, there could be little which escaped their attention. Indeed, if Scotland needed any example other than scripture she had only to look to Germany, England and Scandinavia, and to Switzerland, France and the Netherlands. Narrowing the field somewhat, the claim has been advanced that the earlier polity of the Scottish church had 'a strong Lutheran flavour about it'.[1] Yet, when an examination is made of the many and varied influences to which Scotland was subjected at the Reformation, Calvinism, it would seem, was not the least significant.

In its final form, the Scottish Reformation, it need scarcely be doubted, was characterised by at least a moderate Calvinism in its solution to the challenges of theology and ecclesiastical polity. The Scots Confession of Faith, as the doctrinal statement of the Reformation, and the Book of Discipline, outlining the envisaged structure of the church, forcefully and sometimes eloquently display a firm attachment to Reformed principles. In these documents, little or nothing distinctive of the old Lutheranism which had marked the initial stages of the Reformation can be detected. The span of three decades and more of Reformed teaching and example stood between the first infiltration of

[1] G. Donaldson, *Scotland: Church and Nation through Sixteen Centuries* (2nd edn., Edinburgh, 1972), 58.

Lutheran thought into Scotland and the compilation of the Scots Confession in 1560.

The degree to which the reformed church was doctrinally affected by Calvin's teaching does perhaps lie within the province of the theologian rather than that of the historian, but scholars in both disciplines have long recognised Calvin's remarkable influence as the 'founder of a civilisation'.[2] One who is both an historian and a theologian has indicated how the Scots Confession 'affirms Calvinism with a simple fervour',[3] another has described that work as a 'Calvinistic explication of the Creeds',[4] and earlier a distinguished ecclesiastical historian, clearly demonstrated how passages of that work were directly derived from Genevan sources.[5] It is not surprising therefore that a recent commentator should remark that the Confession of 1560 'affirmed the full Calvinistic doctrine of the Lord's Supper in strikingly realistic language'.[6]

The doctrine of predestination, it is true, was not stressed in the Confession; but neither was it developed in the first edition of Calvin's *Institutes* in 1536, and it was only in later years that the Genevan accorded the doctrine a more central position in his theology.[7] If the authors of the Scots Confession deemed it unnecessary to treat the subject systematically, the kernel of the doctrine was clearly present: the 'elect' who were chosen 'befoir the fundatioun of the warld was laid', are referred to in seven separate passages, though the 'reprobate', so termed, are specifically mentioned only thrice, and the distinctive phrase 'the eternall and immutabill decree of God fra quhilk all our salvatioun springs and depends'[8] appears but once.[9] Yet whatever the deficiencies in the teaching on predestination in the Scots Confession, the standpoint of one leading reformer can be satisfactorily attested. John Knox, whom Beza called 'the apostle of the Scots',[10] left no one in any doubt of his views on the subject. These he had proclaimed in his treatise on predestination, published at Geneva in 1560, in which he sought to assail

[2] E. G. Léonard, *A History of Protestantism*, i (London, 1965), 292.

[3] J. T. McNeill, *The History and Character of Calvinism* (New York, 1967), 299.

[4] G. D. Henderson, *Presbyterianism* (Aberdeen, 1954), 32.

[5] A. F. Mitchell, *The Scottish Reformation* (Edinburgh, 1900), 104–12.

[6] B. A. Gerrish, 'The Lord's Supper in the Reformed Confessions', *Theology Today*, xxiii (1966), 224–43 at 239.

[7] F. Wendel, *Calvin* (London, 1972), 265ff.

[8] *The Works of John Knox*, ed. D. Laing, 6 vols. (Edinburgh, 1846–8), ii, 100 and n.2.

[9] Ibid., ii, 98, 100, 101, 108–9, 114, 119, 120.

[10] T. McCrie, *Life of John Knox* (Edinburgh, 1855), 463.

Calvin's adversaries and to vindicate 'the wordes of this most godlie writer from whose judgement none of us doeth dissent in this mater'.[11] Knox, for one, evidently attached a central importance to the doctrine of predestination, for in his treatise he forcefully explained how 'the doctrine of God's eternal predestination is so necessarie to the church of God that without the same can faith neither be truely taught nether surely established'.[12] Elsewhere in his writings, Knox, it is true, was prepared to adopt and to use to good effect the religious symbolism of the covenants.[13] In some tentative sense, therefore, he may be regarded as a precursor of Robert Rollock and Robert Bruce, two later exponents of covenant thought in Scotland.[14] Yet covenant or federal theology, if carried to extremes, could undermine the doctrine of predestination. It could ultimately shift the emphasis in Calvinism away from the eternal decree of God by focusing attention on the reciprocal obligations of the contract between man and God.[15] Even so, Calvin himself had readily employed the language of the covenants within a wide variety of contexts and evidently understood the matter to be central to his system of theology.[16] Nor did John Knox find any difficulty in reconciling to his own satisfaction the doctrine of predestination with the concept of the covenant.[17]

In scope, the Scots Confession is comparable with other Reformed confessions of the period; and if a parallel is to be

[11] Knox, *Works*, v, 21–468, at 169.

[12] Ibid., 25.

[13] Ibid., ii, 86; iii, 190–7; iv, 123–5, 434, 489, 500, 505–6; vi, 234, 239, 307, 487.

[14] Cf., G. D. Henderson, *The Burning Bush* (Edinburgh, 1957), 68; S. A. Burrell, 'The Covenant Idea as a Revolutionary Symbol: Scotland, 1596–1637', *Church History*, xxvii (1958), 338–49, at 341.

[15] A. C. McGiffert, *Protestant Thought before Kant* (London, 1911), 153–4; E. H. Emerson, 'Calvin and Covenant Theology', *Church History*, xxv (1956), 136–43, at 138.

[16] See index to J. T. McNeill's edition of Calvin's *Institutes of the Christian Religion*, 2 vols. (London, 1961), ii, 1653. Recently, P. A. Lillback has illustrated the inadequacy of interpretations which claim a division between the Rhineland reformers and Calvin on the issue of the mutability and conditionality of the covenant, and indicated Calvin's debt to Zwingli and Bullinger: 'The Binding of God: Calvin's Rôle in the Development of Covenant Theology' (Westminster Theological Seminary, Ph.D. thesis, 1985), 136ff, 184ff, 219ff, 489, 496 and *passim*. The significance of these links is missed in D. Shaw, 'Zwinglian Influences on the Scottish Reformation', *Records of the Scottish Church History Society*, xxii (1985), 132–3. My own former research student, Dr Andrew Woolsey has also taken issue with the central thesis of J. Wayne Baker's *Heinrich Bullinger and the Covenant: the Other Reformed Tradition* (Ohio, 1980) in 'Unity and Continuity in Covenantal Thought: A Study in the Reformed Tradition to the Westminster Assembly' (Glasgow Ph.D. thesis, 1988). In 'The Scots Confession 1560: Context, Complexion and Critique', *Archiv für Reformationsgeschichte*, lxxviii (1987), 314, W. I. P. Hazlett follows Baker.

[17] Knox, *Works*, v, 46–7, 263, 265, 279, 343–5.

sought it may be found in two confessions inspired by Calvin: the French Confession of 1559 and the Belgic Confession written in 1559 by Guido de Brès and published in 1561.[18] But there was also present in the Confession of 1560, as there was in its continental counterparts, a certain body of doctrine which would accommodate protestants of varying ecclesiastical viewpoints and which need not necessarily offend those with Lutheran susceptibilities. An indication of the considerable measure of doctrinal accord between those of differing protestant persuasions had been demonstrated much earlier, in a continental context, in the conference at Marburg in 1529 when Luther and Zwingli reached agreement on fourteen and a half out of fifteen articles and agreed to differ only in their interpretation of the Lord's Supper.[19]

On this latter theme, it has been accurately observed that 'the Scots Confession of Faith of 1560 declared its belief in a Real Presence'.[20] Yet it would seem to be a mistake were one to conclude from this that by rejecting Zwingli the Scots were thereby committed to a Lutheran interpretation of the Lord's Supper. Indeed, on the contrary, there is no evidence, it has been pointed out, that 'an explicitly Lutheran Communion was ever celebrated in Scotland'.[21] Whatever the accuracy of this statement, it is, at any rate, significant that Knox should claim in his *History*, written in the 1560s, that when he celebrated communion at St Andrews in 1547 he did so 'in the same puritie that now it is ministrat in the churches of Scotland, wyth that same doctrin, that he had taught unto thame'. Three years later, in 1550, Knox affirmed the essentially Calvinist tenet that 'when I eat and drink at the tabill, I opinlie confes the frute and vertew of Chrystis bodie, of his blude and passion, to apperteane to my self; and that I am a member of his misticall bodie'.[22] Nor does there seem much substance in the frequently cited claim distinguishing between Knox's readiness to celebrate the Lord's Supper in private houses before establishing proper churches and Calvin's recognition that the sacrament should be dispensed in organised churches. The supposed contrast soon dissolves when Calvin's own judgement is recalled that 'whenever we see the word of God sincerely preached and heard, wherever we see the

[18] P. Schaff, *A History of the Creeds of Christendom*, 3 vols. (London, 1877), iii, 356–436.
[19] *Luther's Works*, edd. J. Pelikan and H. T. Lehmann, 55 vols. (Philadelphia, 1955–69), vol. 38, pp. 85–9.
[20] G. Donaldson, *Scotland: Church and Nation through Sixteen Centuries*, 68.
[21] J. S. McEwen, *The Faith of John Knox* (London, 1961), 55.
[22] Knox, *Works*, i, 201–2; iii, 67.

sacraments administered according to the Institution of Christ, there we cannot have any doubt that the Church of God has some existence'.[23]

Calvinists, no less than Lutherans, believed in a real presence in the Supper, and a study of the eucharistic doctrine of the Scots Confession would suggest that the reformers in 1560 deliberately departed from the distinctive teaching of Luther and consciously adhered to that of Calvin instead. Whereas Luther had asserted that the body of Christ is present not only in the Supper but substantially present in the elements and received by the mouths of believers and unbelievers alike (despite the consequences for the latter),[24] the Scots in their Confession of Faith seem to deny the essence of Luther's teaching and to assert something significantly different. If the Roman doctrine of transubstantiation was rejected outright so too was Luther's belief in what is loosely called 'consubstantiation' implicitly set aside, as was the teaching of the sacramentarians, on the other side of the divide, who affirmed the 'sacramentis to be nothing else but naked and bair signes'.[25] If the beliefs of Rome, Wittenberg and Zürich were regarded in varying degrees as somehow erroneous or inadequate, those of Geneva had evidently more to commend themselves.

Following Calvin, the Scots found no justification for any notion of the ubiquity of the body. Christ's glorified body, they maintained, remains in heaven on the right hand of God and cannot descend so as to be materially present in and under the elements.[26] Instead, believers alone, through faith, are raised up towards heaven to receive what Christ offers in the sacrament.[27] This mystical or sacred union, the Confession plainly taught, 'is wrocht by operatioun of the Holy Ghost, who by trew faith caryes us above all thingis that ar visible, carnall and earthlie, and maikis us to feid upoun the body and bloode of Christ Jesus, whiche was ones brokin and schedd for us, whiche now is in the heavin, and appeareth in the presence of his Father for us'.[28] For the Scots, the body and blood of Christ are clearly not materially

[23] Calvin, *Institutes of the Christian Religion*, ed. H. Beveridge, 3 vols. (Edinburgh, 1845–6), IV, i, 9.

[24] *Luther's Works*, vol. 36, pp.32, 342ff.; vol. 37, pp.29, 87ff., 100–1, 109–10, 354, 367; vol. 38, pp.26, 83, 306.

[25] Knox, *Works*, ii, 114, 115; cf., Calvin, *Institutes*, IV, xvii, 10; Calvin, *Tracts relating to the Reformation*, ed. H. Beveridge, 3 vols. (Edinburgh, 1844–51), ii, 307.

[26] Knox, *Works*, ii, 114; cf., Calvin, *Institutes*, IV, xvii, 16–19; Calvin, *Tracts*, ii, 218–19, 220.

[27] Knox, *Works*, ii, 114–15, 117–18; cf. Calvin, *Institutes*, IV, xvii, 12, 18–19, 31, 36; Calvin, *Tracts*, ii, 280, 373.

[28] Knox, *Works*, ii, 114; cf., Calvin, *Institutes*, IV, xvii, 1, 3, 5, 18–19, 32, 38; Calvin, *Tracts*, ii, 282, 374, 377.

present in the sacrament; they cannot be orally received so as physically to nourish the body. On the contrary, 'in the Supper, rychtlie used, Christ Jesus is so joyned with us that he becumis the verray nurishement and foode of our saullis'.[29] Indeed, as Knox had taught a decade earlier, 'in the sacrament we receave Jesus Chryst spirituallie'.[30] To assert this was not to deny the communion of Christ's person in the sacrament, but only to deny a substantial or material presence in the elements. The Confession itself made careful distinction between Christ's 'naturall substance' and the elements as the sacramental signs, 'so that we will neather wirschip the signes in place of that which is signifeid by thame; neather yit do we dispyse and interprete thame as unprofitable and vane'.[31] Such an interpretation would seem to be patently Calvinist; and Calvin himself had concluded that the[32]

> 'sacred communion of flesh and blood by which Christ transfuses his life into us, just as if it penetrated our bones and marrow, he testifies and seals in the Supper, and that not by presenting a vain or empty sign, but by there exerting an efficacy of the Spirit by which he fulfils what he promises. And truly the thing there signified he exhibits and offers to all who sit down at that spiritual feast, although it is beneficially received by believers only who receive this great benefit with true faith and heartfelt gratitude'.

On each crucial issue when confronted with a choice of following either Luther or Calvin, the Scots seem instinctively to have chosen the latter; and it was scarcely surprising that the general assembly should stipulate that the sacraments should be administered after the manner specified in 'the Book of Geneva'.[33]

Attention, however, need not be confined to the Confession of Faith, for the Book of Common Order,[34] popularly known as 'Knox's Liturgy', is an obvious example of the wholesale importation into Scotland of liturgical forms used by Knox's Genevan congregation. Included in that work was a copy of Calvin's catechism, and in 1562 and again in 1564 the general assembly sanctioned and authorised the Book of Common Order as a serviceable guide to worship in the Church of

[29] Knox, *Works*, ii, 114; cf., Calvin, *Institutes*, IV, xvii, 1, 3 10, 24, 32; Calvin, *Tracts*, ii, 374.
[30] Knox, *Works*, iii, 75.
[31] Ibid., ii, 115; cf., Calvin, *Institutes*, IV, xvii, 11, 19, 21; Calvin, *Tracts*, ii, 215, 224.
[32] Calvin, *Institutes*, IV, xvii, 10.
[33] *The Booke of the Universall Kirk, Acts and Proceedings of the General Assemblies of the Kirk of Scotland* [BUK], 3 vols. and appendix vol. (Edinburgh, 1839), i, 30.
[34] Knox, *Works*, vi, 293ff.

Scotland,[35] but even, earlier, with the very composition of the Book of Discipline, this essentially Genevan publication had already become for Scots 'oure buke of Common Ordour',[36] 'the Booke of our Common Ordour, callit the Ordour of Geneva'.[37] The assimilation had become complete. Contained within the Book of Common Order was a metrical version of the psalms, and some have found it significant that the Scots should look to Geneva, like their French counterparts, and should officially authorise the use of the metrical psalms as an integral part of public worship rather than adopt the hymns of Lutheran churches.[38]

Although some later commentators have been tempted to minimise the extent of Calvin's influence in Scotland, contemporaries themselves were by no means unaware of the influences at work. One former cleric, Thomas Methven, when confronted by the discipline of St Andrews kirk session in August 1561, declared that 'he was nether ane Papist nor ane Calwynist, nor of Paul nor of Apollo, bot Jesus Cristis man',[39] and Bishop Leslie, as a good Catholic, was quite convinced in his own mind that Willock, Goodman and Knox were 'the ministeris of Calvine'.[40] Another Catholic controversialist, Ninian Winzet, in a polemic directed against Knox and the 'Calviniane ministeris', derisively spoke of 'your grete maister Calvin', of the 'lernit theologis of a gret number in Scotland and Geneva', designating Knox as 'principal Patriark of the Calviniane court', and he went on to warn the ministers not to 'mak a monstruous Idoll of your Maister Calvin'.[41] In short, what Winzet was really complaining about was that tendency of Scottish reformed thought which, he felt, 'bindis and astrictis us only to the doctrine and ordour laitlie set furth at Geneva'.[42] Not only had Winzet conferred with what he called 'sum strang Calvinianis' as well as with 'weill leirnit

---

[35] *BUK*, i, 30, 54.

[36] Knox, *Works*, ii, 239.

[37] Ibid., 210. Carswell in his Gaelic translation of the *BCO* likewise acknowledged his debt to 'the Christian brethren who were in the city called Geneva'. *Foirm Na N-Urrnuidheadh*, ed. R. L. Thomson (Edinburgh, 1970), 11, 180.

[38] W. Cowan, 'The Scottish Reformation Psalmody', *RSCHS*, i, 29–47.

[39] *Register of the Minister, Elders and Deacons of the Christian Congregation of St Andrews, 1559–1600*, ed. D. H. Fleming, 2 vols. (Edinburgh, 1889–90), i, 135.

[40] Leslie, *The Historie of Scotland*, edd. E. G. Cody and W. Murison, 2 vols. (Edinburgh, 1888–95), ii, 449; cf., 447, 464.

[41] Winzet, *Certane tractatis for reformatioun of doctryne and maneris in Scotland* (Edinburgh, 1835), 37, 56, 58, 74, 79, 87.

[42] Ibid., 69.

catholikis',[43] but he also professed an acquaintance with Calvin's works,[44] and as there were other Scottish Catholics who found a place for the works of Calvin on the shelves of their libraries, it is safe to assume both that there was a ready supply of Calvinist literature and that it was read by reformers as well as Catholics. Among the pre-Reformation purchases of Adam Bothwell, the Catholic bishop of Orkney who conformed at the Reformation, were Calvin's *Commentaries on Isaiah*, published in 1551;[45] John Duncanson, a canon regular of St Andrews who died in 1566 and who also conformed, possessed a copy of Calvin's *Opuscula*, printed in Geneva in 1552;[46] John Craig, a Dominican friar and later minister at Edinburgh, became converted to protestantism, it was said, by reading Calvin's *Institutes*;[47] and John Row, a Jesuit who subsequently became minister at Perth, was finally won over to protestantism by visiting Geneva *en route* from Italy to France.[48]

Few, it would seem, could disagree with the conclusion that the theology of the post-Reformation church was characterised by at least a moderate Calvinism. This no doubt held good for England, too, but whereas the conservative form of polity retained by the English church was determined in the main by the crown which wished no irrevocable break with the past, in Scotland a differing political situation had enabled a more radical type of church organisation to come into being, a polity which cast aside much of the traditional medieval organisation and one which was therefore moulded not on the example of England, or of the Lutheran countries, but rather on that of the 'best reformed churches'[49] of Switzerland and France. Having adopted a Calvinist theology, and being freed from the restraining influences which even a godly monarch might have wished to exercise, the Scots were able to adopt an essentially Calvinist polity. Indeed, not the least of Calvinism's contributions to the Scottish Reformation was its ability by then to provide to Knox and his colleagues the necessary religious justification for a rebellion in a way in which less assertive, early Lutheranism

[43] Ibid., 55.
[44] Ibid., 74, 79, 89.
[45] J. Durkan and A. Ross, *Early Scottish Libraries* (Glasgow, 1961), 29.
[46] Ibid., 93. For other Scottish Catholics who possessed copies of Calvin's works in their libraries, see ibid., 59, 83, 131.
[47] Spottiswoode, *History of the Church of Scotland*, 3 vols. (Edinburgh, 1851–65), iii, 92.
[48] Ibid., ii, 320.
[49] The phrase occurs in *BUK*, i, 246; Calderwood, *The History of the Kirk of Scotland*, ed. T. Thomson, 8 vols. (Edinburgh, 1842–9), iii, 222; see further below, 334ff.

generally had not (notwithstanding the later example, to which Knox appealed, of the Magdeburg *Bekenntnis* of 1550),[50] and, equally, its ability to provide the religious movement with an ecclesiastical organisation capable of functioning effectively in times of adversity when the church lay under the cross, as well as in more favourable circumstances when the church was established and accorded due recognition by the state.

Wherever a Calvinist polity prevailed, government of the church at congregational level was entrusted to a consistory composed of one or more ministers and a number of elected elders and deacons. In Scotland, the Reformation seems to have followed the Swiss pattern in penetrating the burghs and surrounding countryside. As a result, the 'privy kirks' of the 1550s evolved into the kirk sessions of the 1560s.[51] This peculiar polity observed in Calvinist churches did not escape the attention of Ninian Winzet who asked the reformers to justify their introduction of a 'new ordour of Eldaris' in the kirk,[52] and the difference between the various churches of the protestant persuasion was a subject which also attracted the attention of Winzet who lectured the Scottish reformers accordingly:[53]

> 'your selfis knawis Ingland, Denmark and Alemannie except sum Calvinistis and utheris strange sectis praetending reformatioun alsua by the Romane kirk to dissent in mony heidis fra your doctrine.'

Nor did the impact of Calvin's teaching, it may be added, go unnoticed by Richard Hooker, eleven years the senior of Archbishop Spottiswoode in Scotland, who described how the reformer's writings became 'almost the very canon to judge both doctrine and discipline by' and, after describing how the French churches 'all cast according to that mould which Calvin had made', he added the illuminating, though hardly surprising, comment that 'the church of Scotland in erecting the fabric of their reformation took the selfsame pattern.'[54] Even Archbishop Spottiswoode could scarcely efface, had he wished to do so, the reality of the reformers' debt to Geneva. On his return to Scotland, Knox, we are told, strove 'by all means to conform the government of the Church with that which he had seen in

[50] Knox, *Works*, i, 442–3; ii, 281ff., 425–60; iv, 415–16; Goodman, *How Superior Powers Oght to be Obeyd* (New York, 1931), *passim*; see also above, xv, and below, 246.

[51] Knox, *Works*, i, 300; vi, 78; Calderwood, *History*, i, 333; see above, 12–15.

[52] Winzet, *Certane Tractatis*, 90.

[53] Ibid., 86.

[54] Hooker, *Of the Laws of Ecclesiastical Polity*, Preface, ii, 8, in *Works*, ed. I. Walton, 2 vols. (Oxford, 1865).

Geneva', though in another passage of his *History*, Spottiswoode acknowledged that the first Book of Discipline was 'framed by John Knox, partly in imitation of the Reformed Churches of Germany, partly of that which he had seen in Geneva'.[55]

Whatever the precise meaning which ought to be attached to the phrase 'the Reformed Churches of Germany', the inclusion of Germany in his description has led some to suggest that the origins of some aspects of the Scottish polity 'are to be sought not in Geneva or France but in the Lutheran churches' and that the 'possibility of a debt to Denmark cannot be overlooked'.[56] It is interesting that Cecil, in a letter to the Lords of the Congregation in July 1559, should recommend to the Scots for their attention the Danish financial settlement for the maintenance of the ministry, remarking that he knew of 'no better example in any reformed state than I have heard to be in Denmark'.[57] For the Scots, what exactly Cecil's example amounted to in practice it might be hard to say. What is perhaps more certain is that the response of the Scots was less than enthusiastic. In their reply, Argyll and Lord James Stewart reminded Cecil of the essential difference between the situation in Scotland where the Reformation was carried out in opposition to the crown and that 'which ever favoured you and Denmark in all your reformations',[58] where their form and course had been directed by the crown. The timing of Cecil's advice, in any event, was scarcely opportune. The attention of the Lords of the Congregation was inevitably focused on more pressing issues. Not only so, perceptive Scots were evidently not ignorant of the doctrinal divergence which had emerged between the churches of Scotland and Scandinavia. Each church, it is true, accorded the other recognition of its ministry[59] – it would not have occurred to anyone familiar with Reformation principles to have done otherwise – but it was not until 1587 that Andrew Melville, on the instructions of the general assembly, wrote to congratulate the ministers of Danskene (or Danzig) for 'thair embracing of the trueth in the matter of the Sacrament'.[60] All in all, it is certainly

[55] Keith, *History of the Affairs of Church and State in Scotland*, 3 vols. (Edinburgh, 1844–50), iii, 15, quoting from Spottiswoode's MS. History; Spottiswoode, *History*, i, 371.

[56] G. Donaldson, '"The Example of Denmark" in the Scottish Reformation', *Scottish Historical Review* [SHR], xxvii, 57–64, at 57, 64.

[57] *Calendar of the State Papers relating to Scotland and Mary, Queen of Scots, 1547–1603* [CSP Scot], ed. J. Bain, *et al.* 13 vols. (Edinburgh, 1898–1969), i, no. 506; Knox, *Works*, vi, 51–5, at 53.

[58] *CSP Scot.*, i, no. 525; Knox, *Works*, vi, 65–7, at 66.

[59] *St Andrews Kirk Session Records*, i, 48–50.

[60] *BUK*, ii, 699.

not easy to see why a church which decided to adopt a Reformed theology should seek to imitate features distinctive of Lutheran church polities. Even if Cecil's remark prompted Scots to look beyond the financial settlement[61] to examine the polity operating in the Danish church, there would seem to be slender enough grounds for believing that the Scots deliberately borrowed any of the peculiar features of the Danish church system. Besides, there is no element in the Scottish polity which is paralleled only in Denmark, and indeed evidence can be adduced which would suggest that, despite any apparent or superficial similarities, the polities of the two churches were founded on divergent principles.

In Scotland, unlike most Lutheran countries, the reformers asserted their belief in an autonomous ecclesiastical jurisdiction in no sense exercised at the discretion of the civil power or indeed of any earthly authority. Not only did the general assembly continue to meet without warrant from the secular authorities,[62] but throughout the 1560s the church advanced the claim that its jurisdiction should be separate from that of the state.[63] Moreover, unlike his counterpart in some Lutheran countries,[64] the Scottish superintendent never became a mere royal official or instrument for royal control over the church. Ecclesiastical discipline was not to become a function of the magistracy and

[61] The existence of an extract from the *Ordinatio Ecclesiastica* of the Danish and Norwegian Lutheran church, written in an apparently sixteenth-century Scottish hand, in NLS, Adv. MS. 29.2.8, fo. 51, is doubtless significant (see G. Donaldson, *SHR*, xxvii, 60), but it is also revealing that the portion extracted from the *Ordinatio* should confine itself to the narrow issue of the financial settlement for the church and not deal directly with the wider theme of ecclesiastical polity.

[62] Knox, *Works*, ii, 296, 395–7, 405–6; *BUK*, i, 292; Calderwood, *History*, iii, 305, 307. In the period prior to the 'Black acts' of 1584, assemblies were summoned without reference to the king's consent. The normal method was for the assembly itself to decide the date of its next meeting (*e.g. BUK*, i, 7, 24, 64, 99, 133, 183, 186, 362, 391 *et passim*). In special circumstances, the assembly authorised Knox and the ministers of Edinburgh to intimate the date for the next assembly (*e.g. BUK*, i, 38, 64, 313, 330, 363; ii, 570, 606, 785, Knox, *Works*, ii, 414–5). The regent's proclamation for an assembly, technically a 'convention', to meet in October 1572 to discuss the Catholic menace at home and abroad was exceptional (*Register of the Privy Council of Scotland [RPC]*, 1st ser., edd. J. H. Burton and D. Masson, 14 vols. (Edinburgh, 1877–98), ii, 168–9; *BUK*, i, 250–4); and Throckmorton's report to Elizabeth that the assembly of July 1567 was 'reassembled by the Kynges aucthoritye' (Knox, *Works*, vi, 555) is unsubstantiated (see *BUK*, i, 99). His statement doubtless reflects the events surrounding the deposition of Mary and the accession of her infant son (cf., Knox, *Works*, ii, 563–5), but his phraseology strongly suggests a lack of familiarity with Scottish practice.

[63] *RPC*, ii, 7; *BUK*, i, 140, 146; cf., *BUK*, i, 29, 50, 113, 128.

[64] Cf., M. Roberts, *The Early Vasas* (Cambridge, 1968), 168–9; A. L. Drummond, *German Protestantism since Luther* (London, 1951), 178.

those continental precedents, both Lutheran and Reformed, where it did so become were clearly set aside in favour of what came to be the essentially Calvinist dichotomy of minister and magistrate.

In the regulation of its ministry, the Scottish church found no place either for the *provst*, or dean, of the Danish system,[65] or for the ministerial deacon of the English church. Nor did Scottish reformers assert as did the English that 'from the Apostles' time there hath been these three orders of ministers in Christ's Church: Bishops, Priests and Deacons'.[66] Departing from the examples of Denmark and England, the Scots maintained the scriptural validity of a ministry which included elected elders and deacons (the latter as financial officers). Such an order, it was maintained, God had 'now restoired unto us agane efter that the publict face of the Kirk hes bene deformed by the tyrany of that Romane Antichrist'.[67]

The disinclination to accept magisterial supremacy in the spiritual realm, the emphasis upon the church's sovereignty and the autonomy of its jurisdiction, the introduction of the eldership and the diaconate as advocated by Calvin in his *Institutes* and *Ordonnances Ecclésiastiques*[68] – in all this the Scots followed a course consistent with Calvinist teaching and at variance with Scandinavian or 'Anglican' procedure. Even the adoption of the exercise, a feature familiar to many churches and which can be traced to Zwingli's Zürich, was, it would seem, the product of Genevan contact and of the introduction of the *Forme of Prayers* (used by Knox's Genevan congregation) which contained an exposition of the functions and features of the exercise.[69] Knox's own experience of the Genevan exercise makes it highly probable that it was the latter which acted as a serviceable prototype for Knox and the reformers in Scotland.

Furthermore, the office of superintendent, which the Scots chose to introduce, had numerous parallels and cannot be said to have been a feature peculiar to Lutheran countries. The superintendent of Reformation thought may have originated in

---

[65] Cf., E. H. Dunkley, *The Reformation in Denmark* (London, 1948), 54, 85, 89, where the English rendering 'provost' is used. Both the Danish and English terms are evidently derived from the Latin 'praepositus'. The *Dansk-Engelsk Ordbog*, edd. H. Vintergerg and C. A. Bodelsen (Copenhagen, 1966), i, 213 translates *provst* and *domprovst* as 'dean', the former being a rural dean.

[66] *The Two Liturgies . . . of Edward VI*, ed. J. Ketley (Cambridge, 1844), 16.

[67] Knox, *Works*, ii, 153.

[68] Calvin, *Institutes*, IV, iii, 8–9; *Corpus Reformatorum* [CR], XXXVIII, *Ioannis Calvini Opera . . . omnia*, edd. G. Baum, E. Cunitz and E. Reuss, vol. X (Brunswick, 1871–2), i, 22–3, 100–3.

[69] Knox, *Works*, iv, 178–9; cf., vi, 294.

Saxony,[70] but the need for effective oversight was universally recognised. Whether or not bad Latin replaced good Greek matters little, but what is important is that while 'superintendent' could be equated with 'bishop' it could also mean 'visitor', and indeed in some countries the term 'visitor', or its equivalent, came to be preferred. If Martin Bucer in establishing a church constitution for Hesse made express provision for the office of superintendent,[71] in other parts of Germany where Swiss influence predominated the term 'superintendent', though not the substance of the office, was rejected in favour of another; and if Bucer in England was later to make the customary equation between the office of bishop and that of superintendent,[72] it is also true that in England the office of superintendent came to be identified by others not with a bishop as such, but with the *chorepiscopus* or assistant bishop, or, alternatively, even with the office of rural dean.[73] A diversity in thought and interpretation undoubtedly existed.[74] The superintendent could in fact become the godly visitor[75] just as well as the godly bishop,[76] and this is what happened in Scotland where the superintendent in the early 1570s came to hold office like the commissioner (and unlike the bishop in the commonly accepted sense of that word) for a term from one assembly to another.[77] Finally, in 1576, the office merged into that of the visitor, with any surviving superintendents continuing to act in that capacity.[78]

It is significant, however, that both in Scotland and in France the term 'superintendent' was initially accepted and only later came to be replaced. Not only did the French Confession of Faith in 1559 express its approval of 'those elected to be superintendents'[79] but the view that the French Discipline initially rejected the term in 1559 would appear to be erroneous. This latter document, it has to be borne in mind, was subject to revision by later national synods between 1560 and 1659, and the

[70] *Luther's Works*, vol. 40, pp. 313–14; *The Visitation of the Saxon Reformed Church*, ed. R. Laurence (Dublin, 1839), 24ff.

[71] E. G. Léonard, *A History of Protestantism*, i, 195.

[72] Bucer, *Scripta Anglicana* (Basle, 1577), 259.

[73] *HMC Salisbury MSS*, ii (London, 1888), no. 580; P. Collinson, 'Episcopacy and Reform in England in the Later Sixteenth Century', *Studies in Church History*, ed. G. J. Cuming, iii (Leiden, 1966), 107–9; and *The Elizabethan Puritan Movement* (London, 1967), 181–2.

[74] Cf., J. Pannier, 'Calvin et l'épiscopat', *Revue d'Histoire et de Philosophie religieuses*, vi (1926), 305–35, at 307; see below, 196–206.

[75] Cf., *BUK*, i, 296–7; see below, 229–30.

[76] Cf., Calderwood, *History*, iii, 156–62.

[77] *BUK*, i, 302–3, 318; Calderwood, *History*, iii, 332.

[78] *BUK*, i, 359. see below, 220, 229–30.

[79] P. Schaff, *The Creeds of the Evangelical Protestant Churches*, iii, 378.

section which ultimately condemned 'that custom used in some places of deputing certain ministers from the provincial synods to visit the churches' and which also rejected such titles of superiority as 'elders of synods, superintendents and the like' is nowhere to be found in the earliest texts of the Discipline[80] and is an interpolation found in the much later compilation of Quick.[81] By 1576, the superintendent, as such, had to all intents faded away in Scotland, though the term appears to have survived for longer in France where a national synod in 1603 decreed that the word 'superintendent' was 'not to be understood of any superiority of one pastor above another, but only in general of such as have office and charge in the church',[82] a decision endorsed by the following national synod in 1607.[83]

From a survey of the evidence it seems plain that the precedents of the French Calvinist church cannot lightly be dismissed, and, indeed, the whole pattern of ecclesiastical developments in both France and Scotland merits far greater attention than it has so far received. In each country, the initial wave of protestantism associated with Lutheranism gradually receded as Calvinism gained ground and emerged triumphant. The period of unorganised protestantism was drawing to an end. From the mid 1550s onwards, the first French reformed churches had come into being with their own congregational consistories organised on the model of Geneva and ultimately, as was claimed, on the example of the primitive and apostolic church.[84] The appearance, by 1559, of at least 144 French protestant churches is well-documented: Paris, Poitiers, Loudun and Bayeux, 1555; Tours, 1556; La Rochelle, Bordeaux, Orléans, Rouen and Dieppe, 1557; Caen, Le Havre, Troyes, Amiens, Toulouse and Marseilles, 1558; Nantes, Bergerac, Nîmes and Montélimar, 1559. As Scottish intellectual, cultural and even trading contact was predominantly (though not, of course, exclusively) French, it is scarcely possible to doubt that for every Scot who may have known what was happening in Scandinavia, hundreds more were thoroughly acquainted with developments in France. Indeed, at Châtellerault, where James Hamilton, 2nd Earl of Arran was duke, a protestant church was formed early in 1559 with support from the duke's son, James, 3rd Earl of Arran,

---

[80] E.g. *Histoire Ecclésiastique des Eglises Réformées au Royaume de France*, edd. G. Baum and E. Cunitz, 3 vols. (Paris, 1883–9), i, 215–20.

[81] J. Quick, *Synodicon in Gallia Reformata*, 2 vols. (London, 1692), i, xx.

[82] Ibid., 227; Aymon, *Tous les synodes nationaux des églises réformées de France*, 2 vols. (The Hague, 1710), i, 259.

[83] Quick, *Synodicon*, i, 266; Aymon, *Tous les synodes*, i, 303.

[84] *Histoire Ecclésiastique*, i, 120.

who obtained a minister from Poitiers to preach at his home at Berlandière, and who also organised and attended at nearby Loudun a meeting of the reformed to celebrate the Lord's Supper. At precisely the same point, a parallel development occurred in Scotland with the emergence of the 'privy kirks', which foreshadowed the later organisation of the reformed church on a national basis.[85] Yet the striking similarity of developments in either country does not end here. In 1557 – a year in which Knox travelled through France from Geneva to Dieppe[86] – 'Articles of Polity' for a national church organisation were drafted by the ministers of Poitiers,[87] and in 1559 – a year in which Knox was again in France[88] – the French Discipline and the Confession of Faith were sanctioned and adopted by the first national synod of the French protestant church.[89] In both countries, the higher powers were antipathetic towards the reformed church and just as the Paris synod had provided French protestantism with a central unity and the prospect of a national organisation, so too did a group of protestants meeting together in July 1560 – in what may tentatively be regarded as the first general assembly – take action for the first time on a national level for the appointment (or for the regularisation of appointments) of ministers to reformed congregations. At a point when 'the maist pairt of the cheif Ministeris of the Realme' were present in Edinburgh, 'the haill Nobilitie, and the greitest pairt of the Congregatioun' held a service of thanksgiving in St Giles, for delivery from French domination, after which commissioners from the burghs, with some of the nobility and barons were appointed to approve the distribution of ministers. It is certainly significant that such a meeting should gather in St Giles, that it should be held for an ecclesiastical purpose, that it should have been composed of representatives of the estates and that such a meeting, like later general assemblies, should take place immediately before a meeting of parliament.[90] It would seem, therefore, that this assembly in some tentative sense constituted the first general

[85] S. Mours, *Les Églises Réformées en France* (Paris, 1958), 99ff; A. Lièvre, *Histoire des Protestants et des Églises Réformées du Poitou*, 3 vols. (Paris, 1856–60), i, 62; J. Rondeau, *Les Calvinistes Chatelleraudais (1559–1789)* (Chatellerault, 1907), 5–6; see above, 11–13.

[86] Knox, *Works*, i, 269, 272; iv, 275, 286, 347.

[87] J. T. McNeill, *The History and Character of Calvinism*, 246.

[88] Knox, *Works*, vi, 11, 20, 21; Francisque-Michel, *Les Ecossais en France, les Français en Ecosse*, 2 vols. (London, 1862), i, 529, n.2.

[89] Quick, *Synodicon*, i, viff.

[90] Knox, *Works*, ii, 84–7; Calderwood, *History*, ii, 11; Spottiswoode, *History*, i, 325.

assembly of the reformed church and that it acted as a precedent for the assembly of December 1560, which historians have regarded as the first general assembly of the church.

Like their French counterparts, the Scots also drew up a Confession of Faith and Book of Discipline, and in the first regularly constituted general assembly of which there is record in December 1560, composed of ministers, elders, burgesses, lairds and nobles,[91] a further step was taken towards giving a national church central direction. Yet it is curious that both the French Discipline and the Scottish Book of Discipline were singularly vague on the envisaged national court for each church. The original French Discipline contained a mere two allusions to the national synod with no attempt at elaboration,[92] and the Scottish Book of Discipline was even less forthcoming on the nature of what it called the 'gret Counsall of the Churche'.[93] In practice, the French national synod, it is true, 'consisted of ministers accompanied by one or two elders or deacons who had been elected by the local consistories',[94] and this had led some to deny any identity between the Scottish general assembly and the French national synod.[95] On the other hand, while it is true that ministers and elders constituted the essential element in national synods, it can still be demonstrated that it was by no means unknown for the nobility to be present at, and to vote in, national synods,[96] nor even for the judges, magistrates and council of the town where the synod was held to give their attendance.[97] Indeed, as late as 1607 when the national synod met at La Rochelle the deputies of the community and city demanded to be admitted and to be permitted to cast their vote in the election of the moderator. This resulted in 'a very great debate' and although it was decided that the moderator should be elected by 'such persons as were purely ecclesiastical' the deputies were nevertheless admitted and accorded the privilege of voting in the synod.[98]

The similarity with Scotland is too obvious to be overlooked where nobles, lairds and burgesses are said to have sat side by side with ministers and elders in the general assembly from its

---

[91] *BUK*, i, 3–4; *SHS Miscellany*, viii (Edinburgh, 1951), 105.
[92] *Histoire Ecclésiastique*, i, 219, 220.
[93] Knox, *Works*, ii, 226; cf., 194, 204 n.l., 208, 250–1.
[94] G. Donaldson, *The Scottish Reformation* (Cambridge, 1960), 143; Quick, *Synodicon*, i, 2; Aymon, *Tous les synodes*, i, 2.
[95] G. Donaldson, *The Scottish Reformation*, 143, 148.
[96] *Histoire Ecclésiastique*, ii, 53; Quick, *Synodicon*, i, 116, 129; Aymon, *Tous les synodes*, i, 126, 139.
[97] Quick, *Synodicon*, i, 116, 129; Aymon, *Tous les synodes*, i, 126, 139.
[98] Quick, *Synodicon*, i, 263; Aymon, *Tous les synodes*, i, 299.

inception.[99] Although historians are by no means agreed on the precedents which made for the assembly's creation, evidence of this nature would certainly go some way to confirm the views of at least one historian who has ventured to suggest that the idea of the assembly was:[100]

> 'borrowed from France, where, as in Scotland, an independent Church required an independent central board of control. Without the Assembly the Church would have fallen permanently under the domination of the civil authorities as happened in England. The Assembly remains peculiarly symbolic of spiritual independence.'

If the French Discipline of 1559 was inexplicit on the nature of the national synod, it was scarcely more forthcoming on the subject of the colloquy as a court intermediate between the congregational consistory and the provincial synod. The earlier text of the Discipline contains a single sentence on the 'colloquy or synod'[101] and it seems clear that the sustained discourse on the colloquy in the final version of the Discipline[102] was a later insertion. It is an indisputable fact, however, that colloquies did emerge in the early 1560s, though their existence at first seems sometimes to have been decidedly precarious.[103] Only in areas where six or more ministers from adjacent parishes could conveniently assemble were colloquies able to be formed.[104] In Scotland, the general assembly experienced similar difficulties in its efforts to encourage the 'exercise' as a regular occasion set aside for interpreting scripture by ministers from the surrounding parishes.[105] It was not until 1572 that the French church resolved to amend its Discipline by inserting a section defining the nature of the colloquy as a distinct institution. 'The neighbour-churches', it was accordingly enacted, 'shall assemble themselves in colloquies four times a year, if possibly they can, and each minister shall come accompanied with one elder, not only for this end, that ministers in their respective turns may handle a common place in divinity from the scriptures, but that by mutual common counsel they may compose those emergent difficulties which trouble their churches'.[106] The parallel here with Scotland is too marked to be ignored or lightly cast aside; and it was not

[99] SHS Miscellany, viii, 105.
[100] G. D. Henderson, Presbyterianism, 104.
[101] Histoire Ecclésiastique, i, 216.
[102] E.g. Discipline or Book of Order of the Reformed Churches of France, ed. M. G. Campbell (London, 1924), 25; Quick, Synodicon, i, xxxvii-xxxviii.
[103] Quick, Synodicon, i, 3, 63; Aymon, Tous les synodes, i, 2, 66.
[104] Quick, Synodicon, i, 4; Aymon, Tous les synodes, i, 3.
[105] BUK, i, 26, 57, 270.
[106] Quick, Synodicon, i, 106; Aymon, Tous les synodes, i, 114.

altogether coincidental that this increased emphasis on the colloquy in France should be matched a few years later in Scotland first with the fostering of the exercise as an administrative unit and, in 1578, with its merging finally with the new district presbytery.[107]

While minor differences in procedure inevitably developed as each church made its own rules and regulations, it still seems plain that the conciliar government of each church evolved along fundamentally similar lines, and even in the national assemblies of either church the same device was adopted of introducing the elective office of moderator, with one or more assessors to assist him in his work.[108] Investigations of other polities, including those of Lutheran churches, have failed to produce any parallel as close or as meaningful as that which characterised the organisation of the Scottish and French churches; and apart from the brief interlude of the Leith episcopacy it seems clear that the salient features of the Scottish polity were adopted not from Scandinavia and England but are rather to be traced to those continental churches which could exhibit a polity as well as a theology which was unmistakably Calvinist in the fullest sense of that term.

If the hypothesis is correct that many of the conspicious features of the Scottish polity were derived from Calvinist rather than Lutheran countries, one would expect to find corroborative evidence of contact between Scotland and centres of Calvinism abroad. Mention may be made of Knox's peregrinations through France and Switzerland,[109] of his 'great intelligence' with the French church,[110] and of Andrew Melville's departure by 1564 for France and ultimately for Switzerland.[111] An indication of the lively interest which the Scots took in the fortunes of French protestantism is revealed in the publication of Beza's *Oration* to the colloquy of Poissy in September 1561, which Lekprevik printed in Edinburgh that same year, and equally in the publication of *Ane Answer made the fourth day of September 1561*, which John Baron (a resident with Knox at Geneva and later minister at Galston) translated from French for the benefit

---

[107] *BUK*, i, 265, 357, 430, 439, 465–8; *Wodrow Miscellany*, ed. D. Laing (Edinburgh, 1844), i, 407–8.

[108] *E.g.* Quick, *Synodicon*, i, 2, 12, 129, 136, 143, 157, 174; Aymon, *Tous les synodes*, i, 1, 13, 138, 147, 155, 173, 194.

[109] Knox, *Works*, i, 232, 253, 254; iii, 235; iv, 245; Row, *The History of the Kirk of Scotland*, ed. D. Laing (Edinburgh, 1842), 9.

[110] Knox, *Works*, ii, 137.

[111] Melville, *Autobiography and Diary*, ed. R. Pitcairn (Edinburgh, 1842), 39–42.

of the godly in Scotland and which was published in Edinburgh in 1562 by the same printer.[112]

Contact between Scotland and Geneva, in particular, from a relatively early date, is illustrated in the arrival at Geneva in 1554 – a year in which Knox was resident there[113] – of an unidentified Scotsman who requested the Venerable Company, apparently without success, to license him as a preacher.[114] Among the Marian exiles who sought refuge on the continent were a number of Scots: David Simson, John Willock, John Rough, Alexander Cockburn of Ormiston and John Borthwick.[115] Those known to have been resident in Geneva include John Davidson who is hard to identify but he can scarcely have been the principal of Glasgow university,[116] Sir John Borthwick and 'John Kellye his page',[117] David Lindsay, later minister at Leith,[118] John Baron, who became minister at Galston,[119] Sir James Sandilands of Torphichen,[120] Thomas Drummond,[121] James Lambe *rubantier*, a native of Leith,[122] William Keith and his wife,[123] together with Knox, Marjorie his wife, Elizabeth her mother, James Hamilton his servant, and Patrick his pupil.[124] Other arrivals in Geneva include the godly James Baron and the no less godly James Syme who brought Knox a letter in May 1557 from the Lords of the Congregation inviting him to return to Scotland.[125] In 1559, the Earl of Arran fled from France to Geneva to escape persecution;[126] and six years later the Earl of Moray dutifully made what

---

[112] A. W. Pollard and G. R. Redgrave, *A Short-Title Catalogue* (London, 1956), nos. 2000, 2026. Copies of both works are located in NLS.

[113] Knox, *Works*, i, 231–2.

[114] *Registres de la Compagnie des Pasteurs de Genève au temps de Calvin*, edd. R.-M. Kingdon and J.-F. Bergier, ii (Geneva, 1962), 57.

[115] C. Garrett, *The Marian Exiles* (Cambridge, 1938), 101, 121, 274, 288, 336–7.

[116] Ibid., 141.

[117] Ibid., 101.

[118] *Livre des habitants de Genève*, ed. P.-F. Geisendorf, i, 1549–60 (Geneva, 1957), 139; *Livre des Anglois* in C. Martin, *Les Protestants Anglais* (Geneva, 1915), 334.

[119] C. Garrett, *The Marian Exiles*, 81; C. Martin, *Les Protestants Anglais*, 44, 70, 142, 241, 242, 260; cf., Knox, *Works*, vi, 534n.

[120] *Livre des habitants de Genève*, i, 213; C. Martin, *Les Protestants Anglais*, 47.

[121] *Livre des habitants de Genève*, i, 213.

[122] Ibid., 202.

[123] C. Martin, *Les Protestants Anglais*, 333; C. Garrett, *The Marian Exiles*, 204–5.

[124] C. Martin, *Les Protestants Anglais*, 332.

[125] Knox, *Works*, i, 268.

[126] Ibid., vi, 53; *Papiers d'état pièces et documents inédits on peu connus relatifs a l'histoire de l'Ecosse au XVIe siècle*, ed. A. Teulet (Paris, 1851–60), i, 460–1, and n. 1.

might almost seem to be the customary pilgrimage to Geneva after having conferred with Condé and Coligny in France.[127] Other Scots known to have made the journey to Geneva in the 1560s include Alexander Young, the cousin of James Melville and nephew of Henry Scrimgeour the Scots professor of law at Geneva,[128] Alexander Campbell, bishop of Brechin,[129] and Andrew Polwart, later minister at Paisley.[130] George Gillespie and William Collace were two regents who left St Andrews for Geneva in the 1570s,[131] and even Patrick Adamson had met Beza and studied theology at Geneva.[132] Elements of the Scottish nobility were also attracted to Geneva. Both James Lindsay, son of the Earl of Crawford and minister at Fettercairn, and William Keith, brother of the Earl Marischal, died there.[133] It is notable, too, that after leaving Scotland in 1594, the young Earl of Gowrie should, on Rollock's recommendation, make a point of meeting Beza in Geneva[134] and should thereafter correspond with the Genevan.[135]

It was, indeed, as a centre of learning that Geneva drew a not inconsiderable number of Scottish students and scholars: Melville may have been one of the better known, but he was only following in the footsteps of others. Among the Scots enrolled in the Academy when the register begins was Peter Young, 'Scotus Dundonensis' in 1559,[136] followed by Gilbert Moncrieff, the friend of Melville and later royal physician, in 1567, John Skene in 1569, David Hume, a law student, and James Haldane, a language and theology student, in 1579. Andrew Lamb in 1584–5, Archibald Hunter, a philosophy student, in 1589, Robert Wimeus in 1597, William London in 1598, and John Cameron and James Erskine in 1606.[137] Unlike the many Scots abroad who

---

[127] *Relations Politiques de la France et de l'Espagne avec l'Ecosse au XVIe siècle*, ed. A. Teulet, v (Paris, 1862), 24.
[128] Melville, *Diary*, 30.
[129] Ibid., 42.
[130] Ibid.
[131] Ibid., 51; T. McCrie, *Life of Andrew Melville* (Edinburgh, 1899), 411.
[132] *Dictionary of National Biography*, i, 112.
[133] H. Scott, *Fasti Ecclesiae Scoticanae*, 9 vols. (Edinburgh, 1915–61), v, 461; T. McCrie, *Life of Andrew Melville*, 411.
[134] Calderwood, *History*, vi, 67; J. Scott, *A History of the Life and Death of John, Earl of Gowrie* (Edinburgh, 1818), 109–10.
[135] W. F. Arbuckle, 'The Gowrie Conspiracy', *SHR*, xxxvi (1957), 1–24, 89–110, at 106, 110.
[136] *Le Livre du Recteur de l'Académie de Genève*, ed. S. Stelling-Michaud, 2 vols. (Geneva, 1959), i, 81; C. Borgeaud, *Histoire de l'Université de Genève: L'Académie de Calvin, 1559–1789* (Geneva, 1900), 55.
[137] *Le Livre du Recteur de l'Académie de Genève*, i, 96, 99, 103, 113, 116, 119, 125.

visited the Baltic, the Low Countries and France for trade and commerce, those Scots who can be traced and who made the arduous journey to Geneva did so with one object in mind, to discover themselves what Knox had called that 'maist perfyt schoole of Chryst that ever was in the erth since the dayis of the Apostillis',[138] that 'most godlie Reformed Churche and citie of the warld, Geneva'.[139] Apart from personal visits, contact with Geneva was sustained through correspondence, and although Knox and Goodman are perhaps among the best known of Calvin's correspondents from Scotland,[140] there were other Scots, too, who kept Calvin carefully informed of Scottish affairs during the critical years of the Reformation. In September 1560, an account was despatched to Calvin keeping him abreast of the reformers' progress in Scotland,[141] and in July 1561 no less a person than James Stewart, the half-brother of the queen and a key figure in the political wing of the reforming movement, who, incidentally had Calvin's works in his library,[142] was in communication with the Genevan reformer.[143]

Although Calvin died in 1564, continuing Scottish contact with Geneva is reflected in Beza's letter to Bullinger in Zürich in December 1556 in which the Genevan went so far as to enclose a specimen of the very extensive correspondence of Knox from which you will learn the entire condition of Scotland'.[144] That same year also witnessed the assembly's reply to a letter which Beza had sent Knox requesting the Scottish church to accord its approval of the Helvetic Confession of 1556.[145] In 1569, Beza was again in correspondence with Knox to whom he presented a copy of his treatise on marriage and divorce, along with a second copy which he somewhat inappropriately bade Knox give to that irascible bachelor, George Buchanan,[146] who was also in

---

[138] Knox, *Works*, iv, 240.

[139] Ibid., ii, 16; vi, 16; cf., v, 211–16.

[140] *CR*, XLVI, *Calvini Opera*, XVIII (Brunswick, 1878), nos. 3340, 3377, 3378.

[141] Ibid., no. 3251.

[142] J. Durkan and A. Ross, *Early Scottish Libraries*, 149.

[143] *CR*, XLVI, *Calvini Opera*, XVIII, no. 3435.

[144] Knox, *Works*, vi, 550.

[145] *The Zürich Letters*, ed. Hastings Robinson, 2 vols. (Cambridge, 1842–5), ii, 362–5; Knox, *Works*, vi, 544–50. The critical attitude of Scottish reformers to the celebration of festivals, which led them to take exception to the section on festivals in the second Helvetic Confession, is comparable with that of the citizens of Geneva, who in 1550 in General Council pronounced 'un edict de l'abrogation de toutes les festes, reservant le jour du dimenche, comme il est ordonné de Dieu'. See *Registres de la Compagnie des Pasteurs de Genève au temps de Calvin*, ed. J.-F. Bergier, i, (Geneva, 1964), 74.

[146] Knox, *Works*, vi, 562–5.

correspondence with Beza.[147] For Beza, there was as yet little need for any intervention in a church which from its creation had the closest of ties with Geneva, but with the emergence of a formal episcopate in Scotland, professedly based on English procedure,[148] Beza felt compelled to warn Knox in 1572 of the inherent dangers which he detected within such a system.[149]

Beyond Geneva and France, Scotland's brand of Calvinism was sustained through associations with the Rhineland and the Netherlands as Calvinism spread in Europe. The university town of Heidelberg in the Palatinate, for example, soon established its reputation as an international centre of Calvinist thought.[150] The university which satisfied the intellectual predilections of such English radicals as George Withers and Thomas Cartwright also attracted within its confines an interesting assortment of Scots who weathered the vicissitudes of overseas travel to study at this centre of orthodox Calvinism. In the first half of the sixteenth century, no Scots at all seem to have matriculated at Heidelberg, but as soon as Calvinism made inroads in the Palatinate under Frederick III (1559–73) three Scots arrived to enrol at Heidelberg between 1568 and 1570.[151] Nor was it mere coincidence that no further Scots should venture to attend during the regime of Louis VI (1576–83) who as a Lutheran deposed and exiled the Calvinist ministers and professors. But it is an observable fact that with the subsequent restoration of Calvinism on Louis' death in 1583 no fewer than twenty-five Scots chose to matriculate at Heidelberg between 1587 and 1614,[152] a figure considerably in excess of those identifiable Scots who enrolled in the same period at Oxford with its many constituent colleges. Indeed, if compared with the early seventeenth century when Scots returned in more significant numbers to tread the not unfamiliar path to Oxford,[153] the number of known Scots who went there in the late sixteenth century was apparently meagre if not negligible.[154]

[147] Beza, *Epistolae Theologicae* (1574), no. lxxviii, p. 343; Buchanan, *Epistolae* (1711 edn.), 22–3, 41–3, 72–3.

[148] *CSP Scot.*, iv, no. 149, pp.133–4.

[149] Knox, *Works*, vi, 613–15; Beza, *Epistolae Theologicae*, no. lxxix, p.344–6.

[150] C-P. Clasen, *The Palatinate in European History 1559–1660* (Oxford, 1963), 6, 33, 35.

[151] *Die Matrikel der Universität Heidelberg von 1386 bis 1662*, ed. G. Toepke, ii (1554–1662), (Heidelberg, 1886), 45, 54.

[152] Ibid., 133, 143, 166, 174, 186, 187, 198, 215, 216, 225, 226, 235, 238, 245, 246, 257, 264, 268, 565, 566.

[153] *Register of the University of Oxford*, ed. A. Clark, II, i, (Oxford, 1887), 264, 267, 268, 272, 275, 279, 280, 281, 282, 343–4.

[154] Ibid., 372–3, 388.

If Scottish Calvinists were disinclined to attend in any
appreciable numbers, it is curious that Andrew Melville, despite
his presbyterianism, should keep in touch with Oxford and
should apparently encourage several of his students to continue
their studies there.[155] The number of Scots who decided to send
their sons to England's other university is harder to determine
since the printed register of matriculations and degrees does not
normally distinguish students' nationality or place of residence;
but if John Knox really intended that his sons should go to
Cambridge – they matriculated eight days after his death[156] – he
did at least ensure that they were educated in a radical
environment where Calvinism had evidently left its mark.[157]

Even beyond the environs of the universities, there was in
practice ample scope for through-going Calvinists in both
countries to make common cause. Leaders of the Scottish church
like Knox and Melville seem to have shared a concept of the
church with such English radicals as Whittingham, Humphrey,
Sampson, Gilby and Wilcox and with such later presbyterians as
Cartwright, Field and Travers. Their vision of the church was
one which required a thorough reformation on the model of the
'best reformed churches', with a separate ecclesiastical jurisdiction, to whose discipline all alike, both great and small, would
be subject, a church in which there was no predisposition to
accept lordship in the ministry or any especial need to 'tarry for
the magistrate', a church in which *adiaphora* or things indifferent
would not be enjoined so as become things essential. Contact
between English radicals and ministers of the Scottish church had
of course been longstanding. Willock, Knox and Goodman had
each pursued careers on both sides of the border and the latter
two are known not only to have shown sympathy with the
'puritan' cause in England but also to have criticised aspects of
the Church of England's organisation and worship.[158] Knox's
standing among Marian exiles in Geneva and among later English
puritans was undoubtedly high. His writings were included in
that puritan document *The Seconde Parte of a Register*[159] and to

[155] BL, Harleian MSS. 7004, fo. 5; cf., Calderwood, *History*, iv, 201; Melville,
Diary, 219; *Register of the University of Oxford*, II, i, 372–3.
[156] J. Ridley, *John Knox* (Oxford, 1968), 520; *The Book of Matriculations and
Degrees, 1544–1659*, ed. J. Venn (Cambridge, 1913), 406.
[157] Cf., H. C. Porter, *Reformation and Reaction in Tudor Cambridge*
(Cambridge, 1958); M. H. Curtis, *Oxford and Cambridge in Transition, 1558–
1642* (Oxford, 1959), *passim*.
[158] E.g. Knox, *Works*, v, 515–16, 518–19; vi, 12–13, 83; *CSP Scot.*, i, no. 554.
[159] *The Seconde Parte of a Register*, ed. A. Peel, 2 vols. (Cambridge, 1915), i,
46.

the presbyterian John Field, in particular, who printed one of his sermons and who was anxious to obtain the rest of his works, Knox wrote 'both godly and diligently, in questions of divinitie, and also of Church pollicie'.[160] Scotland, as one of the comparatively few countries where a thorough-going Calvinist discipline had been established, stood in marked contrast with what English puritans felt to be the but half-reformed state of the Church of England,[161] and it therefore afforded English puritans with a place of refuge wherein they could experience that discipline they craved for England: in 1568 the bishop of London criticised that 'wilfull companie' of English puritans who had just returned from Scotland.[162] Equally, as there were also Scots who served in the English church,[163] it was not altogether inappropriate that the Church of Scotland should intervene in 1566 in the vestiarian controversy by urging the bishops and pastors in England to use restraint in their dealings with 'these godlie and our belovit brethren' who, in conscience, had felt bound to reject the 'unprofitable apparrell' which was variously identified with 'Romish ragges' and 'badges of idolaters'.[164]

In later years, while Patrick Adamson sought to enlist the support of the English hierarchy in his attempts at conformity with England,[165] men of a more radical conscience in either land practised their own brand of conformity. In 1583, John Davidson was in correspondence with Field in England on whether the assembly should petition for 'reformatioun of some abuses in your churche and especiallie that sincere men may have libertie to preache without deposing be the tyrannie of the bishops'.[166] Andrew Melville maintained a lasting friendship with Travers and Cartwright, once resident in Geneva in the early 1570s, whom he invited, albeit unsuccessfully, to St Andrews in 1580;[167] and Melville also granted letters of commendation to the Brownists on their arrival in St Andrews in 1584, though the initial friendship soon dissolved into bickering as the latter found themselves engaged in a dispute with Edinburgh presbytery for suggesting that the discipline of the

---

[160] Knox, *Works*, iv, 92.
[161] Cf., P. Collinson, *The Elizabethan Puritan Movement*, 29ff.
[162] BL, Lansdowne MSS. 10, fo.146r.
[163] G. Donaldson, 'Foundations of Anglo-Scottish Union', *Elizabethan Government and Society*, ed. S. T. Bindoff *et al.* (1961), 302ff.
[164] *BUK*, i, 85–88; see further below, 335–41.
[165] G. Donaldson, 'The Attitude of Whitgift and Bancroft to the Scottish Church', *Trans. Royal Hist. Socy.*, 4th ser., xxiv, 95–115.
[166] NLS, Adv. MSS. 6.1.13, fo.42r.
[167] NLS, Wodrow MSS. folio vol. xlii, fos.11v-12r; T. Fuller, *The Church History of Britain* (London, 1842), IX, vii, 52.

Scottish church was altogether amiss.[168] The flight to England of
Scottish presbyterians in 1584 inevitably strengthened the links
with their English counterparts;[169] and this was mirrored in the
large attendance of English puritans at the funeral in London of
James Lawson, the exiled presbyterian minister from Edinburgh.[170]
Not only did John Uddall visit Scotland in 1589,[171] but it was
also symptomatic of the close relations between Calvinists in
either country that John Bonnar should present to Dalkeith
presbytery in 1592 his testimonial 'fra the faythfull brether of the
ministerie in Ingland';[172] that 'Mr Banford minister at the
Newcastle in Ingland' should look to Scotland to seek the
assistance of the synod of Lothian in 1593 'concerning the estate
of thair kirk thair,'[173] and that he should later contribute a sum of
money for the relief of some Melvillian ministers;[174] and that
'Maister Cartwrycht' should be invited to become minister of
Edinburgh in 1596.[175] The relationship established between
fellow Calvinists, in discipline as well as in theology, in both
lands was evidently one of continuing commitment to a common
cause.

The Calvinism which prevailed in Scotland in the period of the
Reformation, it need scarcely be said, was not necessarily a mere
replica of the Calvinism of Geneva which eventually atrophied.
Its ethos had immeasurably transcended the boundaries of that
Swiss republican city. Beyond Geneva, Calvinism had expanded
and matured. Its substance had penetrated France and the
Rhineland as well as much of Switzerland and its theology had
left a deep, and never entirely eradicable, impression on the
Church of England. It was with these practical examples of the
operation of a Calvinist system that reformers were able to adapt
the spirit of international Calvinism to meet their own
requirements. Calvin himself could hardly have approved of the
political theories of 'neo-Calvinists' in either France or Scotland,
but, as an entity, Scottish Calvinism in the late sixteenth century
never underwent such an adaptation or metamorphosis which its
creator would have recognised as a system other than his own.

[168] Calderwood, *History*, iv, 1–3.
[169] G. Donaldson, 'The Scottish Presbyterian Exiles in England, 1584–8',
RSCHS, xiv, 67–80.
[170] BL, Additional MSS. 4736, fo 166v; *Selections from Wodrow's Biographical
Collections*, ed. R. Lippe (Aberdeen, 1890), 231–2; *Wodrow Miscellany*, i, 451–2.
[171] Calderwood, *History*, v, 58, 131–2.
[172] SRO, CH2/424/1, MS. Dalkeith Presbytery Records, 17 Aug. 1592.
[173] SRO, CH2/252/1, MS. Synod of Lothian and Tweeddale Records, fo.55r. 4
Aug. 1593.
[174] Melville, *Diary*, 710; Calderwood, *History*, vi, 660.
[175] SRO, CH2/121/2, MS. Edinburgh Presbytery Records, 7 Sept. 1596.

The theology and discipline which prevailed in post-Reformation Scotland continued to exhibit many of the distinctive traits of Calvin's system.

Admittedly, the indebtedness of one reformer to another, if somewhat intangible, was nonetheless an ever present reality. There was throughout a constant interchange of ideas as reformers shared experiences and borrowed from one another. In particular, Calvin's debt to Strasbourg and to Martin Bucer, whom some have styled the 'father of Calvinism', has been widely recognised;[176] but it is significant that a recent editor of Bucer's works should observe that 'there is virtually no trace of any direct Buceran influence on the Scottish Church in the time of Knox, nor on Knox himself, though of course he, and through him Scotland' fell heirs to Genevan doctrines and institutions which owed their origin in part or in whole to Bucer rather than Calvin.'[177] At the same time, it remains true that much in the Book of Discipline's programme of 1560 was consistent with Bucer's ideals, not least in its discussion on schooling where a debt to Bucer's influential *De Regno Christi* need not be doubted. Nor is this all. Bucer's influence persisted, for the Second Book of Discipline in 1578 borrowed directly from a passage in the *De Regno Christi* on the office of the Christian magistrate.[178] The legacy of the Strasbourg reformer continued to permeate and inform discussion.

Inevitably, explorations in such a field as this are by their very nature apt to be tenuous and never entirely satisfactory, but sufficient evidence has been adduced to illustrate the range and nature of the close relationship with Geneva and other Calvinist centres which Scotland enjoyed at the Reformation and while other influences should not go unnoticed none has yet been shown to have been so sustained or so intimate as those between Scotland and the Calvinist churches abroad.

[176] E.g. W. Pauck, 'Calvin and Butzer', *Journal of Religion*, ix (1929), 237–56.

[177] *Common Places of Martin Bucer*, ed. D. F. Wright, (1972), 29.

[178] *The First Book of Discipline*, ed. J. K. Cameron (Edinburgh, 1972), 133; *The Second Book of Discipline*, ed. J. Kirk (Edinburgh, 1980), 216; see also indices to both works.

4

Recruitment to the Ministry at the Reformation

Historical perspective on recruitment to the ministry at the Reformation is apt to be distorted, if only on the elementary ground that the absence of a contemporary list of the ministers at work in 1560 inevitably leads to much conjecture, speculation and to the formation of what, at best, is a very imperfect picture of the inroads which reformed preaching had made in local communities by the summer of 1560, when the Reformation parliament approved a statement of protestant doctrine and proscribed the Roman mass and papal jurisdiction within the realm. There are evident dangers in generalised assessments of what was happening in the country as a whole; and the deficiency in estimates of the men who had entered the ministry by 1560 is liable to lead to ill-founded assumptions and pronouncements. Besides, too cursory an acquaintance with the seemingly incontrovertible evidence which does survive for later years can sometimes lead to over-hasty judgments and a readiness to minimise the significance of what was taking place as the crisis of 1560 approached.

Whatever the nature of the changeover in the parishes as old priest made way for new presbyter (sometimes by reforming himself and his practices in the process), 1560 as a date was pivotal but indeterminate. Many of the politically active areas of the country had experienced at least a taste of protestant preaching for over a generation before parliament finally declared a break with Rome in 1560. In essence, the Reformation had first taken shape as a clerical revolt in 1517. In Scotland, too, the early movement found its leaders among disaffected clergy who favoured the evangelical message proclaimed on the continent. The men who ended up as protestant preachers were very largely drawn from the old ecclesiastical establishment. Early heretics who had diffused Lutheran or heterodox doctrines ranged from Patrick Hamilton, cleric of St Andrews diocese and commendator of Fearn abbey, in the 1520s, and perhaps friar William Airth, whose preaching in Dundee and St Andrews against the bishops, the abuse of cursing and of miracles was denounced as heresy by the bishop of Brechin (though Knox considered the friar a 'papist in his heart'), to the Aberdeen Franciscan Alexander Dick, the Augustinian canons Alane and Richardson from St Andrews, Robert Logie from Cambuskenneth, and Thomas Forret from Inchcolm; John Gau, the priest who settled in Malmö, George Gilbert a chaplain in Brechin diocese 'dilatit of heresy and marying of ane woman in Rensbrig in Ducheland', the Observant Franciscans Jerome Russell and James Melville (the latter of whom, it was said in 1535, 'had returned from Germany infected with Lutheranism which he attempts to spread among the ignorant people'), Andrew Johnston, prebendary in St Giles, friar Alexander Lindsay in Edinburgh, the Dominicans Seton, MacAlpine, MacDowell, Kelour, Beveridge and Willock; the Carthusian Andrew Charters, the Dominican friar John Craig, Henry Henryson, master of Edinburgh grammar school, Thomas Cocklaw, curate of Tullibody, Duncan Simson, chaplain at Stirling, John Wedderburn, chaplain in Dundee, David Hutchesoun, provost of Roslin, and William Kirk, chaplain apparently in Dunfermline and then in Leith (who recanted), during the 1530s.[1]

---

[1] *John Knox's History of the Reformation in Scotland*, ed. W. C. Dickinson, 2 vols. (Edinburgh, 1949), i, 13–21, 23, 26–8, 56–7; D, Calderwood, *History of the Kirk of Scotland*, ed. T. Thomson, 8 vols. (Edinburgh, 1842–9), i, 93–5, 113–14, 123–8, 132–4, 142–3; *Acts of the Lords of Council in Public Affairs, 1501–1554*, ed. R. K. Hannay (Edinburgh, 1932), 371–2, 426–7, 437, 482, 484; *Calendar of Letters and Papers, Foreign and Domestic, Henry VIII [Cal. L P]*, edd. J. S. Brewer, *et al.* (London, 1864–1932), XII, i, nos. 5, 305; ii, no. 1138; IV, ii, nos. 3019–21, 3348; VIII, no. 469; *Letters of James V*, ed. D. Hay (Edinburgh, 1954), 275–6, 315–16; *Criminal Trials in Scotland*, ed. R. Pitcairn, 3 vols. (Edinburgh, 1829–33), i, 213*–14*; J. Gau, *The Richt Vay to the Kingdom of Heuine*, ed. A. F. Mitchell (Edinburgh, 1888), pp. xx, xxiv; J. Durkan, 'Some Local Heretics', *Transactions of the Dumfriesshire and Galloway Natural History and Antiquarian Society*, 3rd ser., xxxvi (1957–8), 67–77; J. Spottiswoode, *History of the Church of Scotland*, ed. M. Russell, 3 vols. (Edinburgh, 1847–51), i, 183; iii, 91–4; *A Diurnal of Remarkable Occurents*, ed. T. Thomson (Edinburgh, 1833), 18–19; *Registrum Secreti Sigilli Regum Scotorum [RSS]*, edd. D. H. Fleming, *et al.*, 8 vols. (Edinburgh, 1908–82), ii, nos. 2858, 3612; *Accounts of the Lord High Treasurer of Scotland*, ed. T. Dickson, *et al.*, 12 vols. (Edinburgh, 1877–1970), vii, 77, 79–80, 153; *Extracts from the Records of the Burgh of Edinburgh, 1528–1577* [vol. ii], ed. J. D. Marwick (Edinburgh, 1871), 69.

By the 1540s, the Dominicans Gwilliam, Rough, Roger, Hewat and Thomson, the Augustinian canon of Holyrood William Forman, the secular priests John Knox, Henry Elder in Perth, Robert Richardson and James Skea, chaplain in Kirkwall, the Cistercian MacBriar, John Melville, 'a very sedytious' Scots preacher in England, and John Lyn, a Franciscan friar, were won over to protestant doctrines, and most became active preachers of the Reformation.[2] During the 1550s, further recruits were found in John Douglas, a Carmelite friar, Walter Milne, curate of Lunan, Thomas Jamieson, chaplain at Cupar, friar John Christison, and the priests John Petrie and John Knox (on his return).[3] Their immediate impact may have been neither great nor sustained; some were executed, others emigrated. Yet, their disputations, their novel preaching, their defiance of authority, their convictions, their obstinacy and the punishments they endured created attention, discussion, rumour, scandal: it all made news, and, in the process, helped transmit the message of the Reformation.

As the Reformation crisis deepened in 1559, with the rising of the Lords of the Congregation, clerical conversions to protestantism became more pronounced. In May 1559, the authorities in Ayr had dispensed with the services of the chaplains, who offered masses for the souls of the dead and who were expected to reform their ways; in June 1559, a number of Augustinian canons in St Andrews renounced the mass, an action consistent with the initiative taken by their commendator, Lord James Stewart, who in the preceding month, had signed the band of the Congregation 'so that God may be trewlie and puirelie wirschipped';[4] by August some Augustinian canons in Cambuskenneth had also 'forsaken Papistry'; and by December 1559, the council in Crail had required 'the hayll chaplannis of this toun to apply thame selfis to Goddis word and lyf godly, conform to the Congregatioun', and 'to renuns the papis lawis and all uther

---

[2] Knox, *History*, i, 26, 42–3, 48, 55–6, 67, 69, 81–3, 87; Calderwood, *History*, i, 124, 142; *Essays on the Scottish Reformation*, ed. D. McRoberts (Glasgow, 1962), 205; *Criminal Trials*, i, 330*, 352*; *Cal. L P Henry VIII*, XVIII, i, nos. 354, 358, 361, 389, 390, 478, 638, 696; ii, no. 392; *RSS*, iv, no. 916; *Calendar of State Papers relating to Scotland and Mary Queen of Scots [CSP Scot.]*, i, no. 206; *Acts of the Lords of Council*, 601; *Acts of the Privy Council of England*, new ser., ed. J. R. Dasent (vols. i–xxxii) (London, 1890–1907), iv, 330, 429.

[3] Knox, *History*, i, 118–19, 125, 138, 153; Calderwood, *History*, i, 337–42; R. Lindesay of Pitscottie, *Historie and Cronicles of Scotland*, ed. A. J. G. Makay, 3 vols. (Edinburgh, 1899–1911), ii, 130, 132, 138–9; *Wodrow Society Miscellany*, ed. D. Laing (Edinburgh, 1844), i, 55.

[4] Scottish Record Office [SRO], B6/12/3, Ayr Burgh Court Book, 22 May 1559 [now transferred to Carnegie Library, Ayr]; *The Works of John Knox*, ed. D. Laing, 6 vols. (Edinburgh, 1846–64), vi, 26; i, 344.

abominatiounis'.[5] Adam Heriot, vicar of St Andrews, who had been troubled by the doctrine of transubstantiation, renounced popery, joined the Congregation and, in 1559, became minister of the reformed congregation there.[6] John Davidson, principal of Glasgow University and vicar of Alness, Nigg and Colmonell, and Patrick Cockburn, student of St Andrews and Paris and parson of Pitcox (a prebend of Dunbar collegiate kirk) had each adopted protestantism by the summer of 1559; Alexander Gordon, bishop elect of Galloway, joined the Congregation by September 1559 and a few weeks later was reported to be preaching daily; and John Campbell, bishop elect of the Isles, attached himself to the protestant cause by November 1559.[7] Commenting on 'the subdane change' which had been wrought among 'the faythfull' in '1559', the Catholic priest and schoolmaster of Linlithgow, Ninian Winzet, drew attention to the behaviour of conformist priests: 'at pasche and certane soundays efter, thai techeit with grete appering zele, and ministrate the sacramentis til ws on ye catholik manere: and be witsonday yai change yair standart in our plane contrare'.[8] The rising of the Congregation was evidently not without effect.

By 1560, other clerics and teachers had evidently conformed: Spottiswoode, Winram, Douglas and Row, at any rate, were all considered sufficiently reformed to be associated with Knox and Willock in preparing the Book of Discipline; William Cornwall, chaplain in Linlithgow, conformed to serve as reader there by April 1560; and James Archibald, vicar of Lintrathen in Angus, on joining the Congregation by May 1560, caused the common prayers and homilies to be read weekly in his parish kirk. More generally, by February 1559/60, the clergy, it was noted, had begun to fail the Archbishop of St Andrews, who it was said 'desires some poor place to retire to'.[9]

All this, at any rate, is clear from the casual and fragmentary evidence which remains. What is also arresting is the readiness of

[5] Knox, *Works*, i, 391; SRO, B10/8/2, Crail Town Clerk's Scroll Book, 1554–60, 4 Dec. 1559 [now transferred to St Andrews University Archives].

[6] Spottiswoode, *History*, ii, 197; *Register of the Minister, Elders and Deacons of the Christian Congregation of St Andrews [RStAKS]*, ed. D. H. Fleming, 2 vols. (Edinburgh, 1889–90), i, 31.

[7] J. Durkan and J. Kirk, *The University of Glasgow, 1451–1577* (Glasgow, 1977), 232, 244; N. Winzet, *Velitatio in Georgium Buchananum circa dialogum* (1582), 222; *CSP Scot.*, i, nos. 550, 566.

[8] N. Winzet, *Certane Tractatis for Reformation of Doctryne and Maneris in Scotland*, ed. D. Laing (Edinburgh, 1835), 54.

[9] Knox, *History*, i, 343; *Protocol Books of James Foulis, 1546–1553, and Nicol Thounis, 1559–1564*, ed. J. Beveridge and J. Russell (Edinburgh, 1927), 3, no. 10; *Spalding Club Miscellany*, ed. J. Stuart, iv (Aberdeen, 1849), 120–2; *CSP Scot.*, i, no. 647.

some 28 chaplains of St Salvator's collegiate kirk and other priests in St Andrews to renounce their Catholicism between February and March 1559/60,[10] which well supports the claim of desertions among the archbishop's clergy. Few of these defectors, so far as is known, were ready to enter the reformed ministry; but as similar recantations occurred in other towns, a sizeable pool of potential recruits for the new ministry was soon formed. As 'the reformatioun of the protestantis'[11] (as Ninian Winzet ambivalently put it) took effect, some curious trends emerged: thus, in July 1560, the Catholic queen of Scotland and her husband the most Christian king of France informed the provost and bailies in Edinburgh of the rights which Simon Blythe, prebendary of Tain, had acquired to three altarages in St Cuthbert's, St Giles and in Holyrood, and to the rents accruing from his tenants which he ought to enjoy for life 'since the said Simon has renounced all papistry and superstition'.[12]

Yet it is not in tracing the careers of individual reformers or conformers, but in the activities of whole communities that something of the dynamism of protestantism can be appreciated. By 1558, Catholic authorities, aware of the dangers, attributed to reformed preaching, which slandered the sacraments, the authority of the church and articles of the Catholic faith, 'sic tumulte and uproir amangis the peple, that thay culd not be conteaned within the boundis of lauchfull obedience'.[13] Even the crown, in seeking reconciliation with the Lords of the Congregation in 1558, was forced to concede the religious issue when it asked the lords to remain obedient to their sovereigns 'as evir thay war wount befoir this truble and controversie, except in that quhilk concernis the religeone',[14] a statement which rather suggests a recognition that attachment to the cause of religious reform was more than just a matter for political manipulation. During 1558, 'the tumult incressed dalie within the realm', it was candidly admitted, as reformers began 'to preche opinlie in divers partis, and principallie within sum houssis of the toun of Edinburgh', and as 'sindre Inglis buikis, ballettis and treateis' were spread 'amangis the people, to move thame to seditione'.[15] The prelates themselves, who warned their clergy 'to reject vain novelties and doubtful opinions', acknowledged in 1559 the alarming spread of protestant heresies 'propagated everywhere in

[10] RStAKS, i, 10–15, 191–2.
[11] Winzet, Certane Tractatis, 55.
[12] SRO, GD122, Craig Millar Writs, vol. 3, no. 813.
[13] J. Leslie, History of Scotland, ed. T. Thomson (Edinburgh, 1830), 266.
[14] Ibid., 277.
[15] Ibid., 296.

this realm by heretics, heresiarchs, and by the patrons, authors, promoters, and followers in this realm of the heretical corruptions of Lutheranism, Calvinism, and other nefarious heresies, who daily and continually strive with all their care, effort and industry directly and utterly to disturb, destroy and subvert the ecclesiastical liberty' of the established church.[16] In short, the stress which the party of revolution had consistently placed on religious reform,[17] in the expectation that it would bring them popular backing, was evidently not misplaced; it proved sound strategy; and it is hard to resist the findings of one recent writer who remarked:

> 'the notion that the Reformation was not a popular movement but something carried through by a clique of nobles making religion a cloak for their own selfish ends and in defiance of majority opinion, and that Protestantism took root only after a parliament had legislated in its favour, cannot be entertained'.[18]

By May 1559, the brethren of the Congregation of the Mearns, Angus, Fife and Strathearn, with the towns of Dundee and Montrose, began to mobilise to defend their preachers summoned to stand trial before the court of justiciary in Stirling on 10 May. Their plan was to meet at Perth, and then 'to pass forward to Sterling with their preachers, there to consult what wes to be done'. The court summons focused on protestant activities in the north-east where Paul Methven, the former baker, William Harlaw, the Canongate tailor turned minister in the Edwardine Church of England, John Christison, described as a 'friar' (perhaps a kinsman of William who had studied in Lutheran Norway and Denmark before joining the reformers by 1560), and John Willock, the renegade friar from Ayr, were charged with usurping the ministerial office, administering communion in a manner different from the Catholic church during Easter in Dundee, Montrose and elsewhere in Forfar and Kincardineshire, and with convening the people to hear erroneous preaching and seditious doctrine.[19]

In response, the 'whole multitude and number of brethrein' from Dundee (of unknown size) accompanied their preachers to Perth; other communities sent contingents; their strength at Perth was placed at between 4,000 and 5,000 men. The issue which directly affected protestants north of the Tay had clear

---

[16] *Statutes of the Scottish Church, 1225–1559*, ed. D. Patrick (Edinburgh, 1907), 162; 150.
[17] Knox, *History*, i, 136–7, 178–9, 206–7, 314–16.
[18] G. Donaldson, *All the Queen's Men (London, 1983)*, 34.
[19] T. McCrie, *Life of John Knox* (Edinburgh, 1855), 360.

implications for protestants elsewhere. From the south west came reinforcements, 2,500 men on foot and horse, under Glencairn from the Congregation of Kyle and Cunningham. Even then, the 'whole Congregation was not assembled'; some considered the protestants capable of ministering between 10,000 and 12,000 men on the field; but the government, able to call on French troops, commanded an estimated force of 8,000 soldiers. At the same time, many who sided with the queen regent (including Châtelherault), it was said, were 'of like religion and kindred with the other faction'; a truce was called, and the protestants dispersed, singing 'psalmes and spirituall songs', and purging kirks they came across, as they made their way home.[20] Protestantism was no longer to be found in 'the priuat conuenticules of schismatikis and heretikis'[21] but in the crowds which rallied to the Congregation's call in 1559 and in the action taken by communities, defying both church and crown, in establishing godly preachers ready to proclaim the 'true Word of God'. The expectation in July 1559 was that 'a general reformation conform to the pure word of God' would be conceded by the government. Indeed, at that point too, the Congregation considered bestowing church property on 'faithful ministers', a proposal which may help explain the chorus of complaints voiced by kirkmen in 1561–2 of their parishioners' consistent failure to pay them their revenues for the last three or four years.[22]

What all this meant was that, by one means or another, a reformed ministry with public worship was established in the main burghs and centres of population during 1559; Dundee, the first burgh to exhibit the face of a reformed kirk as early as 1558, chose not a renegade cleric of the established church but a former baker for its first minister; admittedly he was a somewhat remarkable baker, for he had been brought up by Miles Coverdale in England and indeed (like Willock) had chosen an Englishwoman for his wife;[23] and by the summer of 1559 Dundee's kirk session operated under the magistrates' protection. Perth, which had received 'the Order of Common Prayers' by May 1559, had its own minister by September.[24] The protestant

[20] Knox, *Works*, vi, 22–6; *Calendar of State Papers, Foreign, Elizabeth, 1558–1559*, ed. J. Stevenson (London, 1863), no. 877; *Wodrow Miscellany*, i, 57–60; *CSP Scot.*, i, nos. 455, 457, 464, 465, 469, 474, 480; Knox, *Works*, i, 335–40; Leslie, *History*, 271–5.
[21] Winzet, *Certane Tractatis*, 44.
[22] *CSP Scot.*, i, no. 480; see below, 320–21, 325.
[23] *CSP Scot.*, i, no. 1163.
[24] Knox, *Works*, vi, 36, 78.

congregation in Edinburgh had publicly elected Knox as minister in July 1559 and was already worshipping in St Giles; and the other churches within the burgh and its environs were reported to be duly 'purged' by the end of June 1559, 'images and monuments of idolatry' were removed, mass was prohibited, and the Edwardine prayer book encouraged.[25] By September 1559, if not earlier, St Andrews also had acquired a reformed ministry, and the surviving record of its session dates from October 1559. The reformed congregations in Montrose, Brechin, Stirling and Ayr had all obtained ministers by September 1559, and protestant preaching had extended south into Jedburgh and Kelso.[26] Indeed, by December 1559, it was reported that the towns of Linlithgow, Jedburgh, Glasgow, Dumfries, Lanark, Ayr, Irvine, Dumbarton, Stirling, Kirkcaldy, Kinghorn, Dysart, Pittenweem, Anstruther, Crail, St Andrews, Cupar, Dunfermline, Perth, Dundee, Brechin and Montrose had openly declared themselves against the French:[27] all were centres where protestant opinions circulated, and the appeal by the insurgents to resentment of the French suggested a solution that only with help from England, whose policy was to promote the reforming cause, would the French be removed from Scotland. Glasgow was already accustomed, by January 1559/60, to 'the ordre of the commen prayers, which are the verie same or dyffer verie lyttle, from those of England', though it may have had to wait a little longer than some burghs for a regular minister; yet in 1560 the city acquired a minister in Willock, who arrived in August; and soon afterwards (perhaps with Willock's appointment as superintendent of Glasgow in September 1561), the town, it seems, gained a second minister in John Davidson, the university's principal and convert of 1559, for both are described early in 1562 as 'ministeris in Glasgw'.[28]

The itinerant preachers, whose inflammatory sermons had once aroused the suspicions of magistrates, had evidently found

[25] *Extracts from the Records of the Burgh of Edinburgh, 1557–1571* [vol. iii], ed. J. D. Marwick (Edinburgh, 1875), 46–48; *Wodrow Miscellany*, i, 63; 61; *CSP Scot.*, i, no. 480; cf. Leslie, *History*, 275.
[26] Knox, *Works*, vi, 78; *RStAKS*, i, 5; Knox, *Works*, vi, 78.
[27] *Cal. S. P. For. Eliz., 1559–60* (1865), no. 485. p. 226.
[28] R. Keith, *History of the Affairs of Church and State in Scotland*, ed. J. P. Lawson, 3 vols. (Edinburgh, 1844–50), iii, 10; *CSP Scot.*, i, no. 616; Durkan and Kirk, *University of Glasgow*, 231–3; *Charters and Documents relating to the Burgh of Peebles, 1165–1710*, ed. W. Chambers (Edinburgh, 1872), 275. (There is mention, too, of how the 'minister of Glasgow departit in Ingland' apparently during the winter of 1560 and of the elders' refusal in his absence to give judgment in the Earl of Eglinton's divorce case. W. Fraser, *Memorials of the Montgomeries*, 2 vols. (Edinburgh, 1859), ii, 184.)

willing and responsive audiences in the towns to such a degree
that magistrates, once reluctant to countenance their preaching,
were prepared by 1559 not just to tolerate them but to recognise
them as the town's official preachers and to finance their ministry
from the public purse. The communities which took this decisive
action could be under no illusion that they were openly defying
and challenging the established church, whose chaplains found
themselves prohibited from fulfilling their time-honoured duties.
As Kirkcaldy of Grange explained to Cecil in June 1559, 'open
defiance is now given to all who maintain idolatry'.[29] By insisting
that the priests who lived among them renounce the papacy and
the mass, town councils and individual congregations were seen
to take the initiative in a manner which bears far more eloquent
testimony to the work of Reformation than any belated
legislation issued by parliament in 1560 could hope to demonstrate.

The identity of some of these early ministers remains obscure:
the efforts of the magistrates in Ayr, in May 1558, to secure the
services of the curate of Prestwick, Robert Leggat, suggest the
introduction of a reforming programme in the town; but when it
came to recruiting a protestant minister for the burgh, Ayr
ultimately looked to Edinburgh: two commissioners attending a
court case in Edinburgh returned home with 'ane precheour', as
an entry in the town's accounts for the financial year September
1558–9 laconically records; this was followed by joinery on the
pulpit, as the new preacher began his work.[30] The demand to
secure a godly preacher clearly came from within the community,
which, with the council's blessing, approached the preacher with
an invitation to become their minister. In seeking to satisfy the
town's religious needs, the council had patently rejected the
existing ecclesiastical structure; and it had also disregarded the
proclamation in March 1558/9 forbidding anyone on pain of
death to preach or minister sacraments who had not been
authorised by a bishop or ordinary.[31]

The unnamed preacher was probably John Willock who as a
temporary preacher was no stranger to Ayr. As a son of the town
since his days as a friar, which may have attracted some civic
pride, Willock had the added appeal of a seasoned preacher,
equipped with an exceptional breadth of experience of reform in
Edwardine England and in East Friesland, and with first-hand

---

[29] *CSP Scot.*, i, no. 471.
[30] SRO, B6/12/3, Ayr Burgh Court Book, 22 May 1559; *Ayr Burgh Accounts,
1534–1624*, ed. G. S. Pryde (Edinburgh, 1937), 130.
[31] *Wodrow Miscellany*, i, 56.

knowledge through his preaching tours of protestant communities at home in the west, in Edinburgh and in Angus. He was certainly active in the burgh by March 1559, when his sermons on the mass sparked off an exchange of polemical letters, dated from Ayr, with Abbot Quintin Kennedy of Crossraguel at Maybole.[32] The town's accounts for the financial year September 1559 to September 1560 also record expenses incurred in conveying the 'minister' to Edinburgh; by then, however, Willock was no longer resident in Ayr. In July 1559 he had replaced Knox as minister in Edinburgh for a year, and in August had ministered communion in St Giles.[33] Yet he evidently returned to visit Ayr, perhaps to collect his effects, for he was entertained with wine by his old town, indicating that he was a guest of the burgh and not its resident minister; the occasion was perhaps the town's farewell to its former preacher.[34]

At the same point, furnishings were bought for 'the ministeris chalmer', which suggests the arrival of a new incumbent; some silver was allocated to 'the minister'; and soon afterwards, a gown was purchased for Christopher Goodman, who had come to Scotland in September 1559, was present with Willock in Edinburgh in October for the election of the protestants' council, and was certainly minister in Ayr by November 1559 when the town made arrangements for its schoolmaster, John Orr, to act as temporary minister, during Goodman's absence, 'quhilk salbe bot viij or ix dayis at the maist at aneis', by reading 'the commoun prayaris' and ministering 'the sacrament'. (Perhaps Orr had earlier officiated as interim minister in the months between Willock's departure and Goodman's arrival.) At that stage, too, the council decided to appoint a chaplain as church officer, 'he keipand the paroche kirk of the said burght honest and clein, ringand the bellis yeirlie and on ilk day neidfull to the commoun prayaris and precheing', on condition that he first 'renunce the devill, the paip and all thair workis' before 'the haill congregatioun' of the parish.[35]

For the second time, Ayr had succeeded in attracting an outstanding preacher in the Englishman who had been Knox's colleague in Geneva. The burgh, which also assumed responsibility for buying wheaten bread for communion, was evidently anxious to retain Goodman's services: it paid for conveying 'the minister to the lordis of Secrete Counsale' in Edinburgh and was

[32] Ibid., 265–77.
[33] Knox, *History*, i, 211; *Wodrow Miscellany*, i, 65, 67.
[34] *Ayr Burgh Accounts*, 30.
[35] Ibid., 30; *CSP Scot.*, i, no. 554; Knox, *Works*, vi, 78; *CSP Scot.*, i, 550; SRO, B6/12/3, Ayr Burgh Court Book, 20 Nov. 1559.

even prepared to pay Goodman's expenses 'quhen he raid to the Ile of Man', in August 1560 where he remained '10 days and preached twice'.[36] The duration of the visit was more or less consistent with the town's contract to its assistant minister: Goodman's absence in spreading the Word elsewhere was viewed as a temporary secondment. But then came news of the decision reached in Edinburgh to transfer Goodman to St Andrews, where his academic and preaching skills could best be used as minister of the city and member of the university.[37] Not to be outdone, Ayr quickly found a replacement in the obscurer figure of Robert Acheson, who may be identified with the Augustinian canon of St Andrews, later accused in 1563 of massmongering at Cranston.[38] As the town's new minister, whom the burgh was anxious to please, Acheson obtained a new pulpit and desks for the kirk, and the council even hired nightwatchmen to keep the kirk secure. In the following year, a Bible was purchased for the kirk, and the new minister, active in travelling to parliament and to St Andrews at the burgh's expense, was suitably attired by the town with 'black clothes', a canvas gown, shirts and black silk buttons for his coat.[39] As the burgesses of Ayr appreciated, the progress of reform could easily suffer a setback were the burgh to lose its minister. After experiencing the services of a succession of three ministers within a year, Ayr hoped to avoid finding a fourth.

It was not merely the larger and bustling burghs, however, which commanded the attention of protestant preachers. Even so small a community as Dalmellington, fifteen miles south east of Ayr, had been able to attract the services of Leonard Clerk, at work as minister by November 1559; and on the east coast, the little seaport of Crail, where Knox had preached in June 1559, was evidently accustomed to reformed worship by December 1559 when the council ordered a conforming chaplain, Sir John Brown, who was ready to renounce papistry to profess his protestantism on 'Sunday nixt to cum publyk in the kyrk off Crail be his awyne hand wret'.[40] Certainly, Crail's initiative in introducing reformed service was later recognised when its minister, elders and deacons were invited to participate with their

---

[36] Ayr Burgh Accounts, 30–1, 33; CSP Scot., i, no. 891.

[37] Knox, History, i, 334; RStAKS, i, 4; St Andrews University Archives, MS. Rector's Book, fo. 71.

[38] SRO, B65/22, St Andrews Charters, no. 323 [now transferred to St Andrews University Archives]; BUK, i, 40.

[39] Ayr Burgh Accounts, 33, 132, 134.

[40] SRO, B6/12/3, Ayr Burgh Court Book, 30 Nov. 1559; SRO, B10/8/2, Crail Town Clerk's Scroll Book, 4 Dec. 1559.

colleagues from Perth, Cupar, Anstruther, Kirkcaldy and Dunfermline in electing a superintendent by April 1561. Yet the example set by Crail was not unusual: to the south west of Crail, the small rural parish of Kilconquhar in the East Neuk of Fife could even claim the services of a graduate minister from 1559 in the form of a reformed Augustinian canon of St Andrews; Kirkcaldy possessed a minister and flourishing kirk session in 1560; the nearby parish of Aberdour, along the estuary of the Forth, had gained a minister by 1560 (later demoted to reader); in the north of Fife, rural Collesie had an exhorter in 1560; the neighbouring parish of Abdie, which had a vicar's house reserved, in May 1559, for a 'minister of the Word of God', was duly equipped with a minister in 1560 and, across the estuary of the Tay, the coastal parish of Monifieth, six miles from godly Dundee, had its own minister at work by April 1560.[41]

In the north east, even Aberdeen, which showed understandable hesitancy in associating with any act of defiance against the crown, had two protestant ministers actively preaching in the burgh in December 1559, at a point when the provost was urging the council to defend the burgh's churches and the buildings of the religious houses against the rebellious Congregation approaching from Angus and the Mearns. The two protestant preachers, Paul Methven and Adam Heriot, 'travailing with them in the Evangel', had been recruited, it was disclosed, by the bailies of the burgh; three months earlier, the chaplains had petitioned the town council, 'offering thaimselffs to do the service of God', a remark which rather suggests that their services may have lapsed; and by December, it was reported how in Aberdeen 'they have already reformed their kirks, destroyed their altars, promised the destruction and abolishment of the dens of idolatry' and seemed ready to support the protestant party, whose adherents from Angus and the Mearns, arriving in January, attacked the religious houses, and persuaded the council to confiscate the revenues of the religious houses for other uses. Soon afterwards, the council openly identified itself with the cause of the Congregation and agreed to suppress idolatry.[42]

Events had clearly overtaken the belated efforts which the

[41] *RStAKS*, i, 74; *BUK*, i, 58; SRO, CS7/45, Acts and Decreets of the Court of Session, fos. 229r–231r; *RStAKS*, i, 54, 56, 132; *Registum Magni Sigilli Regum Scotorum* [*RMS*], ed. J. M. Thomson *et al.*, 11 vols. (Edinburgh, 1882–1914), v, no. 595; New Register House, Edinburgh, OPR.310/1, Monifieth Parochial Records, fo. 2r (6 April 1560).
[42] *Extracts from the Council Register of the Burgh of Aberdeen, 1398–1570*, ed. J. Stuart (Aberdeen, 1844), 322, 325–6; *Cal. S. P. For. Eliz., 1559–60*, no. 485, p. 226; Keith, *History*, i, 265–6 and n. 1.

bishop of Aberdeen had made, in January 1558/9 in consulting
his dean and chapter 'for reformatioun to be maid and stancheing
of hereseis pullelant within the diocie of Aberdene'.[43] Nor can
the Earl of Huntly, a leading magnate in the north with interests
in Aberdeen, be convincingly considered to be then a champion
of Catholicism. By February 1559/60, it was observed how
Huntly had begun to reform religion in his country'[44] (which, of
course, may have given the burgh an added impetus to declare
where its allegiance lay); and the Earl Marischal, the other
dominant magnate in the area, was staunchly protestant. None of
this, it would seem, lends much support for the claim that
Aberdeen was 'the most determinedly Catholic of the major
burghs', supported by its patron 'the even more resolute
Catholic earl of Huntly',[45] a remark which surely stands history
on its head, for Huntly's irresolution and inconstancy at the
Reformation were so pronounced that he had temporarily joined
the insurgent Lords of the Congregation, and his later profession
in 1561, a year before his death, to 'set up the Mass in three
shires' if commanded by Queen Mary[46] merely strengthens the
case for Huntly's vacillation.

South of the Tay, the town of Perth, whose craftsmen had
shown such solicitude for the Reformation, seems to have
experienced difficulties similar to those of Ayr in keeping its
minister: whoever was the burgh's minister in September 1559,
the town had to rely on the services of a temporary preacher,
William Harlaw, by April 1560, who left the burgh later in the
year to become minister at St Cuthbert's, beside his native
Edinburgh, and by July 1560 Perth was assigned to John Row,
whom Lord James Stewart and Knox had newly recruited from
Rome and of whom it was later said that 'in the time of blindness,
the Pope was to him as an angel of God'. Yet, if his Paul-like
conversion discomfited some, Row was esteemed 'a wyse, grave
father' by colleagues in the ministry, was four-times moderator
of the general assembly, and served the burgh of Perth for twenty
years till his death in 1580, 'much lamented', it was said, 'by the
people whom he served'.[47]

[43] *HMC 5th Report, App.* (London, 1876), 640.
[44] *CSP Scot.,* i, no. 647, 661.
[45] M. Lynch in *Early Modern Town in Scotland,* ed. M. Lynch (London, 1987),
19.
[46] *CSP Scot.,* i, no. 1023.
[47] See above, 13–14; Calderwood, *History,* iii, 479; *The Autobiography and
Diary of Mr James Melvill,* ed. R. Pitcairn (Edinburgh, 1842), 83; Spottiswoode,
History, ii, 273–4.

Stirling, with a reformed ministry operating by September 1559, was able by Easter 1560 to hire the services of a chaplain in the burgh, Thomas Duncanson, 'for reiding of the commoun prayeris' daily on week days and twice on Sundays, for which he later received a stipend of 40 merks, and also acted as schoolmaster; but the burgh also promptly obtained its own 'mynister', John Duncanson, an Augustinian canon from St Andrews, who was assigned a 'luggion and houss' by the burgh in October 1560,[48] and who had presumably been handpicked for the job soon after Lord James Stewart and the Congregation had drawn up their band for religion at Stirling in the summer of 1559 and then had repeatedly returned to the town during the autumn and winter of 1559.[49] Stirling, therefore, acquired as its minister an outsider of some distinction (a man versed in Erasmus' Annotations on the New Testament, and with an interest in the early fathers,[50] who seems to have arrived at protestantism through Catholic reform) in preference to a local chaplain like Patrick Gillespie whom the council had so recently presented in 1557 to the chaplainry of the Blessed Virgin Mary in the Holy Rood and who subsequently conformed to become minister at Kirkton (St Ninians), near Stirling.[51] The town's pre-Reformation schoolmaster, William Gulane, himself a chaplain, also conformed to protestantism, and, as he had the 'thirds' of the revenues he derived from St Ninian's chaplainry and St Laurence's altar in Stirling remitted by the crown in 1564 for the years from 1561 onward, the possibility cannot be excluded that he undertook reformed service in one capacity or another.[52]

The absence of council records from June 1557 to April 1560 obscures the progress of reform in Stirling; but the composition of the council in October 1560 contained at least one novelty, namely, the inclusion of half a dozen minor lairds under the leadership of the provost, James Stirling of Keir, who far from being a nonentity, had adhered to the party of revolution and

[48] *Extracts from the Records of the Royal Burgh of Stirling, 1519–1666*, ed. R. Renwick (Glasgow, 1887), 74–6; *BUK*, i, 44.

[49] Knox, *History*, i, 181, 206–7, 228–9, 232, 265–71.

[50] J. Durkan and A. Ross, *Early Scottish Libraries* (Glasgow, 1961) 175. (The library included works by the early father Clement of Alexandria; Albert Pighius, Royard and Gerson.)

[51] SRO, B66/25/637, Royal charters to the burgh of Stirling and related documents (28 May 1557) [now transferred to Central Regional Archives, Stirling].

[52] SRO, B66/25/707, (13 Jan. 1563/4). The entry is not recorded in *Thirds of Benefices*.

attended the Reformation parliament in August.[53] An active kirk
session was to be found at work within the burgh in 1560, and
culprits who slandered 'the magistratis and elderis of the town'
were duly rebuked in February 1560/1. The chalices from the
altars of St James and St Peter, which no longer served any useful
purpose, were sold by the council in April 1561, and much of the
proceeds devoted to the more mundane purpose of road
repairs.[54]

By May 1560, the town council in Edinburgh had made
provision for its minister, John Knox, and its reader, John
Cairns; in June it decided seating in the kirk should be made
available for parishioners attending 'the sermoun and prayarris',
and when the Reformation parliament was held in August, the
council took care that its proposals for submission to parliament
should conform tò 'Goddis trew ordinance for the manteinance
of the trew religioun';[55] and a glimpse of a hitherto unnoticed
record of the members of the kirk session in 1561–2 reveals the
powerful friends of protestantism within the burgh's establishment.[56] Edinburgh's seaport of Leith, which had won a
reputation for godliness in the 1540s, also had the services of a
minister by 1560.[57]

Further south, the bailies in Peebles, careful to dissociate
themselves from any religious change effected in defiance of the
queen regent, discharged an 'appostat', John Wallace, in March
1559/60, from using 'ony new novationes of commoun prayeris
or preching' because Wallace 'wes nocht electit be the saidis
baillies and parochyn'; the bailies, therefore, 'wald nocht assist to
him nor nane of his sect nor opinioun' but 'wald stand vnder the
faith and obedience of thair Prince berand authorite for the tyme,
nocht beand dischargit be ane ordour and in na contemptioun of
the Lordis of Congregatioun'. In Peebles, the magistrates
hesitated to associate themselves with rebels against constituted

[53] SRO, B66/15/4, Burgh of Stirling, Court and Council Records (4 Oct. 1560)
[now transferred to CRA]; Acts of the Parliaments of Scotland, edd. T. Thomson
and C. Innes, 12 vols. (Edinburgh, 1814–75), ii, 526.
[54] Stirling Burgh Records, 77–8.
[55] Edinburgh Burgh Records, iii, 63–5, 67, 71.
[56] Fraser, Montgomeries, ii, 185: John Knox, minister; Mr John Spottiswoode,
superintendent of Lothian; Mr John Spens [merchant], Alexander Guthrie [town
clerk], Mr Richard Strang [advocate], Mr John Marjoribanks [merchant], Mr
Clement Little [advocate], Mr Robert Glen [merchant], Alexander Park
[merchant], Andrew Slater [merchant], Andrew Armstrong [merchant], William
Harlaw [saddler], Alexander Hope [merchant], James Aikman [merchant],
Robert Johnston [merchant], John Frier [skinner], John Weir [pewterer],
Alexander Lyall, John Cairns [reader], elders and deacons. (My identification of
the occupations is supplied in brackets.)
[57] BUK, i, 3.

authority; at the same time, they had no wish to antagonise the Congregation. In particular, news that the Master of Maxwell 'had come to the aid of the Lords of the Congregation' caused alarm and some soul-searching in Peebles: in March 1559/60, the head of the Trinitarian house in the burgh, fearful of the future (and mindful, no doubt, of his friary's destruction by the English a decade earlier), prudently 'changed his dress by changing his white habit for a gray keltour gowne and putting on a how black bonnet but not from any hatred of his old religion', curious phraseology which almost suggests he had abandoned his religion along with his habit, an impression strengthened by the admission in 1560 by one of his subordinates that the friars as a community in Peebles 'had been in times past from the day of the insurrection of the lords of the congregation obedient in all things to the said lords, likeas they would be still obedient in anything they should require of them'.[58]

In the end, the death of the queen regent in June 1560 helped resolve the political dilemma facing the magistrates in Peebles; yet the adherence to the Congregation by September 1559 of Châtelherault, heir presumptive to the throne, had been sufficient to convince the town council of its propriety in sending men to the host called by the duke in April 1560 and then in November 1560 in applying, in name of the 'baillies and communite', to the Lords of the Congregation in Edinburgh 'to provide ane minister and precheour' for the burgh. A week later, with what looks like exceptional haste, the council assigned a stipend of £40 (paid from the parson's effects) to John Dickson, a former prebendary of St John's altar in St Andrew's kirk in the town, as 'minister of the commoun prayeris in our kirk of Pebles'. Whatever the nature of the discussions with the Congregation in Edinburgh, the town opted for a local man, aged about thirty and born in the burgh; they then sought authorisation for their action from the protestant privy council 'conforme to the consuetude of vtheris burrois'. As the parish kirk had been burned by the English twelve years earlier, the burgh gained the privy council's approval to adopt the friary's Cross kirk (which, unlike the friary itself, had escaped the devastation wrought in 1548 and which lay a quarter of a mile east of the ruinous St Andrews kirk) as the new parish kirk for 'preching of Goddis word and ministerie of the sacramentis as appirtenis to christianis to half', a move approved by the dean of

---

[58] *Peebles Charters*, 258; cf. Leslie, *History*, 276; *RMS*, iv, no. 3037; *Peebles Charters*, 259–60, 271.

Christianity of Peebles, John Colquhoun, one of the petitioners, who had evidently conformed to protestantism.[59]

The divisive religious issue affecting the parishioners of Peebles, at that point, was not the competing claims of protestantism and Catholicism, but a dispute about which church should be used for protestant worship; and this, in turn, saw the emergence of rival candidates for the job of minister: the agreement to make the friars' kirk the parish kirk displeased the rural parishioners led by Dionysius Elphinston of Henderstoun, who had been a party to the decision to use the friars' kirk but who changed his mind in December 1560, arguing that either the parson 'if there was one', or 'the vicar or his minister' should 'perform the service of common prayers and sacraments in their parish church of St Andrew', according 'the rite of the kingdom of Scotland now observed', apparently a tacit admission that the vicar had conformed to protestantism and was open to persuasion to enter the ministry. The propriety of Dickson's admission as minister (who, it was said, had entered office without formal election either by the lords of council or by the parishioners) was also challenged by Elphinston, who forgot about persuading 'the vicar or his minister' to take up office and, instead, advanced his own claims 'to minister by himself in the same way as Johne Dikesone had ministered'. Faced with the need to secure agreement within the community (not only within the burgh but within the wider parish), the council showed a readiness to disregard both contenders by seeking a fresh candidate: the bailies were to go to 'the lordis' in Edinburgh (where the general assembly was then in session) 'and get ane minister to schaw the trew word of God' for 'ane ressonable fee'.[60]

Part of the difficulty, of course, was that no uniform procedure had then been adopted for electing protestant preachers. After all, the Book of Discipline which did contain guidelines, as it took shape during 1560, had yet to be submitted for approval. The initiative, at this stage, was still left largely to local communities, acting as they thought best, with advice from the nearest reformed town or from the Lords of the Congregation or their successors on the protestant privy council. There does seem to have been some recognition, however, that the parishioners' consent was a necessary part of the process; hence, the emphasis sometimes found on holding public elections, whose outcome

[59] *Peebles Charters*, 260, 263, 305; SRO, NP2/1, Register of Admissions of Notaries, fo. 44r–v; *Peebles Charters*, 260, 263–5.
[60] *Peebles Charters*, 267–9; see below, 113.

was often announced from the tolbooth of a burgh to give the proceedings the full weight of public authority.[61] In Peebles, the desire to secure common ground among parishioners had led to a search for a third minister. The council had tried to play its part in finding an appropriate candidate; but with the introduction of a kirk session in the burgh (with jurisdiction over the entire parish, burghal and landward), which the council had instituted by February 1561/2, the way was open for the session to assume responsibility for 'chosing Johne Allane to be thair minister in tymes cuming'. Again, the preference was for a son of the burgh, whose crudentials were known to all, not an incomer who may have aroused suspicion or distrust. Allan, a former chaplain, aged about 43 and unmarried had been born in Peebles and like so many priests in search of a living had become a notary in 1556. His career bore a remarkable resemblance to the displaced Dickson's: both had served as priests and notaries in the burgh, each aspired to the office of minister, and both became common clerks of the burgh; neither held a master's degree.[62]

In arriving at its decision in favour of Allan, the kirk session took the precaution of consulting the wider church, as indeed it was obliged by then to do: the Book of Discipline, adopted by the general assembly, had laid down procedures for admissions which involved examining a candidate's doctrine and aptitude by 'the learned Ministers and next reformed church', that is 'the Church of the Superintendent with his councell'. Peebles, however, lay within the new province of Jedburgh which had no superintendent. Faced with this difficulty, the session (mindful of the old ecclesiastical links with Glasgow in whose diocese Peebles once belonged) looked to the ministers of Glasgow (one of whom had become superintendent) to admit their new minister; their approval was gained, and Allan's admission duly authorised.[63]

Yet, Peebles was remote from Glasgow, the journey was over 55 miles; Edinburgh was far more accessible, within a distance of 30 miles. Anxious to forge closer links with Edinburgh and no doubt mindful of its famous minister, the session sought further 'corroboratioun of the superintendence of Glasgw admissioun' of Allan to the ministry from John Knox, 'superintendent of Edinburgh' (unaware of Knox's refusal to accept that office). To assist their new minister's education in the new theology, the

[61] *Wodrow Society Miscellany*, 63.
[62] *Peebles Charters*, 275–6; SRO, NP2/1, Register of Admissions of Notaries, fo. 41r, 44r–v; *Peebles Charters*, 289–91.
[63] *First Book of Discipline*, ed. J. K. Cameron (Edinburgh, 1972), 99; 96; *Peebles Charters*, 275–6.

session arranged to pay his expenses in travelling to Edinburgh to attend 'the preching and exercise' for training ministers to interpret and expound the scriptures.[64] The minister of Peebles was to be trained at the feet of Knox and his colleagues in the capital where he would also receive instruction on kirk session discipline.

It is a remarkable picture of fortitude and endeavour by the protestant community in Peebles and its fledgling minister. Such indeed was the thirst for knowledge by the godly in Peebles that not content with acquiring a minister to expound the Word, the town decided to retain the services of John Dickson (whose rôle as 'minister' had earlier ended in squabbles) in the subordinate capacity as 'redare and exhortare of the commoun prayeris', but with the same stipend as before (which exceeded the Book of Discipline's scale for a reader or exhorter). Duly appointed 'to continew in Peblis' by the superintendent of Glasgow in June 1562, Dickson lost no time in declaring his support for the stricter sort of discipline (which may have been a factor, combined perhaps with an inexperience in preaching, in his earlier replacement or demotion). A month after his admission, to the probable consternation of the council, Dickson as reader (and not Allan as minister) placed the failure to exact discipline (in particular, punishment for cohabitation) on the magistrates, whose 'tovne salbe ane verray Sodome and Gomor, and all becaus na correctioun is put thairto be your maisterschippis, and sua gif ye omit this vndone God will pvnis yow'. The town council might seek to assert its dominance by electing the kirk session and prescribing attendance at prayers for all parishioners; it even had its way by transferring the seats from St Andrew's kirk to the Cross kirk, and one of the bells 'to rigne to the commoun prayeris'; but it was hard for any council to restrain a mesenger of God's Word (even a demoted one) who treated the bailies as erring Christians whose shortcomings he exposed that they might submit themselves to 'the will of the Eternale Judge quha hes set yow in authorite'.[65]

Yet it was the town's minister and not the exhorter who fell from grace. Allan's work in reforming the lives of others did not extend to his own, and therein lay his downfall: if the minister and common clerk who shared the same name were indeed the same man, Allan found himself disgraced in 1563 and dismissed as clerk (and presumably as minister) for keeping 'in his

---

[64] *Peebles Charters*, 276.
[65] *Peebles Charters*, 278; *First Book of Discipline*, 108ff; *Peebles Charters*, 275, 279, 288.

company ane vnclene persone nocht beand joynit with him in the band of matrimonye in contrair all godly order of crystiane', presumably his pre-Reformation mistress whom he neglected to marry with the change of rules in 1560, for his son and daughter were legitimised in 1566.[66] It is certainly possible to detect in Dickson's protest to the magistrates a thinly veiled denunciation not only of the sin of cohabitation in general but of Allan's in particular. Dickson's sermonising, at any rate, was not without effect. In all, the burgh might have been better advised to have retained as minister its original choice in 1560, for the displaced Dickson, who had evidently profited from his years as reader and exhorter, was again recognised by 1566 as the burgh's minister;[67] and Allan continued his career as notary until the burgh had a change of heart in 1570, forgot his earlier scandal and reinstated him as common clerk; but his other 'clerical' career – the ministry – was not, it seems, resumed, and when a new minister was sought in 1571, 'the maist part of the communitie of the burgh' looked beyond the confines of the town in choosing Thomas Cranstoun, a graduate and preacher at Borthwick and Liberton, whose son agreed to serve as schoolmaster.[68]

The small, provincial town of Peebles, which played no crucial rôle in national issues (and sent no commissioner recorded in parliament between 1526 and 1567), well illustrates the struggles and setbacks which a community experienced in securing a protestant ministry at the Reformation. It also says something of the human frailty, even among ministers, with which the reformers had to contend.

At the Reformation, the emphasis on finding a minister usually lay with local communities, and preachers in short supply could look to parishes which offered more promising conditions of employment. Yet many communities cared sufficiently about obtaining a resident preacher that they were ready to sustain him from their own resources in the absence of a benefice. The unsettled conditions during the Reformation and the lack of formal records in rural parishes (beyond perhaps a written contract of service for the minister) have largely obscured what seems to have been the prevailing practice in reformed congregations to chose their ministers without seeking any further mandate for their action.

This becomes all the more evident in the action of

[66] RSS, v, no. 2798; Peebles Charters, 291–2. He remained unmarried in Feb. 1563/4: SRO, NP2/1, Register of Admissions of Notaries, fo. 41r.
[67] SRO, CS7/36, Acts and Decreets of the Court of Session, fo. 374r.
[68] Peebles Charters, 325, 327, 333, 334, 339; Fasti Ecclesiae Scoticanae, ed. H. Scott et al., 10 vols. (Edinburgh, 1915–81), i, 170, 285, 301.

superintendents from 1561 in deposing unqualified ministers and readers who had attached themselves to congregations in the phase before stricter controls on admissions, introduced in the Book of Discipline, were applied. In the small rural parish of Ballingry near Loch Leven in Fife, the parson, it was discovered, had acted as minister of the parish 'sen the Reformation', and had continued in that capacity after the appointment of a superintendent for Fife who at a visitation of the parish in 1561 declined to recognise the parson as minister. The parson, afraid perhaps of being demoted from minister to reader, protested that he had been 'lawfullie chosyn and providit tharto, and that he wald not be ane readar to Jhon Knox nor ony other in Scotland', but he lost the argument by attempting to defy the superintendent (whose earlier career, he truthfully but tactlessly recounted, had been dedicated to oppressing protestants) for which he was deposed.[69]

Another irregular preacher and former priest was pursued by the superintendent of Fife in 1564, 'for takyng upon hand to prech and minister the sacramentis wythowtyn lawfull admission, and for drawyng of the pepill to the chapell of Tulebarne fra thar parroche kyrk'. Amid the muddle and uncertainty, there were former priests, admitted readers who, in fulfilling parishioners needs and expectations, took upon themselves to administer the sacrament of the Lord's Supper 'in privat howsis, as also in the kyrk yard, about the kyrkyard dykis' and to officiate at baptisms and weddings 'efter the Papisticall fasson'. In some cases, the changeover in 1560 must have been as bewildering to the old priest turned new minister as it was to some of his parishioners. Yet what is truly remarkable is not the few readers, as former priests, suspected of lapses into papistry, but the record of the rest who seem to have fulfilled the exacting standards set by the general assembly and superintendents.

As well as a tradition of lingering Catholicism for reformers to combat and guard against, the kirk heard rumour of anabaptists at work, of soul seekers, and exponents of a middle way between Catholicism and protestantism like Robert Ramsay, an unauthorised preacher detected in Angus in 1563, who had borrowed money for books from the town of Inverness (itself reformed by 1560) which he had omitted to repay, and who was 'suspended from his ministrie till further triell war taken'.[70] At the same time, the widespread availability and use within

[69] RStAKS, i, 82–3.
[70] Ibid., i, 226–7; CSP Scot., i, nos. 1023, 1041; Knox, Works, ii, 109; BUK, i, 376; 44.

reformed communities for worship of the English and Genevan prayer books curbed the growth of heterodox expressions in protestant doctrine. The need, however, for an ordered ministry, examined by competent ecclesiastical authorities and not recruited at the will or whim of local leaders, was never greater. The advantage, of course, in introducing readers instead of ministers of uncertain quality minimised the tendency towards doctrinal deviation and helped preserve a consensus in favour of the standards laid down in the Scots Confession and Book of Discipline. In 1560, however, the preference was for ministers who could truly preach the Word; only gradually were some of the men who were recognised as ministers at the Reformation downgraded to exhorters (whose primary duty lay in preaching) and to readers (who might read sermons but not compose them) as the Reformation settlement took fuller effect. But if the reformed ministry as it expanded by 1574 had become substantially staffed by readers, the kirk of 1560 was served by men who all but invariably were depicted as 'ministers'.

In the burghs where a greater emphasis was placed on written record (or, at any rate, on the preservation of documents), a somewhat clearer picture emerges of the steps taken at the Reformation to attract protestant preachers. Again, much depended on local action. During the initial phase of confusion and considerable laxity, magistrates had recognised the part they ought to play in recruiting and hiring (and, if necessary, firing) a preacher whose doctrine they hoped would find approval from the community. In this sense, the minister received a call to officiate within the community; his position was transformed and regularised from that of a wandering preacher of indeterminate status, accustomed to addressing open-air gatherings, to that of the burgh's recognised preacher, financed by the town, with the exclusive right regularly to occupy the pulpit of the burgh's church, and afforded the magistrates' protection. The previously harrassed preacher who lived a hand-to-mouth existence, ever on the move, had at last gained settled and secure employment. A town council, in nominating him, was no doubt satisfied it had gained a powerful preacher who would plainly proclaim the right way to the kingdom of heaven, a man whom it still might be able to remove were he found unsuitable; but beyond this, magistrates generally found themselves unable to halt the pace and direction of reformation (which lay largely beyond their control), just as they failed to exercise control over the content of reformed preaching and, instead, discovered they themselves were not exempt from reformation, rebuke or censure.

Even with the meeting of protestants in Edinburgh in July 1560, no uniform system for appointing ministers seems to have been contemplated, far less to have operated, and the work of that gathering, it appears, concentrated on confirming or regulating local appointments of ministers in some of the major burghs: Aberdeen, Perth, Dundee, St Andrews, Dunfermline, Edinburgh, Leith and Jedburgh. The matter, it is true, was carried further when the general assembly of 'the kirks conveinit', in December 1560, attempted to co-ordinate the enterprise already displayed by local communities when it recognised the service of a further 44 individuals deemed qualified to undertake a regular ministry, eight of whom were thought competent for the subsidiary work of readers, who conducted worship by reading prayers, homilies and sermons but were not expected to preach or minister the sacraments.[71]

So far, recruitment to the reformed ministry had received a promising start. Apart from a knowledge of appointments to the ministry in their own particular areas, on which they could speak with some authority, the commissioners who attended the assembly in 1560 (drawn largely from Angus and the Mearns, Perth, Stirling, Fife, Lothian, Nithsdale and Kyle) must have had, at best, a hazy impression of what was happening elsewhere. They were unlikely to be aware, for example, that small communities remote from their personal experience such as Inchcailloch on Lochlomond or even Renfew had parsons who had conformed to the Reformation by undertaking reformed service.[72] There were even vicars who, if not inclined to enter the new ministry themselves, were certainly ready to ensure that others did. The vicar of Inverkip, who seems to have been too elderly to contemplate a new career in the kirk, was conscious of an obligation to provide for the cure of souls within his parish, even if that meant protestant service: after leasing his vicarage at Candlemas 1558 (that is, 2 February 1558/9) for five years to Bishop John Campbell, 'pentionar of the Ileis' (and a reformer in 1559), David Christison redefined the terms at Stirling in December 1560, which obliged the bishop to 'sustene ane curat or ane minister at the kirk', until the lease expired, 'safar as pertenis to the vicar to do'.[73] The vicar's action was by no means unusual: the beneficiaries of revenues assigned for the cure of souls, whether churchmen or tacksmen, frequently recognised their duty to set aside a portion of the fruits they enjoyed to

---

[71] Knox, *Works*, ii, 87; *BUK*, i, 3–5.
[72] See below, 119–20.
[73] SRO, B66/15/4, unfoliated, 1 Jan. 1560/1.

sustain service in the parishes,[74] and after 1560 that service was understood to be reformed. Conscious of his obligation to pay a substitute, if he himself did not serve, the parson and vicar of Luss on Lochlomondside dutifully affirmed in 1563 (when he was then aged 65) that he had 'furneist and sustenit ministeris for reading and edifeing of the parochinaris thairof yeirlie sen the alteratioun of the religioun, conforme to ordour takin thairanent, lyke as he yit does'.[75] In this way, the rural parish of Luss was able to sustain its minister at the Reformation.

If no one (apparently not even the assembly) in 1560, considered creating a record of the ministers already at work in the parishes (a step which might have been dismissed as impractical in a period of upheaval and confusion), the crown had certainly a financial interest in knowing the income (and therefore the personnel) of the benefices which, of course, continued in being regardless of the Reformation and of the reformers' aims to dismantle them. Besides, unlike the kirk, the crown had also the capacity for compiling such a survey. In February 1561/2, an annual levy amounting to a third of the revenues derived from every benefice was exacted by the crown, to be paid from 1561 onward, for maintenance of the queen and reformed ministry. Existing holders of benefices were required to produce their rentals for inspection, on pain of confiscation of the entire revenues of their benefices. From 1561, therefore, a somewhat clearer picture emerges of beneficed men who conformed to serve in the protestant ministry (and who had their 'thirds' allowed as part of their stipend) as well as incidental mention of benefice-holders who supported ministers from a portion of their revenues.

The survey records the active service in 1561 of 40 beneficed men who had conformed to the Reformation: one archdeacon, three cathedral treasurers, nine parsons, twenty-three vicars and four prebendaries, found at work as ministers, exhorters and readers in areas as far apart as Shetland in the north and Penninghame in Wigtownshire, Thurso in Caithness and Morton in Nithsdale, Inchcailloch in Lennox and Maryton in Angus; and by 1562 an additional two dozen beneficed men, besides those on record in 1561, had undertaken reformed service.[76] Most officiated in an ancillary capacity, either as reader or exhorter, but at least seven were qualified as ministers who served not only

---

[74] See below, 121–30.
[75] SRO, CS7/27. Acts and Decreets of the Court of Session, fos. 32r–33r; *Fasti*, viii, 281; Durkan and Kirk, *University of Glasgow*, 183–4.
[76] *Accounts of the Collectors of Thirds of Benefices*, ed. G. Donaldson (Edinburgh, 1949), 91–3, 149–51.

in a city charge like Brechin but also among remoter communities like Ecclesmachan, Auldhamstocks and Preston-kirk in the Lothians or Renfrew and Inchcailloch in the west. Instead of receiving a retirement pension of two-thirds of their revenues for inactivity, these men opted for the strenuous work of active service in the new ministry and so retained an entitlement to the whole fruits of their livings.

The men, however, whose names do not appear in the survey for 1561 are those who entered the ministry without access to a benefice and who were sustained by the benevolence of their parishioners. (At best the record of the 'thirds' merely alludes to ministers at work by 1561 at three churches appropriated to Fail and five churches belonging to Culross.) The financial hardship facing ministers who lacked a regular income was real enough: some had to support their families from 'that which freindes haue given us, and that which we have borrowed of cheritable persones until God send it us to repay them'.[77]

Some preachers were recruited from occupations outside the established church: Andrew Simson, minister at Cargill, was previously schoolmaster at Perth, Ninian Dalyell, schoolmaster at Dumfries, was recruited as reader at Colvend, Thomas Jack, exhorter at Rutherglen, was earlier schoolmaster at Cambuslang, William Harlaw, minister at St Cuthbert's had been a tailor to trade, and David Fergusson, minister at Dunfermline in 1560 was a former skinner, with associations in Dundee, where he had been cited with others in 1558 to answer a charge of 'wrongous using and wrestling of the Scripture, and disputting upon erroneous opinions, and eiting of flesche in Lenterone'; he was skilled enough in 1562 to compose a reply (printed in 1563) to an attack by René Benedict, a French Doctor of Divinity and chaplain to Queen Mary, on Knox and the ministers; his reply reveals a knowledge of church history and the early fathers as well as a firm grounding in scripture and doctrine, and an acquaintance with Latin, an unusual accomplishment, by any standard, for a former skinner.[78] Other recruits to the ministry were former curates and unbeneficed chaplains who might be hired and fired almost at will, outside the ranks of beneficed men. Some were ready enough to side with parishioners in resenting the appropriation of revenues from the parishes to support their ecclesiastical superiors, at their expense, and who saw a remedy to their plight in the reforming programme which aimed at

[77] *Thirds of Benefices*, 95, cf. 151; *Tracts by David Fergusson*, ed. D. Laing (Edinburgh, 1860), 11.
[78] Fergusson, *Tracts*, p. xiv, 7ff.

redirecting resources to where they mattered in the parishes. In addition, the burghs usually made their own arrangements for financing their ministers.

Reliance on voluntary contributions was the most obvious means of support for protestant ministers until at least a temporary settlement to the financial problem took effect. A tradition was already established, as John Major had observed, for lairds of any substance to have their own private chaplains; many of them were the men in whose homes, as Knox depicted, 'might have been seen the Bible lying almost upon every gentleman's table'.[79] It was a small step, therefore, for enterprising lairds, imbued with religious fervour, to reform their chaplains or sustain protestant preachers for public worship in their place. In 1560, eight nobles, a bishop and over 40 lords and lairds had pledged themselves to 'sett fordwart the Reformatioun of Religioun, according to Goddes word';[80] and in Ayrshire alone, over ninety signatories among the nobles and gentry contracted in 1562 to maintain and assist the preaching of the Word, and its ministers, against any who opposed the doctrine propounded.[81]

At an informal level, voluntary support might take the form of freewill offerings from the lairds and principal parishioners to provide a stipend sufficient to attract a minister;[82] or, more formally, the benefice-holder, or the tacksman who farmed the revenues, might undertake to sustain a preacher from a portion of his revenues. The later course of action, which seems to have been widespread in the immediate aftermath of the Reformation, was clearly consistent with the pre-Reformation practice for a non-resident parson, or even a vicar, to secure a substitute to attend to the cure of souls. Many a parson and vicar, who may have been unwilling or unable to serve in the new church, had no doubt about the propriety of paying a protestant minister. It was, after all, a small price to pay, they may well have reflected, for continued possession of the greater portion of the fruits of their benefices. George Hay, who did conform to serve as minister, held several benefices under the old regime, which he did not readily relinquish under the new, but he recognised his duty to provide a reader at Eddleston in Peebles-shire, where he held the benefice. Reformed service, he understood, had first claim on the

---

[79] J. Major, *A History of Greater Britain*, ed. A. Constable (Edinburgh, 1892), 30; Knox, *History*, i, 45 *Registrum de Panmure*, ed. J. Stuart, 2 vols. (Edinburgh, 1874), i, p. xxxii.

[80] Knox, *Works*, ii, 61–4.

[81] Fraser, *Montgomeries*, ii, 192–3.

[82] *BUK*, i, 61.

fruits, which 'sustenit ane readar according to the ordour and buik of disciplyne'; but, somewhat incongruously, a second claim on his revenues was the payment of 12 merks 'to ane priest of the choir of Glasgw'. The new obligations had begun to compete with the old.[83]

The Book of Discipline, as George Hay appreciated perhaps more than most, had pointed the way ahead by advancing claims to the teinds as the proper patrimony of the kirk. Besides, the privy council and protestant lords who gave the Book of Discipline their blessing in January 1560/1 added the provision that existing beneficed men who conformed to protestantism should retain their revenues for life on condition they sustained ministers from these revenues. Here was a further stimulus for clergy of the old order to support the new. Many appreciated only too well what they stood to lose financially by belatedly resisting religious change. Of this, some had a foretaste in 1560, when kirkmen failed to gain legal redress for arrears in rents owing them, unless 'thai subscrivit the Articlis of the new religioun'; any feus or tacks they made after 6 March 1558/9 were held to be of no avail; and possessors of teinds (usually laymen) were instructed to withold payment until the privy council determined whom the teinds should sustain.[84] All this helps explain the readiness of some beneficed men to support protestant preachers.

Whatever his religious disposition, the parson of Dolphinton in Lanarkshire recorded his contribution in February 1561/2 of more than £13 for the stipend of a minister, who evidently was already at work in the parish in 1561. The sum, it is true, was far from generous, for the whole benefice yielded £50; but it was a start; others presumably added to the minister's stipend; and, in any event, the remarkable fact is not the meagreness of stipend, which was the lot of many rural ministers, but that this small parish on the border of Peebles-shire should have recruited and installed a minister with such promptitude.[85] Whether the parson's action was the outcome of conviction or persuasion, there is scarcely a hint: the parson himself was later escheated in 1568 for siding with Mary at Langside (as many protestants as well as Catholics did); the superior of the lands in the parish was James, 4th Earl of Bothwell, who was no opponent of the

---

[83] SRO, E48/1/1, Books of Assumption, fo. 249v; E48/1/2, fo. 181v.

[84] *First Book of Discipline*, 112, 156–64, 210–12; Keith, *History*, iii, 8–10; i, 324–5.

[85] Edinburgh University Library [EUL], MS. Dc.4.32, Books of Assumption, fo. 111r.

Reformation; and, among the lairds, who as a group showed such solicitude for religious renewal, Cunningham of Bonnington, a landowner in the parish whose family had supported the English alliance and cause of reform in the 1540s, was likely to remain susceptible to the reforming lead given by his chief, the Earl of Glencairn.[86]

Irrespective of motive, other holders of parsonages were disposed to support preachers at the Reformation: Scone abbey paid just over £23 to a minister to take charge of the three kirks of Scone, Cambusmichael and Kinfauns, paid £20 to a reader at Kinfauns, £58 to a minister at Logierait, £60 to a minister at Blairgowrie, and assigned stipends for service at Redgorton, Kilspindie, Logie-Dundee, Liff and Invergowrie;[87] Arbroath contributed the stipends 'to the ministeris in every kirk that is sustenit thair' by command of the commendator, with the apparent exceptions of Monifieth (which had a minister in 1560) and Abernethy whose parsonages were held in tack by Alexander Betoun, whom the commendator presumably expected would pay the stipends there;[88] Balmerino in Fife (where the protestant John Hay had become commendator in 1561) assigned, more generously, £100 'to ane minister at the kirkis of Balmerynocht and Logie', £10 to a reader at Balmerino, and £100 to a minister at Barry, north of Dundee 'as presentlie is appointit to thame be the superintendentis';[89] Scotlandwell sustained a reader at Carnock for 20 merks;[90] Holyrood supported ministers at St Cuthbert's, Holyrood abbey church, Falkirk, Liberton and Barro with salaries which ranged from £80 for St Cuthbert's and the abbey kirk, to a mere £3 6s 8d for the minister at Barro.[91]

Blantyre set aside 40 merks which were 'payit to ane minister';[92] Dundrennan paid the stipends of the minister (£30) and reader (£20) of Kirkmabreck as well as those of the minister (£20 6s 8d) and reader (£20) of Dundrennan[93]; but the income from Sweetheart was considered insufficient, through 'evill payment' to 'sustein tua qualifiet ministeris', which sounds almost as if they were already active;[94] Culross (where Argyll

[86] *RMS*, iv, no. 2111; *RSS*, vi, no. 360.
[87] National Library of Scotland [NLS], Adv. 31.3.12, Books of Assumption, fo. 36v; SRO, E48/1/1, Books of Assumption, fo. 311v.
[88] NLS, Adv. 31.3.12, Books of Assumption, fo. 80v; SRO, E48/1/1, Books of Assumption, fo. 333v.
[89] SRO, E48/1/1, Books of Assumption, fo. 71r; E48/1/2, fo. 61r.
[90] SRO, E48/1/1, Books of Assumption, fo. 68r; E48/1/2, fo. 58r.
[91] SRO, E48/1/1, Books of Assumption, fo. 106v, 107v; E48/1/2, fo. 64v.
[92] EUL, MS. Dc.4.32, Books of Assumption, fo. 12v.
[93] Ibid., fo. 85v.
[94] Ibid., fo. 89v.

was bailie) provided for two ministers by 1561, and for reformed service in five churches in 1561–2.[95] Fail disbursed stipends from 1561 to the ministry in the parishes of Galston, Barnwell and Symington in Ayrshire, Torthorwald in Nithsdale and Inverchaolain in Argyll.[96] Further south, the parson of Wigtown by 1561 paid 40 merks to James Woods as minister, and a further 30 merks to the vicar pensionary as reader;[97] and in Galloway, the kirks of Kirkinner and Kirkcowan, held by the subdean and by the sacristan of the chapel royal, each contributed 50 merks a year 'to the minister and precher'.[98]

In Angus, the parson of Logie-Montrose, whose benefice lay in the archbishop of St Andrew's patronage, had a 'vicar and minister' ('habeo vicarium et ministrum') at work in 1561 whom he supported each year by order of the laird of Dun ('ex mandato dominum de Dwn').[99] At Cookston, the subdean's prebend of Brechin cathedral, where the parsonage was set to the reforming laird Sir Robert Carnegie of Kinnaird for £20, it was the parson (himself a Carnegie), and not the protestant laird, who paid 'the minister' £10, half the income from his parsonage.[100] The chanter of Dunkeld, as parson of Kinclaven in Stormont, also gave £10 'to the minister of the said kirk', which was less than half the pension awarded to John Douglas in St Andrews University (and an author of the Book of Discipline), and further payments were made to a staller, and chaplains and choristers of the cathedral.[101] In the parish itself, the presence of the laird of Airntully, who supported the Lords of the Congregation by reforming Dunkeld cathedral in 1560, was beneficial, no doubt, in securing a minister for the small Tayside parish at the Reformation.[102] Again, at Methlick in Aberdeenshire, from a benefice yielding £162, the parson contributed 'to the minister £20 by uther ordinar chairges'.[103]

In West Lothian, the parson of Strathbrock (who held the

[95] NLS, Adv. 31.3.12, Books of Assumption, fo. 20v; Thirds of Benefices, 95, 151.

[96] EUL, MS. Dc.4.32, Books of Assumption, fos. 48, 49, 52; cf., Thirds of Benefices, 95.

[97] EUL, MS. Dc.4.32, Books of Assumption, fo. 78v.

[98] Ibid., fos. 82v–83r.

[99] NLS, Adv. 31.3.12, Books of Assumption, fo. 88r; SRO, E48/1/1, Books of Assumption, fo. 342r.

[100] NLS, Adv. 31.3.12, Books of Assumption, fo. 92v; SRO, E48/1/1, Books of Assumption, fo. 346v.

[101] NLS, Adv. 31.3.12, 30v; SRO, E48/1/1, Books for Assumption, fo. 294r. (The original text (NLS) reads 'minister'; the later copy (SRO) has 'maister'.)

[102] J. H. Burton, History, iii, 354n. 1, citing Statistical Account, x, 976.

[103] NLS, Adv. 31.3.12, Books of Assumption, fo. 130v; SRO, E48/1/1, Books of Assumption, fo. 384r.

commend of Dunfermline and was considered 'neutral' in religion in 1566) provided £40 in stipend 'to the minister' of his parish, from an income of £200 in rent from the Earl Marischal, as tacksman.[104] The minister in question was presumably Michael Smith, whom the assembly regarded in 1562 as the 'pretended minister of Strabroke'.[105] In East Lothian, the parson of Morham, a parish four miles from Haddington, paid 'the redar and minister of the sacramentis' a mere £16 from his income of £50.[106] Yet, when a third was deducted by the crown, the parson himself ended up with just as little as the minister whom he sustained; and presumably the working minister ended up better off than the idle parson, if the parishioners played their part in augmenting so small a stipend.

At Ashkirk, on the border of Roxburgh and Selkirkshire, the parson was absent in France, but his factor (who was also chamberlain to archbishop Beaton, who, too, had gone to France) arranged for 20 merks to be deducted from the rent paid by two lairds as tacksmen of the benefice, to sustain 'the minister yeirlie';[107] nearby, in Peebles-shire, the same factor, acting for the parson of Lyne, deducted £10 from the annual rental of £60 for 'the reader thairof';[108] and in Hawick, the parson, John Sandilands, paid for 'ane minister' from the proceeds of a lease of the property to Dame Janet Betoun, yielding £163 6s 8d.[109] Nor is it surprising that reformed preaching was penetrating the Borders: after all, it had been remarked in 1559, that 'Christ Jesus is begunne to be preached upon the south borders' in Jedburgh and Kelso. It is unclear, however, whether the commendator of Jedburgh intended payment to four vicars pensionary (at Jedburgh, Crailing, Nisbet and Plenderleith), who each received £13 6s 8d, as a reward for entering reformed service, or simply as a retirement pension; no similar fees were recorded for the remaining churches appropriated to the abbacy.[110]

If the position of parsons in maintaining active ministers in 1561 by donating them stipends as well as contributing to the crown's compulsory levy of the 'thirds' (from the crop of 1561) has not hitherto attracted the attention it deserves, the rôle of

---

[104] *CSP Scot.*, iii, no. 601 (misdated); SRO, E48/1/1, Books of Assumption, fo. 159v; E48/1/2, fo. 114v.
[105] *BUK*, i, 15.
[106] SRO, E48/1/1, Books of Assumption, fo. 174v.
[107] SRO, E48/1/2, Books of Assumption, fo. 148v.
[108] SRO, E48/1/1, Books of Assumption, fo. 252v; E48/1/2, fo. 184v.
[109] SRO, E48/1/1, Books of Assumption, fo. 259v; E48/1/2, 187v.
[110] Knox, *Works*, vi, 78; E48/1/1, Books of Assumption, fo. 217v; SRO, E48/1/2, fo. 152v.

vicars in lending ministers a helping hand was no less valuable and should not be underestimated. With usually more limited funds at their disposal than parsons had, vicars often helped to pay ministers' salaries at the Reformation. The vicar of Stirling agreed to pay the reader in the town £16, out of £36 in revenue from which he had to deduct £12 as his 'third', leaving him just £8 in pocket;[111] in Peebles, no doubt at the council's behest, the vicar deducted 20 merks 'to the minister' from an income of £60 in rent from leasing the vicarage to the tenants and inhabitants of Peebles.[112] At Stow, in Wedale on the Midlothian border seven miles north of Galashiels, the vicar pensionary, as well as paying his 'third', valued at £7 6s 8d, also 'delyverit to the reader' there 20 merks in salary, which left just 6s 8d for himself, a remarkable gesture of self-denial.[113] No less arresting is the early appearance of a reader at Stow, for hitherto the first reader at Stow to be traced was placed on record over a decade later in 1574.[114] In the south west, the vicar of Straiton, whose property was leased to the Earl of Cassillis for £46, set aside 20 merks for 'the minister', who evidently had been installed in the parish by 1561;[115] and at Morton in Nithsdale, where the vicarage was 'vacand in the bishopes handis' (before the appearance of a vicar in 1561–2), 'the redar of Mortoun', who was clearly active in 1561 was assigned £10 in stipend.[116] As part of the patrimony of Lesmahagow, the benefice itself had been gifted by the crown in October 1561 to the Earl of Glencairn's son, who was, it may be presumed, sympathetic to reformed service in the parish; and the man who appears as exhorter at Morton by 1563 was the same prebendary of Lincluden who had entered the reformed ministry, in one capacity or another, by 1561 and who then gained possession of the vicarage of Morton.[117]

Some vicars, of course, were willing, and were found able, to work in the new kirk; they therefore put their modest income from their benefices to the service of the kirk: John Stanis at Birnie in Moray,[118] Thomas Christison, vicar pensionary and

---

[111] EUL, MS. Dc.4.32, Books of Assumption, fo. 43v.

[112] See above, 111–14. SRO, E48/1/1, Books of Assumption, fo. 252v; E48/1/2, fo. 184v.

[113] SRO, E48/1/1, Books of Assumption, fo. 133r; E48/1/2, fo. 89r.

[114] Wodrow Miscellany, i, 369; Fasti, i, 163; C. Haws, Scottish Parish Clergy at the Reformation, 1540–1574 (Edinburgh, 1972), 226.

[115] EUL, MS. Dc.4.32, Books of Assumption, fo. 56r.

[116] Thirds of Benefices, 93; SRO, E48/1/1, Books of Assumption, 267v.

[117] See below, 141, 375; Thirds of Benefices, 93; cf. RSS, vii, no. 1967.

[118] SRO, E48/1/1, Books of Assumption, fo. 413v.

minister at Gamrie in Banffshire,[119] David Arrat, vicar of Guthrie and reader,[120] James Bishop, vicar pensionary of Ratho near Edinburgh, who had conformed by 1561 and is variously described as minister and reader there.[121] Besides, judging from the funds assigned to 'vicariis et ministris' of the churches at Ethie, Barry and Lunan in Angus, 'et aliarum ecclesiarum', it looks rather as if some, at least, of the vicars or vicars pensionary at these churches had conformed as ministers by 1561.[122]

Many benefices, however, had been leased to laymen, often those very lairds who had been so enthusiastic advocates of the cause of reform, and who were able to play their full part in securing reformed service in the parishes. The surviving contract between the vicar of Inverkip and the bishop of the Isles in 1560 is merely one indication of what could be done. A much more detailed illustration of this kind of arrangement by which a beneficed man might lease his property for a competent rent to a layman who assumed responsibility for furnishing a minister's stipend occurs in the case of Monymusk. There the parson, John Hay had evidently assumed proprietorial rights over the priory, too, with the death of the prior on 26 March 1558 and 'the place and religion therof distroyit', though he had still to await a formal gift of the priory from the crown, forthcoming in 1562.[123] In a contract to lease his property (from internal evidence to be dated before 'thairbe ane generall reformatioun maid be the estaittis of this realme and ressavit universalie throw the samyn'), Hay granted to Duncan Forbes of Monymusk a lease for three years of the priory and parsonage (a prebend of Aberdeen cathedral) to take effect at Candlemas 1560 (2 February 1560/1) for an annual rent of £400. A novel feature of the contract is the exceptional attention which Hay (himself a cousin of Cardinal Beaton) devoted to acquiring reformed ministers for the kirks appropriated to the priory. If his earlier employment as ambassador to Denmark and France, then as vicar of Brechin and postulate of the Isles had entitled some antipathy towards England, his later career found him counted among the 'godly' by the English ambassador in 1565, considered a man 'most

[119] NLS, Adv. 31.3.12, Books of Assumption, fo. 135v; SRO, E48/1/1, Books of Assumption, fo. 387v.

[120] NLS, Adv. 31.3.12, Books of Assumption, fo. 97r; SRO, E48/1/1, Books of Assumption, fo. 355r (where a separate and later rental for one of the prebends is added in Jan. 1573/4).

[121] SRO, E48/1/1, Books of Assumption, fo. 135r, 142r; SRO, E48/1/2, 90r, 97r.

[122] NLS, Adv. 31.3.12, Books of Assumption, fo. 79r, cf., 79v.

[123] RSS, v, no. 1009; Scottish Correspondence of Mary of Lorraine, ed. A. I. Cameron (Edinburgh, 1927), 413.

affected to Moray', and depicted (albeit belatedly) as a protestant in 1566; but for Mary who had promoted him 'fra ane puir simple clerk, to ane abot and pryor', Hay had become a 'dowbill flattering traytour'.[124] He had changed his political allegiance.

The recipient of Hay's lease, Forbes of Monymusk, also of protestant sympathies and at feud with Huntly, undertook to supply, at his own expense, a 'sufficient precheour as salbe fund qualifiit at the sych[t] and jugment of Adam Heriote, precheour in the new toun of Abirdene, or sic as salbe deputt in his place in caice of his absence'. As yet, no scheme for creating superintendents or commissioners to examine ministers had taken effect; but, in accord with the Book of Discipline (and, indeed, with commonsense), Hay and Forbes looked for guidance to the nearest main centre with a reformed kirk established, twenty miles away, at Aberdeen whose minister was expected to examine the qualifications of a prospective preacher for the charge and perhaps even to recommend a particular candidate. Once installed, the 'precheour', who was expected to make his residence at Monymusk, 'or at ane of the kirkis pertening to the said priorie', was obliged to 'preche upoun ilk festuall day at ane of the said fyve kirkis' appropriated to the priory. As tacksman, Forbes had also to furnish 'ane sufficient minister' of the sacraments to reside at each of the remaining four kirks.

Aware of the presence of several vicars pensionary who continued to draw their salaries from the annexed churches and whom Hay considered had a duty to undertake reformed service themselves or else find others who would, Forbes agreed to repay Hay the amount in stipend which he would save were any of the vicars pensionary (already financed from the benefices) accepted for service as ministers. The main concern, however, was that the ministers selected should be well-equipped for their task. In the event that any of the ministers should be 'fund unhabill and nocht of gud conversatioun to the contentment of the parrochenaris', Hay accorded his tacksman 'be this present contract full powar to outputt and imput utheris in thair places qualifiet and habill thairfoir, at the sycht of the said Adam Heriot or sic uther as salbe present precheour within the said burgh of Abirdene for the tyme'. Inept ministers were to be fired, and replacements hired, almost as if they were Forbes' tenants, though the propriety of consulting the minister in Aberdeen before taking action was duly recognised. In all, the contract exhibited a curious blend of financial accumen and a solicitude

[124] CSP Scot., ii, no. 198; 183; 202, 205; W. Fraser, Memorials of the Earls of Haddington, 3 vols. (Edinburgh, 1889), ii, 270.

for securing true ministers of the Word; at times, it even reveals an imprecise understanding of reformed practice in the prescription for preaching on festival days and in the distinction drawn between the 'precheour and ministeris', almost as if the function of the latter was considered subsidiary to the proclamation of the Word. No less remarkable is the precision with which the contract spelt out the requirements for reformed service in what, after all, was a lease for merely three years.[125]

Few contracts of this sort may have survived to illuminate the process through which laymen as tacksmen 'furnished' the parishes with protestant preachers, but so familiar was the practice that it must have been considered a commonplace. John Stewart, Lord Innermeath, who had sat in the Reformation parliament and, for long, had supported protestant reform, was certainly well-placed as tacksman of Auchterless, in north-west Aberdeenshire, to assign 'ane resonable fie to ane minister' of the parish at the Reformation;[126] and the vicar pensionary, whom he also paid, conformed as reader. The reader at Inchcailloch, employed by 1561, received his salary from 80 merks which a Dumbarton burgess, as tacksman of the parsonage and vicarage, paid annually to the benefice-holder and his 'under reader'. The non-resident possessor of the benefice, James Walker, parson of Inchcailloch and vicar of Stevenston, was also active in the new kirk in 1561 and so was eager, it may be presumed, to see his reader serve the parish, for he settled elsewhere as minister at Stevenston.[127] The parsonage and vicarage of Benvie, situated five miles from godly Dundee, had both been leased for £60, from which, as the parson explained, 20 merks were deducted 'to be payit to ane minister'; nearby in Newdosk, where the parsonage was leased to the Earl of Crawford, the parson, in submitting his rental for 1558–61, noted as the first charge 'the ministeris fie'; and as tacksman of the parsonage and vicarage of Peebles, an Edinburgh burgess, Allan Dickson (probably related to Peebles' minister John Dickson), recognised his duty in February 1560/1 'to mak payment and answer to the minister of the said paroche kirk of his yeirlie fee and stipend'.[128] Similarly, John Hay, who had been so meticulous in securing reformed

---

[125] NLS, Adv. 31.3.12, Books of Assumption, fos. 137v–138v; SRO, E48/1/1, Books of Assumption, fos. 389r–390r.

[126] NLS, Adv. 31.3.12, Books of Assumption, 127v; SRO, E48/1/1, Books of Assumption, fo. 381r; *Thirds of Benefices*, 222.

[127] EUL, MS. Dc.4.32, Books of Assumption, fo. 36v; *Thirds of Benefices*, 92, 150, 261.

[128] SRO, E48/1/1, Books of Assumption, fo. 312r; SRO, E48/1/1, fo. 346v; SRO, CS7/20, Acts and Decreets of the Court of Session, fos. 319r–320v.

service at Monymusk in 1561, was also ready, as parson of
Melville in Midlothian, to contribute £10 'to a curat or a minister'
from £50 in rent paid by the laird of Lugton and John Young in
Lasswade, as tacksmen of the benefice.[129]

In Ayrshire, Cunningham of Caprington, who leased the
parsonage of Tarbolton, paid the curate's fee of £20, and it is
more than a guess that the curate had conformed, for Cunningham's earlier career had shown him an energetic supporter of
protestant reform, a participent in the party of revolution in 1559
and a signatory to the Ayrshire bond in 1562 designed to 'assist
the preaching' and 'maintain the ministers of the same'.[130] At any
rate, elsewhere the curate of Luncarty in Gowrie seems to have
served as reader by 1561, for the parson declared in January
1561/2 that his benefice was 'worth na mair nor fourtie merkis be
yeir, satisfiand the curat and ridar'.[131] The provost of Lincluden
collegiate the kirk near Dumfries, who recorded his obligation to
sustain the curates and maintain five annexed churches, did not
disclose whether the curates' fees were for reformed service; his
kinsmen, however, joined the party of revolution in 1559; and
one of the prebendaries of the collegiate kirk, who conformed to
serve at Morton in Nithsdale, paid 22 merks, from his income of
£20, 'to ane redar and sangster'.[132]

What all this amounts to, quite simply, is that many more
ministers were employed by 1561 than has previously been
appreciated. Besides 44 or so ministers known from casual or
incidental references to have been appointed by 1560 and 40
beneficed men who conformed by 1561, there is to be added at
least another 121 ministers and readers mentioned in rentals
required for submission in February 1561/2 and who presumably
were active in 1561. Not only so, the general assembly in
December 1560 approved a further 40 ministers and readers.[133]
To have recruited a ministry whose number, in all probability,
exceeded 240 men by 1561, or thereabouts, is little less than an
outstanding achievement. Certainly, to have filled about a
quarter of the country's parishes within a year or so of the
Reformation parliament was a remarkable accomplishment
which demonstrates the strength of attachment within the nation
to the cause of reform. Yet it is a feat which curiously has gone

[129] SRO, E48/1/1, Books of Assumption, fo. 131r; SRO, E48/1/2, fo. 87r.
[130] EUL, MS. Dc.31.3.12, Books of Assumption, fo. 64v; Knox, *History*, ii,
55–6.
[131] NLS, Adv. 31.3.12, Books of Assumption, fo. 42r; SRO, E48/1/1, fo. 303v.
[132] EUL, MS. Dc.4.32, Books of Assumption, fo. 98v; SRO, E48/1/1, Books of
Assumption, fo. 267v; see above, 126.
[133] See above, 118–19; and below, 131ff.

unrecognised by writers whose vision has been restricted by the deficiences which accompanied the religious upheaval, and who as a consequence are content to remark that 'less than a quarter of the parishes had a minister even by 1574', a claim which obscures as much as it illuminates.[134]

In part, the technical nature of certain records is apt to mislead. One particular pitfall for the unwary is presented by the most valuable single source for tracing the personnel of the ministry after 1560, the accounts submitted to the crown's new financial office, the collectory, by the various collectors of the thirds of benefices. For a start, it is not always appreciated that although the record begins in 1561, the apparent dearth of ministers entered in the early years arises largely because details of reformed staff and stipends were entered not in the accounts of the collector general (apart, that is, from conforming beneficed men and a few ministers recorded in 1561 and 1562) but in the more informative accounts rendered by the regional sub-collectors, where besides the thirds collected (or remitted or allowed) are to be found the sums allocated individually in stipend. Yet, even here cursory study can create false impressions. The late appearance of ministers for much of Ayrshire in the record arises not from any tardiness in recruiting ministers in an area, which after all, had conspicuously demonstrated its support for reform, but simply from the incomplete record which effectively starts only in 1568. It is, for example, open to speculation when John Cunningham, a minister for 'divers yeris', began his duties at Dailly and Girvan in Carrick: his name is duly entered in the register of stipends which begins in 1567 and he remained there in 1574 (notwithstanding the appearance, at least on record, of another minister in 1568).[135] In fact, it emerges that he was already minister before 1567, for in that year he gained (as he later explained in 1573) an augmentation in stipend from the collector of thirds, on the instruction of the visitor for Ayrshire.[136] Even in parishes financed by the unsympathetic abbacy of Crossraguel, where Cassillis was tacksman, ministers were evidently recruited despite the small stipends they initially received.

If the ministry in Ayrshire is poorly recorded in the surviving

---

[134] M. Lynch, 'Calvinism in Scotland, 1559–1638', in *International Calvinism, 1541–1715*, ed. M. Prestwich (London, 1985), 248.

[135] *Register of Ministers, Exhorters and Readers, and of their Stipends after the period of the Reformation*, ed. A. Macdonald (Edinburgh, 1830), 40; *Wodrow Miscellany*, i, 387; *RSS*, vi, no. 366.

[136] SRO, CS7/45, Register of Acts and Decreets of the Court of Session, fos. 453r–454r.

accounts, Aberdeen, Angus, a portion of Fife, the far south-east, along with Stirling, Dunbarton, Renfrew and Lanark are better served with accounts beginning in 1563, but the record for Moray survives only from 1566, Orkney is later in 1567, Lothian and Perth each becomes available in 1568 and Inverness in 1569.[137] A detailed picture of the ministers recruited in the early 1560s across the country is yet again frustrated.

A further drawback, for which due account has to be taken, stems from the fact that not all ministers known to have been at work were necessarily entered in the collectors' accounts. This arose partly through administrative inefficiency: it took time for the claims of ministers and readers to stipends derived from the thirds to be entered by superintendents or commissioners who, at the very earliest, had only begun their duties from 1561 onwards. Again, where ministers were sustained by freewill offerings or where beneficed men had previously undertaken to make a contribution to their stipends, there seems to have been no urgency in recording the stipends in the collectors' accounts. At any rate, one may search in vain in the defective collectors' accounts for mention of most of the reformed staff discussed above who were, it seems, initially financed by means other than the 'thirds' in over a hundred parishes just after the Reformation: indeed, the only exceptions among these examples where reformed service is recorded in the accounts are the meagre handful of entries for three parishes attached to Fail (1561), five belonging to Culross (1561), Murroes (1561), Stevenston and Alness (1562), Morton (1562), Benvie and Morham (1568), Lunan (1569), and Dunbog (1572).[138] This being so, the limitations of placing too great a reliance on the collectors' accounts, which are after all an imperfect record, in tracing how the kirk was staffed in and after 1561 become all the more apparent.

Besides, there is the obvious danger in assuming too readily that the first appearance of a minister or reader in the collectors' accounts for a particular year is indicative of the start of that individual's service in the ministry. How unwarranted this assumption can be is easily demonstrated in the case of several ministers who, after years of service, only belatedly made their appearance in the accounts. John White, curate at Tullicheddill in

---

[137] Two accounts, SRO, E46/3/6, the sub-collector's accounts for Fife, Fothrick and Kinross for the crop of 1565 (discovered in 1959) and E46/6/3, fragments of accounts for Linlithgow, c.1566, are not printed in *Thirds of Benefices*.

[138] *Thirds of Benefices*, 95; 93, 250, 274; 230, 242.

July 1560, is entered on the first occasion in the collectors' accounts as reader there in 1568, though the register of ministers' stipends (which starts in 1567) shows him installed at nearby Kinkell.[139] What neither source discloses is that White (or conceivably another reader who shared his name) was active at least as early as 1562 as reader and exhorter at Clackmannan, where the Earl of Mar was responsible for paying his stipend. His service there comes to light simply because the reader took the earl to court in Febraury 1566/7 for failing to provide 40 merks in salary for the four years 'or thairby' preceding April 1566.[140]

For Dunino in Fife, there is no early entry whatsoever in the 'thirds'; yet David Guild, recorded as minister in the register of stipends for 1567, was minister of the parish at least as early as 1563, when he sought payment from the parishioners in March 1563/4 for the teinds of the crop, in his capacity as 'persone, vicare and minister' of the parish. This was a particularly fortuitous entry, as in other instances his title of parson (which of course need not entail reformed service) was invariably used.[141] Nor is there any mention in the accounts of a stipend for a minister at Libberton (who nonetheless does occur in the register of stipends for 1567); and the first entry for a reader in the parish is as late as 1569; but, in truth, Libberton had a serving minister, William Livingston, himself a graduate, as early as 1562 with a stipend as 'precheour' of £50, provided by Lord Somerville as tacksman; and neighbouring Quothquan, again in 1562, had an exhorter, George Alexander (the reader for Libberton in 1569), who received from Lord Somerville an annual salary of 20 merks.[142] Thomas Scott, however, does belatedly appear in the 'thirds' as exhorter at Findogask, ten miles from Perth, in 1568; but another source discloses how much earlier, in July 1564, he was serving nearby as 'curat and exhortar in the paroche kirk of Trinitie Gask'.[143] Yet again, it ought not to be assumed that John Leslie, who occurs as reader at Carriden (near Bo'ness) in the register for 1567 and as minister there in the 'thirds' for 1568 was a new recruit: as other evidence shows only too plainly, he was already installed as 'reidar and exhortar in the paroche kirk of

[139] RMS, iv, no. 2046; Thirds of Benefices, 254; Register of Ministers, 28.

[140] SRO, CS7/38, Register of Acts and Decreets of the Court of Session, fo. 413r; SRO, NP2/1, Register of Admissions of Notaries, fo. 95r–v.

[141] SRO, CS7/29, Register of Acts and Decreets of the Court of Session, fo. 95r; cf. ibid., 359r–360v; SRO, CS7/28, fo. 299r; SRO, CS7/32, fos. 11v–12r.

[142] Thirds of Benefices, 264; SRO, CS7/41, Register of Acts and Decreets of the Court of Session, fos. 4r–5r.

[143] Thirds of Benefices, 254; SRO, CS7/32, Register of Acts and Decreets of the Court of Session, fo. 72v.

Carridin and actuallie duelland at the samyn' in February 1563/4 when he took his oath as notary public under the new regime.[144]

When charged by the superintendent of Fife and Strathearn to provide Thomas Drummond, as minister, with the principal manse and glebe of Findogask, as legislation in 1563 had prescribed, the archdeacon of Dunblane argued in court in March 1563/4 that Drummond 'reparis as minister in Dunblane, Methill [Muthill] and divers utheris kirkis and nevir as yit usit the office of minister at the said paroche kirk of Findogask'; but of Drummond's early labours there is no trace in the thirds of benefices nor in the register of ministers' stipends.[145] Again William Barbour occurs as exhorter at Lasswade in 1568, when the sub-collector's account for Lothian begins; and he is entered as exhorter in the register of stipends for 1567; but, in fact, was already serving as 'minister and exhortar' on 27 March 1565 when he, along with the superintendent of Lothian, took action in the court of session against the vicar for access to the 'gleib, mans, houss, yardis and kirklandis of Leswaid', so that he might 'remane at the said kirk to dewlie use his office of ministratioun and exhortatioun thairin'; and much earlier, of course, he had served as minister in 1559 to the Hammermen in Edinburgh. Similarly, the minister at Morham in East Lothian, listed in the register of ministers in 1567, was active in his parish, it emerges, in 1565 as 'persone, vicar and minister of Morhame', and reformed service there can of course be dated from 1561.[146] It has not previously been recognised that ministers were active in these parishes from so early a date; and such evidence would go some way to dispelling the prevalent notion that a considerable time-lapse ensued before ministers were widely recruited.

Indeed, the facile old assumptions that a pre-Reformation lethargy was followed by a dearth of reformed service in many a rural parish for years after the Reformation[147] requires essential revision in the light of this sort of fresh evidence. Stray references (of which there is no scarcity) to early ministers in a miscellany of judicial proceedings (of somewhat unmanageable proportions and altogether lacking indices), deeds and testaments well illustrate the distortions which too narrow a reliance on records of stipends produce when taken as a guide to the expansion of the

[144] *Register of Ministers*, 6; *Thirds of Benefices*, 277; SRO, NP2/1, Register of Admissions of Notaries, fo. 55r–v.

[145] SRO, CS7/29, Register of Acts and Decreets of the Court of Session, fos. 170r–171r; cf. *Thirds of Benefices*, 254.

[146] *Thirds of Benefices*, 276; *Register of Ministers*, 8; SRO, CS7/34, Acts and Decreets of the Court of Session, fo. 36r–v; see below, 283; SRO, CS7/36, fo. 46v.

[147] Lynch, 'Calvinism', 245–6.

ministry. The work of reformation in the parishes had yielded a remarkable harvest of ministers within a very short space of time.

Even with their very evident limitations, the accounts of the collectors of thirds support the underlying trend of a rapid recruitment of ministers in and after 1561. As a source, they are capable of exploitation, not only from the incomplete lists of ministers entered at varying dates, but also from the finance disbursed in stipend for different areas of the country. This aggregate expenditure on stipends, which has survived in the collector general's accounts, for years when the sub-collectors' returns are often missing, testifies to an early, steady expansion of the ministry in many areas in the immediate aftermath of the Reformation.

In the northern isles, the sums paid in stipends rose from £220 in 1561 to £380 in 1562; Inverness (which seems to have included the rest of the northern mainland) gained £379 in 1561 and £646 in 1562; stipends in Moray amounting to £214 in 1561 rose sixfold to £1,241 in the following year, which testifies, by any standard, to a remarkable expansion in the ministry in a very short space of time. Aberdeen and Banff more than doubled their quota in stipend from £1,092 in 1561 to £2,551 in 1562; and from the sub-collectors accounts, which begin earlier there than most of the areas, a reformed staff, at the very least, of 11 ministers, 8 exhorters and 66 readers was already installed by 1563. In all, the figure of £2,514 paid in stipend in 1563 for Aberdeen and Banff represents a slight fall from the total for 1562; and, on the basis of these sums it looks rather as if a ministry of 85 or so was at work in the area during 1562 and perhaps three dozen in 1561. Angus and the Mearns, an area reputed for its godliness gained £3,144 in stipends for 1561 and a further £792 in 1562, which again is indicative of the early provision of staff. The kirks of Fife and Kinross were also suitably supplied with staff from an early date: £2,912 were disbursed in stipends in 1561, and the slightly lower sum of £2,698 was paid in 1562. The three divisions of Ayrshire received £1,289 in 1561 and a little more, £1,493, in 1562, which suggests a rapid recruitment in staffing. The vast area stretching from Stirling, Lanark, Renfrew and Dunbarton to Wigtown, Dumfries, Kirkcudbright and Annandale (but excluding Ayrshire) had a ministry which was paid £2,699 in 1561 and £3,174, in 1562. The sub-collector's accounts for Dumfries, Annandale, Kirkcudbright and Wigtown, which survive for 1563, record expenditure of £1,565 in stipends for a reformed staff of 39; and when this sum is added to the corresponding figure of £1,830 for Stirling, Dunbarton, Renfrew and Lanark in 1563, it emerges that the total sum spent on stipends for the entire area was merely £221 more than the figure for 1562. Much of the recruitment, is is clear, was undertaken without delay. Expenditure on stipends in Lothian, however, rose from £2,401 in 1561 to £3,183 in 1562; and Roxburgh, Berwick, Selkirk and Peebles managed to double the sums allocated in stipend from £428 to £848.[148]

This financial record is added testimony to the success of early efforts to recruit a reformed ministry, and it is all the more remarkable that so much was achieved so quickly, for there was then little central, and virtually no regional, co-ordination. The general assembly, at the centre, could at best give encouragement, but there were few signs, as yet, of any overall strategy: of the five superintendents whose task it became to admit men to the ministry, only two had been admitted to office by the spring of 1561, a third accepted office in September 1561, and the remaining holders of the office are to be found at work only in or after 1562. Again, the assembly's device of appointing commissioners for other areas to supervise admissions can hardly have taken effect before 1562. The earliest response to reformed preaching came not from administrators whose task it subsequently became to 'plant ministers' but from local communities which assumed the responsibility of finding qualified preachers. The basic work of recruiting so many ministers (before an organisation of officials took over) had been very largely the product of private enterprise by numerous nobles, lairds, town councils and even the occasional conforming bishop who demonstrated their attachment to the reforming cause by seeking the services of a reformed ministry.

Among the nobles, the Earls of Glencairn, Argyll, Morton and Arran, Lord James Stewart (the queen's half brother and later Earl of Moray) and Lords Ochiltree and Boyd were early enthusiasts for protestants reform and most were leading members of the Congregation by 1559;[149] Châtelherault, Huntly, Rothes, Menteith, Ogilvie of Airlie, Ruthven and Somerville lent their support by April 1560.[150] Then in the Reformation parliament, the Earl Marischall, who confirmed his earlier 'suspitioun of the Papisticall religioun', declared for protestantism; Lord Erskine, who followed his example, acknowledged, with others, that 'this was the faith wherein they ought to live and die'; and the elderly Lord Lindsay of the Byres rejoiced that he had lived to 'see thys daye wher so maynie nobles and other have allowed

---

[148] *Thirds of Benefices*, 94, 152, 219, 221–4, 286; 256.
[149] Knox, *Works*, i, 344–5.
[150] Knox, *Works*, ii, 63–4; *CSP Scot.*, i, no. 751.

so worthie a work'.[151] Apart from a significant body of opinion unresolved in religion, of which it was remarked in 1560 that some nobles, as yet uncommitted, had attended 'daylie to the prechynges',[152] there were, at best, merely half a dozen nobles who remained Catholic in 1560, and even the 'Catholicism' of the Earl of Erroll found curious expression when he supported the preachers and helped to expel the friars from Perth in May 1559.[153] Dispersed, disorganised and possibly demoralised, these conservatives were no match for the Lords of the Congregation, among whose ranks were to be found almost three times as many peers. These protestant lords had clearly the capacity to mould opinion in their territories through the extensive influence they wielded as patrons, tacksmen of benefices and feuars of ecclesiastical properties, and through the lordship they exercised over lesser men.

It was customary for nobles to act as bailies of the abbacies, whose commendators were frequently well-disposed to protestantism and ready to finance reformed service in their appropriated parishes. The canons of St Andrews priory, where Lord James Stewart was commendator, were prominent in entering service in the new kirk. The ministers and readers who served the 27 parishes attached to the priory are found at work between 1562 and 1567; many (perhaps 20) were the priory's own canons, who in all likelihood had conformed at the Reformation. At any rate, they give the appearance of espousing the Reformation with enthusiasm; all 33 parishes appropriated to the priory had reformed staff operating, at the very latest, by 1567. Another Stewart, Lord Robert (also an illegitimate son of James V), was installed at Holyrood; he, too, joined the Congregation by 1559, and openly repudiated his old faith in favour of the new in the Reformation parliament.[154] All but three of Holyrood's 27 parish churches are on record as possessing reformed staff in the 1560s. Insular Inchcolm, on the Firth of Forth, was controlled by a third Stewart, the son of the laird of Beath, who had joined the Congregation by 1559 and proclaimed his protestantism in the Reformation parliament.[155] His half-dozen or so churches were quickly filled with protestant incumbents. Such, indeed, was the commendator of Holyrood's readiness to employ his canons in the service of the kirk that he commended to the assembly in 1566 'diverse godlie and learned

[151] Knox, *Works*, ii, 122; *CSP Scot.*, i, no. 886.
[152] *CSP Scot.*, i, no. 881.
[153] Ibid., i, no. 455.
[154] *RPC*, xiv, 167–8; Knox, *Works*, ii, 88; *CSP Scot.*, i, no. 885.
[155] *RPC*, xiv, 168; Knox, *Works*, ii, 88.

men of his awin place of Halyrudehous, sick as Alexander
Forrester and Peter Blackburn, who are men of good conversation and literature'; and, as they were already admitted to the
ministry, they ought, he argued, to serve his appropriated kirks.
The assembly, however, after consulting the elders, rejected his
plea that the existing ministers at Tranent and St Cuthbert's
should be redeployed elsewhere but invited Stewart to provide
'godlie ministers' for 'preaching of the true word of God' at any
of the abbey's charges then vacant.[156]

At Culross, where Argyll was bailie, William Colville adhered
to the party of reform by May 1560, publicly renounced his
Catholicism and professed his protestantism in the Reformation
parliament, and lent his support to the Book of Discipline.[157]
From 1559 onwards, his protestant sympathies were evident in
his attitude towards his monks: five monks who conformed to
protestantism continued to enjoy their portions as pensions but
the four who refused to recant received no further sustenance
from the commendator until they took him to court in May 1563
for arrears in payments due since 1559, and obtained a partial
settlement of £20 each, until further order should be taken by the
privy council. Pressure and inducements of this sort were
certainly applied; and the commendator showed resolution in
supporting protestant preachers.[158]

The abbacy of Tongland, annexed to the bishopric of
Galloway, was held by the conforming bishop, Alexander
Gordon, whose strenuous efforts helped secure, with a minimum
of delay, a reformed ministry in his diocese;[159] and he had also
Inchaffray abbey in Perthshire, whose appropriated churches
(apart from two in Argyll where information is lacking) had
reformed service by the early or mid 1560s. Another protestant,
John Campbell, who held the abbacy of Iona on the eve of the
Reformation as well as the commend of Ardchattan, may
conceivably be the same clerk of Lismore diocese who asserted a
claim to Coupar Angus as well.[160] The existing abbot of Coupar
Angus, Donald Campbell who was evidently his kinsman, was
observed to have 'put on secular weed' in May 1559 and he
agreed to reform his abbey and support the Lords of the
Congregation in parliament. Although the abbot's death by 1562

[156] BUK, i, 78. Forrester was minister at Liberton by 1562, and Blackburn
minister at Aberdour in 1567.
[157] Knox, Works, ii, 53, 88; First Book of Discipline, 211.
[158] SRO, CS7/26, Register of Acts and Decreets of the Court of Session, fos.
382v–383v; see above, 123.
[159] G. Donaldson, Reformed by Bishops (Edinburgh, 1987), 1–16.
[160] Vatican Archives, Register of Resignations, vol. 186, fo. 131v.

may have been reckoned something of a loss to protestants, the abbacy fell to the crown which delayed appointing a successor till 1565 and so had a particular responsibility for ensuring that stipends were available for reformed staff, whose names occur on record between 1563 and 1567, at the annexed churches, including one monk of the abbey who became minister at Bendochy.[161]

Two Hamiltons, both sons of Châtelherault, controlled Arbroath and Paisley. Arbroath was prominent in reforming circles as a member of the Congregation in 1559 and of the Reformation parliament in 1560,[162] and his many churches, with few exceptions,[163] were quickly staffed with reformed personnel in the early 1560s. Paisley, if less ostentatiously than his brother, also sided with protestantism,[164] and had therefore no doctrinaire distaste for seeing the 28 appropriated kirks filled with staff: most are to be found equipped with service in the sporadic records between 1563 and 1567; only in 7 parishes (including Paisley itself and two in Argyll) have staff not been traced for the 1560s.

A third Hamilton, at best a kinsman and presumably a client of Châtelherault, was installed at Kilwinning. If, as was reported in 1548, he had been 'clene converted' to Arran's reforming policies, succeeding years had worked a change in outlook: in 1559 Knox considered him one of the 'cheaf ennemeis to Christ Jesus'; yet he sat in the Reformation parliament, conformed and, even by Knox's demanding standards, was 'joyned to the Churche'.[165] The commendator after 1560, it seems, proved no enemy to the Gospel; ministers, exhorters and readers were planted in a dozen of his churches in the 1560s; many were active in the early 1560s; one monk of the abbey became minister of Kilwinning just after the Reformation;[166] only in two kirks, Beith and Pierstoun, has service not been identified before the early 1570s; and there is, of course, no evidence for Cill Mo Charmaig in Knapdale, Argyll.

In Fife, the abbot of Lindores, who rather curiously assisted, so it was said, the murderers of Cardinal Beaton in 1546, reformed himself and his house in 1559, and publicly repudiated

[161] *CSP Scot.*, i, no. 455; 'Two papers from the Argyll Charter Chest', *Scottish Historical Review*, xxi (1923/4), 142–3.
[162] *RPC*, xiv, 167–8; *APS*, ii, 525.
[163] Exceptionally, service at Ethie in Angus and Forgue in Aberdeenshire has not been traced before 1574.
[164] *CSP Scot.*, iii, no. 601 (misdated).
[165] Ibid., i. no. 336; *APS*, ii, 525; Knox, *Works*, i, 325, 400; ii, 320.
[166] M. H. B. Sanderson, 'Kilwinning at the time of the Reformation', *Ayrshire Collections*, x (1970–2), 102–3, at 118.

his old faith in favour of protestantism at the Reformation parliament.[167] He made provision for protestant service, and, indeed, remained a protestant, as was noted in 1566.[168] His action in resigning the abbacy in the hands of the pope[169] (while retaining a fat pension) was no more an indication of a drift towards incipient Catholicism on the abbot's part than was Alexander Gordon's decision, as reformed bishop of Galloway, to return Iona to the papacy a sign of the bishop's zealous attachment to the old faith.[170] (Similarly, Gordon's later claim that he was reduced to parting with ecclesiastical property to clear debts incurred in seeking bulls for his bishopric[171] was not a sign of the bishop's imminent return to Rome, as some have imagined,[172] but simply an excuse for dilapidating his patrimony even further, as clerics under the old regime had done so effectively, ostensibly on the ground of resisting heresies for the church's wellbeing or on some such pretext.[173]) In so favourable a climate, it is not surprising that thirteen of Lindores' churches had protestant service by 1563; Kinnethmont in Aberdeenshire was certainly staffed by 1567; only in Exmagirdle is there no mention of staff till 1574.

Dunfermline abbey (whose abbot, George Durie, had left for France by 1561 and where Robert Pitcairn remained as commendator) had responsibility for 17 annexed churches, which were mainly filled by protestant staff in the early 1560s; only Moulin, in northern Perthshire lacks record of reformed personnel before 1574; but it is doubtful if any of the credit for planting the new ministry belongs to Pitcairn, who had evidently not declared for protestantism in 1560, was compelled in 1563 to contribute towards the upkeep of the parish kirk of Dunfermline, and was thought to be neutral in religion in 1566, though the general assembly of 1567, which invited him to attend its meeting, evidently considered him no enemy of the Reformation.[174]

---

[167] *Treasurer's Accounts*, ix, 45; Knox, *History*, i, 213, 335.
[168] *RMS*, v, no. 595; *CSP Scot.*, iii, no. 601 (misdated).
[169] Vatican Archives, Register of Resignations, vol. 238, fo. 266.
[170] See below, 216.
[171] *RMS*, iv, nos. 1719, 1743.
[172] M. Lynch, Introduction, 'Mary Stewart, Queen in three Kingdoms', *Innes Review*, xxxviii (1987), 21.
[173] *Registrum Episcopatus Glasguensis*, ed. C. Innes (Edinburgh, 1843), ii. no. 526; *Glasgow City Charters*, i, pt. ii, 125–6; W. Fraser, *The Red Book of Menteith*, 2 vols. (Edinburgh, 1880), ii, 362; *RMS*, iv, no. 1615 (where even George Hay could reiterate the stereotyped phraseology).
[174] Keith, *History*, iii, 9; *RPC*, i, 246–7; *CSP Scot.*, iii, no. 601 (misdated); *BUK*, i, 96.

Mark Ker, who held Newbattle, identified himself, like his father the laird of Cessford, with the party of revolution in 1560; he subscribed the Congregation's band, repudiated his old faith and openly proclaimed his attachment to the new.[175] At least four of his five kirks (with the curious exception of Newbattle itself for which there is no evidence before 1574) were filled with ministers by 1567. Another Ker, by 1559, had gained control of Kelso abbey[176] (in whose town protestant preaching had begun in 1559). Eleven of the abbey's kirks had gained protestant incumbents by 1567; five more, in 1574, were vacant in the unsettled border territory of Teviotdale, Eskdale and the Merse. The dependent cell of Lesmahagow, where Glencairn's son had an interest, was financed by a dozen kirks which (with the possible exception of Carluke) had all gained reformed staff by the early or mid 1560s.

Like the commendators of Culross and Arbroath, John Hay, on acquiring Monymusk, demonstrated what could be done to assist reformed preaching; and he proceeded, in 1561, to gain Balmerino, too, whose three annexed kirks were speedily filled with ministers and readers. Kinloss was administered by the protestant Walter Reid; and Deer was in the possession of Robert Keith, a son of the staunchly protestant Earl Marischal, whose four kirks were staffed by 1563 (when the sub-collector's record begins) and no doubt earlier, for the assembly had noted the minister of Deer's appointment in 1562.[177]

In the far south west, Holywood, near Dumfries, was administered by an illegitimate son of Campbell of Loudoun, an influential laird and early advocate of the reforming cause, and was leased, with its kirks, to the protestant Maxwell of Terregles who joined the party of revolution.[178] The existing staff at the five annexed kirks readily conformed at the Reformation to serve the new regime with a minimum of dislocation. The enterprising Maxwell had also a lease of Dundrennan, whose commendator took the trouble to attend the Reformation parliament, and on the commendator's death in 1562, the abbacy was granted by the crown to Maxwell's son, all of which facilitated the appointment of protestant staff to Dundrennan's few churches.[179] The abbot

[175] CSP Scot., i, no. 751; Knox, History, i, 316, 335.
[176] RSS, v. no. 1428.
[177] See above, 123, 127–9; RSS, v, no. 845; BUK, i, 29.
[178] RSS, iii, no. 2653; W. Fraser, The Herries Muniments, 1289–1667 (Edinburgh 1865), 102.
[179] Acts of Lords of Council, 1501–1544, 607–8; CSP Scot., i, no. 533; APS, ii, 525; RSS, v. no. 1101.

of Sweetheart, John Brown, had a long record of attachment to the English cause, which aimed at promoting religious reform in Scotland: he had to be pardoned in 1548 for his treacherous negotiations with the English and for fighting against the Scottish regime, and was again to be found among supporters of the English king in 1553; but he was still prepared in 1562 to extend hospitality to an English papist whom Knox had met in Dumfries.[180] The abbot's conduct, at any rate, presented no obstacle to filling four of his five churches with reformed staff by 1563, and the fifth by 1567.

Crossraguel, in Ayrshire, whose able abbot, Quintin Kennedy (son of the 2nd Earl of Cassillis), engaged the reformers in lively debate (and befriended the English papist who arrived at Dundrennan), remained one of the few monastic centres where Catholicism lingered on: the general assembly denounced the abbot as a massmonger and bad payer of his thirds; but by 1564 the abbot had died after leasing the whole property to his uncle, the 4th Earl of Cassillis, who was prepared in 1561 to attend preaching on Sunday and mass on Monday; only marriage, it seems, in 1566 rendered Cassillis, at the least, a nominal protestant who then undertook 'to reform his churches in Carrick, and promised to maintain the doctrine of the Evangel'.[181] This claim accords with the evidence, for just one of Crossraguel's five kirks can be shown to have had protestant service before the earl's 'reforms' were effected; three more were staffed by 1567; only Kirkcudbright-Invertig has no known record of service in the 1560s. Cassillis, however, had also an interest in Glenluce, near Stranraer, where he successfully established his rights as heritable bailie and then tacksman of the abbacy. His rival for possession of the property, Gordon of Lochinvar, whose record was that of an energetic reformer, had ordered his servants at the Reformation forcibly to occupy the abbey and to expel the monks; one monk forged a feu charter in the laird's favour; but, in the end, the earl had his way, and by November 1561 Gordon of Lochinvar resigned possession of the abbacy to the earl (as bailie) and abbot (who was later reckoned a protestant) and removed his servants from the property.[182]

[180] *RSS*, iii, no. 2698; *CSP Scot.*, i, nos. 396, 1152.
[181] *BUK*, i, 4; *Crossraguel Charters* 2 vols. (Edinburgh, 1886), i, no. 77, pp. 137–8; *CSP Scot.*, i, no. 1010; Knox, *History*, ii, 189. [The assertion that the earl was 'firmly protestant' (Lynch, 'Mary Stewart', *IR*, xxxviii (1987), 21) in 1564 is hard to reconcile with his conduct and reputation at that point, and the claim, it seems, lacks substance.]
[182] SRO, GD25/1/587, 601, Ailsa Muniments; GD25/2/118, 120; *First Book of Discipline*, 212; *CSP Scot.*, iii, no. 601.

What such jostling meant for reformed service it might be hard to say, were it not that the abbey possessed merely the church of Glenluce itself, whose vicar opted for the Reformation with apparent enthusiasm. At nearby Soulseat, however, the abbot's resistance to change proved no effective impediment to reform: the vicar at the kirk of Soulseat conformed to the Reformation and was already serving as reader in 1563; and the vicar of Kirkmaiden in Rhinns at the Reformation is later to be found at work as reader of the same parish in 1574, but it would be unsafe to date his conversion only at that point, in the incomplete records, where he first appears as reader.[183] Similarly, at Inchmahome on the Lake of Menteith, long dominated by the Erskines, the commendator, David Erskine (who also held Dryburgh), conferred in 1562 the coveted office of bailie (already heritable in the family) on the reforming Lord Erskine, who had joined the Congregation and declared for protestantism in the Reformation parliament. The commendator was evidently a firm protestant by 1567, for he later claimed to have 'trewlie servit in the common cause of defence of the religioun'; one of the four appropriated churches, Lintrathen, had reformed service in 1560, two, Kilmadock and Port, had readers on record by 1569, and Leny by 1573.[184]

For the most part, the record of the leading commendators (whose houses held the majority of parishes in commendam) was one of attachment to the reformed cause, which assisted the transition, often without perceptible dislocation, from old priest or monk to new minister, exhorter and reader. Their attitudes helped create or reinforce a climate of opinion in favour of reformed preaching. In many parishes, however, where neither noble, commandator nor patron was resident, the work of lairds in promoting protestant preaching is well-attested. Over 160 lords and lairds from Aberdeenshire, Angus, the Mearns, Fife, Perth and Kinross, the Lothians, the Borders, Ayrshire, Renfrew, Lanark and Galloway took part in the revolution against France and Rome during 1559–60. Many had a long record of loyal support for the reforming cause and of active collaboration with

---

[183] Donaldson, *Reformed by Bishops*, 8–9; Knox, *History*, i, 347.
[184] Fraser, *Red Book of Menteith*, ii, 353–6; *CSP Scot.*, i, no, 886; *RPC*, ii, 347; see above, 99; *Register of Ministers*, 30. (The vicar of Kilmadock, James Kennedy, as chancellor of Dunblane, whose behaviour can hardly be considered orthodox, defied his bishop by appropriating for his own use the chapter's common seal during 'the trublus tyme and invasioun laitlie fallin in the kirk within this realme', which prompted the bishop to secure legal redress in 1564: SRO, CS7/29, Acts and Decreets of the Court of Session, fo. 62r.).

English policies against the regime at home. They flocked in unprecedented numbers to the Reformation parliament not to indulge in tactical voting (a ploy which only the most cynical of historians could invent) but to determine great issues and declare their support for a cause which many had long espoused. These lairds continued to make their presence felt in other ways, by supporting the godly cause as elders in the parishes and as commissioners to the general assembly. In doing so, they established a remarkable tradition of family service in the kirk. Other lairds, who achieved less prominence in pursuing the quest for reformation, could also radiate assurance in their religious convictions: in his testament, Hamilton of Milburn, who died at Fairholm (near Larkhall) in 1564, 'left his saule to the protectioun of the almichtie God to be savit on the merceis of Crist'.[185] The emphasis on salvation only by the merits of Christ and not, by implication, on the works of men, saints or masses, became a characteristic feature of protestant testaments.

Among protestant activists were Wishart of Pittarrow, Whitelaw of New Grange, Graham of Morphie, Ogilvie of Airlie and Erskine of Dun in the north-east; Campbell of Glenorchy, Stewart of Innermeath, Murray of Tullibardine and Murray of Balvaird in Perthshire; Balnaves of Halhill, Learmonth of Dairsie and Balcomie in Fife; Sandilands of Calder, Drummond of Riccarton, McGill of Rankeillor Nether, Cockburn of Ormiston, Douglas of Whittinghame, Broun of Colstoun, Home of Spott, Johnston of Elphinstone and Lauder of Haltoun in Lothian; Douglas of Drumlanrig, Home of Wedderburn, Ker of Faldonside, Ker of Fernihurst, and Ker of Cessford in the Borders; Gordon of Lochinvar and Stewart of Garlies in the south-west; Campbell of Cessnock, Campbell of Kinyeancleuch, Cunningham of Cunninghamhead, Dunbar of Cumnock, Lockhart of Bar, Stewart of Ochiltree, Wallace of Carnell and Wallace of Craigie in Ayrshire.[186]

The list itself, though far from exhaustive,[187] is a reminder of the lairds' attachment to reform in the more politically assertive and articulate parts of the kingdom; and it was from precisely these areas that the strength of opinion in general assemblies was drawn: from the north-east came Guthrie of Halkertoun, Durham of Grange, Fotheringham of Powrie, Douglas of Glenbervie, Guthrie of that Ilk, Haliburton of Pitcur, Barclay of

---

[185] SRO, GD30/2177, Shairp of Houstoun Muniments.
[186] Knox, *History*, i, 136, 173, 181; 294, 315–16; 119–20, 123, 188, 257; 173; 107–8, 299; 182; 69, 183; 122, 201, 356–7; 66, 101, 193, 345; 157; 121; 61, 175, 179, 207; ii, 324; Keith, *History*, ii, 8.
[187] G. Donaldson, *All the Queen's Men*, 161–4.

Mathers, Straiton of that Ilk, Strachan of Thornton, Ogilvie of that Ilk, Ogilvie of Inverarity, Lundie of that Ilk, Strachan of Tullievaird and Ogston of Fettercairn; from Perthshire, Stewart of Innermeath, Stirling of Keir, Murray of Balvaird and Murray of Tullibardine; from Fife, Melville of Raith, Scott of Abbotshall, Kirkaldy of Grange, Wood of Largo, Stewart of Rosyth; south of the Forth, Forester of Garden in Stirlingshire, Stewart of Minto from Glasgow (though his title belonged to Roxburghshire) and Shaw of Greenock in Renfrewshire; from the Lothians, Fairlie of Braid, Douglas of Pittendreich, Home of Spott, Hamilton of Preston, Johnston of Elphinstone, Douglas of Whittinghame; from the Borders, Ker of Fernihurst, Ker of Faldonside, Home of Coldenknowis, Home of Wedderburn, Scott of Haning (a signatory to the Book of Discipline in 1561) and Scott of Thirlestane; from the far south-west, Stewart of Garlies, Gordon of Lochinvar, and Vaus of Barnbarroch; and from Ayrshire, Cunningham of Cunninghamhead, Wallace of Carnell, Shaw of Sornbeg, Fullerton of Dreghorn, Corrie of Kelwood (who subscribed the Book of Discipline in 1561 and the band at Ayr in 1562), Crawford of Kerse, Campbell of Kinyeancleuch, Campbell of Skeldon, Cunningham of Drumquhassill, Cathcart of Carletoun, Chalmers of Gadgirth, Lockhart of Bar, Kennedy of Bargany and Stewart of Ochiltree.[188]

Some had openly associated themselves with the revolution of 1559–60, and their enthusiasm for religious change led then to endure the hardships of travel to be present at assemblies, often in Edinburgh, where they represented the local congregations which they served, in all probability, as elders. Surviving accounts of the assembly, it is true, rarely disclose its composition by listing the men who attended its meetings. Consequently, it is harder to say how regularly these lairds attended; but there is little doubt that the communities which sent lairds as commisioners were substantially those where support for the Reformation had been strongest. They were therefore particularly well-placed to secure reformed preaching at an early date.

Although no lists of Ayrshire ministers survive before 1567 (which is apt to create the false impression that ministers were hitherto lacking), it is scarcely conceivable that those Ayrshire lairds who pursued the reforming cause so determinedly failed to find ministers for their parishes. George Hay, after all, as the assembly's commisioner had preached 'with great fruit' for a month at a time in all the churches of Carrick in 1562; the

[188] *BUK*, i, *passim*; *First Book of Discipline*, 210–12; Fraser, *Memorials of Montgomeries*, ii, 192–3.

superintendent of Glasgow and two other commissioners were also active in Ayrshire that year; and part of their duties was to ensure that the nine kirks of Carrick had protestant staff.[189] In Dalry, for example, where the reforming Ker of Carsland dwelt, an exhorter was duly entered in the earliest lists of 1567; yet a fortuitous entry in the proceedings of the court of session in 1564 discloses that the parish had its own minister soon after the Reformation.[190] Again, the long reforming record and labours of the energetic Lockhart of Bar, a supporter of Wishart in 1546, an active member of the Congregation, associate of Knox and signatory to the Book of Discipline in 1561, had presumably borne fruit in his own parish of Galston. As Lockhart himself figured among the subscribers to the band at Ayr in 1562, which pledged to 'mentaine and assist the preatching of this holy evangell', it looks rather as if his efforts met with success. At any rate, a minister was recruited for Galston by 1563, and Robert Cunningham, who held the priory of Fail and subscribed the Ayrshire band of 1562, contributed 200 merks in stipend to the minister, whose parish was annexed to Fail.[191] Besides, in 1562, John Knox himself was active for a spell as the assembly's commissioner for the kirks of Kyle and Galloway; and in 1562, the assembly itself arranged to appoint James Greig to a charge in Carrick, 'if the Lord Areskine could be moved to consent'.[192] He was presumably active in the area soon afterwards, for he appears on the lists by 1568 (when he obtained the parsonage and vicarage) as minister of Colmonell in Carrick.[193] It is possible, however, that the more promising position of the reformers immediately after 1560 deteriorated somewhat by 1565 when is was remarked that the queen had diverted from Colmonell kirk revenues which previously had supported ministers' stipends; and a similar complaint was voiced by the parishioners of Dalry (where a minister was active in 1564), that kirklands formerly 'assignit to the ministers of the parochin' were disponed by the crown for other purposes.[194]

Dunbar of Blantyre, who undertook to support the reformed ministry in the band of 1562, may well have devoted his energies on the kirk's behalf, though the earliest evidence, so far available,

---

[189] Knox, *History*, ii, 55; *BUK*, i, 17–18.
[190] *Register of Ministers*, 38; *Fasti*, iii, 84.
[191] Knox, *History*, i, 61, 121, 175; ii, 56, 161, 324; Fraser, *Memorials of Montgomeries*, ii, 192–3; Knox, *History*, ii, 55–6; *Register of Ministers*, 39.
[192] *BUK*, i, 55; 29.
[193] *Register of Ministers*, 40; *RSS*, vi, no. 366. He was already minister at Dailly.
[194] *BUK*, i, 58.

of reformed service in the parish of Blantyre (in Lanarkshire) dates only from 1574. Again, it is hard to accept that Riccarton parish was devoid of reformed service until 1570 (when a reader appears on record), for among the parishioners was Cunningham of Caprington who had supported the cause of reform since the 1540s, adhered to the party of revolution in 1559, and swore to 'maintaine the ministers' in 1562. Indeed, in 1565, the assembly had promised satisfaction to the lairds of Carnell, Sornbeg and Dreghorn who sought 'support of a ministrie' (which may suggest they were equipped merely with readers) for Riccarton and Dundonald and offered 'of their awin friewill that they sould provyde stipends sufficient according as the Kirk wald appoint'.[195] In all, the overwhelming impression gained from the activities of the 91 signatories to the Ayrshire bond is of a thirst for the Gospel and an endeavour to 'maintain' their preachers.

Further south, in Nithsdale, Sir James Douglas of Drumlanrig, who had joined the army of the Congregation and signed the Book of Discipline, was well-placed to recommend his own servitor, John Taylor, parson of Cummertrees, as reader at Penpont in 1561: the appointment at any rate could hardly have been made without the laird's express approval, for Taylor remained a member of the laird's household, acting no doubt as his chaplain and notary: born in the barony of Annandale and aged about 40, the laird's recruit for the kirk continued his notarial duties (which helped supplement a meagre stipend) and served as exhorter and reader in the parish over two decades.[196] The rôle which single-minded lairds could play in recommending men for the ministry could often prove decisive.

On occasion, a minister's duties might extend over more than one parish: the parishioners of Mauchline and Ochiltree, for example, shared the services of one minister in 1562, and possibly earlier; but, later, with the start of the register of ministers in 1567, two different ministers are found at work in these parishes.[197] This, too, should serve as a reminder that where a vacancy occurs in the lists for 1567, it should not be assumed that the vacancy necessarily existed from the Reformation onward: when a minister died or left for another charge, there was no guarantee an immediate replacement would be found. Kinghorn

[195] Knox, *History*, ii, 56; Fraser, *Memorials of Montgomeries*, ii, 192; *Thirds of Benefices*, 264; *BUK*, i, 61.
[196] Knox, *History*, i, 51, 316, 345; ii, 324, 326; *Thirds of Benefices*, 92, 150, 290; *Wodrow Miscellany*, i, 389; SRO, NP2/1, Register of Admissions of Notaries, fo. 190r–v.
[197] *BUK*, i, 17; *Register of Ministers*, 39.

Wester, whose exhorter in 1563–4, Andrew Kirkcaldy, was a remarkable 76 years of age, was presumably more fortunate than some parishes in securing a coadjutor and successor without delay.[198] Generally, however, the real challenge facing the reformed church was not so much a problem of recruiting ministers at the Reformation, which, on the whole, was achieved without a significant lapse in time over much of country, but one of replacing the recruits of the early 1560s with a second generation of fully-fledged ministers, educated under the new regime and trained in the universities.

Among the first generation of ministers, so often recruited from the ranks of the pre-Reformation clergy, a sizeable number (including John Knox himself) had served as notaries: priests awaiting benefices frequently gained employment, and an income, by practising as notaries after securing papal authorisation. They were, therefore, not only literate but skilled in Latin as well as in Scots or English. After 1560, many made promising recruits as readers by conducting worship in the parishes; their essential task was to read the common prayers from a service-book and sermons from a book of homilies. Curiously, the work of these notaries who conformed to protestantism by acting as readers and exhorters has not been adequately acknowledged; yet their rôle in staffing the kirk was invaluable and conspicuous. At least fifty notaries demonstrated their support for the Reformation not merely by joining the ranks of the reformers but by displaying a readiness to read, exhort or minister in the new kirk. The figure of 50 is presumably a conservative one, for if more were known about the men who staffed the kirk in the years immediately after 1560, the number of notaries who joined the ministry would in all probability rise.

These men who provided such sterling service, for very little financial recompense, were, on the whole, not a new breed of revolutionary young priests, impatient with the apparent inability of the old church to effect much-needed reform, but men of mature experience, who came to protestantism and to serve the new kirk in their middle years (and, in some cases, even in old age); they were professional men of repute and standing in their communities, men often at the height of their careers. Few, it would seem, had spent their formative years consciously imbibing protestant doctrines, though in the end the message of the Reformation gained powerful support among all social groups, and its earliest recruits and protagonists had been clergy

[198] SRO, NP2/1, Register of Admissions of Notaries, fos. 182v–183r; *Thirds of Benefices*, 244–5.

of the established church itself. The revolt, after all, had been initiated by dissatisfied clerics.

Not many septuagenarians, it is true, were likely to follow the example of the notary, Andrew Kirkcaldy, who in his mid-seventies forsook the prospect of a life of ease and retirement at Wester Wemyss in Auchterderran parish in Fife by becoming exhorter at nearby Kinghorn Wester; certainly, his assistant and successor as reader, John Brown, who was also a notary, was a much younger man in his late 30s, and married, though, unlike Kirkcaldy, he had not a master's degree.[199] On the other hand, the reader and exhorter at Monikie, Matthew Greif, who had been born in neighbouring Monifieth parish, was indisputably a man of advancing years, in his sixties, with an established record of service as vicar pensionary and notary at Monikie.[200] Again, the men who agreed to serve after the Reformation as readers or exhorters at Creich, Carnock and Anstruther in Fife, at Tullibody in Clackmananshire, Pentland in Lothian, Symington in Lanark and Auchinleck in Ayrshire were all in their fifties in the early 1560s, and to that extent, regardless of the enthusiasm they exhibited for the Reformation, were past the peak of their intellectual and physical powers.[201]

Those notaries who served the kirk as readers and exhorters at Essil, Belhelvie, Little Dunkeld, Kenmore, Eassie, Kilmadock, Carriden, Manor and Penpont were all in their forties in the early 1560s, when, for the most part, they seem to have entered ecclesiastical office (though the readers at Little Dunkeld, Essil, Eassie and Kilmadock, listed somewhat later in the 1570s, when they were then men in their fifties, may well have been later recruits; at any rate, of their earlier service no knowledge exists).[202] Younger men, who by the early 1560s were still in their thirties, were recruited for service in the parishes of Killearnan, Cullen, Menmuir (where the notary Andrew Eldar, a graduate, 'duelland with Johne Erskeyn of Dwn', was presum-

[199] SRO, NP2/1, Register of Admissions of Notaries, fos. 182v–183r, fo. 46r–v; *Thirds of Benefices*, 244–5.

[200] SRO, NP2/1, Register of Admissions of Notaries, fos. 39r–v; *Thirds of Benefices*, 231.

[201] SRO, NP2/1, Register of Admissions of Notaries, fo. 34r (Creich, John Seton); fo. 63r–v (Carnock, Richard Brown); fo. 65r–v (Anstruther, John Forman); fo. 132r–v (Tullibody, Andrew Drysdale); fo. 171r–v (Pentland, John Brown); fo. 140r–v (Symington, Lanarkshire, John Lindsay); fo. 31r–v (Auchinleck, Adam Landels); *Thirds of Benefices*, 245; 92, 266; 264; *Register of Ministers*, 27; 8.

[202] SRO, NP2/1, Register of Admissions of Notaries, fos. 160r–v; 99r–v, 135v–136r, 203v–204r; 61r–v, 78r–v, 55r–v; 41r, 190r–v; *Thirds of Benefices*, 110, 223, 277, 283; 92; *Wodrow Miscellany*, i, 355; 351; *Register of Ministers*, 29, 82; see below, 150–1.

ably installed in the parish as reader by Erskine as superintendent), Dunblane (where Duncan Nevin, a graduate, notary
and married man, was initially contracted as city schoolmaster
in May 1562,[203] and later undertook work as a reader),
Tullicheddill, Carnwath, Carmichael, Cranston, and Tranent
(where a graduate notary belonging to Lord Borthwick's
household acted as parish minister by 1562).[204] Some parishes,
however, like Kintore in Aberdeenshire (which gained a graduate
notary as reader by 1563), or Kinnoull in Perthshire (which
attracted as minister by 1568 a graduate notary, born in Perth)
gained the services of qualified, if inexperienced, men in their late
twenties; and when the parishioners of Ceres in Fife sought a
successor to Patrick Adamson, who had served as minister for a
spell in the early 1560s, they found as replacement a graduate
notary, William Laing, who hitherto was 'servand to Jhonne
archbischope of Sanctandrois', and then aged about thirty.[205]

Comparatively few of these recruits were the products of an
urban environment: Gavin Nasmyth, at work as exhorter in
Dreghorn by 1568, had previously lived in Irvine where he
practised as a notary, though he had been born in Bothwell in
Clydesdale about 1535; the exhorter and minister at Carnwath,
Thomas King, who was already married and living in Carnwath,
it is true, had been born in Glasgow, twenty-seven miles away;
Ninian Swan, married and living in Lanark by 1564, had been
born in Glasgow where he had served as chaplain and had
studied in the university, before becoming reader, by 1568, at
Carmichael, five miles to the south-east of Lanark; John Leslie,
exhorter and minister at Carriden, was born in Edinburgh,
twenty-three miles to the east of his rural parish; William Rhynd,
minister at Kinnoull, was a native of nearby Perth; from Elgin
came William Hay, reader at Elchies (some fifteen miles to the
south of the city), and Alexander Douglas, reader at Essil, a
parish eight miles or so east of Elgin; and William Gray, exhorter

---

[203] SRO, RD1/5, Register of Deeds, fos. 190v–192r. (As 'schoilmaister of
Dunblane', Nevin contracted in May 1562 to teach grammar to the children of
James Chisholm of Cromlix, Edward Sinclair of Gallwermoir and Robert
Lermonth, bailie of Dunblane, in their homes, with 'friendis barnis, utheris
nychtbouris and citienaris barinis of the toun' on payment annually of 5 merks
each by Chisholm and Sinclair, 2 merks by Lermonth, and 40s. by the
community from the common goods of the city.)

[204] SRO, NP2/1, Register of Admissions of Notaries, fos. 163r–v; 71r–v;
113r–v; 66r–v; 95r–v; 33r–v; 134v; 41r–v; 103r–v; Register of Ministers, 52;
Thirds of Benefices, 221, 231, 254, 264, 266, 274; BUK, i, 13.

[205] SRO, NP2/1, Register of Admissions of Notaries, fos. 42r–v; 102r–v;
93r–v; Thirds of Benefices, 222, 251; 243.

and minister at Dornoch, was born in the cathedral town of Caithness.[206] These apart, most of the notaries who entered service in the kirk came from an explicitly rural background: the graduate, William Ramsay, who conformed at the Reformation to serve as Campbell of Glenorchy's chaplain and minister at Kenmore, had been born at the kirktoun of Fowlis in Strathearn about 1517; in Ayrshire, the exhorter at Auchinleck, Adam Landels, was born in the neighbouring parish of Ochiltree; the minister at Creich, John Seton, born nearby in Collesie parish, had previously served at Creich as vicar and notary before conforming to the Reformation; James Murray, reader at Cranston, was a native of the parish; William Pettillock, a former priest and notary living in Arbroath and born in East Ferry of Portincraig, became reader at Eassie, to the north of the Sidlaw Hills, in Angus by 1574: from birth to death, much of his life's work was performed within the span of twenty miles. Again, Andrew Drummond, born in Strathearn and created notary in 1560, became reader by 1574, when aged 34, at Strogeith, in his own native district. The physical horizons of Andrew Drysdale, a former priest and notary, who found employment in Lord Erskine's household, were no less limited: born in the Mains of Dollar, he dwelt in Alva, and, by 1567, had become reader at Tullibody: he lived and worked within the shadow of the Ochils, and within the confines of three adjoining parishes. Similarly, the notary and reader at Kilbirnie, Robert Crawford, was himself a native of the parish he served. In Ross-shire, Alexander Mackenzie, born at Avoch on the Black Isle, was a graduate who had obviously received his training in the south, but had returned to his own community where he acted, after the Reformation, as reader of the neighbouring parish of Killearnan: in seeking a man to provide for its spiritual needs, the community instinctively looked for a local figure, respected and learned, in whom it had confidence.[207] Most, however, were of a sufficiently humble origin to obviate the need for any record of their parentage when they applied for admission as notaries in 1564; merely a few were duly noted as the sons of lairds: the exhorter at Carriden was the son of Leslie of Innerpeffray, and the reader at Kilbirnie was himself the son of Crawford of Kilbirnie.[208]

[206] SRO, NP2/1, Register of Admissions of Notaries, fos. 70r-v; 33r-v, 134v; 55r-v; 102r-v; 104r-v; 160r-v, 136r-137r; Durkan and Kirk, *University of Glasgow*, 184, 235-6.
[207] SRO, NP2/1, Register of Admissions of Notaries, fos. 203v-204r; 31r-v; 34r, 41r-v, 61r-v, 67r-v, 151r-v, 163r-v.
[208] Ibid., fos. 55r-v, 151r-v.

The diffusion of protestantism in society and, in turn recruitment to the reformed ministry depended on a network of communications: the printed and spoken word of protestant literature helped transmit the ideas of Reform; the public sermon, disputation and singing of hymns, psalms and 'good and godly ballads' attracted attention, comment and conversation. This was the substance of Archbishop Hamilton's complaint in 1556 to the bailies of Edinburgh about 'certane odious ballettis and rymes laitlie sett furth be sum evil inclinit persones of youre town, quha hes alssua tane doun diveris imagis and contempnandlie brokin the samyn, quhilk is ane thing verray sclanderous to the peple and contrarious to the ordinancis and statutis of haly kirk'.[209] Private Bible-study initiated by families and friends fostered a simple, personal faith; itinerant preachers and traders, both merchants and craftsmen, brought news and views, and sometimes English Bibles too, as they travelled among communities. Nor is it any coincidence that protestantism gained its firmest foothold in areas where most of the authorised market centres were concentrated. At local markets and at annual regional fairs, information, opinions and ideas could be exchanged just as readily as any other commodity on offer. The regional organisation of the Lords of the Congregation was itself a product of interaction of this sort; and the work of receptive lairds and communities with a thirst for the Gospel set in motion the search by congregations for a new ministry. All the important burghs engaged in overseas trade – Edinburgh and Leith, Haddington and Dunbar to the east, Linlithgow to the west, Stirling, Inverkeithing, Kinghorn, St Andrews, Cupar, Perth, Dundee, Arbroath, Montrose, Aberdeen, Banff and Inverness, with Dumbarton, Ayr and Dumfries on the west coast – took a lead in acquiring reformed service at the Reformation. Other communities, too, living in close proximity to the main trade routes and lines of communication were likely to be better equipped to secure the services of a protestant preacher at an early date. Again, where parish units were compact and manageable, and preachers energetic, headway was readily made.

How far the cause of reformation in the parishes advanced during the 1560s can be demonstrated, at least in part, by the appearance in those years of reformed staff over wide areas of the country. In Lothian and Tweeddale, 97 (out of 101) parishes were filled during the 1560s; a few parishes, it is true, had still to share personnel. There is also good evidence in the 1560s for

[209] J. C. Lees, *St Giles', Edinburgh: Church, College and Cathedral* (Edinburgh 1889), 355; cf. *Edinburgh Burgh Records*, ii, 251.

reformed staff at work in all but ten of the 92 kirks in Perth, Stirling and Clackmannan. In Fife, all 63 parishes had obtained protestant staff during the 1560s; 87 parishes in Angus and the Mearns were filled by then, and three which were not had the service of ministers from adjacent kirks. With some sharing of resources, in Aberdeenshire, too, 85 out of 91 parishes had reformed service in the 1560s; and a creditable record of staffing at least 52 of the 72 churches in Moray was achieved during the 1560s. All the kirks in Dunbarton and Lanark gained protestant service during that decade; and only in three parishes in Renfrewshire (Houston, Lochwinnoch and Paisley) have no personnel been traced for the 1560s. At least 31 of the 42 parishes in Ayrshire were equipped with reformed service by then; and in the old diocese of Galloway every parish is known to have been filled by 1570, and most considerably earlier.[210] The remaining area around Dumfries eastward through Teviotdale, and some difficult border territory, to the Merse contained about 130 parishes, of which no fewer than 83 kirks had staff who can be traced to the 1560s. Even in the Highlands where the pace of change was slower, but only marginally so, significant headway was made in securing recruits to the ministry in the decade after parliament had abrogated papal authority and proscribed the mass.[211]

Evangelisation, at last, was placed firmly in the hands of the new ministry whose task was to spread the new faith through the personal links forged between preachers and reforming lairds, their families and circle of friends, their tenants and servants, heads of households and, through them, to reach the wider community of parishioners, and, not least, the youth, through catechising and schooling. This, in turn, fostered the growth of protestantism, especially where those with local power and influence favoured reformation and the eradication of the old ways. With what looks like remarkable speed and ease, the reformed kirk had dramatically established its claim for recognition as the national church. The contrast with the circumstances confronting reformers in the 1550s could scarcely have been sharper.

[210] The calculations are based on entries in *Thirds of Benefices, Register of Ministers, Fasti,* i-viii, Haws, *Parish Clergy,* G. Donaldson, *Reformed by Bishops,* and MS. sources discussed above.
[211] See below, 305–33.

5

The Superintendent:
Myth and Reality

I

'Planting kirks':
The existence, by 1560, of inumerable protestant congregations
in town and countryside, linked only by attachment to a
common creed, by a readiness to share the services of itinerant
preachers, and, perhaps, by a visitation from Lords of the
Congregation, invited a solution to the problem of integrating
the work of local churches in manner which gave coherence,
direction and unity to the loose amalgamation of protestant
communities and which guarded against any tendency for
incipient congregationalism to degenerate into mere individual-
ism. Some protestant churches had emerged from inconspicuous
house groups which met for Bible study and devotion. The little
group of burgesses in Cupar, for example, which congregated 'in
the Lady Brakmonthis hous, at the begynnyng of the religion'
and 'communicat at the table of the Lord, Paull Meffen beand
minister''serves as a reminder both of the rôle of godly matrons
in the Reformation and that of the preacher in firing the
imagination of believers and in instilling or reinforcing a sense of
identity and brotherhood.

Some protestant congregations were undoubtedly well-
organised, individually equipped with minister, elders and
deacons. St Andrews had already made the transition from 'privy
kirk' to city church during 1559 when the provost, some
magistrates, university teachers, prominent citizens and ordinary
merchants, craftsmen, and clerics – initially over 300 recorded
names (of men) – declared themselves to have joined 'the

---

¹ *Register of the Minister, Elders and Deacons of the Christian Congregation
of St Andrews [RStAKS]*, ed. D. H. Fleming, 2 vols. (Edinburgh, 1889–90), i, 286,
290, 292.

congregatioun within this cietie', and professed their determination to 'put downe all idolatrie, abhominationess, superstitioness,
and quhatsumever thing dois exalte the self against the majestie
of our God, and maynteyn and sett up the trew religioun of
Christe, his Word and sacramentes, and alswa assist and defend
the trew ministeris therof'.[2] Their example, soon afterwards, was
followed by others including 18 priests in the primatial city –
among them Augustinian canons – who renounced the papacy,
the veneration of saints, the doctrine of purgatory and 'all
traditiones of men sett owt to thirle the consciences of Goddis
people aganis his holy laws', to which list of repudiated beliefs
there was added explicitly, in a subsequent recantation, the
doctrine of transubstantiation itself.[3]

Certainly, the pace of protestant reform had intensified by the
summer of 1559 when, as the prior provincial of the friars
preachers in Scotland lamented, the religious observances of
many of the monastic orders had ceased, 'the places themselves
being utterly overthrown and destroyed'.[4] A no less pessimistic
note was struck by the Catholic primate in 1560 who despairingly placed on record how 'the elderis callit of every town takis
all the causis of our ecclesiastical jurisdiction, and intromettis
with all our office', and it was presumably informed comment
gained from first-hand experience when he observed how the
protestant preachers were installed, in defiance of the established
church, 'be force, or tane in be townis at thair awin hand, sa that
thai will not thol ony maner of service in the kirk, oder Mess,
preching, using ony Sacramentis bot alanarlie be thai men, and all
utterly opposis all utheris, baith Bischopis, Abbotis, Parsonis,
Vicaris, that will not use all thyngis of thair manner as thai
prescrif'.[5] Beyond the towns and main centres of reform, some
protestant congregations, presumably, were less well served by
their existing pre-Reformation curates who had reformed themselves and their practices at least to the extent that they were
equipped, if not yet to preach, to read the common prayers from
either the Edwardine or Genevan prayer book, then circulating
in Scotland.[6]

[2] Ibid., i, 6–10.
[3] Ibid., i, 11–18.
[4] Scottish Record Office [SRO], B65/22, St Andrews Charters, no. 430, 1 Aug.
1559.
[5] R. Keith, *History of the Affairs of the Church and State in Scotland*, ed. J. P.
Lawson, 3 vols. (Edinburgh, 1844–50), iii, 5.
[6] G. Donaldson, *The Making of the Scottish Prayer Book of 1637* (Edinburgh,
1954), 1–13; J. K. Cameron, *The First Book of Discipline* (Edinburgh, 1972),
130–1, 182.

Attempts at providing national direction and leadership to bourgeoning reformed communities, which had surfaced in Fife, Strathearn, Angus and the Mearns, Lothian, Ayrshire and Argyll (and which were by no means unknown elsewhere)[7] may be sought in the meetings held by the Lords of the Congregation, notably in Edinburgh but also in Perth, Stirling, Glasgow and even Hamilton (the Duke of Châtelherault's residence), which served as a model for the formation, during 1560, of a general assembly to govern the whole church across the nation.[8] Their deliberations, during the struggle for Reformation, were wide-ranging and are known to have included preparations for the common prayers to be read weekly in every parish either by the curates themselves, if found willing and qualified, or by other parishioners better able to perform these duties, for doctrine and the meaning of scripture to be discussed privately in men's homes, for the recruitment of 'faithful ministers purely and truly to minister Christ's Evangel and sacraments to his people', the adoption of the native tongue in services, the suppression of idolatry, the establishment of the church in Edinburgh, and the distribution of ministers to certain charges, especially in the towns, a measure which, in some cases, may have amounted to no more than an endorsement of the work already done by local congregations in selecting ministers.[9] At any rate, the congregation of Edinburgh, which, in July 1559, had 'elected and chose John Knox publiquely in the Tolbooth of Edenburgh for their minister' had its proceedings confirmed in July 1560 when 'the greatest part of the Congregation' assembled in Edinburgh (where the 'most part of the chief ministers of the realm' had also gathered) to sanction *inter alia* the election of Knox, who had been advised to reside for a spell in St Andrews, as minister of the capital and to approve the appointment of ministers in the east-coast towns of Aberdeen, Dundee, Perth, St Andrews, Dunfermline and Leith, and in the Borders market-town of Jedburgh where the commendator of the abbey proved no enemy to reform.[10]

Although it provides very little impression of the extent to which protestant congregations were already equipped with reformed service (and it wholly excludes the initiative of

[7] See above, 1–15, 96ff.

[8] *John Knox's History of the Reformation in Scotland*, ed. W. C. Dickinson, 2 vols. (Edinburgh, 1949), i, 136–8, 148–79, 188, 198, 206, 229–30, 232, 244, 247–9, 265, 276, 298, 332–4.

[9] Ibid., i, 136–8, 148–58; 125, 127–9; 198, 334.

[10] *Miscellany of the Wodrow Society*, ed. D. Laing (Edinburgh, 1844), i, 63; Knox, *History*, i, 332–4.

protestants in the west), the list of ministers assigned to specific burghs by the Congregation does at least serve to emphasise the strategic significance which reformers attached to the towns. As centres not just of commerce but of education, culture and conference, the towns were seen to act as agencies for carrying forward the work of evangelisation throughout the countryside. Towns, of course, could, and did, react differently in their response to protestantism, depending, in part on the extent to which ruling élites were prepared or able to sponsor the propagation of protestant doctrine within their communities. Yet such was their perception of the leadership which the 'best reformed Citie and Towne' could provide to the surrounding countryside that the reformers warned the government to 'disappoint not your chief townes and where learning is exercised of such ministers as more may profit by residence in one place than by continuall travell from place to place'; they also proposed that recruits to the ministry be examined by 'men of soundest judgement remaining in some principal town next adjacent unto them'; and there, too, it was expected, meetings of the exercise for interpreting scripture would be held to impart theological instruction, not least, to the 'ministers of the parish kirks in the landwart adjacent to every chiefe town'. Besides, in the 'great towns', daily services were to be made available; and 'in every notable town', a weekday, as well as the Sabbath, was to be set aside for preaching and prayer. The towns were to act as a kind of theological powerhouse to equip ministers for their task in fulfilling the church's wider mission to the nation.[11]

Whatever their tentative plans to establish a measure of co-ordination from the centre, the Lords of the Congregation had already effected a mechanism for communicating their instructions to congregations by commissioning delegates to make known their wishes in particular localities. In August 1560, the Congregation directed two lairds to purge Dunkeld cathedral of 'all kinds of monuments of idolatry'[12]; similar instructions were sent to supporters in Glasgow,[13] and, presumably elsewhere; and, in the case of St Andrews, the Lords of the Congregation in 1560 are known to have appointed as their local agents or commissioners two men from the university, John Douglas and

[11] *First Book of Discipline*, 97, 101, 127, 181, 190.
[12] *Old Statistical Account of Scotland*, x, 976.
[13] J. Durkan and J. Kirk, *The University of Glasgow, 1451–1577* (Glasgow, 1977), 231 and n. 45.

John Winram, to extract a recantation from a former priest.[14] Clearly, by 1560, as a result of local initiative assisted by some central co-ordination, a reformed ecclesiastical organisation was operating with some effect in many parts of the country.

So far, however, no impetus had emerged to give reformed congregations any semblance of regional cohesion or identity. Between congregational kirk sessions in localities and the general assembly, of somewhat indeterminate composition, at the centre, the new church in 1560 was bereft of any intermediate structure for leadership or government. Much of the reformers' energies had been directed towards meeting the needs of parishes; but the more parochial ministries were established, the greater the urgency became to regulate procedures for co-ordinating the heady work of Reformation in the provinces and for bringing coherence to the piecemeal and fragmented process of reform in specific districts. The reformers' emphasis on the right of congregations to select ministers of their own choosing was never carried so far as to deny that a minister's doctrine should first be tested and acknowledged by several fellow ministers. Besides, regardless of whether a precise mechanism had then been formulated for removing a minister from a parish, it was clearly understood that deposition for erroneous doctrine or scandalous behaviour involved more than merely a congregational decision; it required the judgment of neighbouring ministers, the consent, that is, of the wider church beyond the parish.[15] A national, protestant church (which, as early as October 1559, saw itself as 'the Church of Scotland'[16]) could not concede complete autonomy to individual congregations to act as they saw fit without reference to an authority beyond the confines of the parish.

Initially, if understanding of the content of the 'Book of Reformation', drafted in the spring of 1560, is correct, the reformers had envisaged linking loosely the work of rural ministries to that of 'the best reformed church', located in the nearest sizeable town, where assistance from 'men of soundest judgement' could be had for examining entrants to the ministry; hence the recurring emphasis on the need to secure 'the judgement of the godly and learned'.[17] In practice, some

---

[14] *RStAKS*, i, 137–8. The dating of the commission in 1560 evidently preceded July when Adam Heriot, described in the document as minister of St Andrews, was appointed to Aberdeen.

[15] *First Book of Discipline*, 96ff, 177.

[16] Knox, *History*, i, 255.

[17] *First Book of Discipline*, 96, 98, 99, 101–2.

direction in appointing ministers from the Lords of the Congregation was scarcely unavoidable, and Lord James Stewart's rôle in selecting recruits from his Augustinian priory in St Andrews to serve as ministers and readers for reformed parishes in Fife and beyond is unlikely to have been unique.[18] As early as May 1559, when the Congregation appeared in his district, the commendator of the Tironensian abbey of Lindores proved a friend to reform and assigned a vicar's manse for a 'minister of the Word of God', who presumably was placed in the rural parish of Abdie (or Lindores) with the Congregation's authority.[19] At any rate, the commendator's decision to 'put some reformation' to his abbey was evidently not without effect, for the earliest minister of Abdie on record by 1561 was himself a former monk of Lindores. Whether the commendator was permitted to exercise his traditional right of patronage to the parish church or whether this was eclipsed in preference to a congregational decision in this the parish's first reformed appointment is not disclosed; but preachers, in any event, were in short supply and, so long as 'this rarietie of true ministers' remained, parishioners could not afford to be unduly demanding.[20]

On what were the essential requirements for entry to the ministry, the reformers stood in no doubt. The inward call of God and the outward call of a congregation, with an attestation of the candidate's fitness in doctrine and life were the salient characteristics sought for admission to the reformed ministry. The doctrine of apostolic succession, and its transmission through bishops, was curtly dismissed 'seeing the miracle is ceased', and any belief in 'lineall discente' ('a successione perpetua episcoporum', in the Latin text) discounted.[21] Repudiating, as they did, any notion of a personal succession, the reformers were not obliged to recognise the bishop's traditional rôle in presiding at ordinations and in conferring holy orders. Ordination, as customarily conceived, was eschewed at the Reformation, and, in its place, emphasis was placed on 'inaugurating' ministers to particular charges. In other words, the validity of the ministry was understood not to rest on authorisation from a bishop. Thus, given the nature of the reformers' concept of the pastoral ministry, considerable latitude might be allowed on the

[18] See below, 417–18.
[19] The Works of John Knox, ed. D, Laing, 6 vols. (Edinburgh, 1846–64), i, 391–2; ii, 87–88; Registrum Magni Sigilli Regum Scotorum [RMS], edd. J. M. Thomson et al. 11 vols. (Edinburgh, 1882–1914), v, no. 595; Fasti, v, 123.
[20] First Book of Discipline, 104.
[21] Ibid., 96ff, 102, 207; Knox, Works, ii, 110; P. Schaff, The Creeds of Christendom, 3 vols. (New York, 1882), iii, 461.

methods by which ministers came to receive their congregational charges. At the Reformation, the kirk in Scotland had concentrated its energies and resources on the pastoral ministry and, like many other churches of the Reformation, had simply abandoned diocesan episcopacy which then was regarded as constituting neither the *esse* nor even *bene esse* (nor, for that matter, *plene esse*) of the church. For the most part, the existing episcopate had acted as an impediment to protestant reform; and the retention of an episcopal structure in a church reformed was understood not as a requirement but as inessential, to be kept or discarded as reformers thought fit and as local conditions dictated.

By audatiously casting aside the familiar edifice of ecclesiastical offices from archbishop to acolyte, Scottish reformers sought to restore to prominence the ministry of the Word and sacraments as the highest function within a corporate priesthood of believers. In so proceeding, from an austere biblicism which rejected man-made accretions 'because in Gods Scriptures they neither have commandement nor assurance',[22] the kirk, as it emerged in 1560, proved hostile to much medieval paraphernalia and was disposed simply to recognise the duties and work of preachers, teachers (both in schools and universities), elders and deacons, functions for which Calvin had earlier sought scriptural warrant, in serving the Christian community.[23] The pastoral ministry was understood ordinarily to be exercised within a congregation; but its scope might as readily be extended to include the work of itinerant preachers who carried the Gospel to communities devoid of reformed service; hence the readiness to assign particular duties 'to him that travels from place to place, whome we call Superintendent'.[24] So strict, indeed, was reformed opinion on the maintenance of 'wholesome doctrine' that it was deemed preferable to leave congregations without a settled ministry than to provide them with 'a vain shadow' which might delude them into thinking that 'they have a minister when in

---

[22] *First Book of Discipline*, 88–9.

[23] Knox, *History*, i, 148, 337; ii, 277–9; *First Book of Discipline*, 96ff, 129ff, 174ff; *Corpus Reformatorum*, XXXVIII, i, *Ioannis Calvini Opera . . . omnia*, edd. G. Baum, E. Cunitz and E. Reuss (Brunswick, 1869–96), X, i, 15–17; Calvin, *Institution de la religion chrestienne*, ed. J.-D. Benoit, 5 vols. (Paris, 1957–63) [another edition, Calvin, *Institutes of the Christian Religion*, ed. H. Beveridge, 3 vols. (Edinburgh, 1846)], IV, iv, 1; IV, iii, 4–5, 8; Calvin, *Commentary on the Epistles of Paul, the Apostle to the Corinthians*, ed. J. Pringle (Edinburgh, 1848–9), i, 414–15; Calvin, *Commentaries on the Epistles of Paul to the Galatians and Ephesians*, ed. W. Pringle (Edinburgh, 1854), 280.

[24] *First Book of Discipline*, 109.

verie deed they have none'.[25] Readers of scripture and the
common prayers, who performed a subsidiary service, were no
substitutes for ministers. In a bid, therefore, to reach communities
lacking reformed service, the proposal in 1560 was to assign to
experienced ministers, as 'chiefest workmen, not onelie townes
to remaine in, but also provinces that by their faithfull labours
churches may be erected and order established where none is
now'.[26]

From such a prosaic and inauspicious start, the idea took root
that some preachers might exercise their ministry over an entire
district; and, as the Book of Reformation underwent revision and
expansion in the course of 1560, the authors of the report felt
obliged to explain why they now considered it appropriate 'to
make difference betwixt Preachers at this time' by proposing to
have superintendent ministers. The reasons adduced in the Book
of Discipline, as it finally took shape, for appointing superintendent ministers were purely practical, not theological, and
indicate, incidentally, that no differentiation among protestant
preachers had previously emerged. Besides, the basis for the
distinction was located in the geographical areas for their
ministry. In an effort to meet the emergency which confronted
them, the reformers realistically proposed not to restrict the
ablest ministers to individual congregations but to distribute the
ministry across the nation, as best they could despite a severe
shortage of staff, by selecting, as 'a thing most expedient for this
time', ten or twelve ministers as superintendents, with responsibility 'to plant and erect Kirkes, to set, order and appoint
Ministers' so that the message of the Gospel might be carried to
'all Inhabitants of this realme' and that 'the simple and ignorant,
who perchance have never heard Jesus Christ truely preached,
shall come to some knowledge'. As a reminder of the urgency of
their task in evangelising the wider community across parochial
boundaries, the superintendents were instructed in their duties to
preach, at least, thrice weekly (unlike the bishops of the old
church who had been urged in 1549 'to preach in person at least
four times in the year'[27]), to reside in no one place for more than
twenty days during visitations, and to re-enter visitation after
three or four months' residence 'at most' in the chief town of the
province. Beyond a concern for the poor, and for education over

---

[25] Ibid., 104; cf., Bucer, *De Regno Christi*, in *Martini Buceri Opera Latina*, xv,
ed. F. Wendel, (Paris, 1955), 2 vols., i, 128 (*Melanchthon and Bucer*, ed. W. Pauck
(London, 1969), 293).
[26] *First Book of Discipline*, 105.
[27] *Statutes of the Scottish Church, 1225–1559*, ed. D. Patrick (Edinburgh,
1907), 104.

which the superintendent was to exercise some supervision, no further claims were advanced, nor duties enumerated, for the office in the Book of Discipline which broadly received approval, apart from some misgivings on finance, from the privy council and convention of lords in January 1561.[28]

The concern expressed by the compilers in justifying the expediency of their proposal to differentiate among preachers at a time when preachers were so scarce is doubtless to be explained by the criticism anticipated from congregations who found themselves deprived of preachers selected as superintendents. A complaint, not wholly unrelated, at any rate, was voiced soon afterwards by the parishioners of Mid Calder whose minister exceptionally sought to combine, with the general assembly's blessing, a congregational ministry with the duties of superintendent of Lothian, to the evident distaste of his parishioners.[29] Even so, whatever the exact objection to their scheme which the authors of the Book of Discipline may have sought to assuage, the general purport and direction of their argument almost suggests that, had there been no shortage, they would not have found it appropriate to make such a distinction among preachers. But whether different circumstances would have resulted in an exclusive emphasis on ecclesiastical courts or councils, it would be idle to speculate, for the reality was that the councils devised by the reformers in and after 1560 to govern the church both locally and nationally were less applicable in the regions where missionary work had to be undertaken by individuals, not courts or committees. Nonetheless, the Book of Discipline expressed clearly enough the need to subordinate the superintendent to the wider judgment of the kirk: he was to be subject to correction by the ministers and elders of the province; he could not change his area except 'by the consent of the whole counsell of the Kirk'; and he was obliged to present for inspection audited accounts of congregational finance to 'the great councell of the Kirk'.[30] Nowhere does the document even so much as hint that superintendents were to be entrusted with the full government of the church.

---

[28] First Book of Discipline, 97, 115–28, 131, 145, 148, 152, 164, 210–11; Calendar of State Papers relating to Scotland and Mary, Queen of Scots, 1547–1603 [CSP Scot.], edd. J. Bain et al., 13 vols. (Edinburgh, 1898–1969), i, no. 959; Knox, Works, i, 344–5.

[29] The Book of the Universall Kirk. Acts and Proceedings of the General Assemblies of the Kirk of Scotland, 1560–1618 [BUK], ed. T. Thomson, 3 vols. and appendix vol. (Edinburgh, 1839–45), i, 42.

[30] First Book of Discipline, 127, 164.

II

'Watchmen and pastors of the flock':
The picture presented in the Book of Discipline of superintendents' duties is complemented and amplified in a second statement, conveying a further impression of the reformers' conception of some salient characteristics of the office, the 'Form and Order of the Election of Superintendents', composed by the spring of 1561 and used at the election of Spottiswoode as superintendent of Lothian in March 1561 when Knox himself, having declined the offer of superintendent, acted as presiding minister. In the document, Spottiswoode was presented as 'Christis Minister' to the gathering who were invited either to name an alternative or accept him with obedience 'as becumethe the scheip to give unto thair Pastour, sa lang as he remains faythfull in his office'. In replying to the presiding minister's questions, the superintendent was obliged to affirm that he undertook the office not for 'warldly commoditie, riches or glory', that as 'a man subject to infirmity, and ane that hes neid of correctioun and admonitioun', he remained 'subject to the Discipline of the Kirk, as the rest of your Brethrein', for, as he was required to acknowledge aloud, 'the vocatioun of God to bear charge within his Kirk makethe not men tyrantes, nor lordis, but appoynteth thame Servandis, Watchemen, and Pastoris of the Flock'. Thereafter, the process of admission was concluded with an exhortation to the superintendent to act as a 'trew servand' and 'usurpe not dominioun nor tyrranicall impyre over thy brethrein'.[31]

In all, the pastoral responsibilities of the office could scarcely have been more strikingly conveyed. Again, if further reminder were necessary of the essential unity of the pastoral ministry, in which both superintendent and minister were seen to serve, it can be found in the phraseology attached to the title of 'The Form and Order of the Election of Superintendents' which discloses that the same procedure for admitting superintendents 'may serve also in electioun of all uther Ministers'.[32] In other words, the one formula for inaugurating ministers and superintendents offers testimony of how their functions differed neither in their essential nature nor in their authorisation by the church. Their shared task was to serve congregations through their ministry of the Word and sacraments.

The notion, then, that superintendents were to be lords and princes of the church receives not support but rather refutation

---

[31] Knox, *Works*, ii, 144–50; *CSP Scot.*, i, no. 967.
[32] Knox, *Works*, ii, 144.

from this source; and it is difficult to explain why historical accounts of the superintendent's office have not always disclosed the evidence from this particular document. It is only fair to add, however, that the whole subject has attracted more controversy and misunderstanding than most. But, another example, of what looks like the uneven presentation of evidence occurs over the seemingly simple matter of the superintendent's form of address. One writer eager to emphasise the 'lordly dignity' of the superintendent's office drew attention to his style 'dominus superintendens',[33] and to the extent that the words quoted were reproduced accurately from the source, the information imparted was correct; but evidence from the same source which reveals that the superintendent was described as 'my lord' only on three occasions, and as 'dominus superintendens' in merely seven instances – ten occurrences in all amid almost 200 entries naming the superintendent between 1561 and 1572 – was not presented for appraisal; nor was it disclosed that in the same source a minister and kirk session, in an instance, were addressed by a petitioner as 'my lords' and 'your lordschipes'.[34] That, presumably, would merely have detracted from conveying the impression that the title was reserved for superintendents and not assigned to humble parish ministers. But the omission of this additional information is liable to obscure a wider truth, and to create so misleading impression that the partial truth conveyed may be of exceedingly little worth.

Now it is perfectly true that chancery clerks, addicted as they were to traditional styles and formularies, were sometimes apt to address a superintendent by such archaisms as 'venerabilis pater' rather oddly, for this been used in the past as a customary form of address for abbots, rather than bishops, and to which legitimate exception might therefore be taken by reformers, and, again, as a 'reverend father in God' (presumably a vernacular rendering of the customary pre-Reformation form of address to a bishop, 'reverendus in Christo pater'), to which (as a purely descriptive title) there was presumably less ground for serious objection (especially so when a presbyterian minister later detected no incongruity in addressing the general assembly as 'fathers and brethren' and as 'reverend and loving brethren'); but in so far as the phrase may have instilled a sense of continuity

---

[33] G. Donaldson, 'The Scottish Episcopate at the Reformation', *English Historical Review*, lx (1945), 349–64, at 352; G. Donaldson, *The Scottish Reformation* (Cambridge, 1960), 125–6; G. Donaldson, *Scottish Church History* (Edinburgh, 1985), 69.

[34] *RStAKS*, i, 81, 131, 299, 313–15, 332; 63–4.

with the pre-Reformation episcopate, there was adequate ground for objection to the epithet, especially as the reformers themselves at the outset had avoided adopting any such title.[35]

Possibly the very novelty of the office contributed to uncertainty, at least among the uninitiated, on an apposite form of address. At any rate, the diversity of styles employed is all too evident in the case of Erskine of Dun who, regardless of ecclesiastical rank, was himself a baron and eligible to be called a 'lord'. In practice, Cardinal Beaton, in 1544, had recognised Erskine as 'the rycht honorable and our rycht traist cousin, the Lard of Dvn', and surviving fragments of correspondence in later years testify to the superintendent's being addressed by a minister as 'honorabill scir' and the letter directed to 'the richt honorabill lord of Dwn, superintendent of Angus and Mearns'; by another minister as 'the right honourable lard of Dune, superintendent of Anguse and Merns'; by the laird of Dunipace as 'my lord'; by James Scrimgeour, constable of Dundee, as 'the reuerend in God, Johnn Erskin of Dun, superintendent of Anguiss, Gowrie and Starmouth'; in 1584, by the assuredly conservative Earl of Montrose as 'my lord and fader'; and in 1585, during what has been called a 'conservative reaction', by the archbishop of St Andrews, and by the brethren of the 'exercise' in Angus (at a point when presbyteries were proscribed), as 'your lordship'.[36] Yet, honorific titles of this sort were not reserved for superintendents: a similar sort of style was adopted in the case of an ordinary minister appointed by the assembly to act as commissioner (or visitor) who was addressed (in 1571) by a minister as 'rycht honorable', and another commissioner was greeted (in 1575) as the 'rycht venerable commissioner of the kirk of God'.[37]

For Winram, the evidence which survives among the university's records resembles that contained in the kirk session register for St Andrews. Though variously mentioned in five dozen entries from 1562 onward as prior of Portmoak, subprior of St Andrews, and, without adornment, as superintendent of Fife and Strathearn, only twice was he accorded an epithet (and not once as 'father' or 'lord'); in 1570, he was styled 'the rycht

---

[35] G. Donaldson, *Scottish Reformation*, 126; *St Andrews Formulare*, edd. G. Donaldson and C. Macrae, 2 vols. (Edinburgh, 1942), ii, e.g. nos. 376, 403(b); *BUK*, iii, 914; see below, 186–7, 194, 219.

[36] *Historical Manuscripts Commission* [*HMC*], *5th Report* (London, 1876), App., 635ff; *Miscellany of the Spalding Club*, ed. J. Stuart, iv (Aberdeen, 1849), 45, 63–6, 69–72.

[37] R. Bannatyne, *Journal of the Transactions of Scotland*, ed. J. G. Dalyell (Edinburgh, 1806), 306; *HMC, 5th Report*, 101.

worschipfull Mr Johnne Wynram, superintendent of Fyffe' (an
epithet shared by other ministers and commissioners of assembly)
and, as prior of Portmoak, in 1582, he was depicted as
'venerabilis et egregius vir Mr Joannes Wynram',[38] an accurate
enough description, which bears comparison with the kirk
session's description of John Douglas, rector of the university, as
'venerabilis et circumspecti viri' ('a venerable and discreet man')
and of other university teachers as 'venerabill and godlie lernit
men'.[39] Yet, the minister and kirk session of Kinghorn addressed
a testimonial in 1565 unostentatiously 'unto the Superintendent
of Fyff and to the minister eldaris and diaconis of Sanctandrois,
for salutacion', who thereafter were fraternally greeted simply as
'brethren'. In his legacy and will, Winram described himself in
1582 simply as 'sumtyme superintendent of Fyf', though the
commisary clerk in recording his testament chose to designate
him as 'ane honorabill man', as doubtless he was.[40]

At the same time, a minister and session might be addressed
not only as 'my lords' but as the 'ryght reverend ministeris,
elderis and deaconis of the kirk of Edinburgh' or as 'your
wisdomes', 'maist honorabill ministre', 'honorabill sirs, minister,
eldaris and diaconis', 'richt worschiphull minister and eldaris',
'richt venerable minister and eldaris', and the general assembly in
1571 as the 'ryght honorable superintendentis, ministeris
and kirk of God presentlie assembled within this burgh
for reformatione'. By contrast, John Knox addressed the
superintendent of Lothian simply as 'superintendent', without
embellishment.[41] Yet, regardless of individuals' preferences in
employing epithets which seemed appropriate for the circumstances, it surely ought to be placed on record that there is not
one trace in the general assembly's proceedings of any disposition
to accord superintendents a lordly or honorific title, a pattern
consistent with the record of the superintendent of Lothian's
visitations of Canongate, where he received the simple nomenclature of 'superentendent', or 'superentendent of Lowdiane'.
Similarly, the councillors of Ayr and Peebles used the unadorned

[38] St Andrews University Archives, MS SL110.P1 (31.10.1570); SL516
(14.9.1582). I am grateful to Mr Robert N. Smart, Keeper of Muniments, for
providing me with a sample of more than 60 references to Winram.
[39] RStAKS, i, 169, 103.
[40] Ibid., i, 249; SRO, CC8/8/11, Register of Edinburgh Testaments (14 Dec.
1582), fos, 254v–257v.
[41] Bannatyne, Transactions, 32, 72, 100, 103, 306; 84; RStAKS, i, 19, 30, 37, 47,
60, 63.

appellation of 'superintendent'.[42]

In all, it needs admitting that the designations 'my lord', 'dominus superintendens', and 'venerabilis pater' were atypical and not at all representative of reformed ecclesiastical opinion. Indeed, the very variety of styles adopted for superintendents, the disinclination of ecclesiastical courts to accord a superintendent any special or consistent appellation, and the simple fact that a commissioner might also be designated as the 'rycht venerable commissioner of the kirk of God', all suggest that the evidence, adduced from styles of address, for the supposedly 'superior dignity' of the superintendent's title is somewhat strained and unconvincing. Besides, one superintendent, who then saw no need, as superintendent, to resort to fanciful titles, himself spoke plainly in 1564 of 'my brethren the minister of Edinburgh and Superintendent of Glasgo';[43] but, significantly, when promoted to a bishopric, by gift from the queen in 1565, over which the kirk had no say, he found himself addressed, in 1570, by a notary (though not by the kirk) as 'reverendus in Christo pater'.[44] Such a title, of course, was shared with the conforming bishops, among whom one was criticised for departing from the title assigned him at the Reformation as 'over-looker or over-seer' and for resuming his pre-Reformation title of 'bishop', which to a seasoned eye was another example of the sense in which 'proud ambitious men take the name of Bishop'.[45] Expressions conveying the essential brotherhood of the ministry were evidently to be preferred to titles reminiscent of lordly and arrogant dignity.

A similar difficulty, sometimes encountered in distinguishing fact from fiction, is revealed over comprehension of the Book of Discipline's statement that the superintendent was adjudged to be 'most expedient for this time' and accusations of distortion have been, and continue to be, directed[46] (erroneously, as it turns out) against those, including Alexander Petrie in the late seventeenth century, who have rendered the wording in the Book of Discipline as 'most expedient at this time'. Yet simple

[42] *The Buik of the Kirk of the Canagait, 1564–1567*, ed. A. B. Calderwood (Edinburgh, 1961), 16, 24, 32–3, 36, 42, 62, 70; *Ayr Burgh Accounts, 1534–1624*, ed. G. S. Pryde (Edinburgh, 1937), 132; *Charters and Documents relating to the Burgh of Peebles*, ed. W. Chambers (Edinburgh, 1872), 275, 278.
[43] *Wodrow Society Miscellany*, i, 285–6.
[44] SRO, GD112/5/10, Breadalbane Muniments, Protocol Book of Gavin Hamilton, 1.
[45] Knox, *History*, ii, 189.
[46] G. Donaldson, *Scottish Church History*, 93.

reference to the record discloses not disingenuousness on the part of those who have rendered accurately a variant reading of the text,[47] but carelessness by the instigator of the charges.

III

Salaried supervisors:

The salaries assigned to superintendents have proved another fertile area of needless confusion among commentators whose opinions have ranged from expressions of surprise that a parity in stipends was not upheld (unmindful perhaps that parity applied to ministry, not financial recompense) to the peculiarly modern, but no less erroneous, idea that aptitude or 'ability' determined the level of stipend a superintendent or minister received.[48] The reformers themselves, however, were astute enough to avoid either solution; and in the Book of Discipline, conscious of practical realities, they purposely rejected equal stipends 'by reason that the charge and necessitie of all will not be alike'; their reasoning was sound: for 'some will be continuers in one place, some will be compelled to travel, and oft change their dwelling place (if they shall have charge of divers kirkes)'; some would be married with children, others single, so that 'if equall stipends should be appointed to these that in charge should be so unequall, either should the one suffer penurie, or else should the other have superfluitie and too much'.[49] Instead, they proposed equitable stipends to be adjusted on the basis of needs, a step which it proved much harder to achieve.

It may however have been faultering logic on the reformers' part in the Book of Discipline to assign the same level of stipend to all superintendents, regardless of any variation in domestic circumstance or in expenses incurred in the performance of their duties which were just as liable to vary as those of parish ministers. It is by no means unreasonable to consider that the work of a superintendent in Argyll would be markedly more arduous than a superintendent in Lothian. Even the obligation for superintendents to attend meetings of the general assembly in or near Edinburgh imposed an unequal burden and expense in travel. Yet both were to receive a fixed annual salary, recommended in the Book of Discipline as 600 merks (or £400 Scots) plus victual, which, it may be reckoned, was worth at least another £300 allowing for fluctuations in price and local

---

[47] *First Book of Discipline*, 115.
[48] D. Mullen, *Episcopacy in Scotland* (Edinburgh, 1986), 25.
[49] *First Book of Discipline*, 108–9.

variation.[50] Although the component in ilver of the envisaged minimum stipend for ministers was not disclosed in the Book of Discipline, the minimum recommended payment in victual was set at a level which, if converted into cash terms, amounted to no more than a third of the value of victual accorded to superintendents; and, in reality, in the early years few ministers could command a stipend in excess of £100 a year.[51]

Proposals on paper, of course, had to be put into practice; some disparity in stipend among superintendents and a modest adjustment in annual rates of pay, which did ensue, were no doubt unavoidable; and none of the superintendents' salaries, assigned in practice, quite matched the quotas in victual and silver which the Book of Discipline had prescribed. Even the highest-paid superintendent, Angus and the Mearns, fell short of the Book of Discipline's ambitious target: when the victual assigned in stipend was commuted into cash, his salary for Angus only once reached £765 (the recorded payment from the crop of 1561, though his formal election to office is dated early in 1562); in subsequent years he enjoyed a reduced but still handsome competence for his work in Angus.[52] Yet, it did not give him wealth. Nor was the salary strictly comparable with the income which a bishop might expect to acquire from the small see of Brechin which straddled the bounds of the superintendency and yielded over £1,800 a year, in gross (or over £1,200 with the 'third' deducted).[53] No doubt a bishop had potentially many more calls on his resources than a superintendent, who, unlike a bishop, escaped taxation by the crown: a bishop, either of the reformed or unreformed variety, had secular lordship to exercise and patronage to dispense, sizable household establishments and property to maintain; and, of course, there were always others only too ready to spend his income for him.

If the superintendent of Angus managed at the outset to attract what looked like an adequate, even ample, salary for his

---

[50] Ibid., 109–10; *Accounts of the Collectors of Thirds of Benefices, 1561–1572*, ed. G. Donaldson (Edinburgh, 1949) provides the prices which victual fetched in various localities.

[51] *First Book of Discipline*, 109; *Thirds of Benefices*, for calculations of the value of victual, and ibid., 204ff (for stipends); *Register of Ministers, Exhorters and Readers, and of their Stipends, after the period of the Reformation*, ed. A. Macdonald (Edinburgh, 1830).

[52] *Thirds of Benefices*, 95, 128, 131, 213; *Register of Ministers*, 1 (where the increase in the money component in Erskine's stipend for 1567 offset the lesser value which victual fetched; he was also assigned a further £100 for undertaking the visitation of Stormonth and Gowrie outside his superintendency); *Wodrow Society Miscellany*, i, 355.

[53] The calculation is based on the entries in *Thirds of Benefices*, 11, 12, 33, 36, 62, 67–8.

strenuous labours, somewhat less generous financial treatment seems to have been accorded the superintendent of Fife who had to make do, it seems, in 1563 with two chalders of wheat and three of bere, worth perhaps no more than £200, with no hint of any additional payment in cash. His salary, it is true, gradually improved over the years; but, in 1563, it was comparable with John Knox's stipend of some £200 as a parish minister in the capital, and it was less on paper than John Hepburn's (£266 13s 4d, in 1563) as minister in Brechin;[54] and it is tempting to speculate whether his lesser allocation in stipend was connected with his position as a recipient of separate income, in his pre-Reformation capacity, as prior of Portmoak (St Serf's, Lochleven),[55] a dependent cell of St Andrews where he also held office as sub-prior. Some, indeed, may have considered him sufficiently reformed to put such additional (albeit modest) income to appropriate use in service of the kirk. Further south, in Lothian, the superintendent there obtained, as recompense in 1561, assorted victual worth around £200, but he was presumably entitled to claim (though he may not have received) a further £333 in silver which is not recorded. In the far west, nothing whatsoever is known of the superintendent of Argyll's stipend; but in Glasgow, the superintendent for what might be called the mid-west received a salary from the crop of 1563 of £333 6s 8d in silver, plus victual worth a further £340 or thereabouts, which still fell short of the Book of Discipline's target, and, of course, bore little comparison to the archiepiscopal income valued at no less than £4,400 in 1561.[56]

By any appropriate reckoning, a superintendent's salary hardly justifies the epithet of 'princely'. To a peasant, of course, £700, or even £300, a year represented undreamt riches; to the labourer worthy of his hire, a mason, at work, might expect 18s a week, at a time when a minister's lodgings, in chamber mail, could cost 10 merks (£6 13s 4d) a year, and a gunsmith's annual wages, in 1579, could rise to more than £60 (which surpassed some ministers' stipends); but compared to the income from all but the poorest Scottish sees, the sum allotted to a superintendent must have seemed meagre, if not paultry; certainly far from lavish. It also bore some comparison to the fees the crown might

[54] *Thirds of Benefices*, 128, 131, 137, 141, 246 (Winram); 54, 72, 128, 131, 141, 180, 191 (Knox); 232 (Hepburn); *Register of Ministers*, 2 (Knox), 14 (Hepburn).
[55] *Thirds of Benefices*, 12, 33, 40, 242.
[56] Ibid., 54, 61, 67, 72, 128, 130 (Spottiswoode); 128, 131, 137, 261 (Willock); *Medieval Religious Houses Scotland*, edd. I. B. Cowan and D. E. Easson (London, 1976), 202.

pay a keeper of Liddesdale (in 1579). In truth, it represented neither a fortune nor penury but a satisfactory income for a professional man.[57]

Whatever the yardstick used to measure the worth of a superintendent's stipend, it is beyond dispute that the salaries they received were not themselves an attractive enough inducement to persuade the superintendents to remain in office: from 1563 onwards, one superintendent after another asked the general assembly's permission to demit his post.[58] Besides, one superintendent (who had the highest salary) disclosed how he was sometimes obliged to live with friends while conducting visitations, and he later recounted his great expenses incurred in service of the kirk,[59] a remark which may well suggest that the hospitality he received in visitation was less than lavish; certainly less than that which the commendator of Arbroath claimed to dispense to 'grit lordis and utheris strangeris and siclyk the superintendant cumis yeirlie, tuyis or thryis', though the substance of the commendator's comments, in any event, was designed to impress on the government his high level of expenses thereby to secure a reduction in taxation. Again, a second superintendent, by 1576, also claimed to have 'growne grettlie in utheris menis dett and danger'.[60]

By the nature of his office, a superintendent was not confronted by some of the pressures facing bishops of whatever variety, unreformed, conforming or reformed. As a salaried servant, shorn of much episcopal privilege and power, retaining neither church property of his own to administer nor a place in parliament to occupy, the new superintendent lacked the familiar means of exercising local authority which were available for bishops to use. Without the customary symbols of power and

[57] SRO, GD1/413/3, fo. 191 (minister's rent); *Register of the Privy Council of Scotland [RPC]*, 1st ser., edd. J. H. Burton and D. Masson, 14 vols. (Edinburgh, 1877–98), iii, 206 (gunsmith); iii, 252, 347 (Liddesdale).

[58] See below, 230.

[59] BUK, i, 65; *HMC 5th Report*, App., 636. Although Erskine had a lease of property in 1546 from the abbacy of Scone (*HMC 5th Report*, App., 640) and had an interest in the temporality of the bishopric of Brechin (*Registrum Secreti Sigilli Regum Scotorum [RSS]*, edd. M. Livingstone et al., 8 vols. (Edinburgh, 1908–82), v. no. 134), his finances after the Reformation were subject to fluctuation: added to difficulties in securing prompt payment of his stipend were the debts incurred by his son, which 'burdenis me above my awin', for which he sought a loan of £300 from the Countess of Crawford (John Rylands University Library, Manchester, Crawford Muniments, MS 3/1/4, John Erskine of Dun to the Countess of Crawford, n.d.).

[60] National Library of Scotland [NLS], MS Adv. 31.3.1, Books of Assumption, fo. 80r; SRO, GD150/3439/8, Morton Papers (Winram to Douglas of Lochleven, 14 April 1576).

influence which, as landholders, bishops possessed, the superintendent, as such, had neither a distinctive social nor political
leadership to offer which, in certain areas, diminished his scope
for independent action, and underlined the dilemma, which
confronted the kirk, of discovering how exactly a reformed
conception of ministry eschewing traditional patterns of lordship
and dominion could hope to bring about a reformation in
society, still dependent on the mechanisms associated with good
lordship. None of the superintendents, once fully installed in
office, occupied any of the episcopal palaces; and, as a group,
their modest station as preaching supervisors was familiar
enough to contemporaries who well appreciated just how far the
superintendents lacked that social authority enjoyed by diocesan
bishops, and which led the general assembly to lament that not
sufficient respect was accorded superintendents. Indeed, so
ineffectual or misunderstood was their power that even ministers
had to be reminded of their obedience to superintendents.[61] All
in all, the reality of the distinct positions occupied by reformed
bishops and superintendents in local society was abundantly
plain, which only an abstract or academic exercise in semantics,
in which contemporaries occasionally indulged, on the issue of
'episcopus seu superintendens' can contrive to obscure.

The distinctive bounds assigned to superintendents was a
further reminder, if such were needed, of how a reformed
superintendent was not expected to be confused with a diocesan
bishop of either the Catholic or protestant variety. By abandoning
the old diocesan structure, the reformers were certainly able to
assign territory for the superintendents' provinces on a more
rational basis. By delineating fairly well-defined geographical
units, the reformers avoided the old problem of detached
parishes which had afflicted the ancient dioceses of Dunkeld, St
Andrews and Dunblane. To that extent, the new system offered
the prospect of more effective supervision. Yet, by replacing
thirteen dioceses with plans for ten provinces for superintendents,
the Book of Discipline looked like reducing rather than
increasing the manpower available for efficient oversight.[62] In
practice, as only five superintendents were ever appointed, the
work of supervision had also to be undertaken by further
ministers who though usually retaining their congregational
charges were commissioned by the general assemblies to serve
for a spell as overseers for an additional stipend usually between

[61] *BUK*, i, 8; Knox, *Works*, ii, 342, 344; *BUK*, 15, 19, 65–6.
[62] See below, 208.

£100 and £200.[63] Although sometimes popularly (though inaccurately) called 'superintendents',[64] these ministers whom the assembly chose as visitors were correctly, and technically, known as 'commissioners'.

Oversight was thus understood to reside with the whole church which might commission ministers to undertake the superintendence of a region for a period; it was certainly not understood to be restricted to a permanent order or degree of bishops. Besides, the superintendents, who were elected to office for an unspecified period, and the commissioners, appointed for a specific term, normally renewed, were themselves subject to vigilant superintendence from the general assembly which exercised ultimate authority and oversight over those to whom superintendence at a lower level was entrusted. In explaining, how 'now every where throughout the realme commissioners and superintendents' were placed, the general assembly in 1567 actually gave priority to the work of commissioners who, of course, numerically exceeded the original five superintendents; and such was the latitude of one superintendent on the subject of episcopē that he advanced the exceedingly modest claim in 1571 that admission to the ministry lay simply in the hands of 'sic of the ministerie as hes commissione' to examine entrants.[65] Superintendence or inspection was seen to involve nothing more than a simple commission to individual ministers from the wider church, which might be held for a shorter or longer term as the whole church thought fit. It was not then seen to reside exclusively or essentially in a recognised system of bishops. Indeed, the structure which the Scots devised in the 1560s deserves greater credit than it has usually received: it was both practically and theologically uncomplicated and effective.

---

[63] *Thirds of Benefices*, 193, 208, 217, 290; *Wodrow Society Miscellany*, i, 334, 347, 384.

[64] SRO, NP1/11, Protocol Book of James Colvill, fo. 45v ('Mr David Lindsay, minister in Leith, superintendent of the sheriffdom of Ayr', 1572); *BUK*, i, 29; *RSS*, vi, nos. 545, 622, 642, 644, 1034, 1059, 1264, 1275, 1795; *RPC*, ii, 381–2, 659; *The Autobiography and Diary of Mr James Melvill*, ed. R. Pitcairn (Edinburgh, 1842), 47, 50. (One of the five superintendents (Spottiswoode) retained a congregational charge; and, unlike most commissioners who remained parish ministers, at least one commissioner (Pont) appears, for a spell, to have acted as overseer in the north without the responsibility of a particular congregation.)

[65] *BUK*, i, 121; *Spalding Club Miscellany*, iv, 100.

IV

Election to office:

The method by which superintendents were appointed again serves to illustrate dissimilarity with established procedures from the middle ages onward for episcopal election. The Book of Discipline had entrusted nomination of superintendents 'in this present necessity' to the provisional government or their commissioners but had also acknowledged the need for the participation of the 'gentlemen and burgesses' of the province whose presence was required at the superintendent's election in order 'to bring the kirk in some practise of her liberty'. In giving effect to these recommendations, the privy council (as the executive arm of government) ordered the ministers, elders and deacons of Lothian, Fife, Angus and the Mearns, Glasgow and Argyll 'to propone be publict edict certan men' as superintendents, namely, Spottiswoode for Edinburgh, Winram for St Andrews, Erskine of Dun for Brechin, Willock for Glasgow and Carswell for Argyll. At Winram's election in St Andrews on 13 April, 1561, which took place 'according to the ordor provydit in the Buk of Reformacion', the ministers elders and deacons of St Andrews, Perth, Cupar, Crail, Anstruther, Kirkcaldy and Dunfermline had first selected the date and place for the election and had then instructed the earls, lords, barons, burgesses, ministers, elders and others in the area not only to attend but to give their votes. Nor was this considered a mere formality. As voters, they were recognised explicitly to possess the right either 'to consent to the same, or ellis to oppone aganis the lyff and doctrin of the person nominated'.[66]

Similar evidence of the widespread consent which was sought in a superintendent's appointment is forthcoming in Spottiswoode's election to Lothian in March 1561. There the privy council evidently considered itself responsible for having formally 'elected' the superintendent, but Spottiswoode himself, as the new superintendent, revealingly affirmed in the same month that 'be the consent of the kirkis of Lautheane and be the commandement of the nobilitie I am appoyntit superintendent oure the same and *be vertew thareof be the lordis of secreit consale I am straitlie chargeit to visey the kirkis* for establissing of ane uniforme and godlie ordour in the same'.[67] Spottiswoode regarded his commission to act as superintendent as valid and effective, first, because he possessed the approval and support of

---

[66] *First Book of Discipline*, 123ff; *RStAKS*, i, 72–5.
[67] G. Donaldson, *Scottish Reformation*, 226–8 (my italics).

the churches in his province; secondly, because he was so charged and ordered by the 'nobility' (which might signify either the Lords of the Congregation; or the godly great council of the realm, that is, the provisional government which the Lords of the Congregation had established; or, again, the earls and lords of the area who were deemed in the Book of Discipline to have vote in his election); and, thirdly, because, as a consequence of this authorisation so to act, he had received from the privy council endorsement and added authority for effecting a visitation of his province.

All this, no doubt, was consistent with the Book of Discipline's acknowledgment that 'in this present necessity, the nomination, examination and admission of the Superintendent cannot be so straight as we require and as afterwards it must be'. But once immediate needs had been met, and the superintendent's office had been established for three years, the Book of Discipline, in a step which is not without significance, proposed to reform the method of superintendents' election by entrusting power to local communities and by excluding the privy council from any say in future appointments. Nomination of prospective candidates for the job was to reside equally in the kirk session and town council of the chief town of the province and in any individual congregation which wished to make recommendations. After the list of candidates was publicly proclaimed throughout the province, 'all men that have any exception against the persons nominate' were to be invited to voice their objection on the day assigned for examination and election, at which 'the whole ministers of the Province' were expected to assemble, with three or four neighbouring superintendents, and provision was made for ministers to 'bring with them the votes of them that were committed to their care'. The purpose of granting the godly government the initial right (later withheld) of nominating superintendents was explained in the Book of Discipline on account of the urgent need 'that Christ Jesus bee universally once preached throughout this Realme, which shall not suddenly be, unless that by you, men be appointed, and compelled, faithfully to travell in such Provinces as to them shall be assigned'.[68]

The procedures adopted are worth both detailed description and examination, if only to avoid conflated claims that the superintendents 'derived their authority from the civil power' or that they were later to be 'chosen by the clergy of the diocese'.[69]

[68] *First Book of Discipline*, 116, 123–8.
[69] G. Donaldson, *Scottish Reformation*, 137; G. Donaldson, *Scottish Church History*, 69.

In theory and in practice, the form of election was much less restrictive than either of these assessments conveys; and in a further statement on the subject, not previously cited, Spottiswoode expressed his own belief that he was 'chosin by the kirk superintendentt of Lotheane'.[70] The reformers' intention was plainly to ensure, as they themselves explained, that the form of 'election should be the more free'.[71] This being so, a system of congé d'élire, of the sort devised for episcopal appointments in England, was unlikely to be favoured by Scottish reformers in 1561 as their preferred method for a superintendent's appointment.

V

Holders of the office:

The men elected to the superintendent's office were again distinguished by their social origins from many of the men accustomed to be advanced to episcopal office, who were apt, perhaps because of the attractions of episcopal wealth (denied to superintendents) and the operation of a different method of appointment, to be near kinsmen of the nobility. In the selection of superintendents, however, more prominence was accorded ability than birth. To the extent that he was a laird, indeed, 'a barrone of your graces realme'[72] with the distinction of a seat in parliament, Erskine of Dun was certainly conspicuous, and of sufficient standing to marry, first, Elizabeth Lindsay, a younger daughter of the 8th Earl of Crawford, and, then, on her death, a Frenchwoman from Picardy;[73] but far more remarkable than either his social background – which, after all, he shared with some ministers who belonged to the gentry – or even his tenure of the provostship in Montrose, heritable in his family, was the outstanding leadership he provided to protestants in Angus from so early a date which singled him out as the appropriate choice for superintendent of a region he could successfully administer from his house at Dun near Montrose as well as from Brechin.

Although unable to match Erskine's social status, John Winram, superintendent of Fife and Strathearn, was also entitled to sit in parliament (which he did in August 1560) as prior of

---

[70] SRO, GD1/371/1, Warrender Papers, fo. 92r.
[71] *First Book of Discipline*, 126.
[72] *HMC 5th Report*, App., 636.
[73] *The Scots Peerage*, ed. J. B. Paul, 9 vols. (Edinburgh, 1904–14), iii, 27; *Fasti Ecclesiae Scoticanae*, edd. H. Scott *et al*, 10 vols. (Edinburgh, 1915–81), v, 388.

Portmoak, a legacy from his pre-Reformation days.[74] A product of St Leonard's college, St Andrews where he was described as 'pauper' in 1515 and of the Lothian 'nation', Winram was related to the Winrams of Ratho and Gogarmylne; but it was his clerical career as vicar of Dull, sub-prior of the Augustinian house at St Andrews, canon regular and then vicar-general of the archdiocese, participant in the provincial councils of 1549 and, apparently, 1559 which brought him to prominence.[75] He had attended the trial of George Wishart for heresy in 1546, had heard Knox preach his first sermon in 1547, which resulted in a rebuke from his archbishop (for permitting Knox to preach heresy) and in a disputation with Knox; he later witnessed the burning of Adam Wallace in 1550 and Walter Milne in 1558 for heresy.[76]

With remarkable agility, Winram remained long enough within the old church to see the last heretic executed and to attend that church's last provincial council and yet was an early enough convert to the new to attach himself, as a doctor of theology, to 'the new preaching and doctrin of soutteris, tailzeouris, skynneris, baksteris' and others, which he had earlier opposed, to help draft the Confession of Faith and Book of Discipline and to be adjudged by the general assembly in December 1560 as most qualified for 'ministreing and teaching'.[77] It was not for nothing, then, that the abbot of Crossraguel, with a surprising generosity in view of Winram's defection and with some sarcasm, depicted him in 1561 as 'wonderfullie learnit in the New Testament, Auld Testament, and mekle mair'.[78] Whether academic distinction alone as doctor (and indeed dean) of theology would have guaranteed preferment as superintendent may be doubted: it may not be capable of proof but it would be unreasonable to deny that Lord James Stewart, commendator of St Andrews priory, with whom Winram had secured licence to

[74] *The Acts of the Parliaments of Scotland* [*APS*], edd. T. Thomson and C. Innes, 12 vols. (Edinburgh, 1814–75), ii, 525. He also attended parliament in 1567 and 1568, and was present at a convention of estates in 1575 (ibid., iii, 3–4, 46, 84, 89).

[75] *Early Records of the University of St Andrews*, ed. J. M. Anderson (Edinburgh, 1926), 211, 104; SRO, CC8/8/11, Register of Edinburgh Testaments (14 Dec. 1582), fo. 256r; *RMS*, iv, no. 2934; v, no. 1159; *HMC 14th Report*, iii, 86 no. 71; R. Wodrow, *Collections upon the lives of the reformers*, ed. W. J. Duncan, 2 vols. (Glasgow, 1834–48), i, 455; Knox, *Works*, i, 193; *Statutes of the Scottish Church*, 86, 163.

[76] Knox, *Works*, i, 150, 168, 192–3; J. Foxe, *Acts and Monuments*, 8 vols. (London, 1853–70), v, 627–8, 637, 644–5.

[77] R. Lindesay of Pitscottie, *The Historie and Cronicles of Scotland*, ed. A. J. G. Mackay, 3 vols. (Edinburgh, 1899–1911), ii, 142; Knox, *Works*, ii, 128; *BUK*, i, 4.

[78] Knox, *Works*, vi, 167.

visit France in 1550 and whom he accompanied (with archbishop Hamilton) in 1559 on a preaching tour of Fife, was instrumental in securing Winram's appointment as superintendent of Fife.[79]

Others, at any rate, with claims for consideration included a co-author of the Book of Discipline and Confession of Faith, John Douglas, provost of St Mary's college in St Andrews, whom the assembly also considerd qualified in 1560 for ministering and teaching and the Englishman, Christopher Goodman, then minister in St Andrews, a 'greyt freynd' of Lord James Stewart, and once Knox's colleague in Geneva. Douglas, instead, continued to teach in the university but, a decade later, his claims were not forgotten (and, indeed, were evidently considered superior to Winram's) when he was promoted, despite his advanced years, to the archbishopric of St Andrews.[80] Goodman, who shared Knox's distaste for protestant 'lord-like' bishops and his preference for exercising an energetic pastoral ministry, had, of course, no objection to the office of superintendent, and just as Knox had presided at the election of the superintendent of Lothian, so too did Goodman, in the same month, make preparations for Winram's election in Fife.[81]

Once installed as superintendent, Winram at the age of 70 settled down to married life, after taking as his wife in 1562 Margaret Stewart, the legitimised daughter of a pre-Reformation bishop of Moray and widow of John Aytoun of Kinnaldy, and continued to occupy 'the superintendentis chalmer within the abbay of St. Androis'. In fact, he had two residences (though not by virtue of his superintendent's office): as well as his 'duelling hous within the abbay of Sanctandrois', where, as his testament discloses, he had his chamberlain, servants and even an 'undircuik', he had also his 'dwelling hous of Kirknes' at Lochleven. Yet, despite his old age, and the acquisition of a wife, Winram was by no means disposed to tarry in St Andrews and displayed surprising energy and vigour in visiting churches in his province. His services on the kirk's behalf extended over two decades; and after his death (in his ninetieth year) in 1582, at a point when St Andrews had an archbishop who argued the novel concept of bishops by divine right, a tombstone was erected in St Leonard's college kirk to Winram's memory depicting him as 'Fifanorum episcopo' (bishop of the people of Fife), a legend for which

---

[79] RSS, iv, no. 879; Pitscottie, Historie, ii, 142.

[80] BUK, i, 4; Knox, Works, ii, 87; RStAKS, i, 4; CSP Scot., ii, no. 316; Knox, Works, iv, 66–8; vi, 27, 78; D. E. R. Watt, Fasti Ecclesiae Scoticanae Medii Aevi (Edinburgh, 1969), 299, 382.

[81] Knox, Works, vi, 559; CSP Scot., i, no. 554; RStAKS, i, 75.

Winram of course had no responsibility, and in his testament for whose composition he had some say he modestly described himself as 'sumtyme superintendent'. With net assets at his death of £396 13s 4d, he was financially a far poorer man than his colleague, John Douglas, provost of St Mary's college and archbishop of St Andrews, whose net estate at his death in 1574 was valued at £3,925 18s 4d, and who (unlike the superintendent) was accorded the title in his testament of 'the maist reverend father in God'.[82]

In Lothian, where Knox had declined to serve as superintendent, choice fell on John Spottiswoode whose qualification, as a younger son (orphaned at four) of a Berwickshire laird, lay not in his family's pedigree but in his early adherence to the cause of reform and his association with the party which favoured accommodation with England. As a young Glasgow Arts graduate, intent on studying divinity but disturbed by the persecution of heretics, Spottiswoode had left for England, was converted by Archbishop Cranmer, returned home to stay 'a long time' with the Earl of Glencairn, a friend of reform, who introduced him to the Earl of Lennox, a supporter of the English cause, who, in turn, employed Spottiswoode in his negotiations with Henry VIII.[83] When Lennox, in the west, took to arms, at Henry's bidding, in an unsuccessful effort to overthrow the government, Spottiswoode was present at Dumbarton castle, as servitor to Lennox's brother, Robert Stewart, bishop elect of Caithness, who became another exile in England and temporarily lost his bishopric. On receiving a pardon, enabling him to return home, Spottiswoode was already known to Sir James Sandilands of Calder, himself a supporter of George Wishart and 'assured' to the English cause, which had involved him in plans for sacking Arbroath abbey and in imprisonment for his activities in 1544.[84]

[82] *Papal Negotiations with Mary, Queen of Scots*, ed. J. H. Pollen (Edinburgh, 1901), 38; *RMS*, iv, nos. 157, 2934; v, no. 681; D. H. Fleming, *The Reformation in Scotland* (London, 1910), 613; D. Calderwood, *The History of the Kirk of Scotland*, ed. T. Thomson, 8 vols. (Edinburgh, 1842–9), iv, 53); *RStAKS*, i, *frontispiece* (for illustration of Winram's tombstone); SRO, CC8/8/11, Register of Edinburgh Testaments (14 Dec. 1582), fos. 254v–257v [Winram]; CC8/8/3 (14 Feb. 1574/5), fos. 213r–215v [Douglas]; for Winram's wife, Margaret Stewart, see SRO, CC8/8/3, Register of Edinburgh Testaments, fos. 127r–128v, 220v–221r (5 Aug. 1574 and 18 Feb. 1574/5).

[83] *CSP Scot.*, i, no. 967; *Munimenta Alme Universitatis Glasguensis*, ed. C. Innes, 4 vols. (Glasgow, 1854), ii, 160, 167, 286; J. Spottiswoode, *History of the Church of Scotland*, ed. M. Russell, 3 vols. (Edinburgh, 1847–51), ii, 336.

[84] *RSS*, iii, nos. 1758; 399; 2358; *Calendar of Letters and Papers, Foreign and Domestic, Henry VIII*, edd. J. S. Brewer et al., 21 vols. and addenda (London, 1864–1932), XVIII, ii, no. 424; XIX, i, nos. 350, 389; *A Diurnal of Remarkable Occurrents*, ed. T. Thomson (Edinburgh, 1833), 35.

Accepting Sandiland's offer of the parsonage of Calder in West Lothian, Spottiswoode lived sometimes at the laird's home, and, in 1550, as servitor accompanied his son, James Lord St John, also of protestant sympathies, to France as part of Mary of Guise's retinue which included Lord James Stewart, John Winram and the bishop elect of Caithness.[85]

In all, Spottiswoode had been moving in reforming and anglophile circles for a generation before his appointment as superintendent in 1561 when a Catholic controversialist scoffed at how he was 'sa profundlie learnit in the misteriis of the New Testament'; and he was plainly well-placed, when invited in 1560, to offer his ideas on reform by contributing to the Book of Discipline and Confession of Faith. Nor does his history of constancy lend any substance to the claim that 'if indeed a sincere Protestant before 1560, he must have kept his counsel for there is no indication of an earlier outspoken commitment to the cause', a comment which might best be met by simple contradiction.[86] As was the case with not a few ministers, themselves the sons of lairds, Spottiswoode married the daughter of a laird of middling means, Patrick Crichton of Lugton in East Lothian, whose family was later to supply elders and commissioners to the general assembly.[87] Yet, as a superintendent who retained his parish ministry at Mid-Calder (and who found himself described only a decade earlier by the less than prestigous title of servitor), Spottiswoode may have felt himself somewhat disadvantaged by Knox, who occupied the pulpit of St Giles in the capital, had inaugurated him to his superintendency, had authority to call general assemblies, was prepared to act as a visitor (with duties of a temporary superintendent), and, of course, had the ear of the English ambassador, who in all his despatches during Mary's personal rule seems only once to have alluded to Spottiswoode (and even then only in the context of Knox's activities, without so much as mentioning his name) when he remarked in 1562 how 'Mr Knox with the superintendent of Lodian is ridden to the west'. Such, indeed, was Knox's prestige that some mistook him for superintendent of Edinburgh.[88]

In the west itself, the reformers' choice as superintendent of

[85] Knox, *Works*, i, 139, 142; *Diurnal of Occurrents*, 41–2; Spottiswoode, *History*, ii, 336; *RSS*, iv, no. 882; Spottiswoode, *History*, ii, 336 *RSS*, iv, no. 882.

[86] Knox, *Works*, vi, 167; D. Mullen, *Episcopacy in Scotland*, 22.

[87] J. Kirk, *The Second Book of Discipline* (Edinburgh, 1980), 262–3.

[88] *RSS*, iii, no. 2358; *CSP Scot.*, i, no. 1136; *Peebles Charters and Documents*, 275. (Knox's name also took precedence over Spottiswoode's in the decree granting the Earl of Eglinton's divorce in 1562: W. Fraser, *Memorials of the Montgomeries*, 2 vols. (Edinburgh, 1859), ii, 185.)

Glasgow, John Willock, was a man of modest origin, like Winram, but whereas Winram had attained some prominence by pursuing a clerical career Willock had gained notoriety as a renegade Dominican friar in Ayr, driven from Scotland for heresy, who sought sanctuary in the south by 1539 as a curate in London, chantry priest in Somerset, chaplain to the Marquis of Dorset in Edward VI's reign, a Master of Arts, who had visited Oxford and was 'well skilled in Greek and Latin', and a follower of Bullinger's doctrines, who gained the wealthy parsonage of Loughborough yet, by the early 1550s, was preaching in the Scottish border country, joined the Marian exiles and returned twice to Scotland from Emden in 1555 and 1558 to preach in Dundee, Edinburgh, Ayr and elsewhere.[89] Though again absent for a spell in 1559, Willock could count on support from the Earl of Glencairn (with whom he was associated in 1559 and who may have been influential in securing his appointment to Glasgow), and presumably from Châtelherault, though he was hardly likely to have obtained unqualified approval from either Argyll or Lord James Stewart whom he had earlier accused of inconstancy. His undoubted leadership, however, was duly attested in his contributions to the Book of Discipline and Confession of Faith and in contemporary comment which variously depicted him as 'Primat of thair religioun' and, less flatteringly, as the man who pulled the plough which Knox steered.[90]

Although he was nominated in March 1561, Willock's final election as superintendent of Glasgow and the west did not take place until September, when Châtelherault, Arran, Glencairn and Lords Ruthven, Boyd and Ochiltree gave their attendance; but, as early as August 1560, he had been appointed to preach in Glasgow and by the summer of 1561 had engaged in a public disputation there with a Dominican friar, John Black. Far from disdaining, as has been claimed, 'any controversialist of lower rank than the archbishop of St Andrews', Willock undertook debates with the masters of Linlithgow and Glasgow grammar schools, though he failed to keep his appointment for a disputation with the abbot of Crossraguel.[91] His abode in Glasgow by August 1560 is confirmed by the chamberlain to the

[89] *Calendar of Patent Rolls, Edward VI*, 5 vols. (London, 1924–7), i, 183; iv, 17; Knox, *Works*, vi, p.xxviii; D. Shaw, 'John Willock', in *Reformation and Revolution*, ed. D. Shaw (Edinburgh, 1967), 42–69.

[90] Knox, *Works*, i, 342–3; ii, 128; *Wodrow Society Miscellany*, i, 267; *Satirical Poems of the time of the Reformation*, ed. J. Cranstoun, 2 vols. (Edinburgh, 1891–3), i, 337.

[91] *CSP Scot.*, i, nos. 967, 1023; 891; G. Donaldson, *Scottish Reformation*, 126; J. Leslie, *The History of Scotland*, ed. T. Thomson (Edinburgh, 1830), 295; *Wodrow Society Miscellany*, i, 264–77.

Catholic archbishop of Glasgow who imagined, mistakenly, that with his installation in Glasgow as preacher, presumably in the cathedral, his residence in the dean's house, and an allowance, supposedly £1,000 (no longer verifiable), from the archbishopric, 'Johne Willokis is maid Bischop of Glasquo, now in zour Lordschipis absens, and placit in zour place of Glasquo'. But to the abbot of Crossraguel, Willock in 1561 was merely one of 'thar pestilent Precheouris'. Once settled at Glasgow, Willock, who was already married, made arrangements in 1560 for bringing his wife, Catherine, north from England.[92] As superintendent, he is on record as once receiving the hospitality reserved for important personalities and 'other great men', presumably during his visitation, from the magistrates of Ayr in 1561, but the inference that he was eligible for entertainment only because he was superintendent ignores the evidence that as a preacher he had earlier obtained the town's customary hospitality in 1559; and Knox, too, is on record as a recipient of the burgh's hospitality in 1562.[93]

In the far west, where Archibald 5th Earl of Argyll had identified himself with the party of reform and with the work of the Congregation, it was no doubt appropriate that his own protégé, John Carswell, emerged as superintendent of Argyll. As was the case with Winram and Willock, Carswell came not from a prominent or wealthy family but from one which was inconspicuous and of modest means. But he secured sufficient schooling to enable him in 1540 to enter St Andrews university where, as a poor student, he graduated in 1544, equipped to embark on a clerical career, first, as a notary public in the diocese of the Isles, and later as treasurer of Lismore and parson of Kilmartin where the Campbell keep of Carnassery castle was situated and whose custody, with some lands, he obtained from his patron, the Earl of Argyll, in 1559. Although no date for Carswell's election as superintendent has been traced, he was active in that capacity in the early 1560s; and it is scarcely open to doubt that Argyll was responsible for securing his appointment.[94]

VI

The work of watchmen:

The duties entrusted to the superintendents in the Book of Discipline of preaching, visiting congregations and appointing ministers and readers in the parishes were gradually amplified, or

---

[92] Keith, *History*, iii, 7n., 10; Knox, *Works*, vi, 165; *Diurnal of Occurrents*, 281.
[93] *Ayr Burgh Accounts*, 30, 132, 134.
[94] See below, 290–1.

at least clarified, once the five superintendents set about their work. That they played a principal part in the examination, admission and deposition of ministers and readers need hardly be doubted; and, indeed, when a minister proceeded to depose the reader of an adjacent parish on the basis of unfounded accusations, he was duly rebuked by his superintendent in 1563 for exceeding his office.[95] Although kirk sessions had previously acquired a competence to determine actions for divorce,[96] the general assembly in 1562 sought to restrict judgment in cases of divorce to the superintendents and to those from whom they had received a 'speciall commissioun', evidently as a temporary measure, until such time as secular judges were appointed (which occurred in 1564).[97]

Of more lasting significance was the superintendent's duty, defined by the assembly in 1562, to convene synods twice yearly, though, by 1563, the rôle assigned him in the selection of commissioners to the general assembly (which required his own presence at its meetings) was merely to 'warn' the shires, towns and parish kirks to send their representatives, and to ensure his own attendance.[98] By 1563, the assembly also held superintendents responsible for ensuring that churches were repaired, that books were censored before publication, that burials were conducted in proper form, and that ministers and readers obtained stipend, manse and glebe.[99] Then, too, it was envisaged that superintendents might be authorised to give collation to candidates presented to benefices, which, despite the reformers' intention of dissolving them, still remained in being; and, in 1565, the assembly reiterated its claim that persons presented to benefices should be examined 'be the judgement of learned men of the kirk, sick as presentlie are the superintendentis appointed therto'.[100] As a consequence, when the assembly's claim was recognised by the crown in 1566, and by parliament in 1567, presentations to the lesser benefices were directed to superintendents or other commissioners of the general assembly.[101] At that

---

[95] RStAKS, i, 75–6, 82ff, 84; BUK, i, 15–16; Calderwood, History, ii, 208; RStAKS, i, 175–6.
[96] J. Riddell, Scottish Peerages and Consistorial Law, 2 vols. (Edinburgh, 1842), i, 392, 443; RStAKS, i, 19–27, 37–41, 49–53, 59–60.
[97] BUK, i, 30; Selections from the Records of the Kirk Session, Presbytery, and Synod of Aberdeen, ed. J. Stuart (Aberdeen, 1846), 11; BUK, i, 19, 23, 34; cf., SRO, GD1/371/1, Warrender Papers, fo. 95r.
[98] BUK, i, 29, 36.
[99] Ibid., i, 34, 35, 40–1, 43.
[100] Ibid., i, 34, 70.
[101] RPC, i, 487–8; APS, iii, 23; RSS, vi, nos. 82, 95, 108, 112–13 et seq.; SRO, CS7/42, Register of Acts and Decreets, vol. 42, fos. 299r, 361v, 395r.

point, too, parliament affirmed the right of superintendents and other 'visitors' of the kirk to examine all teachers in schools and universities, a function which the assembly had wished to see superintendents exercise from at least as early as 1565.[102] None of these specific duties, however, was evidently understood significantly to augment the powers of superintendents; and when, much later, the question was canvassed whether or not superintendents' powers should be enlarged, the assembly determined in 1570 that the extent of a superintendent's jurisdiction was that originally defined in the Book of Discipline to which, as the assembly reiterated in 1571 perhaps to underline the point, superintendents remained 'subject'.[103]

The superintendent, then, had certainly his part to play in disciplinary proceedings both within the structure of ecclesiastical courts and within areas where a reformed system of discipline had not been fully established; but the claim, initially advanced by Archbishop Spottiswoode and too hastily accepted by some subsequent commentators, that, in the 1560s, as the church's highest censure, excommunication, could be authorised only by a superintendent is not supported, but rather contradicted, by the surviving evidence.[104] Calvin, of course, had criticised entrusting excommunication 'to single pastors' and had commended 'calling in others to deliberate with him' before passing the sentence; and in Scotland, where the Book of Discipline had approved that excommunication should proceed 'by the mouth of the minister, with the consent of the Ministry and commandement of the Kirk', the sentence in practice was determined by the 'ministerie' of the kirk session (the 'minister eldaris and diaconis of Cristis kyrk and congregacion'), acting on behalf of the congregation, and delivered publicly by the minister before the whole congregation.[105] In all of this, the superintendent's participation (however desirable) was not considered essential. Not only did St Andrews kirk session pass sentence of excommunication in 1564, when Christopher Goodman was minister, and again in 1566, when it was expressly affirmed that the minister and elders, and not the superintendent, were the

---

[102] APS, iii, 24, 38; BUK, i, 108; RPC, i, 535, cf., 675; BUK, i, 60; Knox, Works, ii, 458–61.

[103] BUK, i, 179, 195.

[104] Spottiswoode, History, ii, 167; G. Donaldson, Scottish Reformation, 123–4.

[105] J. Calvin, Letters, ed. J. Bonnet, 3 vols. (Edinburgh, 1855–7), iii, 67; First Book of Discipline, 170; RStAKS, i, 202–5. Zwingli had also recognised that pronouncing excommunication belonged not to any individual, whether pope or bishop, but to the church or congregation (W. P. Stephens, The Theology of Huldrych Zwingli (Oxford, 1986), 271–4).

competent authority, but the general assembly itself in 1565 had plainly distinguished between 'townes wher ordour is established' and 'kirks reformed without the superintendent', on the one hand, where the kirk session was considered the appropriate agent for resolving cases which might result in excommunication, and, on the other, rural areas without strict disciplinary machinery where the superintendent, 'with advyce of the nixt reformit kirk' might pronounce the sentence on unrepentant offenders.[106]

That this is a correct understanding of the assembly's act which one writer has considered 'confused' is supported by the definition of the act offered in the Order of Excommunication of 1569 (a revised version of Knox's original draft of 1563) which recognised that 'reformed townis and uther places where the Ministerie is planted with Minister and Eldaris' might determine cases involving excommunication and repentance without re-course to the superintendent; and elsewhere the Order affirmed that either the 'Sessioun or Superintendent' might command a minister to proceed by stages to pass the sentence.[107] Besides, the general assembly, which in 1567, had found no fault with 'the brethren of the kirk of Machlen' who had excommunicated a former elder of their kirk, itself proceeded, in 1569, to instruct 'superintendents or ministers to proceid to excommunicatioun' against contumacious offenders guilty of capital crimes.[108] Again, when the question arose in 1571 of whether superinten-dents alone or all ministers, even in rural areas, might pronounce excommunication, the assembly gave the consistent reply that only in cases where ministers were unaccustomed to pronounce the sentence should the superintendent 'or some uther sufficientlie qualified and authorized' undertake to execute the censure.[109] Little mystery, therefore, need surround the church's attitude on this issue.

In contrast to an episcopal system where, as Richard Hooker observed, the power to excommunicate normally resided in a bishop, and not as puritans contended in the hands of many,[110] the Scottish solution in the 1560s was to authorise any minister and established kirk session, practising effective discipline, to exercise collectively the church's highest censure. Indeed, after

[106] RStAKS, i, 203–5, 266–76; BUK, i, 74–5.
[107] G. Donaldson, Scottish Reformation, 123; BUK, i, 37; Calderwood, History, viii, 173; Knox, Works, vi, 449–70.
[108] BUK, i, 98–9, 145.
[109] Ibid., i, 195.
[110] R. Hooker, Of the Laws of Ecclesiastical Polity, VII, xiv, 13 (in R. Hooker, Works, ed. I. Walton, 2 vols. (Oxford, 1865), ii, 405–6).

1572, when the church acquired what has been described, not inappropriately, as an 'effete episcopacy',[111] an effort was made in 1573 to restrict sentences of excommunication to those which had the assent of bishops, superintendents or commissioners[112] (as was later to recur under the episcopal regime of 1610[113]), a decision which, when challenged in 1573, was justified in the belief that some earlier excommunications had lacked 'due order of law'.[114] But if such a restriction were enforced after 1573, it did not endure; and by 1576 the assembly merely required ministers 'that *unadvisedly* they proceed not to excommunicat; and if difficultie arise herein that the Visiter and the rest of the countrie be advised with; and sicklyk in absolution'.[115] This resolution, in turn, prepared the way for the Second Book of Discipline's renewed emphasis in 1578 on excommunication as a function of the eldership.[116]

As one who was 'called to that office as ane watcheman over hys [Christ's] flok', the superintendent had broadly similar disciplinary duties to perform over a wider area to those exercised by a minister and kirk session over a congregation where 'the face of ane perfyt reformed kyrk' had been established and who, therefore, appropriately also considered themselves to be 'called as watchemen ower his flok'.[117] The wider jurisdiction entrusted to superintendents no doubt entailed the assignment to them of wider powers than those enjoyed by parish ministers; but it would be difficult to determine any function performed by a superintendent which could not also be undertaken by another minister who received a short-term commission from the general assembly to that effect. Nor was this all. The subordination of ministers to superintendents, which the assembly felt obliged to remind forgetful ministers on more than one occasion, was complemented by the subordination of superintendents to ministers in a manner which has not adequately been recognised and which might be hard to reconcile with what is generally accepted as the principles of episcopal government.[118]

A superintendent had not only to renounce lordship and dominion over the ministry and promise obedience to the order prescribed in the Book of Discipline, but had to submit himself

---

[111] P. Collinson, *The Elizabethan Puritan Movement* (London, 1967), 110.
[112] *BUK*, i, 272.
[113] Ibid., iii, 1105; Calderwood, *History*, vii, 100, 167.
[114] *BUK*, i, 284.
[115] Ibid., i, 358 (my italics).
[116] *Second Book of Discipline*, 200.
[117] *RStAKS*, i, 167; cf., Knox, *Works*, ii, 147, 149, 203, 274, 311.
[118] *BUK*, i, 15, 29, 65–6.

to correction by the ministers and elders not just of his principal town but of his whole province;[119] he was held accountable to the church's conciliar government, and was especially subordinate to the general assembly which rigorously reviewed each superintendent's performance and praised critics for registering their complaints. The device adopted was for the assembly at every meeting to remove the superintendents, in turn, and in their absence to invite criticism from the ministers and others present. Indeed, such was the significance attached to this procedure for censure and correction to which the superintendents were obliged to submit themselves that the matter was given priority over all other business facing the assembly (an action which could conceivably be construed as a comment on the 'superior dignity' and greater 'honour than ordinary ministers',[120] which one writer has accorded superintendents).

As early as 1562, the assembly had decided that congregations should be made aware of the practice to which all 'superintendents, ministers, elders, and deacons doe willingly subject themselves to discipline; and if any man have any thing to lay justly to thair charge, that they doe the same at the next Assembly'. Even so late as 1573 the assembly still considered it appropriate to circulate to all ministers 'the extracts of the Superintendent's office registred in the Book of Discipline' so that 'the Superintendents may be tryed thereby' and as they were 'found dilligent, to be continued or changed'.[121] At every level, a superintendent was liable to find his actions scrutinised in a manner designed to obviate any prospect that he might succumb to the temptation, which the Book of Discipline had castigated, of seeking 'to live as your idle Bishops have done heretofore'.[122]

In one instance, a superintendent in 1561 readily submitted to the jurisdiction of his kirk session which he had empowered, presumably as his court, to give judgment in an action he brought before it for determination. In other cases, superintendents' complaints against ministers were themselves referred by the assembly for resolution in 1563 and 1565 to a group of ministers or university teachers. A similar arrangement of setting up a committee of ministers and teachers was used to investigate complaints against a superintendent in 1567 and instructions were issued to 'all ministers, elders and deacons of kirks' within

[119] Knox, *Works*, ii, 207.
[120] G. Donaldson, 'The Polity of the Scottish Church, 1560–1600', *Records of the Scottish Church History Society* [*RSCHS*], xi (1955), 212–26, at 215; G. Donaldson, *Scottish Church History*, 69.
[121] *BUK*, i, 14, 266.
[122] *First Book of Discipline*, 122.

the superintendent's province to voice their grievances at an inquiry to be held in Cupar.[123] Final authority in the church plainly lay not with superintendents; and it was consistent with the kirk's efforts to balance individual initiative within a framework of conciliar government that the assembly should establish in 1563 a procedure for appeals from kirk session through superintendent and synod to general assembly. Indeed, as befitted such system of representative government, the introduction of an appellate jurisdiction seems to have worked effectively in appeals to church courts against superintendents' decisions; and it guarded against vesting undue authority in individual overseers.[124]

VII

Collegiality and conciliar government:

Accountable to the graded series of ecclesiastical courts, the superintendents were expected to act, wherever practicable, with the consent of their brethren. The Book of Discipline had no doubt pointed the way when it assigned to 'the best reformed Church, to wit, the Church of the Superintendent with his councell' the right of presenting a candidate to a parish whose congregation had been negligent in electing its minister. In practice, the machinery established provided a fair measure of consultation and deliberation. Where a superintendent encountered a disobedient minister or reader, the assembly resolved in 1565 that 'some of the neerest discreit ministers' should take part in the trial. Earlier, in 1562, the assembly had expected 'every superintendent, with the ministers and elders within his dyocie', presumably at a meeting of synod, 'to note the offences and crymes that they know', in order that a remedy might be had. At that point, too, it required the examination of serving ministers to take place in the presence of 'the superintendent and of the best reformed kirk' located nearest the parish whose minister was due for 'trial', to enable 'the judgement of the best learned' to be had in both 'the examination and admission', and it empowered superintendents 'with consent of the maist pairt of the elders and ministers of kirks', at meetings of synods to translate ministers from one parish to another.[125]

The insistence that superintendents consult and deliberate with their fellow ministers was again underlined in 1571 when the assembly ordered all superintendents, 'with the advyse of their

---

[123] *RStAKS*, i, 83–9; *BUK*, i, 36, 73; 113.
[124] *BUK*, i, 32–3, cf., 158, 264; *RStAKS*, i, 334–5.
[125] *First Book of Discipline*, 96; *BUK*, i, 65; 14, 15, 29.

ministers' in synods to admit ministers to vacant charges, appoint fast days and seek reconciliation among the nobility, and the practice that superintendents and commissioners admit ministers to benefices 'be advice of a certain number of Ministers nixt adjacent' was recognised once more in 1572. Similarly, as early as 1564, the assembly decided to remit certain questions placed before it to the provinces for resolution by the superintendents 'with ane certain number of the ministers', who were then to report their answers to the next assembly. Again, in 1571, it proposed that questions submitted from the provinces ought more properly to be determined by superintendents or commissioners 'with the assistance of their Ministers' in synods.[126] The assembly also considered it appropriate in 1571 that all superintendents and commissioners, 'with such as they shall choose in their Synodall conventiones' should scrutinise the accounts of the collectors of the thirds of benefices, and have collective power to appoint and dismiss collectors. Besides, in pronouncing sentence on stubborn offenders, superintendents were required by the assembly in 1565 to act 'with advyce of the nixt reformit kirk', and either a superintendent or 'nixt reformed kirk' was considered an appropriate agency by the assembly for administering the relevant ecclesiastical censure in cases of murder (in 1568), and of other capital crimes including adultery (in 1569).[127]

Clearly, no superintendent was left unaware of the importance attached to acting with 'the advice of ministers and elders who ought to be his counsellors'. One superintendent, indeed, found himself censured in the assembly of 1572 for his failure 'in so far as he consulted not with the Ministers and Elders touching things to be reformed'; and the same superintendent who, in the following assembly, was judged 'to have done wrong' in refusing a reader collation had his actions reviewed by 'the Ministers, elders and deacons of the congregation of Sanct Andrews', whom the assembly empowered to investigate the reader's complaints.[128] Consistent with the reformers' disinclination to entrust individuals with powers which were better shared, the assembly ordered superintendents and other overseers in 1574 neither to grant collation to benefices nor admit ministers 'without the assistance of thrie of thair qualified Ministers'; and earlier the preference for collective action was again evident in selecting a colleague and successor for Knox in Edinburgh,

[126] *BUK*, i, 193–4, 241; 32; 191–2.
[127] Ibid., i, 178; 75; 124–5, 144–5.
[128] Ibid., i, 195; 237, 264.

where the superintendent was instructed by the assembly, in 1572, to act 'with so many Ministers of the province as he should choose, with advice also of Mr Knox and the Session of the Kirk of Edinburgh'.[129]

The subordination of superintendents to the merciless scrutiny of the assembly and the requirement that they worked, where appropriate, with the approval of their brethren were not the only methods adopted for ensuring that superintendents remained vigilant and accountable. In 1564, the assembly decided to make the superintendents visitors of one another's provinces; and from at least as early as 1562 the assembly had chosen ministers as visitors to help superintendents fulfil their duties.[130] At that point, too, no further appointment to the office of superintendent, beyond the original five, was made; and although the full complement of ten was still sought, the assembly remained sufficiently ambivalent in its attitude toward nominees to fill the vacancies that, in 1562, it questioned the propriety of appointing a superintendent in Galloway and sought guidance from the kirks of Galloway 'whither they required any superintendent or not'.[131] Such an attitude almost suggests that the assembly then regarded the office as expendable, to be adopted or declined as regional requirements demanded, especially where an overseer or commissioner was already at work in the area, which might be held to render the appointment of a superintendent super-fluous.[132] It is true that, in 1567, it was still expected that 'superintendentis be appointit quhair neid requiris'; but as late as 1571 when Caithness (with its conforming protestant 'bishop') asked for 'a superintendent or commissioner', the assembly's response was simply to assign to the area yet another commissioner.[133]

Plainly, flexibility was a keynote of the assembly's attitude toward regional oversight – a flexibility, indeed, which was implicit in the claim in 1565 that ministers should be admitted to benefices by 'the Superintendents and Overseers', other ministers, that is, whom the assembly had authorised so to act. This expedient, indeed, was recognised both by the crown, which afterwards directed presentations indeterminately to superintendents or commissioners, and by the privy council, which required 'the Kirk, Ministery, and Superintendentis', in

[129] Ibid., i, 294; 245; cf., Bannatyne, *Transactions*, 386–7.
[130] Ibid., i, 54; 17, 54, 113; *CSP Scot.*, i, no. 1132.
[131] *BUK*, i, 53–4; 15.
[132] See below, 229–30.
[133] *APS*, iii, 37; *BUK*, i, 189–90.

1571, to admit a candidate to the parsonage of Glasgow. Yet the adaptability displayed was tempered by the assembly's recognition that too great powers ought not to be committed to too few; hence its resolve to choose from 1563 onward an elected moderator (and not the superintendents who were merely eligible for election with the rest) to preside at its meetings. This satisfied the need for order without sacrificing ministerial parity at the highest level by placing one individual permanently above his brethren.[134] Nor was this all.

The assembly also introduced the device of providing assessors to act with superintendents in resolving particular matters: the superintendent and ministry of St Andrews were assisted in 1566 by 'assessoris' or 'collegis, commissaris deput be the Generall Kyrk'; the assembly in 1570 commended 'the assistance of such assessors' as the superintendents and commissioners should select to set the yearly price of victual; and the Order of Excommunication in 1569, a revision of that in 1563, referred to what seems to have been accepted practice when it assigned some offenders for trial by 'the Superintendent and his assessors' in the chief town of the province. The device of assessors, later adopted by the assembly for preparing its own agenda, was thus applicable to the work of superintendents. Even after the demise of superintendents, the merits of the scheme ensured that the practice of associating assessors with visitors was continued by the assembly which ordered all synods, by 1580, to name 'certaine Assessours' to assist commissioners of provinces 'in all weightie and great matters'.[135] Collective responsibility taken by courts and committees seemed to the assembly to be preferable to placing excessive reliance on the judgment of a single individual.

Further testimony, if such were needed, of the reformers' emphasis on collegiality is forthcoming from the remarkable register of St Andrews kirk session, which claimed to exhibit 'the face of ane perfyt reformed kirk', and which also contains the record of the superintendent's council or court, where cases were heard and determined, and judgments issued on matters affecting either parish or province by the superintendent, minister, elders and (sometimes) deacons – 'the holl ministerie'. Both session and

[134] Knox, *Works*, ii, 485 (which Knox claims is an accurate rendering; *BUK*, i, 59 differs); *RPC*, ii, 80; cf., i, 487–8; *BUK*, i, 38; cf., A. C. Cochrane, *Reformed Confessions of the 16th Century* (London, 1966), 155, 212, 274; J. Calvin, *Commentaries on . . . Titus*, ed. D. W. & T. F. Torrance (Edinburgh, 1964), 359 (Titus I, 7).

[135] *RStAKS*, i, 257; *BUK*, i, 161; Knox, *Works*, vi, 450; *BUK*, ii, 460; cf., 441, 456.

superintendent had their seals, and summonses issued either by
superintendent or session. After a case was heard, a decision was
made frequently by superintendent and session acting together[136]
('the Superintendent and ministerie'; 'Superintendent, minister
and eldaris'; the 'holl session of Superintendent and ministerie';
'Superintendent and seat', 'Superintendent and assemblie'), or by
the superintendent, with the advice of the session,[137] (with 'the
consall and sentement of the ministerie of Sanctandrois'; 'wyth
the avyis of the holl ministerie'; 'wyth his consall beand heirwyth
avysed') or by the session itself ('the ministerie being convenit in
thar sessione'; 'the seat'; 'the sessioun') in the superintendent's
absence.[138]

Only in comparatively few cases is the superintendent on
record as taking cognisance, without mention of his court's
assistance,[139] in matters such as matrimonial causes, where
he possessed a particular but not exclusive competence. Even
here, the omission, in these instances, of the court's advice may
be attributed simply to scribal idiocyncrasies, an impression
strengthened by the fact that further entries to the same cases
often disclose that the court's advice was indeed sought.[140] But
none of this ought to obscure the essential truth that matrimonial
cases were heard by the superintendent in the presence of the
other members of the court, and that this court or session by
itself, in the superintendent's absence, had also a competence to
determine a range of matrimonial causes: divorce, contracts and
promise of marriage, impediments to matrimony, the solemnisa-
tion of marriage, cohabitation and adultery.[141] It is therefore
plainly an over-simplification, and possibly an error, to suggest
that the exercise of this consistorial jurisdiction was vested in
superintendents alone. Here as elsewhere, the conciliar emphasis
in reaching conclusions is all too apparent.

Apart from hearing matrimonial suits, this, too, was the court

---

[136] *RStAKS*, i, 75, 123, 202–5; 148, 200–1, 264, 283, 287 (seals); 1, 75, 101, 104,
123, 133, 135–6, 138–9, 141–2, 145, 151–6, 168–9, 173, 176–8, 182, 184, 186,
192–3, 210, 229–30, 233, 235–8, 240, 272, 284, 294, 298, 303, 307–9, 313–14, 316,
318–20, 329, 335, 337–8, 343.

[137] Ibid., i, 77, 110, 131, 140, 143, 145–6, 151, 183–4, 188–90, 221, 231, 233,
251–4, 277, 308, 315, 318–19, 343.

[138] Ibid., i, 87, 141, 149, 185, 195, 201–6, 213, 219–21, 224, 232, 266, 309–13,
322–4, 330, 337.

[139] Ibid., i, 128, 139–40, 148–9, 155, 158–68, 172, 179–82, 184–6, 188–9, 193,
207ff, 222, 234–5, 243–4, 246–9, 252, 256–7, 278–84, 285–93, 295, 301, 328, 331,
336–8.

[140] Ibid., i, 129–31, 140, 154–5, 210, 235–8, 252–4, 284, 293.

[141] Ibid., i, 141, 213, 224, 232, 330, 337; *Buik of the Kirk of the Canagait*, 6–7,
12, 15–18, 20, 28–30, 34, 36–8, 40, 44, 46–7, 55–6, 63–4, 67, 77, 79.

which heard the more serious disciplinary cases, encountered by a superintendent on his visitations, which he had remitted to the chief town of his province for collective determination. Only with the approval of this (or a higher) court, it would seem, was a superintendent empowered to depose a minister or reader; and even during visitations a superintendent was expected to hear disciplinary cases not by himself as sole judge but, wherever possible, in association with the minister and session of the parish or, failing this, with the nearest reformed kirk.[142] Corporate action and conciliar government were clearly the approved method of procedure. At every stage, the work of overseers – superintendents, commissioners and visitors – was carefully subordinated to the graduated series of representative courts, so familiar a feature of the Calvinist system.

In conducting visitations, a superintendent was sometimes assigned assistance from a minister whom the assembly selected as visitor: thus, in 1562, the assembly appointed a minister to assist the superintendent of Glasgow for a spell in overseeing his province, which, incidentally, serves as an example of how authority to make such appointments lay not with individual superintendents (as in an episcopal system) but was understood to reside collectively in the general assembly, which also recruited the superintendent of Angus with two ministers as his 'associats' to visit Aberdeen and Banff; similarly Knox was assigned by the assembly to help the superintendent of Lothian visit the area from Stirling to Berwick in 1567. Nor was Erskine of Dun the only superintendent to receive from the assembly a commission of visitation beyond his own bounds: the super-intendent of Glasgow in 1563 was commissioned to visit Nithsdale for a year. Added to this, the assembly arranged in 1571 for the books of visitation kept by superintendents to be reviewed regularly by ministers and others who attended its meetings.[143] Sometimes, too, it was the turn of the superintendent to assist the ministry: in 1570, at St Andrews, 'the sessioun, wytht avis of the Superintendent', resolved the problem of its aged minister; and much earlier, in 1562, the assembly had commissioned John Knox with some of his elders and deacons, and not the superintendent of Lothian (whose duties extended to the Merse), to investigate the delinquency of the minister of Jedburgh (where no superintendent had been provided), who was sentenced by Knox, 'with advyce of the Kirk of Edinburgh,

[142] Ibid., i, 145–6; 172, 175–6, 189; BUK, i, 195; 75; Buik of the Kirk of the Canagait, 16, 24, 32–3, 36, 62, 70.
[143] BUK, i, 17, 19, 113; 35; 184, 237–8, 256–7.

superintendent of Lowthiane and collegues', to be deposed from the ministry and to be excommunicated from the church he had sought to serve.[144]

In this context, too, it was apt, no doubt, that the kirk should resolutely abandon the language of the pre-Reformation church (retained in England) which distinguished the higher from the inferior clergy. Modern writers, therefore, who transfer the old phraseology of 'inferior clergy' to depict the reformed ministry under a superintendent's care are in danger of imposing not only language which the reformers rejected but, with it, assumptions alien to their thought.[145] Nor will it suffice to restrict application of 'chief ministers' or 'chiefest workmen', two phrases which they did employ, solely to superintendents. The Book of Discipline, it is true, had spoken of the rôle of 'learned ministers' in examining entrants to the ministry and that of the 'chief minister' (or presiding minister) who declared a candidate admitted to his charge. There, too, in the section on the election of ministers, the Book of Discipline had recommended assigning to the 'chiefest workmen, not onlie townes to remaine in, but also provinces that by their faithfull labours churches may be erected and order established where none is now'. Similarly, at his election as superintendent of Fife in 1561, John Winram was acknowledged one of the 'cheef ministeris', an accurate enough description.[146]

Yet both before and after the election of superintendents, ordinary ministers were also eligible to receive the epithet: in July 1560, 'the maist pairt of the cheif Ministeris of the Realm' had congregated in Edinburgh; in the Form and Order for the Election of Superintendents of 1561 the 'cheif Minister' (again in the sense of presiding minister), was instructed to pronounce the benediction after 'the rest of the Ministers, if ony be, and the Elders of the Kirk' had extended the right hand of fellowship to the entrant; in 1564 the assembly considered the presence of

---

[144] *RStAKS*, i, 334; *BUK* i, 29, 31; Knox, *Works*, ii, 364–5.

[145] G. Donaldson, *Reformed By Bishops* (Edinburgh, 1987), ix. A rare survival of the phraseology (employed not by a reformed minister but by a clerk of chancery) occurs at a point when, without advising the kirk, the government decided in 1571 to make appointments to certain bishoprics on the supposition that the candidates advanced would 'have the charge and oversicht of the inferiour ministeris' (*RSS*, vi, no. 2810). In 1573, parliament reverted to the old terminology in its decision that 'all inferiour persounis' should appear 'befoir the archebischoppis, bischoppis, superintendentis or commissionaris of the dioceis or provinces within the quhilkis thay dwell' to subscribe the articles of religion (*APS*, iii, 72).

[146] *First Book of Discipline*, 102 n.24; 105; *RStAKS*, i, 74; cf., *The Two Liturgies . . . of Edward VI*, ed. J. Ketley (Cambridge, 1844), 170, 340.

'thair Superintendantis and cheif ministeris' so necessary at its own meetings that, at first, it declined an invitation for superintendents 'and sum of the leirnit ministeris' to confer with Queen Mary's court; later, the question of whether 'the consent of the chiefest ministers' was needed before a superintendent could admit or depose a minister was raised in the assembly of 1571; and Knox himself, not inappropriately, was described as 'cheif preacher at Edinburgh'. The use of such epithets was clearly designed to signify the more learned and experienced ministers and was not intended to denote superiority of office.[147]

The novelty of the superintendent's office in Scotland lay precisely in its freedom from traditional concepts of superiority and lordship, and also in the ability of the reformers, in possibly unprecedented fashion, to combine individual initiative and leadership within the wider government of a national church committed to a concentric series of representative courts which ensured the continuation of mutual correction and fraternal admonition among ministers and superintendents alike. In none of the three functions of ministry – in preaching the Word, administering the sacraments, and in government and discipline (the last of which in an episcopal system is normally reserved to bishops and their delegates) – did the Scottish superintendents possess an exclusive jurisdiction. Thus, to characterise such a polity (which reserved neither the admission of ministers nor the power to discipline and excommunicate to superintendents alone) as 'congregationalism tempered with episcopacy'[148] does less than justice to the superior government entrusted neither to single congregations nor to individual overseers of whatever rank but to a series of graded courts linking the local to the national church in a manner fatal both to congregational autonomy and to full episcopal government.

Indeed, unlike the episcopal structure of the Elizabethan church, where only the bishop or archdeacon had legal power to apply ecclesiastical discipline,[149] the kirk in Scotland recognised its jurisdiction (derived directly from God and not intermediately through the prince[150]) to reside collectively within its system of representative government. Thus, in distinction to an episcopal structure where bishops might delegate certain powers to their

[147] Knox, *Works*, ii, 84, 149, 423; *BUK*, i, 195; *The Historie and Life of King James the Sext*, ed. T. Thomson (Edinburgh, 1825), 69; cf., Knox, *Works*, ii, 479: 'Superintendants and other learned men'.

[148] G. Donaldson, *Scottish Reformation*, 247; G. Donaldson, *Church and Nation through Sixteen Centuries* (Edinburgh, 1972), 63.

[149] P. Collinson, *Elizabethan Puritan Movement*, 348.

[150] *Spalding Club Miscellany*, iv, 88–92; *Second Book of Discipline*, 59ff.

subordinates, the Scottish superintendents (and commissioners) had no such right to devolve their duties on others: by 1562, if not before, authority to assign individuals supervisory tasks was reserved to the collective determination of the ecclesiastical courts, as manifestations of the wider church, especially the general assembly, embodying the authority of the whole church. The peculiar, even original, features of the Scottish polity have thus not always been fully recognised by those who have sought, sometimes with limited success, direct parallels with England or even with the continent. Nonetheless, the model, at least in outline, for the Scottish superintendent is to be found not in the bishops of Elizabethan England but in the ministry of protestant churches on the continent.

VIII

Supervising preachers and preaching supervisors:

There need be no dubiety that the office of superintendent originated in the Lutheran churches of Germany, and was introduced to the Lutheran churches of Denmark and Norway (though not the different ranks of special and general superintendents to be found in some German territories), where the 'provst'[151] (sometimes rendered 'provost', but more appropriately 'dean', despite its derivation from the Latin 'praepositus') was assigned a subordinate rôle as an assistant visitor. Even in Sweden, where episcopacy was retained, attempts were made in the 1540s to replace bishops with 'seniores', empowered to ordain entrants to the ministry and conduct visitations, assisted by lay conservators, and with ordinaries or superintendents at the top.[152] Uncommitted to any particular polity, Luther initially had considered the possibility, in 1520, of a German evangelical church equipped with bishops, archbishops and even a 'primate of Germany'; but when this proved not to be feasible, supervisory duties were assigned to visitors ('visitatores') and their subordinates, the superintendents ('superintendenten' or 'superattendenten'), who were apt to be seen (as in the Saxon Visitation instructions of 1528) as executive officials of the secular authority.[153]

[151] Cf., E. H. Dunkley, *the Reformation in Denmark* (London, 1948), 54, 86.
[152] *Episcopacy in the Lutheran Church?*, edd. I. Asheim and V. R. Gold (Philadelphia, 1970), 57–62; Dunkley, *The Reformation in Denmark*, 77–9, 84–8; M. Roberts, *The Early Vasas* (Cambridge, 1968), 116–19, 167–8.
[153] *Luther's Works*, vol. 44, 160; vol. 36, 158; vol. 40, 296–320; 40–1; vol. 45, 174; cf., H. H. Kramm, 'The "Pastor Pastorum" in Luther and Early Lutheranism', in *And Other Pastors of Thy Flock*, ed. F. Hildebrandt (Cambridge, 1942), 124–34; *Episcopacy in the Lutheran Church?*, 52–5.

The nature of the superintendent's office, however, found different expression in different lands; and those Reformed churches which utilised the office succeeded in avoiding the 'caesaropapism' of the evangelical churches which threatened to depress the superintendent's office into that of a royal official.[154] The possibility that Denmark acted as a model for the Scots has been examined and indeed re-examined; but, disappointingly, not one of the six of the authors of the Book of Discipline responsible for introducing the superintendent's office can be shown to have had any Danish contact: their assorted intellectual background was essentially French, Swiss, Netherlandish, English and Italian; not Scandinavian. It can be enlightening, too, to have a Scandinavian perspective in the matter: in declaring his judgment, to which it would be hard to take exception, one Danish historian has remarked that 'it may be difficult, if not impossible, to give conclusive evidence of Danish influence on the polity of the Scottish church'.[155]

A much more promising direction has been sought in the example of Cologne where the office was promoted as part of a reformist, if unsuccessful, programme initiated by archbishop Hermann von Wied and inspired by Philip Melanchthon and by Martin Bucer,[156] who had based the Cologne Ordinances of 1543 on the Brandenburg–Nürnberg Ordinance of 1533, the Saxon Ordinance of 1539 and the Cassel Ordinance of 1539.[157] In disciplining the obstinate, the Cologne experiment proposed that 'the whole matter be brought before the superintendaunte by the pastoure and one of them whych shall be ioyned wyth the pastoure by the appoyntmente of the congregation', that 'the superintendaunt muste come to that congregation where suche an obstinate wicked person shalbe', and that 'the superintendant, the pastoure and other deputed to thys ministerie, muste use excommunication onely against open il-livers, whiche will not amende'. The rôles of 'visitors' in confirmation and oversight of parishes, 'examiners' in the admission of pastors, of the 'suffra-

---

[154] M. Roberts, The Early Vasas, 117, 119, 168–9.

[155] G. Donaldson, ' "The Example of Denmark" in the Scottish Reformation', SHR, xxvii (1948), 57–64; G. Donaldson, Scottish Church History, 60–70; Thorkild Lyby Christensen, 'Scoto-Danish relations in the sixteenth century: the historiography and some questions', SHR, xlviii (1969), 80–97, at 95; see also above, 43, 79–81.

[156] J. K. Cameron, 'The Cologne Reformation and the Church of Scotland', Journal of Ecclesiastical History, xxx (1979), 39–64.

[157] H. E. Short, 'Bucer and Church Organisation' (Hartford Theological Seminary Ph.D thesis, 1942), 88–98, esp. 96.

gane' in institution were also recognised.[158] Elsewhere, Bucer
had approved the adoption the superintendent's office for
Augsburg and for Hesse. Yet, he found no place for it in his
organisation of the ministry for Strasbourg's seven parishes;[159]
and the Marian exiles in Frankfort, with whom Knox was soon
to be associated, declining to 'have any superintendent to take
the chief charge and government', declared their preference in
1554 'to have the church governed by two, or three, grave godly,
and learned, ministers of like authority, as is accustomed in the
best reformed churches', and appealed to the example of the
English congregation in Geneva; with Cox's ascendancy, however, the issue of selecting a 'bishop, superintendent or pastor'
had again come to the fore in 1555, despite the efforts of
Christopher Goodman to avoid dissension.[160]

At the same time, among the Reformed the office was
sometimes considered appropriate for congregations within
individual cities, as was so at Emden, of whose church order à
Lasco, the Pole, and John Willock, the Scot, had experience
during their residence there, and in London where à Lasco's
stranger churches had found refuge,[161] and of whose organisation Knox and Willock would have had knowledge. In establishing 'a regular plan of government' by electing elders, 'according
to the apostolic ordinance', and deacons, by the imposition of
hands 'which the apostles observed with their deacons', to assist
'the pure ministry of the word and sacraments, according to
apostolic form', the strangers had appointed à Lasco as their
superintendent,[162] an office which he understood to differ only
from a minister's in the greater work and charge, and he
expressly acknowledged his debt to Geneva and Strasbourg as

[158] *A simple and religious consultation of us Herman by the grace of God
Archbishop of Collone and prince Electoure etc.* . . . (London, 1548), fos. clxxiii[r]–
clxxx[v], ccxxi[r]–ccxxii[v], cclxxi[r], cclxxiii[r]–cclxxiv[r].

[159] J. Courvoisier, *La Notion d'Église chez Bucer* (Paris, 1933), 25–37; H.
Strohl, 'La théorie et la pratique des quatres ministères à Strasbourg avant l'arivée
de Calvin', *Bulletin de la société de l'histoire du protestantisme français*, lxxxiv
(Paris, 1935), 123–40; F. Wendel, *L'Église de Strasbourg, sa constitution et son
organisation, 1532–1539* (Paris, 1942), 37ff, 45, 50–1, 56, 75, 91, 141ff; M. U.
Christman, *Strasbourg and the Reform* (New Haven, 1967), 203.

[160] *A Brief Discourse of the Troubles begun at Frankfort, 1554–1558 A.D.*, ed.
E. Arber (London, 1908), 31, cf., 165; 72, 77.

[161] F. A. Norwood, 'The Strangers' "Model Churches" in Sixteenth-Century
England', in *Reformation Studies, Essays in Honour of Roland H. Bainton*, ed.
F. H. Littell (Richmond, Virginia, 1962), 181–96; P. Collinson, *Archbishop
Grindal* (London, 1979), 125–52; A. Pettegree, *Foreign Protestant Communities
in Sixteenth-Century London* (Oxford, 1986), 47, 49, 137.

[162] *Original Letters relative to the English Reformation, 1531–1538*, ed.
H. Robinson, 2 vols. (Cambridge, 1846–7), ii, 567–8, 570–1 (Micronius to
Bullinger, Aug. and Oct. 1550).

models for his stranger churches.[163] (Nor were the Danish impressed when Superintendent à Lasco, with his congregation, as Marian exiles, had attempted to settle in Denmark where he was received 'with much harshness, not to say barbarity: not indeed, I suppose, through the fault of the king, but of the doctors and ministers of the church, by whose preaching and attacks he and his friends were at length driven away from that kingdom' to seek sanctuary again in Emden.[164]) The similarities between the Scottish and à Lasco's superintendents have accordingly attracted comment, not without reason, for in parts the Scottish 'Form and Order for the Election of Superintendents' appears to pharaphrase à Lasco's 'Forma ac Ratio'.[165]

Among Calvinist churches, the utility of superintendents was recognised for more extensive territories, too: in northern Germany, for example, the Reformed churches, following the Lutheran precedent, adopted the office; and French protestants also showed an awareness of the value of superintendents ('surintendants') in their Confession of 1559, which professed it 'desirable and useful that those elected to be superintendents devise among themselves what means should be adopted for the government of the whole body'.[166] Yet the French practice of deputising some ministers at meetings of the provincial synod to visit churches provoked censure in the national synod at Orléans in 1562, which determined that 'this new-found office is condemned because of its dangerous consequence'; and the criticism which emerged of 'tous noms de supériorité comme anciens de Synodes, surintendants, et autre semblables' was resolved, in the end, with the decision in 1603 that superintendent ought 'not to be understood of any superiority of one pastor above another, but only in general of such as have office and charge in the church'.[167] As the country with which Scots of learning had the closest cultural and intellectual ties, it may yet emerge, that France, in these initial years, was capable of giving a lead to Scots on methods of superintendence, in outline if not in detail, as it undoubtedly did on patterns for conciliar government.

In both etymology and function, the identity of the reformed

---

[163] *Joannis à Lasco Opera*, ed. A. Kuyper, 2 vols. (Leiden, 1866), ii, 51.
[164] *Original Letters*, ii, 512–13 (Martyr to Bullinger, Feb. 1554).
[165] A. F. Mitchell, *The Wedderburns and their Work* (Edinburgh, 1867), 80–8.
[166] P. Schaff, *The Creeds of Christendom*, iii, 378.
[167] F. de Schickler, *Les Églises du refuge en Engleterre*, 3 vols. (Paris, 1892), i, 40; J. Quick, *Synodicon in Gallia Reformata*, 2 vols. (London, 1692), i, 24, 227; J. Aymon, *Tous les synodes nationaux des Églises réformées de France*, 2 vols. (The Hague, 1710), i, 26, 259; *Discipline de l'Église Réformée de France*, ed, F. Méjan (Paris, 1947), 201–2.

bishop with superintendent, in the sense of a preaching supervisor, was such a commonplace at the Reformation as to be scarcely a matter for dispute. As he found no biblical basis for dividing the ministry into a full and limited (or essential and dependent) ministry, Luther saw every minister as a bishop and successor to the Apostles; but supervision might still be legitimately committed, as a human arrangement, to superintendents or 'bishops, that is, inspectors and visitors', phraseology later borrowed by Martin Bucer.[168] Other lively expositions of episcopē followed. In Zürich, during the First Disputation, Zwingli discussed 'the little word bishop which, when one translates it into German properly, means nothing else than a guardian or supervisor, who should direct attention and care towards his people, being entrusted to instruct them in the divine faith and will, that is, in good German, a pastor'.[169]

After illustrating how pastor, bishop and elder in the New Testament were interchangeable, denoting 'the ministers of one master, co-equal in all things touching office or charge', Zwingli's colleague and successor, Heinrich Bullinger, readily acknowledged that 'bishops are called superintendents, seers, keepers, watchmen and rulers'. The significance of this he explained by citing St Jerome who had shown how in the primitive church congregations had been governed 'with the common counsel and advice of the elders', from whose company one of the elders might be chosen as 'superintendent, and to have the oversight of ministers and the whole flock', yet without 'dominion over his fellows in office or other elders: but, as the consul in the senate-house was placed to demand and gather together the voices of the senators, and to defend the laws and privileges, and to be careful lest there should arise factions among the senators; even so no other was the office of a bishop in the church: in all other things he was but equal with the other ministers'. This emphasis and exposition was shared by Martin Bucer, who in identifying superintendent and bishop, had drawn the same analogy of the 'consul in the senate' to depict the work of the bishop in presbytery.[170]

There were, therefore, ample precedents for the Henrician reformers' claims that 'the office of preaching is the chief and

---

[168] *Luther's Works*, vol. 29, 17; cf., M. Bucer, *Scripta Anglicana* (1577), 280: 'episcopi, hoc est, inspectores'.

[169] R. C. Walton, *Zwingli's Theocracy* (Toronto, 1967), 25; cf., W. P. Stephens, *Theology of Zwingli*, 19, 275, 279.

[170] *The Decades of Henry Bullinger*, ed. T. Harding, 4 vols. (Cambridge, 1849–52), iv, 106–111; Bucer, *Scripta Anglicana*, 259; 194; cf., Calvin, *Institutes*, IV, iv, 2; Calvin, *Comm. Titus*, 357–8.

most principal office, whereunto priests or bishops be called by the authority of the gospel; and they be also called bishops or archbishops, that is to say, superattendants or overseers, to watch and to look diligently upon their flock, and to cause that Christ's doctrine and his religion may be truly and sincerely conserved'. In any event, Archbishop Cranmer had observed that 'bishops and priests' had both occupied 'one office in the beginning of Christ's religion'.[171] Later, when the Catholic controversialist Thomas Harding dismissed the protestant bishops of the Church of England as mere superintendents and not proper bishops, Bishop Jewel protested by demonstrating the antiquity of the name 'superintendent' which he traced through the medieval scholastics to the early fathers – Augustine, Chrysostom and Jerome – who had used bishop and superintendent as synonyms for overseer.[172] Yet, to reformers (including the first generation of Elizabethan divines, despite the wording of the Ordinal) no inherent difference in order distinguished bishop from minister, and the retention of episcopal succession was not then considered a mark of catholicity.

IX

Episcopē:
Modern writers who have investigated the issue have usually proceeded thus far and not beyond, having satisfied themselves by illustrating how 'superintendent' was simply an alternative designation for 'bishop'. In doing so, they have often failed to observe that this was by no means the sole Reformation equation or expression of the ideal of superintendence. To put it another way, the words 'bishop' and 'superintendent' were not the only terms employed to signify an overseer in the churches of the Reformation. Luther himself had favoured supervision by visitors (composed of pastors and laymen), appointed *ad hoc*, as well as 'superattendenten' or superintendents. Yet, even in Germany variant titles for superintendent were employed: 'archpriest' in Prussia, 'pröpste' or dean in Schleswig-Holstein; 'senior' in the Hanseatic cities, 'dekane' or dean in southern Germany and even 'metropolitan' in Hesse. Elsewhere, among the Reformed churches in different parts of Switzerland,

---

[171] C. Lloyd, *Formularies of Faith* (Oxford, 1825), 109–10; cf., *Luther's Works*, vol. 29, 32, 173; vol. 37, 367; T. Cranmer, *Works*, ed. J. E. Cox (Cambridge, 1844–6), ii, 117.
[172] *The Works of John Jewel*, ed. J. Ayre, 4 vols. (Cambridge, 1845–50), iv, 903, 906.

'inspector', 'dekan', 'antistes' and 'visitor'[173] had been introduced to maintain the duties of episkopē. It would be difficult to
deny, therefore, that all of these titles, as legitimately as 'bishop'
or 'superintendent', might signify the essence of the 'godly
bishop' (or 'godly overseer').

Besides all this, 'superintendent' need not be equated with
'bishop' *per se*. It could also denote a variety of overseers. This
diversity is well exemplified in England, where, apart from a
bishop, 'superintendent' could mean an assistant bishop or
alternatively a rural dean under episcopal supervision. Not only
did Bishop Ponet prefer 'superintendent' to 'bishop', but Bishop
Latimer had advocated assigning bishops auxiliaries in the form
of 'chorepiscopi' or 'superintendents'; and Bishop Hooper
recommended the deployment of lesser superintendents over
smaller, manageable districts, akin to rural deaneries. Others like
Bishop Aylmer went even further in claiming for 'every city his
superintendent, to live honestly and not pompously'.[174] Again,
the Marian martyr, John Rogers, considered a superintendent
should be placed over every ten churches 'which should have
under him faithful readers such as might be got'.[175] It was wholly
apposite, therefore that Valerand Poullain should adopt 'superintendent' in a context indistinguishable from that of minister
('superintendent ou pasteur') to denote his position as pastor of
the stranger congregation at Glastonbury.[176] The equation of
bishop and superintendent was thus far from complete and not
nearly so straightforward as it may superficially appear, a point
which Zanchi's remark on bad Latin replacing good Greek has
served merely to obscure. In other words, even though superintendence was episkopē a superintendent need not be identified
with a diocesan bishop. The imprecise image of the 'godly
bishop' – was he a supervising preacher or a preaching
supervisor? – conveyed different pictures to different men in the
ever-changing kaleidoscope of radical reform. The truly reformed
bishop might manifest himself not only in the guise of a diocesan
bishop, but as an archdeacon, a rural dean (where he existed) or a
minister of a congregation. Each, after all, was a watchman of his
flock.

[173] *Luther's Works*, vol. 40, 269–320; Kramm, 'The "Pastor Pastorum"',
128–9; *Episcopacy in the Lutheran Church?*, 62; H. Vuilleumier, *Histoire de
l'Église Réformée du Pays de Vaud*, 4 vols. (Lausanne, 1927–33), i, 281; *Calvini
Opera*, X, i, 45–8, 97–100.
[174] P. Collinson, *Godly People* (London, 1983), 164, 169, 171–2; cf., Calvin,
Institutes, IV, iv, 2.
[175] J. Strype, *Annals of the Reformation*, 4 vols. (Oxford, 1824), I, i, 265.
[176] Schickler, *Les Églises du refuge en Angleterre*, i, 61–2, 65–6.

In distinguishing the true from the false bishop, reformers had been at pains to commend the preaching office and to condemn bishops who were pastors in name but not in action. In protestant eyes, the unreformed church had merely maintained the episcopal title (the dignity and lordship) while forfeiting the substance (the duties and work). A few national protestant churches – England and Sweden – had sought to make the defective effective once more by preserving the name and office of a diocesan bishop and reforming, at least in part, the medieval practice of a bishop's duties. Elsewhere, experiments in oversight and supervision led other churches of the Reformation to reject the name, and sometimes even the office, of bishop as they found other modes of expressing the principles of episcopē. In Lutheran churches, this could be carried so far as to entrust ultimate oversight to the prince either as Luther's emergency bishop or as the 'summus episcopus' of later Lutheranism. As the Lutheran pastor of Zwickau explained in 1525 for the Elector of Saxony's benefit, 'the work of supervising (May we say bishoping?) is a noble work', to be undertaken by princes and visitors following the example of Jehosaphat.[177]

Yet, in their different ways, the English bishop, the Lutheran superintendent, the Swiss dekan, antistes, and visitor, the Scottish superintendent, commissioner and visitor, and, initially at least, the French superintendent or visitor all conveyed the essential function of episcopē, regardless of whether or not a church was episcopally governed. Nor was it of consequence whether these overseers served for a term or for life so long as they diligently discharged their duties. After all, if reformed thought made the bishop primarily a preacher and watchman, there was no longer any valid reason (except perhaps custom and orderliness) why pastoral oversight and government should not be shared with the full ministry. This, at any rate, was the pattern which prevailed in Scotland. Indeed, the more reformers contrasted contemporary bishops with the primitive bishops of the New Testament and early church, the greater their perception of the bishop as preacher and pastor.

In distinction to a papal bishop adorned with a 'bishop's mitre and staff and other pride and pomp, which are only meant to amaze the stupid', Luther had taught that 'in Paul's view he is certainly a bishop who takes the lead in the preaching of the

[177] *Episcopacy in the Lutheran Church?*, 55–6, 64–5; J. O. Evjen, 'Luther's Ideas Concerning Church Polity', *The Lutheran Church Review*, no. 3 (1926), 207–37, 339–73, at 351; 230.

Word'.[178] Similarly, Bullinger was later to emphasize how the Lord had 'appointed no princes in the church, but ministers and elders, who with the word of Christ should feed Christ's flock'. The example of the primitive church undeniably had a powerful and sustained appeal to reformers who sought to jettison medieval accretions and to return to apostolic models as the basis for organising their churches. After illustrating how the temporary offices of apostle, evangelist and prophet had served the church 'at the beginning', Bullinger explained, in language almost identical to Calvin, how the church was then 'enlarged and maintained' through the ministry of 'bishops, pastors, doctors and elders: which order hath continued most stedfastly in the church: that now we cannot doubt, that the order of the church is perfect and the government absolute, if at this day also there remain in the church of God bishops or pastors, doctors also elders'. In commenting on the original 'equality between bishops and elders', the Zürich reformer also indicated how 'in the order of bishops and elders from the beginning there was singular humility, charity and concord, no contention or strife for prerogative, or titles, or dignity; for all acknowledged themselves to be the ministers of one master, co-equal in all things touching office or charge. He made them unequal, not in office, but in gifts, by the excellency of gifts'. In commending such an order, Bullinger remarked:

> 'oh happy had we been, if this order of pastors had not been changed; but that that ancient simplicity of ministers, that faith, humility and diligence, had remained uncorrupted. . . . But in process of time all things of ancient soundness, humility, and simplicity, vanished away; while some things are turned upside down . . .'.

On the admission of ministers, the advice from the Züricher was unambiguous: the call by God and by men was essential; 'bishops alone had not power to make ministers', for 'the apostles did not exercise tyranny in the churches'; and both Paul and Titus 'made it no great matter whether discreet men chosen of the church, or the whole church itself, do ordain fit ministers; and that either by voices, either by lots, or after some certain necessary and holy manner . . .'.[179] It was not therefore Geneva alone but the powerful voice of Zürich, too, which advocated a return to apostolic simplicity for 'the best reformed churches'.

In Scotland, where early Lutheranism had gradually yielded

---

[178] *Luther's Works*, vol. 40, 41.
[179] Bullinger, *Decades*, iv, 106–9, 128–34.

foremost place to Swiss influences, what was understood to be the model of the New Testament church had not escaped reformers' attention. Captured in the aftermath of Wishart's martyrdom and shipped with Knox to France, Henry Balnaves, whose earliest protestant insights had been Lutheran, dismissed as deception the Roman doctrine of apostolic succession and in his 'confession' of 1548 (revised by Knox) he attempted to convey the essence of the pastoral office by appeal to primitive Christianity: bishops, he explained, were properly called to undertake 'a great charge and worke', and 'not a greate dignitie or lordschippe', which had led them to neglect their vocation; the work incumbent on a man 'called to the office of a Bishop or Minister of the Worde of God', he affirmed, was to 'preach the pure and syncere worde to the flocke', to comfort the weak, minister the sacraments according to the Word and 'follow the example of the Apostles in all ryghteousnesse':

'This was the order in the church of Christ in the beginning: The minister of the worde to teache and preache, and the auditors to reade, that therby they might take the teaching the better; as the Thessalonians did at the preaching of the Apostle . . .'.

Again, in discussing the election of bishops (whom he regarded as occupying the same office as minister), Balnaves commended the practice of how 'in the primitive church, the bishops were chosen' from godly, honest householders. 'When this order was kept in the Church of Christ', he exclaimed, 'the Worde of God flourished'. In his 'summary' of Balnaves' work, John Knox, in turn, gave further weight to the reformed ideal that 'the principall office of a Bishop is to preach the true Evangell'. The instruction was, no doubt, salutory in discerning a 'true' from a 'false' bishop; and much of the reformers' argument was directed, of course, at their Catholic adversaries who, Knox claimed, had departed 'from the puritie of Chrystes doctrine and from the simplicitie of his Apostillis and primative kirk'. Indeed, the persecution endured by believers in the early church and in his own time enabled Knox to affirm that 'our cause is one this day with the cause of the primitive kirk' and to observe how 'the Kirk at all tymes to be under the Cross'. Such, indeed, was the example of the early church, to whose testimony Knox repeatedly appealed, that Scottish protestants in their first petition of 1558 sought a restoration of 'the grave and godlie face of the primitive Churche'.[180]

[180] Knox, *Works*, iii, 460, 531-5, 538; 26; cf., i.194; iv, 311; 301; i, 306; cf., iii, 50, 131; iv, 514; v, 24.

Yet if the Catholic bishop, negligent in his duties, was assuredly, in protestant eyes, the false bishop, – the proud prelates, dumb dogs, idle bellies tyrants and wolves, thieves and murderers of Reformation polemics – it was not a self-evident truth that a protestant bishop was necessarily a true bishop.[181] Set against the perspective of the New Testament church, even protestant bishops were sometimes seen to stand in need of further reform.

In a catalogue of complaints directed at the more serious short-comings of the Elizabethan church, the Englishman, Christopher Goodman, in a letter from Edinburgh in October 1559 to Elizabeth's chief adviser, had sharply censured the practice of 'making lordly bishops before the realm is provided of necessary ministers'. Similar misgivings were voiced, no less emphatically, by John Knox in 1568 when he vigorously contrasted the protestant 'lord-like Bishop' with the 'painfull Preacher' of the Evangel, who fulfilled the duties of the pastoral ministry. Again, shortly before his death in 1572, Knox recalled his own refusal to become 'a great bischope in England' and declared his satisfaction with the original Reformation polity which he had helped to shape in Scotland.[182] Others who remained to serve in England sometimes offered radical yet constructive criticism. Not only were far-reaching proposals later drafted for redrawing the ecclesiastical map of England and Wales by replacing the 27 existing bishoprics with 150 smaller sees, but earlier schemes devised by Hooper among others by the early 1550s had urged the creation of new units of oversight by placing every ten churches under the care of a superintendent. Even bolder was William Turner's advice for every shire to be equipped with at least four bishops chosen annually by the ministry of the district.[183]

Within this framework of radical attempts to remodel traditional concepts of oversight and to experiment with new expressions of supervision, John Knox in 1558 had formulated his own proposals, when resident in Geneva, for the reform of diocesan episcopacy in England by subdividing each bishopric by ten 'so in every citie and great towne there may be placed a godly learned man, with so many joyned with him, for preaching and instruction, as shalbe thoght sufficient for the bondes

[181] Ibid., i, iv, 443, cf., 468; Knox, *History*, i, 10 (proud prelates); 9, 20–1; ii, 31 (dumb dogs); i, 243, 363; ii, 31 (idle bellies); Knox, *Works*, iii, 26; Knox, *History*, i, 243, 363 (tyrants and wolves); i, 337, 363; ii, 90 (thieves and murderers).
[182] *CSP Scot.*, i, no. 554; Knox, *Works*, vi, 559, 633.
[183] P. Collinson, *Godly People*, 169–72.

committed to their charge'.[184] In advocating this radical restructuring, Knox avoided disclosing the appropriate name for his godly supervisor; but the emphasis of his thought was not only on the provision of effective pastoral supervision for every substantial town and its environs but on collegiality, on the team-work of a preaching supervisor supported by other preachers for the district entrusted to their collective charge. Such a primitive model adapted to meet the evangelising needs, as Knox perceived them, of contemporary England drew much of its inspiration from the example of the early church: the groups of presbyters in the first century who ruled and instructed congregations, the presbyteral colleges serving house congregations, especially numerous in the larger cities which had a particular relevance to sixteenth-century reformers. But, as yet, in Knox's plans for England, there was no advocacy for the eldership, as such, which he had experienced in Frankfort and Geneva, and which he later considered appropriate for Scotland, not only when the church lay under the cross but even after it was accorded the prince's protection and support.

If Knox's remedies proved too strong a medicine to administer in England, the substance of his vision was applied in Scotland where the Book of Discipline revived his plans by commending the allocation of perhaps a dozen 'godly and learned men' to the chief towns of the land as centres for spreading the reforming work of evangelising the dependent country areas, grouped into provinces, in order that 'Christ Jesus bee universally once preached throughout this Realme'. Towns in Scotland were of course less numerous and less developed than they were in England. Kirkwall, Fortrose, Aberdeen, Brechin, St Andrews, Edinburgh, Jedburgh, Glasgow and Dumfries were the regional centres chosen; and while it would have been possible to have increased the number by adding perhaps Lerwick, Dornoch, Perth, Stirling, Ayr and even Dunoon, it would have been harder, if not impossible, initially to have found sufficient men of distinction to fill so many charges; the Book of Discipline itself had reflected on the difficulties in finding suitable candidates for the work. The reformers were noticeably sensitive to the issue of recruiting superintendents from congregations with an established ministry; they therefore justified the expediency of an itinerant ministry of superintendents in the expectation that a greater proportion of the population would thereby receive the services of the kirk; but, at the same time, they recognised the nation's

---

[184] Knox, *Works*, v, 518.

needs ought not to be met at the expense of the main centres of population, and therefore urged in the Book of Discipline that care be taken to 'disappoint not your chief townes and where learning is exercised, of such ministers as more may profit by residence in one place than by continuall travell from place to place'.[185] This inherent tension was not readily resolved.

In size, most of the new provinces were only marginally smaller than the old dioceses, apart, that is, from the new province of Glasgow, whose extent was merely a third that of the old diocese, and with the exception of Ross (and possibly Argyll) whose bounds actually exceeded the size of the former dioceses; by contrast, the parishes within the old dioceses of St Andrews, Dunkeld, Dunblane (with a portion of Brechin) were redistributed and absorbed within merely two new provinces. Nor, for that matter, were the geographical bounds of the new provinces markedly at variance with the dimensions of many English dioceses whose extent Knox was intent on cutting down to a size sufficient for one man's charge. With perhaps four times the population of Scotland, England and Wales had only twice as many dioceses (27) as Scotland had at the Reformation in 1560 (13); and apart from the undoubtedly large sees of York, Lincoln, Norwich and Exeter, many English sees, in geographical terms, were no greater, and some much smaller, than their Scottish counterparts. But the significant difference between the two countries lay not in the extent of diocesan boundaries but in the number of parishes comprehended within a diocese which in England could exceed a thousand parishes (the total for the whole of Scotland).

In Scotland, by contrast, the new superintendents' provinces, as depicted in the Book of Discipline, rarely had more than a hundred churches grouped within a province; the province with the largest collection of parishes, Fife and Strathearn, quite exceptionally had around 125 churches; Glasgow, Aberdeen and Ross had each around one hundred parishes; Angus and the Mearns, Lothian and Jedburgh had slightly less; whereas Argyll and Orkney had each as few as three or four dozen parishes. The proposed divisions, in any event, were far from sacrosanct; the scheme was never fully operational, was subject to modification from the outset; and fifteen years later, as ministers became more numerous, though still not plentiful, the general assembly reduced the units for supervision by establishing more than 26 visitors (or commissioners) for 20 specified areas. Such an

[185] *First Book of Discipline*, 115–27.

arrangment, of course, involved no change of principle; not only did it realistically take account of the increased size of the reformed ministry in the years between 1560 and 1576 but it fulfilled the Book of Discipline's original requirement for more effective supervision; it was also consistent with the reformers' understanding of episcopē, restated with further clarity in the Second Book of Discipline (1578), which recognised that superintendence, entrusted to the whole church, might be legitimately exercised by individual visitors commissioned by the courts of the church so to act. Such a solution, while fatal to diocesan episcopacy, did not condemn the episcopal principle, or, more exactly, the principle of episcopē.[186]

The belief, then, that superintendence should be exercised not by a distinct order or degree of bishops but merely by such individuals as happened to receive a commission from the church to discharge these duties (either for a shorter or longer interval, though evidently not for life) can be traced not only to prevailing practice in the 1560s, which had the general assembly's full support, but to Erskine of Dun's claim in December 1571 that such duties should be discharged simply by 'sic of the ministerie as hes commissione'[187] and to the Second Book of Discipline's reiteration, in 1578, that church courts were the appropriate agencies for commissioning visitors. The failure of some assessments, therefore, which characterise the polity of the 1560s as essentially episcopal can be traced to an inability to distinguish episcopē from episcopal government. In 1561 (and again in the Second Book of Discipline in 1578) the Scots accepted the need for inspection, superintendence and oversight by individual visitors but they firmly declined to commit the church to government by a hierarchy of individuals on the English model and instead entrusted final authority and supervision to its courts and assemblies which acted on behalf of the whole church and to which all individuals were subordinated.

Such an approach, which they considered consistent with the teaching of scripture, enabled Scottish reformers to retain within their church order the New Testament identity of minister and bishop. Not only did Henry Balnaves, John Knox and Erskine of Dun use the words interchangeably, but David Fergusson, minister of Dunfermline, illustrated his acceptance of the equation in 1563 when he described the 'poore preachers of the Gospel, or Bishopes call them as ye list', an identity affirmed by the general assembly in 1565 and again in 1575, and restated in

---

[186] *BUK*, i, 358–9; *Second Book of Discipline*, 196–7.
[187] *Spalding Club Miscellany*, iv, 100.

the Second Book of Discipline which denied that 'the name of ane bischope be attributit to the visitor onlie'. At the same time, Fergusson sought to avoid any ambiguity in vague appeals to the primitive church by warning in 1563 how the original purity of the early church was not for long preserved with the appearance of a monarchical hierarchy in the form of archbishops, patriarchs and, finally, the primacy of the papacy and with it the papal claim to be the 'universal Bishop or head of the Church'.[188]

Here, too, is another significant contrast with England. The concept that a minister was also a bishop proved unattractive to leaders of the English church. The earlier Elizabethan divines, following the example of their predecessors, were prepared to admit the identity of minister and bishop in the New Testament, and also to recognise no difference in order. What they did distinguish were the separate functions of bishop and minister. Thus the example of the New Testament church (which men of precise conscience sought to imitate and restore), a church labouring under the cross and subject to persecution, was considered an inappropriate model for post-Reformation England where the church, blessed with a godly Deborah, was established and protected by the Christian magistrate, who legitimately might prescribe the church's external government since none had been commanded by scripture.[189] The crown's preference, therefore, for a hierarchy of individuals in governing the church was then recognised as an order instituted by human appointment. To have argued otherwise, at that stage, for the existence of diocesan episcopacy *iure divino* (as Bilson, Bancroft, Hooker and Saravia did later) would have been contrary to almost all contemporary thought. In its organisation, therefore, the Elizabethan church more closely resembled the medieval church than 'the best reformed churches' elsewhere. In Scotland, however, where efforts were made to restore the grave and godly face of the primitive church, the kirk's government, from the start, ultimately resided in courts and councils, and in continuing to advance the claim that 'every true preacher of Jesus Christ is a Christian bishop', the reformers had formulated a different method for exercising episcopē to that adopted in England. In other words, within the kirk at the Reformation a corporate episcopē was exercised partly by individuals and partly by superior councils. This superintendence could be administered in

---

[188] Knox, *Works*, iii, 531; vi, 434; *Spalding Club Miscellany*, iv, 96; *Tracts by David Fergusson*, ed. J. Lee (Edinburgh, 1860), 13–14.

[189] *The Works of John Whitgift*, 3 vols. ed. J. Ayre (Cambridge, 1851–3), i, 21ff, 153, 184–6, 243–4, 252, 363, 369, 389–92, 472; ii, 263–4.

different ways at different levels, but, in the final analysis, was held in a united capacity by all called to perform a ministry.

In their interpretation of supervision, the Scots were indebted partly to Bucer and particularly to Calvin, copies of whose *Institutes* were readily available. In his writings, Calvin had emphasised the unity of the ministry and had discussed the emergence of the bishop in the early church in the context of a president (moderator, or chairman) in a company or senate of presbyters. In examining the ministry of the New Testament church, in which he distinguished the 'extraordinary' and 'temporary' offices of apostle, prophet and evangelist from the ordinary and 'perpetual' offices of pastor and teacher, 'who preside over the government of the Church according to the institution of Christ', Calvin had illustrated how 'in giving the name of bishops, presbyters, and pastors, indiscriminately to those who govern churches, I have done it on the authority of Scripture, which uses the words as synonyms. To all who discharge the ministry of the word it gives the name of bishops'. Having discerned 'the order of church government as delivered to us in the pure word of God and of ministerial offices as instituted by Christ', Calvin observed how, with the expansion of the ministry in the early church, the method of government adopted had then 'not strayed far' from 'the divine institution' in as much as the bishop, selected from the presbyters of a city, was no more than 'one of their number to whom they gave the special title', lest dissension should arise, and was 'subject to the meeting of the brethren':

> 'The bishop, however, was not so superior in honour and dignity as to have dominion over his colleagues, but as it belongs to a president in an assembly to bring matters before them, collect their opinions, take precedence of others in consulting, advising, exhorting, guide the whole procedure by his authority, and execute what is decreed by common consent, a bishop held the same office in a meeting of presbyters. And the ancients themselves confess that this practice was introduced by human arrangement, according to the exigency of the times'.

Later, the church 'greatly degenerated from ancient purity', and its government became concentrated in the hands of individuals; a corporate episcopacy was gradually replaced by monarchical episcopacy, even though 'the Holy Spirit designed to provide that no one should dream of primacy or domination in regard to the government of the Church', and the ancient government was finally corrupted by the tyranny of the papacy 'and the whole of that hierarchy', which ought properly to be contrasted with 'the primitive and early Church'.[190]

The lesson which Calvin and other reformers had spelt out with such clarity was not lost on the Scots who not only devised a form of government which, unlike the English system, avoided placing undue authority in the hands of individuals but who also declined to recognise the title of those bishops who joined their ranks. Their attitude towards the five bishops who conformed at the Reformation, three of whom undertook, without delay, active service in the reformed church, is particularly significant and reveals a further difference in aims and intention between the Scottish and English Reformations.

X

'Them that are callit bischops':

Far from commending episcopal government as an appropriate structure for the new church, the conversion of five bishops to protestantism did not at that stage deflect reformers in Scotland from pursuing a programme aimed at dissolving the bishoprics and establishing superintendents. The reason why reformers at the Reformation did not seek to appoint bishops on the English model is sometimes attributed to the success of the remaining six Catholic bishops (for two sees were then vacant) in retaining their bishoprics; they simply could not be readily dispossessed. Yet the reformers' resolution in abandoning the old structure, and their reluctance to modify their proposals even with the adherence to their cause of several bishops, suggests that their action had a deeper significance than merely an inability, through historical accident, to preserve diocesan episcopacy.

After all, irrespective of their prospects for success, had they wished to replace the six recalcitrant Catholic bishops at the Reformation with protestant successors, and to utilise as bishops the five conformists, it would have been no more difficult for reformers to have advanced this claim than it was for them to have pursued their embarrassing, and far less attainable, campaign for inheriting much of the old church's wealth, which they thought could be achieved by dissolving the old financial system. Plainly, adherence to the reforming cause by almost half of the existing episcopate was not itself considered a compelling reason for setting up protestant bishops on England's example where, two years earlier, Elizabeth's government had resorted to a wholesale forfeiture of the Marian episcopate. Nor was the attitude of the Scottish crown an insurmountable obstacle here. Not only had the Reformation parliament in 1560 given

[190] Calvin, *Institutes*, IV, iii, 4–8; IV, iv, 1–3; IV, v, 1.

unprecedented countenance to the religious revolution effected in defiance of the crown, but Queen Mary herself was no religious bigot, and her largely protestant council could have advised just as readily on protestant episcopal appointments as they did on candidates for selection as superintendents.

If the creation of protestant bishops was not even an issue at the Reformation, the practical problem which presented itself was how exactly the conforming bishops should be absorbed within the very different structure of the new church whose general assembly declined to acknowledge them either as bishops or even as superintendents. There was good reason for the assembly's cautious attitude in accepting the labours of these men to reform their dioceses. After all, it could hardly have escaped contemporary comment that the bishops who defected included men who had experienced difficulty in the unreformed church in securing full or effective title to their sees: two of the reforming bishops, Robert Stewart, elect of Caithness, and Alexander Gordon of Galloway had been competitors in the 1540s for Caithness; and although Gordon succeeded Stewart first, it would seem, to the provostry of Dumbarton in 1543 and then, with Stewart's temporary forfeiture, as bishop elect to the see of Caithness in 1544, Stewart's claim ultimately prevailed and, by 1548, Gordon had agreed to renounce his rights in Stewart's favour.[191]

Gordon had therefore to look elsewhere. His hopes of finding a bishopric had again been frustrated in 1550 when, with support from the king of France and cardinal of Guise, he had journeyed to Rome to gain the archbishopric of Glasgow, but he was then in minor orders and lacked licence from the Scottish crown, was declared a barrator and resigned the see in 1551, for which loss his titular appointment as archbishop of Athens was no recompense; but by 1553 he had become bishop elect of the Isles, with the abbacy of Iona, and by 1559 was nominated bishop elect of Galloway, to whose see the abbacy of Tongland was annexed; and in the interval, he had also acquired the commendatorship of Inchaffray in 1551. If Gordon's pre-Reformation career had something of the flavour of a none too successful careerist, his decision to join the Lords of the Congregation in 1559, which enabled him later to boast, perhaps not idly, that he 'was the first

---

[191] Watt, *Fasti*, 61, 353; *RSS*, i, no. 919; *The Scottish Correspondence of Mary of Lorraine*, ed. A. I. Cameron (Edinburgh, 1927), 10; *Acts of the Lords of Council in Public Affairs, 1501–1554*, ed. R. K. Hannay (Edinburgh, 1932), 553–4; *RSS*, iii, no. 2561; *L & P Henry VIII*, XXI, ii, no. 284. Gordon's title to the provostry may not have been effective; he is not recorded as provost in Watt, *Fasti*.

that publickly preached Christ in face of the Authority', had for him a beneficial outcome in so far as the Reformation parliament, which he attended, took the unusual step of confirming his legal rights to the bishopric of Galloway.[192]

Yet, neither bishop, even allowing for Gordon's boast, had significant pastoral experience; and the same defect was apparent in the career of the third conforming bishop who undertook an active ministry. Adam Bothwell, a canon of Glasgow and the son of an Edinburgh burgess, had only acquired the bishopric of Orkney in 1559 as the struggle for Reformation intensified, though earlier, it emerges, he had visited Orkney, at the government's expense, in 1555.[193] Whether the disadvantage of pastoral inexperience extended to James Hamilton, bishop elect of Argyll (once a candidate for the see of Glasgow in 1547) and subdean of Glasgow was of less consequence; he was reckoned a convinced protestant by 1560 but despite his conformity he remained an absentee bishop, avoided the work of a bishop beyond discharging some duties associated with granting collation to benefices, and, in the end, undertook no known ministry in the new church.[194] Somewhat more promising was the case of the fifth conforming bishop, John Campbell, elect of the Isles, who had identified himself with the Lords of the Congregation during 1559, had sat in the Reformation parliament and was considered a committed protestant; he relinquished his claims to be a bishop, settled for life in the reformed ministry, as a 'preacher of the Word of God', until he found himself once again promoted to the bishopric of the Isles, this time as a protestant bishop, by 1573.[195]

Even more significantly, these bishops proved to be absentees. After arriving in his new diocese by April 1560, Bothwell of Orkney, in conventional posture, recorded in a charter issued in June 1560 the debts he had incurred in resisting 'tumults, battles and wars, heresies, errors and schisms'; he belatedly attempted by February 1560/1 to put an end to the celebration of mass in his church, and by March was on record as beginning the task of reforming his diocese and of preaching in person.[196] In later

---

[192] Watt, *Fasti*, 150, 205; 132; *Acts of the Lords of Council*, 604, 638; *Mary of Lorraine*, 239; *CSP Scot.*, i, no. 566; *BUK*, i, 276.

[193] Watt, *Fasti*, 254; *Accounts of the Lord High Treasurer of Scotland*, edd. T. Dickson *et al.*, 11 vols. (Edinburgh, 1877–1916), x, 284.

[194] Watt, *Fasti*, 28, 149, 168; *CSP Scot.*, i, no. 891, cf., no. 885; see below, 470.

[195] Watt, *Fasti*, 205–6; *CSP Scot.*, i, no. 566; *APS*, ii, 525; see below, 473.

[196] *RMS*, iv, no. 1668; M. Napier, *Memoirs of John Napier of Merchiston* (Edinburgh, 1834), 67–70; *CSP Scot.*, i, no. 967.

years, he recalled how 'when idolatry and superstitione was suppressed, he suppressed the same also in his bounds, preached the word, administered the sacraments, planted ministers in Orknay and Shetland, disponed benefices and gave out stipends out of his rents to ministers, exhorters and readers'.[197] Yet, such an auspicious start, which had as its sequel the winning over to protestantism of many clergy in the diocese,[198] was not wholly sustained. Bothwell soon showed little disposition for the life of a resident bishop. By April 1561, he had left his diocese to visit France; and his appointment (contrary to reformed standards), first, as a judge in the Court of Session in 1564 and, then, from 1566 as a privy councillor necessitated prolonged periods of absence in Edinburgh, as did his attendance at parliament and at numerous general assemblies.[199] Nonetheless, his services as an overseer were sought by the assembly which granted him several short-term commissions to serve as visitor; and Bothwell himself placed on record that he had, 'when he was a Commissioner, visited all the kirkes of Orknay and Shetland tuice' in the period before his suspension in 1567. To have visited, in often difficult circumstances, all three dozen or so churches in his far-flung diocese on at least two occasions as the assembly's commissioner was by no means a discreditable performance, and, of course, it must have required numerous visits, presumably in the summer months, over these years to have achieved such a target.[200]

In neighbouring Caithness, Bishop Stewart was present in his diocese at the Reformation and therefore able to assist in laying the foundations of a reformed ministry in the area. His reputation for deviating from Roman orthodoxy had been established fifteen years earlier when he showed a readiness to endure papal wrath for transferring his allegiance to that 'rapacious wolf', Henry VIII, the schismatic 'tyrant of England'. His visit to Edinburgh, in 1561, elicited favourable comment in protestant circles; and by 1564 it was said that he 'sometimes preaches'. Yet, in later years, he increasingly detached himself from the work of the ministry in Caithness, devoted more attention to affairs in the south, sitting in parliament and council,

---

[197] *BUK*, i, 165.
[198] G. Donaldson, 'Bishop Adam Bothwell and the Reformation in Orkney', *RSCHS*, xiii (1959), 85–100.
[199] Ibid., 91; G. Brunton and D. Haig, *An Historical Account of the Senators of the College of Justice from its Institution in MDXXXII* (Edinburgh, 1832), 119–22; *RPC*, i, 477, 485, 488, 490–1 et seq.; *APS*, ii, 546; iii, 46, 65, 77, 115, 127, 194, 290, 326, 328, 373, 424, 427, 523; *BUK*, i, 32, 38, 60, 77, 90, 112, 165, 207.
[200] *BUK*, i, 165.

and spent much of his time living in St Andrews where he ultimately retired.[201]

A similar drift is detectable in the career of Bishop Gordon of Galloway whose lack of experience under the old regime in governing the diocese (where during the technical vacancy the prior of Whithorn had acted as vicar general) was likely to have affected his work of reform after 1560. Although he was undoubtedly discharging the duties of a reformed overseer of Galloway by 1561, Gordon was nonetheless prepared in 1562, almost in spite of the Reformation, to resign the abbacy of Iona, acquired in 1554, into the hands of 'sanctissimi domini nostri papae', or so the legal jargon ran.[202] His attachment to protestantism, of course, was not in question; but his enthusiasm for reforming his diocese was tempered by a worldly recognition that his presence was required outside his diocese, notably at Inchaffray in Perthshire, whose commend he retained until 1565, as well as at Stirling, where as dean of the chapel royal his seal might be needed to authenticate documents, and not least at Edinburgh where he served as a courtier, privy councillor and a senator of the College of Justice, which incurred the general assembly's grave displeasure. Like his colleagues, Gordon remained too often an absentee bishop.[203]

While welcoming the initiative which they had shown, no doubt at the prompting of the Lords of the Congregation, in introducing reforms in their dioceses, the general assembly retained reservations about the activities and demeanour of the conforming bishops who sometimes gave the impression of being less than thoroughly reformed. Although, *quoad civilia*, these bishops retained a legal title to their bishoprics, the general assembly was disinclined to recognise their title within the reformed church. Accordingly, it referred sometimes disparagingly to 'them that are callit bischops' who had undertaken reformed service (1562), to 'Mr Alexander Gordon entituled Bishop of Galloway' (1562), or 'stiled Bishop of Galloway' (1563), to 'Adam called Bishop of Orkney, Commissioner for Orkney' (1567) and to 'Alexander called Bishop of Galloway, commissioner' (1567). [204] In the assembly's eyes, the conforming

[201] See below, 312–13, 455, 458; Vatican Archives, Minutes of Briefs (Armarium, XLI), vol. 32, fos. 332–335v.; *CSP Scot.*, ii, no. 110.

[202] *RSS*, v, no. 725; *Thirds of Benefices*, 146; Vatican Archives, Register of Resignations, series A, vol. 212, fo. 96.

[203] G. Donaldson, 'Alexander Gordon, Bishop of Galloway (1559–1575) and his work in the Reformed Church', *Transactions of the Dumfriesshire and Galloway Natural History & Antiquarian Society*, xxiv (1945–6), 111–28.

[204] *BUK*, i, 27–8, 31, 38, 112, 114; cf., the assembly's later attitude to Adamson 'callit Bishop of Sanct Androes' (1577), ibid., i, 385–6.

bishops who had undertaken a reformed ministry were legitimately empowered to conduct visitations only as the assembly's commissioners, appointed for a term effective either for a year or from one assembly till the next, and not by virtue of their episcopal office in the pre-Reformation church for which, of course, the reformers had assigned no place in their constitution for the new church. That this is a correct reading of these developments is supported by the distinction which the assembly itself drew in 1569 between Bothwell's appointment as bishop in the Catholic church and his appointment 'in Christis Kirk' to 'the charge of preaching of the evangell' and 'to be also Commissioner in Orknay, quhilk he accepted and executed for a certain space thereafter'.[205]

Now, it is perfectly true that in the fragmentary record of the early assemblies, the first mention of the three actively conforming bishops receiving commissions of visitation and oversight from the assembly date merely from 1563. It may not be capable of proof but it would be unreasonable to doubt that the commission of 1563 was not the first assignment of this kind which the conforming bishops obtained from the assembly. For a start, in 1562 Gordon of Galloway was assigned a stipend as 'owirsear their'; and in 1563, when he is known to have been appointed commissioner, he was again styled 'ourseair' of Galloway. Not only this, the assembly's record for 1563 discloses that Gordon was the recipient of an earlier commission: he had obtained, it was said, a 'commission *before* to plant ministers, exhorters, readers, and other office-bearers requisite for a reformed kirk within the bounds of Galloway', which the assembly presumably had granted him in 1562 or earlier. It is also clear that Bothwell of Orkney was allotted a stipend for 1562 (and retrospectively for 1561) 'for his visitatioun, owirsycht and labouris tane upon the kirkis of Orknay and Zetland in place of a superintendent'.[206] In the absence of any evidence that parliament or the privy council commissioned the bishops as overseers in the reformed church, it looks rather as if the general assembly, having failed to secure superintendents for these areas in 1561, was the agency which then authorised them, possibly in 1562, to act as overseers, or commissioners, in the absence of superintendents.

[205] Ibid., i, 162.
[206] *BUK*, i, 32; *Thirds of Benefices*, 146, 150, 290; *BUK*, i, 31 (my italics); *Thirds of Benefices*, 152.

This impression is fortified by the contemporary comment that Gordon of Galloway had at first accepted work as overseer but subsequently 'being promoted to great dignity, as to be of the number of the Lords of Privy Council, and likewise one of the Session, he would no more be called Over-looker, or Over-seer of Galloway, but Bishop'.[207] Here, too, was added reason why the assembly should look with such disfavour on his title as bishop. Besides, a further illustration of the assembly's defective record is afforded in later random references to Bothwell, Stewart and Gordon which seem to imply that they were expected to conduct visitations in certain years for which no renewal of their commissions has survived in the assembly's proceedings.[208]

At the same time, it is clear enough from the assembly's act of 1562, requiring all who had already entered the ministry to undergo examination by superintendents, that the assembly intended this measure to apply to 'them that are callit bischops as uthers pretending to any ministrie within the kirk'.[209] This suggests an attempt by the assembly in 1562 to regularise the position of the conforming bishops not by recognising them as superintendents but by subordinating them to the assembly's legislation and to examination by superintendents. What is less clear is whether this enactment was specifically directed at Bothwell and Gordon, already active in 1561 (and who may – or may not – have been authorised or confirmed in their ministry after trial by a superintendent, which could readily have been obtained in Edinburgh during their visits there), or possibly at Stewart, who was slower to seize the initiative, or even at Hamilton of Argyll and Campbell of the Isles whose involve-ment or otherwise as preachers, at this stage, remains shadowy.

Yet, regardless of the precise date when the conformists first received their commissions, it is surely significant that the general assembly declined to recommend any of the conforming bishops for office as superintendent and preferred, instead, to issue them with short-term commissions of visitation, which could readily be terminated. After actively canvassing for the post of superintendent of Galloway, Gordon conspicuously failed in his bid: the assembly declined to recognise him as superintendent but encouraged him to continue in his work; and Knox's account of Gordon's predicament after his attempt to

---

[207] Knox, *History*, ii, 189.
[208] *BUK*, i, 162–3, 165–8 (Bothwell); 130, 136, 190 (Stewart); 65, 112, 114 (Gordon).
[209] Ibid., i, 209.

bribe the electors to accept him as superintendent is not, in essence, inconsistent with what is known of the episode.[210] Nor, in the end, did these bishop-commissioners succeed in matching the standards set by the superintendents, who, though subject to the assembly's constant criticism, assuredly avoided suspension or deposition, a fate which all too readily overcame some of the conforming bishops.

In 1567, Bothwell of Orkney received the assembly's censure for his negligence in preaching and oversight, and was then deposed for transgressing 'the act of the Kirk in marrying the divorcit adulterer', namely, Bothwell to Queen Mary. Restored, after repentance, 'to the ministrie of the word' in 1568, he denied in 1570 that 'he had abandoned absolutely the preaching of the word' but was rebuked by the assembly for styling himself 'with Roman titles, as Reverend Father in God, which pertaineth to no Ministers of Christ Jesus, nor is given them in Scriptures', to which he replied that he had 'never delighted in such a stile, nor desired any such arrogant title; for I acknowledge myself to be a worm of the earth, not worthy any reverence; giving and attributing to my God only, all honour, glory, and reverence, with all humble submission'.[211] Gordon of Galloway, whom the assembly repeatedly charged with negligence, and with devoting his time to affairs of state 'quhich cannot agree with the office of a pastor or bishop' had his commission of visitation withdrawn in 1568, was suspended from the ministry in 1569, a sentence repeated in 1573, and was threatened with excommunication in 1574 before effecting a reconciliation in 1575.[212] By contrast, none of the superintendents was subjected to such humiliation.

It also remains a valid observation, despite efforts to obscure the issue, that parliamentary recognition in 1567 for the work of overseers in granting collation to benefices extended only to superintendents and commissioners and was withheld from the conforming bishops *qua* bishops.[213] In other words, parliament was then prepared to follow the assembly's lead in acknowledging this work of the conforming bishops only in so far as they continued to receive commissions from the assembly and not in respect of their episcopal titles, a not unimportant distinction.

---

[210] Knox, *History*, ii, 72–3, 188–9, 210.
[211] *BUK*, i, 114, 131, 162, 165–8.
[212] Ibid., i, 65, 112, 114, 150, 261, 309, 319.
[213] *APS*, iii, 23.

XI

Experiments in oversight:

If none of the conforming bishops was permitted to become a superintendent as such, none of the superintendents achieved recognition as a bishop when a protestant episcopate was finally (though briefly) introduced as the product of a financial compromise between crown and kirk in 1572. Not only so, but the one superintendent who had received a simple gift from the crown, without the assembly's approval, of the property of a bishopric in 1565, at a point when Queen Mary had sought to win over protestant support, was himself dead by 1572. Before that point, however, the kirk had succeeded in rejecting episcopal government while affirming its belief in the need for episcopē or supervision. If the superintendent were the 'godly bishop' as some have argued, it is decidedly odd that not one superintendent was appointed bishop when the general assembly somewhat reluctantly accepted a protestant episcopate in 1572. Instead, the remaining superintendents were assigned the new and humbler task of acting as suffragans. But, in any event, the assembly accepted this experiment in diocesan episcopacy for no more than four years, and by 1576 had reverted to a system of oversight by visitors or commissioners into whose hands, of course, much of the work of supervision had been committed during the 1560s.[214] Conventional definitions of superintendents or individual overseers as bishops dissolve even further when it is observed that commissioners or visitors (as distinct from diocesan bishops) were not then considered incompatible with the presbyterian programme of the Second Book of Discipline in 1578.

This being so, it was the missionary, evangelising and pastoral or supervisory duties of ministry (and not, of course, any claim for *iure divino* episcopacy) which the reformers had sought to convey at Winram's election as superintendent when it was remarked (presumably in the sermon of induction possibly by Christopher Goodman) that 'wythowt the care of superintendentis, neyther can the kyrk be suddenlie erected, neyther can thei be retened in disciplin and unite of doctrin; and farther seing that of Crist Jesus and of his apostolis we have command and exempill to appoynt men to sic chergis'. The exercise of this apostolic commission is thus manifested in the ministry. As the reformers appreciated, the apostles themselves were superintendents of individual churches, and, as the Gospel spread, so some

[214] *Second Book of Discipline*, 31–2, 54.

established congregations assigned disciples who each lived for a spell in a particular place to direct the activities of the church there.[215]

Both Luther and Calvin had taught that in the apostolic writings 'presbyter' and 'bishop' were different descriptions of the same office[216] and recognised that it was a later age which represented Timothy as bishop of Ephesus and Titus as bishop of Crete. Only in the former sense do the comments at Winram's election become readily intelligible, and identifiable with the Scottish concept of superintendence (which need not denote episcopal government), and with Knox's belief that all true ministers of the Word were the successors of the apostles. Besides, the earlier reformers did not then consider diocesan bishops, as bishops, to be the apostles' successors. In England, for example, John Bradford, chaplain to Edward VI, canon of St Paul's and Marian martyr, had denied that the apostles were bishops. As another English divine, Thomas Becon, had explained in his catechism, a bishop is 'an overseer or superintendent, as St Paul said to his elders or bishops of Ephesus', and by the term 'bishop', he elaborated, the apostle 'meaneth every spiritual minister'.[217] It is only within this context too, that the statement at Winram's election can be reconciled with the reformers' official pronouncements in the Book of Discipline and Form and Order for the Election of Superintendents, each of which promoted the essential unity of the pastoral ministry and sought to efface distinctions beyond those which were apt to arise in respect of the geographical bounds assigned for a particular ministry.

The familiar, if solitary, Scottish utterance (by Erskine of Dun in 1571) in favour of the identity of bishop and superintendent, for which scriptural warrant was adduced by appeal to Timothy and Titus, occurred in unusual circumstances and requires closer examination than it has usually received to resolve the ambiguities surrounding his remarks. In seeking to repel the government's action in appointing candidates of its own choice to several vacant bishoprics of the old church (without consulting the new), Erskine vigorously protested to the Regent Mar in November 1571 at the intrusion of 'that misordered creation of bishops'.

---

[215] *RStAKS*, i, 75 (where the entry is oddly inserted in a minute of 1568); cf., J. B. Lightfoot, 'The Christian Ministry', in *Saint Paul's Epistle to the Philippians* (London, 1888), 199.

[216] See below, 223–4, 226.

[217] *The Writings of John Bradford*, ed. A. Townsend, 2 vols. (Cambridge, 1848, 1853), i, 506; *The Catechism of Thomas Becon*, ed. J. Ayre (Cambridge, 1844), 319.

Such candidates for spiritual office, he argued, ought not to be appointed solely by the government, for the power of admission 'is committed by the kirk to bishops or superintendents' in accordance with scripture. Here was no claim to diocesan episcopacy *iure divino* in its later sense of the bishop as the successor to the apostles. The furthest Erskine was prepared to argue in his heated exchange with the Regent was that among the duties assigned to those whom scripture called bishops was the admission of men to the ministry; and the Scottish superintendent, as an overseer, had exercised this power not by any intrinsic virtue of his office but because 'by the kirk spirituall offices are distributed, and men admitted and receaved thereto. And the administration of the power is committed by the kirk to bishops or superintendents', and he could have added (as he did elsewhere) to other ministers commissioned for a spell to act as temporary visitors.[218]

In employing the weight of scripture itself to resist the government's policy of filling the ancient bishoprics with its own men instead of dissolving them as the reformers had campaigned, Erskine drew attention to the example of Timothy and of Titus, 'Bishop of Creet'. This, in turn, raises the question of Erskine's understanding of the New Testament 'bishop' depicted in the pastoral epistles. As he is known to have read Oecolampadius, it need hardly be doubted that he was also familiar with the writings of other leading reformers including Luther and Calvin. In his lectures on the Epistle to Titus in 1527, Luther had taught that 'in Paul bishop is the same as elder'; 'a bishop', he explained, 'is a minister of the Word'; and he expounded how it was Paul's ordinance that Titus in Crete:

> 'should select "elders" (in the plural) in each city, and they are called bishops and elders. Therefore at the time of the apostles every city had numerous bishops. Then Christianity was in outstanding condition. This meaning of the word "bishop" disappeared, and it was subjected to very long and very distored abuse. Now it is called the human ordinance by which a man is in charge of five cities. Thus human traditions are never harmless, no matter how good they may be'.

In applying the significance of this message to contemporary circumstances, Luther argued that:

---

[218] For Erskine's identity of bishop and superintendent, see my introduction to *The Second Book of Discipline*, 78; Calderwood, *History*, iii, 156–62; *Spalding Club Miscellany*, iv, 100.

'every city ought to have many bishops, that is, inspectors or visitors. Such an inspector should be the parish clergyman along with the chaplain, so that they may share the duties and see how the people live and what is taught. He would see who is a usurer, and then he would speak the Word of healing and correction. This apostolic type of episcopacy has long since been done away with'.

Here, in Luther, was not only an exposition of 'bishop', as found in Titus, but a commendation of episcopē quite dissociated from diocesan episcopal government of the church.[219]

At Strasbourg, Martin Bucer had taught how 'the Holy Spirit has appointed two distinct degrees in the Church's ministry', first 'the senior pastors, whom the Holy Spirit styles overseers and elders (Tit. 1. 5, 7; Acts 14. 23; 20. 28), and to whom he entrusts the ministries of teaching, the holy sacraments, and Christian discipline, that is to say, everything concerned with the cure of souls'; and, secondly, the deacons, as assistants to the elders, to aid the poor. Again, in his *De Regno Christi*, in which he urged Edward VI to undertake 'a reformation of the order of bishops', Bucer explained how 'from a review of the churches since the time of the apostles', it became the practice for 'the name of bishop' to be attributed to the elders who presided as 'chief administrators of the churches', but he nonetheless affirmed, by reference to Titus, how all presbyters 'are called bishops in the Scriptures because of this common ministry'. In England, too, William Tyndale, for example, whose vernacular New Testament had appeared in 1526, had commented on how 'bishop', 'priest' and 'elder' were the names for the same office in the apostolic church:

'they were called elders, because of their age, gravity and sadness, as thou mayest see by the text; and bishops, or overseers, by the reason of their offices. And all that were called elders (or priests, if they so will) were called bishops also, though they have divided the names now: which thing thou mayest evidently see by the first chapter of Titus and Acts xx and other places more'.

In the Epistles to Timothy, Tyndale understood 'the bishop' as 'an overseer and an elder' and declined to describe Timothy as '*episcopus* properly: for those overseers, which we now call bishops after the Greek word, were always biding in one place, to govern the congregation there'. It is hardly surprising, therefore, that Thomas Becon, citing Acts xx, should define the bishop as 'an overseer or superintendent, as St Paul said to the elders or bishops of Ephesus'. [220]

Similarly, Calvin in his commentary on Timothy had observed that 'we should also note what Paul means here by the office of bishop, especially in view of the fact that the early generations were led away from the true meaning by the custom of their times. Paul includes in the designation "bishop" all pastors, while they mean one who was elected out of each presbyteral college to preside over his brethren. Let us therefore bear in mind that this word means the same as minister, pastor or presbyter'. Again, in his exposition on Titus, the Genevan returned to this theme, which he had illustrated elsewhere, by observing how Titus, who had 'the additional burden of organising churches whose affairs were not yet rightly ordered and of giving them a fixed method of government and discipline', also presided 'as moderator at the appointment of pastors'. Even here, however, there was 'no differences between a presbyter and a bishop', for in Paul's letter 'he uses both names indiscriminately with the same meaning, as Jerome has also noted'. For his part, Calvin could find:

> 'no fault with the custom which has prevailed from the very earliest days of the Church whereby each assembly of bishops has one man as moderator. But to take the title of the office which God has given to all and to transfer it to one man and deprive the rest of it is both unjust and absurd. Besides to pervert the language of the Holy Spirit so as to make the very words have a different meaning from the one He has chosen smacks of excessive and unholy temerity.'

Patristic scholar that he was, Calvin was only too familiar with Jerome's judgment that in Titus 'presbyter is the same as bishop' and with his explanation that 'Timothy and Titus are instructed about appointing a bishop and deacons, while nothing is said about presbyters, for "presbyter" is included in "bishop" ', an interpretation supported by Pelagius and Chrysostom. [221]

With such an exegesis the common property of so many reformers (quite apart from the 'presbyterian' legacy of the middle ages), it is scarcely open to doubt that Erskine of Dun was aware of this identity when he cited the examples of

---

[220] *Common Places of Martin Bucer*, ed. D. F. Wright (Appleford, 1972), 83–4; Bucer, *De Regno Christi*, in *Martini Buceri Opera Latina*, xv, 117ff; cf., *Melanchthon and Bucer*, 284; W. Tyndale, *An Answer to Sir Thomas More's Dialogue*, ed. H. Walter (Cambridge, 1850), 17–18; Tyndale, *Expositions and Notes on Sundry Portions of the Holy Scriptures, together with the Practice of Prelates*, ed. H. Walter (Cambridge, 1849), 253; Tyndale, *Doctrinal Treatises . . .*, ed. H. Walter (Cambridge, 1848), 229, 518; Becon, *Catechism*, 319.

[221] Calvin, *Commentaries on . . . Timothy . . .*, edd. D. W. & T. F. Torrance (Edinburgh, 1964), 223; *Com. Titus*, 356–7, 359–60; cf., *Apostolic Ministry*, ed. K. E. Kirk (London, 1946), 221.

Timothy and Titus in his argument with the Regent Mar. What is only open to doubt is that he accepted this equation. Further light on Erskine's thinking, however, is forthcoming in 'ane epistill wrettin to ane faythfull brother', in December 1571, composed in more reflective tone in the aftermath of his heated exchange with the Regent in November. In this more carefully considered and fuller exposition of the church and its ministry, Erskine considered the work of the apostles, prophets, evangelists, pastors, teachers and deacons in the apostolic church but significantly nowhere did he allude to any distinctive office of bishop. This is all the more significant in so far as Erskine claimed that the method for admitting ministers in the primitive kirk ought to be 'the samin ordour observit at this present' by the kirk in Scotland where simply 'sic of the ministry as hes commissione and cuir to exeme' were entrusted with supervising admissions to the ministry, provided that 'the pastouris of the kirk do all thingis concerning the publict efferis of the kirk with the consent of the congregatione, and that the admissioun be publict, be impositione of handis be the pastouris'. Nor is there any hint here that Erskine considered reserving these functions to bishops. Instead, the superintendent showed a readiness to accept the conventional reformed understanding of the passage in I Timothy requiring 'the bishop' to provide hospitality and so interpreted Paul's injunction to apply interchangeably to 'a bischop or ministere'.[222]

In other words, Erskine was fully familiar with the identity of the New Testament 'bishop' and 'presbyter' as two terms for the same office. This being so, on the reasonable assumption that he had not radically revised his ideas on the early ministry within the space of a couple of weeks, Erskine's heated utterances on bishops in his letter of November 1571 need interpreting in the light of his more academic exposition in December 1571, which seems to prove conclusively enough that Erskine at that point was far from being the enthusiastic advocate of *iure divino* episcopacy which some writers have portrayed him.[223] When reality is distinguished from myth (and due allowance made for the special pleading and understandably exaggerated language of his letter to the Regent), Erskine is seen to have shared the common Lutheran and Calvinist conception of episcopacy as a human, not divine, arrangement in the church.

All in all, to cite the former letter, and conceal the latter, as can so readily be done, is liable to misrepresent Erskine's attitude to

[222] *Spalding Club Miscellany*, iv, 92–101.
[223] G. Donaldson, *Scottish Reformation*, 125.

ministry and to isolate him from the generality of reformed thinking on the subject. Erskine's understanding of the Pauline bishop, which made it possible for him to contribute to the Second Book of Discipline of 1578, was wholly compatible with the reformers' exegesis, which was such common property that even an aspirant to the archbishopric of Glasgow recognised in 1581 that 'sic ane bischop as Paull teichis in his epistillis to Titus and Timothie' was none other than 'a minister and preichour of the Word of God'.[224] Nor should it be overlooked that Erskine was a signatory to the general assembly's report to Beza in 1566 on the Second Helvetic Confession in which no exception was taken to the Confession's identity of 'episcopi vel presbyteri' and its depiction of the superiority of ministers above ministers as a human arrangement.[225]

The kirk of Scotland being what it was in the 1560s, it is hard to see how Erskine could have dissented from Calvin's strictures here, expressed in his commentary on Philippians, where he had pronounced:

'The titles, therefore, of *bishop* and *pastor* are synonymous. . . . Afterwards there crept in the custom of applying the name of *bishop* exclusively to the person whom the presbyters in each church appointed over their company. It originated, however, in a human custom, and rests on no Scripture authority. I acknowledge, indeed, as the minds and manners of men are there cannot be order maintained among the ministers of the word without one presiding over the others. I speak of particular bodies, not of whole provinces, much less of the whole world. Now, although we must not contend for words, it were at the same time better for us in speaking to follow the Holy Spirit, the author of tongues, than to change for the worse forms of speech which are dictated to us by Him. For from the corrupted signification of the word this evil has resulted that, as if all the presbyters were not colleagues called to the same office, one of them, under the pretext of a new appellation usurped dominion over the others'.

Calvin's ideal of the presiding minister was the moderator of an assembly or company of presbyters, a device which the Scots had adopted by 1563; his model was manifestly not a distinctive and

---

[224] *Second Book of Discipline*, 46, 48–51; *Stirling Presbytery Records, 1581–1587*, ed. J. Kirk (Edinburgh, 1981), 19; Spottiswoode, *History*, ii, 282.

[225] Knox, *Works*, vi, 459; Schaff, *Creeds of Christendom*, iii, 283; A. C. Cochrane, *Reformed Confessions of the 16th Century* (London, 1966), 274. (Despite the disparity between the kirk's attempts to restore the godly face of the primitive and apostolic church, as revealed by reformed exegesis, and its acquiescence for a spell in the compromise of 1572 (which utilised the medieval structure), it still required ministers placed in bishoprics should possess the kind of qualities depicted in Timothy and Titus.)

permanent degree of bishops, divinely authorised, in whom resided the full government of the church. In other words, authority might be delegated by the church or an assembly, at its behest, to an individual to undertake certain duties for a spell; and in Scotland it is plain that the general assembly understood that the authority delegated to individual overseers (moderators, superintendents, commissioners and visitors) was derived from the whole church and did not reside intrinsically in the office or function itself. This view had also been expressed in 1561 by Spottiswoode, as superintendent; it was repeated by Erskine of Dun in December 1571; and was reaffirmed in the Second Book of Discipline in 1578.[226]

Given their pragmatic attitude to oversight, the Scots did not regard bishops as the essential custodians and guardians of authentic doctrine. In as much as individual overseers, of whatever description, had a rôle in ensuring, with others, that candidates admitted to the ministry exhibited sound doctrine and that in visitation they might legitimately report to the church courts any cases of unsound doctrine, they had a duty to conserve the faith, as the address at Winram's election makes plain. Yet, the predominating belief which Scottish reformers expressed was that unity of doctrine was preserved not by individuals, however eminent, but by the councils and assemblies of the faithful gathered together from the whole church.

This view, which owed much to the reformers' perception of the early church up to Chalcedon, was expounded in the Scots Confession of Faith in 1560, which explained that the purpose of general councils 'was partlie for confutatioun of heresyes, and for geving publict confessioun of thair faith to the posteritie following'; it was reiterated in 1561 by Knox who defended the freedom of general assemblies in the belief that they were essential for the retention of 'good ordour and unitie in doctrine' (a rôle which neither the Book of Discipline nor the Form and Order for the Election of superintendents reserved for particular ministries); and, when again under attack in 1574, the assembly itself argued its existence *iure divino* 'for preservatioun of the

---

[226] Calvin, *Commentaries on . . . the Philippians . . .*, ed. J. Pringle (Edinburgh, 1851), 23–4; see above, 174, 209–10, 220, 222.

holie Ministrie and Kirk in puritie'.[227] This emphasis on councils for maintaining unity of doctrine did of course complement the kirk's approach to ecclesiastical jurisdiction and disciplinary authority, assigned to collective government.

The distinctive contribution of superintendents and commissioners as supervising preachers in the 1560s was blurred with the creation of a protestant episcopacy in 1572 which had as its model the example of England; yet, beyond the appearance of diocesan bishops, it proved impossible for the crown to persuade the church to imitate the English system where government, under the prince, lay with individual archbishops, bishops and their subordinates. In Scotland, the government failed to supersede the church's system of government through courts which, it discovered, could not so readily be removed to make way for English practice. Instead, the general assembly remained supreme, to which the new bishops were required to recognise their subordination in all things spiritual. As for the old superintendents who had served the church well, the Regent Morton contended that with the appearance of bishops as overseers the rôle of superintendents (and by implication that of the assembly's commissioners) was no longer necessary.[228]

XII

Parting of the ways:
The introduction of episcopacy, not presbyterianism, was thus responsible for eclipsing the work of superintendents in those areas where bishops were immediately appointed to the ancient dioceses. The elimination, not perpetuation, of superintendents was thus the intention once this diocesan organisation took final form; but unpredictably, the new bishops, and not the superintendents, found themselves under attack and soon superseded: by 1575, the general assembly reverted to its earlier position in the 1560s by again approving, at a critical juncture, that 'the name of Bischop is common to all them that hes a particular flock over the quhilk he hes a peculiar charge, asweill to preach the

---

[227] Knox, *Works*, ii, 113, 296; *BUK*, i, 292. In the Scots Confession, chapter xx, 'Of Generall Counsallis, of thair Powar, Authoritie and causes of thair Convention' bears some general similarity to the more succinct article xxi, 'Of the aucthoritie of generall Counselles' in the Thirty-Nine Articles of Religion, in the Church of England (Schaff, *Creeds*, iii, 500–1), and to Beza's 'Confession de foi du chrétien', art. xi, 'L'autorité des conciles universels' (*La Revue réformée* (1955), 96ff). (The most recent study of the Scots Confession curiously ignores this entire chapter of the confession, W. I. P. Hazlett, 'The Scots Confession 1560: Context, Complexion and Critique', *Archiv für Reformationsgeschichte*, 78 (1987), 287–320.) See also, Calvin, *Institutes*, IV, ix, 1–2, 8.

[228] Spottiswoode, *History*, ii, 196.

word as to minister the sacraments, and to execute the ecclesiasticall discipline with the consent of his elders; and this is his cheife functioun of the Word of God'. Beyond individual congregations, supervision might still legitimately be exercised over 'reasonable bounds' (but not the old dioceses) by any whom 'the Generall Kirk sall appoint'. This prepared the way, in 1576, for the assembly to scrap the short-lived experiment in diocesan episcopacy and to return to visitors or commissioners for manageable areas on a basis similar to the practice of the 1560s with the remaining superintendents, as well as some bishops, receiving short-term commissions to act as overseers with the same authority and duties as the superintendents and commissioners had enjoyed in the 1560s. This administrative expedient was again approved by the Second Book of Discipline in 1578 which recognised that the power to appoint visitors resided collectively in the ecclesiastical courts, representing or expressing the wishes of the whole church. Here, not for the first time, was an acclamation of episcopē but a rejection of diocesan episcopacy.[229]

Yet the survival of superintendents as visitors is not itself an argument for the permanence of the superintendent's office. Beyond the short and enigmatic phrase that superintendents were 'a thing most expedient at this time' (which may suggest that they were not thought expedient for all time), the Book of Discipline had expressed no view on whether the office was designed as a temporary expedient or, alternatively, as a permanent ministry, 'a continual fixture', as one writer has quaintly put it. That untidy document cannot therefore be expected to offer further enlightenment on this issue. Nor is it a convincing argument to claim that if the duties of oversight were permanent, the office of superintendent was also essential and lasting, for although the work attached to the office might readily be considered permanent, the agencies for performing that work might just as readily change. This, after all, had been conceded by the assembly itself, from the early 1560s onward, with the creation of commissioners; and the adoption of alternative agencies to do the work of supervision was implicit in the assembly's decision in 1565 that candidates presented to benefices should undergo examination by 'learned men of the kirk, sick as presentlie are the superintendentis appointed therto', and later in Erskine of Dun's comment in December 1571 that the examination and admission of candidates lay simply in 'sic of the ministerie as hes commissione'. Besides, the Scots Confession in 1560 had dismissed the notion that 'ane policie, and ane ordour in Ceremonies can be appointit for all aigis, tymes, and plaicis'.[230]

Just as the assembly had found other, complementary means for exercising regional supervision through commissioners and visitors, so too the superintendents had regarded their tenure of office as temporary, in the sense that they did not consider the post to be held for life, and one superintendent explicitly stated in 1563 that he had accepted the work 'onlie for a time'. From 1563 onwards, the superintendents as a whole repeatedly sought to be released from their supervisory rôle and to resume (or, in some cases, possibly assume) a parish ministry. The assembly, as best it could, might urge them to persevere in their work, but one, superintendent, Willock, had departed for England in 1565 where he remained till 1568 when he temporarily returned north; and another, Winram, by 1571 in a 'charter of reces', decided formally to terminate his duties and so refused further attendance at the session, later tendered his resignation to the assembly and considered himself as 'sumtyme superintendent', which (notwithstanding his acceptance of short-term commissions for visitation) hardly lends support to the assertion that 'once a superintendent was inaugurated he was never permitted to resign his diocesan responsibilities'.[231] At the same time, the effect of the superintendents' continued appeals during the 1560s to lay aside their office must only have reinforced, in the assembly's mind, the need to rely more fully on the labours of commissioners as alternatives, a further illustration of the permanence of episcopē and of the changing modes for expressing the idea in practice.

In the end, several of the old superintendents soldiered on as visitors during the 1570s and beyond, in much the same capacity as before; none had become a bishop in 1572, and the surviving superintendent, though still ready to act as a visitor, did not become a bishop when diocesan episcopacy was reasserted by the crown in 1584. Amid the political struggles for control of the church, the superintendents had displayed a dignified attachment to duty as brothers among brethren, their supervisory powers checked and matched by their ready subordination to inspection

---

[230] D. Mullen, *Episcopacy in Scotland*, 19; see above, 173; Knox, *Works*, ii, 113.
[231] *BUK*, i, 39, 65, 77, 92, 120, 239, 242, 296–7, 302–3; *RStAKS*, i, 346–7; *BUK*, i, 297, 318, 337, 359; SRO, CC8/8/11, Register of Edinburgh Testaments (14 Dec. 1582), fos. 254v, 256r; D. Mullen, *Episcopacy in Scotland*, 19.

and admonition by their fellow ministers. As the political conflict between crown and kirk intensified, with some archbishops beginning to deny their subordination to the general assembly,[232] it was hardly surprising that neither side should seek to recreate the eirenic model of the Scottish superintendent whose fate was simply that of lapsing into disuetude (though not oblivion) without prospect of revival.

[232] *BUK*, ii, 337.

6

Ministers and Magistrates

I

Two Kingdoms:

In essence a theological revolt, the Reformation challenged many of the old dogmas and assumptions. Its anticlerical characteristics, fortified by Luther's royal priesthood of believers, had a distinctive part to play in effacing the accepted medieval distinction between the clergy, as the spiritual estate, and the laity, relegated to the temporal estate. Luther's emphasis, instead, on two distinctive governments or kingdoms, the spiritual government, exercised through God's Word, and the worldly kingdom or government of earthly princes and magistrates had a sustained appeal, with far-reaching repercussions in Scotland as elsewhere.

In 1548, the early Scottish Lutheran, Henry Balnaves, whom an admirer described as that 'devine Lawier and honourable Sessioner', found time as a prisoner in Rouen, after the fall of St Andrews castle to French troops, to reflect on his understanding of the religious life from a protestant perspective. Affirming that 'by Faith only in Christ we ar made just, without the law and workes thereof', Balnaves saw good words simply as 'the right fruits of repentance and faith' exhibited in a Christian's life. For him, 'blinde reason' had misled man to magnify his own good works to the neglect of scripture and of 'the good worke of God' who offered unmerited salvation through faith in Christ alone. This path to salvation was the same for all, regardless of rank and occupation. In the 'generall vocation, by the which we ar called by Christ and his Word to a Christian religion', there existed 'no distinction of persones, for all men are equall before God, of one estate', all participants in the royal priesthood of believers, all 'the holy people of God', 'free heirs of eternal life'.

In discussing a Christian's calling, Balnaves distinguished several vocations through which the Christian served society. Each calling had its own setting, whether within the family and household, or between master and servant, judge and judged, ruler and ruled. In everyday life, the faithful Christian might exercise his particular calling or 'speciall vocation' through his relationship with his neighbour, so that 'every one serveth other in their owne place', prince and people, minister and congregation, parents and children, masters and servants. In affirming the religious character of ordinary occupations, at the expense of medieval clericalism, Balnaves indicated how 'if we will looke dayly to this Christian vocation, we shal have perfite knowledge of what works we shuld doe and what works we should leave undone'. Among the 'vaine workes invented by man', which ought to be eschewed as unprofitable, were 'the superstitious worshipping of Saintes; going in pilgrimage; purgeing in purgatorie; hallowing of water, or other elements; foundation of masses to publike or private idolatrie; offering or sacrifices making, not commanded in the Word of God; choice of meats; forbidding of marriage in the church of God; and abominable abuses of the whole Christian religion by the shaven, oincted, or smeared priests, bishops, monkes, and friers; having onely there vocation of man by man'. Just as a Christian's salvation was not dependent on the performance of good works as prescribed by traditional teaching, so too was the individual freed from the clerical domination of the institutional church; everyone belonged to the spiritual estate.

As the means enabling men to fulfil their particular vocations, the offices of prince, magistrate and judge were consequently endowed with a religious dimension comparable with the office of bishop or minister. For Balnaves, the princely office was 'created and ordained' by God; its occupants were thus the very 'ministers of God', who according to scripture, because they exercised 'the power of God' committed to 'princes of earthly kingdomes', might even be called 'gods' themselves. Yet, in the spiritual kingdom, before God, an earthly ruler remained but 'the creature of God, equal to the poorest of thy kingdom or dominion; his brother by creation and naturall succession of Adam, and of nature a rebell to God'. To govern wisely and righteously in his vocation, a king must act 'as thou art taught by the Worde of God; and decline not therefrom', for as a mortal man he, too, was accountable for his administration to Christ, 'your king, ruler, guider, and governour who shall rule you with an iron rod'. In ruling his subjects 'in all goodnesse and sweetnes', a just prince will govern impartially, without thought of coveting others' lands or goods; he will defend the oppressed and poor, and recognise that 'the poorest and most vile within your jurisdiction is thy brother, whom thou shouldst not despise nor contemne, but love him as thy self'.

To the prince, too, belonged the *ius reformandi*, to 'restore the true, pure and syncere Christian religion; abolish, destroye, and put downe all false worshippinges and susperstitions, contrarie to the Worde of God, and not commanded therein'. Beyond recognising the prince's vital right of intervention in reforming a church corrupted, Balnaves was evidently not disposed to accord the prince extensive authority in a church reformed and specifically limited the prince's ordinary power to the administration of the commonwealth and the 'jurisdiction of people in the civil ordinance', in recognition of 'the office of the administration of the Word of God, under whom we comprehend all power ecclesiastical'.

Beyond distinguishing ecclesiastical from temporal authority by virtue of the different offices and work to which men are called, Balnaves gave little thought to the visible or institutional church; he merely touched on the example of the primitive church and on defective practice in the existing church. This, of course, was wholly consistent both with the failure of the protestant revolt in Scotland in 1547, and with it the end to any prospect of readily overturning the established order, and also with Luther's own earlier emphasis on the invisible church or 'communio sanctorum', the gathered spiritual community of true believers, known only to God. The Scot's indebtedness to Luther (whom he prudently never mentions) is apparent throughout; and despite the brevity of the work, more than an echo is detectable of Luther's doctrine of the two kingdoms, the spiritual kindom which God rules through the uncoercive Word, committed to his ministers as preachers, without the sword, and the secular or temporal kingdom which God also rules through the coercive law and punishments imposed by earthly governments in whose hands the sword is placed to restrain the wicked, just as a child needs correction from his father. The two kingdoms necessarily have two governments, for they confront sin and the work of the devil by different means, namely, the application of the law in one realm and of the Gospel in the other. All this is implicit in Balnaves' treatise; and present, too (in a manner so familiar in Luther's discussion of God's two kingdoms which complement each other), is the juxtaposition of two other, contradictory forces, the kingdoms of Christ and the devil

locked in cosmic combat in which God employs the governments of both his kingdoms as weapons in the struggle.[1]
   A sharper definition of the distinction between the spiritual
and the temporal or secular jurisdictions was forthcoming a
decade later in May 1559 when the protestant Lords of the Congregation wrote to the queen regent, Mary of Guise, at a point
when the government had summoned the preachers to answer
for their actions, in the aftermath of its apparently unsuccessful
attempts to restore the Easter mass in several protestant strong-
holds. In their letter, the Congregation expressed their initial
hope that Mary of Guise herself might have effected reformation
by suppressing 'all idolatre, abhominatioun, and superstititioun
in this realme', an expectation not wholly unreasonable in view
of her earlier conciliatory gestures; but, subsequently they
discovered that her real intention was 'the downputting of Godis
gloir, his wird, and trew wirschiping'. They therefore reminded
Mary that she was God's 'minister and servand', to whom was
committed the 'office and ministratioun of ane kingdome
temporall'. In discharging the duties of that office she ought to
take care, that nothing 'be dwn contrair the will of God expressit
in his word' and that her actions did not exceed the bounds of her
office and vocation by trespassing into 'Christis kingdome
vsurpeand further powr vnto you nor he hes gewin', as God's
two kingdoms possessed distinctive governments:

   'ffor thocht all kindomes bayth temporall and spirituall pertenis to
   God, yit hes God distributit the ministerie diuerslye, that is the
   temporall kingdomes in the gouerment of mortell men, and makis
   thame princes of the erthe, for the mentenance of commown
   welthis and ciwill polaceis. Bot the gouerment of the spirituall and
   hewinlie kindome, the kirk of God we mein, he hes onlie
   committit to his sone Christ, ffor he is the heid thairoff, all wther
   ar her memberis vnder him'.

   In Christ's kingdom, as the reformers reminded her, the regent
was 'ane seruand and na quein, hawand na preheminence nor
authoritie aboue the kyrk, or onye power in that kingdome'; the
prince's rôle was to administer 'iustlie the authoritie temporall
gewin to your maiestie, and suffer Christ trewlie be his word to
rewill his awin kingdome'; and subjects, in rendering their duty,
should 'knaw the difference betwix God and Cesar', and 'obey
God before men'; they ought also to observe the example of 'the
prophetis and the apostlis, and all the marteris' who 'did disobei

[1] *The Works of John Knox*, ed. D. Laing, 6 vols (Edinburgh, 1846–64), iii, 433–
542; *Luther's Works*, edd. J. Pelican and H. T. Lehmann, 55 vols (Philadelphia,
1955–69), vol. 45, 81–129; vol. 46, 93–137, 161–205.

the commandimentis of imperouris and princeis' in fulfilling that
'quhilk God commandis'. The allegiance of all 'trew memberis of
Christis kirk' must therefore lie with the cause of reform by
assisting and defending true preachers of the Word 'thocht all the
poweris of the erthe will command the contrair'.[2] Notably, the
reformers' argument was not that Mary should be denied the
exercise of ecclesiastical authority because she was an 'ungodly'
prince, but that as a prince she remained a member of the church,
ineligible to assume greater ecclesiastical powers than any other
member. Even in a church reformed, the direction of ecclesiastical government was evidently not considered a princely duty.

This unambiguous statement of the doctrine of the two
kingdoms, which Andrew Melville a generation later could not
surpass, has curiously not received the attention it deserves. Its
significance is twofold. Not only does it expose the fallacy of
claims to establish Melville as the Scottish innovator of the two
kingdoms' doctrine but it suggests a continuity in thought
linking earlier and later generations of reformers. Certainly, a
belief in two separate ecclesiastical and temporal governments,
whose administration was not held to be united in the prince's
office, an emphasis on vocation, and on the need to avoid
exceeding the limits of one's calling are central themes shared by
Balnaves in the 1540s and by supporters of the Congregation's
letter in 1559, whose authorship may be attributed to Erskine of
Dun, a steadfast reformer whose earlier Lutheran insights were
later matched by an interest in the Swiss reformers. It is not
unreasonable to believe that, like Balnaves, Erskine readily
borrowed from Luther's teaching on the two kingdoms, though
Erskine's explicit identification of 'Christis kingdome', 'the
spirituall and hewinlie kingdome', with 'the kirk of God' was
narrower than Luther's understanding.

In any event, Erskine was also familiar with the ideas of
Oecolampadius,[3] the reformer of Basel, who, in acknowledging
the 'great difference between the temporal power and the
spiritual power', had advocated the adoption of a system of
ecclesiastical discipline, including the use of excommunication,
administered independently of the magistracy. Elsewhere,
Martin Bucer in Strasbourg had also expressed the need for an
autonomous ecclesiastical jurisdiction, arguing that 'the Church
of Christ should have her own discipline and punishment
beyond the common discipline and punishment of the secular
authority, even though it is entirely Christian and diligent and

[2] *Spalding Club Miscellany*, ed. J. Stuart, vol. iv (Aberdeen, 1849), 88–92.
[3] *Early Scottish Libraries*, ed. J. Durkan and A. Ross (Glasgow, 1961), 95.

eager in exercising discipline'. In developing this tradition of ecclesiastical independence, Calvin, too, had criticised those who failed to observe 'the distinction and dissimilarity between ecclesiastical and civil power', and who imagined that the exercise of an independent jursidiction by the church was merely 'temporary as magistrates were still strangers to our profession of religion', whereas, in reality, 'the Church cannot dispense with the spiritual jurisdiction which existed from the beginning'.[4] There were, therefore, ample precedents, both Lutheran and Reformed, for the Scots to consider when they formulated their doctrine of the two kingdoms in 1559.

The concept of two kingdoms 'bayth temporall and spirituall', over which, as his own creation, God chose to exercise his powers diversely as sovereign ruler, presented no more of an anomaly than the earthly rule of two separate kingdoms by the same monarch: at the end of the thirteenth century, the kingdoms of Bohemia and Poland had been ruled by the same monarch; at the end of the fourteenth century, in the Scandi-navian kingdoms, it was possible for one king to rule not two but three realms; at the end of the fifteenth century, a dynastic marriage had united the rulers of the two Spanish kingdoms; and later James VI was able to demonstrate how two separate kingdoms could share one head, and how inhabitants from each realm should become subjects of both kingdoms yet still be governed through different agencies.

Apart from acknowledging the undisputed sovereignty of God, the Congregation's letter contains no trace of what one modern writer has considered to be the reformers' aim of 'introducing the concept of a single authority over ecclesiastical and secular affairs'.[5] In expounding their doctrine of the two kingdoms, the reformers, of course, were not so naïve as to deny that God ruled both realms. After all, the reformers had consistently emphasised their conviction that princes were the ministers and servants of God within the bounds assigned to their office. Christ's headship was understood to extend over commonwealth as well as church. What they did reject was precisely the belief that God had delegated earthly government to a single authority responsible for directing both ecclesiastical and secural affairs; instead they acknowledged that God had

---

[4] Akira Demura, 'Church Discipline according to Johannes Oecolampadius in the Setting of his Life and Thought' (Princeton Theological Seminary, Th.D. disssertation, 1964), 16, 79, 87–8, 99, 102, 154–5; M. U. Christman, *Strasbourg and the Reform* (New Haven, 1967), 207–8; Calvin, *Institutes of the Christian Religion*, ed. H. Beveridge, 3 vols (Edinburgh, 1846), IV, xi, 3–4.

[5] G. Donaldson, *Scottish Church History* (Edinburgh, 1985), 235.

diffused his power (he had 'distributit the ministerie diuerslye') by vesting authority in different agencies.

Consequently, when Erskine of Dun, at the Congregation's behest, told the queen regent in 1559 that in Christ's kingdom, 'the kirk of god we mein', she was but a member, 'ane seruand and na quein', he intended not to convey (and would only have ridiculed) any suggestion that Christ was not also lord of the commonwealth, but to affirm that the direction of the church on earth belonged not to an individual, either pope or prince, but was diffused among its members, and their representatives, who were receptive to the message of the Word. The point, of course, was not that the same community or body should develop two heads but that the different facets of society (not all of whose members shared the same religious faith) should be served with forms of government best suited to meeting particular needs: in the spiritual dimension or realm, Christ was seen to rule through the preaching of the Word, a function committed not to princes but to the ministry of men called to hold office in his church; and in temporal affairs, the prince as God's lieutenant in this sphere, was responsible for fortifying faith, not by nurturing men's souls with spiritual food but by regulating men's outward conduct and behaviour, enabling them to serve their neighbour (as Balnaves had remarked) in accordance with the teaching of the Word. Distinctive jurisdictions were thus the necessary product of the different forms of government; and two kinds of government, in turn, denoted or, at least, implied *regna* or kingdoms.

Such an affirmation by the Lords of the Congregation also coincided with Calvin's own understanding of the problem where he observed how:

> 'in man government is twofold: the one spiritual, by which the conscience is trained to piety and divine worship; the other civil, by which the individual is instructed in those duties which, as men and citizens, we are bound to perform. To these two forms are commonly given the not inappropriate names of spiritual and temporal jurisdiction, intimating that the former species has reference to the life of the soul, while the latter relates to matters of the present life, not only to food and clothing, but to the enacting of laws which require a man to live among his fellows purely, honourably and modestly. The former has its seat within the soul, the latter only regulates the external conduct. We may call the one spiritual, the other the civil kingdom'.[6]

In Edwardine England, John Hooper adopted a not wholly dissimilar conception of dual government; his understanding was that:

[6] Calvin, *Institutes*, III, xix, 15.

'Whereas every commonwealth ought to have but two governors God and the prince, the one to make a law for the soul, the other for the body: all the king's officers to be ministers of the law made to the conservation of the commonwealth, and the bishops to be ministers in the church, of the law that is prescribed by God; as all justices, mayors, sheriffs, constables and bailiffs, be ministers of the law made unto them, to govern the commonwealth; so must the bishops, priests, and all other preachers, be ministers of Christ, and govern the people in their vocation according unto the law prescribed by God'.[7]

At a practical level, too, there was certainly no novelty in subjecting the community to different forms of government. For a start, the exercise of lordship, itself a mode of government, operating at a variety of levels, meant that an individual could find himself the client of more than one lord; an individual might even have an appreciation of 'local' and 'central' government, at least in the sense of distinguishing delegated authority from the authority personally exercised by the king wherever he happened to reside; and he could scarcely have been unaware, at one point or another, of the competing and overlapping, even rival, jurisdictions of privy council and court of session, of parliaments and conventions of estates, of conventions of royal burghs, merchant gilds and craft incorporations, town councils, burgh courts, dean of gild courts, commissary courts, barony courts and sheriff courts, not to mention the extensive jurisdiction formerly exercised by the courts of the pre-Reformation church, with their allegiance to an authority beyond the realm. It was therefore wholly conceivable to contemporaries that the different aspects of the same community should have, if not several heads, at least, distinctive governments under the sole headship of Christ.

At the same time, Christ's headship could be interpreted variously. As second person in the Trinity, Christ could be understood to share God's kingship, his sovereignty or kingly rule over the entire world he had created, 'the kingdom of God'; as mediator, Christ was believed to have a particular relationship not with earthly kingdoms but with his church, the people whom he rules with his spirit and who therefore form his kingdom. This was the identification between 'Christis kingdome' and 'the kirk of God' which 'the professouris of Christis ewangell in the realme of Scotland' made in 1559; it recurred in Erskine's distinction in 1571 between 'the ciuile policie . . . of a commone wealth' and the 'kirk of God' which was 'the bodie of Christ', the 'spous of the Almychtie', 'the inheritance of the Lord, his proper

[7] J. Hooper, *Early Writings*, ed. S. Carr (Cambridge, 1843), 142.

possessioun and kingdome', the 'citie and habitatione quhairin the Lord delytis to duell'; and the same reasoning was responsible for the assembly's recognition of 'our two states of Church and Common Wealth' (1595), of 'Chrystis kingdom better established in our congregatiouns' (1596), and for commissioners to an assembly to speak of 'the kirk and kingdome of Jesus Christ established within this Realme' (1604).[8]

II

The Higher Powers:
The political theories espoused by the reformers complemented their adherence to a theology in which God was perceived as ruling the ecclesiastical and temporal jurisdictions by different methods. In affirming Christ's distinctive kingship and headship 'of his Kirk', John Knox in 1550 had implicitly recognised that the church formed Christ's kingdom, in which 'yf he be King, then must he do the office of a King; whilk is not onlie to gyd, reule, and defend his subjectis, but also to mak and statute lawis, whilk lawis onlie, ar his subjectis bound to obey, and not the lawis of any Forrane Princes'. Accordingly, it belonged to 'the Kirk of Jesus Chryst to advert what he speiketh, to receave and imbrace his lawis', for 'all the power of the Kirk is subject to Godis Word'.[9]

In opposing the pope and prelates of the old order whom he wished to see swept from power, Knox initially had turned, as had reformers throughout Europe, to the prince and civil magistrate whose duty as God's lieutenants, he emphasised, was to reform and maintain the church in accordance with God's Word.[10] In December 1557, Knox was ready to recognise:

> 'that na power on earth is above the power of the Civill reular; that everie saule, be he Pope or Cardinall, aught to be subject to the higher Poweris. That thair commandementis, not repugnying to Godis glorie and honour, aught to be obeyit, evin with great loss of temporall thingis'.[11]

Yet he was not prepared to concede to the prince that freedom or latitude to establish whatever form of religion the prince thought

---

[8] *Spalding Club Miscellany*, iv, 88–101; *The Booke of the Universall Kirk, Acts and Procedings of the General Assemblies of the Kirk of Scotland, 1560–1618* [*BUK*], ed. T. Thomson, 3 vols and appendix vol. (Edinburgh, 1839–45), iii, 854, 867; Holy Trinity Parish Church, St Andrews, St Andrews Presbytery Records, 9 August 1604; *The Autobiography and Diary of Mr James Melvill*, ed. R. Pitcairn (Edinburgh, 1842), 563.

[9] Knox, *Works*, iii, 41.

[10] Ibid., iv, 79, 443, 445–6, 485ff, 513.

[11] Ibid., iv. 324.

fit. Nor was it acceptable to the reformer that religious practices should be adopted merely because they did not contradict scripture; they ought, Knox believed, to have the positive warrant and command of scripture, for 'in religioun thair is na middis: either it is the religioun of God, and that in everie thing that is done it must have the assurance of his awn Word, and than is his Majestie trewlie honourit, or els it is the religioun of the Divill, whilk is, when men will erect and set up to God sic religioun as pleaseth thame'.[12] By 1558, in his 'Exhortation to England' (published in 1559), Knox reminded English pro-testants (as Andrew Melville was later to remind King James) that the prince had no greater authority in religious affairs 'then becometh a membre of Christ's body'; he therefore sharply admonished them:

> 'Let not the King and his proceadinges (whatsoever they be), not agreable to his Worde, be a snare to thy conscience. O cursed were the hartes that first devised that phrase in matters of religion, whereby the simple people were broght to one of these two inconveniences: to wit, That either they dyd esteme everie religion good and acceptable unto God, which the King and Parliament dyd approve and commande; or els, that God's religion, honor, and service, was nothinge els but devises of men'.[13]

In countries where the Reformation was effected through the crown, the prince might readily seek to determine the religious allegiance of his subjects, but in Scotland, where the Reformation was achieved in defiance of the wishes of the crown, the rôles were reversed as reformers sought to impose their religious values on the prince. If he had earlier been tempted to place his faith in princes, as a counterpoise to the papacy, Knox soon saw around him princes unwilling to repent and prepared to act in a manner unworthy of God's vicegerents; he therefore looked elsewhere to other elements in the constitution for support. His observation that 'oft it is that Princes ar the most ignorant of all otheris in Goddis treu Religioun' had driven him to the painful conclusion that princes must either be reformed or all good men must depart from their service. If he attempted to usurp God's rule and contradict divine law, the prince should be considered an enemy of God, unfit to reign, even deserving punishment by death as an idolater and destroyer of God's true religion. Knox therefore developed his argument from his original contention that reformation pertained to more than bishops and clergy by claiming, in turn, that the cause of religion concerned more than

[12] Ibid., iv, 232.
[13] Ibid., v, 515.

princes, and by appealing to the nobility as born councillors and lesser magistrates to bridle the fury and rage of idolatrous and ungodly monarchs.[14]

Yet, to his disgust, Knox realised that nobles, too, could reveal themselves as uncommitted or untrustworthy; they were as liable as pope or prince to abrogate God's law and frustrate his work on earth, claiming for themselves the patrimony which properly belonged to the church alone.[15] He, therefore, turned to the people, the community at large, and urged them to action so that they might play their rightful part in bringing about a Reformation in defiance of the higher powers.

In his rousing 'Letter to the Commonalty of Scotland', Knox boldly affirmed in 1558: 'Neither would I that ye should esteme the Reformation and care of Religion lesse to appertain to you, because ye are no Kinges, Rulers, Judges, Nobils, nor in auctoritie'. As God's creatures, for whom Christ's blood was shed, subjects as much as sovereigns were recipients of the Gospel; and 'albeit God hath put and ordened distinction and difference betwixt the King and subjects, betwixt the Rulers and the commune people, *in the regiment and administration of Civile policies*', in the spiritual kingdom God had made all men equal 'in the hope of the life to come'. It was therefore the duty of ordinary people, as much as kings and princes, to ensure that 'Christ Jesus be truely preached amongest you, seing that without his true knowledge can neither of you both attaine to salvation'. If the superior powers failed to provide true preachers, it became the people's responsibility in cities, towns and villages to establish, maintain and defend protestant preachers against their adversaries. To plead that simple subjects were unable to redress the faults of rulers was no excuse in the sight of God who required subjects and rulers alike to remove all superstition and idolatry.[16] Here was a clarion call to action and an end to vacillation.

A further insight into the developing struggle between the advocates of revolution from below and the attempts of government to retain political control was revealed, in a later episode, in Maitland of Lethington's debates with Knox who firmly insisted that the right to take the life of an idolatrous prince lay with 'the peopill of God'. Once more, however, Knox

[14] Ibid., ii, 281; iv, 327; v, 516; cf. C. Goodman, *How Superior Powers Oght to be Obeyd* (Facsimile Text Society, New York, 1931), 58–9, 139–40; Knox, *Works*, iv, 490; i, 411; cf. Goodman, *Superior Powers*, 35.

[15] Knox, *Works*, ii, 128.

[16] Ibid., iv, 523–38; iv, 501, 507; ii, 442–3, 452; cf. Goodman, *Superior Powers*, 142.

feared and distrusted the unpredictable actions of the populace; his 'beloved brethren the communaltie of Scotland' could readily degenerate into 'the rascal multitude' whose worst excesses and wanton violence made him appreciate the people's limitations. His final aim was therefore, through discipline, to raise the church supreme over all. 'My travell,' he declared in 1561, 'is that boyth princes and subjectis obey God', for all mortals alike must be subject 'unto God, and unto his trubled Churche'.[17] Such an aphorism sums up Knox's whole approach.

The progression in Knox's political thought can, of course, be traced in a manner which it is not possible to undertake so readily for other reformers whose ideas are less fully documented. Nonetheless, it was the collective decision of the Congregation in 1559 'to tak the sweard of just defence aganis all that shall persew us for the mater of religioun'. By distinguishing between 'the authoritie quhiche is Goddis ordinance, and the personis of those whiche ar placit in authoritie', whose 'injust commandimentis' should not be obeyed, the protestant insurgents swiftly organised themselves into an army of the Congregation, threatening violent action in their confrontations with opponents. Charged by the queen regent with plain rebellion 'under pretence and colour of religioun', the Congregation protested that their action was directed solely at promoting God's glory by defending true preachers and eliminating idolatry and abuse, to which the regent was invited to contribute 'as is the dewetie of everie Christiane Prince and good magistrat'.[18]

Protestant preachers might well 'commend to God all Princeis in generall, and the Magistrattis of this our natyve realme in particular', but they strictly qualified the obedience of subjects to magistrates by approving the right of 'the Nobilitie, sworne and borne Counsallouris', in free kingdoms, and also of 'the Barronis and Pepill' to restrain the unlawful actions of princes. They therefore argued 'gif wickit personeis, abusing the auctoratie estableischet be God, command thingis manifestlie wickit, that sick as may and do brydill thair inordinatt appetyteis of Princeis, can not be accusit as resistaris of the aucthoratie, quhilk is Godis gud ordinance'. After summoning two preachers, Willock and Knox, to discourse on the bounds of the magistrate's authority and on the just causes for deposing princes, the protestant nobles, barons and burgesses in convention at Edinburgh, on

[17] Knox, *Works*, ii, 441 ('the pople of God' is a recurring theme in the writings of Knox and Goodman, e.g. Knox, *Works*, ii, 453; Goodman, *Superior Powers*, 35); Knox, *Works*, i, 322; cf. ii, 155, 164, 396; ii, 283.
[18] Knox, *Works*, i, 326; cf. 344; i, 332–3; i, 363; i, 335–6, 344, 351–66.

recounting the enormity of her alleged crimes, solemnly 'suspended' Mary of Guise from her regency in October 1559 and sought to transfer power to a protestant provisional government. In doing so, the insurgents maintained the legal fiction that they acted 'in name and authoritie' of their sovereigns, Queen Mary and her husband Francis II of France, to whom they professed continuing obedience.[19]

Mary's return home to rule in person in 1561 raised in more urgent form protestant reaction to the rôle of a supreme magistrate whose religious preferences were not those of all her subjects. Yet such was their esteem for the ruler's office that the reformers in their Confession of Faith assigned to the magistracy 'cheiflie and maist principallie the conservatioun and purgatioun of the Religioun'.[20] Their expectation that Mary would maintain 'the true Religioun' and suppress, not practise, 'idolatrie and superstitioun whatsomever' may not have been fully realised; but, in the event, Mary came much closer to observing those duties placed upon her than is usually appreciated: far from resolutely defending Catholicism as a creed or even the interests of the generality of her co-religionists, Mary opted as her official policy to maintain protestantism; she repeatedly prohibited any change in religion or worship; she granted the reformed ministry financial support in the form of manses, glebes and a share in the revenues of parochial benefices; she recognised the need to legislate for the repair of churches for protestant worship; and she even rewarded a superintendent of the kirk with the property of a bishopric. Nor did she set her mind against occasional attendance at public preaching and even granted audiences at court to protestant preachers, including Knox, to the dismay of Romanists.[21] At the same time, the queen studiously withheld effective support for a counter-reformation; as emphatically as any protestant monarch, she approved firm action against Roman Catholic worship (her own household excepted) and countenanced the prosecution of priests for celebrating the outlawed mass. As things stood, under Mary Stewart Scottish protestants enjoyed a freedom of expression both in worship and in governing their church which assuredly was denied to Catholics and unknown to the subjects of Elizabeth Tudor.

---

[19] Knox, *Works*, i, 410–11, cf. 424; 441–8.

[20] *Acts of the Parliaments of Scotland* [*APS*], edd. T. Thomson and C. Innes, 12 vols (Edinburgh, 1814–75), iii, 534; Knox, *Works*, ii, 118; cf. iv, 485–6.

[21] Cf. *Calendar of State Papers relating to Scotland and Mary, Queen of Scots, 1547–1603* [*CSP Scot.*], edd. J. Bain *et al.*, 13 vols (Edinburgh, 1898–1969), i, no. 1017.

The effect of Mary's conciliatory policies towards the reformed church accentuated the division in protestant opinion on whether subjects might justifiably restrain by force a monarch who wished to have the mass in her private chapel. Knox, who in 1561 had expounded 'the duty of all kind of magistrates in a good reformed commonwealth', was no stranger to arguing that women who ruled deserved deposition. In recognition that 'subjectis ar not bound to the Religioun of their Princes, albeit thei ar commanded to geve thame obedience', Knox quickly qualified the limits of obedience by affirming, in his interview with the queen at court in 1561, that princes who 'exceed thair boundis' might legitimately be 'resisted, evin by power'; and later, in 1563, when he again considered it no sin before God for 'otheris then cheaff magistrattis' to constrain and bridle kings who 'stryck innocent men in thair raige', Knox drew the queen's attention to the 'mutuall contract' under God between prince and people and the reciprocal obligations of each, a theme which was to re-emerge at Mary's deposition or enforced abdication in 1567.[22]

However forthrightly expressed, Knox's opinions were, of course, those of one individual; they were shared by some and rejected by others; but the underlying issue of whether 'subjectis mycht put to thair hand to suppresse the idolatrie of thair Prince' was hotly debated at a meeting of influential protestants in the home of James MacGill, the clerk register, in 1561 when the leading politicians present (a group which comprised Lord James Stewart, the Earl of Morton, the Earl Marishcal, Maitland of Lethington, the queen's secretary, Bellenden of Auchnoul, the justic clerk, and MacGill) argued in favour of the queen's right to worship privately in her chapel, as she chose, and that 'subjectis mycht not lauchfullie tack hir Messe frome hir', an opinion opposed by the 'principall ministeris' present, whose number included John Knox, John Row, minister at Perth and an author of the Confession and Discipline of 1560, Robert Hamilton, regent in St Mary's college and minister at St Andrews, and George Hay, of whose standing there is evidence in Knox's measured comment in 1564 that he was 'callit the Minister of the Court'. On that occasion, as Knox conceded, the wishes of the lords prevailed at the expense of the ministers; but when Maitland of Lethington, in 1564, expressed further disapproval of Knox's 'extremitie aganis hir Messe' and asked him to moderate his language both in his prayers for the queen and in

[22] Ibid., i, no. 1023; Knox, *Works*, iv, 415–16; ii, 281–2; ii, 372–3.

his doctrine of obedience, the preacher responded, steadfast in his convictions, by reasserting the distinction between the office of kingship, which was God's ordinance, and the person occupying the office, whose unlawful actions subjects ought justifiably to resist without fear of violating the ordinance of God. For Knox, 'the peopill assembled togidder in one bodie of ane Commounewealth' were empowered by God 'nocht onlie to resyst, but also to suppres all kynde of opin idolatrie' even if practised by the prince himself. 'The peopll', he believed, 'may put Godis lawis in executioune' against their king 'having no farther regaird to him in that behalf, than gif he had bene the moist simpill subject within this Realme'.[23]

When invited by Maitland to contradict Knox's views on obedience, George Hay not only declined but sided with Knox, revealingly adding, in Knox's words, that 'monie utheris', presumably in Scotland, shared his beliefs. If Maitland in his argument appealed to the teaching of Luther, Melanchthon, Bucer, Musculus and Calvin, whose views Knox claimed he had distorted by taking them out of context, Knox, for his part, cited the Lutheran example of the Magdeburg *Bekenntnis* of 1550 which justified resistance by inferior magistrates against oppressive rule; and, among the Reformed of whom he had knowledge, he might also have added the judgment of Pierre Viret in 1547 (to whom Calvin had given Knox a letter of introduction in 1554) and of Theodore Beza in 1554, who each had justified the resort of godly magistrates to resistance by force.[24]

When the opinions of other ministers were canvassed, John Douglas, provost of St Mary's college in St Andrews, and John Winram, superintendent of Fife, agreed that 'gif the Quene oppone hir self to oure religioun, whilk is the onelie trew religioun', then the nobility and estates of the realm, as professors of true doctrine 'may justlie oppone thame selffis unto hir' but they remained unresolved on whether Mary might be denied her mass 'be violence'. Knox's colleague in Edinburgh, John Craig, assented to the belief he had heard debated at Bologna that 'All Reuleris, be thay supreame or be they

[23] Knox, *Works*, ii, 291–2, 423–54.
[24] Ibid., ii, 434–5, 442, 453; O. K. Olson, 'Theology of Revolution; Magdeburg, 1550–1551', *Sixteenth-Century Journal*, iii (1972), 56–79; *Corpus Reformatorum*, 43, *Ionnis Calvini Opera . . . omnia*, edd. G. Baum, E. Cunitz and E. Reuss, XV (Brunswick, 1876), no. 1909, 38–9; R. D. Linder, *The Political Ideas of Pierre Viret* (Geneva, 1964), 127ff, 140; R. M. Kingdon, 'The First Expression of Theodore Beza's Political Ideas', *Archiv für Reformationsgeschichte* [ARG], 46 (1955), 88–100; Knox, *Works*, iv, 31, 35; v, 38, 184, 229; vi, 119, 544, 550, 562, 613.

inferiour, may and aucht to be reformed or deposed be thame be whom thay ar chosin, confirmed, or admitted to thair office, as oft as they brak that promeis maid be the oath to thair subjectis'. With opinion divided, it was left to Knox to seek Calvin's advice in Geneva, in much the manner in which a decade earlier he had submitted to Bullinger at Zürich a series of questions on obedience to lawful maigstrates.[25]

It would be unreasonable to deny that opinions at variance with Knox's utterances were also held among ministers. Indeed, it is possible that the ideas expressed by John Carswell in Argyll diverged from the theories which prevailed in the general assembly, which he seems infrequently to have attended. Nor need it be doubted that Alexander Gordon's adherence in 1571 to the doctrine that 'na inferiour subiect hes power to deprive or depose their lauchfull magistrate' was indicative of attitudes which he had earlier espoused. But the cause to which he, as a Marian, was attached to defending proved a lost cause by 1572; and the revolutionaries of 1567 had already secured a further tactical advantage in having their accusations against Mary reviewed at an English conference during 1568.[26]

Not surprisingly, other exponents of the right to active resistance were far from silent. Knox's Genevan colleague, Christopher Goodman, minister first at Ayr and then for five years at St Andrews, had earlier argued that to obey an ungodly prince was to disobey God, to resist such a prince was not to oppose God but Satan; a prince's duty was to advance the glory of God; 'by the ordinance of God, no other kinges or Rulers, oght to be chosen to rule ouer vs, but suche as will seke his honor and glorie'; princes and magistrates who abused their powers by countenancing blasphemy, idolatry and oppression ought no longer to be recognised as 'kinges or lawfull Magistrats, but as priuate men', and punished accordingly. In defending true religion, it was the duty not only of nobles and magistrates to ensure that 'their Princes be subiect to Gods Lawes' but of 'the comon people also', 'the whole multitude', to whom 'a portion of the sworde of iustice is committed' and who 'oght not to suffer all power and libertie to be taken from them'.[27] In academic circles, too, the return to Scotland of George Buchanan by 1562, lent intellectual vigour, from a standpoint which was

[25] Knox, *Works*, ii, 459–60; iii, 221–6.
[26] See below, 303; *Journal of the Transactions in Scotland*, ed. J. G. Dalyell (Edinburgh, 1806), 181; G. Donaldson, *The First Trial of Mary, Queen of Scots* (London, 1969), 106ff.
[27] Goodman, *Superior Powers*, 34–5, 47, 58–9, 103, 110, 122, 139–40, 142, 149, 180–4.

not theological but classical and humanist, to the cause of tyrannicide and of a limited, elective kingship. Reaffirming the notion of a 'mutual contract between the king and the people', Buchanan defended the historic right of the people, 'to create kings and to keep them within due bounds' by calling them to account and by passing judgment on the magistracy, for ultimately 'in the people, to whom belongs the supreme power, lies the enactment of laws'; and just as the prince, who at his coronation should swear to uphold the constitution, ought to be subject to the law, and not be above it, so too should he accept the discipline of the church in spiritual matters.[28]

In the midst of formulating these theories (which later circulated in manuscript in 1569 and finally in print by 1579), Buchanan found himself elected moderator of the general assembly which met in June 1567. The meeting took place in troubled times, ten days after Mary's surrender at Carberry to the confederate lords whom the assembly (in Argyll's perception as a queen's man), was understood to support. Like some others, Argyll absented himself from a second, hastily summoned assembly which met in July, at a point when Mary, at Lochleven, was constrained to demit the crown in favour of her infant son, prince James. Nor was it unforeseen that the assembly would give its blessing to the unprecedented action of the lords in deposing a reigning monarch by substituting her son as king while she still lived.[29]

Whether they based their contractual theories on the 'ancient Scottish constitution' which Buchanan had thoughtfully revived (or rather contrived), or, more comprehensively on biblical precedents, supported by historical examples, the laws and practices of the realm, and the conditions attached to the prince's coronation oath which John Knox and his colleague John Craig had provided, the general assembly readily justified the lords' proceedings in the belief that 'it hes pleasit Almightie God of his mercie to give ane native prince to this countrey, appeirand to be our soveraigne'. Besides, the assembly considered that the relationship between God, prince and people constituted a 'band and contract to be mutuall and reciproque in all tymes comeing betuixt the prince and God, and also betuixt the prince and

---

[28] G. Buchanan, *De Jure Regni apud Scotos*, translated by D. H. MacNeill, in *The Art and Science of Government Among the Scots* (Glasgow, 1964), 64, 69, 71, 78, 84–5, 88, 96; cf. H. R. Trevor Roper, 'George Buchanan and the Ancient Scottish Constitution', *English Historical Review* (Supplement 3, 1966), 8, 42, 45, 47.

[29] I. D. McFarlane, *Buchanan* (London, 1981), 392–3; *CSP Scot.*, ii, no. 560, p. 351; *BUK*, i, 93, 101, 106–10.

faithfull peiple according to the word of God'. Accordingly, 'all kings, princes, and magistrates', before entering office, should be required to 'make ther faithfull league and promise to the true kirk of God', which they must pledge to maintain and defend. The assembly, it would seem, was intent on dictating to princes the terms of their rule.[30]

The implications of the 'covenant' or 'contract' theory which the assembly reaffirmed in 1567 were conveniently vague and ill-defined; but at least they did suggest clearly enough that sovereignty was delegated to the prince by God through the people to whom he remained accountable for his actions. Unlike James VI who, when freed from Buchanan's domination, later denounced 'this mutuall and reciprock band' and declared that 'kings were the authors and makers of the Lawes, and not the Lawes of the kinges',[31] the heirs of the Scottish revolution came to profess their belief in a strictly limited 'constitutional' monarchy, in an age when kings sought to magnify their powers. From different premises, Buchanan and Knox, with support from Craig, Goodman (by then in England) and other radically-minded ministers, had arrived at the same conclusion that kings were responsible not to God alone but, in a very real sense, to their subjects, too; any king acting against God's will and the people's interests was deemed to have broken the basic covenant and, as a tyrant, deserved deposition.

Such a philosophy infuriated Queen Elizabeth who considered the Scottish revolutionaries to have 'no warrant by God's or man's law to be as superiors, judges, or vindicators over their prince'; nor was it 'consonant in nature that the head shuld be subject to the foote'; it was strenuously repudiated by leading English divines, and was utterly disclaimed by the majority of continental reformers including Calvin who cautiously recognised that it was perhaps permissible for the estates of the realm as inferior magistrates to check the licence of tyrants.[32] Yet to those Scots who welcomed the revolutions of 1560 and 1567 justification for resistance and rebellion seemed self-evident.

[30] CSP Scot., ii, no. 563; BUK, i, 108–9.
[31] The Political Works of James I, ed. C. H. McIlwain (Cambridge, Mass., 1918), 55–6, 62.
[32] CSP Scot., ii, no. 577; T. Cranmer, Works, ed. J. E. Cox, 2 vols (Cambridge, 1844–6), ii, 185, 188; The Works of John Jewel, ed. J. Ayre, 4 vols (Cambridge, 1845–50), iv, 974; The Works of John Whitgift, ed. J. Ayre, 3 vols (Cambridge, 1851–3), ii, 407–8; R. Bancroft, Dangerous Positions and Proceedings (1593); The Works of . . . Richard Hooker, ed. I. Walton, 2 vols (Oxford, 1845), ii, 583–6; T. Bilson, The True Difference Between Christian Subjection and Unchristian Rebellion (1585); Calvin, Institutes, IV, xx, 31; J. T. McNeill, John Calvin on God and Political Duty (New York, 1950), xviii.

Indeed, although a great many protestants supported the queen's cause, it was impossible for those who had opposed Mary to approve her deposition, on the one hand, and to assert, on the other, as Elizabeth did in England and as James VI later attempted in Scotland, that kings were responsible to God alone, that rebellion was altogether wicked and unjustified, and that subjects could appeal only 'by sobbes and teares to God'.[33]

Nor will it suffice to attribute the contractual theories of monarchy elaborated in the assembly of 1567 merely to the extravagant delusions of the clerical mentors of the new king, for not only had the nobles, barons and others present in the assembly individually subscribed to these beliefs but the first parliament of the new reign, meeting in December 1567, expressly approved and 'ffund gude' the assembly's observations on the coronation oath.[34] Contemporaries were then evidently ready to concede that royal authority, of its very nature, was far from unlimited. This being so, if as reformers contended the prince's rule within the commonwealth was firmly limited by divine and human law alike, it was no historical accident that reformers should express a no less critical view of any claims, even by a godly prince, to supremacy over the church. The decent English precedent of acknowledging the prince as supreme governor of the protestant church was not to be readily repeated in Scotland. Nor is this surprising, for it is sometimes necessary to recall that even in England the royal supremacy was acknowledged only with misgiving.

In his 'Admonition to England and Scotland' in which he warned the Scots to 'folow not the example of your brethren of England', Anthony Gilby, a Genevan exile with Knox in 1558, had attacked, with particular ferocity, Henry VIII's title to headship of the English church, thereby 'displacing Christ our only head of the church,' an attitude which had found earlier expression in Hugh Latimer's criticism of Henry's headship as 'a chargeable dignity'. The milder Thomas Sampson sought advice from Zürich in 1558 on how 'to act with respect of allowing or disallowing the title "after Christ supreme head of the Church of England"', when 'all scripture seems to assign the title of head of the Church to Christ alone'; and Thomas Cartwright considered that 'although the godly magistrate be the head of the common-wealth, and a great ornament unto the church, yet he is but a

---

[33] *Political Works of James VI*, 61.
[34] *BUK*, i, 110; *APS*, iii, 39; cf. 23-4.

member of the same', a remark which invites comparison with Scottish reformers' claims in 1559.[35]

III

Royal Supremacy rejected:

What looks like a clear enough indication of the kirk's hostile attitude towards the emergence of any theory of royal supremacy over the church occurred in 1568 when the Edinburgh printer, Thomas Bassandyne, without the magistrate's licence or kirk's permission, printed a book on the 'Fall of the Roman Kirk', in which James VI was depicted as 'supreme head of the primitive kirk', a title to which the assembly took such exception that it ordered the printer to 'call in againe all the saidis bookes that he hes sauld, and keip the rest unsauld untill he alter the forsaid title'. The futility of arguing that the assembly's objection was not to the crown's supremacy, as such, but merely to the peculiar phraseology 'supreame head of the primitive kirk' (at a point, be it noted, when the kirk sought to restore 'the grave and godlie face of the primitive Churche') is amply demonstrated six years later when the Regent Morton failed to persuade the church to accept the crown's supremacy in matters ecclesiastical.[36]

In a conference, specially convened for the express purpose of gaining acceptance of the royal supremacy, Morton invited representatives from the church (whose number comprised James Lawson, Knox's successor in Edinburgh, superintendents Erskine and Spottiswoode, and David Lindsay, minister at Leith) in March 1574 to debate with representatives of the government the proposition 'whether the supreame magistrate should not be head of the church was well as of the commonwealthe'; but the meeting ended, without agreement, when the Regent discovered there was 'no appearance of obtaining that point', as the ministers rejected his claims. Although no account of the conference has survived in the defective record of the assembly's proceedings, there is significantly mention in that month of the assembly's selection of commissioners to discuss with the Regent and privy councillors the issue of 'the jurisdictioun and policie of the Kirk, and sick uther heids and articles as salbe proponit be his Grace and Counsell to them'. The accuracy and authenticity of

---

[35] Knox, *Works*, iv, 561–4; Latimer, *Works*, i, 152; *Zürich Letters*, ed. H. Robinson, 2 vols (Cambridge, 1842–5), i, 1; Whitgift, *Works*, i, 390; see above, 235–6.

[36] *BUK*, i, 125–6; Knox, *Works*, i, 303, 306; ii, 264; *BUK*, i, 94, 107, 267, 311; ii, 419; *Register of the Minister, Elders and Deacons of the Christian Congregation of St Andrews* [*RStAKS*], ed. D. H. Fleming, 2 vols (Edinburgh, 1889–90), i, 311.

the report that the supremacy was both discussed and rejected at the meeting can therefore scarcely be doubted. Besides, another, strictly contemporary source also testifies to the church's refusal in March 1574 to acknowledge any claims to the crown's supremacy, and records the Regent's insistence that 'the king and his counsall sould be suppreme heid of the kirk under god', and the ministers' assertion that they were 'supreame heid of the kirk and that nane sould have jurrisdictioun ovir thame bot thair sellffis and generall counsall under God'.[37]

Here was a further indication of the church's unwillingness to vest ecclesiastical authority in the crown, privy council or parliament, or indeed in any other organ of temporal government, and of its resolve that the general assembly, representing Christian communities, should continue as the appropriate means for governing the church. In any event, it is clear that the continued existence of the general assembly (whose jurisdiction and right to convene were not recognised either to emanate from or be dependent upon the authority of the crown) remained an obstacle to the emergence of royal headship over the church. As contemporaries were aware, the assembly as the church's highest court limited and impaired the king's jurisdiction, so preventing him from becoming 'a frie King and monarche, haiffing the rewell and power of all Esteates'. To separate the government of the church from the government of the commonwealth, as Whitgift explained in England, was 'to divide one realm into two, and to spoil the prince of the one half of her jurisdiction and authority'.[38]

The attitude of reformers in Scotland towards the rôle and rights of the crown in the church readily accorded with beliefs expressed by leading continental divines. Luther's claim that 'on earth there is no head of spiritual Christendom other than Christ alone' rendered it difficult to substitute royal supremacy for papal headship. Martin Bucer, if anything, was even more explicit in his condemnation of the concept when he observed:

> 'None of the earthly members of the Church becomes its head; it has its head in Christ in heaven. The princes and magistrates of each local church may of course be called "heads", but only in the body politic and in political government, not in the ecclesiastical sphere.'[39]

[37] D. Hume of Godscroft, *History of the Houses of Douglas and Angus* (Edinburgh, 1644), 334; *BUK*, i, 295–6; R. Lindesay of Pitscottie, *The Historie and Cronicles of Scotland*, ed. E. J. G. Mackay, 3 vols (Edinburgh, 1899–1911), ii, 313–14.

[38] Melville, *Diary*, 61; Whitgift, *Works*, ii, 264.

[39] *Luther's Works*, vol. 39, p. 72; *Common Places of Martin Bucer*, ed. D. F. Wright (Appleford, 1972), 203.

It was not for nothing, therefore, that Calvin censured the 'blasphemies' by which Henry VIII had asserted his claim to be 'sovereign head of the church' in England, a criticism evidently shared by Bullinger, who, in repelling papal demands, recognised that the titles 'head of the church' and 'supreme governor of the faithful' should be bestowed on 'no creature without blasphemy and sacrilege'. The French reformed church, which also displayed an antipathy to magisterial control, condemned at its national synod at La Rochelle in 1571 the opinions of a doctor in Bordeaux, accused of having 'maintained the Supremacy of the Magistrate as Head of the Church', a subject which had earlier engaged the attention of the Genevan Company of Pastors in 1564 when the threat of tyranny inherent in the claims both of the papacy and of the monarch in England to act as 'head of the church' had been expounded.[40]

The Scottish dimension to this European debate is apparent not least in Erskine of Dun's outspoken criticism in 1571 of the magistrate's unwarranted interference in the church by 'medling with suche things as apperteane to the ministers of God's kirk', when he pronounced that 'of old the Papists called the truth heresie; and some now call the truthe treasoun'.[41] In Erskine's estimation, royal control could prove as detrimental as papal headship to the church's welfare. The inescapable conclusion would seem to be that ministers in Scotland found no difficulty in denying the claim that the prince as head of the commonwealth should also be recognised as head of the church within his realm.

As Erskine of Dun had distinguished in 1571, 'there is a spirituall jurisdictioun and power which God hath givin unto his kirk, and to these who beare office therin; and there is a temporall power givin of God to kings and civill magistrats'; the two powers were separate yet complementary; just as the prince ought to defend and maintain the integrity of the kirk, so the church should strengthen the proper powers of the magistracy. In the language of the Scots Confession of 1560, 'to Kingis, Princes, Reullaris, and Magistratis, we affirme that cheiflie and maist principallie the conservatioun and purgatioun of the Religioun apperteanes; so that not onlie thei are appointed for

[40] R. H. Murray, *The Political Consequences of the Reformation* (London, 1926), 96; *The Decades of Henry Bullinger*, ed. T. Harding, 4 vols (Cambridge, 1849–52), bk. v, 85–6; J. Quick, *Synodicon in Gallia Reformata*, 2 vols (London, 1692), 92; E. Choisy, *L'état chrétien calviniste à Genève au temps de Théodore de Bèze* (Geneva, 1902), 20–4.

[41] Calderwood, *History of the Kirk of Scotland*, ed. T. Thomson, 8 vols (Edinburgh, 1842–9), iii, 158–60.

civile policey, bot also for mantenance of the trew Religioun, and for suppressing of idolatrie and superstitioun whatsomever', an affirmation which, of course, accorded with the beliefs of virtually all the influential continental reformers, was accepted by English puritans and their opponents alike, and repudiated only by the anabaptists, spiritualists and separatists who eschewed, and declined to submit to, all temporal power. Indeed, it was Beza, no less, who advised his Scottish correspondent that a Christian king should be accounted, 'next after God, the keeper and defender of churches'; and in a previously overlooked letter, the pastors of the French refugees in London replied in 1574 to a Scottish inquiry by advising that 'toutesfois où le Magistrat est fidelle, le Ministre ne doit rien attenter sans son advis', while maintaining 'la différence entre la discipline Ecclésiastique et la police civile'.[42]

For Scots to assign to the magistracy 'the conservatioun and purgatioun of the Religioun' did not of course imply a recognition of royal supremacy over the church. This was made manifest in 1572 when the kirk, in negotiating a scheme for utilising the ancient system of benefices as a means of finance, declined to accept the forthright phraseology of the Elizabethan supremacy (itself modified by Henrician or Edwardine standards). In devising an oath of obedience for benefice-holders to swear, which otherwise followed English practice, the Scots meaningfully substituted the wording of the Scots Confession acknowledging King James as 'supreme governour of this realme, als weill in things temporall as in the conservatioun and purgatioun of the religioun'. By doing so, they avoided the terms of the English oath affirming Elizabeth as 'supreme governor . . . as well in all spiritual and ecclesiastical things or causes as temporal', an aphorism they evidently considered distasteful. Also incorporated in the oath was a repudiation of all foreign jurisdictions, a measure considered particularly apposite amid heightened tension following Elizabeth's excommunication by the papacy in 1570; hence perhaps the readiness of Scots in 1572 to adopt a modified version of the Elizabethan oath renouncing the authority of all foreign princes, prelates, states or potentates in spiritual or temporal affairs.[43]

[42] Knox, *Works*, ii, 118 and n. 1; *John Knox's History of the Reformation in Scotland*, ed. W. C. Dickinson (Edinburgh, 1949), 271, and n. 2; *APS*, iii, 22; *Scottish History Society Miscellany*, 3rd ser., viii (Edinburgh, 1951), 109; F. de Schickler, *Les Églises du Refuge en Engleterre* (Paris, 1892), iii, 87–8.

[43] Knox, *Works*, ii, 118; *APS*, ii, 534; *BUK*, i, 220; *Statutes of the Realm*, edd. A. Luders, *et al.*, 11 vols (London, 1810–28), IV, i, 350–5; *BUK*, i, 231.

The general assembly, by adopting this solution, may be seen to have pursued a policy consistent with its earlier criticism of Bassandine's epithet on the royal supremacy in 1568 and with the subsequent refusal of its own commissioners to recognise the crown's claim to ecclesiastical supremacy in 1574. There was plainly neither novelty nor originality in the Second Book of Discipline's verdict in 1578 that earthly headship of the church 'aucht not to be attributtit to angell or to mane, of quhat estait soevir he be'.[44]

Besides revising the text from the English oath of obedience (an action whose significance can so readily be overlooked), the Convention of Leith in 1572 also devised a formula which required all future bishops to recognise a dual allegiance: they were to be 'subiect to the Kirk and Generall Assembly thairof in spiritualibus, as thay ar to the King in temporalibus'. Earlier, in 1569, the privy council readily distinguished ecclesiastical from secular authority by recognising that Robert Pont, as commissioner of Moray, should admit a candidate to a benefice 'as he will answer to God and to the Generall Assembllie of the Kirk'; and later in 1573 the Bishop of Galloway, formerly a Marian supporter, was conscious not only of his previous disloyalty to King James' cause but of his divided allegiance to two superiors when he professed a readiness, with others, to become 'obedient subjects to the King and Kirk'.[45]

Such language, it may be fairly considered, looks less than promising for the emergence of a 'concept of a single authority over ecclesiastical and secular affairs' which, it is sometimes said, was the reformers' true objective.[46] The reality is that, from the outset, the reformers consistently argued for the separation, not unification, of the ecclesiastical and temporal jurisdictions, a standpoint only too well appreciated by King James himself who, from a position of strength as king in England, succeeded only in 1612 in securing a redrafting of the oath of obedience to conform to English practice by insisting that Scots recognise his supremacy in 'matters spirituall and ecclesiasticall', wording which finally replaced the earlier adherence to the crown's rôle in the 'conservation and purgation of religion'.[47]

---

[44] See above, 251; J. Kirk, *Second Book of Discipline* (Edinburgh, 1980), 167.
[45] *BUK*, i, 209; *RPC*, ii, 68; *BUK*, i, 276.
[46] See above, 237, n. 5; G. Donaldson, *Studies in Scottish Church History*, 233.
[47] Calderwood, *History*, vii, 173; see below, 433.

IV

Spiritual and Temporal Government:

To a modern mind theorising on the identity of church and nation it may be beguiling to imagine that the supreme governor of the realm, the sovereign, must also be supreme governor of the church. After all, if the people of a nation ideally and legally belonged to one national church and owed allegiance as subjects to that nation's monarch, it might seem hard to deny that the same authority, the king (perhaps in association with the privy council or parliament), should also direct the ecclesiastical affairs of a church which consisted of his same subjects. It was not so in sixteenth-century Scotland. There prevailing opinion in the general assembly (which had also claims, perhaps superior claims, to represent Christian communities) favoured the recognition of two distinct governments and jurisdictions for church and commonwealth. Even after the accession of a 'godly' prince in 1567, the general assembly continued its campaign in March and July 1569 that 'the jurisdictioune of the Kirk may be separate fra that quhilk is civill'.[48]

To Scottish reformers, the separation of ecclesiastical and civil (or temporal) power was considered neither improper nor artificial in a commonwealth whose members were also eligible for membership of the one national church. With impeccable logic, the general assembly in 1565 had sought to distinguish ecclesiastical matters from temporal by recognising that 'civill things we remit to the civile magistrate'; and even earlier the logical deduction had been made that if there were civil magistrates there ought also to be what contemporaries described as 'ecclesiastical magistrates', in the form of elders, whose disciplinary powers one Catholic (forgetful of the extensive jurisdiction wielded by his own church) considered usurped those of the civil magistrate, a remark wholly at variance with the belief expressed by his own ordinary, Archbishop Hamilton, in 1560 that the elders of the reformed kirk had assumed 'our ecclesiasticall jurisdiction, and intromettis with all our office'.[49]

The related issue of whether these elders were 'laymen' or 'clergy' (regardless of the reformers' repudiation of this antithesis) has attracted much muddled thinking. In particular, the popular misconception of contrasting the elder of 1560 as a

---

[48] *BUK*, i, 140, 146.
[49] *BUK*, i, 74; A. Maxwell, *History of Old Dundee* (Edinburgh, 1884), 72; N. Winzet, *Certane tractatis for reformation of doctryne and manneris in Scotland*, ed. D. Laing (Edinburgh, 1835), 72.

'genuine layman' with the later elder of the Second Book of
Discipline, considered a 'clerical figure' because his office was
defined as 'ane functioun spirituall, as is the ministrie', not only
fails to distinguish clerical from spiritual but does no justice to
the historical evidence from the record of St Andrews kirk
session which from the outset in the 1560s recognised the elder
was part of 'the ministerie' (not 'clergy').[50] In 1561, the
'ministerie' of the kirk session was defined as the 'minister and
eldaris of the reformed kyrk and cite of Sanctandrois'; the variant
expression of the 'holl ministerie' was also adopted; in 1562 the
'ministerie of Sancandrois', at one meeting of the session,
consisted of the minister and three elders; even the seal of the
session was portrayed in 1562 as 'the sayll of the ministerie'.[51]
Rarely has there been such needless confusion or misunderstanding of an issue.

There is danger, too, in imaginaing that the theory of the
crown's supremacy in ecclesiastical affairs was compatible with
any belief vesting ecclesiastical authority in representatives of the
Christian community (be it in general assembly or in parliament). The argument, sometimes advanced by modern writers,
that parliament, representing the entire nation, had also claims to
represent the church by directing ecclesiastical affairs is not
simply a different way of expressing the idea that ecclesiastical
and secular government was united in the person of a Christian
prince. The two approaches, as some contemporaries appreciated,[52] are significantly different; and any attempt to present
them as statements of the same concept would have been
dismissed as unsound thinking. In other words, the idea that the
crown should rule the commonwealth (with advice from privy
council and parliament) by delegating its inherent powers
derived from God to its magistrates and that it should govern the
church by entrusting administrative powers to its ecclesiastical
officers, the bishops, had the effect of preserving the crown's
supremacy intact. But the understanding that only the crown in
parliament, where bishops had a seat, represented the entire
Christian commonwealth, which alone had authority to legislate
on ecclesiastical matters, marked a radical departure from the
former concept of royal supremacy by threatening to undermine
or, at least, severely to curtail powers attributed to the crown
itself.

[50] *Second Book of Discipline*, 152.
[51] *RStAKS*, i, 75, 131, 133, 138, 143, 147.
[52] Whitgift, *Works*, ii, 246; Hooker, *Of the Laws of Ecclesiastical Polity*, VIII,
ii, 17; VIII, vi, 10–11, in Hooker, *Works*; cf. G. Donaldson, *Scottish Church
History*, 232–3.

As it was, neither theory carried much conviction in Scotland in the 1560s, where the reformed church claimed an autonomy for its ecclesiastical courts which were considered not to be dependent on the powers of either the crown or parliament and which, therefore, met without tarrying for the magistrate's permission. Besides, not only did the kirk severely disapprove of its ministers involving themselves in secular affairs (and so sought no place for its superintendents in parliament or council) but it found a more appropriate and distinctive forum for determining ecclesiastical affairs in the general assembly whose continued existence, irrespective of the monarch's religion, was resolutely defended in the belief, first that it was necessary for preserving good order and unity of doctrine in the church, and later, in 1574, on the elevated claim that it had been sanctioned by divine right.[53]

V

Patterns for Scottish Practice:
The contention that ecclesiastical and secular government ought to be united in the person of a Christian prince (or, alternatively, in the body of a parliament, in some sense representing the Christian community) – ideas which rest more on simple logic than on the subtleties of theology – is peculiarly reminiscent of the various arguments advanced by Whitgift, Jewel, Bancroft, Saravia and Hooker, as apologists for the Elizabethan supremacy where the *potestas jurisdictionis*, including the *ius liturgicum*, which belonged to the church was conceived as emanating from the authority of the crown. There the ecclesiastical courts for administering discipline owed their existence and jurisdiction to the powers held by the crown; the courts were not autonomous in the Calvinist sense. After all, the Henrician act for the restraint of appeals had declared that all jurisdictions, spiritual as well as temporal, proceeded from the monarch; and successive acts of supremacy had underlined the same approach by endowing the prince with those non-priestly ecclesiastical powers previously exercised by the pope.[54] Archbishop Cranmer, a confirmed 'erastian', has readily conceded that:

    [53] Knox, *Works*, ii, 296–7, 395–7, 405–6, 479; *BUK*, i, 38–9, 292; Calderwood, *History*, iii, 306–7; Melville, *Diary*, 45, 61, 68, 209–10, 233; *BUK*, i, 7, 24, 99, 133; see above, 228, n. 227.
    [54] E. T. Davies, *Episcopacy and the Royal Supremacy in the Church of England in the XVI Century* (Oxford, 1950), 61; J. V. P. Thompson, *Supreme Governor* (London, 1940); F. J. Smithen, *Continental Protestantism and the English Reformation* (London, 1927); *Zürich Letters*, ii, 149.

'all Christian princes have committed unto them immediately of God the whole cure of all their subjects, as well concerning the administration of God's word of the cure of souls, as concerning the ministration of things political and civil governance. In both these ministrations they must have sundry ministers under them, to supply that which is appointed to their several offices'.[55]

Whether the church possessed the right to excommunicate, which for Bucer and Calvin was fundamental and exclusive, was for Cranmer a matter for the prince's discretion; and he was therefore prepared to acknowledge the propriety of excommunication by the civil authorities. Adhering to Cranmer's example, Richard Bancroft was later able to argue approvingly in Elizabeth's reign that 'the excommunication now used by Chauncelors in England, is but a signe of civill punishment, and hath greate resemblaunce of that good order, which is practized by the Magistrates in the reformed Churches of Helvetia'.[56]

In Edward VI's reign, the *Reformatio Legum Ecclesiasticarum* has reaffirmed the belief that the church's jurisdiction derived from the crown, while an act for consecrating bishops in Elizabeth's reign had vested the queen with all 'jurisdictions, power and authorities over the state ecclesiastical and temporal, as well causes ecclesiastical as temporal, within the realm'.[57] That the government and jurisdiction of the English church was dependent on the royal prerogative was evident in both theory and practice. In 1566, Bishop Jewel had observed that 'the queen at this time is unable to endure the least alteration in matters of religion', and, in similar vein, Pilkington of Durham, in 1573, admitted that 'we are under authority, and cannot make any innovation without the sanction of the queen, or abrogate any thing without the authority of the laws; and the only alternative now allowed us is whether we will bear with these things or disturb the peace of the church'.[58] In England, therefore, it looked almost as if the church was placed under, and not as Calvin would have wished alongside, the temporal power.

Within this context, Archbishop Whitgift was able to express the underlying concept of the indivisibility of sovereignty, during his protracted controversy with the presbyterian Thomas Cartwright, by arguing from the standpoint that:

[55] Cranmer, *Works*, ii, 116.
[56] M. Bucer, *Opera Latina*, ed. F. Wendel, vol. xv (Paris, 1954), i, 77; Calvin, *Institutes*, IV, xii, 4–5; Calvin, *Letters*, ed. J. Bonnet, 3 vols (Edinburgh, 1855–7), i, 353–4; Cranmer, *Works*, ii, 117; *Tracts ascribed to Richard Bancroft*, ed. A. Peel (Cambridge, 1953), 128.
[57] J. W. Allen, *A History of Political Thought in the Sixteenth Century* (London, 1967), 162; E. T. Davies, *Episcopacy and the Royal Supremacy*, 77.
[58] *Zürich Letters*, i, 149, 287–8.

'I perceive no such distinction of the commonwealth and the church that they should be counted, as it were, two several bodies, governed with divers laws and divers magistrates, except the church be linked with an heathenish and idolatrous commonwealth'.[59]

Unlike Calvin, therefore, Whitgift maintained that 'God hath given the chief government of his church to the christian magistrate, who hath to consider what is most convenient', for in a church established 'in place of elders and seniors are come christian princes and magistrates'. As was so with Cranmer, Whitgift was drawn to the conclusion, in recognition of the royal supremacy, that even an 'archbishop doth exercise his jurisdiction under the prince and by the prince's authority. For, the prince having the supreme government of the realm, in all causes and over all persons, as she doth exercise the one by the lord chancellor, so doth she the other by the archbishops'.[60] In a further expression of the unity of church and nation, Richard Hooker, in developing his ecclesiology, accepted that 'civil and ecclesiastical functions may be lawfully united in one and the same person', a belief which more radical protestants like John Hooper had earlier censured for confounding the two jurisdictions.[61]

As three Tudor monarchs had effectively demonstrated through their exercise of kingship, royal supremacy extended over spiritual no less than temporal affairs; ecclesiastical and temporal government remained two aspects of the one society, so that within England, it may be said, the 'one kingdom theory' prevailed. Such a theory, however, which invites comparison with the teaching emanating from Zwingli's Zürich and from similar models, was inconsistent with Calvinist theory and practice. It may not, therefore, have been wholly fortuitous that a continental visitor to Scotland, attending a service in St Giles conducted by King James' apologist for the 'one kingdom' notion, Archbishop Adamson (himself no stranger to Switzerland), should imagine that the service he witnessed in 1585 was 'Zwinglian' in character.[62]

---

[59] Whitgift, *Works*, i, 21–2; Hooker, *Of the Laws of Ecclesiastical Polity*, VIII, i, 7.

[60] Whitgift, *Works*, iii, 176; i, 472; ii, 246.

[61] Hooker, *Of the Laws of Ecclesiastical Polity*, VII, xv, 3; Hooper, *Later Writings*, ed. C. Nevison (Cambridge, 1852), 559.

[62] J. K. Cameron, 'Some Continental Visitors to Scotland in the late Sixteenth and Early Seventeenth Centuries', *Scotland and Europe, 1200–1850* (Edinburgh, 1986), 45–61, at 48; 'Journey through England and Scotland made by Lupold von Wedel in the years 1584 and 1585', translated by Gottfried von Bülow, *Transactions of the Royal Historical Society*, new ser., ix (1895), 223–70.

The idealised picture of an entire nation belonging to one visible church does less than justice to the presence in society of unbelievers, nonconformists, and notorious offenders liable to be excommunicated from 'the societie of Christis Church'. Yet excommunicants, in practice, were not necessarily outlawed from the commonwealth by the magistrate, who (so Scottish reformers believed) 'oft winkis at such crymes', which merited severest censure from the church. This perception led thorough-going Calvinists to consider church and state as two separate realms ('regna'), entities or societies, whose relationship to one another Calvin likened to the twins of Hippocrates, a description borrowed by Thomas Cartwright in England and which the Scot John Davidson, by adjustment, later rendered as 'two loving sisters'.[63]

The 'one kingdom' theory, so favoured by leaders of the Elizabethan church and admired by James VI in Scotland, owed its origin neither to the ideas of Luther nor Calvin. For a start, Luther had repudiated the idea that the individuals who composed society could be identified with the members of the Christian community; true believers who made up the invisible church, for whom God had provided the spiritual government of the Gospel 'committed to the preachers', had no need for the temporal government of law and the sword which God had placed in the hands of men not to constrain the conscience and soul, which remained unhurt, but to restrain the wicked actions of unbelievers in order to maintain peace among men. Yet, 'among Christians there is no superior but Christ himself and him alone'; the church, for Luther, was 'not a physical assembly, but an assembly of hearts in one faith'; 'for what is believed is neither physical nor visible'. In the spiritual kingdom, therefore, Christians are 'subjects of no one but Christ', ruled by the spiritual government of his Word, where the sword 'serves no purpose in his kingdom'; but, as men in the world, they are also 'subject to worldly rulers', to whose temporal government they owe obedience. Both governments must thus 'be permitted to remain'; yet temporal government ought not to be allowed too wide a scope 'lest it extend too far and encroach upon God's kingdom and government'; instead it ought to be exercised 'in a Christian and salutory manner'. On this basis, Luther had argued in 1523 that:

---

[63] *Calvini Opera*, xxix, 659; Whitgift, *Works*, i, 23; *BUK*, iii, 915.

'God has ordained two governments: the spiritual, by which the
Holy Spirit produces Christians and righteous people under
Christ; and the temporal, which restrains the un-Christian and
wicked so that – no thanks to them – they are obliged to keep still
and to maintain an outward peace'.

To the German reformer, mindful of how true christians 'are few
and far between', it seemed 'out of the question that there should
be a common Christian government over the whole world, or
indeed over a single country or any considerable body of people,
for the wicked always outnumber the good'.[64] The idea of royal
supremacy over the church, it would appear, was then alien to
Luther's thought, a verdict which is surely strengthened by
Luther's remark in 1529 when he contended:

'The emperor is not the head of Christendom or defender of the
gospel and the faith. The church and the faith must have a
defender other than emperors and kings. They are usually the
worst enemies of Christendom and of the faith'.[65]

In Calvin's perception, too, there existed 'a twofold government in man, . . . the one which, placed in the soul or inward
man, relates to eternal life, . . . the other, which pertains only to
civil institutions and the external regulation of manners'. From
this understanding, Calvin appreciated that the two governments
applied to different entities or societies; hence his belief that just
'as no city or village can exist without a magistrate and
government, so the Church of God . . . needs a kind of spiritual
government', which 'is altogether distinct from civil government'.[66] By adopting a more positive appreciation than had
Luther of the visible church, comprising believers and hypo-
crites, Calvin was able to provide a systematic exposition of the
form which he believed the visible church should assume. 'Our
Lord has instituted for the government of His church', the
Genevan declared, the four ministries of minister, doctor, elder
and deacon, and accordingly 'if we would have the church well
ordered and maintain it in its entirety, we must observe that form
of rule'.[67] Rejecting the claims that an established church in a
nation ruled by a godly magistrate had no need for a separate
ecclesiastical jurisdiction (claims which he dismissed as 'a Jewish
vanity'), and affirming instead the belief that 'the church cannot

---

[64] *Luther's Works*, vol. 45, 81–129, at 90–3, 104–5, 117; vol. 39, 65, 75; vol. 46,
93–137, at 99–100, 108.
[65] *Luther's Works*, vol. 46, 185.
[66] Calvin, *Institutes*, IV, xi, 1.
[67] *Calvini Opera*, X, i, 15–17.

dispense with the spiritual jurisdiction which existed in the beginning', Calvin insisted on the necessity of an independent disciplinary authority based on the eldership as part of 'the order in which the Lord has been pleased that his Church should be governed'. From antiquity, too, he argued that 'when emperors and magistrates began to assume the Christian name, spiritual jurisdiction was not forthwith abolished, but was only so arranged as not in any respect to impair civil jurisdiction, or be confounded with it'.[68] There was ample substance, therefore, in Richard Bancroft's charge that Calvin had 'laboured to perswade the people and the Magistrates: that as there was a civil *Senate*, for the gouernement of the Citie; and the territories thereof, in ciuile causes; so by the word of God, there should be an ecclesiastical *Senate*, for the gouernment of the same Citie and territories (conteining aboue twentie parishes) in causes ecclesiasticall'.[69]

As the control of churches passed from pope to prince and city magistrate, the significance of Calvin's contribution can be perceived. In recognition that Christ rules his church through the preaching of the Word, and by reasserting the authority of the spiritual ministry as the instrument by which Christ 'exhibits himself as in a manner actually present by exerting the energy of His Spirit in this His institution', the Genevan unmistakably committed the church's external government to the ministry, in association with representative office-bearers drawn from the congregation, not that the ministers might rule but that through 'the gift of interpretation', which they possessed, God's Word might be proclaimed so that Christ in a very real sense was understood to rule the church's life and thought.[70]

Calvin's interpretation of the correct relationship between ecclesiastical and temporal government marked a decided departure from Zwingli's example at Zürich, where ecclesiastical and disciplinary authority had become a function of the magistracy, as well as from English practice which adhered to that example; but his ideas were in accord with the earlier teaching of Oecolampadius in Basel, who considered that 'there is indeed a great difference between the ecclesiastical power and the secular magistrate even if he be Christian', and of Martin Bucer, who remained convinced that, even where the magistrate

---

[68] Calvin, *Institutes*, IV, iii, i; IV, xi, 1, 3–4, 6; IV, xx, 1–2; Calvin, *A Harmony of the Gospels*, edd. D. W. Torrance and T. F. Torrance, 3 vols (Edinburgh, 1972), ii, 274–6.
[69] R. Bancroft, *A Survay of the Pretended Holy Discipline* (1593), 22.
[70] Calvin, *Institutes*, IV, iii, 1–2; IV, vi, 10; IV, xvii, 25.

was Christian, the church should administer its own separate discipline.[71]

VI

Two jurisdictions:
There is abundant evidence that Scottish reformers readily accepted and adopted the Calvinist definition of the respective rôles of minister and magistrate. Their appreciation at the Reformation that princes were appointed 'for the mentenance of commown welthis and ciwill polaceis' and not for 'the gouerment of the spirituall and hewinlie kingdome, the kirk of God' found cogent expression, even under a protestant regime, in the clear distinction drawn between the 'spirituall jurisdictioun and power which God hath givin unto his kirk, and to these who beare office therin', and the 'temporall power givin of God to kings and civill magistrats'.[72] Nor was it merely the ministry which sought to distinguish ecclesiastical from temporal government in an effort to repel undue interference from the magistracy. In language reminiscent of the protestants' letter to Mary of Guise in 1559, the 'barronis and uther protestantis' rallied to the kirk's defence in 1571 by warning the Regent that 'tyranicallie so to impyre above the pure flock' of Christ by denying the church sufficient funds would lead to the replacement of 'prieching pastors' by 'dume dogis', and they demonstrated their own resolve 'to have the pure kirk of Christ Jesus set at fredome'.[73]

To the community at large, part of the appeal of the 'two kingdoms' doctrine lay precisely in the elimination of ministers from all temporal office, and, in particular, from the king's government as royal officers and bureaucrats, thereby creating further scope for 'laymen', of appropriate qualifications, to advance their careers in service of the crown. Gone too were any ancient claims which may have conceived the king's authority to be dependent on the church. Prepared, as it was, for the godly great council of the realm, the Book of Discipline had pointed the way ahead not only when it prohibited ministers from customary attendance at court, from sitting on the privy council and 'from bearing charge in civill affairs' (other than by giving advice when sought) but, more fundamentally, when it distinguished between 'the Ministerie', recognised as 'promoted to the regiment of the Church' (the ministers and other office-

---

[71] R. C. Walton, *Zwingli's Theocracy* (Toronto, 1967), 82, 209, 226; Demura, 'Church Discipline according to Johannes Oecolampadius', 99, 154.
[72] *Spalding Club Miscellany*, iv, 89; Calderwood, *History*, iii, 158.
[73] Bannatyne, *Journal*, 250–3.

bearers, that is, who were understood to govern the church) and the civil magistrate whose rôle in temporal government was acknowledged by his work in applying 'the temporall punishment of the Law'. All this may fairly be contrasted with Archbishop Whitgift's claims in England that 'Christ ruleth in his church by the godly magistrate whom he hath placed over his church and to whom he hath committed his church touching external policy and government'.[74]

If the minister were charged with preaching 'life everlasting', the magistrate was obliged to regulate (and, as punishment, even to forfeit) 'the life temporal' among men.[75] As Calvin had observed, 'he who knows to distinguish between the body and the soul, between the present fleeting life and that which is future and eternal, will have no difficulty in understanding that the spiritual kingdom of Christ and civil government are things very widely separated'.[76] Unlike Luther who, in his earlier career, did not consider the magistrate should enforce religious faith or punish heresy (as distinct from blasphemy), the Book of Discipline adhered to the Calvinist belief that the magistrate's duty towards the church extended to reforming a church corrupted and to defending the liberties of a church reformed.[77] For Calvin, 'in Scripture holy kings are especially praised for restoring the worship of God when corrupted or overthrown, or for taking care that religion flourished under them in purity and safety'.[78] Consistently, the Book of Discipline recognised that the 'duty of the godly Magistrate is not onely to purge the Church of God from all supersitition and to set it at libertie from tyranny and bondage, but also to provide at the utmost of his power how it may abide in some puritie in the posteritie following', a sentiment articulated, yet again, in the Second Book of Discipline of 1578 in language borrowed directly from Bucer's *De Regno Christi*.[79]

In a remark which echoes Calvin's distinction between ecclesiastical and temporal jurisdiction in appreciation that the church, like a city, needs its own government, the Book of Discipline in 1560 advanced the argument that as 'no Commonwealth can flourish or long indure without good laws and sharpe execution of the same, so neither can the Kirk of God be brought

---

[74] *First Book of Discipline*, 100, 178; Whitgift, *Works*, iii, 232.
[75] *First Book of Discipline*, 100.
[76] Calvin, *Institutes*, IV, xx, 1.
[77] *Luther's Works*, vol. 45, 114–17; vol. 46, 186; vol. 53, 39; vol. 36, 311–28; *First Book of Discipline*, 129.
[78] Calvin, *Institutes*, IV, xx, 9.
[79] *First Book of Discipline*, 129; *Second Book of Discipline*, 216.

to purity neither yet be retained in the same without the order of Ecclesiastical Discipline', instituted for those misdemeanours which 'appertaine to the kirk of God to punish',[80] and administered not by the civil magistrate but by the minister and kirk session on the congregation's behalf.

Each jurisdiction had thus its own officers or magistrates. Just as the civil magistrate's primary concern (apart from maintaining the faith) lay, as the name of the office implies, with the administration of justice and rule of law in the commonwealth, so too were the elders and deacons of the kirk session, assuming the rôle of ecclesiastical magistrates, deemed by the Book of Discipline to have 'authoritie to judge in the kirk of God'; and the elders, who were explicitly charged 'to assist the ministers in all publicke affaires of the kirk', were assigned particular responsibility in 'judging causes', 'giving admonition', and 'having respect to the manners and conversation of al men within their charge'.[81] A Christian in Scotland was therefore subject to two sets of government, for the jurisdiction exercised by the kirk did not become absorbed within the authority wielded by the prince.

In its twofold division of offences, the one set which 'ought not properly to fall under censure of the Kirk' but 'ought to be taken away by the civill sword', and the other which 'doe openly appertaine to the kirk of God', the Book of Discipline distinguished the magistrate's reliance on the 'civill sword' to punish offenders from the church's ability to use the spiritual sword of excommunication 'which of God she hath received', not least in cases where the magistrate neglected his duty in punishing by death adulterers whom the church should ex-communicate as 'wicked and to repute them as dead members'; and it recognised the separate duties of minister and magistrate as complementary, not contradictory.[82] Much of the reasoning here was reminiscent of Calvin's belief that, even where the magistrate was godly, authority in church and commonwealth was 'widely different, because neither does the Church assume anything to herself which is proper to the magistrate, nor is the magistrate competent to what is done by the Church'.[83]

Also consistent with Calvin's emphasis on the separation of spiritual and temporal office was the concern of Scottish reformers to avoid the former abuse which permitted ecclesias-

[80] *First Book of Discipline*, 165–66.
[81] Ibid., 174–6.
[82] Ibid., 165, 167, 186, 196–7.
[83] Calvin, *Institutes*, IV, xi, 3–6.

tics to hold offices of state. Even in a Scottish context, this reformed belief had long been cherished. In 1548, Balnaves had remarked that 'no bishope should mixt him selfe with temporall or secular busines, for that is contrarie his vocation', an opinion which coincided with Luther's comment in 1529 that 'what I want to do is to keep a distinction between the callings and offices, so that everyone can see to what God has called him and fulfil the duties of his office faithfully and sincerely in the service of God'.[84] The Tetrapolitan Confession in 1530, composed by Bucer with help from Capito, also condemned the practice of promoting churchmen to secular office. Elsewhere, Bucer's advice to Edward VI in England was to end the mixing of civil and ecclesiastical administration, by following the example of the early church, so that bishops might 'concentrate on taking care of religion only and leave all other matters' to the concern of others.[85]

There were those in England who were similarly minded: Tyndale, Coverdale and Latimer were characteristic of early reformers who adhered to the belief that secular and ecclesiastical office should not be united in the same person; and their pioneering efforts subsequently found support, among others, from John Knox, who pointedly exclaimed, in his 'Exhortation to England', 'Let none that be appointed to labour in Christes vineyearde be entangled with Civil affaires'.[86] The opposing viewpoint, which contradicted these first principles in the Reformation, was represented, in Elizabeth's reign, by Archbishop Whitgift who complained that the ideas of the presbyterian Cartwright would make 'ecclesiastical and civil government so distinct that they can by no means concur in one and the self-same persons', and he justified English practice which regarded a minister in the church as 'not so distinct that he may exercise no such civil office wherein he may do good'; for the archbishop, it was appropriate that 'the ecclesiastical person in some causes use civil jurisdiction, and deal in matters of the commonwealth, if it shall be thought expedient or necessary by the chief magistrate'.[87]

By contrast, in the Scottish church, which not only disapproved of the confounding of the two jurisdictions but actively campaigned for their separation, the general assembly, in 1564

[84] Knox, *Works*, iii, 26, 532; *Luther's Works*, vol. 46, 166.
[85] A. C. Cochrane, *Reformed Confessions of the Sixteenth Century* (London, 1966), 82; *Melanchthon and Bucer*, ed. W. Pauck (London, 1969), 290.
[86] Tyndale, *Doctrinal Treatises*, 207; Tyndale, *Exposition*, 247, 273; Coverdale, *Remains*, 244; Latimer, *Sermons*, 67, 176; Knox, *Works*, v. 519.
[87] Whitgift, *Works*, i, 20–1, 153.

and, again, in 1567, censured two conforming bishops, who had agreed to serve as its commissioners, Bothwell of Orkney and Gordon of Galloway, for their acceptance of secular office as privy councillors and as senators of the College of Justice, appointments which the assembly considered 'cannot agree with the office of a pastor or bishop'. For a start, it detracted from their pastoral work as shepherds of the flock; it left 'the sheep wandering without a pastor'; it also made pastors susceptible to undue royal influence, a point which had not escaped the attention of the assembly when it charged Gordon with attending court (Mary's court) 'too much', in defiance of the Book of Discipline (which, be it noted, he had approved in January 1560/1). In submitting to the assembly, Gordon acknowledged his offence (though he absented himself from some future assemblies and further investigation); but Bothwell, in conducting a spirited defence, attempted with some ingenuity to repel the charges on the basis that acceptance of both kinds of office was 'not repugnant or contrariouse to any good order as yet established in the Kirke' and that 'as the office itself was allowable, so it should be profitable for the Kirke, that many preachers of the evangell were placed in the Sessione'. His contention, which perhaps betrayed an inappropriate attachment to his unreformed heritage, fell on deaf ears in the assembly; yet his claim that 'diverse others having benefices have done the like, and are not condemned for so doing' may have carried a measure of conviction.[88] Archibald Douglas, at any rate, was both a senator of the College of Justice and parson of Douglas and later of Glasgow; but he was simply a benefice-monger who held no office in the reformed ministry;[89] and, apart from Gordon and Bothwell, no minister in the kirk had then either a place on the bench or in council. At the same time, so far as is known from the defective record of the assembly, there was, for example, neither criticism nor censure of superintendent Erskine of Dun for holding the heritable provostship of Montrose or for continuing to sit in parliament as a baron in his own right (or in 1569 as commissioner for Montrose), or for that matter, of John Winram's attendance at parliament in his capacity as prior of Portmoak (and not, of course, as a superintendent who had no right to representation).[90]

[88] *BUK*, i, 52–3, 112, 114, 131, 162, 166; *First Book of Discipline*, 178, 211.
[89] G. Brunton and D. Haig, *An Historical Account of the Senators of the College of Justice from its Institution in MDXXXII* (Edinburgh, 1832), 125–8.
[90] *APS*, ii, 536; iii, 30, 35, 37, 38, 57, 424 (Erskine); ii, 525; iii, 3, 4, 46, 84 (Winram), Erskine's appointment by parliament in 1579 as privy councillor was ineffective (*APS*, iii, 150).

Somewhat later, it is true, the assembly was persuaded to make an exception to its rule when, in response to a request from the Regent, it allowed one minister, Robert Pont, who seemingly had legal skills, to become a senator of the College of Justice (whose pre-Reformation constitution had specified half its members should be churchmen), provided he did not desert the ministry; and it insisted that such an exceptional dispensation should not be misinterpreted as a 'preparative to other ministers to procure sick promotioun'. When the Regent repeated his request in 1573, the assembly refused to make further concessions and resolved, instead, that 'nane was able or apt to beare the saids two charges, and therefor inhibits that any Minister occupying the vocatioun of the Ministrie take upon him to be a Senatour; Mr Robert Pont only excepted'. This, in turn, led the assembly to reaffirm its judgment that:

> 'it is neither aggrieable to the word of God nor to the practise of the primative Kirk, that the speciall administratioun of the Word and Sacraments, and the ministration of the Criminall and Civill Justice be so confoundit, that ane person may occupie both the cures.'

Just as a minister should not assume civil office, so the magistrate ought not to 'passe the bounds of his office, and enter within the sanctuarie of the Lord, medling with suche things as apperteane to the ministers of God's kirk'. As Erskine reminded the government in 1571, 'when the corruptioun of man entereth in, confounding the offices, usurping to himself what he pleaseth, nothing regarding the good order appointed of God, then confusion followeth in all estats'.[91]

In keeping with its efforts to distinguish the ecclesiastical from the secular, the assembly recognised that, in spiritual matters, ministers should be subject to the ecclesiastical courts and that, in all temporal affairs, they were responsible to the civil and criminal courts. The Roman claim to clerical immunity from lay jurisdiction, which Calvin among others had attacked,[92] was therefore not revived, an issue which commentators have sometimes failed to grasp; and although the general assembly asked the Regent in 1569, at a time of civil war, for temporary immunity for its members (who, of course, comprised more than ministers) 'that during the time of the Generall Assemblies they be not molested in civil actions', it still held good, and was reiterated in 1570, that ministers found guilty in civil actions

---

[91] *BUK*, i, 206, 264, 267; Calderwood, *History*, iii, 158.
[92] Calvin, *Institutes*, IV, xi, 15.

should be punished by the magistrates.[93] But such a recognition, of course, did not prevent disputes arising when ministers, accused of exceeding the bounds of their text, declined the king's, or privy council's, jurisdiction in the belief that the matter was doctrinal and properly a case for the ecclesiastical and not the civil courts.[94]

There was logic in the ministers' position. After all, if bishops, as accepted by kirk and crown in 1572, were to be 'be subiect to the Kirk and Generall Assembly thairof in spiritualibus, as they ar to the King in temporalibus',[95] there could be no denying that every minister was bound by the same convention; and the implications of the 'two kingdoms' theory were spelt out, not for the first time, by the king's advocate when he candidly acknowledged, in 1606, that the practice of ministers' declining the privy council's jurisdiction exempted 'ane great pairt of your Maiesties subiectis, from your Maiesties jurisdictioun and obedience *in maters of doctrine and discipline*'.[96] Here was an unambiguous claim by the king's legal adviser that the crown had a jurisdiction in doctrine and discipline. King James' notion of 'one kingdom' threatened to be a very one-sided affair in which church and community would have little say.

VII

A Godly Discipline:
What exactly the church's jurisdiction ought to comprise, beyond the true preaching of the Word and administration of the sacraments, had been suggested in the Scots Confession of Faith in 1560 which elevated discipline to the rank of one of the marks or signs by which the true church, visible before men, might be distinguished from the false.[97] It was wholly meaningful, too, that the accompanying document for a reformed ecclesiology should take as its title *The Book of Discipline*, a strategy consistent with French reformed practice where a Calvinist Confession of Faith and Discipline had won acceptance in 1559. The recognition of discipline as a note of the church can too readily be seen to represent 'a departure from Calvin', who distinguished two notes; but such a perspective ignores Calvin's own approval for the Confession adopted by the Genevan congregation of English exiles, with whom Knox and Goodman

[93] *BUK*, i, 146, 179.
[94] Calderwood, *History*, iv, 5ff; v, 457ff.
[95] *BUK*, i, 209.
[96] *Original Letters relating to the Ecclesiastical Affairs of Scotland*, ed. D. Laing, 2 vols (Edinburgh, 1851), i, 31–2 (my italics).
[97] *APS*, ii, 531; Knox, *Works*, ii, 110.

were associated, which unambiguously affirmed discipline as the third note. Nor does such a perspective sufficiently do justice to Calvin's own teaching on Luke where he discerned 'four marks by which the true and genuine appearance of the Church may be distinguished'.[98] Besides, not only had Calvin been prepared to leave Geneva until the church's right to administer its own discipline was recognised, but earlier Luther himself, by 1539, had come to recognise the power of the Keys (which had implications for discipline) and also the ministry as two of the notes, or 'public signs', of the church.[99] John Knox, who had witnessed in Geneva, the application of the very discipline for which Calvin had fought so strenuously, was understandably appreciative of the magnitude of Calvin's achievement when he readily extolled the virtues of a properly congregational method of ecclesiastical correction administered through a consistory of minister and elders representing the whole congregation.[100] Through fraternal admonition and correction, ecclesiastical discipline, properly applied, was seen to offer a remedy for sinners and a safeguard for the sacraments from profanation. Its action was intended to be remedial or restorative rather than repressive; repentance by the offender was the understood objective.

The necessity of discipline, regardless of whether it was formally accorded as one of the church's marks, did not in itself resolve the issue of how exactly it should be administered. After all, in a Christian commonwealth, it was possible, taking the Zwinglian or prevailing English view, to allow discipline, including excommunication, to be exercised by the magistrate, if conscientiously discharged, as part of his responsibilities for ensuring the church's wellbeing. Yet, the argument sometimes presented that the dominant theory among reformers denied the need in established churches for any disciplinary authority other than the civil power[101] remains valid only if the Zwinglian tradition practised in Zürich, Bern and other German-Swiss

---

[98] W. I. P. Hazlett, 'The Scots Confession 1560; Context, Complexion and Critique', ARG, 78 (1987), 287–320, at 310–11; Knox, Works, iv, 155, 172; Calvin, Commentaries on the Acts of the Apostles, edd. D. W. Torrance and T. F. Torrance, 2 vols (Edinburgh, 1965), i, 85, (Acts 2: 42). Calvin also considered ecclesiastical discipline to be the church's 'sinews', an obviously essential attribute (Institutes, IV, xii, 1). Beza's Confession of Faith in 1558 recognised discipline as the third note of the church (Beza, Confession de foi du chrétien, V, vii, in Revue réformée, 1955, 92–4).

[99] D. Martin Luthers Werke; Weimarer Ausgabe, 58 vols (1883–1948), vol. 50, 628–36. I am grateful for discussions of this text with Dr Ian Hazlett.

[100] Knox, Works, iv, 149, 151, 153, 161, 172; v. 211–16.

[101] G. Donaldson, The Scottish Reformation (Cambridge, 1960), 80.

cities, and adopted in England, is accepted as the norm at the expense of the other Reformed attitude to discipline, represented by the teaching of François Lambert, Oecolampadius, Bucer, Capito, Viret, Calvin and Beza who unanimously asserted the church's right to a discipline independent of the godly magistrate.[102] The inherent tension between the Zwinglian and Calvinist disciplinary systems was demonstrated in the Palatinate at the disputation in 1568 at Heidelberg between the Englishman George Withers, who favoured Genevan discipline, and Thomas Erastus, who maintained that the Christian magistracy had charge of discipline.[103] Yet, even before this episode, it was the Calvinist concept and practice of discipline which had triumphed in Scotland.

Unlike Bullinger who contended that the 'venerable elders' of the civil magistracy were the admonishing body envisaged in the passage in Matthew assigning the unrepentant offender to be heard by the church,[104] the Scottish Book of Discipline, addressed to the godly government, adopted the Calvinist argument that an offender who failed to respond to private admonition should be called before 'the Minister, Elders and Deacons' of the church in the expectation that he may then make public repentance before the whole congregation, seeking forgiveness and reconciliation. If an offender remained 'stubborn' and 'hard-hearted', with no sign of repentance or amendment of life, 'the Ministry' must notify the kirk and seek its judgment. Finally, after 'the Minister' had assigned the obdurate offender for examination 'by the whole Ministry' of the kirk session, the sentence of excommunication might be pronounced 'by the mouth of the Minister, and consent of the Ministry and commandement of the Kirk'.[105]

The Book of Excommunication, revised and issued under a godly regime in 1569, upheld the Book of Discipline's attachment to a separate system of ecclesiastical discipline exercised on Calvinist principles, which in some ways paralleled and complemented the work of the civil magistrate in punishing crime.[106]

---

[102] R. L. Winters, *Francis Lambert of Avignon* (Philadelphia, 1938), 83–5; Demura, 'Church Discipline according to Johannes Oecolampadius', 16–18, 79, 87–8, 99, 102, 154–5; M. U. Chrisman, *Strasbourg and the Reform* (New Haven, 1967), 207–8; Calvin, *Institutes*, IV, xi, 3–4; Calvin, *Harmony*, ii, 187; 228–29; Beza, *Confession de foi du chrétien*, V, xxxii, in *Revue réformée*, 127ff; R. D. Linder, *The Political Ideas of Pierre Viret* (Geneva, 1964), 68–81, 117–25.

[103] J. N. Figgis, *The Divine Right of Kings* (Cambridge, 1914) 293ff.

[104] Demura, 'Church Discipline according to Johannes Oecolampadius', 112.

[105] *First Book of Discipline*, 168–70.

[106] Knox, *Works*, vi, 449ff.

In a process determined by the ecclesiastical courts independently of any punishment inflicted by the civil magistrate for breaking the laws of the land, an offender could be convicted for transgressing God's law and subjected to ecclesiastical censure and admonition in the expectation of securing his unfeigned repentance for slandering God and the kirk. For the unyielding, excommunication remained the church's weapon of last resort. Thus, just as 'the civil sword is in the hand of God's Magistrat', who sometimes failed to punish crimes for which God's law exacted death, so, the reformers claimed, 'we having place in the Ministery, with grief and dolour of our harts, ar compelled to draw the sword granted be God to his Church; that is, to Excommunicat from the society of Christ Jesus, from his body the Church'.[107] In the exercise of this spiritual sword, the Christian magistrate in Scotland had manifestly no part to play. This remarkable achievement of the kirk in establishing its claims, without rebuff from the magistracy, to apply its own discipline and excommunication has not always been adequately appreciated, though few have been so misguided as to imagine that in Scotland 'only the civil magistrate had power to excommunicate'.[108]

Though ready to enlist the magistrate's support in reinforcing its censures or in securing obedience to its authority, the kirk was careful to distinguish the discipline administered in its courts from the civil punishment applied by the magistracy. In St Andrews, the kirk session from the outset separated 'ecclesiasticall disciplyne' from 'forthir correctioun civilie' which the 'ballies and civile magistrates' were expected to apply in the secular courts. The ecclesiastical sanction employed might take the form of requiring penitents to take their place before the congregation on several Sundays 'clethit wytht sek-claitht, and thair in presence of the hael peple stand in sum opin place of the kirk, as the minister sal appoint, in tyme of preching; and eftir the preaching the secound Sunday sal upon thair kneis ask God and the congregatioun forgevenes, quhom they have offendit and sclanderit'. In admonishing an offender, the kirk's intention was 'to repres his stubburnes and be al meanis posseble to wyn him'; social sanctions (or even fines which Perth kirk session 'ordained' the bailies to extract), might be used to secure his conformity; but inflicting physical punishment on a miscreant properly lay in the 'handis and power of temporall magistratis havyng pouer to punys hym, according to the law of God and

[107] Ibid., vi, 451.
[108] M. Lynch, *Edinburgh and the Reformation* (Edinburgh, 1981), 42.

ordor of this realm'; hence the customary practice for kirk sessions, after applying discipline, to hand the disobedient 'to the magistratis to be punist civile according to the law'.[109]

In 1567, the general asembly urged the bailies and councillors of Lanark to assist the minister of the burgh in punishing offenders; while in Canongate kirk session, it was even thought advisable to have a bailie or two on hand, 'assestane with the assemble of the kirk', not, of course, in recognition that the magistrates had any jurisdiction in affairs of the session but in the expectation that they would assist the kirk in upholding its authority by administering civil punishment to offenders who had undergone ecclesiastical censure. An indication of how this dual government was meant to operate occurred in 1565 when the superintendent detected negligence in punishing 'huris and harlottis' in the burgh: the elders and deacons blamed the bailies who deflected criticism by reminding the elders that their task was to ensure culprits 'be callit befoir the kirk and conwickit, and thair efter, be writ, presentit to the baillies, the quhilk the minister, elderis and diocunis promissis to do in tyme to come'.[110] Two bailies, named as assisting the Canongate session, were themselves elders of the kirk; and it was not uncommon for a bailie, as an influential and responsible member of the community, to find himself elected to hold office as an elder of the kirk, in much the same way as in more modern times an assessor for a district or regional council may find himself elected to sit on the university court of his city; and just as it remains the university court (and not the council) which alone administers academic property and finance, so too did the kirk session retain its own separate ecclesiastical jurisdiction, irrespective of whether a bailie happened to be elected an elder. Precisely because of its varied composition, the Scottish kirk session of the sixteenth century skilfully avoided any threat of magisterial dominance emerging through a majority of councillors securing

---

[109] *RStAKS*, 36, 41, 44, 51, 71, 131, 141, 146, 150–1, 152, 191–2, 195, 222–3, 232, 244, 246, 251, 254–5, 260, 270, 277, 297, 307, 319; cf. *BUK*, i, 97, 111, 124–5, 135, 145, 343–44; *RPC*, ii, 61; *Selections from the Records of the Kirk Session, Presbytery and Synod of Aberdeen*, ed. J. Stuart (Aberdeen, 1846), 17, 21, 24; *Extracts from the Council Register of the Burgh of Aberdeen, 1570–1625*, ed. J. Stuart, vol. 2 (Aberdeen, 1848), 203; *Extracts from the Records of the Royal Burgh of Stirling*, A.D. *1519–1666*, ed. R. Renwick (Glasgow, 1887), 77; Scottish Record Office, Edinburgh [SRO], CH2/521/1, Perth Kirk Session Records, fos. 9v, 11v; *Court Book of the Regality of Broughton and the Burgh of the Canongate, 1569–1573*, ed. M. Wood (Edinburgh, 1937), 254.

[110] *The Buik of the Kirk of the Canagait, 1564–1567*, ed. A. B. Calderwood (Edinburgh, 1961), 32.

appointment as elders.[111] That magistrates were not permitted to gain the upper hand is all the more remarkable when it is recalled how even in Geneva the composition of Calvin's consistory, headed by a syndic, was largely drawn from the small council and council of two hundred.[112]

The reformers' objective in devising this system for censure and correction found clear expression in the Book of Discipline's claim that 'to discipline must all the estates within this Realm be subject as well the Rulers, as they that are ruled; yea and the Preachers themselves, as well as the poore within the Kirk'.[113] Far from being a dead letter, this aphorism was applied with some effect; and it plainly carried implications for both ministry and magistracy. Delinquent ministers soon found themselves denounced by the courts of the church as relentlessly as any other offenders;[114] and John Knox, who had extolled the strictness of Genevan discipline,[115] played the leading part in the trial of Paul Methven, minister at Jedburgh, who was deposed and excommunicated for adultery in 1563.[116] The disciplining of ministers (which according to Catholic teaching was an episcopal power) held good for bishops, too: the general assembly ordered the bishop of Galloway in 1573 to 'make publick repentance in sackcloth three severall Sundays', required the bishop of Moray to undergo discipline in 1574, and deposed the bishop of Dunkeld in 1576.[117] Elsewhere, the church's expectation that the same standards of discipline should be meted out to all and sundry, irrespective of rank or position in society, was illustrated in 1563 when the English agent in Edinburgh reported to his government how 'the Lord Treasurer of Scotland, for getting a woman with child, must on Sunday next, do open penance before the whole congregation' in Edinburgh, and listen to Knox's sermon as a corrective for his conduct, a sentence interpreted as 'a note of our greate severitie' towards offenders.[118] No less remarkable was the readiness of the queen's half-sister, the Countess of Argyll, to submit herself to the discipline of the kirk by confessing before the assembly in 1567 her fault in

---

[111] For the social composition of St Andrews and Stirling kirk sessions and Edinburgh general session, see J. Kirk, 'The Development of the Melvillian Movement in late sixteenth-century Scotland' (Edinburgh Ph.D. thesis, 1972), ii, 734–84.

[112] *Transition and Revolution*, ed. R. M. Kingdon (Minneapolis, 1974), 105.

[113] *First Book of Discipline*, 173.

[114] *BUK*, i, 14, 45, 150, 252–3; *RStAKS*, i, 172, 175–6, 186, 189, 334–5.

[115] Knox, *Works*, iv, 240; ii, 16; vi, 16; v, 211–16.

[116] See above 193–4.

[117] *BUK*, i, 227, 288, 295, 350–2.

[118] *CSP Scot.*, ii, no. 45.

assisting at the Catholic baptism of prince James, and thereafter by making public repentance in the chapel royal at Stirling.[119] At that point too, on learning how her estranged husband, the 5th earl, 'was content to submit himselfe to the discipline of the Kirk at all tymes most willinglie', the assembly ordered the superintendent of Argyll to investigate the 'slanders committit be the said Erle, and therafter to cause sick satisfaction be made as Gods law appoints, and to report the ordour therof to the nixt Generall Assemblie of the Kirk'.[120] The kirk's discipline had certainly the potential to humble the mighty.

The disposition of Scottish reformers to require both prince and magistrate, as members of the kirk, to be subject to its discipline and even to excommunication carried far-reaching implications for the existing social and political order. There was, of course, nothing new, and much which was intensely medieval, in the competing claims of temporal and ecclesiastical government, but the novel dimension of ecclesiastical discipline, conscientiously exacted by the kirk, in contrast to the prevailing laxity of the previous regime, introduced amid political upheaval, religious change and uncertainty, posed a threat to the stability of the existing order. The new mechanisms for promoting virtue and punishing vice were designed, of course, to reform and not overturn society; but they carried with them the disruptive danger that once the reformation of society was found to be less readily attained, the prospect of effecting its transformation through revolutionary action seemed an increasingly attractive option. At any rate, something of the momentum contained within the far-reaching changes the reformers sought was appreciated, first, by Mary of Guise who warned the reformers not to speak 'irreverently and slanderously' of princes, complaining that they intended to overthrow the existing political, as well as the religious, order; then by Queen Mary herself who argued that subjects should not presume to dictate to their sovereign a law in matters of religion; and, yet again, by her son who clung tenaciously to the doctrine of one kingdom, in the expectation that as a 'universal king', superior to the discipline of his subjects, James would emerge as governor of both church and nation.[121]

King James' outlook was plainly sympathetic to the standpoint of those leaders in the English church who accepted that the Christian prince, as supreme governor of the church, was

[119] BUK, i, 117.
[120] Ibid., i, 114.
[121] Knox, History, i, 175, 193, 217–19, 367; CSP Scot., vi, no. 523.

exempt from excommunication and, indeed, from all significant ecclesiastical censure and correction. As the highest magistrate in the land, the prince could have no earthly peer and so ought to be judged by none save God. In England, Archbishop Whitgift vigorously denied the puritan contention that the prince should be subject to the church's discipline, a position reinforced by Richard Hooker's judgment that 'it cannot therefore stand with the nature of such sovereign regiment that any subject should have power to exercise on kings so highly authorized the greatest censure of excommunication, according to the platform of Reformed Discipline'.[122]

The 'platform of reformed discipline' which Hooker dismissed was the puritan programme associated with the presbyterian Cartwright and Travers, who argued that kings (in Cartwright's words) 'must remember to subject themselves unto the church, to submit their sceptres, to throw down their crowns, before the church, yea, as the prophet speaketh, to lick the dust of the feet of the church'; hence Cartwright's avowal: 'that princes should be exempted from ecclesiastical discipline and namely excommunication, I utterly mislike'.[123] This attitude of mind was inherited from Calvin's teaching that none should be exempt from the church's discipline, precisely because 'it is the discipline of Christ, to whom all sceptres and diadems should be subject'. In his widely-circulated writings, Calvin unreservedly disclosed how:

> 'Great kings should not think it a disgrace to them to prostrate themselves suppliantly before Christ, the King of kings; nor ought they to be displeased at being judged by the Church. For seeing they seldom hear anything in their courts but mere flattery, the more necessary it is that the Lord should correct them by the mouth of his priests. Nay, they ought rather to wish the priests not to spare them, in order that the Lord may spare'.[124]

For the Genevan, 'the magistrate, if he is pious, will have no wish to exempt himself from the common subjection of the children of God, not the least part of which is to subject himself to the Church, judging according to the word of God'.[125]

This pattern of reformed discipline, to which Calvin was attached, was the model which found favour among Scottish

---

[122] Whitgift, *Works*, iii, 189–92, 231–2; Hooker, *Of the Laws of Ecclesiastical Polity*, VIII, ix, 6.

[123] Whitgift, *Works*, iii, 189; W. Travers, *A full and plaine declaration of ecclesiastical discipline* (1574), 185; *Puritan Manifestoes*, edd. W. H. Frere and C. E. Douglas (London, 1907), 18; A. F. S. Pearson, *Church and State* (Cambridge, 1928), 27.

[124] Calvin, *Institutes*, IV, xii, 7.

[125] Ibid., IV, xi, 4.

reformers. Even before the Book of Discipline had required the submission of 'the Rulers' to the church's practice of correction, John Knox had placed his belief on record in 1558 that no-one, whether of high or low estate, should be exempt from the yoke of discipline and that Christ's ministers had a duty to admonish the prince and subject him to ecclesiastical correction if he attempted to usurp authority or alter one jot of 'the true religion' commanded by God. Again, in 1561, Knox voiced his conviction that the prince was subject both to God and his 'trubled Churche'; in 1562 he bluntly informed his queen that, as a minister, he had been 'appointed by God to rebuk the synnes and vices of all' alike: 'ye shall fullie understand', he explained to Mary, 'boyth what I like and myslike, als weall in your Majestie as in all otheris'. No less trenchant was Knox's comment in 1564: 'I heir nocht Kingis and Quenis exceptit, but all unfaithfull ar pronounced to stand in one rank, and to be in bondage to ane tyrant, the Devill'.[126]

This attitude, expressed by Knox, was strikingly reflected in the proceedings of the general assembly which gave the church's corporate assent in 1562 and again in 1571 to the belief that the civil magistrate, being subject to the rule of Christ, was not exempt from excommunication.[127] Erskine of Dun, underlining this approach, claimed that the powers of the world existed for the benefit of the church to whose jurisdiction all men should submit: the ministers, he argued, held an office above that of others; kings had no power to alter God's order for the church; it was the duty of ministers to reprove and withstand princes and magistrates who sought to interfere in matters affecting the church's jurisdiction.[128] So firmly held was this attitude among ministers that even the moderate-minded minister of South Leith since 1560, David Lindsay (apt to be dubbed a 'court minister') reiterated so late as 1592 the opinion he held with other ministers that King James was not exempt from liability to excommunication if he disobeyed God's will.[129] Unwittingly or otherwise, in one sentence, George Buchanan captured prevailing opinion in the general assembly when he remarked (at a point when there were still bishops in the kirk) that 'just as bishops are subject to kings in their capacity of citizens, so kings ought to accept the admonitions of bishops in regard to spiritual matters'.[130] Nor

[126] First Book of Discipline, 173; Knox, Works, v, 516–20; ii, 283, 334, 432; cf. 441.
[127] BUK, i, 16, 195.
[128] Spalding Club Miscellany, iv, 93, 99; Calderwood, History, iii, 156–62.
[129] Calderwood, History, v, 162, 129, 179.
[130] Buchanan, De Jure Regni Apud Scotos, LXVII.

was there novelty in the Second Book of Discipline's adherence in 1578 to the view that 'all men, alsweill magistrattis as inferiouris', were subject to the judgment of the general assembly as the supreme court in ecclesiastical causes.[131] Reformed opinion in Scotland conceded neither to prince nor magistrate immunity from church discipline and in accord with this belief denied him supremacy over the church.

Reverence for individual monarchs, as distinct from the institution of monarchy, was not always a discernible trait among reformed ministers who all too readily in the decades after the Reformation preferred to cultivate the practice, though scarcely the art, of plain-speaking to a degree which princes found alarming, insufferable and ultimately treasonable. From the outset, the kirk claimed its own jurisdiction, its own discipline, its own king. When King James undertook to remodel both the theory and practice to accommodate his own ideas on how church and commonwealth should be ruled, he embarked on the most sustained campaign of his long reign. The obstacles were formidable; and although he ultimately achieved a measure of acquiescence, compromise and outward conformity in his reconstructed church, even a king endowed with such ingenuity was unequal to the task of stifling ideas. That strand of Reformation thought in Scotland which professed to champion ecclesiastical independence had a remarkable resilience which defied the crown's efforts at eradication. The patterns of reform which prevailed among protestant thinking in 1560, 1567 and 1578 remained a peculiarly potent, enduring force which helped colour mental attitudes towards covenanting opposition, in all its varied forms, to successive Stewart sovereigns during the seventeenth century and beyond, surfacing in the National Covenant of 1638, the Queensferry paper and Sanquhar declaration of 1680, the Claim of Right and Articles of Grievances in 1689. Even then this pedigree was far from ended.

---

[131] *Second Book of Discipline*, 233.

7

John Carswell,
Superintendent of Argyll

On 24 April 1567 Robert Lekprevik, the Edinburgh printer, completed work on a book which must have been as strange to its compositor as it is significant in the history of the Scottish Reformation. This was the translation into Gaelic of the *Book of Common Order*[1] by John Carswell, superintendent of Argyll and bishop of the Isles.[2] In the 'lawful apology' which he appended to his work, Bishop Carswell referred to the printer's complete lack of familiarity with Gaelic, which he thought should be taken into account if anyone should notice its orthographical defects, and he forestalled criticism of his own ignorance of the best form of diction.[3] Neither defence was necessary, for the book is a testimony to the painstaking accuracy of Lekprevik and to the literary expertise of Carswell himself. It was, in fact, the first book to be printed in either Scottish Gaelic or Irish, and it is therefore an important literary landmark; but it was also the first attempt to provide a working basis for the presentation of reformed principles in the Gaelic-speaking areas of the north and west, and particularly in Argyll where Carswell had held the parsonage of Kilmartin since 1553.[4]

That the translation of the *Book of Common Order*, or *Foirm na n-Urrnuidheadh* ('The Form of Prayers'), as Carswell called it, should have come from the heart of Gaelic Argyll suggests – though it does not necessarily prove – that the reformed faith had considerable vitality in that area, compared with some other

---

[1] *The Works of John Knox*, ed. D. Laing, 6 vols. (Edinburgh, 1846–64), vi, 293–380.
[2] *Foirm na n-Urrnuidheadh*, ed. R. L. Thomson (Edinburgh, 1970).
[3] Ibid., 8, 177; 112.
[4] Inverary Castle, Argyll Transcripts [AT], v, 29.

parts of Gaeldom which were slower in assimilating reformed ideals; and an examination of the factors which permitted the rise of protestantism elsewhere in Scotland helps to explain why this should be so. In its initial stages, the Reformation movement was primarily an east-coast phenomenon, sustained by close trading links with Scandinavia and the Low Countries and by a ready accessibility to the chief continental centres of protestantism by North Sea routes. The importance of trading links is underlined by the support which the movement derived from the burghs and fishing ports of the eastern seaboard. Parliament's decision in 1525, repeated in 1535, to ban the importation of Lutheran literature had, of course, a special relevance to the coastal burghs and fishing ports, the obvious centres for the distribution of heretical and subversive works; and the act itself was to be 'publist and proclamit outthrow this realme at all portis and burrowis of the samin'.[5] The government, plainly, was well aware of the nature of the threat which confronted both church and state, and its action in 1525 merely emphasised the strategic importance of the burghs to the development of Scottish protestantism. Contemporaries themselves were conscious of the influences at work. John Knox largely attributed the spread of protestantism in the 1530s to the activities of 'merchantis and marinaris, who, frequenting other cuntreis, heard the trew doctrin affirmed and the vanitie of the Papisticall religioun openly rebucked: amongis whome war Dundy and Leyth principalles'.[6] By the 1550s, all the evidence suggests that the foundations had been laid in many lowland burghs for the emergence of reformed congregations,[7] which provided the reforming movement with a spearhead for further penetration into the surrounding countryside, where lairds such as Erskine of Dun and the 'gentilmen of the Mernse', and others like Pittarrow, Brunstane, Longniddry, Ormiston and Calder exhibited a steadfast commitment to the godly cause, and provided the movement with an additional impetus and source of strength.[8]

In the west, a similar pattern, if less developed, can be detected. One of the main west-coast burghs in which incipient protestantism took root was Ayr, itself a seaport trading with England and overseas. Evidence of iconoclasm at Ayr can be

---

[5] *Acts of the Parliament of Scotland* [*APS*], ed. T. Thomson, 12 vols. (London, 1844–75), ii, 295 c. 4, 342 c. 2.
[6] Knox, *Works*, i, 61.
[7] See above, 12ff., 96ff., 154ff.
[8] Knox, *Works*, i, 136–42, 215, 237, 249, 250, 251, 273; see above, 144–5.

traced back to the 1530s,[9] and the missionary activities of George Wishart who preached there in 1545 can only have contributed to this mood of criticism and discontent.[10] Eleven years later, John Knox himself 'taught in ... the toune of Air',[11] as did John Willock in 1559.[12] In the surrounding countryside, lairds like John Lockhart of Bar, Robert Campbell of Kinyeancleuch, Hugh Wallace of Carnell, Andrew Stewart, Lord Ochiltree, and James Chalmers of Gadgirth fostered the spread of reforming ideas, thereby creating a more effective basis of support in rural society for the developing politico-religious movement.[13]

Such a picture, however, is less applicable to the Highlands, where the preached and printed Word of the Reformation took longer to circulate. In the country as a whole, the protestant movement developed piecemeal, and, before the Reformation took full effect, it was largely concentrated in certain clearly defined geographical areas. The greatest fervency, it was said, was to be found in the Lothians, Fife, Angus and the Mearns, and Kyle, though even earlier John ab Ulmis, on crossing the border in 1551, formed the impression that 'as to the commonalty, it is the general opinion that greater numbers of them are rightly persuaded as to the true religion than here among us in England'.[14] The Highlands and the Borders, on the other hand, proved less susceptible to reforming influences. They remained areas with poor communications and less effective government. Although Carswell would have been familiar with the state of protestantism in the Lowlands, the conditions which he faced in Argyll were markedly different. In contrast to the south and east, the Gaelic seaboard had few developed trading connections. Nor did it possess the organised town life which undeniably facilitated the spread of protestantism. In the towns of the Lowlands, religious ideas were readily transmitted not only by people hearing a powerful preacher expound the Word at public assemblies but also, informally, at markets, fairs, festivals, in taverns and private houses and at the workplace.

The structure of merchant and craft gilds, themselves a

---

[9] Calderwood, *History of the Kirk of Scotland*, ed. T. Thomson, 8 vols. (Edinburgh, 1842–9), i, 104; *St Andrews Formulare*, ed. G. Donaldson, 2 vols. (Edinburgh, 1944), ii, 59–60; cf. *Ayr Burgh Accounts, 1534–1624*, ed. G. S. Pryde (Edinburgh, 1937), 97.

[10] Knox, *Works*, i, 127.

[11] Ibid., 250.

[12] *Ayr Burgh Accounts*, 30; see above, 104–5.

[13] Knox, *Works*, i, 250, 257.

[14] *Wodrow Society Miscellany*, ed. D. Laing (Edinburgh, 1844), i, 54; *Original Letters relative to the English Reformation*, 1537–58, ed. H. Robinson, 2 vols. (Cambridge, 1846–7), ii, 434.

product of townlife, whose proceedings were discussed behind closed doors, could also be used as a means of protecting and fostering the growth of protestant opinion. In Perth, which lay to the immediate south of the highland boundary, the chance survival of evidence reveals the firm attachment of craftsmen to protestantism, and to issues of social justice, brotherhood and reform, and resentment at the consumption of material resources by idle 'kirkmen, papis, cardinalis, bischoipis, abbottis, prioris, dennis, arsdennis, personis, vicars, curatis', and by kings, princes, earls and landowners, at the expense of the producers. These concerns clearly circulated within the context of the craft incorporations, which showed themselves ready also to address 'the estaittis of parliament, nobilite and haill congregatioun of this realme'; and the attachment of 258 names and signatures to a document, composed by the bailies, council and deacons of crafts, electing two commissioners (at the behest of the protestant lords, with help from their minister for redressing craft grievances) to attend a meeting of the privy council and convention of lords, held in January 1560/1, which substantially approved the Book of Discipline, is again indicative of the interaction of forces in shaping organised opinion within the institutions of the burgh.[15] Even in Edinburgh, where the person of the monarch may have predisposed conservatives to adhere to old observances, the 'Catholicism' of the crafts is sometimes apt to be exaggerated: it is clear that the Hammermen, by November 1559, had appointed a minister, William Barbour, himself a notary, to their Magdalen chapel; and there seems no reason to adopt the ingenuity of one writer who, unable to believe Barbour was a 'reformed minister', decided he was just a 'replacement chaplain'; Barbour, in fact, soon afterwards, became minister at Lasswade, seven miles to the south.[16] Those structures which afforded protestantism access to the towns were, of course, all but absent in the Highlands. As reformers gradually worked their way into the west by mainland routes, they found their path barred by mountain ranges; and their sense of frustration would also have increased as they encountered the linguistic barrier, one of the principal sources of misunderstanding between highlander and lowlander.

The spread of protestantism was, however, helped or hindered, as the case may be, by yet another factor – the attitude of the

[15] Perth Museum and Art Gallery, MS Original papers and letters of the Convener Court of the Incorporated Trades of Perth, nos. 23a, 30, 34–5. I am grateful to the Director of the Museum for kindly depositing this collection, and related material, in Glasgow University Archives for my inspection during 1977.

[16] J. Smith, *The Hammermen of Edinburgh* (Edinburgh, 1905), 171–3, 177; M. Lynch, *Edinburgh and the Reformation* (Edinburgh, 1981), 57; see above, 134.

nobility. In the years preceding 1560, the protestant reformers may be considered a minority pressure group; and to gain the ascendancy they required the support of at least a section of the nobility. The political backing which a number of nobles gave to the religious movement was of particular importance in the isolated Gaelic west where clan chiefs held land and distributed it on what was still – in a strict legal sense at least – an essentially feudal basis modified by a strong kin element. The comparatively late acceptance of protestantism in the west Highland area north of Argyll was due in no small measure to the resistance offered by some local chiefs who saw the new faith as an integral part of the external threat to their accustomed way of life.

In Argyll, the homeland of clan Campbell, the key figure was Archibald, 5th earl of Argyll, who took up the astute, aggrandising policies of his predecessors with great enthusiasm. As early as 1556, his father, the 4th earl, had invited Knox to preach at Castle Campbell, near Dollar,[17] and by 1558, he had installed John Douglas, a renegade Carmelite friar, as his domestic chaplain.[18] Earlier, in 1557, father and son alike had publicly committed themselves to the reformed cause by subscribing the first band of the Lords of the Congregation.[19] As a contribution towards the survival of protestantism, the 4th earl in his testament exhorted his son to 'study to set fordwarte the publict and trew preaching of the Evangell of Jesus Christ, and to suppress all superstitioun and idolatrie to the uttermost of his power'.[20] Nor was he to be altogether disappointed in his expectation. Although radical reformers complained of the 5th earl's ambivalent attitude to outright protestant defiance of the higher powers,[21] his real allegiance was soon demonstrated by his reluctance to return to the queen regent's party on grounds of conscience.[22] Instead, in 1559, he chose to confer with the brethren at St Andrews 'for Reformatioun to be maid thair',[23] and with the ascendancy of the reformers by 1560, he was active in destroying 'places and monumentis of ydolatrie' in the west.[24] During Mary's personal rule, Argyll sought to combine his protestant enthusiasm with his earlier deference to civil government.[25] Nevertheless, his continuing support of protestantism created a framework probably

[17] Knox, *Works*, i, 253.
[18] Ibid., 256, 276.
[19] Ibid., 273–4.
[20] Ibid., 290.
[21] Ibid., 337, 342–3.
[22] Ibid., 346–7.
[23] Ibid., 347.
[24] Ibid., ii, 167–8.
[25] Ibid., 481–2.

unequalled elsewhere in the Highlands, within which Carswell could further the work of the reformed ministry. Beyond the earl's immediate sphere of influence, however, the ecclesiastical situation in Argyll during Carswell's lifetime is harder to assess than it is for many other areas of Scotland. The main sources for studying the reformed ministry in Scotland – the Accounts of the Collectors of Thirds, and the Register of Assignations and Modifications of Stipends[26] – do not extend to Argyll and the Isles, and in their absence reliance has to be placed on other relevant, though not primarily ecclesiastical, sources which have survived. Throughout the sixteenth century, the Argyll charters provide a continuous body of information which sheds a good deal of light on the local situation. Even the names of those who witnessed charters, and of the notaries public and scribes who drew them up, are of primary importance.

Approximately twenty of these notaries appear on record in the Argyll muniments in the thirty years before the Reformation, and many of them, it may be assumed, were also in orders. Some, like Archibald Ramsay, Alexander Dougall, and William Hegait,[27] though not readily identifiable as holding any ecclesiastical office, may nevertheless have been clerics. A dozen or so are known to have held benefices within the diocese, or are mentioned as priests, or yet again, as dignitaries of the cathedral church of Lismore. Mr Neil Campbell, for example, who comes on record as vicar of Kilmartin in 1528, dean of Lochawe in 1533 (an office which he held conjointly with the vicarage of Kilmartin), parson of Kilmartin in 1545, and parson of Kilmolew in 1552, was acting as a notary from at least 1533.[28] Equally, Mr Gilbert Macolchallum, latterly parson of Craignish was vicar of Lochgoilhead and notary public in 1529,[29] and Mr Cornelius Omey, another active notary, held the offices of parson of Kilberry and dean of Kintyre simultaneously during a lengthy ecclesiastical career extending probably from before 1550 to around 1577.[30] All this demonstrates that before 1560, there was in Argyll a conspicuous group of literate clergy. In addition to these, the names of another thirty-five clerics, many of whom held benefices, are attested in the Argyll charters for this period.

---

[26] See, in general, G. Donaldson, 'Sources for the Study of Scottish Ecclesiastical Organisation and Personnel', *Bulletin of the Institute of Historical Research*, xix (1942–3), 188–203.
[27] AT, v, 13, 105, 121.
[28] Ibid., iii, 212; iv, 22, 23, 156; v, 13.
[29] Ibid., iii, 223; iv, 153.
[30] Ibid., iv, 217, 218; v, i; vii, 20.

Such evidence helps to provide something like a picture of the parochial structure in the pre-Reformation diocese of Argyll. Among the benefices on record are those of Lochawe, Innishail, Luing, Kilmaluag, Kilmolew, Killean, Lochgoilhead, Kilmodan, Craignish, Kilmore, Kilmorich, Muckairn, Melfort, Kilberry, Kilmartin, Kilcolmkill, and Strachur.[31] There is also mention of the collegiate church of Kilmun, with its provost and chaplains.[32] Although it cannot be said with certainty how far, if at all, the holders of these benefices attended to their primary concern, the cure of souls, appointments to benefices continued to be made, and were seldom allowed to lapse. Even in the decade after 1560, there is remarkably little evidence of any dislocation. Mr Cornelius Omey's record of long service is rivalled, if not actually exceeded, by that of Mr Gilbert Macolchallum, for example, who was vicar of Lochgoilhead from about 1529 to 1544, and parson of Craignish from 1544 to 1571.[33] These men, like numerous others, survived the Reformation crisis unscathed; and only in 1573 was a religious test imposed on the holders of benefices.[34] Carswell himself possessed the parsonage of Kilmartin from 1553 until his death, sometime before 20 August 1572,[35] while his immediate predecessor as parson of Kilmartin, Mr Patrick Graham, held the parsonage of Kilmore, again from 1553 to 1576.[36]

One factor which contributed to the regularity of appointments to parishes in Argyll was the extent to which they were subject to secular control. It is quite apparent that in Carswell's day the church in Argyll was dominated by the Earls of Argyll and other landowners whose property rights included presentation to benefices. Inevitably, the right of presentation gave rise to disputes between different parties, even within clan Campbell itself, and the earl was careful to safeguard his own interests. One such dispute, between Archibald, Master of Argyll, and Sir Colin Campbell of Glenorchy, about presentation to benefices in Lorn occurred in 1553, when it was resolved that Campbell of Glenorchy should present to the chancellory and chantory of Lismore, and the earl and master to the deanery and treasurership of Lismore, as well as to the parsonage of Kilmore.[37] The

[31] Ibid., iv, 22, 44, 128, 129, 152, 153, 217; v, 11, 13, 27, 79, 104, 105, 149.
[32] Ibid., iii, 85; iv, 44; v, 81, 165.
[33] Ibid., iv, 44, 153.
[34] *APS*, iii, 72 c.3.
[35] AT, vi, 193B.
[36] Ibid., v, 20; vii, 2.
[37] Ibid., v, 21; *Origines Parochiales Scotiae*, ed. Cosmo Innes, ii (pt. 1), (Edinburgh, 1854), 161.

uncertainty of the situation at Kilmore is demonstrated by the fairly rapid succession to the parsonage of three individuals – Alexander MacAlister, Mr Neil MacArthur, and Neil MacTavish.[38] When the earl's presentee, Mr Patrick Graham, was appointed after the settlement of the dispute, he remained in office until 1576.[39] The influence exerted by successive earls is also manifest in Carswell's own parish of Kilmartin. After his death, his brother, Donald, formally resigned the parsonage into the 5th earl's hands, 'promising to deilver to the earl all writs which he had containing the said parsonage'[40] – a point which sufficiently demonstrates the earl's continuing ecclesiastical power in the post-Reformation period.

Presentation by the earl and other lay patrons did not necessarily mean that poorly qualified candidates were appointed to benefices. There were certainly cases of nepotism – Iain Campbell, for example, who was provost of Kilmun from at least 1559 to 1573, was an illegitimate son of the 4th earl[41] but the average cleric would seem to have been no worse, and possibly no better, than his counterpart elsewhere in pre-Reformation Scotland. The title, 'Master', signifying a graduate in Arts, which was given to a number of priests (twenty out of the forty or so identifiable clergy in Argyll for the period 1530–60), indicates that they had received what was the normal university training for aspiring clerics. A number of these can be positively identified as graduates of St Andrews, while a few others can be traced with less certainty. Among the latter are Mr Patrick Graham, *Angusiensis*, who studied at St Leonard's, and who obtained his M.A. in 1543,[42] Mr Robert Lamont, *Angusiensis*, a fellow student at St Leonard's, who graduated M.A. in 1542, and who probably appears as parson of Kilmodan in 1556, and as provost of Kilmun in 1557;[43] and Mr Robert Montgomery, at St Salvator's, who received his M.A. in 1534, and who may be on record as archdeacon of Lismore in 1556 and 1557.[44] The former include Mr John Campbell, *nationis Britanniae*, who matriculated at St Salvator's in 1533, and who was one of Carswell's predecessors in the parsonage of Kilmartin;[45] and Mr Cornelius Omey, later parson of Kilberry and dean of Kintyre, who

[38] AT v, 1; v, 10, 13.
[39] Ibid., vii, 2.
[40] Ibid., vi, 193B.
[41] Ibid., vi, 124.
[42] *Early Records of the University of St Andrews [RStAU]*, ed. J. M. Anderson (Edinburgh, 1926), 146, 148, 246.
[43] Ibid., 144, 146, 246; AT, v, 64, 81.
[44] *RStAU*, 129, 132, 233; AT, v, 64, 78.
[45] *RStAU*, 232.

attained the B.A. standard at St Leonard's in 1528.[46] Another
Omey, Patrick, is mentioned as priest of Killean in 1557,[47] and,
indeed, as late as the seventeenth century, Omeys are found
holding ecclesiastical offices in Argyll and Perthshire.[48] The
career of Cornelius Omey illustrates well how members of
Gaelic families became integrated into the structure of the
sixteenth-century Scottish church, and equally, how they received
their formal university education in the Lowlands.

Carswell's own education conformed to this pattern. It is with
his matriculation at St Salvator's College, St Andrews, in 1540,
that he first appears on record,[49] an indication that he probably
meant to follow an ecclesiastical career. Thereafter, he attained
the B.A. standard in 1542, and graduated M.A. in 1544.[50] Indeed,
the college rolls contain the earliest evidence about his origins,
where he is described as *nationis Britanniae* and *pauper*.[51] All this
suggests that he came from the west of Scotland and that his
family was not particularly well-to-do, a point which contrasts
with Cornelius Omey, described as *dives*,[52] and descended from
a landowning family. Although tradition has it that he was born
at Kilmartin in Argyll, which is only a short distance from
Carnassery castle where his family were said to have been
constables or captains under the house of Argyll,[53] no evidence
has yet been brought forward to substantiate either claim. The
close connection of his family with the Earls of Argyll and their
tenure of Carnassery castle at this point are highly suspect. The
status accorded to Carswell in the St Andrews records scarcely
suggests a castle-holding background, and the apparent absence
of the names of any earlier members of his family in the Argyll
charters may also indicate that he came from a family which was
comparatively insignificant. Indeed, it would seem that the
Carswells were not originally natives of Argyll. The name itself is
territorial, and in its distribution, it is lowland rather than
highland.[54] The view that the Carswells came to Argyll in the
train of Campbells who had settled in Corsewall in Wigtownshire

[46] Ibid., 122; AT, iv, 217; v, 1.

[47] AT, v, 79.

[48] *Fasti Ecclesiae Scoticanae*, ed. H. Scott, 9 vols. (Edinburgh, 1915–61), iv, 34,
48, 54, 66, 105, 188, 204, 206, 222, 224, 246.

[49] *RStAU*, 245.

[50] Ibid., 146, 149.

[51] Ibid., 245, 149.

[52] Ibid., 122.

[53] A. Matheson, *Transactions of the Gaelic Society of Inverness* [*TGSI*], xlii
(1953–9), 183.

[54] G. F. Black, *The Surnames of Scotland* (New York, 1965), 140.

is hard to resist[55] – all the more so as in a charter dated at Wigtown, 14 December 1511, Alexander Campbell of Corsewall sold to Archibald, 2nd Earl of Argyll, 'the forty shilling lands of Knokbrek and the twenty shilling lands of Arge' in the parish of Kirkcolm.[56] The arrival of the Carswells in Argyll on the present evidence is probably not to be dated much before the early sixteenth century. As for the tenure of Carnassery castle, no member of the family is known to have been in possession before John Carswell himself obtained the '8 merklands of old extent of the two Carnasseries, with custody of the castle' in blench ferm from the 5th earl in 1559.[57] The earliest reference so far traced to the landholding interests of the Carswells occurs only in 1556, when John Carswell, acting on behalf of his brother, Donald, disputed the ownership of the lands of Barindryne in Argyll.[58]

Carswell left St Andrews in 1544, the year before the outbreak of the rebellion headed by the Earl of Lennox. The claim has been advanced by Robert Wodrow, writing in the eighteenth century, that Carswell actively supported the rebellion,[59] and this assertion has been repeated by successive historians who seem scarcely to have considered its validity.[60] Carswell, it is true, as notary public, witnessed a charter on 28 July 1545, at Ellencarne near Eigg, in which Donald, called 'Lord of the Isles', undertook 'to deal with Henry VIII as shall be commanded them by Matthew, Earl of Lennox, second person of the realm of Scotland'.[61] Shortly afterwards, on 5 August 1545, Carswell, this time styled 'notary public of the diocese of the Isles', drew up a notarial certificate witnessing an oath taken by Donald and his barons at Knockfergus in Ireland 'to be the king's subjects at the command of the Earl of Lennox, and to support the king touching the marriage of the Princess of Scotland and all other affairs'.[62] The inference from this might be that Carswell supported the policy of Donald Dubh to restore the Lordship of the Isles by connivance with Lennox, but there is no firm evidence that he committed himself to the Lennox cause, or

[55] A. Matheson, *TGSI*, xlii, 183.

[56] AT, iii, 163.

[57] *Registrum Magni Sigilli* [*RMS*], ed. J. M. Thomson, iv (Edinburgh, 1886), no. 1592).

[58] AT, v, 69.

[59] R. Wodrow, *Collections upon the Lives of the Reformers*, 2 vols. (Glasgow, 1848), i, 472.

[60] Cf. T. Maclauchlan, *Carswell's Liturgy* (Edinburgh, 1873), xiv; A. Matheson, *TGSI*, xlii, 184; *Foirm na n-Urrnuidheadh*, ed. R. L. Thomson, lxxix.

[61] *Letters and Papers, Foreign and Domestic, of the Reign of Henry VIII*, xx (pt. i), ed. J. Gardner and R. H. Brodie (London, 1905), no. 1298.

[62] Ibid., xx (pt. ii) (London, 1907), no. 42.

indeed, followed him into England, as has often been claimed.[63] Some have even expressed surprise that he should have been 'on the opposing side to his feudal chief',[64] the Earl of Argyll. Yet not only is Carswell's allegiance uncertain, but his links with the house of Argyll, in any event, appear to have been tenuous at this point.

No further information has come to light about Carswell's activities as notary public in the Isles. In March 1549, however, he witnessed a marriage contract in Argyll,[65] and had clearly changed his diocese by September 1550, when he appears as treasurer of Lismore, his first major ecclesiastical appointment.[66] By August 1553, he was in possession of the parsonage of Kilmartin in succession to Mr Patrick Graham, who had been transferred to Kilmore, having held the Kilmartin benefice for only a matter of months.[67] The significance of the benefice of Kilmartin may be suggested by the frequency with which Carswell's predecessors appear as witnesses to Argyll charters, compared with the other parsons of the diocese.[68] Perhaps the strategic position of the parish beside the Campbell keep of Carnassery, which, situated on a rocky eminence overlooking the glen, commanded one of the main routes through mid-Argyll, helps explain its distinction. At any rate, Carswell's appointment there rather than to Kilmore can hardly have been fortuitous. During those critical years which led up to the Reformation, Carswell appears to have lent his support to the ecclesiastical policies of his patrons, the Earls of Argyll. Precisely when he conformed is not clear, but the first significant grant of land, including the custody of Carnassery castle, which he received from the 5th earl in February 1558/9,[69] might well be interpreted as an acknowledgment of his reformed position, and perhaps as a guarantee of his further support. By March 1560, he had obtained three more heritable grants of land.[70] The most important of these included the custody of Craignish castle and the 'produce of the whole barony of Craignish'.[71] The peninsula of Craignish lies immediately west of Carnassery, and, all in all,

[63] R. Wodrow, *Collections*, i, 472; A. Matheson, *TGSI*, xlii, 184; *Foirm na n-Urrnuidheadh*, lxxix.
[64] A. Matheson, *TGSI*, xlii, 184; *Foirm na n-Urrnuidheadh*, lxxix.
[65] AT, iv, 200.
[66] Ibid., iv, 214.
[67] Ibid., v, 26, 29.
[68] E.g., ibid., iv, 61, 63, 85, 91, 95, 108, 137, 156, 174, 182, 196, 201, 217; v, 9, 13, 20, 26.
[69] RMS, iv, no. 1592.
[70] Ibid.
[71] Ibid.

Carswell's influence extended over a fairly wide area of mid- and west-Argyll. No other parson in the district received a comparable amount of land, and, indeed, his appointment as superintendent in Argyll after 1560[72] could scarcely have come as a surprise to his contemporaries.

Yet, on the eve of the Reformation, Carswell's position in Argyll was not entirely unorthodox. He was a cleric whose attitude to the church and its benefices was in some respects typical of the time. In 1558, for example, sir George Clapperton presented him to the parsonage of Southwick and Kingarth in Bute, where he dilapidated the teinds, glebe and kirklands of Kingarth.[73] The parsonage and vicarage fruits of both these benefices had been erected into the chancellory of the Chapel Royal in 1509, and Carswell himself, probably in 1558, was appointed chancellor.[74] In 1562, one of his tenants, a Sinclair, took Carswell to court over rights to the five merkland called the glebe and kirkland of Southwick where Carswell had the benefice; three years later, it was Carswell's turn, as parson and vicar, to proceed against William Bell in Stirling, who asserted a claim to the kirkland and glebe of Southwick on the ground that Carswell's predecessor, sir Michael Dysart, had feued him the property, but the claimant was unwilling or unable to produce any charter for inspection by the Lords of Council; then, in January 1569/70, Carswell was engaged in a dispute with Sinclair of Auchinfranko, the expiry of whose lease for three years of the teinds of Southwick, which Carswell had granted him in March 1566/7, led Carswell to believe that he was free to dispose of the teinds as he saw fit.[75]

Plurality and dilapidation of benefices are clearly attested in Argyll before and after 1560,[76] and Carswell himself abandoned neither practice. Indeed, he succeeded in holding his pre-Reformation benefices until his death in 1572.[77] He seems also to have continued his notarial interests, although the comparatively few instances of his signature in Argyll charters after 1560[78] might suggest that his activities lay in other areas.

[72] The date of his appointment is unknown.
[73] *Origines Parochiales Scotiae*, ii (pt. i), 211.
[74] I. B. Cowan, *Parishes of Medieval Scotland* (Edinburgh, 1967), 112, 186; *Registrum Secreti Sigilli Regum Scotorum* [*RSS*], edd. M. Livingston et al., 8 vols. (Edinburgh, 1908–82), vi, no. 1716.
[75] SRO, CS7/25, Acts and Decreets of the Court of Session, fo. 39v; CS7/35, fos. 135v–136v; CS7/46, fo. 139v.
[76] Cf., AT, v, 21, 64; vi, 6, 43, 154.
[77] Cf., *RSS*, vi, nos. 1716, 1756, 1906.
[78] AT, vi, 32, 42, 44, 45, 62, 67, 85, 98, 137.

Carswell acquired more land in the period after 1560. Three further heritable grants by the earl are on record between 1562 and 1564[79] and two other grants in the Cowal and Lochgoilhead areas appear to have been made before 1571.[80] The previous holders of the Lochgoilhead lands evidently resented their transfer to Carswell, and he had to enlist the support of the earl himself in order to remove 'thameselffis, with the pertinentis, thair servandis and gudis fra all and haill the landis of Laggan and suffer me and my servandis entir therto according to my infeftment and saising of the same'.[81] Evidence of Carswell's business transactions with other parties comes to light in an instrument of reversion of 15 September 1560, whereby he renounced all claims to the lands of Glenliever on their redemption by John Campbell of Inverliever for £100 Scots.[82] But although in this instance Carswell was the creditor, he also accumulated debts of his own. On 24 March 1569/70, both he and his wife, Margaret, herself a Campbell, registered in the books of Council their promise to pay an Edinburgh merchant burgess and his wife the sum of £1,175 8s 7d Scots.[83] Four days earlier, Carswell was involved in dealings of another sort, an agreement for honouring payment of a pension from the bishopric of the Isles to John Hay, commendator of Balmerino, granted by his predecessor, John Campbell, pensionary of the bishopric.[84]

Financial considerations, no doubt, had been uppermost in his mind when Carswell originally accepted the gift of the bishopric of the Isles from Mary in January 1564/5. Later, he was formally presented to the bishopric, and to the annexed abbacy of Iona, in March 1567.[85] What has not hitherto been recognised, however, is that Carswell was already in effective possession of another bishopric and abbacy, namely Argyll and Saddell, both spirituality temporality, which the conforming bishop and commendator, James Hamilton, had leased to him in 1563 for six years in return for payment of 420 merks a year, to be rendered in Glasgow (where Hamilton had associations as subdean and whose location was obviously within convenient reach of his own residence in Monkland). The transaction gave Carswell full power to grant leases of the teinds and lands of the two properties, to utilise

[79] *RMS*, iv, no. 1592.
[80] AT, vi, 144, 155.
[81] Ibid., 155.
[82] Ibid., v, 142.
[83] SRO, RD1/11, Register of Deeds, fo. 176v (24 March, 1569/70).
[84] Ibid., fo. 175r-v (21 March 1569/70).
[85] *RSS*, v, no. 1885; vi, no. 3373.

benefices, and appoint depute commissaries; but he also became responsible, in place of the bishop, for paying the crown's levy of a third of the fruits of both bishopric and abbacy. The prudent bishop had inserted in the contract a clause to the effect that if the crown should dispense with the levy, Carswell should pay an increased annual rent of 625 merks; and the careful Carswell added a rider that if the crown should impose a new exaction, the bishop should relieve him of all further taxation. The document was also witnessed by the bishop's kinsman or client, William Hamilton, parson of Cambuslang, sir Thomas Knox, chaplain and notary (later reader at Eastwood), Alexander Dickie, vicar choral of Glasgow, and Archibald Campbell of Inverraw, with whom Carswell presumably had contact. It is fortuitous, too, that the terms of this remarkable contract survive because Carswell himself failed to make prompt payment to the bishop's factors and chamberlains, which, in turn, forced Carswell's cautioners, three prominent Glasgow burgesses (Archibald Lyon, George Herbertson and William Hegait), to take the superintendent to court in July 1565.[86]

Nor is this all. It looks rather as if, at any early date, Carswell had come to a similar arrangement with John Campbell over property pertaining to the bishopric of the Isles and abbacy of Iona. This, at any rate, would seem to be the inference from Carswell's later action against Campbell before the Lords of Council in June 1567 for recovery of a debt of £100 (acknowledged in Campbell's obligations of 26 July 1564 and 1 August 1565) and also for delivery of 'the auld rental buik of the said abbacie of Icolmkill and bischoprik of the Ilis that wes wount to ly in the said place of Icolmkill and wes than in the said Maister Johnne Campbellis keping'.[87] Although Campbell was styled commendator of Ardchattan (which had held since 1545, long before his acquisition of the Isles and Iona), the action Carswell instigated related to the recovery of rents and victual from the temporality of Skeirchenzie (Kilchenzie) in Kintyre for 1561 and 1562, and of revenues from the kirk of Kilchenzie in 1561. All this was the patrimony of the Isles and Iona (not Ardchattan), in which Carswell had evidently a financial interest long before his acquisition of the bishopric of the Isles in 1565.

Carswell's political support for the Earl of Argyll, who was then still a firm supporter of Mary, can scarcely be overestimated in explaining many of his earlier grants and privileges. In 1564, he and two others, James Campbell of Ardkinglass and John

[86] SRO, CS7/33, Acts and Decreets of the Court of Session, fos. 439v–441v.
[87] Ibid., CS7/37, fos. 441v–442r.

Campbell of Inverliever, were engaged in administering the earl's justice to a party of the Stewarts of Appin who had attacked some of Argyll's officers. The number who were to be kept in ward in Inchconnel castle had previously been determined by Carswell in negotiations with John Stewart of Appin.[88] Later, in April 1567, when John Lamont of Innerrin failed to adhere to the settlement of a dispute with Carswell by decreet arbitral determined by the Earl of Argyll, Carswell took the matter to the Lords of Council who agreed that Lamont was obliged to pay Carswell the teinds for lands belonging to the kirk of Dunoon from 1557 to 1563.[89]

In national affairs, Carswell believed, like Argyll himself, that commitment to protestantism need not preclude political support for the queen. A few days after his election in parliament to the Committee of the Articles in April 1567,[90] he followed Argyll in approving Mary's marriage to Bothwell,[91] although two years later he was prepared to oppose the queen's wishes by voting against her divorce from Bothwell.[92] In July 1569, he was particularly active in coming to her defence after her escape from Lochleven,[93] and in attending the Convention of Estates held at Perth to discuss, *inter alia*, Elizabeth's relations with Mary and her son.[94] The mood of the general assembly which, on 5 July, had rebuked him 'for accepting the Bishoprik of the Isles not making the Assemblie foreseene, and for ryding at and assisting of parliament holden by the Queen after the murther of the king'[95] had clearly done nothing to dampen his spirits. Indeed, the assembly itself, while it censured him, was still prepared to appoint him one of its commissioners to petition the Regent and nobility at Perth.[96]

If Carswell's political manœuvrings had thus incurred some criticism, it is also clear that he laid himself open to charges of cupidity. Rumours that he was acting out of self-interest, and making the most of the teinds and revenues of his churches, were

[88] AT, vi, 25.
[89] SRO, CS7/37, Register of Acts and Decreets of the Court of Session, fos. 398v–399r.
[90] APS, ii, 546.
[91] Calderwood, *History*, ii, 354.
[92] *Register of the Privy Council of Scotland* [RPC], 1st ser., edd. J. H. Burton and D. Masson, 14 vols. (Edinburgh, 1877–98), ii, 8–9.
[93] R. Keith, *History of the Affairs of Church and State in Scotland*, 3 vols. (Edinburgh, 1844–50), ii, 807–10.
[94] RPC, ii, 2–6.
[95] *The Booke of the Universall Kirk, Acts and Proceedings of the General Assemblies of the Kirk of Scotland* [BUK], 3 vols. and appendix vol. (Edinburgh, 1839), i, 144; Calderwood, *History*, ii, 490–1.
[96] BUK, i, 145–6; Calderwood, *History*, ii, 493–4.

evidently current by 1564. In May of that year, he wrote to Robert Campbell of Kinyeancleuch, in an attempt to dispel the rumours in circulation:[97]

> 'In your letter directit unto me (beluiffit Brother in the Lord), it apperis to me that yer ar sinisterlie informit towardis me, or ellis in jugement and credit sum part facill. Becaus ye writt as ane mening that ye think the warld and induellaris thairof turnand to[o] fast; and in deid I fear the samin to be maist trew in generall: God forbid it be so in all speciallis ... I commonit with our brother George [probably George Hay, commissioner of Aberdeen] at lenthe, and gif he had informit yow as I informit him and for my parte offerit him occasioun, I beleiff he culd have declarit unto you my part, for latt thame saye quhat thai list, my conscience will nocht lat me use rigour bot aganis the stubburne. Bot in this mater of Teindis, it is nocht myne bot the factouris. . . .'

This letter rather suggests that the traditional Gaelic view of Carswell as a somewhat harsh and grasping individual[98] is not wholly ill-deserved. Nevertheless, the same letter contains evidence that Carswell, as superintendent of Argyll, was taking his duties with some seriousness. He excused himself from attending the general assembly:[99]

> 'becaus I pas presentlie to Kyntire, and thaireftir to the Ilis, to veseit sum kirkis ... and my brethren the minister of Edinburgh and Superintendent of Glasgo hes written unto me, that thai will excuse me at the Generall Assemblie and thinkis that my travell now in the Ilis may do mair gude to the Kirk nor my presens at the Assemblie; because the Ilis can nocht be travellit wele throwch in Wynter. . . .'

That he fulfilled the essential requirements of his office – if not always to the exacting standards of the general assembly – is by no means inconceivable. Considering the wide bounds of his province, and its remoteness from Edinburgh, it is not altogether surprising that he attended the assembly less regularly than might have been wished,[100] but there is at least some indication that he carried out such routine duties as visitation and collation to benefices. Detailed investigation is prevented by the fragmentary nature of the surviving evidence. One instance of his activities, however, is on record in June 1572, in which he granted collation to the vicarage of Kilmolew to Donald Macvicar, Argyll's presentee, who was to receive institution from the parson of

[97] Wodrow Miscellany, 285.
[98] A. Matheson, TGSI, xlii, 188.
[99] Wodrow Miscellany, 285–6.
[100] Cf., BUK, ii, 13, 114, 144, 145.

Lochawe.[101] The difficulties which he encountered in overseeing his province may well have been formidable, for in June the general assembly had to enlist the support of the justice-clerk, to take order with 'James Mackverit in Boote for disobedience to the Superintendent of Argile'.[102] Though not disclosed in the assembly's record, the substance of the disagreement, it seems, was revealed in 1564, when the parishioners of Kingarth complained of the rival claims by Carswell, as parson and vicar of Kingarth, and Macveratie, as vicar pensionary (for 30 or 40 years), to the teinds for the crops of 1562 and 1563.[103] Again, Carswell's ability to visit the churches of his province was no doubt interrupted in January 1565/6 (admittedly not the most hospitable season for journeying), when a band of Macaulays and others including the parson of Killearn, violently stole the superintendent's best horses: 'ane suilyeart horse, quheit tallit and quhete manit, ane mirk gray hors, ane quhete gray hors, ane bassound broun hors, ane uther basound broun hors', from Orchard in Argyll.[104] To financial and personal problems of this sort were added political and pastoral problems, particularly when, he was charged by the assembly, in December 1567, 'to trie and take satisfactioun' concerning the separation of the Earl and Countess of Argyll.[105]

Carswell's difficulties were by no means solved by his acceptance of the bishopric of the Isles. The removal of the bishop elect, Mr Patrick Maclean, in Carswell's favour[106] should perhaps be seen against a background of strained relations between the Campbells and the Macleans.[107] Indeed, it would appear that two years later there was a further claimant, again in the person of a Maclean. On 21 May 1567, two months after Carswell's appointment had been confirmed, 'Mr Lachlan Maclean' appeared before the Lords of the Privy Council, and 'maid fayth that he nevir obtenit licence of oure Soverane Ladie to pas to Rome for purchessing and impetratioun of the Bishoprik of the Ilis, nor na uther benefices pertening to Maistir Johne Carswell Bischope of the Ilis, nor nevir purchest the said bishoprik, nor the abbacie of Ycolmkill or utheris benefices, in ony tyme

---

[101] SRO, GD112/5/10, Breadalbane Papers (Protocol Book of Gavin Hamilton), 5r (21 June 1572), Dr John Durkan kindly supplied this reference.
[102] BUK, i, 19; Calderwood, History, ii, 192–3.
[103] SRO, CS7/32, Register of Acts and Decreets of the Court of Session, fo. 36r.
[104] Ibid., CS7/37, fo. 398r.
[105] BUK, i, 114; Calderwood, History, ii, 397.
[106] RSS, v, no. 1885.
[107] AT, v, 107; Calendar of the State Papers relating to Scotland, and Mary, Queen of Scots, 1547–1603 [CSP Scot], edd. J. Bain et al., 13 vols. (Edinburgh, 1898–1969), ii, no. 728; RPC, ii, 491–2, 710, 728.

bigane'.[108] He also promised never to 'vex nor molest the said Maister Johnne in the peciabill brouking and posseding of the said bishoprik and utheris his benefices, move nor intent actioun pley nor questioun aganis him for the samyn during his lyftyme'.[109] Although this charge was clearly not without foundation, Maclean was released from further prosecution. It may well be that with a disputed succession to the bishopric, Argyll took the opportunity of recommending his own candidate whose jurisdiction as superintendent already covered the islands south of Skye. The move may not have been wholly distasteful to an assembly which was as eager to extend the area of protestant influence as Argyll himself was to increase his political power under Mary.

Carswell's appointment as bishop of the Isles bound him to provide a pension for Mr Patrick Maclean, and to pay the stipends of ministers planted within the diocese.[110] In the formal confirmation, he was given jurisdiction in actions relating to benefices, churches and their lands, and teinds, as well as the right to dispose of vacant benefices.[111] In April 1567 he exercised his authority as commendator of Iona by proceeding against Hew MacKegane from Coll, who was imprisoned in Edinburgh tolbooth for not finding surety to answer before the town council 'for allegit intramission with the mailles of the kirklandis of Coll and teinds of the samyne be the spaice of sax yeiris last bypast allegit pertenand to him by virtew of tak and assedatioun maid be him thairof be the provest of Ycolmekill, extending yeirlie be the said space to sevin scoir bollis of beir, price of the boll or heid yeirlie thretty shillingis'.[112] Carswell subsequently obtained MacKegane's release, but the latter had still to appear before the sheriff of Argyll or his deputies the following month.[113] It also seems likely that Carswell was active in the Outer Isles. In August 1566 he witnessed a paternity confession involving Hucheon, brieve of Lewis,[114] and in February 1567, the crown confirmed Carswell's authorisation of collation in August 1566 to two benefices, in Argyll's patronage, in Harris and Skye.[115] These, however, were fairly routine duties, and there is so far no explicit evidence besides this to show him

[108] *RPC*, i, 511.
[109] Ibid.
[110] *RSS*, v, no. 1885.
[111] Ibid., vi, no. 3373.
[112] SRO, RD1/7, Register of Deeds, fo. 425, 11 April 1567.
[113] Ibid.
[114] *Highland Papers*, ed. J. MacPhail, 3 vols. (Edinburgh, 1914–20), ii, 280–1.
[115] *RSS*, v (pt. ii), no. 3246.

engaged in propagating the reformed faith, or in organising reformed congregations in the diocese. The only other record of his activities in the Isles indicates that he granted a feu charter of some lands belonging to the bishopric to Maclean of Duart.[116]

Carswell's standing in the eyes of the reformed church must have been enhanced by the appearance of his Gaelic translation of the *Book of Common Order* shortly after his election to parliament as one of the Lords of the Articles. It was a work of major literary and liturgical significance, and the fact that it was undertaken during three busy years in Carswell's life adds to his achievement. There is no evidence that either the general assembly or the Earl of Argyll actually commissioned Carswell to carry out the translation, but the dedicatory epistle to the earl indicates that at the very least his patronage was an important stimulus. The *Book of Common Order*, which drew its inspiration from the English congregation at Frankfort and from Calvin's Geneva, was intended to regularise worship in the protestant areas of Scotland. Accordingly, in December 1564, the general assembly ordained that 'everie minister, exhorter and reader sall have one of the Psalme bookes latelie printed in Edinburgh, and use the order contained therein in prayers, mariage and ministration of the sacraments'.[117] It was thus intended as a serviceable guide, or manual, for those who were in the reformed ministry, but the inclusion of certain items such as graces indicates that it did not neglect the ordinary person who might be expected to learn these for daily use. The immediate question with regard to Carswell's translation is whether he envisaged a similar purpose for the book in Argyll.

In Argyll, the Reformation caused little noticeable dislocation in the ecclesiastical structure in the years immediately following 1560, and many of the pre-Reformation clergy simply continued to hold their benefices as before. The Argyll charters, however, throw little light on the activities of ministers in that area, but Carswell himself, in his dedicatory epistle to the earl, speaks of 'your ministers'.[118] Indeed, he states that one of his reasons for undertaking the translation was 'to help my Christian brethren who need teaching and comfort, and who lack books'.[119] This statement, whether taken to apply to the ordinary people or to the ministry – and the latter seems the more likely – presupposes

[116] *Collectanea de Rebus Albanicis*, ed. Iona Club (Edinburgh, 1847), 17–18.
[117] *BUK*, 54.
[118] *Foirm na n-Urrnuidheadh*, 10, 179.
[119] Ibid., 9, 178.

the existence of a literate group of Gaelic-speaking ministers, however small that group may have been. These ministers, in the main, would have been drawn, like Carswell himself, from the ranks of the pre-Reformation clergy, and they would have been bi-lingual, if not tri-lingual, with a Gaelic, Scots, and probably Latin, background. Carswell's emphasis on a 'lack of books' would therefore appear to be somewhat exaggerated. In his epistle to the reader, however, he made it clear that the lack was of specifically Gaelic (and the term to him included Irish Gaelic) books, which he considered to be a great disadvantage.[120] Referring to the circulation of Gaelic manuscript histories, he commented particularly on the lack of a Gaelic translation of the Bible, comparable with those already existing in Latin and English[121] – a point which indicates that he acknowledged what has been called 'the explosive and renovating and often disintegrating effect of the Bible'[122] in contributing to the spread of the reformed faith. Indeed, he viewed his own translation as nothing more than the beginning of a programme which he was not spared to carry through.[123] It is apparent from this that while there were reformed ministers in Argyll, the overall situation was very different from that for which the original *Book of Common Order* had been intended, particularly among the ordinary people. Although what were essentially Irish translations of parts of the Bible appeared from the early seventeenth century, more than two centuries were to pass before a vernacular Scottish Gaelic translation of the complete Bible was made available. Even then, the other great problem which Carswell, very significantly, does not mention, that of non-literacy among the ordinary people, had not been fully overcome.

The indispensability of ministers, literate in Gaelic, as organisers of the reformed faith in Argyll is further emphasised by the language of Carswell's translation. This was not the ordinary, everyday language of the people, but the literary language shared by the *literati* of Ireland and Gaelic Scotland, and therefore known as Classical Common Gaelic. It has been argued convincingly that 'by the fifteenth century at least . . . there was already a fairly free movement between professions and learned orders: clergy, bards, scribes, and medical men', all of whom would have been 'at home in reading and writing Classical

---

[120] Ibid., 10, 179.
[121] Ibid.
[122] G. R. Elton, *Reformation Europe* (London, 1972), 52.
[123] *Foirm na n-Urrnuidheadh*, 12, 181.

Common Gaelic'.[124] John Carswell clearly occupied a prominent place within this group, but his conservatism in using Classical Common Gaelic, rather than the vernacular, as his medium of expression may well have made it difficult for ordinary congregations to understand fully the contents of his book. It is possible, however, that the differences between Classical Common Gaelic and the vernacular were less in practice than has been supposed, particularly when ministers read passages from his book aloud to their congregations, though Carswell may have expected them to simplify, as a matter of course, the archaisms inherent in the language of his translation.

It is evident that Carswell's translation was based on the 1564 edition of the *Book of Common Order*,[125] although he claimed to have had access to both the English and the Latin texts.[126] By this he must be referring to the Latin translation of the Geneva Book, the *Ratio et Forma*, and it is of some significance that as well as acknowledging the importance of 'the Christian brethren who were at Geneva', he gave his translation the title of the Geneva Book itself, 'The Form of Prayers'.[127] Even so, the contents of the translation indicate a closer connection with the Scottish edition of the *Book of Common Order* than with the Geneva Book or its Latin rendering; the Latin phrases which Carswell occasionally uses are not from the *Ratio et Forma*.[128] The overall format of the translation, however, with a dedicatory epistle to the Earl of Argyll,[129] an epistle to the reader,[130] and a tail-piece (the 'lawful apology')[131] suggests, that Carswell viewed his translation as a new, and even original, contribution which had to be accommodated to the literary conventions of the time – a view which would allow him to alter the text of the *Book of Common Order* where he thought this necessary. Numerous alterations do occur, and it is quite apparent that Carswell did not aim at producing a literal translation of the *Book of Common Order*. He was well aware that Argyll, and the Gaelic areas generally, presented a situation in sharp contrast to that for which the original *Book of Common Order* had been compiled, in that much of the groundwork had still to be prepared even

[124] D. S. Thomson, 'Gaelic Learned Orders and Literati in Mediaeval Scotland', *Proceedings of the Third International Congress of Celtic Studies*, ed. W. F. H. Nicolaisen (Edinburgh, 1968), 68.
[125] *Foirm na n-Urrnuidheadh*, lxv-lxvi.
[126] Ibid., 1.
[127] Ibid., 1, 11, 180.
[128] Ibid., lxviii.
[129] Ibid., 3–10.
[130] Ibid., 10–13.
[131] Ibid., 112–3.

after the formal establishment of the reformed church by 1567. There were plainly some purely practical considerations which had to be taken into account. It is scarcely surprising that he did not attempt to translate the psalms, since, quite apart from the time-consuming problem of fitting them into Gaelic metre,[132] they were meant primarily for devotion rather than instruction. In any event, the Psalm-book was appended to the *Book of Common Order*, and did not necessarily form an integral part of it. This emphasis on basic instruction is also indicated by the replacement of numerous sections of Calvin's little Catechism (which Carswell chose to use in place of the large Catechism of the *Book of Common Order*) by long passages apparently of his own composition.[133] In these, he tried to communicate the fundamental principles of the reformed faith, as well as to remove any obvious traces of Catholicism which might remain in the minds of the people.

These are the most apparent divergences from the text of the *Book of Common Order*, but, while they are generally consistent with the substance of protestant doctrine, a closer examination reveals that Carswell had not completely dissociated himself from earlier traditions, and may well have retained some affection for certain aspects of the old order. Whereas the doctrine of election as enunciated in the *Book of Common Order* explains how God 'hath ordeyned some, as vessels of wrathe, to damnation and hathe chosen others, as vessels of his mercie, to be saved',[134] Carswell reinterpreted this by emphasising the doctrine of good works, and stating that there were 'some who have damned and condemned themselves by their deeds and unworthy works, and others who believe the church appropriate unto their salvation through his great loving mercy'.[135] In other words, the emphasis at this point was on man rather than on God. Yet, elsewhere he faithfully reproduced the Reformed view of such central doctrines as justification by faith,[136] and even predestination itself, where the elect are said to have been chosen 'before the foundation of the world was laid'.[137] Again, although he condemned the invocation of 'saints and female saints',[138] he

---

[132] Ibid., lxvii.
[133] Ibid., lxxv.
[134] Knox, *Works*, iv, 171.
[135] *Foirm na n-Urrnuidheadh*, 17.
[136] Ibid., 5, 175.
[137] Ibid., 66; Knox, *Works*, iv, 196.
[138] *Foirm na n-Urrnuidheadh*, 19.

nevertheless included a purely superfluous allusion to 'the saints and archangels',[139] and he found it justifiable to insert a formula with liturgical responses for the blessing of a ship,[140] a practice at variance with protestant thinking.

If Carswell was therefore prepared to countenance ideas of this sort, and to carry over a number of minor observances, he manifestly repudiated the cardinal doctrines of Catholicism. He discredited the 'popish mass without substance in its words',[141] and affirmed the belief that 'the substance of the bread or the wine remains unaltered'.[142] He rejected the Catholic doctrine of the necessity of baptism as a prerequisite for salvation,[143] eschewed what he cautiously termed 'inappropriate idolatry',[144] and condemned 'the tyranny of the pope and other false prophets',[145] and prayers to saints and for the souls of the dead, as well as the holding of feast days, idolatrous services, and 'the vows of celibacy unkept'.[146] Although Carswell, for reasons best known to himself, chose to omit the references to purgatory, *limbus patrum*, and free-will, which were singled out for condemnation in the *Book of Common Order*,[147] he was plainly no crypto-Catholic in spite of his innate conservatism.

His caution was again apparent in matters of church government, where he displayed a marked deference to the civil magistrate – an attitude not wholly surprising in view of the hierarchical structure of Gaelic society as well as Argyll's influence in national politics and over the church in the locality. In the dedicatory epistle to the earl, Carswell argued from the example of the patriarchs that knowledge of the law of God and the suppression of false worship were both an integral part of the prince's rôle and also essential to the welfare of the church. The earl, he claimed, had succeeded in fulfilling his function, in acquainting himself with the scriptures from his youth, and in destroying idols.[148] No reformer, radical or otherwise, need have taken exception to this; indeed, such an attitude can be traced in the writings of both Knox and Melville.[149] But Carswell went

[139] Ibid., 16.
[140] Ibid., 110–11.
[141] Ibid., 19.
[142] Ibid., 107.
[143] Ibid., 106.
[144] Ibid., 19.
[145] Ibid., 6, 175.
[146] Ibid., 19.
[147] Ibid., Knox, *Works*, iv, 173.
[148] *Foirm na n-Urrnuidheadh*, 4–7; 174–7.
[149] See J. Kirk, 'The Development of the Melvillian Movement in Late Sixteenth-century Scotland', (Edinburgh Ph.D. thesis, 1972), 74–184; see also above, 236, 240ff.

much farther. In his translation – or, rather, adaptation – of the Confession of Faith employed by Knox's Genevan congregation, and inserted in the *Book of Common Order*, he altered the church's political doctrine. Whereas the Genevan Confession of Faith contained within the *Book of Common Order* expounded a theory which required the church member to state, 'I acknowlage to belonge to this church a politicall Magistrate',[150] Carswell, in translating the same passage, inverted the relationship to read: 'The church ought to have a lord or secular noble over it, called in Latin, *magistratus civilis*, and that magistrate ought to deal fairly with all men, in such matters as giving honour and protection to the good and in punishing the bad; and the church ought to render obedience and honour to those nobles in anything that does not conflict with the will or command of God'.[151] Such a standpoint, while not devoid of support, was altogether inconsistent with what became the dominant view within the church of the relationship between the two jurisdictions.[152]

It may be this somewhat rigid concept of secular control over the church, or simply the difficulty of setting up reformed congregations in Argyll, that led Carswell to limit the congregation's participation in church government. In laying down the procedure for the election of a minister, it is certainly true that he retained the reference to the candidate's examination by a minister and elders, but it is scarcely accidental that he omitted any mention of the congregation's rôle in advising the minister and elders, as the *Book of Common Order* directed, 'who may best serve in that rowme and office'.[153] In Carswell's adaptation, the initiative lay entirely with 'the ministers and learned elders, whom the care and the increase of the church concerns', to indicate 'the potential minister who will be most suitable ... and who is most likely to do God's services unfailingly.'[154] Again, Carswell recast the section in the *Book of Common Order* dealing with the enquiry into the life and conversation of the candidate by the ministers and elders, with a recommended trial period of at least eight days,[155] so that it read: 'Let those who choose him give a delay of some time until all may ascertain that he is of good morals'.[156] It would also seem

[150] Knox, *Works*, iv, 173.
[151] *Foirm na n-Urrnuidheadh*, 18–19.
[152] J. Kirk, 'The Melvillian Movement', 74–184; see above, 234ff.
[153] Knox, *Works*, iv, 175.
[154] *Foirm na n-Urrnuidheadh*, 21.
[155] Knox, *Works*, iv, 175.
[156] *Foirm na n-Urrnuidheadh*, 22.

that Carswell minimised the function of the elders. Where the *Book of Common Order* prescribed that 'In assemblying the people, nether they withoute the ministers, nor the ministers withoute them, may attempt anything',[157] Carswell wrote: 'In an assembly of the people, the elders can do nothing without the ministers'.[158] In the section dealing with the interpretation of the scriptures, he stated that ministers alone may settle theological disputes,[159] whereas the *Book of Common Order* stipulated that judgment should be referred to both ministers and elders.[160] Although this would appear to reflect Carswell's concept of a church controlled from the top, his failure to mention the kirk session at any point seems to reflect the problems facing the reformed church in Argyll.

It is hard to estimate what impression Carswell's translation of the *Book of Common Order* made on Argyll and the Isles, far less on the Gaelic-speaking west as a whole. Even after his death, the book had yet to make its full impact in many parts of his province. On a journey through Lorne and Cowal in July, 1574 the 6th Earl of Argyll found it still necessary to urge the adoption of 'the prayaris, ministratioun of the sacramentis and forme of discipline after the ordour of Genevay translatit out of Englis in the Erische toung be Maister Jhone Carsuale lait beschoppe of the Ylis'.[161] Yet, although Carswell's book may not have met with the response initially envisaged, the fault may have lain less in the translation itself than in the formidable obstacles facing organised religion in the Gaelic west.[162]

---

[157] Knox, *Works*, iv, 176.
[158] *Foirm na n-Urrnuidheadh*, 23.
[159] Ibid., 25.
[160] Knox, *Works*, iv, 179.
[161] *CSP Scot.*, v, 34.
[162] See below, 305ff., 449ff.

8

The Kirk and the Highlands at the Reformation

To the historian, the Church in the Highlands for almost any period in Scottish history, except perhaps for comparatively modern times, is a subject fraught with quite exceptional difficulty.[1] Apart from the readily recognisable, and therefore relatively straightforward problem of ecclesiastical loyalties among historians, which certainly can bedevil the subject, there is the more fundamental issue of the source material itself. The record evidence, the building blocks on which the historian relies to reconstruct a picture of the past and which for most lowland areas has survived in usually sufficient quantity to yield something like an adequate understanding of the past, is by contrast seriously deficient for most of the highland area. The Gaelic emphasis on oral tradition offers only a partial explanation for this deficiency, for there were undoubtedly ecclesiastical records written in Latin, and even in Scots, which were kept but which simply have not survived – records perhaps no longer retained when their evident utility had ceased. This dearth of material is particularly acute for the period of the Reformation. For a start, there is a complete absence of kirk session, presbytery and synod records for the highland areas throughout the late sixteenth century; and in their default reliance in tracing the progress of the Reformation has to be placed essentially on two series of financial records kept by the crown for recording the rentals of ecclesiastical benefices and for assigning stipends to ministers and others serving in the reformed church – surveys which extend over most of the country including much of the Highlands but which nonetheless effectively exclude the dioceses of Argyll and the Isles.

[1] The substance of this chapter formed a paper delivered at the Centre for Scottish Studies, University of Aberdeen on 14 May 1985.

These records, then, which consist of the accounts of the collectors of the thirds of benefices from 1561 to 1595,[2] the books of assumption,[3] initially prepared in the early 1560s, and the registers of stipends,[4] extant in one form or another for most years from 1567 to 1615, provide the main sources for tracing the work of the reformed church in the Highlands in the decades after 1560. Their contents reveal not only the names and revenues of the existing beneficed clergy (who, of course, may or may not have conformed to the Reformation) but also the personnel of the reformed church, the men who served either as ministers or, in a lesser capacity, as exhorters and readers in those early years, as well as the financial recompense assigned to them for so doing. None of these sources, of course, reveals the thinking behind the action of those men who chose, often in difficult circumstances, to enter the ministry of the new church; but the very existence of this material constitutes a record of commitment, and presumably of conviction, on the part of those who undertook the often arduous and financially unrewarding work of serving in the reformed church in the years following 1560. Conversely, of course, it may also be a testimony of resolution on the part of the clergy who declined to conform to the new regime in 1560 and who continued to enjoy an entitlement to most of the fruits of their livings without undertaking service of any kind. At the same time, the prospect of a life of ease with the added benefit of financial security may have held attractions for some. Again, the standards expected from entrants to the new ministry may have had the effect of dissuading others from offering themselves for active service in the protestant church.

However exploited, records of this kind clearly have their limitations and the resulting picture clarifies at best only one dimension in the highly complex situation which existed in and after 1560. Nor are there even adequate ancillary sources of the sort which do exist for the Lowlands, such as histories and diaries, to reveal the more personal reminiscences and attitudes of contemporaries to the developments they depict. Too frequently, then, the tendency among commentators has been to

[2] Scottish Record Office [SRO], E45/1-27 (Accounts of the Collector-General); E46/1-11 (Accounts of sub-collectors). The accounts between 1561 and 1572 are calendared in *Accounts of the Collectors of Thirds of Benefices, 1561-1572*, ed. G. Donaldson (Edinburgh, 1949).

[3] SRO, E48/1/1-2; National Library of Scotland [NLS], Adv. MS. 31.3.12; Edinburgh University Library [EUL], MS. Dc.4.32.

[4] SRO, E47/1-10; E48/2 [printed in *Register of Ministers, Exhorters and Readers, and of their Stipends, after the period of the Reformation* (Edinburgh, 1830)]; E48/3; NLS, Adv. MS. 17.1.4 [printed in *Miscellany of the Wodrow Society*, i, ed. D. Laing (Edinburgh, 1844), 329-96].

·

circumvent the problem by conveniently ignoring it. Too few studies of the Reformation have paused to assess the rôle of the new kirk in Highland areas. A. R. MacEwen wrote dismissively of the Highlanders who, at the Reformation, 'were as yet untouched by the religious movement'; and Hay Fleming, in his more detailed study of the Reformation, showed little awareness or appreciation of this dimension; but not so Professor Gordon Donaldson, who, in a couple of pages devoted to the subject in his study of the Reformation, suggests, significantly enough, that the apparent dearth of reformed clergy in parts of the Highlands in the years after 1560 may have been largely illusory, and he is altogether inclined to take a more optimistic view of the recruitment of candidates to the ministry in parts of the north and west. In decidedly different vein, however, Professor Ian Cowan in his recent synthesis sombrely concluded that 'much of the Western Highlands and Islands was to lack ministers for more than half a century after the Reformation'.[5]

Nor are matters exactly helped if guidance is sought not from the conflicting views of ecclesiastical historians but from the works of highland historians themselves. Donald Gregory offers no enlightenment beyond the unhelpful comment that the Reformation's 'progress is to be traced almost exclusively in the history of the Lowlands; at least, the history of the Highlands and Isles presents little that is interesting on this subject'; and to W. C. Mackenzie, it was 'abundantly clear that the Reformed Church was too much occupied with its own priestly concerns in the South to attempt the religious renovation of the North'. Even a recent commentator, content to reiterate received wisdom, has remarked that the effect of the Reformation 'left the Highlands largely Catholic or without religion at all'.[6] Yet despite such discouraging appraisals, there is in a very real sense a history to be uncovered here; and the starting point lies with the structure of the late medieval church itself.

Of Scotland's eleven mainland dioceses, no fewer than six – Argyll, Dunblane, Dunkeld, Moray, Ross and Caithness – straddled the length and breadth of the geographical Highlands, though, in each case, with the exception of Argyll, all these dioceses contained some lowland features too, represented

---

[5] A. R. MacEwen, *A History of the Church in Scotland*, 2 vols. (London, 1913–18), ii, 113; D. H. Fleming, *The Reformation in Scotland* (London, 1910); G. Donaldson, *The Scottish Reformation* (Cambridge, 1960), 88–9; I. B. Cowan, *The Scottish Reformation* (London, 1982), 168.

[6] D. Gregory, *The History of the Western Highlands and Isles of Scotland* (Glasgow, 1881), 186; W. C. Mackenzie, *A Short History of the Scottish Highlands and Islands* (Paisley, 1906), 123.

geographically in the coastal and lower-lying portions of the
dioceses, which contrasted with the mountainous hinterland, and
were exemplified culturally in the cathedral cities of Dunblane,
Dunkeld, Elgin, Fortrose and Dornoch on the periphery of the
Highlands proper, where the Scots language and the customs of
the Lowlands took precedence over the culture of the Gaidhealtachd. These cities were the headquarters, the centres of
leadership within the system, and the wholly Gaelic-speaking
dioceses of Argyll and the Isles, which lacked these features,
based as they were on Lismore and on Skye or Iona, remained
far weaker and less developed, and to that extent presumably less
effective.

In these cities, the bishops and cathedral dignitaries, the
secular church's clerical leaders, held office. They were usually
ambitious men, fully conversant with political and religious life
in the Lowlands. For a start, many of them possessed a lowland
background or upbringing, having been schooled at a centre in
the Lowlands and trained at a lowland university, and often at a
continental one, before seeking promotion in the church. Those
who attained the rank of prelate were frequently in attendance at
court or parliament in the south or otherwise employed in royal
service. This being so, they could not be other than aware of the
inroads of protestantism elsewhere; and their reaction to its
continued development within the realm was at least one
determining factor in the spread, or otherwise, of reformed
opinions within their own dioceses. After all, the bishops of
Moray, Argyll and Dunblane, the commendators of Strathfillan,
Kinloss and Pluscarden, the archdeacon of Argyll, the dean,
subdean and a canon of Dunkeld, the precentor of Moray, the
provost of Tain and the parson of Conveth had all attended the
provincial council of the Scottish church in Edinburgh in 1549
which *inter alia* had called for the extirpation of heresies. Even
earlier, the bishop of Ross had been empowered by Cardinal
Beaton to proceed against heretics; and later the bishops of
Dunblane and Moray were present at Adam Wallace's heresy
trial in Edinburgh in 1550: indeed, the bishop of Dunblane could
also recall witnessing Patrick Hamilton's execution in St Andrews
in 1528 and the execution of other heretics in 1544. Again, the
bishops of Caithness, Moray, Dunkeld and Dunblane were
among those present at the execution of Walter Miln for heresy
in 1558; and it is altogether probable that representatives from
highland dioceses took part in the provincial councils of 1552,
1555 and again in 1559 (whose sederunts have not survived),
when it was candidly acknowledged that 'Lutheranism, Calvin-

ism and very many other nefarious heresies are being propagated everywhere in this realm'.[7]

The men in charge of highland dioceses, then, were by no means remote figures cut off from, or unmindful of, ecclesiastical developments within the country as a whole. Roderick Maclean, after all, who occupied the bishopric of the Isles from 1544 to 1553, had not only a taste for Latin and Gaelic scholarship but had studied at Lutheran Wittenberg, where he matriculated in 1535.[8] Further north, Robert Stewart, bishop of Caithness (a diocese which included the mountainous regions of Sutherland as well as the lower-lying terrain of much of Caithness) was himself a son of the 3rd Earl of Lennox and had been first presented to the see in 1541, having already acquired the provostry of Dumbarton collegiate kirk in 1539 to which he added a canonry of Canterbury in 1546, when in exile in England, before accompanying Mary of Guise to France in 1550.[9] In neighbouring Ross, Henry Sinclair, dean of Glasgow and president of the college of justice, had received a gift of the temporalities of the bishopric in 1558 and later was provided to the see as bishop in 1561.[10] Sinclair, whose origins lay in the Lothians, had studied at St Andrews, had later travelled in Flanders and France, and his evident antipathy to aspects of life in the Highlands is revealed in his description of the precautions he was forced to take to defend and garrison his episcopal castle at the Chanonry 'quhilk lyis in ane far heland cuntrie'. His castle had been taken over and robbed by some 'brokin men' who had occupied it for nine months, while Sinclair was absent in Edinburgh at the College of Justice, and they caused such damage in the neighbourhood that the bishop was forced to retain 'ane guid company of men in my absence in the said place' to protect it from marauding Highlanders.[11] Stewart of Caithness seems to have shared Sinclair's sentiments, and, indeed, anticipated some of his problems, for in 1557 he had appointed the Earl of Sutherland constable of the episcopal castle at Scrabster and palace of

[7] *The Statutes of the Scottish Church*, ed. D. Patrick (Edinburgh, 1907), 85–8; *St Andrews Formulare, 1514–1564*, ed. G. Donaldson and C. Macrae, 2 vols. (Edinburgh, 1942–4), ii, no. 416; J. Foxe, *Acts and Monuments*, ed. J. Cumming, 3 vols. (London, 1875), ii, 250, 717, 722; R. Lindesay of Pitscottie, *The Historie and Cronicles of Scotland*, ed. E. J. G. Mackay, 2 vols. (Edinburgh, 1899), 130–6; *Statutes of the Scottish Church*, 150.

[8] J. Durkan, 'The Cultural Background in Sixteenth-Century Scotland', *Innes Review*, x (1959), 428.

[9] *The Scots Peerage*, ed. J. B. Paul, 9 vols. (Edinburgh, 1904–14), v, 355; D. E. R. Watt, *Fasti Ecclesiae Scoticanae Medii Aevi ad annum 1638* (Edinburgh, 1969), 61; G. Donaldson, *All the Queen's Men* (London, 1983), 160.

[10] Watt, *Fasti*, 156, 270.

[11] EUL, MS. Dc.4.32, fo. 103r.

Dornoch, which he depicted as 'situated among the wild and uncivilised Scots and in a wintry region'.[12] Both bishops, in fact, seemed happier outside their dioceses than in them. But what they did find more to their liking were the revenues which they derived from their sees.

As property, the predominantly highland bishoprics, as a group, were not noticeably poorer than their counterparts elsewhere in Scotland; and this meant that careerists from the south seeking promotion found them financially rewarding to accept. What the bishoprics yielded in revenues at the Reformation it is impossible to say with any exactitude, for most of the revenues forthcoming were paid not in silver but in victual; and what the cash equivalents of this unsold victual represent can only be approximated on the basis of the various prices which victual fetched in different areas. No suitable figures are available for Argyll and the Isles, which probably ranked among the poorer bishoprics. Caithness, however, which yielded around £1,300 annually, was admittedly low in the scale, but not significantly at odds with Orkney at £1,350 or with Galloway (and Tongland) or Dunblane at £1,500. Next came Brechin at, perhaps, £1,800, Ross and Aberdeen each around £2,000, followed by Glasgow at £3,000 and Dunkeld at £3,400, which left Moray the second richest see at £4,500, surpassed only by St Andrews, worth around £6,000.[13] These figures, of course, are merely estimations calculated on the basis of variable rates for the sale of victual, but they do convey an impression of the valuation and financial standing of the respective sees.

The wealth of the bishoprics, therefore, was conspicuous, especially when contrasted with the resulting poverty of the parishes. After all, it could hardly have been otherwise under a system which financed the higher reaches of the church very largely at the expense of the parishes through the diversion of the bulk of parochial revenues for the upkeep of the higher clergy. All the parishes of Caithness and Ross – some 59 in all – were devoted to supporting the bishops and other dignitaries at Dornoch and Fortrose.[14] Thus, in Wester Ross, the parsonage and vicarage revenues of the remote and mountainous parish of Applecross in the far west were appropriated to Fortrose

[12] *Origines Parochiales Scotiae*, ed. C. Innes, 2 vols. (Edinburgh, 1851–5), ii, 611.

[13] These calculations are based on information in *Thirds of Benefices*; for Moray, cf., A. L. Murray, 'The Revenues of the Bishopric of Moray in 1538', *Innes Review*, xix (1968), 40–56, at 48.

[14] This information is derived from the entries in I. B. Cowan, *The Parishes of Medieval Scotland* (Edinburgh, 1967).

cathedral, the best part of a hundred miles away at the other end of the diocese; and in Easter Ross, at Alness on the Black Isle, the parsonage revenues of the parish, which yielded 100 merks a year, were allocated to supporting the needs of the cathedral at Fortrose, and even the remaining vicarage income of £20, which ought to have provided for the cure of souls in the parish, was assigned instead to the non-resident vicar, John Davidson, the principal of Glasgow University.[15]

In the neighbouring diocese of Moray, 62 annexed churches provided income for Elgin cathedral, a further eleven maintained monastic houses, a single parish financed the work of a hospital, leaving only five independent, unappropriated parishes in the whole diocese. Yet even in these free parishes, revenues could readily be diverted. At Glass in Strathbogie, for example, the benefice-holder, on the eve of the Reformation, had an income of 105 merks from the combined parsonage and vicarage fruits, but he evidently felt no obligation to undertake service in the parish and instead hired as his substitute a vicar pensionary for a mere twelve merks a year. Not content with this, the same individual held the neighbouring vicarage of Kirkmichael, which supplemented his income by another 60 merks, apart, that is, from the outlay of £10 a year to employ a curate in the parish.[16]

Further south, the picture was very much the same. More than half of Dunkeld's 63 or so parishes supplied the stipends of the cathedral staff, 20 parishes contributed to the maintenance of monastic houses and just five remained unannexed. Among Dunblane's 38 parishes, matters were no better. There the cathedral clergy were sustained by about a dozen parishes; the finances of twice as many parishes in the diocese were lavished on monasteries, leaving only three parishes unappropriated. In the west Highlands, this concentration of the church's material resources on cathedrals and abbeys to the detriment of the parishes is again apparent. Thirteen of Argyll's 46 parishes upheld the cathedral establishment of Lismore, 26 were allocated to religious houses and collegiate kirks and 15 stayed independent. Finally, the diocese of the Isles, with at least 16 free parishes, possessed another 17 or so churches associated with the bishopric of the Isles and the annexed abbacy of Iona, with the revenues of a further eight parishes attached to other institutions.

The story, then, is a uniformly depressing one: it is a catalogue of the systematic exploitation of parochial resources and of the

[15] EUL, MS. Dc.4.32, fos. 117r, 121v, 123v; J. Durkan and J. Kirk, *The University of Glasgow, 1451–1577* (Glasgow, 1977), 244.
[16] SRO, E48/1/1, fo. 413r.

consequent neglect of that essential feature in the church's life which might best have benefited from a retention of these same resources. The protestant reformers, of course, had their remedy for redistributing the church's wealth in favour of the parishes. But such a scheme, if comprehensively applied, threatened too many vested interests, for it was not merely the bishops and higher clergy who coveted ecclesiastical property. Laymen, too, at almost every level had become thoroughly entrenched in ecclesiastical finances and so the church's fate at the Reformation directly effected many interested parties.

In Caithness, where the conservative Earl of Sutherland had a financial interest in the bishopric and where his opponent the no less conservative Earl of Caithness also held sway, the bishop himself took a different line by joining the ranks of the reformers. Why he adopted a reformed position is not immediately apparent, for Robert Stewart's earlier record had been decidedly unreformed. His apparent lack of holy orders could scarcely be said to have impeded his career in the pre-Reformation church, rising as he did to become a prelate without ever having served as a priest; but it did mean that he could not be consecrated bishop. He therefore remained as postulant or bishop elect, but this mere technicality had not prevented him from dilapidating his bishopric in characteristically unreformed fashion. In 1553, the bishop granted the entire lands of the bishopric to his brother-in-law and hereditary bailie, the Earl of Sutherland, who by 1557 had also obtained the heritable office of constable of the episcopal castle of Scrabster and palace of Dornoch.[17]

Even after 1560 it proved hard for Stewart to measure up to the requirements of a 'godly bishop', and one critic who had no love for bishops, reformed or otherwise, depicted the bishop in his later years as squandering kirk rents from St Andrews priory, whose commendatorship he had acquired and whose proceeds he is said to have spent, to the detriment of ministers' stipends, with his friends at golf, archery and good cheer.[18] By then, however, the bishop-commendator had also become Earl of March (having resigned the earldom of Lennox acquired in 1578), which may well explain, if not excuse, his pursuits and expenses.

Yet it remains an indisputable fact that the man who had witnessed the burning of Walter Miln as a heretic in 1558 and who in 1560 had sought the Earl of Sutherland's protection 'in this most perilous time' was duly attending protestant services in

[17] *Origines Parochiales*, 610–11.
[18] *The Autobiography and Diary of Mr James Melvill* (Edinburgh, 1842), 126.

Edinburgh by 1561 and was reputed by the reformers themselves to be 'honeste inoughe'.[19] No doubt one factor which helped shape his thinking was the anglophile outlook of his brother, Matthew, 4th Earl of Lennox; and the bishop himself, of course, may have sampled protestantism in England. Perhaps the recognition of clerical marriage which the Reformation made respectable may also have counted for something here, though the aging bachelor bishop, it must be admitted, showed no great haste in entering matrimony. He did so only in 1579 after becoming Earl of Lennox and his wife, Lord Lovat's widow and the Earl of Atholl's daughter, promptly divorced him for impotency, though Stewart, it seems, had fathered at least one illegitimate daughter.[20] The bishop, therefore, must be one of the earliest Scottish examples of clerical marriage ending in clerical divorce.

Factors such as these, though they may help to explain the bishop's conversion to protestantism, do not explain his decision to enter the reformed ministry. After all, Stewart could readily have accepted protestantism and, indeed, belated matrimony for that matter, while retaining a legal title to his see and to its finances, as some of his colleagues did, without the inconvenience of undertaking active and energetic service in the reformed church. It is no doubt a testimony to his conviction that he chose to further the work of the Reformation in his diocese, but it is no easy matter to uncover the reasons which lay behind his actions. It is quite possible that he was influenced here by the example of his kinsman, Lord James Stewart, a leader of the protestant Lords of the Congregation and the queen's half brother; and some wider significance beyond mere familial affection may be attached to the bishop's succession to St Andrews priory as commendator on Lord James Stewart's death in 1570,[21] promoted as he was by his brother Lennox, the new Regent, possibly in belated recognition of his services to the Reformation.

That Stewart took the work of reforming his diocese with some earnestness is suggested by his residence in Caithness for much of the 1560s. His rôle did not exactly coincide with the First Book of Discipline's plans to unite Caithness with Orkney and Shetland under the jurisdiction of a superintendent based at Kirkwall; but, in the absence of a superintendent for the area and

[19] Foxe, *Acts and Monuments*, ii, 722; *Origines Parochiales*, 613; *Calendar of State Papers relating to Scotland and Mary, Queen of Scots* [*CSP Scot.*] ed. J. Bain et al., 13 vols. (Edinburgh, 1898–1970), i, no. 1049.

[20] *Scots Peerage*, v, 355.

[21] *Register of the Privy Seal of Scotland* [*RSS*], ed. M. Livingstone et al., 8 vols. (Edinburgh, 1908–82), vi, no. 930.

with the bishop of Orkney's decision to join the reformers and to reform his diocese, the general assembly gave its blessing to the work of these reforming bishops.[22] How effective Stewart's efforts were may be judged by the fact that within a decade nearly all 24 parishes possessed the services of the reformed church.[23] This in itself is a not inconsiderable achievement, especially when it is recalled that it took the best part of ten years to reform, say, King's College, Aberdeen, well over a hundred miles (even by sea) to the south.

The first surviving register of reformed clergy – and it is not necessarily a full or exact record – dates only from 1567, though an earlier register, no longer extant, undoubtedly existed.[24] What the record of 1567 reveals is that the personnel of the reformed church in Caithness then stood at 16; but since only one new recruit is recorded as entering office that year, it is reasonable to conclude that the remainder must have joined at an earlier date, perhaps soon after the Reformation, and it is known that the vicar of Thurso conformed and was already at work as minister there in 1561.[25]

Yet the surviving evidence suggests that the recruitment of candidates to serve in the reformed church was not noticeably forthcoming from the ranks of the existing beneficed clergy within the diocese. None of the cathedral dignitaries, for example, appears to have followed the bishop's example. By 1563 the dean had died and the others, as benefice-holders, simply continued to draw their revenues without undertaking work of any sort, and from 1562 they were legally entitled for the duration of their lives to retain two-thirds of the income derived from their benefices. There was, therefore, little enough financial incentive for these men to volunteer as ministers when all that they stood to gain financially in return for the energetic labours required of parish ministers was a possible restoration of the deducted 'third' of their income which the government had levied. The stipends which the kirk initially could offer, ranging within the diocese from around £66 for a minister to £20 a year for a reader, were generally small and unattractive to men already assured of a guaranteed income from their benefices for doing

[22] *The First Book of Discipline*, ed. J. K. Cameron (Edinburgh, 1972), 116; *The Booke of the Universall Kirk: Acts and Proceedings of the General Assemblies of the Kirk of Scotland [BUK]*, ed. T. Thompson, 4 vols. (Edinburgh, 1839–45), 28, 31–2.

[23] *Register of Stipends*, 53–4.

[24] G. Donaldson, 'Sources for the Study of Scottish Ecclesiastical Organisation and Personnel, 1560–1600', *Bulletin of the Institute of Historical Research*, xix (1944), 188–203, at 192.

[25] *Register of Stipends*, 53–4; *Thirds of Benefices*, 92.

nothing in return. The archdeacon of Caithness, whose stipend was paid from the teinds of the parishes of Bower and Watten, evidently saw no incentive to enter the reformed ministry but the vicar pensionary at Watten did accept office as exhorter in the same parish with a stipend in 1569 which amounted to the equivalent of about £38 in cash; he conformed soon after 1560 as his pension from the archdeaconry was allowed in 1561 'for serving of the cuire' as exhorter.[26]

Invariably, the parsons, whose endowment derived from the parsonage revenues of the parishes, were not resident parish priests known to their parishioners; usually they were cathedral canons stationed at Dornoch. Not only did they live in comparative comfort and security, which they were unwilling to relinquish, but they had no detailed knowledge of the parishes whose benefices they held, and in their absence parochial work had been entrusted to vicars, though they too might delegate their duties in the parishes to other priests and unbeneficed curates whose very lack of a benefice makes them shadowy and elusive figures to identify in the records.

At Wick, where the parsonage fruits formed part of the bishop's income, the vicar was the non-resident Andrew Graham (an adventurer who achieved the distinction of becoming the first protestant bishop of Dunblane without first having served as a minister) but, again, the vicar pensionary of Wick who did provide service in the parish is on record as reader of Wick in 1574; and Alexander Patrick Grahamson, who appears as his factor in 1562, was also at work as exhorter at Canisbay in 1567.[27] In the parish of Kilmalie (now Golspie), it was the existing curate who opted to serve the parish as exhorter with a stipend in 1567 of 50 merks contributed by the bishop himself in recognition, no doubt, that revenues from the parish formed part of the bishop's income. This being so, it is not wholly unreasonable to suggest that the bishop may also have supported the initial upkeep of exhorters or readers at his other mensal churches at Durness, Latheron, Loth, Reay and Wick, all of which were equipped with staff by 1567. At any rate, from 1567 Stewart was allowed his additional 'third' from the bishopric,

[26] Register of Stipends, 53 (where the entry of the exhorter's stipend confusingly bears the date 1570, though other sources reveal that his initial stipend as exhorter had been assigned from the crop of 1561); Thirds of Benefices, 60–1; Origines Parochiales, ii, 782.
[27] Visitation of the Diocese of Dunblane and other churches, 1586–89, ed. J. Kirk (Edinburgh, 1984), x-xi, and notes 12–14; Thirds of Benefices, 211; Wodrow Miscellany, i, 333; Register of Stipends, 53.

which, it was claimed, he used to finance the ministers of his own kirks.[28]

There were advantages, no doubt, for the reformed church in recruiting suitable men from the ranks of ordinary parish priests who could claim a knowledge of the parishes they intended to serve after 1560. Familiar as they were with parish work, they would be more likely to possess the necessary linguistic qualifications, a thorough command of Gaelic, which the new emphasis on preaching demanded, and which many of the canons at Dornoch, trained as they were in Latin and Scots, in all probability lacked. Indeed, the need for what looks like bilingual instruction in the parish of Dornoch itself seems to have been recognised in the appointment of an 'exhorter in the Irsche toung' to supplement the bishop's own preaching, presumably in Scots, in the cathedral.[29]

By no means all staff were recruited locally; some came from further afield, illustrated not least by the exhorter at Olrig, Mr Francis Wright, on record in 1570, whose relatively uncommon name may reasonably be identified with the Dominican friar of that name in Elgin.[30] Others, again, whose antecedents have not been traced to offices in the pre-Reformation church were presumably found elsewhere.

Whatever the considerations which deterred many beneficed clergy in the diocese from undertaking an active ministry after 1560, religious dissent seems to have counted for very little. Initially in 1560, no legal penalty had been exacted on possessors of benefices for nonconformity; there was then no compulsion for them to accept the protestant Confession of Faith, which the Reformation parliament had affirmed. But when a religious test was applied at last in 1573, there was little indication of any refusal to comply with its terms by the old possessors who were still alive; and no deprivations ensued among benefices in royal patronage within the diocese. A decade of familiarity with ascendant protestantism, and an apparent absence of persecution, had no doubt the effect of reconciling many to the new regime. At the same time, the gradual succession of ministers to vacant benefices, begun in 1566, was designed to harmonise the claims of the ministry with those of existing possessors and so to reduce the amount of disruption which might otherwise have followed

[28] *Register of Stipends*, 53 (a further contribution by the bishop towards the stipend of the exhorter at Loth is recorded in 1567); *BUK*, i, 104; cf., *Thirds of Benefices*, 208.

[29] *Register of Stipends*, 53; cf., *Thirds of Benefices*, 209.

[30] C. Haws, *Scottish Parish Clergy at the Reformation, 1540–1574* (Edinburgh, 1972), 193.

had a more radical policy prevailed. At any rate, determined recusancy is surprisingly little in evidence within the diocese. As religious conservatives, even the Earl of Caithness and the Gordon Earl of Sutherland showed little antipathy to the system then operating; and although Knox had branded Caithness as a papist, the earl's position was sufficiently ambiguous for the queen to find it necessary in 1566 to order the earl, and others, to attend mass in Edinburgh, which he agreed to do. Yet the same earl seems to have placed no impediment in the way of his third son, George Sinclair of Mey, who entered the reformed ministry at Rogart and was elected chancellor of Caithness in 1572.[31]

Within Caithness as a whole, the foundations had been firmly laid for the development of a reformed ministry. But much, of course, remained to be achieved. Besides, the pre-Reformation legacy of two-dozen exceedingly large parishes, which the reformed church initially could staff with something like four ministers and 16 exhorters or readers in the first decade, rising in 1574 to eight ministers and 16 readers, meant that many years would elapse before all the parishes would have their own resident ministers.[32] Nonetheless, a vigorous start had been made under Bishop Stewart's auspices.

The general assembly in the south was by no means unmindful of the size of the task or of its own obligations. In response to a request from Caithness in 1571 for the appointment of a superintendent or commissioner, the assembly selected John Gray of Fordell as its commissioner in recognition of his earlier services; and he was now required to work 'with the assistance of the Bishop' as 'head Commissioner'. Yet it is plain that Stewart, as bishop, increasingly sought the attractions of life in St Andrews and, in his absence, the assembly had to select its own commissioners to supervise the church in Caithness, men who might hope to exercise the jurisdiction entrusted to them but who lacked the status and authority which Stewart, as bishop, could expect to command. The new commissioner, at any rate, evidently found his work overtaxing and by 1574 had presented to the assembly 'a book containing a visitation of the Diocie of Caithnes', together with a request to be excused from his office of visitation on account of his age and meagre stipend.[33]

[31] *Register of the Privy Council of Scotland [RPC]*, 1st ser., ed. J. H. Burton, et al., 14 vols. (Edinburgh, 1877–98), i, 192–4; *The Works of John Knox*, ed. D. Laing, 6 vols. (Edinburgh, 1846–64), ii, 420; *Fasti Ecclesiae Scoticanae*, ed. H. Scott, 9 vols. (Edinburgh, 1915–61), vii, 97; *CSP Scot.*, ii, no. 355.

[32] *Register of Stipends*, 53–4; *Wodrow Miscellany*, i, 332–4.

[33] *BUK*, i, 189–90, 282–3, 287; cf., 311–12, 332.

By that date, the church's complement in the diocese stood at one new commissioner recruited from Ross and two-dozen parish ministers or readers, with two parishes (Assynt and Durness) temporarily vacant. Some earlier personnel had died, a few left office, replacements had to be found, and accusations were forthcoming in 1575 against five of dilapidation of benefices and non-residence, itself a persistent problem when the manses, to which ministers and readers were legally entitled to possess since 1563, were not always in practice available for their use. Again, the recurrence of 'deadly feuds' was another explanation offered for a minister's non-residence.[34] This, then, was the less energetic sequel to the vigorous start under Bishop Stewart's auspices.

The course of the Reformation in Caithness in some ways contrasts with its development in the neighbouring dioceses of Ross and Moray where no conforming bishop came forward to champion the Reformation as Stewart had done in Caithness. In Ross, with its 35 parishes, the vacant see was filled even after the Reformation by a succession of Catholic bishops: Henry Sinclair, who in religious matters was by no means wholly intransigent, and, in 1566, John Leslie, a committed papalist. There the Reformation was plainly denied the official leadership it enjoyed in Caithness, and so was bound to take a different direction. The general assembly, aware of the need for the presence of an overseer in Ross, selected a commissioner in 1563 who was instructed to assist the bishop of Caithness in appointing ministers in the whole region.[35]

Yet there were signs of reforming activity in the diocese well before the assembly's belated intervention. Nor was support for reformed opinions by any means stifled with the election of a Catholic bishop after 1560. The treasurer of Ross, for one, who was no newcomer, having held office from 1548, was already serving as minister in 1561 and is known to have married.[36] Circumstances, therefore, were not wholly unfavourable to the cause of protestant reform. Indeed, the initial vacancy in the see, followed by Sinclair's frequent absence as president of the College of Justice in Edinburgh, evidently enabled some like the treasurer to take an independent line without fear of retaliation. What is more, the treasurer's enthusiasm was not to be dampened by financial considerations. In 1561, or thereabouts, he provided 100 merks for stipends from the endowment of his

[34] *Wodrow Miscellany*, i, 332–4; *BUK*, i, 336, 342.
[35] Watt, *Fasti*, 270; *BUK*, i, 34.
[36] *Thirds of Benefices*, 91, 149; *RSS*, viii, no. 1802.

prebend for the support of ministers who were evidently already installed at the churches of Urquhart and Logie-Wester.[37] Nor was this all. The vicar of Dingwall, who also conformed at this point, served as minister of the burgh; and he, in turn, was related to Munro of Foulis who took the trouble of attending the Reformation parliament in Edinburgh in 1560. Indeed, the vicar's meagre income, which seems to have consisted only of 36 merks from two chaplainries and five merks from his vicarage, led him to seek the queen's support so that he might 'have ane lyf lyk ane minister and be speciallie exercit'.[38] The burgh's schoolmaster also conformed to protestantism;[39] and it seems almost certain that the unbeneficed curate in Cromarty, who continued to be paid after the Reformation, undertook reformed service as reader in 1561, influenced perhaps by the example of the reforming treasurer who held a quarter of the parsonage of Cromarty. At any rate, the later evidence from the register of stipends available in 1567, which shows the curate serving as reader at Cromarty, considerably strengthens the impression that he was active from an earlier date.[40]

It can be demonstrated, too, that similar factors operated at Alness where an exhorter was at work in 1562 and in receipt of part of the parsonage revenues. There the parsonage was divided among four portioners; two further portioners conformed as readers at Suddie and Killearnan on the Black Isle; and it may be no coincidence that the vicar of Alness (and also of Nigg) was John Davidson, the reforming principal of Glasgow University and minister at Hamilton.[41]

No less revealing is the support shown for the cause of reform in the neighbouring parish of Kiltearn, which stretched from the Cromarty Firth westwards towards Ben Wyvis, where the parson (a kinsman of Sandilands of St Monans in Fife) was by the early 1560s contributing financially to sustain a minister in the parish; and by 1574 the minister in charge of the parish is identified as none other than Donald Munro, the former archdeacon of the Isles, who had produced his *Description of the Western Isles* during his tour of 1549, and who, as a conforming

[37] EUL, MS. Dc.4.32, fo. 115r.
[38] Ibid., fo. 117r; *Acts of the Parliaments of Scotland* [*APS*], ed. T. Thomson and C. Innes, 12 vols. (Edinburgh, 1814–75), ii, 526.
[39] *RSS*, vi, no. 657.
[40] EUL, MS. Dc.4.32, fo. 115r, 119r; *Register of Stipends*, 52. The schoolmaster, curate and reader appear to be the same individual, James Burnet (Haws, *Parish Clergy*, 52, 258).
[41] *Thirds of Benefices*, 151; EUL, MS. Dc.4.32, fos. 121v, 123v; Haws, *Parish Clergy*, 125 (Alexander McKenzie), 231 (James Buschart); Durkan and Kirk, *University of Glasgow*, 242–5.

minister, was appointed by the general assembly in 1563 as commissioner of Ross.[42]

The relative promptitude with which these appointments were made in much of Easter Ross reveals a good deal about the spread and reception of reforming ideas in areas such as this, where the Lords of the Congregation could not hope to dominate by their physical presence; and it suggests that there was only pardonable exaggeration in the claims of the provincial council of 1559 which depicted protestantism as 'being propagated everywhere within this realm'.[43] What is also remarkable is that all this activity in and around 1560 should take the form of individual initiative and enterprise, for at that stage there was still no effective central control or, for that matter, regional direction and organisation.

Confronted with these trends, Henry Sinclair, as bishop, seems to have been not entirely unyielding and at times decidedly flexible in his attitude to protestant reform. As parson of Glasgow, he had earlier agreed to supply bread and wine for reformed communion in the parish kirk of Glasgow; and as bishop of Ross not only had he declined to reply to the papal envoy but, as a good lawyer, had also maintained that the queen's laws, including the act forbidding the celebration of mass, must be obeyed and upheld.[44] But this Catholic bishop went even further and from his own funds found £50 a year for 'the prechar of the kirkis of Nyg and Terbat', the two churches whose teinds were assigned to the bishop's prebend.[45]

In Ross there is also some indication that critical, or even hypocritical, laymen within the diocese took advantage of the opportunity which the Reformation presented to cease making payments to some of the existing beneficed clergy. There is, of course, a long history both before and after 1560 of prolonged litigation arising from the failure of the possessors to obtain their entitlement to the fruits of their benefices. At the Reformation, the Earl of Caithness's tenants at Canisbay, for example, failed to pay their teinds, but this, it was recognised, arose simply 'throw default of justice'.[46] But what happened in a number of other instances between 1559 and 1561 when holders failed to obtain their revenues is of a rather different character; and the expropriations which took place were linked to the broader religious upheaval itself.

[42] EUL, MS. Dc.4.32, fo. 113r-v; *Register of Stipends*, 335; *BUK*, i, 34, 40.
[43] *Statutes of the Scottish Church*, 150.
[44] *RPC*, i, 492–3; Knox, *Works*, ii, 379–80.
[45] EUL, MS. Dc.4.32, fo. 102v.
[46] Ibid., fo. 115v.

The vicar of Kilmorack who was accustomed to receive a stipend of £20 a year discovered at the Reformation that there was 'now nothing payit thir tua yeiris quhill universall ordour be tane'. The joint vicarages of Suddy and Kilmuir were hitherto worth 20 merks annually 'and now thir twa yeiris bygane nothing gottin'; the vicarage of Urray used to pay £19 'and now nothing gottin thir thrie yeiris'; and the same complaint was voiced by the vicar of Rosemarkie; while at Kiltearn, where the vicarage fruits were leased for 40 merks a year, no further payment was forthcoming to the vicar 'be reasoun the paroshineris will not pay quhill farder ordour be put to the kirk of the samin'; the wish, that is, to obtain value for money spent on the cure of souls seems to have been the reason or, at any rate, the pretext for the parishioners' withholding their dues. But the parson of Kiltearn, by contrast, who undertook to finance a minister, seems not to have incurred the difficulties which beset the parish's vicar.[47]

Within a decade of the Reformation, Ross's 35 parishes had attracted, on record, over 20 of a staff; 3 ministers, 19 exhorters and readers, some of whom undertook linked charges, superintended by one commissioner. There is, however, some indication that this list may be defective. Not only are some parishes omitted but also excluded are two candidates known to have been considered as exhorters in 1565 but who only appear on record as readers at Kintail and Lochalsh in 1574.[48] Even so, the staffing complement was certainly less than ideal or even desirable, but it was far from being wholly or hopelessly inadequate. Besides, the official policy of the reformers favoured leaving parishes vacant rather than filling them with less than satisfactory candidates. Only in 1573, with the application of a religious test and in recognition that 'the most part of the persons who were Channons, Monks and Friars within this realme, have made profession of the true religion', did the assembly finally decide to urge them 'to pass and serve as readers at the places where they shall be appointed'.[49] Even so, given the relatively slow pace of life when decisions took time to effect and when court cases could and frequently did drag on for years on end, the ability to find so many recruits in so short a period might be reckoned as a measure of the Reformation's success. How many ministers and readers were active in Ross in the early 1560s is probably beyond discovery; but at least one tantalising clue has survived.

---

[47] Ibid., fos, 114r, 116r, 117r, 120r, 122r; 113r-v.
[48] *Register of Stipends*, 51–2; *BUK*, i, 63; *Wodrow Miscellany*, i, 334.
[49] *BUK*, i, 280.

The crown is known to have assigned £379 for paying the stipends of ministers and readers in Caithness and Ross in 1561, a figure which rose steeply to £646 the following year. Now it can be calculated from the register of stipends for 1569 or thereabouts that the average stipend in Caithness and Ross was about £34. Stipends, of course, may have been higher in 1561/2 than they were in 1569, but it is reasonable to assume that fewer ministers than readers were initially at work, and readers were paid at the lower end of the scale. What all this means is that the sums allocated in stipends for Caithness and Ross were capable of yielding something like a staff of 11 ministers or readers in 1561/2, sharply increasing to about 19 recruits in 1562/3, financed directly from the crown's levy of the thirds. To this figure there should be added a smaller group of ministers and readers otherwise financed from the income of a bishop, commendator or other benefactor. By 1569, the crown's allocation for stipends in the area had risen to £1,666 – a sum which, on present calculations, might finance a staff of around 49, a figure not wholly at odds with the staff of 43 recorded in the register of stipends as employed in Caithness and Ross between 1568 and 1572.[50]

The figure for Ross, presented in the register of stipends, of one commissioner and 22 individuals serving 24 of the 35 parishes is in some ways all the more remarkable, in that not more than half the ministry in the region on record in 1569 is known to have held office in the pre-Reformation church; and the presumption is that some of the remainder were recruited outside the ranks of former priests. The eleven parishes omitted from the register, and which might therefore be thought to lack reformed service in 1569, lay partly in south-west Ross from Gairloch and Applecross to Lochcarron and Kintail, and partly in Easter Ross clustered around the Cromarty Firth. Yet, by 1574, this deficiency – if deficiency it were – had been largely wiped out when eight of the eleven omitted parishes were filled; only the parishes of Gairloch in the west and Contin and Lemlair in the east were then vacant. But there were changes in other directions, too: five further parishes filled in 1569 lacked resident readers in 1574 and relied solely on the services of a minister entrusted with the oversight of neighbouring parishes as a result of reorganisation in 1573. Sometimes, it looked like one step forward and two steps back, but despite formidable obstacles headway continued to be made. In 1574, the kirk's personnel in the diocese had risen to 34 (one commissioner, eight ministers

[50] *Thirds of Benefices*, 93, 152, 208; *Register of Stipends*, 51–4.

and 25 readers) in a diocese with 35 parishes.[51] This compared with a staff of 25 (one commissioner, eight ministers and 16 readers) in Caithness with 24 parishes. If Caithness, therefore, had enjoyed an initial advantage from the work of its reforming bishop, Ross with its commissioner belatedly appointed had come close to catching up.

In Moray, whose bishop remained largely aloof from the Reformation, the work of reforming the diocese had again to be entrusted to a commissioner; but whereas the commissioner for Ross was a Gaelic-speaker with little knowledge of Scots – he was said to have been 'not prompt in the Scottish tongue'[52] (which must have added to his problems in attending assemblies in the south) – the commissioner in Moray for much of the 1560s was Robert Pont from Fife who knew no Gaelic. Pont, who had associations with Culross and had served not only as an elder on St Andrews kirk session but also as minister first at Dunblane and then at Dunkeld, by 1563 was entrusted with the care of churches in the diocese of Moray. He accepted a renewed commission for Moray on the undertaking that 'he sould not be burthened with the kirks speeking the Irish tongue', but the assembly seems to have disregarded his plea to find another commissioner 'expert in the Irish tongue', despite the fact that much of the diocese was Gaelic-speaking.[53]

As commissioner, Pont was, of course, responsible not for initiating reformed activity in the area but for co-ordinating, directing and encouraging the support which he found. Inverness, after all, was already equipped in 1560 with a minister recruited from the Dominican friary at Perth, and who presumably had connections with the friary at Inverness; and by January 1560/1, Inverness town council had assigned him a stipend. There, too, the conforming curate took up service as exhorter at the 'Yrische kirk of Invernes'. Reformed activity elsewhere in the diocese is clearly indicated in the payment by the crown of £214 in stipends from the harvest of 1561, which dramatically rose sixfold the following year to £1,241. If the average stipend of £39 for the diocese is applied to the earlier sums paid from the crown's levy in stipend, it emerges that around six of a staff could have been

[51] *Register of Stipends*, 51–2; *Wodrow Miscellany*, i, 334–6.

[52] *BUK*, i, 175. Evidence of commissioner Donald Munro's literacy in Scots, if not of his verbal proficiency in the language, is testified by his *Description of the Western Isles*: R. W. Munro, *Monro's Western Isles of Scotland and the Genealogies of the Clans, 1549* (Edinburgh, 1961).

[53] NLS, Adv. MS. 31.3.12, fo. 19r; *Register of the Ministers, Elders and Deacons of the Christian Congregation of St Andrews*, ed. D. H. Fleming, 2 vols. (Edinburgh, 1889–90), i, 2–4, 8; *BUK*, i, 3, 4, 13, 18, 28, 34, 40, 44.

paid from this source in 1561/2 and, perhaps, three-dozen clergy in 1562/3.[54]

Any enthusiasm for the Reformation which might have been forthcoming from Patrick Hepburn, as bishop of Moray, who after all had initially offered to support the Lords of the Congregation and to vote with them in the Reformation parliament, was effectively dampened when the reformers attacked Scone abbey, which he held as commendator, but he did at least accord the Reformation a measure of tacit support and agreed, in 1569, to pay his share towards the repair of Elgin cathedral 'for hearing the word of God' by the protestant congregation.[55] One friend of the Reformation, however, was Walter Reid, commendator of Kinloss and of the dependent priory at Beauly, who as a convert to protestantism gave his practical support not only by arranging in 1561 to pay the stipend of 'the reidar of the commoun prayeris in the kirk' of Ellon in Aberdeenshire, annexed to Kinloss, but also, as it later emerged, by giving a helping hand to a minister and former monk of Kinloss when his stipend failed in 1565, and who in turn 'enterit in societie with the said Abbot and techit the Evangell to his people of Strathylay and Kinloss, at his chargeis, till sum provisioun wes maid for the sustentatioun of the ministerie'.[56] Such action and assistance may not have been altogether isolated. The vicarage of Moy, it was declared, at the Reformation had insufficient revenues to sustain a minister from the teinds forthcoming from the townships in the parish and if one were to be attracted alternative finance was plainly required; but there the immediate problem seems to have been solved, for a spell at least, with the parson's decision to serve the parish as exhorter.[57]

In other cases, too, the existing vicar showed a readiness to serve and so was financed from his vicarage revenues: by 1562, the vicar of Birnie had conformed and described himself, a little confusingly, as 'vicar and minister of the said kirk and reider and exhortar in the said kirk'. He was, perhaps, a little uncertain of his exact status under the new regime.[58] In all, around twenty parish priests in the diocese are known to have conformed and undertaken service; half a dozen friars also joined the reformed

[54] *Records of Inverness*, ed. W. Mackay and H. C. Boyd, 2 vols. (Aberdeen, 1911–24), i, 50, 52, 54, 58–9, 71, 131, 146, 198; *Thirds of Benefices*, 93, 152; *Register of Stipends*, 58–62.
[55] Knox, *Works*, i, 359–61; *Wodrow Miscellany*, i, 60–1; *RPC*, i, 677–8.
[56] SRO, E48/1/1, fo. 397v; *RPC*, i, 680–1, 684.
[57] SRO, E48/1/1, fo. 404v.
[58] Ibid., fo. 413v.

ministry; and a similar number of monks did likewise.[59] In the main, however, the existing beneficed clergy, as well as most of the monks and friars (protected as they were financially from poverty by their income which they largely retained as retirement pensions), were either unwilling or were considered unsuited to become ministers and readers, though almost all of them still to the fore in 1573 had quietly accepted protestantism.

There was, however, a phase at the height of the Reformation, in Moray as elsewhere, when some of the clergy who did not support the reformed cause suffered a loss of revenues at the hands of the parishioners or the tacksmen as lease-holders of the teinds. The fruits of the kirks of Daviot and Dalarossie at the Reformation were said to be 'waist and nathing payit thir thrie yeiris bypast'. This, of course, may simply have been a consequence of warring clansmen. No revenues had been forthcoming either from the vicarage of Abertarff, again for three years, where Clan Ranald had declined to make payment. The vicar of Ardclach also had problems which he duly reported in February 1561/2, the date for submitting rentals from benefices. This meant that payments had ceased in 1559. Similar statements were reported by possessors of other benefices whose revenues had suddenly ceased over the preceding three years. At Laggan, the vicar declared that his benefices would yield 'nothing quhill generall ordour be tane'. There is, therefore, a wider significance to be attached to this boycott of payments over the three years repeatedly cited.[60]

That this widespread refusal to make payments is frequently to be linked to the Reformation movement is dramatically underlined in a lowland parish where the vicar complained that, 'befoir the rysing of the Congregatioun', he had received his dues but now he was 'payit not ane penny thir last iij yeiris bipast'.[61] Stability, it is true, soon returned; but whatever the precise significance of this phenomenon, it is clear that parishioners in highland areas were fully conversant with ecclesiastical developments in the south.

A further fillip to the reformed cause in Moray came when the protestant leader, Lord James Stewart, succeeded to the earldom in 1562 which had the effect of undermining Huntly's influence in the region, and it no doubt played a part in furthering recruitment to the ministry. Even so, there were at least some

---

[59] C. Haws, 'Continuity and change. The clergy in the diocese of Moray, 1560–74', *Northern Scotland*, v (1983), 95–6.
[60] SRO, E48/1/1, fos. 400r, 414v, 413v.
[61] Ibid., fo. 100v.

ministers already at work in the diocese when the general
assembly rather vaguely instructed the minister of Brechin in
December 1562 to preach the Gospel in Moray 'and if it sall
chance that he sall find anie qualified persons apt to be ministers,
exhorters or readers', he was to refer them for examination to the
commissioner of Aberdeen.[62] By 1568 or so, when the Earl of
Moray was Regent for James VI, the diocese could claim a
recorded staff of 47, financed from the 'thirds', and despite a fall
in the level of stipends, 78 readers and ministers had been
recruited by 1574, with the ministry evenly dispersed over
highland and lowland areas, save for half a dozen or so vacant
churches in the Inverness area.[63] Despite all the obstacles and
setbacks incurred, this looks rather like an initial success story
for the kirk. The oft-repeated claim, therefore, that the new kirk
failed to secure an early foothold in the northern Highlands
would seem to be not supported by the record evidence, and
such claims might best be consigned to the ranks of popular
mythology.

What, then, was the position in the two remaining highland
areas – Perthshire and Argyll? In the dioceses of Dunkeld and
Dunblane, which engrossed the predominantly highland parts of
Perthshire, the two bishops showed little sympathy for protestant
reform. Instead, they trod a cautious path, as well they might,
displaying hesitancy and equivocation in their attitude towards
the reformed Confession of Faith in 1560, which they were
prepared neither to accept nor wholly to condemn – or so it
was reported.[64] Others, however, identified themselves more
assuredly with the cause of protestantism. The treasurer of
Dunkeld agreed to serve as exhorter in the city;[65] the occasional
canon, some vicars and chaplains, and one or two monks and
friars also showed a willingness to enter the new ministry in the
diocese. In August 1560, two local lairds had been instructed by
the protestant provisional government to remove all 'monuments
of idolatry' from the cathedral without damage to the rest of the
fabric. The cathedral was thus secured for protestant service; and
in 1562 Robert Pont, for a spell, served as minister.[66]

Once again, most of the new ministry was recruited from
outside the ranks of the existing beneficed clergy. Over £2,000
was paid in stipends from the harvest of 1561 for Perthshire

[62] *BUK*, i, 27–8.
[63] *Register of Stipends*, 58–62; *Wodrow Miscellany*, i, 337–41.
[64] *CSP Scot.*, no. 885.
[65] *Thirds of Benefices*, 92.
[66] Haws, *Parish Clergy*, passim; J. H. Burton, *History of Scotland*, 8 vols.
(Edinburgh, 1897), iii, 354 n. 1; *BUK*, i, 18.

and Strathearn, which indicates a sizable ministry from an early date, sustained from the 'thirds'. Indeed, a decade later, payments for stipends stood at only £600 more than in 1561.[67] Some ministers in the area, however, were paid from sources other than 'thirds'.

The chanter of Dunkeld in 1561 or so contributed £10 for a minister at Kinclaven.[68] The bishop of Moray, as commendator of Scone, dutifully paid the stipends of ministers and readers at kirks appropriated to his abbacy, including £58 to the minister of Logierait in Dunkeld diocese.[69] So too did the protestant commendator of Arbroath abbey, some of whose churches lay in Perthshire; and the protestant commendator of Culross, by 1561, was paying the minister's stipend at Crombie in the lowland portion of the diocese.[70] The initiative of lairds is sometimes revealing, too: Colin Campbell of Glenorchy agreed to pay the stipend of the minister at Kenmore who had earlier acted as his chaplain at Finlarig castle and as curate at Killin.[71] There is some reason for supposing that other lairds in the area who took part in the revolution of 1559/60 – men like Stewart of Grandtully and Ramsay of Bamff (near Alyth) – may well have offered similar assistance. Moreover in Perthshire an earlier tradition of anticlericalism, which might be expected to have appealed to lairds like Campbell of Glenorchy, is apparent in the pages of 'Makgregouris Testament', where in satirical form the curate is charged with negligence, the vicar with greed, the parson with oppression, the friars with dissimulation, the prior with gluttony, the abbot with pride, the dean with lechery, and the bishop, perhaps most damningly, with failing to preach the Gospel.[72]

From time to time, however, the depredations of some unruly clans made the task of settling ministers all the more difficult. The notorious Clan Gregor, it is true, had laid waste the bishop of Dunkeld's lands of Kilmorlich in 1561 and also the whole parish of Rannoch in 1562, where Menzies of Weem as tacksman had been harried by the Macgregors.[73] But what is also true is that Macgregors undertook to serve as readers at Moulin, Fortingall and Killin; and the parish of Rannoch itself was also served by a reader, possibly by 1567 and certainly by 1574.[74]

[67] *Thirds of Benefices*, 93, 247.
[68] NLS, Adv. MS. 31.3.12, fo. 30v.
[69] Ibid., fo. 36v.
[70] Ibid., fos. 80v (Arbroath); 20v (Culross).
[71] W. A. Gilles, *In Famed Breadalbane* (Perth, 1938), 261–3.
[72] *The Black Book of Taymouth* (Edinburgh, 1855), 151–72.
[73] *Thirds of Benefices*, 114, 149, 160–1.
[74] *Register of Stipends*, 29; *Wodrow Miscellany*, i, 356; *Thirds of Benefices*, 253; Haws, *Parish Clergy*, 93, 126, 186, 203.

Reflection might suggest, therefore, that the activities of clans in disrupting the collection of the 'thirds' was less of an endemic problem than might at first be thought; certainly they figure only occasionally in these records. Much further south, from 1563 to 1565, the produce of the subdean of Glasgow and abbot of Paisley was said to have been 'extremely harried the said years by the Highland men', but here, too, the problem, though serious, did not persist.[75] A much more pressing and persistent problem, in Highlands and Lowlands alike, was the failure of some possessors of benefices, or their tacksmen, to pay the 'thirds' which the crown had levied as a tax.

Nonetheless, with the appearance of the first surviving register of stipends in 1567, it emerges that the new kirk had a presence in almost every parish of Dunkeld diocese, with perhaps four exceptions where record of a serving minister or reader becomes available only as late as 1574. But, of course, it ought not to be concluded from the sudden appearance of a reader in 1567 or 1574 that this was the date at which reformed service in any particular parish began. An illustration of the pitfalls which await the unwary occurs in the case of Logierait in mountainous Atholl and Breadalbane. Now the first occurrence of a reader at Logierait in the register of stipends is an entry as late as 1574; and in his parish survey, Dr Haws duly noted this entry and speculated whether a reader might have served the parish from 1569.[76] Yet an examination of other relevant material discloses that a minister, no less, was active in the parish as early as 1562;[77] and it was presumably this minister who reported the presence of a priest in the parish to the general assembly in 1563.[78] By 1574, the reformed staff of the diocese (including its detached parishes but excluding Muckairn in Argyll) stood at an impressive 74: 54 resident readers and 20 ministers supervising small groups of parishes. Only five parishes, which had previously been served and which lay in Atholl and Breadalbane, lacked readers in 1574, but they could still count on the support of ministers supervising adjacent, though admittedly large, parishes. All in all, 74 readers and ministers for 62 parishes suggests that much of the spadework had been accomplished with some effect during the 1560s in both highland and lowland portions of the diocese.[79]

So far as can be judged, the religious conservatism of the Earl of Atholl, who as tacksman was less than prompt in paying his

[75] *Thirds of Benefices*, 256n. 2.
[76] Haws, *Parish Clergy*, 169.
[77] NLS, Adv. MS. 31.3.12, fo. 36v.
[78] *BUK*, i, 40.
[79] *Wodrow Miscellany*, i, 348ff.

'thirds', seems at most to have presented only a limited obstacle to the growth of a reformed ministry in the diocese. At any rate, Atholl's patronage of six churches in the diocese did not prevent the appearance of readers in two of these churches by 1567 and in the remaining four by 1574.[80]

Further south, in the diocese of Dunblane, the reforming initiative taken by the Earl of Menteith, described as 'one of the most zealous protestants of this country',[81] went some way towards offsetting the conservative influence exercised by Bishop William Chisholm. The earl's request for a Gaelic-speaking minister in Menteith led the assembly in 1564 to translate the minister of Leuchars, who surprisingly was a Gaelic-speaker.[82] Elsewhere in the diocese, there were, of course, earlier recruits like the conforming vicar pensionary of Comrie who served as reader there in 1561[83] and who presumably had some knowledge of Gaelic, though, as mentioned, Robert Pont, who was briefly minister at Dunblane, was not conversant with Gaelic.

By the late 1560s, all but three of Dunblane's 38 parishes are known to have been filled with reformed staff.[84] In some cases, where the vicar or curate of a parish later appears on record in the register of stipends as reader in 1567, it can scarcely be doubted that his conformity had its antecedents in the period preceding 1567. Again, Arbroath abbey, two of whose churches (Abernethy and Dron) lay within the diocese, was contributing stipends as early as 1561 'for the ministeris in every kirk that is sustenit thair be my lordis grace command'.[85] There is little reason, therefore, to suppose that reformed service at Abernethy or Dron dated only from 1567. Similarly, the Augustinian abbey of Inchaffray, whose canons made a notable contribution to the reformed ministry and whose commendator was the reforming bishop of Galloway, succeeded in securing the service of reformed staff at a number of its eleven parishes in the diocese by the early 1560s. The same is also true of Cistercian Culross on the lowland extremity of the diocese. The register of stipends discloses that Culross kirk had its exhorter in 1567; and Dr Haws has taken this as the earliest known date of reformed service in the parish,[86] unaware that the protestant commendator of

---

[80] Killin and Inchaiden, 1567; Blair Atholl, Struan, Kilmaveonaig and Lude, 1574 (*Register of Stipends*, 30; *Wodrow Miscellany*, i, 356).
[81] *CSP Scot.*, ii, no. 153.
[82] *BUK*, i, 47.
[83] *Thirds of Benefices*, 92.
[84] *Register of Stipends*, 26ff. *passim*.
[85] NLS, Adv. MS. 31.3.12, fo. 80v.
[86] *Register of Stipends*, 26; Haws, *Parish Clergy*, 55.

Culross at the Reformation had testified that 'I gif yeirlie to ane minister to serve in the kirk of Culross, conform to the buk of reformatioun, ij^c li.'.[87] Examples of this sort certainly shake one's confidence in the accounts of other historians who seem intent· on stressing the deficiencies in securing reformed service in the parishes, and whose uncritical use of the register of stipends for 1567 is liable to lead them astray in the process. Besides, what is true for Culross, one suspects, may also hold good for the four churches in the diocese appropriated to Inchmahome and Cambuskenneth, where the protestant Erskines held sway and which were unlikely to lack reformed service in the years immediately after 1560.

The one remaining highland area about which it is difficult to offer informed comment on recruitment to the ministry in this period is Argyll. Yet any assessment of the progress of the Reformation in Argyll ought to involve a candid recognition that the evidence available for the rest of mainland Scotland in the form of lists of ministers and their stipends does not exist for Argyll. This does not mean, however, that crown and church turned a blind eye to the problem of providing ministers in the area. Nor does it mean that benefices in the region ceased to provide income for possessors or their tacksmen. Benefices continued to be bestowed. The difficulty here, however, is that while identifying the possessors of benefices in Argyll after 1560 is relatively straightforward, it is considerably harder to discover whether these same benefice-holders served as ministers and readers. Although the reformed ministry from 1566 could claim a legal right to succeed to vacant parochial benefices, it was still not the law, even after the application of a religious test in 1573, that protestant benefice-holders should actually serve in the reformed ministry. Since charters and other legal records invariably deploy the legal terminology of 'parson' or 'vicar' rather than refer to the ecclesiastical offices of 'minister' or 'reader', it is not surprising, in the absence of a register of stipends for the diocese, that all too few ministers have been properly identified in Argyll for those early years.

Dr Haws could find evidence of only one minister at work in Argyll during the 1560s and just three for the 1570s;[88] and others have made much – too much – of this supposed dearth of ministers in Argyll. The printed sources consulted, it is true, have not proved helpful. Yet certain considerations might suggest that the apparent absence of ministers is largely illusory and that

---

[87] NLS, Adv. MS. 31.3.12, fo. 20v.
[88] Haws, *Parish Clergy*, 100; 13, 73, 165.

recruitment to the ministry in Argyll was not markedly at variance with the patterns established elsewhere in the Highlands.

For a start, Archibald, 4th Earl of Argyll, was firmly committed to the cause of reform and so too was his son, the 5th earl, who is said to have 'plucked down the images in divers churches' within the realm.[89] Not only so, but the bishop of Argyll, who was Châtelherault's half-brother (and the 5th earl was the duke's nephew[90]), also conformed to protestantism and accepted the reformed Confession in 1560.[91] All this clearly had its implications for the clergy of Argyll. Yet the conforming bishop who preferred the comparative comforts of living in Glasgow, where he held the subdeanery, to the rigours of life in Argyll, was assigned no office in the reformed church – understandably, perhaps, on account of his scandalous life: by 1562, the godly were shocked to discover that the bishop 'has now two women with child besides his wife'.[92]

If Argyll had thus a conforming, but not a reforming, bishop, it was also one of the few areas of the country to be assigned a reformed superintendent in the person of John Carswell, who enjoyed the support of the earl as his patron and who was based at Carnassery Castle in central Argyll. It would be a mistake, therefore, to consider that the reformers were unmindful of their responsibilities in Argyll. But how far were these responsibilities effectively discharged? The First Book of Discipline had defined the area of the superintendent's jurisdiction as Argyll, Kintyre, Lorne, Lochaber and the southern isles.[93] At the same time, however, Carswell's provision by Queen Mary to the bishopric of the Isles in 1565 enabled him to increase the scope of his work; and he began to style himself superintendent of Argyll and the Isles. That he took his duties with some seriousness is suggested by his journey on May 1564 to Kintyre 'and thaireftir to the Ilis to veseit sum kirkis', as he considered that 'my travell now in the Ilis may do mair gude to the Kirk nor my presens at the Assemblie; because the Ilis can nocht be travellit wele throwch in Wynter'. He is also on record in later years granting collation to benefices in Argyll and the Isles; and, indeed, at his appointment to the bishopric of the Isles, he agreed to pay the stipends of the ministers planted within the diocese. None of these developments, then, seems consistent with the view that the area as a whole was destitute of ministers. Indeed, one observer at the

[89] *CSP Scot.*, i, no. 469.
[90] Ibid., i, no. 464.
[91] Ibid., i, no. 891, p. 471 (cf., *APS*, ii, 525).
[92] *CSP Scot.*, i, no. 1066.
[93] *First Book of Discipline*, 117.

Reformation considered the people of Argyll to have been mainly protestant.[94]

More significantly, it was, of course, from Argyll that the first book to be printed in either Scottish or Irish Gaelic emerged in the form of Carswell's Gaelic adaptation of the Scottish Book of Common Order – his *Foirm na n-Urrnuidheadh* or Form of Prayers – for use in public worship.[95] The appearance of this work in 1567 rather suggests that the reformed faith had considerable vitality in the area. Indeed, the Earl of Argyll pressed forward the advantage already gained by encouraging further use of Carswell's work for worship in Argyll; and, by 1574, it was reported that the 6th earl had secured the services of ministers and readers, with stipends assigned, in every parish in Lorne, central Argyll and Cowal.[96] None of this lends any weight to the claim that Carswell's endeavours were of limited significance and confined to a group of Gaelic ministers whose 'numbers must have been very small and their activity extremely restricted'.[97]

In any case, neither Carswell nor Lekprevik, his Edinburgh printer, is likely to have undertaken such a time-consuming and costly project merely to satisfy the needs of an insignificant number of Gaelic ministers. They had, of course, a potentially very wide market indeed. After all, it was remarked in 1618 that 'Gaelic is the language used in the greater part of Scotland [and] is the language spoken in all but three of the dioceses'.[98]

If detailed investigation of the size of the ministry in Argyll is prevented by the fragmentary nature of the surviving evidence, the general picture elsewhere is rather more revealing. In the essentially highland dioceses of Caithness, Ross, Moray, a section of Dunkeld and also Dunblane, there were 215 kirks which, by 1574, were served by 65 ministers and 158 readers: a staff of 223 for 215 parishes; five ministerial posts were then empty and there were vacancies for 27 readers; but those parishes which happened to lack a reader were, of course, under the care of the local minister who supervised three or four neighbouring parishes. These figures are testimony, indeed, of the sustained assault which the kirk had mounted in the Gaelic north and west in the decade after the Reformation; and they compare mar-

[94] See above, 13; Inverary Castle, Argyll Transcripts, vi, 67; *The Hamilton Papers*, ed. J. Bain 2 vols. (Edinburgh, 1890–2), ii, p. 749.
[95] *Foirm na n-Urrnuidheadh*, ed. R. L. Thomson (Edinburgh, 1970), lxxiv.
[96] *CSP Scot.*, v, no. 28.
[97] I. B. Cowan, *Scottish Reformation*, 169.
[98] *Irish Franciscan Mission to Scotland, 1619–1646*, ed. C. Giblin (Dublin, 1964), 15.

ginally favourably with the figure for Scotland as a whole. In 1574, with the exception of Argyll and the Isles, 988 parishes were equipped with the services of 289 ministers and 715 readers, with 20 ministerial charges then unfilled and 97 vacancies for readers.[99]

Evidence of this sort, which cannot readily be controverted, does nothing to sustain the popular and frequently-repeated opinion that the inhabitants of the Highlands after 1560 found themselves wholly neglected by the kirk. Within a remarkably short interval, the kirk had more or less achieved the startling distinction of having a presence in most mainland parishes in the Highlands. But, if the kirk could not in fairness be said to have neglected the Highlanders, it was still possible for Highlanders to neglect the kirk. The support which the new church commanded, apart from its physical presence in most parishes, is far harder to assess. One legacy which the reformers had inherited from their predecessors and which did not always assist them in their task was the parochial system itself, for in the Highlands each parish, practically without exception, was inordinately large. It is hard to see how any minister then or later could reasonably hope to keep in close touch with all his parishioners or they with him. Besides, too many parishioners had to remain content merely with a resident reader instead of having their own minister living within the parish. There was ample opportunity, therefore, even in more settled times, for parishioners in remoter communities – and even in not so remote communities – to avoid all contact with the kirk. Even so, the kirk's initial response in meeting the challenge presented by the Reformation in the Highlands deserves more recognition than it has customarily received.

[99] *Wodrow Miscellany*, i, 396.

9

'The Polities of the Best Reformed Kirks'

Scottish achievements and English aspirations in church government after the Reformation:[1]

It has become almost a commonplace to regard the presbyterian movements in both England and Scotland as emerging simultaneously in the 1570s, guided if not directed from Geneva by Theodore Beza, and led by his disciples who returned from that Swiss republican city to create a new party with new principles within the respective churches. Yet in Reformation history, as elsewhere, the tendency to concentrate on ready parallels between the neighbouring kingdoms is liable to obscure more than it elucidates. Besides, an examination of the interaction between the objectives of the Scottish reformers from 1560 and the aims of at least a section of the English nonconformists would suggest that most of the programme advocated by English presbyterians in the 1570s had been already achieved in Scotland during the 1560s, long before the return to Scotland from Geneva in 1574 of Andrew Melville, the so-called 'father of Scottish presbyterianism'.

In 1572, the English puritans presented their famous 'Admonition to the Parliament', in which its authors, John Field and Thomas Wilcox, advocated a radical reformation of the Elizabethan Church of England, whose structure of government they sought to subvert and whose patterns of worship they intended to modify in a manner more consistent with what they claimed were the examples of 'all the best reformed churches throwoute Christendome', several models of which already existed in

[1] The quotation in the title is from the general assembly of August 1572 (*Booke of the Universall Kirk of Scotland, Acts and Proceedings of the General Assemblies of the Kirk of Scotland [BUK]* [Edinburgh, 1839–45], i, 246).

London and elsewhere in the exiled strangers' churches organised on Reformed or Calvinist lines.[2] The parliament, for whose members' benefit the 'Admonition' had been penned, had before its consideration in 1572 a bill regarding rites and ceremonies which, if approved, would have undermined the whole policy of enforcing strict observance of the revised Prayer Book and of the Thirty-Nine Articles of Religion, as well as the acceptance of distinctive clerical apparel which puritans found so objectionable. The bill, which was abandoned only on Elizabeth's direct intervention, was designed to champion the cause of what it called the 'lerned pastors and zealouse minysters' who, in contravention of the liturgical observances enjoined by authority, had 'conformed themselves more neerlie to the Imitacyon of thauncyent apostolicall churche and the best reformed churches in Europe'.[3]

Beneath the narrow issue of whether or not prescribed external forms in worship might be accepted simply as *adiaphora*, as things indifferent in themselves, there had emerged (particularly in the aftermath of the vestiarian controversy of the 1560s) a deeper reappraisal of the royal supremacy in ecclesiastical matters, of the magistrate's discretionary power in matters of religion and of the superintendence by bishops whose task it became to enforce the ecclesiastical policies of a queen intent on fulfilling her duties as 'supreme governor' of that church. In the ensuing 'Exhortation to the Bishops', the puritan conviction was again asserted that 'many things are out of order in our Church of England'; and, once more, in 'A Second Admonition to the Parliament' of 1572, compiled perhaps by Christopher Goodman, the campaign was renewed for replacing the ancient structure of church government, retained at the Reformation, with the distinctive polity which 'the best reformed churches doe use'. The persistent appeal, then, was to the model of the primitive and apostolic church and to the practice of the overseas churches in Switzerland, France, the Netherlands and the

[2] *Puritan Manifestoes*, edd. W. H. Frere and C. E. Douglas (London, 1907), 6; J. Strype, *The History of the Life and Acts of . . . Edmund Grindal* (London, 1710), 41ff.; F. A. Norwood, 'The Strangers' "Model Churches" in sixteenth-century England', in *Reformation Studies, Essays in Honour of Roland H. Bainton*, ed. F. H. Littell (Richmond, Virginia, 1962), 181–96; P. Collinson, 'The Elizabethan puritans and the foreign reformed churches in London', *Proceedings of the Huguenot Society of London*, xx (1965), 528–57.
[3] S. D'Ewes, *A Compleat Journal of the Votes, Speeches and Debates, both of the House of Lords and House of Commons throughout the whole reign of Queen Elizabeth* (London, 1693), 207, 212–14; J. Strype, *Annals of the Reformation* (Oxford, 1824), II, i, 185; *Puritan Manifestoes*; 149–51.

Rhineland, which the presbyterians preferred to the existing 'face of an English church'.[4]

From Geneva and from Heidelberg, the English non-conformists won support and encouragement for their cause, but from Zürich there came merely sympathy and the sobering advice that the peace and unity of the church could be best protected only through moderation, forbearance and compliance with the magistrate's injunctions.[5] Yet, besides the responses of these overseas churches, there existed within the same island, as puritans never ceased to recall,[6] another reformed church in Scotland, organised and adapted to meet the needs of a nation. That English puritans should look towards the reformed church in the northern kingdom is scarcely surprising, for there were already links besides a common protestantism and the language which (in effect) they shared: not only did Scots serve as beneficed clergy in the English church, but during the Scottish Reformation the English radical, Christopher Goodman, fresh from Geneva, had deserted his own country, whose church he criticised for retaining 'divers monuments of superstition', in preference for Scotland where he helped to establish a Calvinist discipline both at Ayr and in the former primatial seat of St Andrews itself.[7] Besides, John Knox, who ended his days as minister of the Scottish capital, had earlier won notoriety as a puritan leader in the Church of England, and no less so among the Marian exiles, first as Frankfort and then where he experienced at first hand what he described as that 'most godlie Reformed Churche and citie of the warld, Geneva'.[8]

---

[4] *The Remains of Edmund Grindal*, ed. W. Nicholson (Cambridge, 1843), 201ff.; *Puritan Manifestoes*, 65, 113; *The Seconde Parte of a Register*, ed. A. Peel (Cambridge, 1915), i, 97; *The Works of John Whitgift*, ed. J. Ayre (Cambridge, 1851–3), i, 47, 311, 363, 369; ii, 341, 451; iii, 107, 125; Strype, *Annals*, I, ii, 125–75; II, ii, 392ff.; cf. *A Brief Discourse of the Troubles at Frankfort*, ed. E. Arber (London, 1908), 25, 54, 57, 62, 74, 84, 118, 154–5, 164–5.

[5] *The Zürich Letters*, ed. H. Robinson (Cambridge, 1842–5), i, 341–65; ii, 32–3, 38–9, 47–9, 128–35, 142–6, 185–8, 339–53, 357; *Epistolarum Theologicarum Theodori Bezae Vezelii* (Geneva, 1573), i, 73–87, 103–13, 145–8, 149–67, 267–70; *A Brief Discourse*, 239–50; Strype, *Annals*, II, i, 142ff.

[6] *The Seconde Parte of a Register*, i, 83, 106, 165; ii, 69; *The Marprelate Tracts, 1588, 1589*, ed. W. Pierce (London, 1911), 26; Whitgift, *Works*, iii, 314–16; cf. R. Bancroft, *Dangerous Positions and Proceedings* (London, 1593), 41ff.

[7] C[alendar of the] S[tate] P[apers relating to] Scot[land and Mary, Queen of Scots, 1547–1603], edd. J. Bain, *et al.* (Edinburgh, 1898–1970), i, no. 316; *The Works of John Knox*, ed. D. Laing (Edinburgh, 1846–8), ii, 87; iv, 66–8; vi, 27, 78, 101; *Register of the Minister, Elders and Deacons of the Christian Congregation of St Andrews, 1559–1600 [RStAKS]*, ed. D. H. Fleming (Edinburgh, 1889–90), i, 4–5, 53, 71, 75, 131, 156, 168, 205, 221.

[8] Knox, *Works*, ii, 16; vi, 16; cf. v. 211–16.

Knox's earlier career in England had led him, as a Marian exile, to denounce 'that slackness to reform religion when time and place was granted'. He also declared his distaste for vestments, for ceremonies such as the sign of the cross in baptism and for the practice, enjoined in the Prayer Book, of kneeling, instead of sitting, at the reception of the elements in communion, a practice in which he had earlier acquiesced when resident in England – so as not 'for maintenance of that one thing to gainstand the magistrates' – but only under protest and in the expectation of further reform.[9] Yet, when freed from such constraints, in exile Knox affirmed that 'I do find in the English Book . . . things superstitious, impure, unclean and unperfect'; and when Richard Cox urged its adoption among the exiles at Frankfort so that 'their church should have an English face', Knox's response was that 'the Lord grant it to have the face of Christ's church . . . agreeable in outward rites and ceremonies with Christian churches reformed'. Again, in private correspondence with an Englishwoman, Anna Locke, in 1559, Knox seems to have expressed his inmost feelings when he roundly censured 'these Diabolicall inventiouns, viz., Crossing in Baptisme, Kneeling at the Lord's table, mummelling or singing of the Letanie', and he severely attacked 'the mingle mangle as now is commaunded in your kirks' including the use of the surplice and the commemoration of saints' days, which he considered to be neither 'commaunded by Christ nor found in the prayers of the Apostles, nather yit received in anie weill-reformed Kirk'.[10] The evidence for Knox's puritan convictions – his conception of the apostolic church as a model for his time and the reformed churches as an example to the church in which he exercised his ministry – is unimpeachable. Although some of Elizabeth's earlier bishops shared some of his opinions, they nonetheless sought to apply the queen's injunctions and to impose a measure of conformity, whereas Knox remained a focus for puritan dissenters,[11] who sought to put into practice their programme of further reform.

In Scotland, however, where the Reformation had taken the form of a rebellion – a rebellion effected in defiance of the wishes of the crown – and where no 'godly prince' was forthcoming to dictate or, at least, to temper the pattern and pace of reform, the

[9] Ibid., iii, 279; iv, 11, 33, 36–7, 41–4, 59; vi, 12, 83; P. Lorimer, *John Knox and the Church of England* (London, 1875), 251–65; *A Brief Discourse*, 44ff., 62–9.

[10] Knox, *Works*, iv, 44; vi, 12, 83; *A Brief Discourse*, 54, 62.

[11] *The Seconde Parte of a Register*, i, 46; Knox, *Works*, iv, 92; *The Marprelate Tracts*, 326; see also below, 345.

new church from 1560 enjoyed a remarkable freedom, enabling it
to abandon, as it saw fit, such accretions of medieval thought and
practice which found no firm support from scripture and to
adopt instead practices more carefully attuned to what was
understood to be the purity and simplicity of the apostolic
church. The intention of reformers in Scotland, or so they
declared, was to restore 'the grave and godlie face of the primitive
Churche' in order that the 'the reverent face of the primitive and
apostolick Churche should be reduced agane to the eyes and
knowledge of men'.[12] The austere approach adopted here meant
that the ceremonies and apparel which so offended the puritan
conscience in England found no place in the drastically reconstituted Scottish church.

In worship, the Scots chose to adopt the Genevan 'Forme of
Prayers', which Knox's English congregation had used in exile
there; and since this was the only service book commended by
the Book of Discipline in 1560 and authorised by the general
assembly in 1562, 'the Booke of our Common Ordour, callit the
Ordour of Geneva' soon displaced the second, more protestant,
English Prayer Book which had circulated in Scottish reformed
circles well before the Reformation. Equally, in the First Book of
Discipline, which Knox had helped to draft, the celebration of
saints' days was declared 'utterly to be abolished from this
Realme'; ceremonies such as the sign of the cross in baptism were
repudiated and any who presumed to adopt such practices, it was
noted, 'ought severely' to be punished. At communion, 'sitting at
a table' was judged to be 'most convenient to that holy action';
ordinary bread broken by the minister replaced the unleavened
wafer both of pre-Reformation practice and of English usage, as
redefined in the royal injunctions of 1559. Burials, the Book of
Discipline decided, were to take place 'without all kind of
ceremony' and, as English puritans also contended, funeral
sermons were to be eschewed as serving only to 'nourish
superstition and a false opinion'.[13] Episcopal confirmation of
children was discontinued, and the celebration of sacraments in
private houses was forbidden. After the Reformation, too, the
use of organs in church services seems to have been discontinued
or, at least, discouraged to such an extent that in both Edinburgh
and Aberdeen the organs were dismantled and sold. All this, of

---

[12] Knox, *Works*, i, 306; ii, 264.
[13] Ibid., ii, 210, 239; *BUK*, i, 30, 54; *The First Book of Discipline*, ed.
J. K. Cameron (Edinburgh, 1972), 88–9, 91, 130–1, 200–1; H. Gee, *The
Elizabethan Clergy and the Settlement of Religion, 1558–1564* (Oxford, 1898),
64; Whitgift, *Works*, iii, 82ff.

course, was thoroughly in keeping with the demands of puritans in England. Similarly, the prescription for distinctive clerical outdoor attire – the square cap, long gown, tippet and bishop's rochet – though retained in England, disappeared by 1560 in Scotland, where the black teaching gown – the so-called Geneva gown – replaced the white surplice and cope, which continued to be worn during divine service in England since Elizabeth, as Bishop Jewel explained to the Zürich divines in 1566, 'is unable to endure the least alteration in matters of religion'.[14]

The contrast between prevailing practice within the two churches was indeed marked, and it could scarcely have been otherwise. The initial absence of a 'godly prince' had led to a more radical Reformation in Scotland where, as Jewel remarked with some satisfaction to Peter Martyr in 1559, 'the theatrical dresses, the sacrilegious chalices, the idols, the altars are consigned to the flames; not a vestige of the ancient superstition and idolatry is left'. Certainly, when the English government explored the possibility of achieving what it called a 'uniformity' in religion between the two realms, their ambassador found merely goodwill and a lukewarm response: ministers in the north were 'so severe in that that theie professe, and so lothe to remytte any thyng of that that theie have receaved that I se lyttle hope thereof'. The same diplomat also explained that the reason why the Scottish reformers sought for their Book of Discipline the approval of Geneva and Zürich, but not that of England, was simply that 'I see not their opinion to England to be such that they will "stonde to their judgement herin", yet they will not refuse to commune with any "lerned in our nacion" to hear it'.[15]

The verdict was not ill-considered. In 1562, the ministers in Scotland were said to have 'ronne allmost wylde' at the suggestion that Mary, Queen of Scots, might 'embrace the religion of England'; and Knox in a sermon 'gave the crosse and the candle such a wype' as to eliminate any prospect of accommodation. Somewhat later, in 1568, when there was again talk that Mary might adopt the English Prayer Book, the English ambassador shrewdly observed that the Scots were not likely to revert to 'cornerd cappes and typpets, with surpless and coopes' which had been abandoned 'by order ever since they first received the gospel' in favour of practices more 'agreable with

[14] First Book of Discipline, 182; Edinburgh Records: Dean of Guild's Account, 1552–1567, ed. R. Adam (Edinburgh, 1899), 117; R[egister of the] P[rivy] C[ouncil of Scotland] (Edinburgh, 1877–98), ii, 391; Cartularium Ecclesiae Sancti Nicholai Aberdonensis, ii (Aberdeen, 1892), 385; Zürich Letters, i, 163–5; cf. 178; 149.
[15] Zürich Letters, i, 39–40; cf. 67; CSP Scot., i, no. 891.

divers well reformed churches in Germany, Swyserland, France, and in Savoye'. The point, at any rate, was appreciated years later by Mary's son, who carefully explained to his English bishops in 1604: 'You may now safely wear your caps: but I shall tell you, if you should walk in one street in Scotland with such a cap on your head, if I were not with you, you should be stoned to death with your cap'. Not only so, but in the 1560s the Scots had shown no hesitation in intervening in the English quarrel. The two leading politicians in Scotland – Lord James Stewart, Earl of Moray and the queen's half brother, and William Maitland of Lethington – had warned the English government in 1565 of 'what scandal may ensue among yourselves and your neighbours' if godly preachers were constrained to 'tak on the apparell usit in tyme of papistrie', and they counselled setting aside any policy of enforced conformity.[16] Thereafter, in 1566, the general assembly of the Scottish church interceded with 'the Bischops and pastours of Ingland', in a letter composed by Knox, in which they pleaded for liberty of conscience on whether or not such 'unprofitable apparrell' might be adopted. Their forceful, if less than tactful, argument was simply that 'if surp-claithes, cornett cap, and tippet has bein badges of idolaters in the verie act of ther idolatrie, what hes the preacher of Christian libertie and the open rebuiker of all superstitioun to doe with the dregges of that Romish beast'. The assembly's overwhelming support for the 'godly and learned' in England, the conscience-stricken who had been 'depryvit fra ecclesiastical functioun and forbidden to preach', was scarcely concealed. Even when Bullinger in Zürich produced a work countenancing the English apparel, in St Andrews a master in St Salvator's College, William Ramsay, took a sterner view and wrote an answer or reply to Bullinger which an assembly committee in 1566 was charged to 'reconsider and revise', not because the assembly sought to censure its contents – of that there is no evidence – but rather in recognition of the assembly's claim to supervise and review all religious publications (in much the same way, presumably, as the assembly was later to consider and revise other literature including the Second Book of Discipline).[17] All along, the trend within the two churches had been one of divergence rather than of conformity; and later an archbishop of St Andrews, who himself favoured conformity, drew a not inappropriate contrast between the two countries when he observed that, in Scotland, King James had

[16] *CSP Scot.*, i, no. 1077; ii, no. 743; E. Cardwell, *A History of Conferences* (Oxford, 1840), 201; *CSP Scot.*, ii, nos. 156, 161.
[17] *BUK*, i, 85–8, 90; cf., 289, 383–5.

'not burthened his realme' as Elizabeth had done in England 'with sindrie ceremoneis and injunctions, wherunto their clergie is astricted'.[18]

The diversity of practice, already apparent, was accentuated by the different systems of government regulating the respective churches. Whereas in England the traditional structure was retained and utilised, in Scotland the reformers disregarded the pleas of the Catholic archbishop of St Andrews that the ancient polity – 'the work of many ages' – should not be hastily overturned; and they proceeded to sweep aside the medieval structure of church government in preference for a distinctively reformed church order.[19] The names and offices of archbishop, bishop *per se*, archdeacon, dean of Christianity (or rural dean), of such cathedral dignitaries as chancellor, dean and canons, of provosts and prebendaries of collegiate churches, and even the titles of parson and vicar where denoting ecclesiastical office, were simply jettisoned by a reformed church which sought to concentrate its resources in the parishes – whose earlier neglect had led reformers to criticise the top-heavy superstructure of the unreformed church, a structure which had been sustained very largely at the expense of the parishes through the diversion of parochial revenues to finance the higher levels. Similarly, the legislative activities of provincial councils and diocesan synods and the judicial work of the episcopal and archidiaconal courts were superseded by a series of reformed church courts, endowed with an appellate jurisdiction, from the congregational kirk session through the superintendent's court centred on the principal town of the province and the provincial synod which met twice-yearly, to the general assembly of the whole church which had emerged by 1560 as the supreme court of the church.

Discipline, administered not by the bishop or archdeacon but by the eldership, both in the narrower sense of the correction of offenders by elders and in the wider sense of a graded series of church courts through which mutual censuring and fraternal correction were exercised, became a special feature of the Scottish polity. 'To discipline', the reformers affirmed in 1560, 'must all the estates within this Realm be subject, as well the Rulers, as they that are ruled'; and it was no idle boast when St Andrews kirk session pronounced in 1566 that 'disciplin is ane part of owr relegion'. The elders, who assisted their minister in

---

[18] D. Calderwood, *The History of the Kirk of Scotland*, ed. T. Thomson (Edinburgh, 1842–9), iv, 90.

[19] J. Spottiswoode, *History of the Church of Scotland* (Edinburgh, 1851–65), i, 372.

governing the church, sat with the minister in the congregational consistory or kirk session, together with the deacons who acted as financial officers; they participated in the work of the superintendent's court, which was simply a reconstituted kirk session with an enlarged jurisdiction during the superintendent's residence in the principal town of the province; elders were eligible to be chosen to attend meetings of the provincial synod, and they are known to have formed an element in the earliest general assemblies. Nor was this all. Elders were responsible for submitting a report on their minister's performance to the superintendent's court each year; and the superintendent himself, at his election, was required to acknowledge his subjection to the censure of the elders of his province.[20]

The decision taken by 1561 'to make difference betwixt Preachers at this time' by appointing superintendents, formed no part of the reformers' original strategy; it was added only as an afterthought in the final drafting of the Book of Discipline, where it was justified on the purely practical grounds of expediency. With a severe shortage of ministers, it was recognised that the needs of the whole church could be realistically met only by the adoption of ten or twelve 'godly and learned men', who were 'to plant and erect Kirkes, to set, order and appoint Ministers . . . to the Countries that shall be appointed to their care where none are now'. Somewhat earlier, by 1559, John Knox had recommended reforming and reducing the pattern of episcopacy in England. His plan was to reconstruct the units of pastoral oversight by subdividing by ten the large English dioceses, so that in place of 'proud Prelates' in 'every citie and great towne there may be placed a godly learned man, with so many joyned with him, for preaching and instruction, as shalbe thoght sufficient for the boundes committed to *their* charge'.[21] The superintendence advocated here was decidedly constitutional, corporate and pastoral; not monarchical, regal or narrowly jurisdictional. The substance of this advice, though not accepted in England, was adopted in Scotland where the streamlined provinces assigned to the superintendents bore little resemblance to the antiquated boundaries of the thirteen pre-Reformation dioceses, whose structure, far from being dissolved as reformers had urged, continued to survive intact, although it formed no part of the new church's organisation.

Although he was charged not 'to live as your idle Bishops have done heretofore', the Scottish superintendent could scarcely be

---

[20] RStAKS, i, 270; First Book of Discipline, 177; 127.
[21] First Book of Discipline, 155; Knox, Works, v, 518 (my italics).

confused with either the pre-Reformation or the English bishop. He exercised no civil or criminal jurisdiction and was denied a seat in parliament, on the privy council and college of justice. At his admission, he had to promise to eschew lordship and dominion over his brethren; he was subject to correction by his fellow ministers and elders; he was subordinate to the conciliar system of church government which had developed; and the general assembly, as the supreme governing body, customarily began its deliberations by examining the activities of the superintendents as regional administrators.[22] Even here, however, with the creation of superintendents, the intentions of the reformers were still frustrated: because of political instability and inadequate finance, only five superintendents were ever appointed and elsewhere their work was undertaken by other ministers whom the assembly commissioned for a term to act as overseers; and also by three conforming bishops who undertook to serve in the reformed church, but whose status the general assembly recognised to be that of commissioner and not that of bishop or even superintendent, a not unimportant qualification.[23]

If the government of the Elizabethan church was both royal and episcopal in form, the government of the Scottish church might be best described as conciliar and anti-erastian. The graduated series of representative courts, reaching its fullest expression in the general assembly, where a presiding moderator was elected for order's sake from 1563,[24] provided a system of checks and balances which permitted individual initiative while obviating the need for raising one man permanently above his brethren. The greater responsibilities which were the lot of the superintendents (though even they understood that their tenure of office was not for life)[25] no doubt infringed any narrow notion of a strict equality in jurisdiction among ministers, but all this was effectively counterbalanced by the greater accountability of superintendents both to those within their jurisdiction and to the wider church; and it is plain that any notion of imparity or inequality was firmly rejected by reformers at national level in their institution of an elective moderator's office in the church's supreme court.

An expression of the reformers' anti-erastian sentiments, their disinclination to accept magisterial control, was evident as early

---

[22] *First Book of Discipline*, 122; Knox, *Works*, ii, 147; *BUK*, i, 25ff., 266; see further above, 188ff.
[23] *BUK*, i, 15, 26–32, 34–5, 39–40, 42, 44, 51–2; see further above 212ff.
[24] Ibid., 38.
[25] Ibid., 39, 65, 77, 92, 120, 239, 296–7, 302–3.

as 1559 when the protestant Lords of the Congregation formulated a classical exposition of the 'two kingdoms' theory, which was to be borrowed and expounded by Superintendent Erskine of Dun in 1571 and then by Andrew Melville himself.[26] From the outset, the disciplinary machinery of the Scottish church was exercised in a capacity quite separate from the jurisdiction of the civil magistrate. The elders, whom contemporaries described as 'ecclesiastical magistrates', were intended to complement in the spiritual sphere the work of the civil magistrate in temporal affairs. Excommunication, which might be executed by a lay official in the Elizabethan church, was administered independently of the civil authorities in Scotland, where the sentence was pronounced by the ministry and kirk session in name of the whole church; and in reaction to the unreformed practice of cursing for trivial offences, the Scottish reformers restored and restricted excommunication to be a sentence of ultimate resort, applied only in the case of heinous offenders who remained obdurate and unrepentant. The magistrate's exclusion from exercising ecclesiastical discipline, and notably excommunication, was markedly at variance with the emphasis in England and elsewhere on magisterial control, but it was certainly consistent with Knox's defence of excommunication in 1559 on the grounds that 'our Churche, and the trew ministeris of the same, have the same power which our Maister, Christ Jesus, granted to his Apostles'.[27]

Under the rule of Queen Mary, a sovereign unsympathetic to the reformed church, it was perhaps inevitable that church and state should remain separate, but even after the accession in 1567 of a 'godly prince' in the person of James VI, the general assembly continued to claim that the church's jurisdiction should be separate from that of the state, and the church courts continued to operate without licence from the crown until the 'Black Acts' of 1584 sought to curb this tradition of ecclesiastical independence. Church and nation might be coextensive, but in Scotland it was far from being a foregone conclusion that church

[26] *Spalding Club Miscellany*, iv (Aberdeen, 1849), 88–92; Calderwood, *History*, iii, 158; v, 440; *The Autobiography and Diary of Mr James Melvill*, ed. R. Pitcairn (Edinburgh, 1842), 370; see further above, 235–6.

[27] A. Maxwell, *The History of Old Dundee* (Edinburgh, 1884), 72; P. Collinson, *The Elizabethan Puritan Movement* (London, 1967), 40–1; F. D. Price, 'The abuses of excommunication and the decline of ecclesiastical discipline under Queen Elizabeth', *EHR*, lvii (1942), 106–15; Grindal, *Remains*, 451ff.; *A Brief Discourse*, 247–8 (for letter from the Genevans, including Henry Scrimgeour, the Scots professor of law there, to ministers in the Church of England, 1567); Knox, *Works*, vi, 449ff.; *First Book of Discipline*, 169–71; *RStAKS*, i, 99–101, 203–5; Knox, *Works*, i, 333.

and state should be united under the rule of a 'godly prince' claiming supremacy over both jurisdictions; and even in 1574, in the aftermath of the civil war, the church still declined to acknowledge any explicit claims to royal supremacy in ecclesiastical matters.[28]

In any event, the reformed polity which operated in Scotland, and which had its parallels in the French reformed churches,[29] was exactly the sort of system to which English puritans appealed in their efforts to adopt a similar structure in the southern kingdom. 'Is a reformation good for France?', the English presbyterians demanded in 1572, 'and can it be evyl for England? Is discipline meete for Scotland? and is it unprofitable for this Realme? Surely God hath set these examples before your eyes to encourage you to go foreward to a thorow and a speedy reformation'. Another English puritan underlined the point when he remarked in 1572 that 'by a brief comparison you may see how the state of our Church is, and how it ought to be, both by the Word of God and example of the primitive Church, as allso of Geneva, France, Scotland and all other Churches rightly reformed'.[30] Somewhat earlier, in 1568, the bishop of London had criticised that 'wilful company' of English puritans who had come north to sample the Scottish discipline and to confer with Knox, to whom they later confided, on returning home, 'we desire no other order than you hold'. But when they sought to achieve this by seceding – by severing their connection with the Church of England – and by establishing their own 'reformed church', Knox soon withdrew his support and counselled perseverance within the one, national church.[31]

In these English controversies, which centred first on worship and then on government, the Scots were by no means impartial observers. After all, long before Thomas Cartwright and the English puritans pressed in the early 1570s for the introduction of a drastically reformed church polity, the cardinal aspects of their programme already had been achieved and effected in Scotland during the 1560s. Bishop Sandys, writing to Zürich in

[28] BUK, i, 140, 146; Knox, Works, ii, 296, 395–7, 405–6; BUK, i, 292; Miscellany of the Scot. Hist. Soc., viii (Edinburgh, 1951), 105; Hume of Godscroft, History of the Houses of Douglas and Angus (Edinburgh, 1644), 334; BUK, i, 295–6; Lindesay of Pitscottie, The Historie and Cronicles of Scotland (Edinburgh, 1889), ii, 313–14.
[29] See above, 82–7.
[30] Puritan Manifestoes, 19; Seconde Parte of a Register, i, 83; cf. Bancroft, Dangerous Positions and Proceedings, 41ff.
[31] Grindal, Remains, 295–6; Strype, Grindal, 121–2; Lorimer, Knox and the Church of England, 298–300. Like Knox, Beza is also reported to have expressed disapproval of the behaviour of the English separatists (Strype, Grindal, 119).

1573, saw the main contentions of English prebyterians to be these. Firstly, that the civil magistrate was merely a member of the church and not supreme over it, a view wholly consistent with the claims of the Scottish general assembly since the 1560s that the magistrate was subject to ecclesiastical discipline, and with the church's refusal to concede the crown's claim to ecclesiastical supremacy. Secondly, the English prebyterians' belief that the government of the church ought properly to be committed to the ministry had its antecedents in the Scottish Book of Discipline which recognised in 1560 that ministers were 'promoted to the regiment of the Church'. The English 'Admonition to the Parliament' likewise had remarked, in 1572, that 'to these three jointly, that is, the Ministers, Seniors and deacons, is the whole regiment of the church to be committed'. This claim that the church ought to be governed by presbyteries of ministers, elders and deacons had a direct and obvious parallel in the work of the Scottish kirk session, for the English presbytery, it has to be recalled, simply denoted the congregational consistory and not the classis or presbytery in the later Scottish sense. This was made clear in the requirement that 'each parish should have its own presbytery'.[32]

There seems to be no convincing evidence that the Scots adopted the eldership only as a device when their church lay 'under the cross' and was persecuted, or that they intended the eldership to be superseded by the establishment of an episcopal system once the church was finally accorded protection and recognition by the state. To contend thus, as some have done, is merely to import the arguments advanced by Archbishops Whitgift and Bancroft in their encounters with their opponents in England. The eldership, after all, was commended in the Book of Discipline at a time when Scotland possessed a 'godly' provisional government in the great council of the realm, and the office was justified by reformers as an order which 'O Lord, thow of thy mercie hes now restoired unto us agane efter that the publict face of the Kirk hes bene deformed by the tyrany of that Romane Antichrist'. In similar manner, the English 'Admonition to the Parliament' in 1572, it may be noted, also defined the eldership as 'an order left by God unto his church'.[33] The

---

[32] *Zürich Letters*, i, 295–6; cf. 280–1; *First Book of Discipline*, 100; *Puritan Manifestoes*, 16; *Zürich Letters*, i, 296.

[33] Whitgift, *Works*, i, 389–95, 472; iii, 160–7, 180, 214; *Tracts ascribed to Richard Bancroft*, ed. A. Peel (Cambridge, 1953), 108–10, 112–15; T. Bilson, *The Perpetual Government of Christ's Church* (1593; Oxford, 1842 edn.), 399, 460; *First Book of Discipline*, 174ff.; Knox, *Works*, ii, 153; *Puritan Manifestoes*, 16.

reformers' belief in the centrality of the eldership in a reformed polity, professedly modelled on the primitive church, seems to be irrefutable. Thus, in 1574, long after the accession of a 'godly prince', the general assembly continued to regard elders and deacons as 'necessar and requisite for erecting of a perfect reformed Kirk'.[34]

A further aim of English presbyterians, as Bishop Sandys observed, was that the 'names and authority of archbishops, archdeacons, deans, chancellors, commissaries, and other titles and dignities of the like kind, should be altogether removed from the church of Christ'; but such a hierarchical structure the Scots had succeeded in sweeping aside in and after 1560. The Scots, of course, were well aware, as were their counterparts in England, that the name of bishop was scriptural; but there were bishops and bishops, and in Scottish eyes a bishop need not be identified with a diocesan bishop. The Scottish superintendent was certainly an overseer, but an overseer of a somewhat distinctive and unusual kind: he was a pastor of pastors, and yet subject to these same pastors. The office, so termed, had been adopted in a number of reformed church orders; and if it originated in Lutheran churches, it was soon commended by Bucer; the name, if not the species, appeared in the French Confession of Faith, while in England some identified the superintendent with the *chorepiscopus*, an auxiliary overseer to the bishop, or even with the office of rural dean.[35] A variety of interpretations existed. Yet, in Scotland, the general assembly avoided any ambiguity and made its own attitude towards episcopacy very clear in 1565 when it pronounced that 'every true preacher of Jesus Christ is a Christian bishop'.[36] Here was an authoritative identification of the parish minister and bishop, an equation which Andrew Melville was to reiterate in 1575. Such a statement certainly

[34] *BUK*, i, 311.

[35] *Zürich Letters*, i, 295–6; *Luther's Works*, edd. J. Pelikan and H. T. Lehmann (Philadelphia, 1955–69), xl, 313–14; *The Visitation of the Saxon Reformed Church*, ed. R. Laurence (Dublin, 1839), 24ff.; J. K. Cameron, 'The Cologne Reformation and the Church of Scotland', *Journal of Ecclesiastical History*, xxx (1979), 39–64 (at 49ff); Hermann von Wied, *A simple and religious consultation* (London, 1548), fos. cxlviii^v, ccxx^v, ccxxii^r, cclxvi^v; Bucer, *Scripta Anglicana* (Basle, 1577), 259; *Common Places of Martin Bucer*, ed. D. F. Wright (Appleford, 1972), 278; *The Creeds of Christendom*, ed. P. Schaff (London, 1877), iii, 378; see also J. Quick, *Synodicon in Gallia Reformata* (London, 1692), i, 227, 266; J. Aymon, *Tous les synodes nationaux des églises réformées de France* (The Hague, 1710), i, 259, 303; Historical Manuscripts Commission, *Salisbury MSS*, ii (London, 1888), no. 580; P. Collinson, 'Episcopacy and reform in England in the later sixteenth century', *Studies in Church History*, ed. G. J. Cumming, iii (Leiden, 1966), 91–125 at 107–9; see further above, 196–204.

[36] Knox, *Works*, vi, 434.

echoed the ideas of Tyndale and others in England but it nonetheless antedated by at least half a decade the claims of the English presbyterians on this score. 'Instead of an Archbishop or Lord bishop, you must make equalitie of ministers' was the advice of the 'Admonition to the Parliament', and in the accompanying 'Exhortation to the bishops' in 1572 the English radicals contended that 'there oughte to be no Lordlinesse in the ministerie: Bishops livings ought to be abated: their great circuites cutte shorter: and themselves made equall to their brethren'.[37] By all accounts, the Scottish polity of the 1560s would have gone far towards satisfying all but the most fastidious of English presbyterians.

English radicals and Scottish reformers likewise affirmed that ministers ought not to be ordained at large into a priestly order and, while the Anglican ordinal recognised that 'from the Apostles' time there hath been these three orders of ministers in Christ's Church: Bishops, Priests and Deacons', reformers in both countries were agreed that a minister should be called to serve a specific vocation in a particular congregation and that that congregation ought to have its say in the choice of candidates appointed.[38]

One further area where the ideals of English presbyterians had been anticipated by the Scots in 1560 lay in the intended confiscation of episcopal and cathedral revenues, and the envisaged redistribution of these finances to meet the needs of the wider church. In attempting to reorganise the unsatisfactory state of ecclesiastical finances, the Scottish Book of Discipline in 1560 had called for a drastic reallocation of ecclesiastical endowment. The intention was to claim, and to utilise, much of the patrimony of the pre-Reformation church on a radically different basis by dissolving the benefices and redistributing the revenues at the hands of the deacons to meet the needs of the parishes, the schools and universities, and the poor.[39] But here the Scots failed to carry through their financial programme in its entirety. The crown and nobility who had acquired church

[37] Spottiswoode, *History*, ii, 200; Tyndale, *Doctrinal Treatises*, ed. H. Walker (Cambridge, 1848), 229–31; Hooper, *Early Writings*, ed. C. Carr (Cambridge, 1843), 19; *A Brief Discourse*, 31, 154–6, 163–5; *Puritan Manifestoes*, 63.
[38] *The Two Liturgies . . . of Edward VI*, ed. J. Ketley (Cambridge, 1844), 16; *Puritan Manifestoes*, 10, 96–100; Travers, *A full and plaine Declaration of Ecclesiastical Discipline* (1574), 36; *A Directory of Church Government* (1644), sig. A 2 verso, ff.; *Seconde Parte of a Register*, i, 70ff, 87, 151; ii, 41, 70, 214; *Zürich Letters*, i, 1, 280, 296; *First Book of Discipline*, 96ff.
[39] *Zürich Letters*, i, 296; *Puritan Manifestoes*, 12, 100, 103ff., 132; *Seconde Parte of a Register*, i, 255–6; ii, 21, 211; *First book of Discipline*, 108ff, 112, 150, 156–64.

property before the Reformation saw no reason to relinquish their hold on this profitable new source of income. The deacon's activities were thus largely restricted to poor relief; and the pre-Reformation system of ecclesiastical patronage remained in uneasy association with a polity devised to uphold congregational rights.

All this had important and far-reaching implications. The failure to secure an adequate measure of finance to fulfil this ambitious programme led the church to acquiesce in a series of financial compromises: firstly, in a scheme of 1562 whereby a third of the revenues from benefices was withheld from existing benefice-holders and assigned instead, though in unequal measure, to the crown and kirk for their maintenance; then from 1566 ministers were permitted access to the lesser, including parochial, benefices in their entirety, as they became vacant, so that instead of dissolving the old structure of benefices, the reformers had been forced to make use of it; the next step came in 1572 at the Convention of Leith when the church gained added finance, this time from the greater benefices or prelacies, where the earlier trend had been towards their secularisation.[40] Yet, by succeeding to vacant bishoprics after 1572, ministers acquired the title and office of bishop – a development unforeseen in all its implications in the 1560s. It had the effect of deflecting the reformers' original strategy. As late as 1571, the church's objective was still to dissolve the bishoprics, as the Book of Discipline had recommended in 1560. But by then, instead of subverting this ancient structure, the reformed church looked almost as if it might be prepared, under pressure, to integrate this structure – a structure which it had earlier condemned – within its own organisation. Such a financial expedient, if accepted, was clearly bound to have consequences for the church's polity.[41]

The solution on endowment which inaugurated the appearance of bishops, so styled, within the kirk was devised and adopted at Leith by officials representing government and church who met for negotiations, and it was a solution which arose fortuitously and not as part of a coherent policy to identify the reformed church with the old ecclesiastical structure. It arose essentially as an unexpected sequel to an episode in magnatial politics, and it had the effect of allowing the government a share in ecclesiastical finances, which it urgently required in the midst of the 'civil war' between the king's men and the queen's men. In

[40] RPC, i, 201–3, 487–9; APS, iii, 230; BUK, i, 207ff.
[41] Calderwood, History, iii, 159; cf. BUK, i, 151; see further below, 403ff.

1571, at a point when the church still displayed no interest in acquiring the bishoprics as financial and administrative entities, the government chose to promote its own candidates to the archbishoprics of Glasgow and St Andrews, which were declared to be vacant through the forfeiture of one Catholic archbishop and the execution for treason of the other. As the two archbishoprics did not form part of the organisation of the new church, the government felt quite entitled, without consulting the church, to appoint two candidates of its own – candidates who thus acquired legal titles to their bishoprics and thereby gained access to the revenues; but it could scarcely have been entertained at that point that the two titular archbishops, so appointed, would play any active part in ecclesiastical administration, though they were certainly eligible to take their seats in parliament as their Catholic predecessors had done. After all, earlier governments had provided titular bishops to Brechin and the Isles in 1566 and in 1567 (and had also approved an appointment to Ross by 1567), and in all of these elections the reformed church had played no part. Indeed, it was only when confronted by criticism of the unilateral appointments of 1571 that the new government accepted the need to make arrangements for examining the aptitude of the two archbishops and only then, in September 1571, was it finally acknowledged that the new archbishops ought to play a part in ecclesiastical administration, though neither had suitable pastoral experience. It was not yet explained how their duties would be reconciled with the work of the existing superintendents.[42]

The Glasgow candidate, John Porterfield, described at Glencairn's 'servitor', seems to have been sponsored by the Earl of Glencairn; and the nominee for St Andrews, John Douglas, found support from his kinsman, the Earl of Morton, himself a prominent member of the government. The milking of the bishoprics by magnates through the simple device of filling a see with a relation of a particular noble family was a practice which both crown and nobility had richly and adeptly exploited to their financial advantage long before 1560, and it was far from easy to prevent the continuation of this practice even after the Reformation, particularly so as the new church had no voice in the disposal of the greater benefices. At the same time, the kirk did

---

[42] *BUK*, i, 207ff.; R[egistrum S[ecreti] S[igilli Regum Scotorum], ed. G. Donaldson, vi (Edinburgh, 1963), nos. 1107, 1228, 1473–4, 1535, 2142, 2810; Calderwood, *History*, iii, 58–9, 135, 138; A[cts of the] P[arliaments of] S[cotland] (Edinburgh, 1844–75), iii, 65, 70; D. E. R. Watt, *Fasti Ecclesiae Scoticanae Medii Aevi ad annum 1638* (Edinburgh, 1969), 41, 150, 206, 270, 299.

lay claim to the patrimony of bishoprics which it aimed to dissolve and whose finances it wished to reform and reorganise. It could therefore scarcely afford to remain a distinterested spectator of a procedure which looked like facilitating, rather than impeding, the process towards the secularisation of both episcopal and abbatial property.[43]

Faced with this dilemma, the church found a spokesman in Erskine of Dun, superintendent of Angus and the Mearns, who urged the government to reverse its policy and to accede to the church's requests for a dissolution of the bishoprics. If such a drastic and comprehensive solution could not be immediately adopted, Erskine then proposed that in the short term only candidates approved by the church should be eligible for promotion to the bishoprics, as had been the case with the lesser benefices from 1566. Moreover, as possession of a benefice ought to incur a responsibility by the holder for the cure of souls, Erskine contended that future episcopal appointments ought to entail an obligation to perform the spiritual office attached to the living. In this way, by restricting episcopal appointments to qualified ministers and by reasserting a measure of ecclesiastical control over this machinery, it was hoped to halt the secularisation of episcopal property and to reallocate these resources for the work of the reformed church.[44]

The outcome of Erskine's intervention, then, was the Convention of Leith in 1572, which provided recognised and agreed procedures for disposing of episcopal and abbatial revenues to the benefit of both church and crown. Yet the compromise, so achieved, of identifying the old bishoprics with the work of the reformed church was precipitated largely by the government's persistent refusal to adopt the solution preferred by the general assembly, which favoured a thorough reform of ecclesiastical endowment 'according to the booke of God and the ordour and practise of the primitive kirk'.[45] The government, instead, chose to imitate English practice, where the protestant church had taken over the old ecclesiastical structure. Thus in 1572, by a curious paradox, in the year in which the English puritans' 'Admonition' appealed to the example of Scotland, the decision was taken at Leith – or so the English ambassador reported – that 'in the order of admission of bishops and others entering to

---

[43] *Fasti Ecclesiae Scoticanae*, ed. H. Scott (Edinburgh, 1915–61), iii, 5, 340, 350; *BUK*, i, 132, 153–4; Melville, *Diary*, 31; R. Bannatyne, *Journal of the Transactions in Scotland* (Edinburgh, 1806), 246, 250–5, 279–93, 296–7.

[44] Calderwood, *History*, iii, 156–65.

[45] *BUK*, i, 107.

spiritual promotions, so far as may be, the order of the kirk of England be followed'.[46] Conformity with England was now being seriously canvassed. Yet 1572 was also the year in which Theodore Beza wrote from Geneva to Knox advising against the introduction of episcopacy. The letter was too late to affect the Convention of Leith, but Knox was scarcely in need of Beza's advice, for he had already protested that the church should not be subject to 'that ordour', the Leith episcopacy.[47]

Again, the general assembly had still to give its considered judgment on an agreement negotiated by only a few individuals. There were already signs of disquiet even before the assembly finally declined to accept the Leith episcopacy as a permanent settlement. All that the assembly was prepared to entertain in 1572 was that the compromise should operate as 'ane interim' measure, a temporary expedient until a solution more acceptable to the church was devised. This led Knox to acquiesce in the assembly's verdict, despite his preference for the order of 1560 which he had helped to introduce. Already, in 1572, members of the assembly condemned as 'slanderous and offensive' the adoption of such titles as archbishop, dean, archdeacon, and chapter, and the titles of abbot and prior were ordered to be changed to 'other names more agreeable to Gods word, and the polities of the best reformed Kirks'.[48]

At the very point when the church was under pressure from the government to adopt a policy of conformity with England, the assembly showed a decided determination not to depart from the tradition of 'the best reformed churches'; and in succeeding years much of the assembly's energy was devoted to accommodating the old financial structure with a reformed and effective system of church government. Knox himself had died in 1572, and shortly afterwards it fell to Andrew Melville to help guide the church back towards a stricter adherence to the Reformation principles of 1560.

'The John Knox of mythology', it has been claimed, 'is very largely compounded of the Andrew Melville of history, for it was Melville', one is assured, 'and not Knox, who was the originator of Scottish presbyterianism'.[49] There are, of course, myths and myths in Scottish history, and one of the myths which ought so to be recognised is the belief which attributes the outbreak of strife in the reformed church to the arrival from

[46] CSP Scot., iv, no. 149, pp. 133–4.
[47] Melville, Diary, 45, 60–1; Knox, Works, vi. 613–15; Bannatyne, Journal, 375.
[48] BUK, i, 238, 244–9.
[49] G. Donaldson, Scotland: Church and National through Sixteen Centuries (Edinburgh, 1972), 71.

Geneva in 1574 of Andrew Melville who, it is said, disturbed good order in the church by undermining an episcopacy to which the Scots were singularly attached, and by substituting in its place his own brand of presbyterianism, doctrinaire and innovating, wholly contrary to the principles and aims of the earlier reformers. Such a claim, which Archbishop Spottiswoode first advanced, might best be made by an appeal to fiction rather than to fact, for it is by no means easy to find reliable contemporary support for such a view.

It is true that, as one of Melville's severest critics, Archbishop Spottiswoode, writing in the early seventeenth century, accused Melville of 'labouring with a burning desire to bring into this Church the presbyterial discipline of Geneva', but the trouble with Spottiswoode is that he was simply not consistent, for elsewhere he criticised Knox for attempting 'by all means to conform the government of the Church with that which he had seen in Geneva'.[50] The testimony of Spottiswoode, therefore, suggests not a divergence but rather a continuity in belief and purpose between Knox and Melville. The Earl of Morton, as a more strictly contemporary critic, also commented on what he claimed were Melville's 'new opiniones and owersie dreames anent the Kirk Discipline and Polecie', and he proceeded to criticise the 'conceats and owersie dreames' of those ministers who sought to imitate 'Genev discipline and lawes'.[51] Yet, Morton himself was no dispassionate observer of ecclesiastical developments. He fully appreciated the government's utter dependence on England for political support, and this, in turn, affected his attitude towards the church. After returning from a visit to England in 1571 where he had stressed the common religious cause, Morton became an enthusiastic supporter of the Leith episcopacy of 1572, and on assuming the regency later in 1572 he practised an ecclesiastical policy of 'conformity with England'. His intention was to curb the tradition of ecclesiastical independence which had grown up, and thereby to strengthen the authority of the crown whose initiative in ecclesiastical matters had suffered something approaching an eclipse since the Reformation. His programme therefore involved an assertion of royal supremacy over the church, which commissioners from the church in the spring of 1574 resolutely refused to concede; and he aimed at putting the government of the church into the hands

[50] Spottiswoode, *History*, ii, 200; R. Keith, *History of the Affairs of Church and State in Scotland* (Edinburgh, 1844–50), iii, 15 (citing Spottiswoode's MS History).
[51] Melville, *Diary*, 54, 68.

of bishops who were to be directly subordinate to the crown and not subject, as the Leith bishops promised to be, in spiritual matters to the oversight of the general assembly which Morton hoped to suppress.[52]

With Scotland under the rule of a 'godly prince', the Regent Morton believed that the assembly no longer served a necessary purpose and that it ought to surrender its powers to the crown in parliament and to bishops as delegates of the crown; he charged the assembly with convening illegally; he declined to attend or to send representatives, and preferred that the church should remit certain matters for determination to an ecclesiastical committee of the privy council. Such an undisguisedly erastian policy was plainly moulded on English practice where the Tudors had undermined convocation's traditional rôle as an independent ecclesiastical legislature. But in adapting English practice to suit Scottish circumstances, Morton was less than successful. His ecclesiastical programme was said by the English ambassador to have caused 'misliking' among the ministers, and this he attributed not to the appearance of Andrew Melville but, significantly, to Morton's own attempts to

'induce into the Church of Scotland, the liberty used by the magistrates and bishops of the Church of England, which they [the ministers] like not of, and so it stands between them as yet undecided. In the meanwhile, the Church fast holds her own. . . .'

Morton's policy of conformity with England had clearly met with opposition from the church. Not only was the church unwilling to accept the crown's supremacy in ecclesiastical matters, but the general assembly saw no sound reason to abdicate its responsibilities, and in March 1574 it responded to Morton's attack by justifying its permanence on the exalted grounds that it existed by divine right.[53]

Despite Spottiswoode's urgent advocacy to the contrary, the truth would seem to be that Melville's homecoming in the summer of 1574 took place only after the church had expressed its dissatisfaction with the Leith episcopacy – an arrangement which the assembly was prepared to tolerate merely as a temporary expedient. Equally, Melville's return occurred at a point only after the church had declared its opposition to Morton's policy of seeking to subordinate the church to the machinery of the state. Controversy and conflict, then, already

[52] Calderwood, History, iii, 306; Melville, Diary, 59, 61; BUK, i, 207; see also above, 251–2.
[53] BUK, i, 365, 392–4; RPC, ii, 346–9, 434–5; CSP Scot., v, no. 187; BUK, i, 292.

existed before the appearance of Andrew Melville. Melville's ideas, when he came to formulate them, were certainly contrary to Morton's plans for the church – he even declined an offer to become Morton's chaplain at court – but it would be hard to demonstrate convincingly that Melville's views were either novel or inconsistent with the declared intentions and priorities of the general assembly. Clearly, the abandonment of the view which attributes to Melville the whole responsibility for initiating controversy in the church is long overdue, for Melville was no ayatollah who engineered and masterminded a revolution in the kirk in defiance of the earlier generation of reformers. In practice, most of the earlier reformers, the veterans of 1560, concurred in drafting the contents of the Second Book of Discipline in 1578 – a document which is regarded, not inappropriately, as an authoritative statement of Scottish presbyterianism. None of this, then, would seem to suggest hostility to a presbyterian polity by such prominent earlier reformers as Erskine of Dun, the superintendent of Angus; William Christison, minister at Dundee; John Duncanson, the minister of Stirling; John Craig, then minister at Aberdeen; George Hay, commissioner in the north; and his brother, Andrew Hay, commissioner in the west and also rector of Glasgow University who, it was said, 'lyked never those bischopries, and wha specialie was the earnest suttar for Mr Andro Melvill'. David Lindsay, minister at Leith, who had earlier given support to the Leith settlement, also contributed to the Second Book of Discipline, as did two of the surviving authors of the First Book of Discipline – John Row, minister of Perth, and John Winram, superintendent of Fife. By contrast, it emerges that John Spottiswoode, the father of the archbishop, was one of the few leading reformers of 1560 who were not associated with producing the Second Book of Discipline in 1578.[54]

The evidence, therefore, would seem to indicate that most of the advocates of the Reformation polity in 1560 readily gave their support to the presbyterian programme of the Second Book of Discipline, designed to replace the financial expediency of the Leith episcopacy of 1572; and Melville's rôle lay not in advocating novel policies at variance with the principles of 1560 but rather in reinforcing the assembly's determination to resist Morton's own intended revolution in church government. In any event, the claim that the presbyterians were intent on disturbing good order in the church by effecting a revolution was one which was first voiced in England, not in Scotland. In the southern kingdom, Bishop Cox, writing to Zürich in 1573, denounced the presbyterians as 'innovators' and as 'disturbers of the state of the Anglican church', as no doubt they were; men 'who are labouring to bring about a revolution in the church'; and Bishop Sandys was equally convinced that the presbyterian challenge would not 'make for the advantage and peace of the church, but for her ruin and confusion'.[55]

To apply these observations to Scotland, however, would be less than meaningful. The essential difference between the two countries after all, was that Scotland had already devised a system of church government in the 1560s which, in essentials, the English presbyterians still sought to adopt. The Scottish polity of the 1560s had served as a model for the English presbyterians in 1572 in their campaign to transform the ancient structure in accordance with the pattern of the 'best reformed churches'. In Scotland, by contrast, the innovating policy was that of 'conformity with England', in which the Regent Morton, it was said, 'bure forwart his Bischopes, and pressed to his injunctiones and conformitie with Eingland'.[56] Disagreement and discord in the Scottish church arose only after the attempts of 1572 to merge the old ecclesiastical order with the new were seen to have the detrimental effect of undermining the reformed polity. Such a device adopted in the interests of securing additional finance was seen to carry with it implications fatal to the survival of a polity moulded in the tradition of 'the best reformed churches'. All this, then, goes far towards explaining the church's dissatisfaction with the Leith agreement of 1572.

It is, of course, well known that Melville both studied and taught at Geneva under Calvin's successor, Theodore Beza, at a point when Walter Travers and Thomas Cartwright, the two aspiring leaders of English presbyterianism, were also resident there; and the presumption is that they were acquainted, for Melville is known to have had a copy of Travers' treatise on presbyterianism, his *Ecclesiasticae disciplinae ... explicatio*, published in 1574, which Melville presented in 1575 to Alexander Arbuthnot, the principal of King's College in Old Aberdeen. Even so, in Scotland, unlike in England, no settled polity approved by the crown and confirmed by parliament had yet been achieved. As late as 1571, the Regent Mar had observed that 'the policie of the Kirk of Scotland is not perfyte'; in 1574, even

[55] *Zürich Letters*, i, 280–1; cf. 322.
[56] Melville, *Diary*, 60.

after the Convention of Leith, the Regent Morton was still aware of the need for 'setling of the Policie of the trew Reformit Kirk'; and, again, in 1576 Lord Glamis informed Beza that 'we are striving to establish some ecclesiastical constitution'.[57] In Scotland, therefore, no lasting agreement acceptable to both church and crown had yet been devised. After all, during the 1560s the reformed church had grown up independently of the civil power, without experiencing any need to tarry for the magistrate; and the First Book of Discipline, as a whole, though approved by a convention in January 1561, had never been recognised by parliament, except for the section on the admission of ministers which parliament approved in 1567.[58] Besides, the need for securing adequate finance had led reformers to depart, at least for a spell, from some of the ideas of the First Book of Discipline. On the other hand, if the reformed polity of the 1560s was denied parliamentary sanction, it is also true that, even in the aftermath of the civil war, the Leith arrangements of 1572 were equally devoid of parliamentary approval. This is all the more surprising, for in 1572 the expectations were that the Leith settlement would be submitted to parliament for ratification. That this was not achieved is a measure of the disagreement which emerged and of the general assembly's determination not to accept the settlement as a lasting solution.[59]

The critical reception which the assembly accorded the negotiations of 1572 is not least apparent in the formal protest issued by the assembly later in that year. By utilising (on a temporary basis) the pre-Reformation financial structure and titles until a 'more perfyte ordour' were established, the assembly made it clear that 'they intend not be useing sick names to ratifie, consent and aggrie to any kynd of Papistrie or superstition, and wishes rather the saids names to be changeit into uthers that are not slanderous or offensive'.[60] There may also have been a certain hesitation, as had been demonstrated in England, at protestants succeeding to such offices which their Roman Catholic opponents had so recently vacated.

The adoption from 1572 of the ancient diocesan framework, which the reformers in 1560 had considered to be both obsolete and an obstacle to effective pastoral oversight, also gave grounds for concern in the assembly, for the old structure looked like

[57] A. F. S. Pearson, *Thomas Cartwright and Elizabethan Puritanism, 1535–1603* (Cambridge, 1925), 142; Calderwood, *History*, iii, 164; *Wodrow Society Miscellany*, ed. D. Laing (Edinburgh, 1844), i, 290; *Scot. Hist. Soc. Misc.*, viii, 101.
[58] *CSP Scot.*, i, no. 959; Knox, *Works*, ii, 129–30, 257–8; *APS*, iii, 37 c. 5.
[59] *CSP Scot.*, iv, no. 149.
[60] *BUK*, i, 246.

replacing the streamlined provinces devised for the superintendents. Not only this, but none of the superintendents after
1572 was promoted to a bishopric; and if the superintendent was,
in effect, the 'godly bishop', as some have argued, it is at least
curious that those superintendents still active were not appointed
to any of the sees after 1572, for the earlier device which Queen
Mary had adopted of granting to Superintendent Carswell of
Argyll the revenues and property of the bishopric of the Isles in
1565 was not repeated in the case of other superintendents.[61]
Instead, dynastic appointments, often of an unreformed variety,
were made which enabled crown and nobility to indulge in their
traditional practice of milking the bishoprics; and it soon became
evident that the restricted form of episcopal election – consisting,
as it did, of crown nomination and capitular election, excluding
the wider Christian community from any voice – did not always
work to the church's advantage. This was fully revealed in the
failure of chapters to oppose improper or scandalous nominitions
advanced by the crown, and equally with their failure to prevent
the continued dilapidation of episcopal revenues. It was not for
nothing, therefore, that contemporary opinion criticised the
appointment of 'counterfet bischopis', as they were dubbed,
whose financial transactions were seen to benefit the crown and
nobility at the expense of the church in which they had
undertaken to serve.[62]

Amidst such criticisms, and at a point when the assembly
looked forward to supplanting the financial and political device
of the Leith episcopacy by what it called a 'more perfyte ordour',
Andrew Melville decided to return in the summer of 1574 after a
decade's study in both France and Switzerland – first at Paris and
Poitiers, and then at Geneva and Lausanne. His apparent
reluctance to leave Geneva scarcely suggests any missionary
enterprise to impose a new church order freshly imported from
Geneva. His return seems to have been the outcome of earlier
attempts to secure the services of Henry Scrimgeour, professor
of civil law at the Genevan academy. Scrimgeour, however,
declined an appointment at home on the grounds of advanced
years and a lack of familiarity with Scottish practice; but
Melville, as his kinsman, was persuaded to go home, with Beza's
blessing, so that Scotland might benefit from the teaching of a
distinguished scholar. Competition from St Andrews and
Glasgow led Melville to accept the principalship of the sadly
neglected Glasgow college whose fortunes he helped to restore,

[61] Watt, *Fasti*, 206; see above 220.
[62] Pitscottie, *Historie*, ii, 283; cf. Calderwood, *History*, ii, 146.

not least by the new teaching methods and specialised training which he offered in both Arts and Divinity. But six years later, he was transferred, 'sear against his will', as was claimed, to the job which he had earlier declined, as principal of St Mary's College in St Andrews, then newly reconstituted as a school of theology.[63]

The links between university and church were inevitably close and, as theology professor, Melville saw himself as occupying the ecclesiastical office of doctor or teacher commended in the Second Book of Discipline of 1578 as one of the four permanent ministries in the church; and it was as doctor that Melville claimed a right to sit on church courts. His appearance, though hardly as a commissioned member, in the assembly of 1574 which approved his appointment to Glasgow, resulted in his selection in the next assembly to two committees charged with examining the qualifications of the newly appointed bishop of Moray and the bishop-elect of Dunblane, two dynastic promotions of which the assembly was highly critical and not without justification: the new bishop of Moray promoted by his kinsman the Regent Morton was an illegitimate son of the Earl of Angus and had been an adventurer in the unreformed church as postulate of Arbroath Abbey; but he experienced great difficulty in satisfying the church of his suitability for the post. He was said to have spent 'a haill wintar mumling on his pretching af his peapers everie day at our morning prayers, and haid it nocht weill *par ceur* when all was done'; and the chapter which allowed his appointment to go forward without even examining his abilities (or lack of them) was severely rebuked by the assembly for its negligence and precipitate action.[64]

As a member of the committees formed to investigate the two bishops, Melville seems to have voiced, so far as is known, no disapproval of episcopacy as such: his task was to make recommendations, not to reform episcopacy out of existence; and if 'monie knew nocht yit the corruption and unlawfulness of that invention of men', diocesan episcopacy, as his nephew in 1600 was later to allege, Melville at this stage seems to have done very little to enlighten them. In any event, the statement can scarcely be taken at its face value, when it is observed that not only had contemporary comment already condemned the Leith bishops as 'counterfet bischopis' and identified the true bishop with the parish minister, but the assembly itself had shown

[63] J. Durkan and J. Kirk, *The University of Glasgow, 1451–1577* (Glasgow, 1977), 262ff., 334.
[64] *BUK*, i, 288, 300–4, 308, 315, 317, 320–1, 323, 325; Melville, *Diary*, 32.

singular solicitude in seeking to remedy and reform the abuses associated with the office.[65] Advancing years had evidently made Melville's nephew forgetful of these developments.

Melville's initial acquaintance with the Leith episcopate in the persons of Moray and Dunblane was hardly designed to create in his mind a favourable impression of episcopacy in Scotland, but he already had a foretaste of what lay ahead when journeying home in the company of Alexander Campbell whom Queen Mary had appointed bishop of Brechin in 1566; but Campbell had not yet performed the spiritual duties of a bishop and so was required by the assembly in 1575 to be trained in the work of a bishop by the existing superintendent. There are ample grounds, therefore, for believing that Melville's attitude towards the Leith episcopacy, which dated only from 1572, was influenced as much by a practical reappraisal of Scottish circumstances as by any dogmatic beliefs emanating from Geneva, where Theodore Beza had already made plain to Scots by 1572 his aversion to 'pseudo-episcopacy' as he termed diocesan episcopacy.[66]

It was, indeed, on the very practical grounds of whether 'the Bischops, *as they are now in the Kirk of Scotland*, hes thair function of the word of God or not, or if the Chapiter appointit for creating of them aucht to be tollerated in this reformed Kirk' that John Durie, an Edinburgh minister who had been present at the Convention of Leith, raised the whole issue of episcopacy in the assembly of 1575. Durie offered the assembly certain undisclosed 'opiniouns and reasons quhilks he and uther brether of his mynd hes to oppone agains the said office and name of a Bischop'. Melville is said to have supported Durie's criticisms and to have reaffirmed the earlier ideal which identified the preaching pastor with the New Testament bishop. The assembly, after further discussion, agreed that the name of bishop was common to all ministers; yet some ministers might still be chosen by the assembly to act not as diocesan bishops but, for a term, as visitors of more manageable districts.[67] Such a decision was a victory for Reformation principles; it also vindicated the continued existence of a dictinctively reformed church order; and it marked a defeat for the view which favoured merging the old ecclesiastical system with the new. The assembly's programme was clearly fatal to the survival of diocesan episcopacy, and the intention was to return to something like the system of

[65] Melville, *Diary*, 32, 48, 52; see above, 358.
[66] Melville, *Diary*, 42–3, 47; *BUK*, i, 318; Beza, *Epistolae*, 344–6; Knox, *Works*, vi, 614.
[67] *BUK*, i, 331, 340, 342–3, 352ff.; Spottiswoode, *History*, ii, 200–1 (my italics).

the 1560s when the assembly had largely entrusted the duties of oversight not to bishops as such but to ministers commissioned for a term to conduct visitations.

In 1576, the assembly put its plans into effect by charging all bishops to undertake a congregational ministry, to which most of them readily acceded, and also by assigning visitors to more than twenty areas designed to replace the thirteen dioceses, which the bishops on their own admission had been unable to administer to the assembly's satisfaction. The Leith episcopacy was thus to be eclipsed and, faced with the disintegration of his policy of conformity with England, the Earl of Morton is said to have asked the assembly to 'settle upon some form of government at which they would abide'. This led the assembly to formulate its programme in the Second Book of Discipline which took final shape by 1578.[68] The work was initiated by a series of regional committees established by the assembly and it is plain that although he was active in the cause, Melville's personal involvement was scarcely allowed to predominate. Not even his admiring nephew attributed to Melville any greater share in the authorship of the Book than the thirty or so other members of the assembly commissioned to take part in the 'work of establisching a perfyte ordour and policie in the Kirk'. And yet the myth persists that Melville wrote the Second Book of Discipline.[69]

The Book itself was largely the product of ecclesiastical dissatisfaction with the Leith agreement, for which it now offered a remedy; and it was essentially a succinct restatement of earlier ideals and priorities espoused by the reformers. It was a far more systematic document than the somewhat untidy First Book of Discipline, which the assembly as early as 1563 had felt to be in need of revision. It began by reasserting the distinction which the first reformers had drawn between the civil and ecclesiastical jurisdictions; it reiterated the church's repudiation of royal headship over the church; it defined the four Calvinist ministries which Knox's liturgy had recognised, of pastor, doctor, elder and deacon; and it distinguished three ecclesiastical courts within the nation – the local or district eldership, the provincial synod and general assembly. It duly acknowledged the duties of the Christian magistrate in defending and maintaining the church's liberty; but it condemned, as had reformers earlier, the whole system of ecclesiastical patronage and the hierarchical titles and offices borrowed from the medieval church, which were said to

[68] *BUK*, i, 349, 352–61; Spottiswoode, *History*, ii, 202.
[69] *BUK*, i, 362, 390.

'have na place in the reformit kirk'. The original programme of
sweeping aside the old structure and redistributing ecclesiastical
finances under the management of deacons, directly accountable
to congregations, was readopted. The system of benefices, it was·
expected, would disappear; resources would thus be set free for
the wider mission of the church, and the secularisation of
ecclesiastical property would finally be arrested. Congregational
election of ministers was preferred to nomination and presentation by a patron; the intrusion of unworthy candidates for the
ministry was deplored; and the supervision of admissions was
entrusted to the eldership which had responsibility for all
disciplinary matters.[70]

The Leith episcopacy was seen to have suffered from abuses
likely to recur unless the episcopal office was reformed, for 'we
can not allow the faissioun of thais new chosin Bischoppis,
nather of the Chapteris that are the electouris of thame to sic
office as they ar chosine'. True bishops, it was claimed, ought to
undertake a congregational ministry, and only church courts
were to have authority to entrust ministers with additional
powers of oversight. In all this, little novelty can be detected, for
it was strictly in line with the assembly's earlier pronouncements.
Certainly, the Second Book of Discipline found little need to
argue a case for 'equalitie of power' among ministers, since the
assembly itself had already conceded that point.[71]

Changes of emphasis rather than of principle are also apparent
in the recognition that an elder's calling was for life, that he
ought to serve on a permanent basis, but that he might still demit
his duties for a spell to attend to his outside occupation.
Deacons, however, were no longer to have a place on the
eldership, but this restriction had already been applied in at least
some areas, such as Perth where the kirk session was described
merely as 'the assembly of the ministers and elders'.[72] Similarly,
the decision to restrict voting membership of the general
assembly to 'ecclesiasticall personis' (that is, to ministers, doctors
and elders) was far less drastic a step than has sometimes been
imagined. There had, after all, been earlier attempts, notably in
1568, to redefine the assembly's voting membership, and the
proposal in the Second Book of Discipline by no means implied
that the assembly would lose its characteristic composition as a
meeting which reflected the dominant interests in society. As
Lord Glamis explained to Beza in 1576, it became an accepted

[70] Ibid., ii, 488–512.
[71] Ibid., 505–6; 491.
[72] Ibid., ii, 496, 501; Scottish Record Office, CH2/521/1; Perth Kirk Session
Records, 6 Sept. 1577.

practice after the Reformation to send to the assembly elders 'who are chosen among us yearly from the people and also from the nobility'. The idea in 1578 was simply that the burgesses, lairds and nobles who frequented assemblies should attend in future in their capacity as elders; and the device of restricting voting membership to 'ecclesiastical persons' did of course go some way towards obviating the criticism, voiced in the past, that the assembly constituted an illegal convocation of the king's lieges.[73]

One rather more significant change in emphasis is to be detected in the proposal that not every congregation need possess an eldership of its own; the intention was rather that several adjacent parishes should join together to form a communal eldership for the whole neighbourhood. Such a pattern, it is true, already existed in the general sessions of the larger burghs, but the idea here to group parishes together under a single eldership was very largely a response to a particular problem: in rural areas many parishes still lacked full-time ministers and in these circumstances it is hardly surprising that elderships often failed to develop; hence the need to associate these weaker churches with one possessing an established tradition of congregational government. At the same time, the need to strengthen ties between neighbouring churches – to permit conference among ministers and elders – was rendered all the more urgent by the assembly's plans to dispense with bishops.[74] The idea of the district eldership or presbytery, the germ of which is to be found in these proposals, firmly took root – firstly, with the assembly's decision in 1579 that the existing exercise for interpreting scripture should be adopted as a ready-made presbytery, and then in 1581 with the creation of thirteen model presbyteries, designed to act as examples to the rest of the country.[75] So, in the end, the presbytery did not replace the kirk session, as the Second Book of Discipline had intended, but formed an additional and complementary court in its own right.

The need for retaining the eldership had certainly been voiced by Beza as early as 1576 when Lord Glamis had sought his advice on such matters; and it was defended by Melville in 1578 against attack from the government, which advanced a counter claim to review and overrule sentences (including excommunication) delivered by the eldership.[76] Even so, beyond the modest

---

[73] *BUK*, ii, 500; i, 124; *Scot. Hist. Soc. Misc.*, viii, 105; Melville, *Diary*, 68.
[74] For further details, see J. Kirk, *The Second Book of Discipline*, 101–114.
[75] *BUK*, ii, 439, 482.
[76] *Scot. Hist. Soc. Misc.*, viii, 103; National Library of Scotland, Wodrow MSS, fol. vol. xlii, fo. 11r–v.

development of a common eldership or presbytery, which had its antecedents in earlier Scottish practice, there was singularly little originality in the presbyterian programme; and it would be hard to point to any feature of these proposals which was not in accord with the beliefs of earlier reformers. After all, the central themes of the Second Book of Discipline had first found expression in the church of John Knox, and cannot fairly be said to have been introduced by Andrew Melville whose influence lay rather in applying and defending earlier strands of reformed thought at a time when the crown was attempting to regain that control and directive in ecclesiastical affairs which it had lost at the Reformation.

Insofar as the Second Book of Discipline was a reapplication of Reformation principles, it is not surprising that it met a fate similar to that of the First Book of Discipline: it failed to secure support from crown and parliament. The comprehensive claims advanced in regard both to patrimony and to ecclesiastical independence were thus denied statutory recognition. Clearly, the form of government devised for the church was not readily to be divorced from the values attached to the structure of society and politics. The assembly might declare in 1580 that episcopacy was abolished by eliminating bishops from ecclesiastical administration, but the crown continued to assert its legal right to provide candidates to the bishoprics, men who possessed at least the title of bishop, and so were thus entitled to take their places as one of the three estates in parliament, 'to alter or wholly uproot which would be most perilous to the commonwealth'.[77] Besides, both crown and nobility had a financial as well as a political interest in maintaining a system of ecclesiastical patronage which the assembly was intent on subverting.

The assembly had committed the church to the programme of the Second Book of Discipline, which it had endorsed and registered among its acts, but there had not yet emerged within the church an organised opposition to that programme in its entirety. By the 1580s, however, the royal and episcopal challenge to presbyterianism became manifest, particularly so in 1584, during what has been termed the 'anti-presbyterian dictatorship' which characterised the Earl of Arran's conservative administration. Arran's government was formed in reaction to the preceding regime of the ultra-protestant Ruthven lords who for their ten months in power had shown sympathy to the presbyterians, but with the flight to England of the lords and leading presbyterian ministers – including Melville – the way was

[77] *Scot. Hist. Soc. Misc.*, viii, 101.

open for the new government to formulate (and to attempt to impose) a fresh ecclesiastical policy devised in part by Patrick Adamson, the archbishop of St Andrews, who at that time returned to prominence.[78]

Adamson owed his patronage to the Earl of Morton whose chaplain he once had been, and he proved a compliant instrument for advancing royal policy. After his elevation to the archbishopric by 1576, Adamson had initially declined to acknowledge his subordination to the general assembly. He sought to practise conformity with England and seized the political opportunity afforded by Arran's conservative regime of undertaking a diplomatic mission to England in 1583 where he had talks with the English government and archbishops, at a point when Whitgift, the new primate, was preparing to launch an attack on English nonconformity.[79]

While in London, Adamson had undertaken a refutation of the presbyterian programme of the Second Book of Discipline, which he wished to see replaced by an ecclesiology which might best be described as erastian in outlook, royal and episcopal in form and essentially 'Anglican' in spirit. He believed that it belonged to the prince and not to the assembly to assign a form of polity for the church since the prince's judgment was sovereign in ecclesiastical and temporal matters alike. Such a view contrasted sharply with Reformation principles and with the presbyterian programme. Under the supremacy of the crown, bishops – the archbishop claimed – ought to assume control of the church, become permanent moderators of church courts, conduct visitations, and they alone might ordain candidates to the ministry. (The restrictive approach advocated here was quite out of keeping with the flexible attitude of reformers and also with much earlier practice; and it is noteworthy that reliance on such an exclusive form of episcopal oversight had never been a feature of the church's polity since 1560.) Doctors were to play no part in church government and might preach only under licence from a bishop; elders were declared to have no scriptural foundation; and presbyteries were condemned as a source of 'great confusion in the kirk, and an occasioun of continuall seditioun'. The general assembly was to be denied any right to

---

[78] BUK, ii, 487–8; Calderwood, History, iii, 650ff., 716, 751, 763.

[79] BUK, i, 165, 367, 376–7, 385–6; ii, 433; CSP Scot., vi, nos. 684, 691, 696, 703, 705, 707; Melville, Diary, 141; The Historie and Life of King James the Sext, ed. T. Thomson (Edinburgh, 1825), 205; Melville of Halhill, Memoirs, ed. A. F. Steuart (London, 1929), 274–5; G. Donaldson, 'The attitude of Whitgift and Bancroft to the Scottish Church', Trans. Royal Hist. Soc., 4th ser., xxiv (1942), 95–115.

formulate its own enactments except by licence of the prince, and it was to meet only when summoned by the crown for 'a great and weightie occasioun'. Further restrictions in composition were designed to reduce the assembly to a 'conventioun generall of clergie', properly termed; elders and laymen were to be excluded, for the proposal was that the assembly should consist only of 'bishops and clerks' subservient to the crown in parliament.[80] In effect, Adamson's proposals left no room for such regularly constituted aesmblies as had met in the past. The composition of assemblies was to be transformed; their traditional independence was to end, and the elective office of moderator was to disappear.

What Adamson aimed at, in short, was a clerical oligarchy operating under the auspices of the crown; and the criticism that Melville was responsible for narrowing the assembly's composition is somewhat misplaced when it is considered that his episcopal opponent intended to alter the assembly beyond all recognition. As was to be expected, ecclesiastical patronage and the system of benefices were strenuously defended, and the management of ecclesiastical revenues by deacons was repudiated as a 'preposterous imitation of the primitive kirk, without anie kinde of reasoun'.[81] The appeal of his proposals, it is evident, was aimed at the crown and aristocracy who could scarcely fail to be attracted to a programme calculated to consolidate their social and political status in the network of local societies which formed the nation.

Yet the whole drift of Adamson's argument took too little account of Scottish Reformation thought. The tone and emphasis of his proposals were undisguisedly English – not surprising, for his articles were initially formulated for consumption outside Scotland and the English primate was among the recipients. Even so, the substance of Adamson's thinking was given tangible form during Arran's regime in the 'Black Acts' of 1584, which asserted the crown's supremacy over the church, approved of episcopal government and discharged all assemblies from meeting without the king's special licence. The church courts were only to operate at the discretion of the crown and, although kirk sessions were permitted to meet, presbyteries were proscribed and no licence was issued to allow the assembly to meet for the duration of Arran's rule. The assembly, accustomed to meet twice yearly, was thus placed in abeyance and the king became, as Adamson explained, a 'bishop of bishops, and universall bishop within his

[80] Calderwood, *History*, iv, 53–5; 145–6; Melville, *Diary*, 196.
[81] Calderwood, *History*, iv, 55.

realme'; appeals from bishops were to be directed solely to the king.[82]

By the 1580s, then, two clearly defined and contradictory programmes had emerged within the Scottish church, and each had its parallel in the programme of the corresponding party in the Church of England. Adamson and Whitgift shared an attitude which Melville, Cartwright and Travers opposed. But, by the 1590s, the Scottish presbyterians had gained ascendancy in their church, which their English counterparts failed to achieve, not least perhaps because in the northern kingdom, where the power of the crown was weaker than in England, the church from 1560 had sought to follow the example of 'the best reformed churches'.

The conclusion which emerges from a survey of the evidence would seem to be that the Reformation and presbyterian programmes embodied in the First and Second Books of Discipline were based on principles irreconcilable with the defence of episcopal government advanced by Archibshop Adamson in 1583. The two former programmes were effected from below and in defiance of the crown and statute law. Their decisive rejection of a hierarchy in the church remained at variance with the structures of a hierarchical society whose dominant interests continued to favour an episcopal system, imposed and directed from above, which seemed better adapted to satisfy, and indeed to safeguard, the values of the crown and nobility – so long, that is, as these interests remained complementary and not contradictory.

[82] APS., iii, 292–303; Calderwood, History, iv, 258–67.

10

The survival of ecclesiastical patronage after the Reformation

I

The medieval inheritance:

The initial success of the Reformation in 1560 raised in particularly acute form the entire issue of the fate of ecclesiastical property. The trend for long enough – since at least the Indult of 1487 – had been towards the complete secularisation of this very extensive patrimony.[1] After 1560, the protestant reformers, it is true, sought to arrest (and even to reverse) this process with plans for a drastic and comprehensive reorganisation of ecclesiastical finances.[2] Yet the sixteenth-century descendants of pious ancestors who once had lavished so much wealth on the church – property, in principle, inalienable in canon law – were far more intent on recouping and then retaining something of what had been lost in earlier centuries to the 'dead hand'[3] of the church.

During the sixteenth century, the crown and nobility, the lairds and some tenants on ecclesiastical estates had all gained access, by one means or another, to the patrimony of the church at every level. This was achieved through the crown's increasingly onerous taxation of the clergy and through the diversion of

[1] G. Donaldson, *The Scottish Reformation* (Cambridge, 1960), 37–43.

[2] J. K. Cameron, *The First Book of Discipline* (Edinburgh, 1972), 108–13, 156–64; *The Booke of the Universall Kirk: Acts and Proceedings of the General Assemblies of the Kirk of Scotland, 1560–1618 [BUK]*, ed. T. Thomson, 3 vols. and appendix vol. (Edinburgh, 1839–45), i, 5, 7, 21–3, 59–60, 70, 82–4, 107–8, 127–8.

[3] *The Acts of the Parliaments of Scotland [APS]*, edd. T. Thomson and C. Innes, 12 vols. (Edinburgh, 1814–75), i, 612, 614, 725; *The Practicks of Sir James Balfour of Pittendreich*, ed. P. G. B. McNeill, 2 vols. (Edinburgh, 1962–3), i, 142–3. In March 1390/1, parliament had confirmed an act of mortmain prohibiting grants of property to the church without the crown's express consent (*APS*, i, 577).

ecclesiastical property to laymen by the feuing of church lands, the leasing of teinds, the reservation to laymen of pensions from parochial and episcopal revenues, and the appointment to abbacies of an *oeconomus* as steward, or of a commendator, chosen from a particular noble family, as titular head of a religious house ostensibly for the purpose of administering the monastic revenues. The church's wealth, estimated to have yielded £400,000 in annual revenues (ten times that of the crown),[4] had been subject to systematic exploitation in the decades preceding 1560; and it proved far from easy to stem the constant drain of ecclesiastical resources for purely secular purposes in the years immediately after 1560.

As the largest owner of property in the kingdom, the pre-Reformation church also possessed and exercised an extensive patronage of ecclesiastical appointments, often to the exclusion of those laymen whose ancestors had once founded or endowed parish churches and who had thus acquired the right of presenting candidates of their own choice to benefices so endowed. During the middle ages, the appropriation of parish churches to higher ecclesiastical institutions – to collegiate kirks, university colleges, cathedrals and particularly to religious houses – meant that the property rights of patronage, unless specifically reserved, were usually transferred along with the inheritance of the parish so conveyed to the appropriating institution which, on acquiring the property and patronage of a parish church, became responsible by means of the ensuing vicarage settlement for the presentation of a vicar to take charge of the cure of souls and service of the appropriated parish. The benefices of very few parish churches (only 14%)[5] remained independent and unappropriated by the time of the Reformation; and it is safe to conclude that the late medieval church engrossed to itself the patronage of the vast majority of the country's thousand or so parishes. Only at the higher – and more lucrative – levels was the crown successful in its bid to challenge the church's (or rather the clergy's) near monopoly of making ecclesiastical appointments without express regard to lay interests.

Apart from the prelacies, however, where the crown had long established its rights of nomination, and with the exception of chaplainries, altarages and certain prebends where laymen retained their rights of patronage, it does emerge that, on the eve

---

[4] G. Donaldson, *Scotland: James V to James VII* (Edinburgh, 1965), 133; *Accounts of the Collectors of Thirds of Benefices, 1561–1572*, ed. G. Donaldson (Edinburgh, 1949), xv, 170–1.

[5] I. B. Cowan, *The Parishes of Medieval Scotland* (Edinburgh, 1967), v.

of the Reformation, the bulk of ecclesiastical patronage, particularly at the lower levels, still remained firmly entrenched in the possession of churchmen, or at least in the control of ecclesiastical institutions whose titular head, in the case of monasteries, may or may not have been a fully ordained ecclesiastic. The extent to which ecclesiastical patronage had become concentrated in the hands of churchmen can be readily gauged when it is recalled that among the numerous parsonages and vicarages appropriated as permanent unions by 1560 more than 470 benefices pertained to religious houses, over 460 were united to cathedrals, two dozen were assigned to university colleges, some 90 parochial benefices belonged to collegiate kirks and three permanent unions had been made to independent hospitals.[6] In most cases, the patronage of the benefices was likewise annexed, though there are obviously qualifications to be made. For a start, by the fifteenth century it had become not uncommon for laymen to reserve to themselves the patronage of parochial benefices newly erected into prebends of cathedral and collegiate kirks; and where monasteries were held *in commendam*, the titular with the chapter's consent might make presentations to the appropriated churches.[7] Some commendators even appear to have been in minor orders, but this, it would seem, was merely a technicality designed to strengthen their claim to office.

It nonetheless remains something of a curiosity that, at a time when laymen were gaining control of church lands and revenues as never before, there was still little indication of any widespread surrendering to laymen by clergy of the patronage of ecclesiastical, and particularly of parochial, benefices. Before the Reformation, it was certainly unusual for feuars of ecclesiastical estates to acquire the patronage of parish churches which, instead, continued to reside with the superiority of the land in the possession of the ecclesiastical authorities. Laymen, therefore, were still denied a larger say in the selection of parish priests – indeed their participation in appointments may even have diminished – for in only a small minority of parishes in 1559 was the patron still a layman. After all, only 148 out of 1,028 parishes remained unappropriated at the Reformation;[8] and even here the patronage of unattached parishes was not entirely in the possession of laymen. At least 28 independent parsonages lay within episcopal patronage; the patronage of three further

---

[6] These calculations are derived from an analysis of the lists provided in Cowan, *Parishes*.

[7] *Calendar of the Laing Charters*, ed. J. Anderson (Edinburgh, 1899), no. 727.

[8] Cowan, *Parishes*, v, 226.

unappropriated parsonages belonged to religious houses;[9] and of the remainder a proportion pertained to the crown, particularly after the annexation of the lordship of the Isles; all of which amply illustrates how little scope existed before 1560 for laymen to influence parochial appointments by presenting candidates of their own choice. Not many laymen, therefore, were likely to be unduly offended by the reformers' contention in 1560 that the 'election of Ministers in this cursed Papistrie hath altogether bene abused' or by their insistence that 'it apertaineth to the people and to every severall Congregation to elect their Minister'. Indeed, the reformers' aim of abolishing ecclesiastical patronage and of subverting the ancient ecclesiastical structure had obvious attractions for those laymen who wished to eliminate the clerical stranglehold of appointments and to achieve a measure of congregational government.[10]

Although as a legal entity, the old financial system of benefices survived the Reformation and, indeed, continued to exist alongside the new structure of the reformed church which had come into operation by 1560, there was still little or no indication that the two structures might ultimately merge through the systematic appointment to benefices, as they became vacant, of ministers serving in the reformed church. Even though parliament in August 1560 had abolished papal jurisdiction and the celebration of mass, existing benefice holders, irrespective of their religious persuasion, remained in possession of their livings and continued to enjoy the fruits, apart from a portion which they were obliged to assign to the reformed ministry for its support.[11] Similarly, the intention of reformers in 1560 was not to gain access to the benefices, as they stood, but to dismantle the old financial system, abolish patronage, and to reallocate the church's patrimony on a radically different basis by separating the spirituality, consisting mainly of teinds, from the temporality, or lands and their rents. The prospect, therefore, that the two ecclesiastical structures might eventually coalesce remained, at best, remote; and reformers in their Book of Discipline disregarded the appeal by the primate and papal legate to maintain for their use 'the old policy, which had been the work of many ages'.[12]

[9] These figures are based on the lists on the lists in Cowan, *Parishes*.

[10] *First Book of Discipline*, 96ff.

[11] *APS*, ii, 526–35; *Thirds of Benefices*, ixff; *Register of the Privy Council of Scotland* [*RPC*], edd. J. H. Burton and D. Masson, 1st ser. 14 vols. (Edinburgh, 1877–98), i, 201–2.

[12] *First Book of Discipline*, 94, 96ff, 108ff, 115ff, 156ff, 174ff; J. Spottiswoode, *The History of the Church of Scotland*, ed. M. Russell, 3 vols. (Edinburgh, 1851), i, 372.

It is, of course, true that the clergy who conformed to the new regime in 1560 and who accepted service in the reformed church used their benefices in the interests of the new faith, but the majority of clergy, declining to conform, continued to draw their revenues without undertaking service of any kind; and it is plain that the immediate beneficiary of the survival of the ancient financial structure was not the reformed church but the crown which, in the absence of any direct competitor, fell heir to a great deal of patronage formerly controlled and administered by churchmen. As continued countenance of papal provision was hard to reconcile with the protestant ascendancy of 1560, it was easy for the crown to extend its traditional rights of nomination to the prelacies into something more comprehensive. Before the Reformation, most monasteries – with some notable exceptions like Lindores – were held *in commendam*. Not even the Book of Discipline advanced any claims for the reformed church to inherit monastic temporalities, and after 1560 the crown assumed full power to appoint commendators and *oeconomi* with 'the same forme, vigoure and strenth in all respectis as thai micht have gevin upone the bullis, provisioun and executorialis gife thai hade bene obtenit in the courte of Rome'.[13]

In some respects, this development was the culmination of a tendency which had emerged at least as early as June 1548 when Marion Hamilton received from the crown a gift of the priory of Eccles, without mention of papal rights. The circumstances surrounding this grant, however, are complicated, for the prioress ultimately secured papal provision *de novo*, at the petition of the crown, a year later, in May 1549, which suggests that an earlier provision had been made at an unknown date. At any rate, the gift under the privy seal seems to have antedated papal provision. No less remarkable was the crown's contention in 1557 that, with the death of James Stewart as commendator, Kelso abbey was 'becuming in oure soverane ladies handis', thereby enabling the crown to appoint an *oeconomus* to administer the spirituality and temporality of the abbacy.[14] Such comprehensive powers extended well beyond the crown's customary right to dispose of the temporality of abbacies during vacancies. It is, of course, true that when it came to disposing of the property of Pluscarden shortly after the Reformation, Queen

[13] E.g. *Register of the Privy Seal of Scotland [RSS]*, edd. M. Livingstone *et al.*, 8 vols. (Edinburgh, 1908–82), v, no. 845.

[14] *RSS*, iii, no. 2823; v, nos. 227, 276; Vatican Archives, Reg. Supp., 2673, fo. 125v; 2661, fo. 4v; *Essays on the Scottish Reformation*, ed. D. McRoberts (Glasgow, 1962), 45.

Mary noticeably reverted to immemorial usage and claimed merely that the temporality of the monastery was at the crown's disposal 'sen the deceis of umquhile Maister Alexander Dunbar, last prioure thairof', thus allowing the whole temporality to be assigned to Lord Seton, in April 1561, as 'commissar and iconymus of the said prioure'. Yet it is equally true, a mere four months later, that Mary granted Balmerino to John Hay, parson of Monymusk, with power to uplift all its revenues, teinds and temporality alike. In the former grant, admittedly Seton was to enjoy the revenues only until the vacancy was filled, whereas in the second gift, Hay was entitled to possess the fruits for life, though his status was evidently considered to be that of *oeconomus*, and not explicitly that of commendator as such, 'albeit he be nocht specialie providit thairof in the . . . courte of Rome, or uthirwayis namit yconomos thairto'.[15] All this became a pattern for some future grants.

In March 1561/2, William Cranstoun, provost of Seton collegiate church, received a gift of the priory of Pluscarden 'with all and sindrie benefices, rentis, teyndis, fischeingis, woddis, mylnis and all utheris commoditeis belangand thairto, for all the dayis of his liffe, vacand be deceis of umquhile Alexander, last prioure and possessoure of the samin, pertening to oure soverane ladeis nominatioun and dispositioun be the privilege of hir croun'. In the week preceding the crown's gift, Cranstoun had also obtained provision at Rome, which was scarcely surprising as he was understood to be 'a great favorer of papystes' and had been threatened with excommunication by St Andrews kirk session. Indeed, in his supplication to the pope he described himself as doctor of theology, principal of St Salvator's college in St Andrews, 'ac vere religionis et orthodoxe fidei necnon sedis apostolicae in regno Scotie protector'. In the end, however, he owed his title to the queen's grant, 'quhilk gift oure soverane ladie declaris to be als sufficient to the said Maister Williame for his liftyme as and he hade obtenit bullis of the said priorie'. His tenure of the priory, however, was short, and within six months it was reported that he was 'happelie ded in thys myschevous worlde'.[16] John Hay obtained a similar gift of Monymusk from

[15] *RSS*, v, nos. 819, 845.
[16] Ibid., v, no. 1008; *The Works of John Knox*, ed. D. Laing, 6 vols. (Edinburgh, 1846–64), vi, 144; *Register of the Minister, Elders and Deacons of the Christian Congregation of St Andrews* [RStAKS], ed. D. H. Fleming, 2 vols. (Edinburgh, 1889–90), i, 169–70; *Calendar of State Papers relating to Scotland and Mary, Queen of Scots* [CSP Scot.], edd. J. Bain et al., 13 vols. (Edinburgh, 1898–1969), i, nos. 1031, 1139; Vatican Archives, Reg. Supp., 3022, fo. 167r-v; 3032, fo. 36v; 3040, fo. 88r; 3044, fo. 8r.

the crown in March 1561/2 with the right to enjoy for life 'all and sindrie fruitis, proventis, emolimentis, teyndis, grassumes, mailes and dewteis of quhatsumevir landis perteninig to the said priorie usit and wount to be payit to the priouris, commendataris or conventis of oure said priorie in ony tyme bigane', though his title was expressly understood to be that of 'yconomus'. There was, however, no mention of the spirituality or teinds being conveyed in a somewhat different grant of January 1562/3 to the Earl of Argyll of two thirds of the revenues of Coupar Angus abbey (the remaining third being reserved to the crown) which the earl was to enjoy 'als frelie as the said umquhile Donald, last abbot, or ony utheris provydit thairto of befoir mycht have done in tymes bygane'.[17]

The device of appointing *oeconomi*, adopted in certain earlier grants, was repeated in December 1563 when Sir Richard Maitland of Lethington and his son, John, were jointly made 'yconomusis, factouris and chalmerlanis of hir hienes abbacie of Hadingtoun', vacant on the death of Elizabeth Hepburn last prioress, with power to 'dispone and apply' the revenues and teinds for 'thair awne use at thair plesour', and again, in January 1563/4 when John Spens of Condy, the queen's advocate, was chosen *oeconomus* of Coldingham, 'now vacand and being in hir mejesteis handis be deceis of umquhile hir hienes bruder, Johne, Lord Dernlie and commendatore of the said priourie'.[18] Nor was it always easy to distinguish the office of an *oeconomus* appointed, sometimes for life, to act as an administrator or steward of a vacant abbacy from that of a titular abbot or commendator; and although the forms of appointment differed somewhat in the styles adopted, it is nonetheless evident after 1560 that the offices, in practice, were sometimes apt to be confused.

Other vacant abbacies were also at the crown's disposal. In May 1565, the queen granted to Gilbert Brown, 'sumtyme professit bruthir of the abbacy', the whole abbacy of Sweetheart with its revenues, 'kirks, personages and vicarages, teind schaves and utheris teindis', which Brown 'as abbot' was to enjoy, subject to the reservation of certain fruits to the former abbot as usufructary. Again, in July 1565, the Earl of Atholl received a gift of the whole fruits of the abbey of Coupar Angus, 'as the abbot thairof mycht have done' until such time as the vacancy was filled and 'ane abbote be lauchfullie provydit thairto'; and he was

---

[17] *RSS*, v, nos. 1009, 1198.
[18] Ibid., v, nos. 1510, 1524.

further accorded the right of choosing an *oeconomus* to uplift the fruits 'alsweile of the teindis and spiritualitie thairof as of the temporalitie'.[19] Further dispositions of abbatial property followed. With the death of Abbot Quintin Kennedy, Allan Stewart obtained a gift in July 1565 of Crossraguel, with the churches and benefices annexed; in the same month, James Drummond received 'the abbacy and benefice' of Inchaffray on the demission of the commendator, Alexander Gordon, bishop of Galloway; in September 1565, Alexander Seton was promoted to Pluscarden; William Rutherford acquired St Mary's Isle in September 1566; Alexander Colville obtained Culross in February 1566/7; and Marion Maclean was promoted to the nunnery of Iona in the same month.[20] Similarly, the nunneries of St Bothans, Coldstream, North Berwick and Eccles were bestowed by the crown on titular prioresses.[21] Yet, when it came to disposing of the dependent priory of Lesmahagow, a cell of the Tironensian monks of Kelso, the crown simply granted the priory in October 1561 as 'ane pension' to James Cunningham, the Earl of Glencairn's son, with 'jurisdictioun spirituall and temporall' over the lands, teinds, parsonages and vicarages, as if he had been provided at Rome, though the matter of a pension of £190 from the mother house had earlier been the subject of a supplication to the Vatican in January 1559/60 on behalf of Cunningham, described as a scholar in Glasgow diocese, as he was then studying at Glasgow University.[22]

Pensions of various sizes were also assigned by the crown to individuals from the fruits of vacant houses, notably from the Charterhouse of Perth in November 1561 'during oure soverane ladyis will'.[23] The property of friaries was similarly understood to be at the crown's disposal. In February 1561/2, the privy council had assigned the buildings and revenues of the friaries to the town councils of the burghs, specifying those of Aberdeen, Elgin, Inverness and Glasgow, for the maintenance of 'hospitaliteis, scolis and utheris godlie usis'. Yet, as late as October 1566, the crown was prepared to make a grant of the friary of Peebles,

[19] Ibid., v, nos. 2072, 2229.

[20] Ibid., v, nos. 2187, 2211, 2315, 3078, 3201, 3255.

[21] *Register of the Great Seal of Scotland* [*RMS*], edd. J. M. Thomson *et al.*, 11 vols. (Edinburgh, 1912; 1882–1914), iv, no. 1716; *RSS*, v, nos. 2682, 2912, 2917, 3041.

[22] *RSS*, v, no. 871; Vatican Archives, Reg. Supp., 2978, fos. 272v–273r; J. Durkan and J. Kirk, *The University of Glasgow, 1451–1577* (Glasgow, 1977), 233 and n. 63.

[23] *RSS*, v, no. 915.

for individual profit, to Thomas Hay, brother of Lord Yester.[24] The friars themselves, like the monks and nuns, were entitled, of course, still to receive their 'portions' or pensions, but once again this was supervised by the crown collectory after the Reformation; and eventually as survivors died, both commendators and the crown were able to grant the portions as favours and rewards.[25]

II

Royal rights asserted:

Although no detailed legislation survives to illuminate the process whereby the crown assumed greater power after 1560 to dispose of ecclesiastical property, the crown's peculiarly comprehensive rights over certain prelacies are apparent as early as 1562 when Queen Mary asserted a claim that 'the haill patronage of the kirk landis and benefices pertening to the abbacie of Haliruidhous pertenit and pertenis to her hienes as patrimonye of hir croune', despite the fact that her half brother, Robert Stewart, was already commendator, 'providit he hir hienes lauchfullie thairto'.[26] It may indeed emerge that the consolidation of such powers in the hands of the crown was no more than the culmination of a trend, already evident before 1560, whereby the crown, in effect, was assuming further control over monastic patronage by making presentations to a number of appropriated churches. It is clear that out of some 120 presentations by the crown in the decade before 1560 more than 15 pertained to churches annexed to monasteries and whose patronage lay with the religious communities.[27] In each case, the presentation was made by the crown during an episcopal vacancy (which may or may not have been coincidental) and further investigation is required to establish conclusively whether, at this point, the crown continued merely to claim its traditional right to present *sede vacante* to benefices of which the bishop himself was patron or whether it sought to extend its powers during episcopal vacancies to include all benefices in ecclesiastical patronage.[28]

---

[24] *RPC*, i, 202; *RSS*, v, no. 3097. For further examples of the disposition of the property of friaries, see *RSS*, v, nos. 1218, 1275, 1956, 1980, 2009, 2109.

[25] *Thirds of Benefices*, 97–8, 153–4, 157, 212, 220, 228, 256–7, 281; *RSS*, v, nos. 220, 967, 1007, 1011, 1963, 2016, 2178, 2265, 2268, 2830, 2863, 3488; vii, nos. 1049, 1987, 2491.

[26] *RSS*, v, no. 965.

[27] This is based on an examination of the relevant entries, from 1549, in *RSS*, iv and v.

[28] G. Donaldson, 'Crown Rights in Episcopal Vacancies', *Scottish Historical Review*, xlv (1966), 27–35; I. B. Cowan, 'Patronage, Provision and Reservation, Pre-Reformation Appointments to Scottish Benefices', in *The Renaissance and Reformation in Scotland*, edd. I. B. Cowan and D. Shaw (Edinburgh, 1983), 91.

As holders of benefices continued in uninterrupted possession of their livings after 1560, vacancies occurred only through the normal process of demission, death, or, occasionally, escheat. Most benefices annexed to religious houses continued, therefore, to be occupied. Nor is there evidence in the register of the privy seal for the 1560s (other than a gift of the vicarage of Kinghorn Easter in October 1566)[29] of any grants by Mary to parochial benefices pertaining to Holyrood, whose patronage the crown then claimed. Even so, it is clear that the queen considered the patronage of Inverkip, appropriated to Paisley abbey, and that of Bourtie, annexed to St Andrews priory, to belong at that point to the crown, and not to be exercised by the religious houses, as she bestowed both vicarages by simple gift in April 1565 and April 1566 respectively.[30] Again, the vicarage of Dunning, which belonged to Inchaffray, was understood by the crown in April 1566 to be 'now pertening to oure soveranis and being at thair hienes gift and disposition' through the death of the last holder. Yet the candidate to whom the crown granted the vacant benefice in April was evidently unsuccessful in securing his title, for eight months later in December the queen readily acknowledged and confirmed the rights to the benefice of another candidate by virtue of 'the donatioun, provisioun and collatioun ordinar' by the chancellor and vicar general of Dunblane in May 1566. During the vacancy of the see, the vicar general evidently considered that the vicarage was at his disposal as the newly appointed commendator of Inchaffray had still to receive institution to the abbacy. Again, the commendator of Kelso, who duly presented his own candidate, Mark Ker, to the vicarage of Linton, vacant in 1562, found his efforts frustrated by the queen's action in appointing another, Mr John Balfour. In the end, the claims of the competitors were resolved in 1564 when Balfour agreed to demit the vicarage in the queen's hands in favour of Ker, the commendator's client; but the right of appointment was held to reside with the crown, not the commendator.[31]

When the crown chose to appoint commendators and titular prioresses after 1560, there appears to have been no specific recognition of the inclusion in such grants of the 'advocation' (or advowson, in English usage) of appropriated churches, until a

[29] *RSS*, v, no. 3093.
[30] Ibid., v, nos. 2029, 2761.
[31] Ibid., v, nos. 2743, 3155; *Charters, Bulls and other documents relating to the Abbey of Inchaffray*, ed. W. A. Lindsay (Edinburgh, 1908), 160–5, 246–8; SRO, CS7/31, Register of Acts and Decreets of the Court of Session, fos. 6v–7v; *RSS*, v, nos. 1223, 1657.

grant of 1565 expressly acknowledged one commendator's right 'to dispoun all benefices pertening thairto to qualifeit personis sa oft as thai sall vaik',[32] phraseology which Mary does not seem to have repeated in other grants. In some titles, the right of presentation may have been assumed to be incidental to the conveying of 'all and sindrie benefices'[33] with the rest of the abbatial property, but in other titles any mention of benefices or churches is omitted;[34] and *oeconomi* were apparently not accorded the right of exercising the patronage of the appropriated churches.[35] Not only this, but in succeeding decades, the crown acted rather as if the patronage of practically every benefice annexed to the religious houses had come into the patrimony of the crown and, on this basis, proceeded to make presentations to the benefices of appropriated churches.[36]

Even so, royal power over the religious houses – so evident in the assumed power of the crown to appoint commendators – was exercised in a manner which did not entirely disregard the interests of other parties. The crown permitted some appointments to commendatorships to be made on the recommendation of crown servants, whose service the crown wished to reward by promoting a kinsman to a particular religious house. In other instances, the crown allowed the right of nomination to devolve on another party. Queen Mary recognised her mother's gift to Lord Erskine of Cambuskenneth abbacy with the right to nominate an abbot or commendator and, in his favour, provided Adam Erskine as commendator in 1562. In that year, too, Mary granted Dundrennan anew to John Maxwell of Terregles, with 'sufficient title thairto', and 'in his name' promoted Edward Maxwell to the abbacy; and in 1565 Francis Stewart received the commendatorship of Coldingham, with power 'to nominate and elect ane prioure or priouris of the said abbacy als oft as he sall think expedient', though by February 1566/7 the priory had once more come into the hands of the crown 'ob decessum Johannis ultimi commendatarii ejusdem, seu per resignationem Francisci Stewart filii legitimi dicti Johannis', and so was granted for life to John Maitland, son of Sir Richard Maitland of Lethington.[37]

Indeed, in order to safeguard the customary rights enjoyed by some noble houses to nominate their own candidates as abbot or

[32] *RSS*, v, no. 2182.
[33] Ibid., v, no. 1008; cf., nos. 1066, 1656, 2072, 2187, 2211, 2912, 2917, 3041, 3078, 3201, 3212; *RMS*, iv, nos. 1716, 1765.
[34] *RSS.*, v, nos. 1101, 2315, 3255.
[35] Ibid., v, nos. 845, 1009, 1510, 1524.
[36] See below, 393.
[37] *RSS.*, v, nos. 1066, 1101, 2182; *RMS*, iv, no. 1765.

prior, the crown was even disposed in March 1565/6 to annul its
earlier grant of the nunnery of Haddington to William Maitland,
younger of Lethington, and 'to certane personis nominat be him,
yconomusis of the same, quhill the lauchfull provisioun of ane
priores to the said abbay'. The queen also acceded to the Earl of
Bothwell's petition recalling that the nunnery was 'his maist
native rowme and kyndlie possessioun', that it had been once
'possessit for the tyme be his neir kynniswoman last priores
thairof', and had been 'a lang tyme broukit be his freindis,
promovit frome tyme to tyme at the nominatioun of his
predecessouris'; all of which led Mary to appoint to Haddington
yet another Hepburn prioress, Bothwell's kinswoman, Dame
Isobel Hepburn.[38]

Even the claims of the papacy were not completely ignored by
Mary. Not only did Thomas Hay's successful supplication to the
papacy in April 1560 for provision to Glenluce go uncontested
by the crown, but the queen herself considered petitioning the
pope in 1565 that the commend of Inchaffray be granted to James
Drummond, in the belief that 'good men, devoted to learning'
should be appointed to ecclesiastical dignities at a time when the
Catholic church was 'so grievously afflicted' and when 'there
were few who openly professed the true doctrine and sought to
repress the errors and turbulence which everywhere prevailed'.
Yet her claim that the pope should admit free of charge the
resignation of Alexander Gordon, as commendator, on account
of the 'heavy losses' which Gordon had incurred 'in the defence
of the Catholic religion and the Apostolic See' is hard to
reconcile with Gordon's active ministry in the reformed church,
and her petition for the pope to grant two pensions, of £200 and
£100, from the fruits of the abbacy is another indication of the
continued dilapidation of church property by crown and
nobility. But despite her profession 'to preserve and advance the
Catholic faith and the religion of her ancestors', Mary proved to
be a great disappointment to the papacy, and, indeed, proceeded
to 'provide' Drummond to the abbacy in July 1565 'in the
accustomed form' under the privy seal, which was recognised to
be as valid as if provision had been made at Rome.[39]

Occasionally, too, the crown was prepared to confirm
presentations by commendators to the benefices of annexed
churches. In February 1564/5, Queen Mary confirmed a presentation, dated March 1555, to the vicarage of Earlston, which

had been made by her brother, John Stewart, the commendator and by the convent of Coldingham, 'undoutit patronis', to which the archbishop of St Andrews had refused to give collation, thus necessitating appeal to Rome, and which the queen then proposed to resolve by ratifying 'the said presentatioun quhilk wes be the said commendatare and convent for conservatioun of thair rycht of patronage'.[40] Similarly, the commendator of Lindores sought confirmation from the crown in January 1565/6 of his presentation of a candidate to the vicarage of Inverurie and Monkegie. In March 1565/6, a presentation to the vicarage of Kirkcaldy, annexed to Dunfermline abbey, was held to have the same force as if it had been made by the queen's 'awin provisioun, conforme to the ordoure and actis laitlie maid thairanent'; in February 1566/7, the crown also confirmed a presentation of 1566 by the commendator and convent of Whithorn to the vicarage pensionary of Whithorn; and in that month, Mary ratified another presentation, dated December 1566, to the same benefice, which, it was stated, pertained to the 'collatioun, provisioun and dispositioun' of Alexander Gordon, bishop of Galloway, 'be ressoun of the inhabilitie of Malcolme, commendator of Quiterne, patrone thairof, to present and nominat ane qualifit persoun thairto throw his being denuncit rebell and remaning at oure soverane ladyis horne this lang tyme bipast'.[41]

The continued recognition of the rights of other patrons clearly placed limitations on the crown's ability to control presentations to the benefices of churches appropriated to religious houses. It is harder, however, to appreciate the circumstances which permitted the Earl Marischal to present his own candidate on 10 June 1565 to the vicarage of the united churches of Longley and Fetterangus, appropriated to Arbroath abbey, and, then, to have his 'gift and presentatioun' confirmed by the queen on 30 June 1565.[42]

The proprietary attitude displayed by the crown in its bestowal of monastic property is apparent in the crown's policy toward the bishoprics. At the Reformation, the only complete vacancy, as such, among the bishoprics was the see of Brechin,

[40] *RSS*, v, no. 1922.

[41] Ibid., v, nos. 2563, 2607, 3249, 3269.

[42] Ibid., v, no. 2148. In May 1566, the Earl Marischal and Master of Marischal were recognised as patrons of the parish church of Longley (*RSS*, v, no. 2822). In September 1592, the current Earl Marischal and his eldest son received a grant, in life rent and fee respectively, of the barony of Straloch with the advowson of the parsonage and vicarage of Fetterangus and of the vicarage of Longley (*RMS*, v, no. 2176).

though several occupants of the remaining dozen bishoprics had not then secured full provision to their sees: Alexander Gordon was merely bishop elect of Galloway, John Campbell was still elect of the Isles, and Robert Stewart of Caithness retained his title though he was apparently never consecrated.[43] Five bishops readily conformed to the Reformation, and three of them – Orkney, Caithness and Galloway[44] – agreed to undertake an active ministry within the reformed church, but there was still no indication that those bishops who declined to conform to protestantism would (or indeed could) be dismissed from their sees. The survival of the bishoprics after 1560 – in contradiction to the reformers' aims of suppressing or dissolving them – clearly enabled the crown to gain further access to the bishoprics as financial entities, and to ignore the demands of the reformed church, which failed to secure its claims to this patrimony, that the spirituality of the bishoprics should be devoted to the work of the parish ministry and that the temporality should be assigned to support the universities and to pay the stipends of superintendents.[45] Thus, instead of distributing episcopal property to the reformed church, Mary chose, for the most part, to utilise episcopal revenues for the profit of the crown and for the reward of loyal servants.

In accordance with traditional practice,[46] during an episcopal vacancy Mary was entitled to enjoy the temporality of the see and at least the patronage of benefices in the bishop's gift. In November 1561, the crown gifted to David Murray a yearly pension of 500 merks, confirmed in December 1564, to be paid for the duration of his life, and not merely for the duration of the vacancy, from the revenues of the bishopric of Brechin. In Galloway, too, where Gordon was only bishop elect, Steven Wilson received a pension, again for life, from the crown in July 1561 in recompense for his expenses incurred in royal service; and, in January 1562/3, a further pension of 100 merks for life was granted from the bishopric of Galloway and abbacy of Tongland to Thomas Stewart, son of Alexander Stewart of

[43] D. E. R. Watt, *Fasti Ecclesiae Scoticanae Medii Aevi ad annum 1638* (Edinburgh, 1969), 132, 205; 61.

[44] See G. Donaldson, 'Bishop Adam Gordon and the Reformation in Orkney', *Records of the Scottish Church History Society [RSCHS]*, xiii (1959), 85–100; G. Donaldson, 'Alexander Gordon, Bishop of Galloway (1559–75) and his work in the Reformed Church', *Transactions of the Dumfriesshire and Galloway Natural History Society and Antiquarian Society*, 3rd ser. xxiv (1945–6), 111–28; G. Donaldson, *Scottish Reformation*, 58–60.

[45] *First Book of Discipline*, 150, 161–2.

[46] G. Donaldson, 'The rights of the Scottish crown in episcopal vacancies', 26–35.

Garlies.[47] Similarly, when Ross fell vacant, with Henry Sinclair's death in Paris in January 1564/5, Mary without delay rewarded Johannes Franciscus de Busso for his services to the crown, as master of the royal household, with the grant in February 1564/5 of a yearly pension for life of £400 from the vacant bishopric of Ross, a sum considerably less than the £600 earlier promised to him from 'quhatsumevir bischoprik, abbacie, prelacie or uther benefice quhilk sal happin to waik or cum in hir hienes handis and be at hir grace dispositioun'.[48] Again, with the death of Bishop William Chisholm of Dunblane, said to be at the point of death in December 1564, Queen Mary lost little time in granting in March 1564/5 a yearly pension of 200 merks for life to 'Eme de Saunctjean, furrour to oure soverane ladyis body', even though Chisholm's nephew had already been appointed coadjutor by the pope in June 1561, and by the end of March 1565 was present in Scotland as bishop in his own right.[49] All in all, there was no immediate financial incentive for the crown to fill vacant bishoprics without delay.

Although, on the eve of the Reformation, the crown's nominee, Henry Sinclair, had still to receive papal provision to the bishopric of Ross (forthcoming on 2 June 1561), the crown had felt entitled to place Sinclair in possession of the temporality in November 1558 and had granted him, as 'elect of Ross', full power in March 1559/60 to present to all benefices, in the bishop's patronage, which fell vacant 'be deceis, resignatioun, cessioun, dimissioun, permutatioun, inhabilitie, incapacitie, deprivatioun or ony uthir maner of way pertening, or may pertene, to oure soveranis presentatioun, gift or dispositioun be the privilege of thair crowne be ressoun of the vacance of the said seit of Ross during all the tyme of the vacance of the same and ay and quhill ane bischop and pastoure be lauchfullie providit and promovit thairto'.[50] Thereafter, in January 1564/5, Patrick Maclean, bishop elect of the Isles, agreed to transfer his rights to John Carswell, superintendent of Argyll, supposedly on the grounds of the 'impotence of his awne bodie' to discharge the office; but the decision to demit was evidently the product of a dispute between the Macleans and Campbells, each of whom had advanced a rival candidate as bishop elect of the Isles in the preceding decade; and the decision in favour of Carswell, a

[47] RSS, v, nos. 893, 1865; 824; 1198.
[48] Watt, Fasti, 270; RSS, v, no. 1918; cf., no. 3268.
[49] Watt, Fasti, 78; RSS, v, no. 1937; Vatican Archives, Acta Miscellanea, 17, fo. 690.
[50] Vatican Archives, Acta Misc., 17, fos. 690–691v; RSS, v, nos. 507, 768.

superintendent in the reformed church, marked a victory for the Earl of Argyll, whose patronage Carswell had long enjoyed. As the new bishop elect, Carswell was obliged 'to releif the quenis majestie and hir comptrollare' by paying the stipends of ministers in the diocese; and in the royal confirmation of March 1566/7 his right to dispose of vacant benefices was expressly recognised.[51]

The precedent of gifting a bishopric to a superintendent of the reformed church was not repeated, and any prospect that the kirk might eventually benefit from the systematic appointment of superintendents, or, indeed, of other ministers, to bishoprics quickly disappeared. Instead, resort was had to the expedient of granting vacant bishoprics to lay titulars. As had been the case with the abbacies, total secularisation now seemed the ultimate fate of the bishoprics. With Henry Sinclair's death in January 1564/5, Mary gifted the vacant bishopric of Ross in May 1565 to the Earl of Ross for life, as lay titular, with the patronage of all benefices in the bishop's gift, and with power to bestow the whole bishopric or any portion of it on whomsoever he might choose.[52]

Such a trend was interrupted in September 1565 when Mary freed herself from the policies of her protestant advisers and obtained papal provision to Brechin for her nominee, John Sinclair, brother of Henry and president of the College of Justice.[53] The resumed practice of seeking papal provision soon proved transitory. By May 1566, the policy of bestowing bishoprics in favour of laymen was resumed, with the grant to Alexander Campbell, who was still a minor, of the bishopric of Brechin, both spirituality and temporality, with full patronage of benefices in the bishop's gift. Experimental styles were devised during 1566 and 1567 for disposing of the bishoprics of Moray and Dunkeld, in anticipation of a vacancy arising, to nominees of the crown.[54] All this was no doubt consistent with Mary's efforts at conciliating protestant opinion for reasons of political expediency; and it was only towards the end of the reign, as Mary entered her twenty-fifth year when revocations might be expected, that John Leslie was finally appointed to Ross, apparently after papal provision and with royal approval in January 1566/7.[55]

[51] RSS, v, nos. 1885, 3373; see above, 296–7.
[52] RSS, v, no. 2066.
[53] Watt, Fasti, 41; Vatican Archives, Acta Misc., 17, fo. 759r-v (7 Sept. 1565).
[54] RSS, v, nos. 2806, 3099, 3100, 3553.
[55] Watt, Fasti, 270.

Mary's device of appointing titulars to bishoprics with power to dispose of vacant benefices in the bishop's gift meant that the crown deprived itself of additional powers of patronage over certain parochial benefices *sede vacante*. And in cases where the bishop was merely elect, the normal procedure of episcopal provision followed by institution could not take place, and so candidates – who, of course, need undertake no service in the reformed church – were required to be presented by the bishop elect to the vicar general of the see, which technically was still vacant, for collation to be granted before institution could take place.[56] Yet what the crown was prepared to relinquish at one point was offset by gains elsewhere. For a start, the patronage of parochial benefices in the gift of laymen devolved on the crown, from time to time, through wardship (where the heir to the patronage was still a minor), through nonentry (where the inheritor had not been served heir of the property to which the patronage was appendant), and through the forfeiture of the property of a patron.[57] Besides, by an act of the privy council in 1562, the crown was permitted to dispose of benefices whose rentals had not been produced for assessment by the crown, following a decision to allow the crown access to a levy of one third of the revenues of all benefices to be uplifted and assigned to support the crown and reformed ministry.[58]

With the appointment of collectors of the thirds,[59] the crown was able to utilise at least a portion of its undisclosed share of this newly found source of finance by making gifts of the thirds[60] and of the revenues not given up in the rentals,[61] by granting remissions of the thirds,[62] which were sometimes even assigned as fees for the queen's priests,[63] or, again, by approving pensions from the thirds as rewards for loyal service;[64] all of which proved too heavy a drain on this profitable means of finance, and in an effort to husband the depleted resources from this source, the privy council in September 1566 issued a general revocation of all such pensions, with certain exceptions, and all gifts of the thirds

[56] *RSS*, v, no. 768.
[57] Ibid., v, nos. 237, 238, 365, 515, 610, 929, 1196, 1222, 1723; vi, no. 972; vii, no. 613; (forfeiture:) vi, nos 123, 1433, 2815; vii, no. 1767.
[58] *RPC*, i, 199–202, 204–6; *RSS*, v, nos. 2659; vi, no. 2250.
[59] *RSS*, v, no. 998; *Thirds of Benefices*, xi, xv-xvi.
[60] *RSS*, v, nos. 2340, 2401, 2791, 2811, 3013, 3323.
[61] Ibid., nos. 2659, 3279.
[62] Ibid., v, nos. 2548, 3245; *Thirds of Benefices*, 83–91, 147–9, 221, 230, 241, 249, 260, 274, 283, 289.
[63] *Thirds of Benefices*, 86–7, 147, 155.
[64] *RSS*, v, nos. 1127, 1179, 1327, 2283, 2811, 3316; *Thirds of Benefices*, 155–6.

and pensions from the thirds.[65] In addition to its substantial share of the thirds, the crown also assumed control of the property of the 'common churches' belonging to the canons and chaplains of cathedrals, whose entire revenues, along with those of certain collegiate churches, had been uplifted by the crown from 1561 onwards.[66] The numerous grants of these properties by the crown took the form either of a lease in return for a fixed rent or of a simple gift. Thus, in July 1565, Mary leased to Robert Douglas, provost of Lincluden collegiate kirk, and his heirs for nineteen years the parsonage and vicarage of Glencairn, a common church of Glasgow cathedral, 'now being in oure soverane ladyis handis and at hir hienes dispositioun be ressoun of the generall ordour takin that all commoun kirkis, fruitis and rentis thairof sal be intromettit with and applyit to hir hienes use'.[67] Again, in January 1566/7, James Hering received a gift for life of the canonry of Forgandenny, a common church of Dunkeld, on the resignation of John Bertoun, who had earlier petitioned the papacy in 1560 for provision anew to the benefice;[68] and in the same month, John Leslie, bishop of Ross, received from Mary a lease for nineteen years of the whole common kirks of Ross.[69] Even after Mary's reign, the crown continued to claim in 1570 that the benefices formerly held in common by the chantry priests of Dunkeld, 'now vakand be ressoun the singing of the saidis preistis ceassis', still pertained to the king's presentation by full right of patronage, 'becaus of the lait ordinance of the kirk anent the gift and dispositioun of sic small thingis', an apparent allusion to the general assembly's decision by 1569 that chaplainries should be assigned to the support of the colleges and the poor.[70]

III

The claims of the Kirk:

Laymen – other than the crown and the crown's nominees to the prelacies – may have had little enough opportunity to exercise ecclesiastical patronage, but at almost every level they assuredly had gained as recipients of patronage; and all this looked like continuing so long as laymen, and not ministers, were in receipt

[65] *RPC*, i, 477–9.
[66] *RSS*, v, nos. 1709, 1751, 1998, 2092, 2192, 3173, 3286; *Thirds of Benefices*, 2, 4, 6, 8, 16, 21, 24–6, 28.
[67] *RSS*, v, 2192.
[68] Ibid., v, no. 3178; Vatican Archives, Reg. Supp., 3032, fo. 168r-v. (A subsequent supplication to Rome in 1560 by John Leslie, priest of Moray diocese, was evidently ineffective: Vatican Archives, Reg. Supp., 3033, fos. 53v-54r.)
[69] *RSS*, v, no. 3173.
[70] Ibid., vi, no. 955; *BUK*, i, 155; cf., 127–9.

of ecclesiastical property. The prospect of the complete secularisation of the church's patrimony, however, was drastically
modified and ultimately reversed by the inheritance, in effect,
from 1567 of the lesser benefices, as they fell vacant, by ministers
of the reformed church. As early as 1562, the assumption of the
thirds, which had recognised in some measure the financial needs
of the kirk, suggested the possibility that the church's legitimate
claims might be met most readily not by dissolving the structure
of benefices, to which the crown was totally opposed, but by
adopting the old financial system and by utilising it in the
interests of the new church. As it was, some ministers who
conformed in 1560 were already in possession of benefices, and
others, by obtaining a portion of the thirds, were also receiving
some – albeit inadequate – financial support from the existing
structure. At a time when the crown's increased demands upon
the thirds actually had led to a corresponding reduction in
stipends, any scheme designed to provide more satisfactory
stipends was likely to prove attractive to ministers; and the
queen's proposal, for reasons of political expediency, in October
1566 that ministers should finally succeed to the lesser benefices
worth less than 300 merks in annual value, as vacancies arose,
provided sufficient financial inducement to secure the church's
further co-operation in preserving, instead of dismantling, the
existing structure of parochial benefices.

The origins of this scheme are to be traced to the assembly's
novel claim first advanced in June 1565 that the parochial
'benefices now vaikand or hes vaike be disposed to qualified and
learned persones, able to preach Gods word, and discharge the
vocation concerning the ministrie, be the tryall and admission of
the superintendents'. The queen's initial and discouraging reply
in December 1565 was that 'her Majestie thinkis it no wayes
reasonable that scho sould defraude her selfe of sa great a pairt of
the patrimonie of her crowne as to put the patronage of benefices
furth of her awin handis', to which the assembly hastened to
reassure Mary that:

> 'our mind is not that her Majestie or anie uther patron of this
> realme sould be defrauded of ther just patronages; bot we meane
> whensoevir her Majestie or any uther patron does present any
> person to a benefice, that the person presentit sould be tryit and
> examineit be the judgement of learned men of the kirk, sick as
> presentlie are the superintendents appointed therto. And as the
> presentation of benefices pertaines to the patrone, sa aucht the
> collatioun therof be law and reason pertaine to the kirk; and of the
> whilk collatioun the kirk sould not be defraudit, more nor the
> patrones of ther presentation; for utherwayes, if it salbe leisum to

the patrone absolutely to present whomever they please, without tryall or examination, what then can abyde in the kirk of God bot meere ignorance without all ordour'.

The assembly's contention that the system of ecclesiastical patronage should not be scrapped but should survive intact and that the kirk should not only inherit the parochial benefices but also operate the machinery for admission was flatly in contravention of the programme of the First Book of Discipline; and if the intention then was to secure agreement through compromise, the assembly's claim was still not conceded by the crown until political necessity finally dictated the adoption by Mary of a policy designed to win support from the kirk. But even with the crown's belated recognition by October 1566 that ministers should succeed to the lesser benefices, there was no wholesale capitulation to the assembly's claims of 1565, for Mary herself continued to favour the disposition of benefices by simple gift, instead of by presentation, and, partly as a consequence, she avoided transferring the machinery for granting collation and admission to the reformed church, machinery ultimately forthcoming only after the accession of a 'godly' prince in 1567.[71]

The plans announced in October 1566 to finance ministers from the full revenues of parochial benefices were, however, markedly at variance with Mary's earlier policy where benefices at the crown's disposal had been assigned on a basis which disregarded the comprehensive claims to this patrimony advanced by the general assembly. Indeed, immediately after the Reformation, the crown's presentations to the lesser benefices – though on a noticeably reduced scale – continued to be made in traditional form, for not only did the old financial structure remain intact but the titles of benefice-holders were still secure in law. This being so, presentations continued to be directed to the bishops, the majority of whom, of course, by declining to conform to the Reformation were prohibited from performing any spiritual functions, but they still had their part to play in the admission of candidates to benefices. This was done by granting letters of collation in which the bishop indicated that he had conferred the benefice on the presentee and then by initiating the machinery for the candidate's formal institution or induction to the benefice.[72] That the old system of episcopal administration persisted and continued to operate, well after 1560, is also evident in the crown's confirmation of presentations specifying

71 RPC, i, 487–8; BUK, i, 59, 68–70; APS, iii, 23.
72 RSS, v, nos. 827, 869, 876, 965, 1884, 2475, 2786, 3070.

episcopal collation, which had been made by other patrons.[73]

Increasingly, however, Queen Mary found it convenient to resort to the device of bestowing lesser benefices in royal patronage by means of a simple gift without recourse to episcopal collation. Earlier presentations to vicarages, prebends and even to chaplainries were quickly followed by gifts of archdeaconries,[74] deaneries and subdeaneries,[75] chancellories,[76] provostries,[77] chantories and subchantories,[78] canonries and prebends,[79] of certain parsonages and vicarages[80] unattached as prebends of cathedrals and collegiate kirks, and of a number of chaplainries[81] at the crown's disposal. Any dubiety about the propriety of resorting to gifts instead of presentations was overcome by the crown's recognition that such gifts were as valid as any other form of grant. The gift of the vicarage pensionary of Balmaclellan in November 1563 was undestood to be as sound in law as if the candidate had been 'providit thairto be waye of presentatioun and collatioun ordinare eftir the auld maner of provisioun to benefices'; and the candidate who received a gift of the vicarage of Linton in March 1563/4 was held to have as sufficient a title 'as onye utheris vicaris within this realme hes of thair vicaraiges'.[82] Again, in December 1565, a gift of the parsonage and vicarage of Duns was said to be as lawful as if provision had been made at Rome, without:[83]

'ony impediment, clame, questioun, actioun or contradictioun to be maid, movit or persewit ... be ony maner of way in tyme cuming, nochtwithstanding ony law, act, statute or constitutioun, cannoun or civile, quhatsumevir maid or to be maid in the contrar,

[73] *RSS*, v, nos. 1638, 2064, 2148, 2531, 2563, 2607, 2653, 2663, 2721, 2722, 2828, 2836, 2840, 2846, 2852, 2859, 2942, 2946, 2998, 3031, 3042, 3246, 3269, 3270, 3308, 3042, 3091, 3112, 3120, 3155, 3174, 3308, 3383, 3433, 3469, 3498, 3533, 3541, 3551. See also Scottish Record Office [SRO], Register House Charters, RH6/1896 (presentation to Dunscore by commendator of Holywood, Nov. 1562); RH6/1975 (to Tullynessle by bishop of Aberdeen, Jan. 1564/5); RH6/2019 (to prebend of St Dothan, Sandwick by bishop of Orkney, Feb. 1565/6); cf., RH6/nos. 2196, 2313, 2830, 2933 (for later presentations, 1570–87).
[74] *RSS*., v, nos. 1445, 1894, 2025, 2121.
[75] Ibid., v, nos. 1416, 1733, 2036, 2217, 2466, 2478, 2757, 3156.
[76] Ibid., v, no. 1469.
[77] Ibid., v, nos. 3123, 3146.
[78] Ibid., v, nos. 1551, 1785, 2036, 2039, 2978.
[79] Ibid., v, nos. 1321, 1368, 1513, 1660, 1917, 1941, 2314, 2369, 2445, 2446, 2456, 2675, 2691, 2743, 2908, 2973, 3029, 3045, 3049, 3060, 3089, 3144, 3158, 3399.
[80] Ibid., v, nos. 1490, 1657, 1899, 2029, 3044.
[81] Ibid., v, nos. 2313, 2370, 2426, 2676, 2761, 2853, 2918, 3028, 3282, 3283, 3061, 3076, 3355.
[82] Ibid., v, nos. 1490, 1657.
[83] Ibid., v, no. 2511.

anent the quhilkis and provisionis contenit thairin quhilkis may be extendit or tend to the rupture, hurt or prejudice of this present gift in ony wayis. . . .'

Occasionally, too, a gift might be forthcoming in the expectation of a 'presentatioun to be maid under the prive seile'.[84]

By 1 October 1566, however, in anticipation of the privy council's enactment of 3 October, Mary bestowed the vicarage of Inchaiden on William Ramsay, minister of that parish; and, after a lapse of some months, this gift was followed in March 1566/7 with the appointment of David Wemyss, minister of Glasgow, to the vicarage of Glasgow, then 'pertening to oure soverane ladyis gift and dispositioun be the ordour laitlie tane and proclamatioun set furth thairon anent the dispositioun of sic small beneficis to ministeris for thair sustentatioun'. Such a gift was held to be as valid as if provision had been made 'be the ordinare as use was befoir the alteratioun of the stait of religioun within this realme', which may imply a belated admission that the traditional practice of seeking episcopal collation 'eftir the auld maner' was considered to be somewhat inappropriate, particularly so in cases involving the appointment to benefices of ministers in the reformed church; hence the adoption of the simple gift in the disposition of parochial benefices.[85] A further gift to a minister was made in April 1567, when Patrick Creich, minister at Ratho, received a grant of a prebend of Corstorphine collegiate kirk, which he was to possess as freely as if provision 'had bene maid at Rome, nochtwithstanding all actis, lawis or constitutionis, titillis, richtis, presentationis or collationis gevin or to be gevin in the contrar quhatsumevir'.[86]

The access of ministers to the lesser benefices on such a modest scale was, however, completely transformed with the revolution against Mary and the accession, in July 1567, of James VI, for not only was the way now open for the statutory recognition and formal establishment of the reformed church, but parliament also transferred to the reformed church the right to receive presentations to benefices from patrons and to grant collation and institution. The traditional machinery for conveying an indisputable title to a benefice was finally to be operated by the reformed church and in favour of candidates willing to serve as ministers, exhorters or readers in the kirk. By an act of parliament in December 1567, it was recognised that, within six months of a vacancy arising, patrons should direct presentations to the

[84] Ibid., v, no. 2313.
[85] Ibid., v, nos. 3080, 3347; 3213.
[86] Ibid., v, no. 3399.

superintendent or to the commissioner of the province appointed by the general assembly, who was empowered to examine the presentee and to grant, or refuse, admission.

On a patron's failure to present within the prescribed period, the right to fill the vacancy *iure devoluto* fell to the superintendent or commissioner. Where a dispute arose, the patron might appeal to the superintendent and ministers of the province, an apparent allusion to the synod, and finally to the general assembly of the church. Not only was recognition thus accorded to the higher courts of the church, but it looked as if parliament had conceded in such instances that the assembly and ecclesiastical courts (rather than the court of session, privy council or parliament itself) were the appropriate courts of appeal. It is noticeable, too, that statutory recognition at this point was withheld from the conforming bishops *qua* bishops. Indeed, one looks in vain in the act for any acknowledgment of the work of the conforming bishops (as bishops and not merely as the assembly's commissioners) or of the part which they might have been expected to play in admitting candidates to benefices; and it is all too evident that only the superintendents 'or utheris havand commissioun of the Kirk' were authorised to grant admissions.[87] Such a restriction, however, was wholly in accord with the general assembly's policy of regarding the bishops who conformed at the Reformation as acting merely as 'commissioners', ministers commissioned by the assembly to act for a spell as overseers or visitors. The occasional presentation by the crown directed to a bishop in the late 1560s presumably rested on this assumption and understanding, for it would have been hard on any other ground to reconcile such a development with the express terms of statute law.[88]

In the years between December 1567 and January 1572/3, when a further statute required benefice-holders to subscribe the reformed Confession of Faith (though they still need not serve as ministers) and to acknowledge the king's authority or to suffer dispossession for their failure to do so,[89] more than 150 presentations by the crown were directed to superintendents and commissioners in favour of ministers; Mary's earlier device of granting simple gifts was all but eliminated;[90] and thereafter, with the enforcement of the act depriving nonconformists,[91] the

---

[87] *APS.*, iii, 23.
[88] *BUK*, i, 15, 26–32, 34–5, 39–40, 44, 51–2; *RSS*, vi, no. 200.
[89] *APS.*, iii, 72.
[90] *RSS.*, vi, nos. 10, 123.
[91] Ibid., vi, nos. 2030, 2034, 2125, 2130, 2170, 2171, 2198, 2224, 2240, 2241, 2286, 2292, 2419, 2437, 2468, 2532, 2608.

prospect was that all benefices would be assigned to protestants and, in particular, to those willing to undertake active service in the kirk. The first grant of a benefice in the new reign to a candidate serving in the reformed church – the bestowal of the vicarage of Walston on an exhorter in September 1567 – admittedly had taken the form of a simple gift, but the special circumstances of this grant were twofold: for a start, the gift was made three months before the act of parliament setting down the procedures to be observed in presentations; secondly, and more especially, the gift was designed to clarify the anomaly arising from an earlier presentation of the same candidate by the Earl of Bothwell, as patron, in May 1567 which had been directed to the vicar general in the old regime who gave collation 'as use was in tyme of papistrie'. Yet before institution had taken place, Bothwell had been denounced rebel at the horn; the vicarage, which was held still to be vacant, then came into the hands of the king, who by means of a simple gift made good the exhorter's title to the benefice.[92] The first presentation, as such, in James' reign on 25 December 1567 – again of an exhorter to the vicarage of Saline – followed the procedure of 1566 'according to the act maid and set furth be our soverane lordis derrest moder and lordis of secreit counsale thairanent', but thereafter some subsequent presentations explicitly acknowledged the authority of the new, and more comprehensive, parliamentary legislation of late December 1567.[93] Occasionally, too, presentations recognised the general assembly's supervisory rôle, and expressly provided that:

> 'in caice that be decre of the generall assembillie of the kirk, to the jugement quhairof he [the presentee] sal be allwayis subject, he be found ather negligent in doctrine or sklanderous in lyfe for gude caussis worthie and meit to be transportit to ane uthir place and charge this present donatioun and presentatioun with all that sal happin to pas thairupoun to be null, and sum uthir qualifiit persoun to be presentit. . . .'

It is also evident that the ecclesiastical authorities displayed a readiness to take advantage of the new act in order to make presentations *iure devoluto* where patrons had failed to exercise their rights. In one instance in 1568, the crown decided to present a minister to the vicarage pensionary of Bothwell, 'na uthir persoun being presentit be the patroun within the tyme appointit be the law', and to assign to the presentee certain revenues 'quhilk was payit of auld for the furnissing of breid, walx, wyne

[92] Ibid., vi, no. 10.
[93] Ibid., vi, nos. 68, 82, 87.

and wesching of the claithis within the college kirk of Boithuile', now vacant 'be ressoun the samyn hes na wayis bene disponit to ony uthir guid use of befoir sen the tyme of the reformatioun of religioun'. In another case, however, it was the superintendent of Fife and Strathearn who presented, examined and admitted an exhorter in 1569 to the parsonage of Dupplin, on account that the patron, Lord Oliphant, had 'nowthir presentit or nominat ony qualifiit persoun thairto be the space of sex monethis . . . be ressoun quhairof the said nobill lord tint his rycht of the presentatioun thairof as for this tyme, and the rycht thairof pertenit to the superintendent *jure devoluto*. . . .'[94]

The disposition of ecclesiastical property in favour of ministers extended beyond the strictly parochial benefices – the parsonages and vicarages having the cure of souls – to include canonries, prebends, the common kirks attached to cathedrals, and even to certain chaplainries. At the same time, the crown extended its newly acquired, additional rights of patronage considerably beyond the common kirks, to whose disposition Mary had laid claim, to encompass the benefices in the patronage of prelates. The transference of the bulk of ecclesiastical patronage from the control of churchmen, or at least men who were nominally ecclesiastics, into the hands of the crown was finally effected in the early decades of the new reign. This silent revolution, which could scarcely be further deferred, was achieved with little noticeable dislocation. Nor would it have been hard to justify the change on the purely practical ground that it would have been less than prudent to permit prelates, many of whom remained suspect in religion, a continued say in selecting and presenting to so many benefices candidates who were expected to serve in the reformed church.

The assumption of these comprehensive rights by the crown, however, is not attributable (or so it would seem) to any surviving act of parliament or council. Nonetheless, from at least as early as 1569, the crown evidently felt confident systematically to make presentations to benefices in ecclesiastical patronage, and it was later recognised, in July 1578, that 'be the Lawes custome and ordour ressavit within our realme all benefices of befoir at the donatioun and presentatioun of prelatis ar now cum in use and ordinit be Parliament to be at our patronage in tyme cuming'. The existence, therefore, of 'ony actis of parliament or lawes of our realme quhairby the richt of presentatioun of ecclesiasticall benefices may appear to cum in our handis sen the reformatioun of religioun and to appertene to us allanerlie' was

94 Ibid., vi, nos. 95, 214, 582; cf., vii, no. 2689.

evidently considered to provide sufficient justification for the crown's action of invading the traditional rights of patronage exercised by the bishops, abbots and priors.[95]

Thus, in the years between 1568 and 1597, the crown made some 46 presentations to 25 churches annexed to Arbroath abbey, despite a succession of commendators there. Five presentations were made between 1570 and 1583 to the parish of Dun, annexed to Elcho priory; and at Holyrood, whose patronage Mary had claimed, around 51 presentations by the crown were made to 21 annexed churches belonging to the abbey between 1568 and 1598, regardless of the existence of a commendator. A similar pattern is evident, too, in the case of other religious houses such as Kelso, Kilwinning, Lindores, Paisley, St Andrews and Whithorn.[96]

The plenary powers exercised by the crown over ecclesiastical property – adapted, perhaps, from the English model where the king as the supreme ecclesiastical authority was acknowledged as patron paramount of all benefices[97] – were applicable also to the bishoprics where the crown assumed a right to present candidates to churches annexed to prebends (as well as to the common churches) not merely during episcopal vacancies, as custom dictated, but also in cases where the bishop was lawfully provided to the see. From 1569, the crown began to assert its claims to present to prebends annexed to the cathedral churches of all the bishoprics, with the apparent exception of Argyll where the evidence is lacking.[98] What is more, the crown went one step further and, from the 1570s onward, proceeded to make presentations even to independent benefices where the bishop happened to be patron. Presentations were accordingly made to the independent churches of Carrington, Collace, Edzell, Fettercairn, Logie Montrose, Muckhart and Nevay which, hitherto, were recognised to lie within the patronage of the archbishop of St Andrews.[99] Similarly, the unappropriated churches of Castlemilk, Kirkpatrick-Fleming, Kirkton, Lochmaben and Redkirk,

[95] See n. 96 below; *APS*, iii, 106.
[96] This evidence is based on an examination of the relevant entries in *RSS*, vi-viii, and SRO, CH4/1/2, Register of Presentations to Benefices; and SRO, PS1/59–63, Register of the Privy Seal.
[97] J. Mirehouse, *A practical Treatise on the Law of Advowsons* (London, 1824), 130.
[98] See above, n. 96.
[99] *RSS*, vii, no. 156 (Carrington); vi, no. 2084; SRO, CH4/1/2, Register of Presentations to Benefices, fo. 81r (Collace); *RSS*, vi, nos. 1152, 2053 (Edzell); vii, nos. 631, 2458 (Fettercairn); vi, no. 2311 (Logy Montrose); vii, nos. 1229, 2027, 2051; SRO, CH4/1/2, Reg. Pres. Ben., fos. 134v, 145r (Muckhart); *RSS*, vi, no. 1674 (Nevay).

formerly pertaining to the patronage of the archbishop of Glasgow, were understood to be at the crown's presentation.[100]

It is apparent, too, that at the Convention of Leith in 1572, which provided the machinery for future episcopal and abbatial appointments, the crown's rights over 'benefices of cure under prelaciis' were once more affirmed in recognition that 'all benefices (under prelaciis) havend cure of saules, quhilkis ayther of auld pertenis to the Kingis patronage, or newly ar cum in use, and be Parliament ordanit to be at his Hienes patronage, sall sua continew conforme to the Actes of Parliament; and that the lawic patrones alwayes brouke and use thair awin richtis'. While the rights of lay patrons were expressly confirmed, those of churchmen looked like being eclipsed.[101]

IV

The search for a settlement:

All along, the survival of the ancient financial structure after the Reformation had suggested at least three possibilities. One solution – the complete secularisation of the property of the old church – had been averted only with considerable difficulty. Another possibility was that the continued existence of the old structure might have held open – and indeed invited – the prospect of a papalist reaction, particularly in the years before the victory of the king's party and the imposition in 1573 of the religious test for benefice-holders. The third solution – which looked like being achieved in the years after 1567 – was that the financial system of the old church should become wholly identified with the work of the reformed ministry, the needs of the schools and universities, and of the poor. There was even a fourth possibility that by first utilising this financial structure the reformed church might ultimately succeed in its original intention of reorganising the chaotic state of ecclesiastical finances along the lines suggested in the Book of Discipline and earlier general assemblies. Indeed, the new regime after 1567 only increased the assembly's expectation that 'the faithfull kirk of Jesus Chryst profest within this realme salbe put in full libertie of the patrimony of the kirk according to the booke of God and the ordour and practise of the primitive kirk'.[102]

---

[100] *RSS*, vii, no. 358; SRO, PS1/60, Register of the Privy Seal, fo. 84r; PS1/63, fo. 112r (Castlemilk); *RSS*, vii, no. 1442 (Kirkpatrick Fleming); SRO, CH4/1/2, Reg. Pres. Ben., fo. 143v (Kirkton); SRO, PS1/63, Register of the Privy Seal, fo. 263r (Lochmaben); *RSS*, vii, nos. 315, 1964 (Redkirk).

[101] *BUK*, i, 211.

[102] Ibid., i, 107.

So far, the accession of a 'godly' prince had brought full statutory recognition of the assembly's claim in 1565 that the supervision of admissions should belong to the kirk; but, as yet, no agreed solution was forthcoming on the fate of the bishoprics and abbacies. To an orderly, modern mind, it is possibly attractive to regard the access of ministers to the bishoprics, achieved in 1572, as the logical sequel to the statutory inheritance of the lesser benefices by ministers from 1567. Yet this was scarcely the attitude of the assembly which proceeded from petitioning for the adoption of the lesser benefices in 1565 to the demand that:[103]

> 'no bishoprik, abbacie, pryorie, deanrie, provestrie, or any uther benefices havand many kirks annexit therto, be disponit altogither in any time comeing to ane one man, bot at the least the kirks therof be severallie disponit and to severall persons, swa that every man having charge may serve at his awin kirk according to his vocatioun. . . .'

Such forceful language is a clear enough expression of the assembly's attitude toward the prelacies, for whose dissolution it continued to campaign, and it illustrates how the ideals of 1560 were by no means cast aside. Evidently, an acceptance of financial endowment from the parochial benefices still brought no nearer the integration of the prelacies within the structure of the reformed church.

Although the assembly's petition to parliament in December 1567 for a dissolution of the abbacies had met with little positive response, the matter was not allowed to rest; and in the aftermath of the parliament in August 1568, whose detailed enactments have not survived, the Regent Moray reported to the assembly in July 1569 that 'ye know at the Parliament . . . we exped in our travell, and inlaikit only a consent to the dissolution of the prelacies; qherunto althogh we were earnestly bent, yet the estates delayit and wold not aggrie therunto'. That the church continued to contend for a dissolution of the bishoprics, as well as of the abbacies, was understood as late as November 1571, when the government's earlier announcement of appointments to the vacant archbishoprics provoked superintendent Erskine of Dun to defend the assembly's programme in favour of 'the dismembring (as they call it) of great benefices', and to remind the government that 'the kirk hath continuallie suted (of old als weill as now) . . . when ever anie of the great benefices vaiked, having manie kirks joyned thereto, that all the kirks sould be divided, and severallie dispouned to severall men, to serve everie

[103] Ibid., i, 59–60.

one at his owne kirk: of which minde all that beare office in the
kirk continue'. But if this ideal could not be granted until at least
the king attained his majority, Erskine expressed the hope that
'in respect of this confused troublous time', the church might be
prepared to compromise 'whill further order may be tane in these
maters'; and the Regent Mar responded by recognising the need
'to procure the reforming of things disordered in all sorts, als
farre as may be, reteaning the priviledge of the king, crown and
patronage'.[104]

The immediate background to Erskine's intervention had been
the government's decision to fill several vacant bishoprics
without consulting the church, as well it might, as the reformed
church had never asserted a claim to participate in episcopal
elections. The problem of the bishoprics, which arose as a matter
of urgency, had by no means been unforeseen. Indeed, the crisis
was precipitated largely by the government's own action, during
the civil war, by instituting proceedings from 1567 against the
leading papalist or Marian bishops. By December 1567, William
Chisholm, the Catholic bishop of Dunblane, had been forfeited,
and put to the horn as a fugitive from the laws, for 'traffiqueing
in the realme of France certane space and committand certane
crymes in the samin', and as a consequence his goods were gifted
to the Master of Montrose, who later received a gift in August
1569 of the whole fruits of the temporality and spirituality of the
bishopric 'ay and quhill the lauchfull provisioun of ane pastor,
prelate or bischop to the said bischoprik', with the right of
'imputting and outputting of the tennantis of the samin at his
plesoure'. Somewhat later, 'for certain crimes of treason' John
Leslie, the Catholic bishop of Ross, was declared to have been
forfeited in August 1568. At the same point, 'the process and
dome of forfaltour ordourlie led aganis Johnne, sumtym Archbishop of Sanctandrois', and his execution for treason in April
1571, resulted in the primatial see falling vacant. The Lords of
Council, in September 1570, declared the archbishopric of
Glasgow to be vacant through the conviction in parliament and
forfeiture for treason of James Beaton, who had been absent
from his see since his flight to France in July 1560. Thereafter,
similar sentences of conviction in parliament and forfeiture for
treason were passed against four other bishops who
had supported Mary: William Gordon, bishop of Aberdeen;
Alexander Gordon, bishop of Galloway; Robert Crichton,
bishop of Dunkeld; and Patrick Hepburn, bishop of Moray,

---

[104] APS, iii, 37; BUK, i, 151; D. Calderwood, History of the Kirk of Scotland,
edd. T. Thomson and D. Laing, 8 vols. (Edinburgh, 1842–9), iii, 159–60.

though both Gordons were soon pardoned and restored in February 1572/3.[105] In all, the government's action in dispossessing Marian supporters had created vacancies in no less than half the bishoprics which were thus declared to have come into the hands of the crown.

It was by no means a foregone conclusion that successors automatically would be chosen to fill the vacant sees. At any rate, there were obviously obstacles to be overcome before any appointments might be forthcoming. For a start, no agreed procedure existed for making appointments. The traditional method of episcopal appointment by crown nomination and capitular election could scarcely operate as the chapters, where not extinct, still consisted of the unreformed variety. There was always the option open to the crown of disposing of episcopal temporalities by simple gift, as had been practised by Queen Mary; and to a government chronically short of finance in the midst of a civil war, there were obvious attractions in permitting episcopal vacancies to continue thereby enabling the crown to enjoy the fruits *sede vacante*. A further, and no less serious, obstacle in filling the sees with protestant successors was, of course, the general assembly's ill-concealed aversion to any policy at variance with its declared objective of dissolving the bishoprics as administrative and financial entities.

As administrative entities, the thirteen bishoprics with their uneven size and their antiquated and irrational diocesan boundaries were no adequate substitute for the rationalised and streamlined provinces assigned to the superintendents and commissioners. Moreover, the continued existence of the bishoprics, as financial entities, impeded and frustrated the assembly's efforts to separate and disentangle the revenues of the appropriated churches for reallocation to the parishes, and to subvert the remaining episcopal resources so that the finances would be finally released for the maintenance of the universities and superintendents, as the Book of Discipline had contended.

The decision ultimately taken at Leith in January 1571/2 to identify the bishoprics with the work of the reformed church arose in an unexpected way and, as the circumstances show, it was achieved by the government and church almost in spite of their policies and intentions. It was certainly far from being the inevitable outcome of any predetermined plan by the government, far less the church, to complete the process begun in 1567 of identifying the pre-Reformation structure of benefices with

---

[105] *RSS*, vi, nos. 56, 590, 729; 501; *APS*, iii, 54; *RSS*, vi, nos. 518, 2142; 1265;1262; 1254, 1255; *RPC*, ii, 196.

the work of the new church. It came about rather as the accidental by-product of an episode in politics which ultimately had the effect of reconciling the government and church in the aftermath of the strained relations and impasse created by the government's unilateral action in making promotions to the bishoprics without consulting the church. The compromise then achieved was a solution which neither government nor general assembly had predicted: it required the government to abandon its plans to utilise the bishoprics purely as an extension of its system of political patronage, and to recognise that candidates so promoted should undergo examination by the church and should exercise the spiritual office attached to the benefice; and the scheme, in turn, obliged the church to place in abeyance its own plans for subverting the bishoprics and to acknowledge the utility in having placed at its disposal the financial and administrative structure of the bishoprics, until a more comprehensive solution acceptable to the crown, parliament and church was devised when the king came of age.[106]

Hitherto, King James' government had been predisposed to use the finances of vacant bishoprics to reward loyal supporters and to win over nobles who were either wavering in their allegiance or who were even prepared to abandon their adherence to Mary. As the queen's party showed signs of disintegrating in the summer of 1571, Argyll transferred his allegiance to the Regent Lennox, who represented the king, and was rewarded by the succeeding Regent Mar, first with a gift in September 1571 of the escheat of the goods, including the fruits of the vacant bishopric of Dunkeld, which had belonged to the forfeited bishop, Robert Crichton, convicted of treason, and then, in January 1571/2, with a further gift of the temporalities of the bishopric; and a year later, he rose to become justice-general and chancellor of the kingdom. The staunchly protestant and anglophile Earl of Morton, who became leader of the king's party and who, as Regent, resigned the chancellorship in favour of Argyll in January 1572/3, had earlier been in receipt of an escheat of the fruits of the bishopric of Dunkeld in December 1570; another Douglas was chamberlain of the bishopric; Morton also acquired an escheat of the fruits of the archbishopric of St Andrews in September 1571, presumably in recompense for his loss to Argyll of the fruits of Dunkeld; provision was made to one of Morton's natural sons of an annual pension for life of £500 from the bishopric of Aberdeen; and the same individual later

[106] *BUK*, i, 207.

acquired a gift of the whole fruits of the bishopric of Galloway.[107]

In a similar way, the Master of Graham, shortly to inherit the earldom of Montrose, and a privy councillor during the regencies, acquired a financial interest in the bishopric of Dunblane: in April 1569 he had obtained the escheat of the revenues of the bishopric, and of any other benefices, formerly held by Chisholm as bishop, and in August received a grant of the entire temporality and spirituality of the bishopric.[108] In September 1571, the brother of Lord Ruthven, the king's treasurer, received a yearly pension for life of 300 merks from the bishopric Moray.[109] Another adherent of the king's party, Lord Methven, obtained in the same month a gift of the revenues of the bishopric of Ross and goods escheated from John Leslie, the former bishop, and in November secured the full temporalities of the bishopric.[110] The Regent Mar enabled a member of a cadet branch of his family to enjoy a yearly pension for life of £40 from the bishopric of the Isles, in September 1572; an identical pension was assigned to a Stewart; while from the archbishopric of Glasgow, the Boyds received pensions before their kinsman was finally promoted to the see.[111]

In the north, Donald Gormson of Skye – a MacDonald of Sleat – found his inability to write was no barrier to receiving in February 1571/2 a substantial gift under the privy seal of a pension of 1,000 merks from the bishopric of Aberdeen for his service in advancing the king's authority; in the same month, Lachlan MacIntosh of Dunachton, chief of clan Chattan, who had signed a bond of allegiance to King James in 1569, obtained a pension, again of 1,000 merks, from the bishopric of Moray for his assistance in maintaining the king's authority and in pursuing rebels; and, at the same point, Lord Lovat, the king's lieutenant in the north, was made factor and chamberlain of the bishopric of Moray till the see was filled.[112] In addition, numerous lesser men were either rewarded or recompensed for their service in the civil war through the bestowal of pensions from vacant bishoprics.[113]

As early as January 1570/1, a style had been devised for the provision of an archbishop to Glasgow, but no appointment was

---

[107] *RSS*, vi, nos. 1276, 1421, 1820; 1052, 1272, 2448; *RSS*, vii, no. 730.
[108] Ibid., vi, nos. 590, 729.
[109] Ibid., vi, no. 1255.
[110] Ibid., vi, nos. 1277, 1358, 1515.
[111] Ibid., vi, nos. 1736; 1722; 1791; 1874.
[112] Ibid., vi, nos. 1491, 1495; *RPC*, i, 654; *RSS*, vi, nos. 1494.
[113] Ibid., vi, nos. 892, 1004, 1051, 1185, 1186, 1265, 1399, 1459, 1680, 1769, 1785, 1792, 1841, 1843, 2003, 2184, 2446, 2700, 2701.

immediately forthcoming.[114] Perhaps it was deemed prudent not to proceed until Dumbarton castle was secured by the king's party in April when among the prisoners taken was the papalist archbishop of St Andrews, who was promptly executed for treason. Nonetheless, the government's decision by the summer to fill the two richest bishoprics of St Andrews and Glasgow was made without any apparent awareness – at this stage at least – that the candidates so promoted as bishops should exercise an active ministry in the church; and its action certainly denuded the crown of its right to enjoy episcopal revenues *sede vacante*. On the other hand, making appointments to the archbishoprics did at least provide the government with an added source of patronage which could be utilised, far more effectively than could mere grants of pensions during vacancies, to reward particular noble houses. This was readily accomplished through the simple device of bestowing the bishopric on a nominee who, as kinsman of a particular family, was well placed to divert on a generous scale episcopal property by grants not only of pensions but also of feus and tacks, which only a bishop, titular or otherwise, with the consent of his chapter could legally do. By August 1571 – at a point immediately preceding parliament's forfeiture of leading Marian supporters – the government proceeded to make a gift of the archbishopric of St Andrews to Morton's kinsman, John Douglas, the elderly principal of St Mary's college in the university; and John Porterfield, a minister apparently sponsored by the Earl of Glencairn with Lennox's blessing, was named as the candidate for Glasgow.[115] The government made no pretence of its purpose in filling the sees. The reason for the unilateral appointments was not to secure the services of bishops in the reformed church nor even to provide the church with a new source of finance but merely to permit leading members of the king's party access to episcopal revenues on a lavish scale. This was amply recognised by contemporary opinion.

With parliament's rejection, in August 1571, of the assembly's petition that benefices should be bestowed only upon qualified persons duly examined by the church, the barons, rallying to the kirk's defence, complained to the Regent Lennox of the 'corruption begunne' whereby 'the kirk sal be compelled to admitt dumbe dogges to the office, dignitie, and rents appointed for sustentatioun of preaching pastors', and they proceeded to condemn the milking of the prelacies:

[114] Ibid., vi, no. 1107.
[115] Calderwood, *History*, iii, 54–9; *RSS*, vi, no. 1228; cf., no. 2810.

'for whill that earles and lords become bishops and abbots, gentlemen, and courteours' babes, and persons unable to guide themselves, are promoted by you to suche benefices as require learned preachers. When such enormiteis are fostered, we say, what a face of a kirk sall we looke for ere it be long within this realme?'

Their protest ended on a constitutional note when the barons threatened to withdraw their continued service to the crown, 'for we are not ignorant of the mutuall contract that God hath placed betwixt the supreme power and the subjects'. Another contemporary commentator explained, no less vigorously, how 'everie erle lord and barroun tuik up all the landis abbasies bischopries to thame sellfis quhilk sould have sustenit the puir peopill'; and even the superintendent of Fife took action by threatening the titular archbishop of St Andrews with excom-munication if he dared vote in name of the kirk in parliament.[116]

Faced with mounting criticism, the newly installed government of the Regent Mar sought to placate the opposition by agreeing to appoint two superintendents, two of the assembly's commissioners for visiting provinces and two laymen to examine the qualifications of the new archbishops; and it was belatedly acknowledged by the government, in September 1571, that candidates promoted to sees 'ar to have the charge and owersicht of the inferior ministers' so that 'na avowit inyme to the trewth of God, nor ignorantis be sufferit to enjoy the patrimony of the kirk'. The government was clearly anxious to make concessions to satisfy ecclesiastical opinion, but no consideration seems to have been given to working out an agreed formula for admissions. This was dramatically illustrated, on the very day when the government announced its intention to examine the archbishops, with the crown's gift of the bishopric of Dunkeld to James Paton, who had at least served as a minister.[117]

The seemingly continued disregard by the government of the church's right to examine the aptitude of candidates so promoted – candidates whom the government then recognised had the charge and oversight of ministers – drew a sharp response from Erskine of Dun, as superintendent of Angus, who admonished the Regent Mar, in November 1571, for intruding false bishops in defiance of the kirk. In voicing his protest, Erskine argued that

[116] Calderwood, *History*, iii, 137, 144–6; R. Lindsay of Pitscottie, *The Historie and Cronicles of Scotland*, ed. A. J. G. Mackay, 3 vols. (Edinburgh, 1899–1911), ii, 260; R. Bannatyne, *Journal of the Transactions in Scotland* (Edinburgh, 1806), 246, 250–3, 255.
[117] *RSS*, vi, nos. 2810–12; *Fasti Ecclesiae Scoticanae*, ed. H. Scott, 10 vols. (Edinburgh, 1915–81), v, 67.

all benefices possessing tithes had a scriptural office annexed
which belonged to the kirk, whose superintendents had a
scriptural duty to examine all candidates promoted; and he
warned that 'a greater offence or contempt of God and his kirk
can no prince doe, than to sett up by his authoritie men in
spirituall offices, as to creat bishops and pastors of the kirk; for
so to doe, is to conclude no kirk of God to be; for the kirk can
not be, without it have its owne proper jurisdictioun and
libertie'.

The existing superintendents, therefore, must withstand the
intruded bishops who 'have no office nor jurisdictioun in the
kirk of God'; and 'that great misorder used in Stirline at the last
parliament, in creating bishops, placing them and giving them
vote in parliament as bishops, in despite of the kirk and high
contempt of God' must be remedied without delay, 'for if that
misordered creation of bishops be not reformed, the kirk will
first compleane unto God, and also unto all their brethrein,
members of the kirk within this realme, and to all reformed kirks
within Europe'. Such resolution, however, was tempered by a
recognition that if the church's programme for 'dismembring (as
they call it) of great benefices' could not be immediately secured
'in respect of this confused troublous time', then a compromise,
acceptable to crown and kirk, might be achieved, at least 'whill
further order may be tane'. This compromise, it was expected,
would confirm 'the king or others in their patronages' and
recognise 'their priviledges of presentatioun according to the
lawes', on condition that 'the examination and admissioun
perteane onlie to the kirk, of all benefices having cure of soules'.
Erskine was even ready to concede that surplus finances from the
prelacies, beyond the church's immediate needs, should be
assigned for the king's support 'whill further order may be tane
in these maters'. In reply to Erskine's letter, the Regent showed
himself ready to achieve an agreement 'by all possible meanes for
quietting of such things as were in controversie' and especially
'to procure the reforming of things disordered in all sorts, als
farre as may be, reteaning the priviledge of the king, crown and
patronage'.[118]

The outcome was the Convention of Leith where, in what was
reported to be a 'quiet conference', a financial settlement was
negotiated by no more than eight commissioners on either side
from the government and church. As the estates had deferred
discussion on the dissolution of the prelacies until such time as
the king came of age, it became plain that any temporary solution

[118] Calderwood, *History*, iii, 156–62; cf., the Regent's reply, ibid., 164.

on ecclesiastical endowment could be achieved only within the existing financial structure of benefices. From the outset, the Regent Mar had recognised that the settlement, so devised, should operate until 'his Highness perfect age; or while the same be altered and abolished be the three Estates in Parliament', and the general assembly, in turn, regarded the financial compromise devised at Leith not as a comprehensive and lasting settlement on ecclesiastical endowment, but as a temporary expedient to 'be only receivit as ane interim, untill farder and more perfyte ordour be obtainit at the handis of the Kings Majesties Regent and Nobilitie'.[119] Evidently, the church was not even prepared to adhere to the Leith settlement until the king's majority, for the expectation then was that agreement on the 'more perfyte ordour', which the assembly demanded, would be achieved rather more speedily after further negotiations with the new Regent, the Earl of Morton, who, as chancellor, had been one of the main architects of the Leith agreement.

V

The legacy of compromise:
Though subjected to severe criticism almost before it had begun to operate, the concordat of Leith was by no means unstatesmanlike. It offered a practical and practicable solution to the vexed question of the church's endowment, and it appeared to reconcile the needs of the church with the interests of crown and nobility. 'In consideratioun of the present state', it was decided not to alter the diocesan structure which existed 'befoir the reformatioun of religioun: at leist, to the Kingis Majesties majoritie, or consent of Parliament'. As vacancies arose, qualified candidates, of at least thirty years of age, were to be nominated by the crown within a year and a day, and thereafter examined by 'a certane assembly or cheptoure of learnit ministeris', who had power to elect or reject the candidates presented. The bishops, so elected, were to be subject to the general assembly in spiritual matters as they were to the crown in temporal affairs: they were to enjoy no greater jurisdiction in the church than that exercised by the superintendents, until 'the same be agreit upoun'; and they were to act with 'the advise of the best learnit of the Cheptour' in admitting candidates to the ministry.

This, then, was the machinery so provided in order that the church might gain proper access to the finances of the bishoprics. But the settlement also extended to the abbacies and priories,

---

[119] *CSP Scot.*, iv, no. 149; *RPC*, ii, 106ff; *BUK*, i, 207–8, 246.

from whose finances (other than the thirds) the church had been largely excluded. It was agreed that where vacancies occurred no further disposition of monastic property should be made until consideration was given to separating the teinds from the lands and rents of the appropriated churches, so that sufficient stipends might be allocated to the ministers serving at the annexed churches. Thereafter, suitable candidates promoted by the crown, to enjoy 'the remanent proffite and title of the benefice', were to represent the abbatial element, and sit with the bishops in parliament. On the extinction of the old monastic chapters, the ministers who served the annexed churches were to act in a capitular capacity in such matters as the disposition of monastic property; but, in the main, the revenues of the religious houses were not allocated to finance the work of the church, but were assigned instead, to sustain senators of the College of Justice and others employed in royal service who were considered eligible by the ordinary for promotion by the crown as titular abbots or commendators. It certainly was not envisaged that the title and office of abbot should be given to ministers. Such a step was evidently considered to be inappropriate or even improper. At any rate, it would obviously not have been easy, so shortly after the Reformation, to permit the appearance within the church of abbots and priors, whose suppression the reformers so strenuously had demanded in 1560. Besides, there was not even the slender prospect anyway that the crown and nobles, already in effective control of monastic revenues, would be persuaded to surrender their claims for the benefit of the church. If the church looked like acquiring at least a share of episcopal revenues, the crown and nobility seemed intent on maintaining their grip on monastic temporalities.

In the disposal of benefices having the cure of souls, which were attached to prelacies, the principle applied was that all such livings should be bestowed only on candidates for the ministry, of at least twenty-three years of age, who had been examined and found qualified by a bishop or superintendent 'of the true reformit Kirk'. Smaller vicarages, under £40 in yearly rental, were to be assigned not to trained ministers but to readers; and chaplainries were allocated to support bursars at the schools and universities. Common kirks attached to cathedrals were to be given to ministers as benefices; and prebends belonging to cathedrals and collegiate kirks were to be filled only after proper provision had been made for stipends by distinguishing the spirituality from the temporality. Even the poor were not ignored, for a tenth of the teinds was to be set aside for their needs. In all, however, by identifying the old financial structure with the work of the new church, the negotiators at Leith provided the machinery whereby most of the revenues, with the exception of the monastic temporalities, could be inherited by the kirk; and alongside this machinery for endowment stood the ancient system of patronage, which, though modified by the persistent inroads of the crown, was still retained in its entirety.[120]

Insofar as a settlement was achieved, time was obviously necessary before the machinery provided could produce the expected results. At the same time, however, criticism was voiced in the assembly in August 1572 of certain aspects of the agreement which were 'found slanderous and offensive to the ears of many of the brethren, appeirand to sound to papistrie'. Nor was this all. Concern over further dynastic appointments to sees, sometimes of an unreformed variety, over the failure of chapters to prevent scandalous promotions or to curb further dilapidation of episcopal revenues through nobles milking the bishoprics, and over the inability of bishops on their own admission adequately to administer their dioceses led the assembly by 1575 to consider the question 'whither if the Bischops, as they are now in the Kirk of Scotland, hes thair function of the word of God or not, or if the Chapiter appointit for creating of them aucht to be tollerated in this reformed Kirk'.[121] In any event, popular opinion, somewhat harshly, had already stigmatised the new bishops of 1572 as 'the lordis counterfett bischopis and nocht men of the kirk of God nor guid religioun';[122] and by 1576 the assembly itself had resolved to eliminate bishops, as such, from ecclesiastical administration.[123]

The assembly's dissatisfaction with the Leith settlement was said to be such that even the Regent was obliged to recognise that the church ought to devise an alternative solution if it were not prepared to stand by the concordat of 1572.[124] This was done in the Second Book of Discipline of 1578 which reasserted the First Book of Discipline's intention of dissolving the benefices and of abolishing patronage.[125] This programme, after all, had never fully been abandoned by the church; and it wholly accorded with John Knox's farewell advice to the church: before his death in

[120] BUK, i, 209–36.
[121] Ibid., i, 243–4, 246, 249, 261, 269–70, 278, 286–8, 295, 297, 300, 301, 303, 308–9, 314–15, 317–18, 320–1, 323, 325, 326–7, 331–3, 335–6, 340–3.
[122] Pitscottie, Historie, ii, 283; cf., 282.
[123] BUK, i, 353–61.
[124] Spottiswoode, History, ii, 202.
[125] The Second Book of Discipline, 122–4, 209–12, 217–29.

1572, Knox had urged the replacement of the Leith episcopacy by the system devised in 1560, and he was prepared only to acquiesce in further appointments to benefices in the belief that the assembly's policy was to regard the Leith settlement as a temporary expedient pending its supersession by a more satisfactory order.[126]

Nonetheless, the operation of the Leith arrangements had at least enabled, new appointments to be made with little delay to the sees of St Andrews, Glasgow, Dunkeld, the Isles, Dunblane, Moray, Ross and ultimately, in 1577, to Aberdeen, where vacancies had arisen either through the forfeiture or death of the previous incumbents. In Galloway, it seems to have been impossible to extinguish the rights and claims of the family of Alexander Gordon; while in Orkney there was no serious intention of dispossessing Adam Bothwell from the title or Lord Robert Stewart from the property of the bishopric. Argyll continued to be held by the ineffective James Hamilton till his death in 1580; and in Ross, Alexander Hepburn, who died in 1578, had no immediate successor until the provision of David Lindsay in 1600. Among the existing bishops who continued to act, Robert Stewart in Caithness, though ageing, seems to have been fairly respectable; and, in 1575, Alexander Campbell, who had received a gift of Brechin from Mary in 1566, had finally to be instructed in the work of a bishop by superintendent Erskine of Dun.[127]

Some of the bishops experienced great difficulty in obtaining, and then retaining, possession of their property and revenues. Ross was perhaps the worst example. There, the chancellor discovered by 1573 that one of the Mackenzies of Kintail had not only taken up residence in the steeple at the Chanonry, 'quhilk now is becum ane filthie sty and den of thevis', but had 'maisterfully reft' the tenants of the whole fruits of the benefice, and had suppressed the preaching of the Word. By 1579, matters had scarcely improved, for the bishop's widow recalled how Colin Mackenzie had denied even 'a plaid or blankat' to protect her 'bairnis fra cauld', and how he had prevented the bishop from obtaining fuel, 'meit, drink or lugeing' by 'usand sic inhumane and cruell dealing aganis him that for displesour thairof he fell seik and nevir recoverit quhill he depairtit this life'. Nor could Lord Methven, who had received the temporality of the vacant bishopric, obtain peaceful possession of his gift. One of the

---

[126] Bannatyne, *Journal*, 375; *BUK*, i, 248.
[127] Watt, *Fasti*, 299; 150; 100; 206; 78; 217; 270; 4, 132–3, 254, 270–1; 61; 41; *BUK*, i, 318.

bishop of Moray's houses was robbed in December 1573; the bishop of the Isles had some of his rents withheld by the Macleans and others; and James Boyd, the archbishop of Glasgow, had his troubles as well, when he found that his kinsman, Robert Boyd of Badinheath, who was earlier in receipt of a pension from the vacant archbishopric, had begun to demolish the archbishop's fortalice at Lochwood.[128]

Even when they gained effective access to their revenues, the bishops, as a whole, lost little time in rewarding kinsmen, friends and nobles with local interests by granting them feus, tacks and pensions on a generous scale. In Glasgow, where Porterfield's candidature for the archbishopric had been superseded in 1573 by that of James Boyd, the nephew of Lord Boyd, there was substance in the claim that the new bishop had been 'inducit be his Cheiff to tak the bischoprie, the gift wharof the said Lord Boid, being a grait counsallour to the Regent, haid purchassit for his commoditie'.[129] Certainly, the Regent Morton and the Boyds were prominent among the recipients of grants from the bishopric.[130] As Regent, Morton also advanced fellow Douglases to the sees of St Andrews and Moray; and when the St Andrews see again fell vacant, the Regent's former chaplain, Patrick Adamson, was appointed as successor, despite earlier opposition from the electoral chapter.[131] Once installed, Adamson showed his gratitude to the Regent by assigning pensions from the fruits of the bishopric to Morton's retainers and servitors,[132] while in the north, at least one royal confirmation survives of a charter granted by George Douglas, natural son of the Earl of Angus, as bishop of Moray to yet another Douglas.[133]

---

[128] RPC, ii, 276–7; iii, 88–9, 90–1; RSS, vii, no. 2090; RSS, vi, no. 2469; RPC, iii, 124–5; 98–9.

[129] RSS, vi, nos. 2142, 2175, 2192; The Autobiography and Diary of Mr James Melvill, ed. R. Pitcairn (Edinburgh, 1842), 47.

[130] RSS, vii, nos. 180, 2075; SRO, CH4/1/2, Reg. Pres. Ben., 83v, 84r (Boyds); RMS, iv, nos. 2199; 2382 (Boyd); 2407 (Boyd); 2727, 2764 (Morton); 2881 (Boyd); 2937 (Lord Boyd); 2938; 2012; v, nos. 90, 451–2, 463–5, 469, 475, 491, 500; 509 (Lord Boyd); 520–2, 565, 581, 591, 603–9, 616, 618–21, 623–5, 646, 647, 657, 659, 670, 958, 986, 1018–22, 1131; 1900 (Boyd).

[131] RSS., vi, nos. 1473–4, 1535; 2070, 2309, 2407; vii, nos. 789, 819; CSP Scot., v, no. 187, p. 181.

[132] RSS, vii, nos. 824, 862–64, 866–7, 869, 902, 916. For other grants of episcopal property by Adamson, see RSS, vii, nos. 827, 865, 868, 941, 1137, 1139, 1614, 1726, 1746, 2015, 2182, 2226, 2493, 2497; RMS, iv, nos. 2703–6, 2725, 2831, 2967, 3030; v, nos. 585, 632–3, 896, 1272, 1279, 1290, 2267; SRO, PS1/50, Register of the Privy Seal, fo. 49; PS1/51, fo. 86v; PS1/53, fos. 78, 86, 168; PS1/56, fo. 118.

[133] RMS, vi, no. 1800. For other tacks and pensions, see also SRO, PS1/51, fo. 106; PS1/54, fo. 37v.

The Earl of Argyll evidently had an interest in the appointment
to Dunkeld of James Paton, whom the assembly suspected of
having made a simoniacal pact with Argyll. The earl and other
Campbells, at any rate, were prominent beneficiaries of Paton's
financial transactions and, by 1576, the assembly had dismissed
Paton from office for dilapidating the resources of his see.[134]
Successive Earls of Argyll were influential in securing the
appointment of Campbells, first, to the sees of Brechin and the
Isles, and, then, to Argyll, with the death in 1580 of James
Hamilton, the previous bishop, who had rewarded both the Earl
of Argyll and at least one fellow Hamilton from the fruits of the
bishopric of Argyll.[135] All the Campbells, so promoted, were
active in making grants of episcopal property, frequently to other
Campbells including the Argylls; and Brechin showed particular
generosity to the fifth earl and his servitors.[136] The Earl of
Caithness was among the recipients of pensions from Robert
Stewart, as bishop of Caithness, and Gordon of Lochinvar and
Laurence Gordon were two beneficiaries of the dynasty of
Gordons appointed to the bishopric of Galloway.[137] In Orkney,
Adam Bothwell gained a not undeserved reputation as a
dilapidator; he exchanged the fruits of the bishopric for the
commend of Holyrood in 1568; and he was charged with
simony, though not so convicted, by the assembly in 1570.[138]
     A succession of Grahams replaced the former dynasty of
Chisholms in Dunblane, where the family of the Earls of

[134] R. Keith, *An Historical Catalogue of the Scottish Bishops*, ed. M. Russel
(Edinburgh, 1824), 97; *BUK*, i, 270, 300, 314, 332–3, 335–6, 340–1, 350–1; *RSS*,
vi, nos. 2003, 2367, 2446; *RMS*, iv, nos. 2236–44, 2318, 2397, 2504, 2631, 2719,
2871, 2989; v, nos. 122, 205, 542; Inveraray Castle, Argyll Transcripts, vi, 82, 214.
Argyll retained his financial interest in the bishopric even with the restoration of
Robert Crichton, the former Catholic bishop, by the conservative Arran regime
in 1584 (SRO, PS1/52, Register of the Privy Seal, fos. 21v, 51; PS1/54, fo. 125r-v;
PS1/55, fo. 79).
[135] Watt, *Fasti*, 41, 206; 28; *RSS*, vii, no. 341; Inveraray Castle, Argyll
Transcripts, vi, 222, 234; vii, 4, 23.
[136] *RSS*, vii, no. 554; Inveraray Castle, Argyll Transcripts, vi, 175, 209, 214; vii,
107, 208; SRO, PS1/63, Register of the Privy Seal, fo. 127v, (Isles); SRO, PS1/57,
fos. 28v–29; Argyll Transcripts, vii, 159, 176, 186, 193, 194, 262, 310 (Argyll);
RSS, vii, no. 978, 2355; SRO, CH4/1/2, Reg. Pres. Ben., 35v; *RMS*, iv, nos. 1745,
1764, 2228, 2443; v, nos. 138, 139, 242, 279, 786, 862, 890, 1059, 1271, 1278, 2006,
2808, 2833 (Brechin).
[137] *RSS*, vi, nos. 1593, 1721, 2536; vii, nos. 987; 269 (earl); SRO, PS1/55,
Register of the Privy Seal, fos. 53v, 220; PS1/63, fo. 124v; PS1/64, fo. 111
(Caithness); *RSS*, vi, no. 1746; vii, nos. 511; 832 (Lochinvar); 1699, 2222; SRO,
PS1/50, fo. 9v (Laurence Gordon); *RMS*, iv, no. 2694; v, nos. 174, 187, 271
(Galloway).
[138] *RMS*, iv, nos. 1668, 1710; G. Donaldson, 'Bishop Adam Bothwell and the
Reformation in Orkney', *RSCHS*, xiii (1959), 100; *RSS*, vi, no. 506; *BUK*, i,
162–3, 165–8.

Montrose, who already had a financial interest in the bishopric, secured the appointment of their own kinsmen – first Andrew and then George Graham – as bishops. [139] The smaller number of charters granted by Andrew Graham is no indication that he intended to behave as a model bishop. The truth is he set the entire lands of the bishopric in feu to one individual – the Earl of Montrose – whereby (so the petitioners complained to parliament in 1578) 'ane thousand of our soverane Lordis commonis and pure people wilbe put to uter heirschip and extreme beggartie . . . quhen as sa grite rowmes quhairupon so mony ar sustenit salbe reducit in the handis of ane particular man'. When later 'accusit for wasting and delapidatioun of the patrimony of the kirk and setting of takis thairof againis the actis of the generall assemblie', the bold bishop 'desyrit to knaw quhat was dilapidatioun of the patrimony' and was promptly reminded 'that setting of fewis or takis of landis or teindis with diminutioun of the auld dewatty, setting of victuell for small pricis of silvir, geving of pentionis, namelie, to unqualefiet personis, and siclyk, was delapidatioun'. But there were parties besides the courts of the church who continued to complain of Graham's financial transactions. The spokesman for the 'possessuris and tennentis of the kirk landis of the bischoprik' protested in 1582 that Graham had: [140]

> 'nocht onelie to the grit hurt, damnage and skayth of his successuris bot alswa to the extreim hurt of us, possessuris and tennentis of the saidis kirk landis, sauld, delapidat and put away the haill leving of the said bishoprie, or at the lest ane gret part thairof in gret menis handis. . . .'

In Aberdeen, David Cunningham, the former dean of faculty at Glasgow University, had little opportunity to offer financial rewards. His Catholic predecessor, William Gordon, had already exhausted the patrimony of the bishopric, effected by means of the 'lait conventioun, concluded between the bishop and Queen Mary whereby 'the haill thrids of the said bishoprik wes disponit in tak and assedatioun' to Gordon for life, in return for the payment of 1,000 merks. The outcome was that 'the haill patrimony' had become:

> 'delapidat and exhausit . . ., the temporall landis and teindis gevin in fewis and assedationis, the haill victuallis and customes convertit in small pryces of silver and the silver maillis consumet by mony and grit pensionis, quhilk prodigall dispositioun hes bene ratefeit and conservit be his hienes said umquhile moder in

[139] Watt, *Fasti*, 78; *RSS*, vi, nos. 590, 729.
[140] *RSS*, vii, nos. 1795, 2008; SRO, PS1/58, Register of the Privy Seal, fos. 83, 110v; *RMS*, iv, no. 2912; *APS*, iii, 111–12; *Stirling Presbytery Records*, 71.

hir majoritie, be his gracis regentis, and his majesties self,
quhairby the said bischoprik in thrid and twa pairt was altogedder
waistit and dilapidat befoir the successioun and entres of the said
Mr David thairto. . . .'

Cunningham therefore found that he had merely gained 'naikit
titill and enteres to the propertie', which yielded only £400 a
year; yet he was still obliged to pay 800 merks 'in satisfactioun of
his thriddis, quhilk soume exceidis far the rait of his present
patrimony'.[141] There were difficulties, too, at Glasgow, where
Robert Montgomery was promoted to the see in 1581 by an
arrangement which gave the Duke of Lennox a lease of the
bishopric for £1,000 a year, though there was still opportunity
for Montgomeries, and others, to benefit from episcopal gifts.[142]

Any expectation that the church might sufficiently augment its
depleted resources by operating the Leith agreement was soon to
be disappointed. The continued milking of the bishoprics by
noble families had merely led to a diminution in the revenues
available for the work of the church. As it was, the resources of
the bishoprics at the time of the Reformation (it has been
estimated) ranged from a mere £1,300 in annual returns for
Caithness, £1,350 for Orkney, £1,400 for Galloway, £1,500 for
Dunblane, £1,800 for Brechin and up to £6,500 for St Andrews.[143]
Episcopal resources were not inexhaustible; the property was
subject to taxation; and the financial dealings of the Leith
bishops, along with the heritage of earlier gifts from episcopal
property, ensured that the church received far less than its fair
share of finance. All this goes far towards explaining the
assembly's hostile reaction to the operation of the Leith
arrangements and its determination to replace the Leith episcopacy by a 'more perfyte ordour'.

The arrangements devised at Leith, however, were also
applicable to the abbacies; but even if the proposals had been
consistently applied, it would have taken a generation or so to
clear out the existing commendators over whose appointment
there had been no ecclesiastical control whatsoever. Besides, the
retention of the monastic dignities (the offices of abbot and
prior) as legal and financial entities spelt an end, in the

[141] Watt, *Fasti*, 4; Durkan and Kirk, *University of Glasgow*, 309, 338; SRO,
PS1/61, Register of the Privy Seal, fo. 42r-v; PS1/65, fo. 196r-v. See further,
PS1/47, fo. 113v; Ps1/55, fo. 204; PS1/56, fos. 23v, 89; PS1/62, fo. 5v; *RMS*, v,
nos. 555, 876, 1124.

[142] Spottiswoode, *History*, ii, 282; SRO, PS1/49, Register of the Privy Seal, fos.
133v, 138; PS1/50, fo. 9v; PS1/55, fo. 218; PS1/59, fo, 88; PS1/62, fo. 154v;
PS1/63, fo. 5ov, 150; PS1/64, fo. 80.

[143] G. Donaldson, 'Leighton's Predecessors', *Journal of the Society of the
Friends of Dunblane Cathedral*, xii, pt. ii (1975), 7–16, at 7.

foreseeable future at least, to the prospect of dissolving the prelacies, as the assembly had argued. This, in turn, was fatal to the likelihood of satisfactory stipends being assigned to the ministers of the appropriated churches, until at least such time as abbacies fell vacant; and it was contrary to the claim that the teinds were the proper patrimony of the kirk. When a vacancy in an abbacy did occur, however, the proposals at Leith at least provided for an assessment of 'quhat portioun of the rentis consistis in kirkis and teinds, and quhat portioun in temporall landes', so that ministers serving at the annexed churches might be 'sustenit of the fruits belanging to the same kirkis, gif it be possible, be speciall assignatioun of samekle yeirlie stipend as salbe found reasonable', to be decided by the bishop or superintendent of the diocese and privy councillors deputed to that effect.

The provisions for the appointment to abbacies of men of ability and repute were by no means entirely inoperative. Only 'well learnit and qualifeit' candidates examined and approved by the bishop of the province, it had been established in 1572, should be promoted to the abbacies, for they were expected to undertake service in the commonwealth and to vote as part of the ecclesiastical estate in parliament. Recognition of the church's newly acquired right to examine the crown's nominees to abbacies is apparent, not least, in the terms of the gift of Beauly to John Fraser in January 1572/3, which specified that Fraser, found sufficiently qualified by the ordinary, was to receive institution from the superintendent (or commissioner) of Ross. This went further than the earlier gift to Henry Kinneir *in expectationem* of the abbacy of Balmerino in 1569 which had merely recognised that Kinneir was 'sufficientlie qualifeit in lettiris, science and gude behaviour' to hold the office, but significantly enough the charter which finally secured for Kinneir effective possession in 1574 acknowledged the archbishop's testimony of Kinneir's suitability and directed the archbishop to give him institution. Similarly, the gift to Alexander Forbes of the priory of Monymusk in August 1574 recognised Forbes' academic qualifications and his suitability for the post, attested by the commissioner of the diocese of Aberdeen, to whom a mandate was directed to give him institution.[144]

At a convention of estates, however, which met on 5 March 1574/5, the decision was taken that no further dispositions of vacant abbacies, priories or nunneries should be made by the

[144] *BUK*, i, 210; *RSS*, vi, nos. 1801; 635, 2467, 2807; *RMS*, vi, nos. 2232, 2290.

crown until such time as a constitution for the church had been determined and established, not later than Easter 1576. The enactment evidently came too late to prevent the gift of Eccles to James Hume from passing the privy seal on 26 March 1576; but when appointments resumed, the whole trend was for the crown to disregard the provisions reached at Leith for the promotion of suitably qualified candidates duly examined by the church. Certainly, there was no hint in the preferment to Pluscarden of James Douglas, the Regent's illegitimate son, that he had undergone examination by the church; and Thomas Fraser, who was 'nocht of perfyte age', was promoted to Beauly while still a minor in November 1579, though his tenure was short-lived, and in February 1580/1 the priory was gifted to Adam Cuming.[145]

If the principles of 1572, applicable to the abbacies, had evidently fallen into desuetude, the machinery which once more operated looked like safeguarding the proprietary rights established by leading noble families over the disposal of monastic property. The proposals of 1572, intent as they were on promoting men of ability and repute, threatened to undermine the quasi-hereditary rights enjoyed by successive lay commendators of a particular noble family, for the intention had been to make service and ability, rather than birth, the criteria for advancement to the abbacies. That a principle of heredity continued to operate in the control of monastic property well after the Reformation is all too evident in the succession of Hamiltons at Paisley and at Arbroath, though with interruptions through forfeiture, in the succession of Leslies at Lindores, of Campbells at Iona and Ardchattan, Colvilles at Culross, Keiths at Deer, Kers at Newbattle, the Ruthvens at Scone, Frasers at Beauly, and Erskines at Cambuskenneth, Dryburgh and Inchmahome. The Stewarts also came to be well entrenched in St Andrews, Pittenweem, Inchcolm and Arbroath, and, for a spell, at Crossraguel and Whithorn.

This being so, the dilapidation of monastic property continued unabated on a scale which no doubt surpassed even that of the bishoprics, for the checks on alienation were purely minimal; and there was substance in the Second Book of Discipline's complaint in 1578 that the continued existence of conventual chapters 'servis for nathing now bot to set fewis and takis (gif ony thing be left) of kirk landis and teindis in hurt and prejudice thairof, as daylie experience teached'. The assembly, which registered the Second Book of Discipline among its acts in April

[145] *APS*, iii, 90; *RSS*, vii, nos. 140, 885, 2113, 2133; SRO, CH4/1/2, Reg. Pres. Ben., fo. 49v; *RMS*, v, no. 105.

1581, also took the step of summoning all commendators suspected of 'devoreing the patrimonie . . . and daylie diminisching the rents of thair benefices', and it reiterated the old claim that the 'Prelacies be dissolvit'.[146]

The evident failure to secure satisfactory stipends for ministers of the annexed churches, even with the appointment of new commendators, led to parliament's intervention in November 1581. All promotions to prelacies were declared to be null, unless provision were made for ministers' stipends; but in spite of the act, the assembly continued to lament in 1583 that 'abbacies are disponed, without any provisioun made for the Ministers serving the kirks annexed therto, directlie against the act of parliament'. The abbacy of Arbroath granted to Esmé Stewart, Duke of Lennox (and subsequently gifted to Ludovic Stewart in July 1583) was cited by the assembly as one conspicuous example where no provision had been made for ministers' stipends. Nor was this all. Criticism was also voiced at how 'spirituall livings are given to bairnes and translatit in temporal lordschips'. Holyrood had been gifted to the abbot's 'yong sone', John Bothwell, in February 1581/2; Newbattle had been bestowed on the existing commendator's son, under an arrangement whereby Mark Ker had been presented to the abbacy during his father's lifetime; and Scone had been erected into a temporal or secular lordship in favour of William, Lord Ruthven, the Earl of Gowrie, in October 1581.[147]

A temporary dislocation in the landholding pattern which had permitted the abbacies virtually to remain the preserves of particular noble houses is apparent with the onset of the Arran regime's conservative reaction against the ultra-protestant policies pursued by the preceding regime of the Ruthven lords, who, by 1584, had fled for safety to England, along with the leading presbyterian ministers.[148] As was to be expected in the circumstances, Gowrie lost Scone with his forfeiture in 1584, though the property was later restored to the family, after the collapse of Arran's rule, in 1586.[149] The ultra-protestant Erskines temporarily lost Cambuskenneth, Dryburgh and Inchmahome: Cambuskenneth was gifted in August 1584 to the Master of Livingston, an opponent of the Ruthven raiders; Inchmahome,

[146] BUK, ii, 504, 513, 514.
[147] APS, iii, 211; BUK, ii, 632; SRO, CH4/1/2, Reg. Pres. Ben., fos. 91–2; RMS, v, no. 594; BUK, ii, 632, 634, 644; SRO, CH4/1/2, fo. 71; RMS, v, nos. 483, 724; 258.
[148] G. Donaldson, 'Scottish Presbyterian Exiles in England, 1584–1588', RSCHS, xiv (1963), 67–80.
[149] RMS, v, no. 695; APS, iii, 479, 591.

in the same month, went to Henry Stewart, son of Lord Doune, a supporter of Arran; and Dryburgh was granted at the same time to William Stewart of Caverstoun.[150] The Pitcairns were dislodged from Dunfermline in favour of the Master of Gray, a former Marian and promoter of the 'Association' (a scheme of joint rule by James and his mother), who became commendator in September 1585, though his tenure was indeed brief and by May 1587 the Earl of Huntly had secured the property. Kilwinning, somewhat surprisingly, was retained by the Cunninghams: James Cunningham obtained a gift of the abbacy in March 1584/5 in succession to Alexander Cunningham, despite Glencairn's support for the Ruthven raid in August 1582; but there was no surprise in the confirmation in October 1585 of Arran's own rights to the commend of St Andrews priory, after the resignation of Robert Stewart, Earl of March.[151]

The Arran regime (like preceding and, indeed, succeeding administrations) did little to impede the complete secularisation of monastic property, which looked like being achieved either by direct annexation to the crown or by the erection of this not inconsiderable property into heritable, temporal lordships. Either solution, however, completely disregarded any claim for the restitution of this property as patrimony of the church. Scone may have been one of the earliest erections of abbatial property into secular lordships, but others soon followed. By July 1587, Newbattle, Deer and Paisley were all converted into hereditary lordships in favour of the existing commendators, namely, Mark Ker, Robert Keith and Claud Hamilton; and in each case firm provision was made for the ministry either by specifying the stipends or by reserving parochial teinds for the support of the ministry.[152]

July 1587 was also the month in which the act of annexation was approved by parliament. Insofar as it contributed to the eclipse of episcopacy by appropriating to the crown the temporalities of benefices, the act was clearly a victory for the presbyterians, who were once more in the ascendancy, but it by no means satisfied presbyterian principles, which required nothing less than a comprehensive restitution of ecclesiastical property. Following the precedent established by James II's annexation of certain lands in 1455, and on the understanding that the crown had been 'greitly hurte' by the dispositions 'of

[150] SRO, CH4/1/2, Reg. Pres. Ben., fo. 105; *RMS*, v, nos. 720, 723; SRO, CH4/1/2, fo. 128.
[151] SRO, CH4/1/2, Reg. Pres. Ben., fos. 82v–83, 137–8, 173v; 125v–126; SRO, PS1/53, Register of the Privy Seal, fo. 58v.
[152] *RMS*, v, nos. 1307, 1309, 1320.

auld to abbayis, Monasteries and utheris personis of the clergy',
parliament sanctioned the annexation to the crown of the
ecclesiastical temporalities, with the exception of certain specified
ecclesiastical properties already erected into temporal lordships:
the earldom of Gowrie, the lordship of Deer or Altrie, the
baronies of Newbattle, Broughton and Kerse, the burgh of
Canongate and part of Leith, the barony of Whitekirk, formerly
belonging to Holyrood, the lordship of Musselburgh, hitherto
pertaining to Dunfermline, and the temporalities of Paisley,
Pluscarden, Coldingham, Kelso and Lesmahagow, as well as
certain lands of North Berwick priory, were all exempted from
the terms of the act; another category of exemptions favoured
John Hamilton, commendator of Arbroath, John Bothwell,
commendator of Holyrood, and Robert Douglas, provost of
Lincluden, who were expressly confirmed in their livings.
Benefices in lay patronage were also excepted from the terms of
the act; but, at best, all that the church was entitled to receive
from this measure were the teinds which, as spirituality, were
expressly reserved along with manses and glebes for the support
of the ministry.[153]

Designed to augment royal finances, the act considerably
extended royal patronage in the sense that James was better
placed to reward loyal supporters from this profitable new
source of property at the crown's disposal; but any dislocation
which may have been anticipated was not pronounced in
practice, for many properties were merely regranted to their
previous possessors, the former commendators, who benefited
by having their lands converted into hereditary lordships.
Indeed, by the end of the reign, at least twenty-one out of thirty
abbacies had been transferred into secular lordships. At the same
time, the act did nothing to increase the crown's right of
patronage in the sense of presenting candidates to the annexed
benefices; rather the reverse was true. After all, the crown
already enjoyed, and had exercised for at least two decades, the
right of presenting ministers to most churches appropriated to
religious houses and to many prebends attached to cathedrals.

There were, of course, exceptions, for certain commendators
retained, or were granted, rights of presentation to annexed
churches. Andrew Moncrieff, on acquiring the commend of
Elcho in 1570, had been authorised 'to dispoun ony inferiour
benefices, chaiplanreis or alteragis quhen thai happin to vaik',
but, in truth, the only parochial benefice annexed to Elcho was
Dun, and the crown proceeded to present its own candidates to

[153] APS, iii, 431–7.

Dun on at least five occasions between 1570 and 1583. At Glenluce, Laurence Gordon as commendator in 1582 received the right to present to the appropriated churches of the abbacy, a right which indeed had been enjoyed by his immediate predecessors, but the only church was that of Glenluce itself, and the same circumstances applied at Pittenweem, with its appropriated churches, when William Stewart was chosen as commendator in 1583. Although Coldingham had been gifted in 1571 to Alexander Hume, who obtained a confirmation of the patronage of the annexed churches in February 1573/4, the crown assumed the right to make presentations from 1574, and despite gifts of the commend of Paisley, first, to William Erskine in November 1579 and, then, to Claud Hamilton in May 1586, with the patronage of the appropriated churches, the crown continued its practice of making new appointments to benefices attached to the abbey.[154] Nonetheless, the policy which ensued of creating temporal lordships from monastic properties threatened to fragment the rights of patronage to parochial benefices which had come to be consolidated, so substantially, in the possession of the crown.

VI

Patronage and popular election – the unresolved tension:
Hitherto the coexistence, with a minimum of friction, of a system of ecclesiastical patronage with a policy designed to protect congregational rights might best be explained by the concentration of so much patronage in the hands of the crown, which, for the most part, conscientiously discharged its duties in accordance with the legislation of 1567 governing presentations to the lesser benefices. In sharp contrast to the crown's extensive ecclesiastical patronage, the nobility had relatively little control over presentations to parochial benefices. In 1559, David Lindsay, Earl of Crawford, had the patronage of numerous chaplainries, but the only parochial benefices then mentioned were the parsonage and vicarage of Inverarity. A charter in favour of Andrew, Earl of Rothes in 1564 specified the patronage of four parish churches; the Earl of Eglinton was recognised to hold the patronage of two parish churches in 1565; and the Earl Marischal's patronage increased from at least five parishes in 1587 to eight in 1592. Even Esmé Stewart, as Earl of Lennox, was merely assigned in 1580 the patronage of Dumbarton collegiate kirk and, more vaguely, 'ceterarum ecclesiasticarum et capel-

---

[154] *RSS*, vi, no. 911; Cowan, *Parishes*, 217; *RMS*, v, nos. 336; 78, 335; Cowan, *Parishes*, 219; *RMS*, v, no. 593; Cowan, *Parishes*, 223; *RSS*, vi, nos. 1163, 2318; *RMS*, iv, no. 2178; *RMS*, iv, no. 2922; v, no. 995; see also n.96 above.

laniarum dicti comitatus'. Where circumstances permitted, it was possible, of course, for a noble who had lost effective exercise of the patronage of a particular living at one point to recover it at another: in 1567, the Earl of Glencairn, as superior, was able to redeem from Cunningham of Glengarnock certain lands, with the patronage of the island kirk of Inchcailloch on Loch Lomond, which the laird was obliged to resign in the earl's favour. Another patron, the Earl Marischal even succeeded in presenting to the parsonage of Strathbrock in West Lothian the king's secretary, who was no minister of religion, an action which the archbishop of St Andrews duly approved by authorising collation to the candidate (presumably because the parsonage formed a prebend of the collegiate kirk of Kirkheugh in St Andrews and did not directly support the parish ministry). More defensible was the earl's subsequent decision to award the parsonage to a university student in philosophy or Arts, who gained collation in October 1585.[155]

In England, a puritan patron like the 3rd Earl of Huntingdon had the patronage of seven benefices in 1560, only to have acquired anther seven by 1570.[156] A study of the influence of the nobility's patronage in the protestant church, which does exist for the Elizabethan church,[157] has yet to be undertaken for Scotland, but if a Scottish parallel is sought for the Earl of Bedford or for the Earl of Leicester, as a patron of 'godly' preachers, it might be found in Lord James Stewart, the Earl of Moray, who was probably responsible more than any individual for securing key appointments of protestant ministers at the Reformation.

As a leader of the lords of the Congregation and commendator of the Augustinian priory in St Andrews, Stewart had been well-placed to foster the growth of protestantism in the primatial city, which had an organised kirk session at least as early as October 1559, with Adam Heriot, an Augustinian canon, as minister; by 1560 another Augustinian from St Andrews, John Duncanson, was placed as minister of Stirling (a kirk annexed to the Benedictine house of Dunfermline); and a third, Patrick Kinloquhy, served at Linlithgow, which was appropriated to St Andrews

[155] *RMS*, iv, nos. 1353, 1564, 1674, 1587; v, no. 2176; iv, no. 2972; SRO, NP1/10, Protocol Book of James Nicolson, 1545–79, fos. 98v–99r (Inchcailloch); SRO, GD30/1968–74, Shairp of Houstoun Muniments.

[156] M. C. Cross, 'Noble Patronage in the Elizabethan Church', *The Historical Journal*, iii (1960), 1–16, at 3.

[157] M. R. O'Day, 'Clerical Patronage and Recruitment in England in the Elizabethan and early Stuart periods, with special reference to the diocese of Coventry and Lichfield' (unpublished London Ph.D. thesis, 1972).

priory. Stewart was also one of the nobles who had earlier invited John Knox to return from Geneva in 1557; Christopher Goodman, who served for a spell as minister in St Andrews, was considered to be his 'greyt freynd'; and he was instrumental in winning over to protestantism John Winram, the sub-prior, who became superintendent of Fife, and John Row, from the papal curia, who entered the ministry apparently at Kennoway, another parish kirk annexed to St Andrews priory, in April 1560 before moving to Perth. Also associated with Stewart's circle was the group from St Andrews – twenty-one individuals in all – considered by the general assembly in December 1560 to be qualified 'for ministreing and teaching'. Another protégé, commended to the English government in 1560, was Patrick Cockburn, a teacher of theology in St Leonard's college in St Andrews, which had particularly close ties with the priory there. Cockburn earlier had accompanied Stewart to Paris in 1548; he received an annual pension from Stewart in 1552 of £50 from the parish of Leuchars, annexed to the priory; he became a prebendary of Dunbar collegiate kirk, and, finally, served as minister at Haddington, yet another parish appropriated to St Andrews priory. Indeed, Augustinian canons serving most parishes annexed to the priory followed Stewart's lead and conformed, undertaking service as ministers and readers in the reformed church.[158]

The principles which operated in early appointments and the degree of congregational initiative asserted in selecting ministers are not readily to be discerned, but once the initial phase of uncertainty and expediency had lapsed, it is probable that the views of congregations and kirk sessions were widely respected, regardless of the attitudes of patrons to the Reformation. That this proved possible is attributable to the essential moderation of the Scottish Reformation which permitted existing holders of benefices to retain their titles and property irrespective of their religious persuasion. This meant that a majority of benefices were already occupied and therefore unavailable for protestant ministers not already in possession of a benefice under the old regime. This being so, patrons could, and did, continue to present to benefices and, by a different process, ministers were admitted to serve congregations, a distinction which had constantly to be kept in view. Even where a minister secured a

[158] *RStAKS*, i, 3, 5; *Fasti Ecclesiae Scoticanae*, v, 230; iv, 317; i, 214; Knox, *Works*, i, 267–8; *CSP Scot.*, ii, no. 316; i, no. 902; *Fasti*, v, 91; *BUK*, i, 4; *Fasti*, i, 368; *RSS*, v, no. 1576. The annexed churches are listed in Cowan, *Parishes*, 224, and biographical details of the conforming Augustinian canons are provided in the *Fasti*.

benefice, the likelihood was that the benefice which he held was geographically removed from the parish at which he had undertaken service.

This curious situation, which prevailed in many parishes, survived long after the act of 1567, permitting ministers access to the lesser benefices, and even after the act of 1573, depriving nonconformist benefice-holders. Only in instances where a minister was presented simultaneously to the benefice and to the church of the parish where he was selected to serve had the rights of patron and congregation to be reconciled. The tendency in royal presentations from 1567, however, was to assign to ministers the benefices (at first the vicarages) belonging to the parishes where the ministers served, so that the parallel systems of presentation to benefices, as financial entities, and of admissions to congregations ultimately coalesced.

At the same time, the First Book of Discipline had insisted that 'it appertaineth to the people and to everie severall Congregation to elect their Minister', and it even considered that 'the presentation of the people to whom he should be appointed Pastor must be preferred to the presentation of the counsell or greater church'. The superintendents and commissioners appointed by the general assembly to admit ministers were accordingly obliged to respect congregational views. The rights of some parishioners, at any rate, seem to have triumphed at Abernethy (a parish appropriated to Arbroath) when the superintendent of Fife, in 1567, duly arranged for the minister of Longforgan to give institution, following collation, to a new minister, William Haitlye, who had been 'presented and nominated' to the parish kirk (and to a quarter of the benefice) by Crichton of Sanquhar, Boyd of Petkindy, two Drummonds of Smithton, three Boyds and the rest of the inhabitants of the parish. Another presentation in 1568 explicitly sought to respect congregational rights by specifying that the superintendent should give collation to the crown's presentee 'if he finds him sufficientlie qualifit in the premissis and having the benevolence and electioun of the parochinnaris of the . . . parroche kirk of Moneydie'. The unusual rubric here was not without relevance: the successful candidate presented (who was the minister of the neighbouring kirks of Foulis Wester, Kinkell and Madderty) was obliged to contest the title of a rival claimant to the parsonage of Moneydie, in July 1569.[159]

[159] *The First Book of Discipline*, 96, 99; *BUK*, i, 16; SRO, NP1/16, Protocol Book of Duncan Gray, 1554–72, 3 [August] 1567; *RSS*, vi, no. 82; SRO, CS7/45, Register of Acts and Decreets of the Court of Session, fos. 453r–454r.

A similar procedure observed in January 1571/2, at the admission of the minister at Dailly to the vicarage of Kirkcudbright-Invertig (or Ballantrae), also acknowledged parishioners' rights: there the minister of Leith, as 'superintendent' (or more exactly commissioner) of Ayrshire, directed by the 'kirk principal of this realme', arranged for the crown's presentation of April 1571 to be read to the parishioners of Kirkcudbright-Invertig by the neighbouring minister (and parson) of Colmonell who then admitted the presentee on finding none of the parishioners opposed the choice or offered an alternative candidate for consideration. The whole exercise, designed as it was to improve the lot of a serving minister with an established congregation (whose meagre stipend of £20 in 1567 was the subject of litigation in December 1573), was considered only to have due force once the parishioners' opinions had been duly canvassed. Besides, parliament itself had intervened in 1567 by acceding to the request that patrons should be empowered to make new presentations to benefices granted contrary to the 'ordoure' of the Book of Discipline, so that the church might be delivered from 'unproffitable pastouris'.[160]

In all, it was probably at least as true for Scotland as it was for England that 'godly' patrons took the wishes of their congregations into account. In England, archdeacon Lever's demand that the congregation should join with the patron in assenting to the presentation was wholly applicable to Scotland, where a candidate was normally required to preach for three successive Sundays in the church of the parish where he was presented, and only if the congregation was satisfied with the choice would the ecclesiastical authorities proceed to grant collation to the benefice and give admission to the church. Local pressures and family connections no doubt had a bearing on the selection of candidates. A patron's desire to provide a living for a kinsman, friend or servitor, or to advance the cause of a particular preacher were obvious enough motives; and even though a congregation possessed the negative right of objecting to the patron's choice, the initiative still lay with the patron to select a second candidate, within six months, to fill the vacancy. At the same time, however, the patron was no longer able to disregard the valid objections of the people, and the rejection of the patron's candidate either by the examining ecclesiastical authorities or by the congregation was a serious blow to the patron's prestige and

[160] SRO, NP1/11, Protocol Book of James Colville, 1545–78, fo. 45v; SRO, CS7/42, Register of Acts and Decreets, fos. 519v–520r; cf., RSS, vi, no. 1147; APS, iii, 37.

influence in the community. It was therefore in the patron's own interest to secure a choice satisfactory to all. Consequently, in the decades after 1567 – at a time when the patronage of parochial benefices was still, in effect, concentrated in the possession of the crown – a majority of presentations went forward without noticeable friction or controversy.

By the late 1580s, the assumption by presbyteries of powers to supervise admissions and to grant collation, which had won the assembly's approval in 1581 but which was belatedly recognised by parliament in 1592, strengthened the ecclesiastical machinery and helped to check any recurrence of the old abuse, detected in the Second Book of Discipline of 1578, whereby a patron, presumably with the bishop's connivance, had intruded his nominee 'without lauchfull electioun and the assent of the peple ovir quhom the persone is placet'. Although the Second Book of Discipline had affirmed that the 'ordour quhilk Goddis word cravis can not stand with patronagis and presentationis to benefices usit in the papis kirk' and had therefore advocated their abolition, it was far from easy to resolve the inherent tensions between the two systems accentuated in the Book of Discipline. After all, patronage, which had originated in the assignment of land for the foundation of a church (*fundatio*), the erection of a church usually at a landowner's expense (*aedificatio*), and the granting of the means of support for the upkeep of the church and its minister (*donatio*), had long been recognised, and was jealously guarded by patrons, as a heritable property-right, normally conveyed with a barony or lands to which it was appendant. In short, the right of presentation, in the language of the lawyers, was an incorporeal hereditament, upheld by statute law; and the distinction observed in charters conveying property 'cum advocatione ecclesiarum et beneficiorum' and 'cum iure patronatus . . .' would seem to be explained on the basis that the more comprehensive *ius patronatus* also included a title to the patronage of the teinds, where a right of titularity was held to be incidental or accessory to a patron's rights over land held 'cum decimis inclusis' – another important factor in explaining the refusal of patrons to accept the claims of the assembly and Second Book of Discipline; hence the assembly's patient acceptance in 1582 that the rights of patrons should continue to be respected 'unto the tyme the lawes be reformed according to the Word of God'.[161]

---

[161] *BUK*, ii, 514, 568, 602; *APS*, iii, 542; *BUK*, ii, 509; 564–5, cf., 568.

In an effort to introduce a measure of commonsense into the tenure of benefices and to resolve the confused situation still prevalent, the assembly had decreed in 1578, and again in 1580, that presentations to benefices should be restricted to the minister of the parish where the benefice lay.[162] The measure was not ineffective. Archibald Livingston, for example, on being presented to a benefice, indicated in 1583 that 'becaus he was lauchfullie provydit to the parsonage of Cultir, he acknawlegit him self to be bund thairby of his dewatie to serve in the cuir of the ministrie at the kirk thairof'.[163] But the implementation of the assembly's enactment, which meant that sooner or later vacancies to benefices and parish churches would occur simultaneously, also had the effect of making explicit the tensions between the rights of patron and congregation; and the system itself to which presbyterianism was opposed was not without its weaknesses.

Presbyteries were often critical of the calibre of candidates presented by patrons. In 1594, Glasgow presbytery refused a presentation from the 'commendator' of Paisley 'as against the laws of God and man and good conscience'; it also required Stirling of Keir to present three candidates before it finally accepted one as minister of Baldernock.[164] Stirling presbytery also refused to admit a candidate presented by Blackadder of Tulliallan as patron; and Edinburgh presbytery upheld the complaints of the parishioners of St Cuthbert's in 1586 that the candidate had sought the votes of the gentry in the parish contrary to the order observed, and it proceeded to condemn the admission as 'corrupt and not according to the ordour of a reformit kirk'.[165] It is significant, too, that the candidate promoted by a couple of lairds to Kemback in Fife should think is necessary to point out to the presbytery in 1596 that his 'contract wes bot subscryvit be the holl parochineris quhilk he cravit to be don befoir his admissioun'.[166] Yet there were also limits to the extent to which a presbytery was prepared to

---

[162] BUK, ii, 409, 462.
[163] SRO, CH4/722/1, Stirling Presbytery Records, 8 Oct. 1583 [now transferred to Central Regional Archives, Stirling]; Stirling Presbytery Records, 1581–1587, ed. J. Kirk (Edinburgh, 1981), 177.
[164] Strathclyde Regional Archives, Glasgow Presbytery Records, i, fo. 21v, 26 Feb. 1593/4; fos. 8r-v, 9v, 12v, 21v, 32v, 34r-v, 24 April, 8 May, 15 May, 25 July 1593; 12 Feb. 1593/4; 16 July, 30 July 1594.
[165] SRO, CH4/722/2, Stirling Presbytery Records. 6 June, 1 Aug., 12 Sept., 19 Sept. 1599; 16 Jan. 1600; SRO, CH4/121/1, Edinburgh Presbytery Records, 24 May, 31 May, 14 June 1586.
[166] Holy Trinity Parish Church, St Andrews: St Andrews Presbytery Records, 4 Nov. 1596.

champion congregational rights. On a vacancy arising at St Ninians near Stirling, a church annexed to Cambuskenneth abbey, the rights of the patron (be it commendator or crown) were eclipsed in 1587 when a powerful group of lairds on the kirk session presented their own leet of three prospective ministers to the presbytery for examination, so that all three, on being found qualified, might then be 'presentit to the particular assemblie of the said parroche kirk, thair to be voittit be thame quhome thai sould think maist meit to the said offeice'; but when it discovered that the 'particular assemblie of sum of the elderis and deacunis and utheris of the said parrochun' were about to elect and admit a minister without its consent, the presbytery promptly condemned the proceedings as 'plaine repugnant to Godis Word and gud ordur', since 'the admissione of all ministeris is onlie in the handis of the presbyteriis and utheris assembleis of ministeris'.[167]

At Lenzie, where Lord Fleming had 'nominated' to the presbytery in January 1600 two successive candidates as minister, it was nonetheless the commendator of Cambuskenneth, as patron, who finally presented the second candidate, 'nominat be' Lord Fleming and approved by the parishioners, to the vicarage in April.[168] Sometimes a presbytery was persuaded to respect the wishes of a particularly influential patron. When the Earl of Morton presented his own candidate to the parsonage of Newlands in 1592, the presbytery initially declined collation on the ground that another minister already served the parish, requiring that the earl present the minister of Newlands to the parsonage, but as soon as Morton threatened to retain for his own use the fruits of the parsonage, as he was legally entitled to do if the presbytery declined to admit a qualified candidate, the presbytery decided to give the earl's presentee collation to the benefice, provided the candidate, in turn, made financial provision for the minister who served the cure'.[169] A particularly complicated dispute ensued at Eddleston where the parishioners in 1592 appealed for the provision of a minister to the synod, which granted Edinburgh presbytery full power to present a candidate to the benefice iure devoluto, if the patron failed to present, though the parsonage itself was in dispute between Maitland of Thirlestane and Lord Yester; the parishioners

[167] SRO, CH4/722/1, Stirling Presbytery Records, 13 June, 18 June, 4 July, 8 Aug., 17 Aug., 22 Aug. 1587.
[168] Strathclyde Regional Archives, Glasgow Presbytery Records, i, fos. 142v, 144r, 148r-v, 149v, 150v, 152r–153v, 154v–155v, 8 Jan. 1600 – 20 May 1600.
[169] SRO, CH4/121/1, Edinburgh Presbytery Records, 2 May, 9 May, 13 June, 20 June 1592.

declined Yester's kinsman as presentee: Yester was not disposed
to accept the presbytery's nominee; and a third candidate
nominated by the patron and approved by both congregation
and presbytery was finally admitted a year later.[170]

Catholic patrons were obliged to respect the legislation of 1567
and 1573 regulating the conditions of appointments to benefices;
and the evidence suggests that, as the government of James VI
stabilised, even nonconformist patrons were prepared to present
candidates to serve in the reformed ministry. The replacement of
the decrepit Alexander Livingston, minister at Kilsyth, by the
presentation of William Livingston, a presbyterian minister of
some repute, to the benefice of Kilsyth in 1599 looks like a
dynastic appointment, for Lord Livingston was no archetypal
'godly' patron; but the choice was at least respectable and
acceptable. Lord Fleming likewise showed a willingness to
participate in the selection of a minister at Lenzie in 1600.[171] In
the appointment, however, of Andrew Boyd as minister of
Eaglesham, Glasgow presbytery seems to have usurped the
Master of Eglinton's right of presentation, but when Eglinton
complained of Boyd's supposed intrusion in 1592, a majority of
elders (whose names were suppressed for fear of reprisal or
intimidation as Eglinton's tenants) testified in sworn statements
that they had agreed to Boyd's admission.[172] In a possibly
conservative analysis of the religious persuasion of the leading
Scottish nobles and barons, prepared for the English government
in 1592, four out of two dozen nobles were considered to be
convinced Catholics, and nine out of thirty-three lords and
barons were depicted as Roman Catholics.[173] But, at best, their
patronage of parochial benefices was modest, and their influence,
in this sphere at least, may be considered minimal.

What was potentially far more disruptive was the decided
proliferation in the ranks of patrons, achieved largely at the
crown's expense. Increased activity in the land-market, the
exchange of properties by purchase, grant or, occasionally,
forfeiture, and most markedly the crown's transference of
episcopal and abbatial estates, with full rights of patronage over
the annexed churches, to numerous earls, lords and barons – the
so-called lords of erection – following the act of annexation in
1587 led the general assembly, in 1588 and again in 1591, to

[170] *The Records of the Synod of Lothian and Tweeddale, 1589–1596,
1640–1649*, ed. J. Kirk (Edinburgh, 1977), xxv and n. 53; 42, 44, 55.
[171] See above, 423.
[172] SRO, CH4/722/2, Stirling Presbytery Records, 4 July, 25 July, 10 Oct.,
31 Oct., 5 Dec. 1592; cf., *BUK*, iii, 813–14.
[173] *CPS Scot.*, x, no. 713.

protest at this dispersal of the crown's patronage, and to urge an annulment of those rights already alienated. Such a fragmentation of patronage was held by the assembly to constitute an 'evident danger, hurt and prejudice to the haill Kirk', its discipline and patrimony; and so presbyteries were inhibited, in the meanwhile, from accepting presentations by the 'new patrons'.[174] The patronage of 29 churches annexed to Paisley, for example, fell to Claud Hamilton by 1592; Kelso with the right to present to more than 40 churches became the heritable property of Francis Stewart in 1588; Kilwinning, with 16 annexed churches, was assigned to William Melville in 1592; Arbroath, with 37 specified churches, was bestowed in 1608 on the Marquess of Hamilton; and Alexander Lindsay, created Lord Spynie with the erection of the lordship out of the temporality of the bishopric of Moray, came to possess the patronage of some 40 churches.[175] The dispersal of so much patronage complicated the church's task of exercising control and supervision of the system in an effort to reconcile divergent interests.

For the first time since the Middle Ages, the rights of presentation to the parochial benefices had come substantially into the possession of laymen other than the crown. The exercise of ecclesiastical patronage had passed from prelate and crown to noble and laird. Changing patterns in the ownership of former ecclesiastical property made it difficult for either crown or church to recover what had been lost. The continued acquisition by laymen of ecclesiastical patronage (linked as it often was to the ownership of teinds) made it increasingly improbable that these rights would be readily surrendered to either crown or parliament for the benefit of any churchman be he prelate or presbyter.

---

[174] BUK, ii, 733, 746, 784. (In 1600, the synod of Glasgow instructed its commissioners to the general assembly 'to lament that the donatioun of benefices quhilk of befoir be actis of parliament pertenit to his Majestie ar now devolvit in particular menis handis to the hurt of the ministerie, and to lament anent the new erectionis of benefices (decimis inclusis) in temporal lordshipes, specialie of the abbacie of Paslaye. . . .' Strathclyde Regional Archives, Glasgow Presbytery Records, 16 Sept. 1600.)

[175] RMS, v, nos. 2070 (patronage excepted from the earlier grant of 1587, ibid., no. 1320); 1597, 2085; vi, no. 2075; v, no. 1727; APS, iii, 650–6; iv, 653–4.

THE KING'S BISHOP
Archbishop Spottiswoode and the See of Glasgow

In different periods of history, differing significance was apt to be attached to the name and office of bishop. The contrast between the duties exercised by New Testament bishops or presbyters (synonymous terms that is, for the men who watched over the government of a Christian congregation)[1] and the work and wealth of medieval prelates (including some bishops of Glasgow cathedral), with all the prestige, power and patronage in secular and ecclesiastical affairs which such an office automatically conferred, is readily demonstrable and could scarcely have been more marked. Such disparity between early example and later practice also makes intelligible the antipathy exhibited at the Reformation by those who criticised the existing episcopate – the existing body of bishops; and this, in turn, invited a reassessment of the episcopal office itself. In Scotland, this reappraisal was carried so far that the name of bishop was not immediately retained but allowed to lapse by the reformed kirk during the 1560s.[2] The new church, in short, had no use for the old bishops unless they reformed themselves by jettisoning much of their medieval past and by becoming preaching pastors, an implicit recognition that there was no higher office in the church than that of the ministry of the Word and sacraments.

If the precise sense attached to the word 'bishop' had thus undergone radical alteration during 1,500 years of history, it was still possible for different men even within one church in the

---

[1] J. B. Lightfoot, *Saint Paul's Epistle to the Philippians* [which includes Bishop Lightfoot's dissertation on 'The Christian Ministry'] (Cambridge, 1888), 191–8, 227–34.

[2] J. K. Cameron, *The First Book of Discipline* (Edinburgh, 1972), 51–4; J. Kirk, *The Second Book of Discipline* (Edinburgh, 1980), 77–8.

same country to adopt divergent attitudes in their understanding of the correct significance to be attached to this word 'bishop'. Two such churchmen, holding incompatible ideas on episcopacy, were John Spottiswoode, archbishop of Glasgow (and later of St Andrews) in the reign of King James VI, and the principal of Glasgow university, where Spottiswoode studied, Andrew Melville, whose forthright views on the invalidity of diocesan episcopacy were such as to earn him the not inappropriate title of 'episcoporum exactor', the flinger-out of bishops. As a student, John Spottiswoode, might have sat at Melville's feet and dutifully listened to what the principal of the college and theology professor (the two offices which Melville occupied) had to say;[3] but, as sometimes happens, Spottiswoode grew up to reject his former teacher's theorisings on this subject at least, in much the same way as James VI himself had proceeded to denounce the political ideology which his tutor, George Buchanan, a few years earlier had attempted to instil in the young king during his formative years.

Yet in few cases have a teacher's views been so decisively discarded as Melville's objections to the episcopal office by John Spottiswoode. In just two decades after graduating from Glasgow in 1581, Spottiswoode found himself advanced by King James to the archbishopric of Glasgow in 1603,[4] and his younger brother, James, who entered Glasgow university in 1579 (the year preceding Melville's move to St Andrews university) and who graduated in 1583, was later rewarded by King James with the Irish bishopric of Clogher for his faithful service to the crown and Church of England in which he ministered, though he declined Charles I's offer of further preferment as an Irish archbishop.[5] Both brothers, therefore, profited through their service to the crown, and both were buried in Westminster abbey, a fitting tribute to their unstinted work in advancing the claims of episcopacy as the appropriate system for administering the church under the supreme governorship of the crown itself.

In his steadfast advocacy of episcopacy, Spottiswoode repudiated the ambitious claims of popes to be the sole inheritors of the apostles' work by arguing, instead, that all bishops were the apostles' successors. This, in itself, did not commit the archbishop

---

[3] J. Durkan and J. Kirk, *The University of Glasgow* (Glasgow, 1977), 376, 378; J. F. S. Gordon, *Scotichronicon*, 3 vols. (Glasgow, 1867), i, 363.

[4] *Munimenta Alme Universitatis Glasguensis*, ed. C. Innes, 4 vols. (Glasgow, 1854), iii, 4; D. E. R. Watt, *Fasti Ecclesiae Scoticanae Medii Aevi ad annum 1638* (Edinburgh, 1969), 151.

[5] *Spottiswoode Miscellany*, ed. J. Maidment (Edinburgh, 1844), 97–164; *Munimenta*, iii, 4; Durkan and Kirk, *University of Glasgow*, 378, 381, 383.

to any precise theory of the apostolic succession operating through bishops. It is true, he revered the antiquity of the episcopal office in the Christian church; and consistent with such a standpoint, in his *History of the Church of Scotland*, completed in the 1630s, he sought to demonstrate the early succession of bishops in Scotland. He therefore took issue with the claims of John Major and George Buchanan, which the archbishop considered were very ill-informed, that the Scots initially had been 'instructed in the Christian faith by priests and monks, without any bishop' and that the early church in the land we know as Scotland had been 'governed by monks without bishops with less pride and outward pomp but greater simplicity and holiness'.[6] Indeed, many of the early bishops, free from the corrupting influence of the later papacy, were expressly commended by Spottiswoode for their piety and learning. He therefore sought to portray these early bishops stripped of the legends invented by what he called 'idle and ignorant monks'. Admittedly, Kentigern, whom he described as 'commonly called St Mungo', is virtually shorn of his sainthood, but he is nonetheless depicted as the founder of a 'stately church' in Glasgow and 'worthy to have been made a subject of truth to posterity, not of fables and fictions as the legends of the monks have made him'.[7] Yet, it is noticeable that Spottiswoode nowhere attempted to identify himself as a successor to Kentigern in the see of Glasgow.

Nor is this surprising. After all, at the Reformation the reformers had explicitly rejected any notion of a personal succession as the mechanism for conferring the characteristics of a valid ministry.[8] Instead, what counted was a succession of apostolic doctrine, the wholesome faith transmitted since the days of the apostles. In this way, John Knox could claim 'we are able to show the succession of our Kirk directly and lawfully to have flowed from the Apostles'.[9] Although the archiepiscopal seal of Glasgow, even after the Reformation, continued to depict a mitred figure in episcopal vestments, presumably a representation of Kentigern, enthroned and flanked by several crosses with crozier before him (which might suggest some sort of continuity with the past with all its evident appeal to the conservatism of the

---

[6] J. Spottiswoode, *History of the Church of Scotland*, ed. M. Napier and M. Russell, 3 vols. (Edinburgh, 1847–51), i, 13, 38.

[7] Ibid., i, 14–20.

[8] Cameron, *First Book of Discipline*, 102, 207; Kirk, *Second Book of Discipline*, 55–6.

[9] *The Works of John Knox*, ed. D. Laing, 6 vols. (Edinburgh, 1846–64), vi, 498.

lawyers and others involved in the transactions which the seal authenticated), Spottiswoode himself preferred to use his 'round seal', a simpler seal (than the grander vesica-shaped seal), devoid of episcopal emblems, protraying merely a shield, with three trees, a boar's head and salmon with ring, and the legend 'S Iohannis Archiepiscopi Glasvensis'.[10] Again, in common with the other Scottish bishops, he wore neither mitre nor other elaborate episcopal garb, and refused to dress like an English bishop at King James' funeral in 1625. For Spottiswoode, too, what he called a 'lineal succession of pastors' counted for very little; what really mattered was recognition that, regardless of origin, the churches which professed the faith of the apostles and were free from the blemishes and errors of later ages were truly apostolic churches. 'We are not a new Church', Spottiswoode affirmed on the kirk's behalf, 'but one truly apostolical, that we can derive the doctrine we profess from the apostles of our Lord and from their next successors'.[11]

In this, at least, the archbishop was at one with John Knox, whose death in 1572 occurred when Spottiswoode was merely a boy of seven years of age, possessing little personal recollection of the reformer's work but of whose stormy career he had ample record by the time he came to prepare his *History*. Yet, if profession of a common faith, articulated in the various confessions, was a subject which united archbishop and reformer, there were other issues on which Spottiswoode showed a readiness to depart from earlier Reformation standards and practices.

For a start, Spottiswoode was the first protestant archbishop in Scotland to receive consecration in 1610 at the hands of three English bishops, at the king's behest, in London. For James, the issue was a simple one. In the king's eyes, the standing of the Scottish bishops, whom he had so painstakingly restored, was anomalous and defective. After all, at the outset, they owed their precarious position to the king's prerogative power. The bishops, whom James had appointed in the 1600s were, at best, nominal bishops. Their appointments were then largely titular: those ministers, like Spottiswoode, advanced to bishoprics were initially assigned no ecclesiastical power except for the privilege of voting as bishops in parliament. That apart, they had no

---

[10] J. H. Stevenson and M. Wood, *Scottish Heraldic Seals*, 3 vols. (Glasgow, 1940), i, 114–15.
[11] Spottiswoode, *History*, i, p. xxiv.

episcopal functions to perform.[12] These were the men known as the king's 'parliamentary bishops'. But the way was now open for James to advance his bishops to positions of real power and influence. Thus, in 1606, parliament provided the bishops with the prospect of sufficient endowment by recovering lands and rents lost to the crown by the act of annexation in 1587; then, by 1607, James proceeded to assign his bishops an ecclesiastical rôle by placing them as permanent moderators of synods.[13] Two years later, the bishops' old consistorial jurisdiction was restored; and, by 1610, two Courts of High Commission, one for the province of Glasgow and the other for St Andrews, had been created to deal with disciplinary cases, especially the subversive speeches of ministers who, by declaring their preference for the former presbyterian system, were seen to threaten the stability of the new regime, which James had constructed.[14] In that year, too, a carefully-managed general assembly, over which Spottiswoode presided, at Glasgow was induced to accept the powers of bishops in excommunication, absolution and in the supervision of ministers including admissions and depositions; and the substance of its findings received ratification from parliament in 1612.[15] Diocesan episcopacy had been revived.

To place the final seal of approval of his new order in the church, James decided to have Spottiswoode and two other Scottish bishops consecrated in England. Why the king should have required Spottiswoode and his colleagues to submit to such a ceremony in England is less readily determined. It cannot have simply been, as it is sometimes claimed, that until this step was taken the Scottish bishops altogether lacked 'spiritual authorisation'.[16] This is merely to take the king's explanation at its face value. Besides, it ignores the fact that the Glasgow assembly of 1610, which preceded the bishops' visit to London for consecration, had already accorded the bishops the necessary

[12] Acts of Parliaments of Scotland [APS], edd. T. Thomson and C. Innes, 12 vols. (Edinburgh, 1814–75), iv, 130; Scottish Record Office, Edinburgh [SRO], CH4/1/4, Register of Presentations to Benefices, fos. 19v–21v; The Booke of the Universall Kirk of Scotland: Acts and Proceedings of the General Assemblies of the Kirk of Scotland, 1560–1618 [BUK], ed. T. Thomson, 3 vols. and appendix vol. (Edinburgh, 1839–45), iii, 931, 955–6; D. Calderwood, The History of the Kirk of Scotland, ed. T. Thomson, 8 vols. (Edinburgh, 1842–9), v, 693–6.

[13] APS, iv, 281–4; cf., iii, 431–7; Original Letters relating to the Ecclesiastical Affairs of Scotland [OL], ed. D. Laing, 2 vols. (Edinburgh, 1851), i, 104–6; Register of the Privy Council of Scotland [RPC] 1st ser., ed. J. H. Burton and D. Masson, 14 vols. (Edinburgh, 1877–98), vii, 380.

[14] APS, iv, 430; RPC, viii, 417–20; Calderwood, History, vii, 57–62.

[15] BUK, iii, 1096–8; Calderwood, History, vii, 94–118; APS, iv, 469–70.

[16] G. Donaldson, Scotland: James V to James VII (Edinburgh, 1965), 206.

ecclesiastical authority for their work. Yet, as James had learned from painful experience, what an assembly might grant at one point, another assembly as readily could withhold at a later date. As it was, the king was increasingly attracted to English forms of procedure and worship. He was also unwilling to have the powers of his bishops made dependent on the approval of a general assembly whose powers he had striven to curb in the expectation that he might ultimately succeed in suppressing it completely. Indeed, it took all the skill and tact of Spottiswoode's moderating influence to persuade the king to summon an assembly at all and to proceed by securing a measure of consent instead of resorting to confrontation.[17] All in all, to James' agile mind, the bestowal of episcopal consecration had the decided merit of demonstrating the respectability and legitimacy of his bishops in Scotland, as well as ensuring an antidote to the continued supremacy of the general assembly.

Even here, however, Spottiswoode and his two companions, the bishops of Brechin and Galloway, were reluctant to participate in a ceremony of consecration to which their own church had long attached no spiritual significance whatsoever (and whose vestigial survival as terminology in the disposition of titles to bishoprics was designed merely to satisfy the legal procedures devised by the lawyers). In essence, James' persuasive argument was that he had summoned the bishops south for consecration in recognition that no king alone had power to make men bishops, nor could they themselves assume that function, given the dearth of surviving bishops in Scotland to consecrate the newcomers. Even although as ministers, they lacked episcopal ordination, a practice customary in England but not in Scotland, there was no serious suggestion made, despite one English bishop's misgivings, that Spottiswoode and his colleagues should first receive ordination as presbyters, in English fashion, as a pre-requisite to their consecration as bishops. Nor did the king permit the two English archbishops to play any part in the ceremony, thereby allaying Scottish fears of a possible revival of the ancient claims of York and Canterbury to jurisdiction over the Scottish church.[18] If all this looked like mere window-dressing, it was nonetheless symptomatic of James' deeper determination to remodel the church in a direction of his own choosing; and in Spottiswoode he found a pliant instrument to effect his innovations in the church.

[17] Spottiswoode, *History*, iii, 205; cf., *OL*, i, 187–90, 241.
[18] Spottiswoode, *History*, iii, 208–9; Calderwood, *History*, vii, 150.

Even on so minor an issue as the practice of confirming children, for example, which caused far less protest than the king's insistence in 1618 that worshippers kneel at communion, and which had hitherto met with neither recognition nor approval by the kirk, Spottiswoode was ready to advance the king's will and, with it, the power of bishops. Susceptible as he was to English influence, and deferential to the sustained assault by King James to win greater uniformity between the two national churches by imposing his 'Five Articles of Perth' in 1618, Spottiswoode characteristically defended confirmation as 'one of the most ancient customs of the Christian Church', since, so the archbishop claimed, 'it is clear by all antiquity that the power of confirming appertained ever to bishops'.[19] King James might have exclaimed 'no bishop, no king', but his archbishop appreciated that the obverse dictum – 'no king, no bishops' – was no less true. Only the king's exceptional determination had made bishops a reality in Scotland; and Spottiswoode proved himself the king's most faithful of servants.

This episode, however, was by no means an isolated instance in which Spottiswoode sided with the ploys of the king rather than with received practice in the church. As archbishop, Spottiswoode shared King James' distrust of presbyteries, the district courts of the church, whose powers rivalled those of proper bishops. He therefore hoped to reduce the scope of presbyteries for independent action so that, as he told the king in 1610, ultimately they would become 'a bare name, which for the present may please, but in a little time shall vanish'.[20] Yet this dream was beyond his grasp, and so he had to settle instead for controlling presbyteries through the appointment from 1606 onwards of selected ministers on whom he could rely to manage presbyteries as constant or permanent moderators.[21] In later life, Spottiswoode also voiced his misgivings on the nature of the eldership, a characteristic feature of the presbyterian system, by denouncing ruling elders as 'a mere human device', detrimental to both church and state.[22] Here, too, he remained faithful to the claims of his royal master who in 1610, perhaps mindful of the remarks of an earlier archbishop in 1583,[23] had instructed the kirk that 'laic elders have neither warrant in the word, nor

---

[19] *Spottiswoode Miscellany*, i, 65–87, at 76.
[20] *OL*, i, 235.
[21] *BUK*, iii, 1032–8; *RPC*, vii, 299–302.
[22] Spottiswoode, *History*, i, p. cxxxi.
[23] Calderwood, *History*, iv, 54.

example of the primitive church'.[24] Equally, Spottiswoode disapproved of the presbyterian doctrine of a parity or equality in jurisdiction among ministers. The appearance of bishops, even of the notional variety, plainly infringed this doctrine of parity, which he contemptuously dismissed as 'the breeder of confusion'. In a well-ordered church, claimed Spottiswoode, 'I am verily persuaded that the government episcopal is the only right and apostolic form'.[25]

How far such views were compatible with the continued existence of the general assembly, as the church's governing body, it might be hard to say. Certainly, Spottiswoode was far more cautious than his royal master who had little time for assemblies, intent as they seemed to be on thwarting royal policies. More realistically, Spottiswoode persuaded James to work through assemblies; but by 1618, having lost his patience, James had decided to summon no more assemblies; even the decision to call an assembly that year was against the king's better judgment; and in a letter which Spottiswoode read twice to the assembled gathering, King James disclosed that he had been 'fully resolved never in our time to have called any more assemblies'.[26] Perhaps despairingly, Spottiswoode acquiesced in James' policy of holding assemblies infrequently as the prelude to their disappearance. Above all, he implicitly believed James was entitled so to behave: the prince had the right, he maintained, to order the church's external government as he saw fit, and it was therefore the duty of subjects to render him obedience in all matters not inconsistent with God's Word. Accordingly, he readily acknowledged the king's supreme governorship of the church, a sensitive issue on which the general assembly had successfully withheld its express approval. In doing so, he helped enforce royal claims that 'bishops must rule the ministers and the king rule both' to the extent that he was latterly able to quip that 'the king is pope now, and so shall be'.[27] In all of this, the archbishop was a thorough-going erastian.

Whether or not the ideas which he came to formulate in the course of his career were initially so clearly defined as this, it is nonetheless plain that any defence of his new office inevitably brought him into conflict with the presbyterian party. Even his appointment as a nominal or parliamentary bishop in 1603,

[24] Spottiswoode, *History*, iii, 211.
[25] Ibid., i, p. cxxxi; cf. p. cxxxviii; Spottiswoode, 'Refutatio Libelli de Regimine Ecclesiae Scoticanae', in *Spottiswoode Miscellany*, i, 29–62.
[26] Spottiswoode, *History*, iii, 205, 241, 246, 252–4.
[27] *Spottiswoode Miscellany*, 81–7; Spottiswoode, *History*, iii, 241; Calderwood, *History*, vii, 421.

which he combined with his parish ministry at Mid Calder, caused difficulties in the synod of Lothian where in 1604, as a member of Linlithgow presbytery, Spottiswoode was accused of seeking to subvert the established discipline in the kirk and was reminded of his subordination to the assembly.[28] Spottiswoode, it seems, was no stranger to the synod's rebukes: he had earlier been reproved for playing football on a Sunday; and he gave great offence to some, as titular archbishop, by riding out of Haddington on the Sabbath while the people were dutifully resorting to church to hear the sermon.[29] Admittedly, he was heading south to see the king in London, taking with him a letter from the synod of Lothian; but the impression one forms is that Spottiswoode was no Sabbatarian of the more rigid variety.

At what stage he was first drawn to support episcopacy is not easy to determine. If his education at Glasgow under the Melville regime had done little in a positive sense to enhance his perception of bishops, there is still the possibility that family background and upbringing may have left an indelible impression, especially so as his father had been minister since the Reformation of the same parish of Mid Calder to which the son succeeded. In his *History*, the archbishop claimed that his father had held that 'the doctrine we profess is good but the old polity was undoubtedly the better', a remark interpreted as an indication of his father's preference for episcopal rule.[30]

Yet, it is assuredly hard to reconcile this claim made by the archbishop in later life with the reality, first, of his father's participation in preparing the Book of Discipline in 1560, which intended to scrap the old system; secondly, of his father's willingness to undertake work (in addition to his parish duties) as superintendent of Lothian, an office introduced by the reformers to replace the old order; and thirdly, of his father's readiness, at his election as superintendent, to eschew lordship and dominion and accept correction and admonition.[31] All in all, the disparity between the father's deeds and the son's description rather suggests that the archbishop in old age had lost touch with the substance of his father's work.

[28] Calderwood, *History*, vi, 268–9.

[29] Gordon, *Scotichronicon*, i, 375; Calderwood, *History*, viii, 55.

[30] Spottiswoode, *History*, ii, 336–7. The reported remark bears a curious similarity to the advice, preserved by Spottiswoode, of John Hamilton, the Catholic archbishop of St Andrews, to John Knox in 1560 that 'he should do wisely to retain the old policy which had been the work of many ages' (Spottiswoode, *History*, i, 372), see above, 341.

[31] Cameron, *First Book of Discipline*, 115–28, 150, 161–2; Knox, *Works*, ii, 144–50; *BUK*, i, 296–7.

If accurately recorded, Spottiswoode's own entry to the ministry, as assistant to his father in 1583,[32] two years after graduating, occurred at a time when the presbyterians were in power; but, soon afterwards, a reaction set in when a new government, in 1584, declared its hostility to presbyterianism by discharging presbyteries from meeting and by handing over power to bishops instead.[33] The industrious Robert Wodrow, writing in the eighteenth century, thought he had uncovered evidence of Spottiswoode's opposition to bishops, at this point, in a document signed by 30 or so ministers, including one John Spottiswoode, from the synod of Merse, in 1586, denouncing episcopacy.[34] But Wodrow's identification was inaccurate and rests on an unfortunate coincidence. Although Spottiswoode's family came from the Merse,[35] the John Spottiswoode who signed the document opposing bishops was another individual of the same name who was already serving as a minister at Longformacus and Mordington when Spottiswoode, the future archbishop, was still a student at Glasgow.[36]

Whatever Spottiswoode's own thoughts were on the replacement in 1584 of presbyteries by bishops, the experiment did not endure; and after 1586 an essentially presbyterian system soon resumed. At that point, too, Spottiswoode, who seems to have opposed any accommodation with Archbishop Adamson, was selected by the assembly in 1586 as a suitable agent to be entrusted with the task of re-establishing Linlithgow presbytery, and the presbytery and synod, in turn, sent him as a commissioner to the assembly in 1590 and 1593, the years of presbyterian ascendancy.[37] Indeed, his standing with his fellow ministers was such that they elected him moderator of the synod of Lothian in October 1594.[38] Either his distaste for the salient features of presbyterianism still lay with the future or he was remarkably expert in disguising his feelings. In 1597 he lent his support to the stricter presbyterians by approving a reply which Robert Bruce, minister in Edinburgh, had prepared to refute the king's charge that a riot in the capital, in December

[32] Gordon, *Scotichronicon*, i, 363.

[33] *APS*, iii, 293–4, 303; Calderwood, *History*, iv, 259–60.

[34] Gordon, *Scotichronicon*, i, 363–6.

[35] Spottiswoode, *History*, ii, 335–6.

[36] *Register of the Privy Seal of Scotland* [*RSS*], edd. M. Livingstone *et al.*, 8 vols., (Edinburgh, 1908–82), viii, no. 208; *Fasti Ecclesiae Scoticanae*, ed. H. Scott *et al.*, 10 vols. (Edinburgh, 1915–81), ii, 57. He was later minister at Nenthorn, and was presented to the vicarage of that parish in May 1599 (SRO, PS1/70, Register of the Privy Seal, fo. 252).

[37] Calderwood, *History*, iv, 583; *BUK*, ii, 648, 765, 796; *The Records of the Synod of Lothian and Tweeddale, 1589–96, 1640–9*, ed. J. Kirk (Edinburgh, 1977), 59.

[38] *Synod of Lothian*, 74.

1596, had been instigated by the ministers.[39] Again, in 1599, he was sufficiently forthright to warn the ministers of his synod to guard against any 'loss of the liberty of Christ's kingdom', but he was also prepared in 1600 to countenance ecclesiastical representation in parliament, which, of course, helped prepare the way for King James to have his bishops.[40]

Perhaps the moderating influence of his father-in-law, David Lindsay, minister at South Leith and soon to be advanced to the bishopric of Ross in 1600, may have counted for something here. Spottiswoode's marriage, at any rate, had taken place by 1599.[41] In 1600, he figured as one of the influential commissioners of assembly, who advised the king between assemblies, and through whom, susceptible as they were to the king's powers of persuasion, James preferred to work in moulding opinion within the kirk.[42] Spottiswoode's ministry at Mid Calder was interrupted, however, when he agreed in 1601 to act as chaplain to the Duke of Lennox (with whose house his family had longstanding links) on the duke's appointment as an ambassador in France, where Spottiswoode's curiosity appears to have got the better of him to the extent that he witnessed – or so it was said – the celebration of mass in Paris.[43]

The Lennox connection has a particular significance for not only had the duke a financial interest in the lands and rents of the archbishopric of Glasgow, but he was feu superior of the regality of Glasgow, with right of nominating the provost and bailies of the burgh.[44] These rights, however, were temporarily set aside in 1598 when the last Catholic archbishop of Glasgow, James Beaton, long-resident in France since 1560 and ambassador to James VI, was restored by the king to the revenues of the archbishopric till his death in 1603 when Lennox recovered possession.[45] Yet, despite these setbacks for Lennox, it was not for nothing that the town council held a banquet for the duke in 1601 to celebrate his appointment as an ambassador, and thoughtfully provided him with an escort of 40 men to accompany him to Edinburgh, and a surgeon for his journey to

[39] Calderwood, *History*, v, 560–75.
[40] Ibid., v, 738; vi, 2–16.
[41] Gordon, *Scotichronicon*, i, 368.
[42] Calderwood, *History*, vi, 21.
[43] Spottiswoode, *History*, iii, 100; Calderwood, *History*, vi, 136; viii, 52; Gordon, *Scotichronicon*, i, 369–70.
[44] *Register of the Great Seal of Scotland [RMS]*, edd. J. M. Thomson *et al.*, 11 vols. (Edinburgh, 1882–1914), vi, no. 1104; *APS*, iv, 38, 146–7, 284; Spottiswoode, *History*, iii, 82, 225; *Extracts from the Records of the Burgh of Glasgow, 1573–1642* [vol. i], ed. J. D. Marwick (Glasgow, 1876), 225; *RPC*, vii, 141–2.
[45] *APS*, iv, 169–70; *RMS*, vi, no. 1457.

France where he was greeted by Archbishop Beaton in Paris as he journeyed to the court of Henry IV.[46]

Nor need it be doubted that Lennox was appropriately placed to commend his own chaplain, Spottiswoode, as a candidate for archbishop when James decided to make a fresh appointment. Besides, Spottiswoode himself was so well-known to James VI that, in 1603, he accompanied James south to England.[47] With the benefit of having a bishop as his father-in-law, a noble duke as patron and the ear of the king as well, it is stating the obvious to say that Spottiswoode was well-placed for promotion. For Spottiswoode, as for James, that journey to England in 1603 proved decisive. At Burleigh House came news of the death in Paris of James Beaton, the pre-Reformation archbishop of Glasgow, whom James had restored as titular archbishop in 1598. Accordingly, James selected Spottiswoode to fill the vacancy in 1603.[48]

Spottiswoode's position as titular archbishop of Glasgow, with a seat in parliament, and yet still an ordinary member of Linlithgow presbytery and parish minister was, to say the least, anomalous and unsatisfactory. Yet, in heightened form, this apparent paradox merely underlined the tensions between what was expected of a minister and bishop. Different people had often widely differing perceptions and expectations.

In Glasgow, the town council and burgh looked for 'benevolence' and goodwill from their archbishop, who as lord of the regality of Glasgow, exercised a temporal jurisdiction over the lands and people of his regality. He had wide-ranging judicial powers which were delegated to his bailie to discharge; and besides his right to present ministers of his choice to churches in his gift, he had the power and patronage at his disposal to nominate the provost and bailies of the council, though at times the king himself might intervene in a bid to secure his own man as provost.[49] It was not for nothing, then, that Spottiswoode

[46] *Glasgow Burgh Records*, i, 220, 223; Spottiswoode, *History*, iii, 100.

[47] Spottiswoode, *History*, iii, 138.

[48] Ibid., iii, 139–40; SRO, CH4/1/3, Register of Presentations to Benefices, fos. 77v–78r.

[49] SRO, CH4/1/3, Register of Presentations to Benefices, fos. 93v–94r; CH4/1/4, fos. 19v–21v; *RMS*, vi, no. 2084 (churches); *Glasgow Burgh Records*, i, 255–6, 257, 261, 268–9 (magistrates). For details of earlier disputes between archbishop and burgh over the election of magistrates, see SRO, RH11/32/1, Charters, depositions of witnesses and productions relative to the claim of the archbishops to appoint the provost and bailies of the city of Glasgow, 1543–57. See also *Charters and other Documents relating to the City of Glasgow, A.D. 1175–1649*, ed. J. D. Marwick (Scottish Burgh Records Society, Edinburgh, 1894), pt. ii, 269–77. In 1611, the burgh was formally erected into a royal burgh (*RMS*, vii, no. 462).

found himself addressed customarily as 'my lord of Glasgow'.[50] He weilded enviable authority – spiritual, social and political.

To underpin his prestige and power, the archbishop had, of course, his castle or palace, which, like the cathedral, was designed on a scale to overawe lesser men. This was a focal point where local ecclesiastical and other business was concluded, and patronage distributed to the archbishop's clients and friends. Traditionally, the archbishop had several smaller castles or houses, such as Daldowie, Haggs, Lochwood and Partick, most of which were leased to lairds; Lochwood itself, a mere six miles from the cathedral, had fallen into disrepair and had passed into the possession of the Boyds of Badinheath,[51] and Partick was long ruinous; there was even a property in Edinburgh, described as ruinous in 1592. Daldowie, however, is known to have been occupied by Spottiswoode in 1609;[52] and he also acquired accommodation in Edinburgh where he conducted much of his business as a servant of the crown.[53] These residences were still a reminder of the archbishop's extensive, if somewhat diminished, powers and a reflection of the incomes derived from the surrounding lands. Some property was located as far away as the baronies of Carstairs in Lanarkshire, Ancrum, Lilliesleaf and Ashkirk, all then in Roxburghshire, and Stobo and Eddleston in Peeblesshire.[54]

The archbishop's assistance and protection were therefore sought by lesser men. To the tenants on his estates, what counted was good lordship. Bishops were reputedly less exacting landlords than some of their temporal counterparts who prized their rights of heritable tenure. As here-today, gone-tomorrow administrators, bishops may have had less incentive to conserve their patrimony and to resist the temptation to dilapidate in favour of family, kin and servants. But, as members of the reformed ministry there were also conscious of their obligations to act as generous landlords by setting an example in caring for tenants and for 'the poor labourers of the ground', and by avoiding all suspicion of rackrenting or other forms of exploitation, which, as preachers, they condemned in others. Some failed to measure up to such

---

[50] *Glasgow Burgh Records*, i, 256; Strathclyde Regional Archives, Glasgow [SRA], Glasgow Presbytery Records, 26 January 1614.

[51] *RSS*, vi, no. 1874; *RPC*, iii, 99; *RMS*, vi, no. 782.

[52] SRA, Glasgow Presbytery Records, 8 November 1609.

[53] Much of the archbishop's surviving correspondence is dated from Edinburgh. (*OL*, i, 13, 17, 25, 180, 279, 315; ii, 354, 363, 365, 384, 401, 417, 457 (Canongate), 460.) Two letters were dated from Glasgow (ibid, i, 236; ii, 387) and one from Moffat (ibid., i, 442*).)

[54] Edinburgh University Library, MS Dc.4.32, Books of Assumption, fos. 1–3.

exacting standards; others were prodigal in their grants of lands and pensions.[55]

Spottiswoode himself saw the need to preserve a balance between his obligation to dispense patronage at a variety of levels and the need to conserve resources (especially so in a period when episcopal incomes had drastically fallen as a consequence of the inroads of the laity and the pressures of inflation).[56] In some of his earliest enactments, the archbishop granted numerous feu charters to sitting tenants, who were thereby raised to the status of owner-occupiers.[57] Many of them were small, independent men, of modest means, whose relative poverty was recognised in 1606 when parliament exempted certain feuars in the barony of Glasgow from paying their customary composition fee on receipt of their charters.[58] Then again, valued and trusted officials in his own household like the Englishman, Robert Blunt, were rewarded for their service with grants of land.[59]

To the nobility and gentry, the archbishopric, as a source of wealth, offered a variety of potential rewards, in the form of leases, feus and pensions which the archbishop might be induced to grant. Apart from the financial attractions, the promotion of a kinsman or servitor as archbishop might assist a magnate to consolidate and extend his political influence in the region. But there were also the rewards of office which the archbishop had at his disposal – the officials necessary for administering his scattered baronies. The offices of bailie and chamberlain, for example, enabled families to increase their hold over particular areas. The post of bailie, in particular, enabling as it did the holder to exercise lordship over lesser men, was especially prized by nobles and lairds alike. Thus, in 1606, Spottiswoode recognised the Earl of Roxburghe as his bailie and justiciar within the baronies of Ancrum, Lilliesleaf and Ashkirk.[60] Again, in 1607, he affirmed the rights of the Elphinstones of Blythswood as heritable bailies and justiciars of the barony of Blythswood, near Glasgow.[61] Competition for the post of bailie of the regality of Glasgow itself was particularly fierce. Over the decades, a succession of magnates – the Earls of Lennox and Arran, Lord

[55] Kirk, *Second Book of Discipline*, 33–5, 211, 218, 237–9, 243; see above, 407ff.
[56] *APS*, iv, 146–7, 284; Spottiswoode, *History*, iii, 82; *OL*, i, 209; Gordon, *Scotichronicon*, i, 371.
[57] *RMS*, vii, nos. 192–7, 1331, 1884–5; viii, no. 177. See further, ibid., vii, nos. 540, 658, 932, 1025, 1159, 1290, 1752–3, 1855, 2102; viii, 44, 1208.
[58] *APS*, iv, 284.
[59] *RMS*, vii, no. 1290; cf., nos. 1025, 1573.
[60] Ibid., vii, no. 932.
[61] Ibid., vii, no. 540.

Boyd, the Stewarts of Minto and Blantyre – had all aspired to so coveted an office. On Spottiswoode's accession, the Duke of Lennox was in command as bailie, having retrived his family's earlier dominance in the area.[62]

Yet there were potential disadvantages, too. The return to the bishops of sufficient property in 1606 meant that less was available for distribution elsewhere in landed society. Besides, the social status of bishops, as local and national figures, was such that their actions were apt to acquire a political significance which nobles might readily resent. This was all too apparent in 1606, when the archbishops and bishops, dressed in silk and velvet, rode to parliament, it was observed, in great pomp and splendour between the earls and lords, a display which one bishop found so distasteful in ministers of religion that he proceeded on foot instead. At the close of parliament, when the bishops were denied the precedence they claimed was theirs as members of the first estate, the nobles felt it necessary to take a stand, fearing, it was said, that the bishops had been 'set up to cast them down'.[63] Spottiswoode himself seems to have developed a taste for riding in style, and so, at his request, the town council in Glasgow provided him with ten men to ride to parliament in 1609.[64] This apart, other danger signals were there to be read. Thus, in 1609, despite steadfast opposition from the lawyers, Spottiswoode urged the king to appoint a churchman as president of the College of Justice,[65] even although the office had been held by laymen since 1584. Besides, the creation of two courts of High Commission in 1610 alarmed those who resented ecclesiastics being 'invested with such power'.[66] Episcopal pretensions were beginning to stir and to assume an overtly political character, which some found objectionable.

For the king, however, the presence of an archbishop like Spottiswoode, vigilant in supervising an ordered ministry not only in the archdiocese itself but throughout the whole western province, proved an irresistible attraction. In the king's eyes, it made for good government. Besides, as the archbishop was the king's hand-picked man for the job, it offered the crown direct influence and control over the church. It even provided a measure of social cohesion and control by reinforcing respect for

[62] *RPC*, vii, 141–2.
[63] Calderwood, *History*, vi, 493–4; cf., Spottiswoode, *History*, iii, 176. Spottiswoode had earlier ridden to parliament in 1604 (Calderwood, *History*, vi, 262).
[64] *Glasgow Burgh Records*, i, 303.
[65] *OL*, i, 188–90.
[66] Spottiswoode, *History*, iii, 212.

the traditional values of an ordered, hierarchical society in church and commonwealth alike. Spottiswoode thus found that he had an almost bewildering and endless variety of rôles to fulfil. In temporal and ecclesiastical affairs, he – or his deputies – had the task of punishing transgressors and of instilling a healthy respect for his and the king's laws.[67] After all, apart from his lordship of Glasgow, Spottiswoode was expected to act as a lord of parliament,[68] a member of the privy council,[69] an extraordinary lord of session,[70] a principal member of the Court of High Commission for Glasgow,[71] a commissioner, and then president, of the Exchequer,[72] a judge in consistorial matters,[73] a commissioner of the peace,[74] chancellor of Glasgow University, with a voice in the election of the principal and teaching staff[75] and a trusted royal counsellor whose advice ranged from episcopal appointments[76] to James' cherished notion of a union of the kingdoms.[77]

Nor was it easy for the reformed ministry to reconcile the disparate nature of Spottiswoode's work with any pattern of apostolic ministry. If anything, it looked like a reversion to many of the features associated with medieval prelacy which the reformers had condemned in 1560. For many ministers, and for others in secular society too, attempts at reducing the power and wealth of lordly prelates by replacing them with salaried, preaching supervisors – superintendents, commissioners or visitors – had a powerful and sustained appeal. Assailed, as they were, from above and below, the bishops found their position all too precarious; and, on finding his 'burdens insupportable', Spottiswoode as early as 1609 considered resigning his archbishopric, hoping 'the world should see that ambition did not set me on work, but a desire to serve your Majesty in a good work that hath many enemies'.[78]

[67] *RMS*, vii, nos. 1195, 1207.
[68] *APS*, iv, 258, 264, 300, 409, 454, 465, 473, 483.
[69] *RPC*, vii, 52 (admission).
[70] Calderwood, *History*, vii, 53–4; viii, 68.
[71] *RPC*, viii, 418.
[72] Ibid., viii, 743; Calderwood, *History*, vii, 158.
[73] *APS*, iv, 430; SRA, Glasgow Presbytery Records, 19 July 1609; 5 June 1611; 26 January 1614; 2 February 1614.
[74] *RPC*, ix, 75–6, 78 419, 488; x, 72–3, 162, 204, 211, 266.
[75] Ibid., vi, 453.
[76] *OL*, i, 303.
[77] *APS*, iv 264; *RPC*, vii, p. xxxiv. (Curiously, Spottiswoode's participation is ignored in B. Galloway, *The Union of England and Scotland, 1603–1608* (Edinburgh, 1986).)
[78] *OL*, i, 209.

In the church, what counted was effective oversight. Court bishops, immersed in affairs of state, were only too liable to end up as absentee bishops, neglectful of their spiritual duties; and Spottiswoode had many calls on his time. He was often absent in Edinburgh or London; most of his surviving correspondence is dated from Edinburgh, where he regularly attended meetings of the privy council; and by 1621 he recounted how he made no fewer than 41 expensive journeys to court in London.[79] He almost seemed more at home outside his diocese than in it. This largely arose not from his own making but from all the tasks the king placed upon him. Although technically the archbishop of St Andrews, as primate, was senior to Spottiswoode in Glasgow, James had long preferred to work through Spottiswoode as his right-hand man in the church. More than any other churchman, Spottiswoode had prepared the way for the return of episcopal government, enabling James to declare: 'bishops must rule the ministers, and the king must rule both'.[80]

When resident in Glasgow, Spottiswoode acted as constant moderator of the presbytery;[81] he was expected to preside over his diocesan synod twice yearly, to conduct diocesan visitations at least every three years and provincial visitations every seven years; he was the agency for ordinations, confirmations and for presentations to benefices; and his approval was necessary for excommunication and absolution.[82] Although the revelant

---

[79] OL, ii, 644.

[80] Spottiswoode, History, iii, 241.

[81] RPC, vii, 302; SRA, Glasgow Presbytery Records, e.g. 25 March 1607, 6 July 1608, 29 March 1609 (absent), 28 June 1609 (Sharp, 'moderator for the time'), 7 February 1610.

[82] OL, i, 104–6; Spottiswoode, History, iii, 210–12; BUK, iii, 1096–7. The MS Register of Presentations to Benefices by the crown sheds some light on the archbishop's rôle in examining candidates and in granting collation to benefices. During the 1600s, presentations by the crown to benefices in the archdiocese were normally directed to the presbytery alone (SRO, CH4/1/3, Reg. Pres. Ben., fos. 99v–100r, 133r–v; CH4/1/4, fos. 9v, 23v, 24v, 28r, 30r–v) or, alternatively, to the commissioner alone (SRO, CH4/1/3, fos. 92v–93r) or in other cases, to the presbytery or commissioner (e.g. SRO, CH4/1/4, fo. 10r–v [three entries]) as the specified agents for supervising admissions. By July 1609, however, a presentation by the crown was directed to the archbishop or presbytery (SRO, CH4/1/4, fos. 31v–32r); some subsequent presentations continued to specify the presbytery or commissioner as the recognised agency for examination and collation (SRO, CH4/1/4, fos. 32v 33r–v); but by April 1610, royal presentations were invariably directed to the archbishop as the recognised authority (SRO, CH4/1/4, fos. 44r, 45r–v, 45v–46v, 48r–v, 48v–49r, 56v–57r, 64r–65r, 67r–68r, 69v, 69v–70r, 78v, 79v–80r, 81r, 82r–v, 98v, 99r, 104v, 108v, 109r). As a consequence, between 1610 and 1615, Spottiswoode had to supervise admissions to the benefices of Peebles, Kirkpatrick-Durham, Hownam, Hassendean, Kelso and Maxwellheuch, Bowden, Morebattle and Mow, Dryfesdale, Staplegorton, Southwick and Colvend, Dalgarnoch and Closeburn, Innertig, Oxnam, Lessudden, Kirkpatrick-Irongray, Lanark, Maybole, and Ayr and Alloway (ibid).

ecclesiastical records are largely lost, incidental glimpses are afforded of the archbishop's work in his diocese. Admittedly, the start to his work was so inauspicious that, in 1607, Glasgow presbytery had ordered the archbishop to compear before the synod to answer charges of nonresidence and negligence.[83] The presbytery's powers were still sufficiently strong in 1608 to enable it to appoint the archbishop as one of its four commissioners to attend the general assembly at Linlithgow, and again, in 1609, to order the archbishop with two other members to conduct a presbyterial visitation of the cathedral.[84]

Although exceedingly few traces of the archbishop's work are to be found in the presbytery records, a working relationship was established between archbishop and presbytery, though by 1610 the tables had been turned: it was then the task of the presbytery to consult the archbishop on a wide range of matters, from stipends and vacant charges to the seemingly timeless problem of squabbles in congregations.[85] Within the archdiocese as a whole, Spottiswoode is known from other sources to have presided over a synod at Peebles, and another at Irvine, in 1611 when he was then engrossed with the case of the nonconformist minister of Ayr, George Dunbar, who was imprisoned in Dumbarton castle for praying publicly for the banished ministers, and whose parish the archbishop considered filling with an Englishman.[86] Again, his attention to detail is apparent at a synod in Glasgow in 1612, when Spottiswoode approved a series of rules and procedures to be observed in disciplinary cases by every kirk session and presbytery in the area.[87]

Also in his thoughts was the case of the outspoken presbyterian minister of Kilsyth, William Livingston, whose behaviour had infuriated the king but on whose behalf the archbishop had nonetheless interceded with the king.[88] This was the man who had earlier preached at Glasgow in 1605 to the effect that 'it is a sin to call a bishop lord bishop and he may as well be called a moderator as lord bishop', which drew from the presbytery the

[83] SRA, Glasgow Presbytery Records, 24 June 1607.

[84] Ibid., 6 July 1608, 2 August 1609.

[85] Ibid., 28 Jan. 1607 (stipend); 29 March 1609 (ratification of Barony parish); 3 July 1611, 4 Aug. 1613, 17 Aug. 1614, 26 July 1615 (visitations); 14 Aug. 1611, 21 Aug. 1611, 30 Oct. 1612, 19 May 1613, 17 Aug. 1614 (admission of ministers); 22 April 1612 (ordination); 8 Nov. 1609 (suspension of minister); 4 April 1610 (bishop on exercise); 8 May 1611 (appeal); 8 Jan, 1614 (deposition from ministry); 28 June 1615 (excommunication); 7 Dec. 1614, 25 Jan. 1615, 8 March 1615, 28 June 1615 (recusancy).

[86] OL, i, 279–82; RPC, ix, 258, 276, 351.

[87] Gordon, Scotichronicon, i, 403–6.

[88] OL, i, 387*; 283; SRA, Glasgow Presbytery Records, 31 Jan. 1608.

mild rebuke that his expression was uncharitable, but he nonetheless refused to retract.[89]

The problem of presbyterian nonconformity was a serious one which confronted the archbishop from the outset of his rule. In 1607, he encountered 'in the beginning great opposition' from ministers to his appointment as constant moderator of the synod of Clydesdale; and it took the presence of the Earl of Abercorn, as the king's commissioner, at the synod for royal policy finally to prevail. Even then, the ministers of Dumbarton and Drymen walked out of the synod rather than acknowledge the archbishop as moderator.[90] As best he could, Spottiswoode sought to resolve the difficulties which beset him with a display of firmness rather than undue severity.

He was familiar enough, however, with James VI's tactics to outwit and browbeat the presbyterians into submission. After all, he had taken part in the conference at Hampton Court in 1606 which the king had arranged to interrogate eight presbyterian ministers, including the Melvilles, who had disobeyed royal wishes in 1605 by approving a general assembly at Aberdeen in defiance of the king. As a consequence, they, and others, were punished with imprisonment and banishment.[91] In Spottiswoode's own diocese, the minister of Ayr, John Welsh was summoned before the privy council for having attended the Aberdeen assembly, and in the archbishop's presence was sentenced to imprisonment, and was later banished to France.[92] The sentence was undeniably severe and even Spottiswoode's father-in-law, the bishop of Ross, spoke out in council against the treatment of the banished ministers which he considered was harsher than that accorded to Jesuits or murderers.[93] Even so, further prosecutions followed and, within the archdiocese of Glasgow, the ministers of Craigie, Loudoun, Beith and Hawick found themselves summoned before the privy council for approving the proceedings of the Aberdeen assembly.[94]

If royal policy was plainly to intimidate the opposition, the archbishop's rôle was rather to conciliate. Yet James Melville,

[89] SRA, Glasgow Presbytery Records, 21 Aug. 1605, 4 Dec. 1605.

[90] OL, i, 105; SRO, CH8/59, Miscellaneous Ecclesiastical Papers, Extract from the records of the synod of Clydesdale accepting John, archbishop of Glasgow, 18 August 1607.

[91] Calderwood, History, vi, 279–94, 342–54, 374–91, 477–80, 559–84, 586–600; Spottiswoode, History, iii, 157–64, 177–82; RPC, vii, 82–3, 92–3, 101–3, 104–5, 109–10, 112–15, 120–1, 123–5, 128–9, 134–7, 257–64, 474–6, 478–86.

[92] RPC, vii, 104; Select Biographies, ed. W. K. Tweedie, 2 vols. (Wodrow Society, Edinburgh, 1845–7), i, 14–31.

[93] RPC, vii, 105.

[94] Ibid., vii, 109, 128–9, 135, 199, 260–4, 370, 406, 478, 480, 492, 495.

warded in Newcastle, saw Spottiswoode's tactics in another light and, at first, declined even to meet his former pupil 'because he had left the right course and followed the world'.[95] Undeterred, the archbishop continued to seek reconciliation, urging the ministers to submit and receive the king's clemency. He even held out hope that their leader, Andrew Melville, languishing in the Tower of London, might be released 'to teach in Glasgow, if he pleased'.[96] But, intercede though he did on the ministers' behalf, Spottiswoode soon discovered that James was in no mood for leniency.

Thereafter, his work on the High Commission for Glasgow, created in 1610 by the king's prerogative power, helped cast the archbishop in the rôle of judge and inquisitor. Despite the absence of the records of these courts, some four dozen recalictrant ministers are known to have been summoned before the High Commission by the time of James' death in 1625. Certainly, within the archdiocese of Glasgow, between 1620 and 1622, the ministers of Ayr, Lanark, Ochiltree, Dailly and Irvine were all deposed from their ministry by the united Court of High Commission, over which Spottiswoode then presided as archbishop of St Andrews.[97] Yet earlier, as archbishop of Glasgow, Spottiswoode had shown himself prepared to act as mediator between the king and recalcitrant ministers. It is perhaps a measure of his success that, in 1611, the king agreed to free four offending presbyterian ministers imprisoned in Glasgow; then, in 1612, the archbishop secured the release from prison of the outspoken William Livingston whom the king agreed should become minister at Lanark, and, by 1613, he was ready to allow the imprisoned ministers of his diocese to attend meetings of synod and presbytery, provided the ministers acknowledged their obedience to the king.[98]

Other issues attracting Spottiswoode's attention were the routine tasks of improving ministers' stipends,[99] raising funds for the university[100] and effecting repairs to his cathedral and palace, in which was to be found 'a silk bed' and even a 'chamber within the dungeon of the castle of Glasgow hung with tapestry', once the property of the Countess of Lennox (and possibly of the crown) which the archbishop had acquired.[101] By 1614, however,

[95] Calderwood, *History*, vi, 732.
[96] Ibid., vii, 4, 5ff, 46.
[97] Ibid., vii, 256, 425, 427–33, 436, 531, 533–42, 549, 553, 567–8.
[98] *RPC*, ix, 600–1; *OL*, i, 283; SRO, CH4/1/4, Register of Presentations to Benefices, fo. 104v; *RPC*, ix, 550–1; Calderwood, *History*, vii, 181.
[99] SRA, Glasgow Presbytery Records, 28 Jan. 1607; *APS*, iv, 300; *OL*, i, 101.
[100] Cf., *OL*, ii, 364; *Munimenta*, i, 188–9, 197–9.
[101] *Glasgow Burgh Records*, i, 301, 308; *RPC*, x, 521.

the question of Catholic recusancy had come to the fore in a synod at Glasgow which led both archbishop and synod to petition the king for urgent action in suppressing recusancy.[102]

This was the prelude to the sensational trial for treason of the Jesuit, John Ogilvie, in whose arrest, examination and trial Spottiswoode played a leading part. The trial, in Glasgow, took place not in the ecclesiastical courts nor even in the court of justiciary but before a special commission established by the king; and it was for treason in affirming papal supremacy and declining King James' authority that Ogilvie was tortured (by depriving him of sleep), then tried and convicted by a jury and executed in 1615, amid heightened feelings in the aftermath of the Gunpowder plot, ten years earlier, and the attempted assassination of the king and his English parliament.[103] The moderation and restraint which characterised his archiepiscopal rule in Glasgow could not be extended to those who repudiated the king's authority.

In all, Spottiswoode by 1614 believed that he had 'sure information' of 27 Jesuits at work in Scotland;[104] and in prosecuting recusants, the secular and ecclesiastical courts had each their part to play. In Ayr, the presbytery sought the archbishop's assistance in dealing with a priest, Gilbert Kennedy, and his associates; and the archbishop himself instructed Paisley presbytery to secure a confession of faith from individuals suspected of unsound religion.[105] In Glasgow, the presbytery showed vigilance in pursuing Ogilvie's associates: one culprit, who denied he knew Ogilvie was a Jesuit and thought him a soldier, was ready to testify to his own religious orthodoxy by observing that he had satisfied the Archbishop of Canterbury of his rectitude by embracing the religion professed in England and, for good measure, affirmed that his wife had taken communion in Glasgow 'out of my lord of Glasgow's own hands'.[106] Another offender who offered to make amends to the presbytery

---

[102] *OL*, ii, 400.

[103] SRO, JC26/Box 7/59, 63, 66, 93, Justiciary Court Records, Indictment and process against John Ogilvie, priest; SRO, Books of Adjournal (Old Series), vol. 5, fos. 179 (14 July 1615), 184 (5 Sept. 1615), 194 (6 Dec. 1615); *RPC*, x, 284–6; *OL*, ii, 385–91, 424, 796; Calderwood, *History*, vii, 193–4, 196; Spottiswoode, *History*, iii, 222–6; *Ancient Criminal Trials in Scotland from A.D. 1488 to A.D. 1624*, ed. R. Pitcairn, 3 vols. (Edinburgh, 1833), iii, 330–52. See also 'Relatio incarcerationis et martyrii P. Ioannis Ogilbei natione Scoti, e Societate Iesv presbyteri', in *Miscellaneous Papers, principally illustrative of events in the reigns of Queen Mary and King James*, ed. W. J. Duncan (Maitland Club, Glasgow, 1834), 79–108.

[104] *OL*, i, 400.

[105] SRA, Glasgow Presbytery Records, 7 December 1614.

[106] Ibid., 25 Jan. 1615.

for entertaining Ogilvie was referred to the archbishop and was subsequently convicted (with another burgess) in the justiciar's court held in Glasgow by Spottiswoode and three others, only to obtain from the crown a remission for life for his crime.[107] As privy councillor, high commissioner, justiciar and archbishop, Spottiswoode saw it as his duty to suppress Catholicism whenever detected.

Outside his diocese, Spottiswoode earlier had confronted the problem of Catholic recusancy from his seat on the council where he had prosecuted several Jesuits, denounced the Marquess of Huntly and the Earls of Erroll and Sutherland for popery, approved enactments for suppressing recusancy and accepted that a priest under interrogation might be subject 'to the torture of the boots'.[108] Besides, during a visitation of the Borders, commissioned by the king in 1609 for repairing churches and appointing ministers, the archbishop had arrested one priest and after breaking into the residence of the last Catholic abbot of Sweetheart, Gilbert Brown, had publicly burned most of the 'popish trash' uncovered, for which he won the king's approval.[109] As a reward, he received from the crown a gift of some of the abbot's confiscated books,[110] and five years later he found himself the recipient of the more lucrative prize of the abbacy of Kilwinning, which a grateful king had conferred on him for life in August 1614.[111] Nor was this all. In 1612, the archbishop's younger son, Robert, had won from King James the abbacy of Sweetheart itself;[112] and, in 1613, his elder son, John, gained from the crown the attractive gift, for life, of the abbacy of Holyrood, a fitting reminder of the need (as some of his protestant predecessors had discovered) for the archbishop, as a married man, to secure appropriate provision for his own immediate family.[113]

[107] Ibid., 8 March 1615; *RMS*, vii, nos. 1195, 1207.
[108] *RPC*, viii, 230–2, 276, 405, 444; ix, 111–12, 117–18, 124, 160, 162, 212, 217–18, 278, 331, 350, 400–1, 407–8, 514, 534; x, 118, 169, 251, 284–6, 336–7, 815.
[109] Ibid., viii, 266–7, 301, 564–5, 584–5.
[110] Ibid., viii, 301, 584–5.
[111] SRO, CH4/1/4, Register of Presentations to Benefices, fo, 110r–v (Kilwinning, 9 August 1614).
[112] Calderwood (*History*, vii, 164) and Gordon (*Scotichronicon*, i, 403) record that Archbishop Spottiswoode himself was the recipient of Sweetheart (or New Abbey) in 1612; but the Register of Presentations to Benefices discloses that it was his son, Robert, who received a gift of the abbacy from the crown in 1612 (SRO, CH4/1/4, Reg. Pres. Ben., fos. 68r–v (29 February 1612), 77r–78v (20 September 1612).
[113] SRO, CH4/1/4, Register of Presentations to Benefices, fo. 92r–v (Holyrood, 4 March 1613). See also *APS*, iii, 471, for protest in favour of Archbishop Boyd's widow and family that Beaton's restitution to the archbishopric did not prejudice their rights.

For his unstinted service to the crown, Spottiswoode was elevated by the king in 1615 to the archbishopric of St Andrews.[114] His work in Glasgow had amply prepared him for his rôle as primate. Yet it was with reluctance that he left Glasgow.[115] In the years ahead, Spottiswoode and his royal master set off along the road that was ultimately to lead to the Covenanting revolution of the 1640s and the repudiation of episcopacy by the Glasgow assembly of 1638. They need not have continued to tread that path to the bitter end. Indeed, there were signs that James knew when to retreat. Yet he bequeathed a bitter legacy to his hapless successor, Charles I, and under his new royal master, Spottiswoode found himself advanced to the chancellorship of the kingdom.[116] Although king and archbishop appeared to be winning all the battles, their victory was a singularly pyrrhic one, and ultimately they lost the war. Lamenting how 'all that we have been doing these 30 years past is thrown down at once',[117] Spottiswoode retreated to England and, in his absence, was deposed from his archbishopric and excommunicated by the Covenanting general assembly, which met in Glasgow cathedral during November and December 1638.[118]

Even in death, the archbishop's wishes were not respected. In his testament drawn up in 1639, he asked to be buried 'without all manner of pomp', beside his wife in the country church at Dairsie in Fife which he had painstakingly restored.[119] Instead, he was buried in Westminster abbey, amid great ceremony, and attended by many mourners and torchbearers including nobles from both England and Scotland who were then at court.[120] In a way, this epitomises Spottiswoode's whole career and the contradictions which made him a reformed minister yet a lord bishop, a leader of souls yet a servant of the crown. In that contradiction may be detected the kernel of his ultimate failure.

[114] Calderwood, *History*, vii, 197–9; Watt, *Fasti*, 299.
[115] Calderwood, *History*, vii, 197.
[116] *RMS*, ix, no. 260 (14 January 1635); J. Row, *History of the Kirk of Scotland*, ed. D. Laing (Edinburgh, 1842), 385; cf. *Handbook of British Chronology*, edd. E. B. Fryde *et al.*, (3rd edn., London, 1986), 183, where the date of Spottsiwoode's appointment as chancellor is wrongly given as 1634. He relinquished the office in 1638.
[117] Spottiswoode, *History*, i, p. cx.
[118] *Records of the Kirk of Scotland*, ed. A. Peterkin (Edinburgh, 1838), 26–7.
[119] Spottiswoode, *History*, i, p. cxxxiii.
[120] *Spottiswoode Miscellany*, i, 6–7; Gordon; *Scotichronicon*, i, 578.

The Jacobean Church in the Highlands 1567–1625

The state of the church in the Highlands in the decades immediately before and after the Reformation is a subject conveniently shrouded in some mystery. The surviving evidence, though somewhat tenuous and, at times, obscure, is not wholly inconsiderable. Yet, in plain disregard of the documentation which does exist, the prevailing picture in the popular imagination – and in some more serious minds alike – is one in which the observances of a pious and devout church, overtoppled at the Reformation, are seen to have been replaced, in highland parishes, with nothing other than irreligion and apathy. Thus, it is concluded, 'the fifty years following the Scottish Reformation in 1560 saw the people of the Hebrides and the adjacent Highlands lose contact with religion because, for the most part, they were left severely alone, to pray and believe as they wished, without priest or minister'.[1] After 1560, the 'inhabitants of the Hebrides and Highlands', it is confidently asserted, 'found themselves neglected by both churches'. Nonetheless, they pertinaciously 'clung to the beliefs and practices of the Catholic faith, the memories of which grew more blurred and indistinct as the years passed by'.[2] Other commentators have either contented themselves by reiterating observations of this sort[3] or by making similar strictures on 'the failure of the Kirk to establish itself in the highland area'.[4] Accordingly, 'far from stimulating religious fervour', the Reformation is understood merely to have 'removed

[1] *Irish Franciscan Mission to Scotland, 1619–1646*, ed. C. Giblin (Dublin, 1964), vii.

[2] Ibid.

[3] I. B. Cowan, *The Scottish Reformation* (London, 1982), 168; C. W. J. Withers, *Gaelic in Scotland, 1698–1981* (London, 1984), 23.

[4] J. Wormald, *Court, Kirk and Community* (London, 1981), 164.

the old props of religion in the Highlands without substituting others of equal efficiency'.[5]

Though tenacious in their persistence, interpretations of this sort are inconsistent with the facts of history and might best be consigned to the ranks of popular mythology. Such claims are doubly misleading: not only do they idealise late-medieval ecclesiastical life but, more seriously, they studiously ignore the remarkable achievements of the kirk in the Highlands in the decades after 1560. By contrast, the work of the kirk in the Highlands during James VI's long reign from 1567 to 1625 is, in a very real sense, not one of negligence and failure but of commitment and success, so that, far from being a period of sterility and ineffectiveness, so popularly portrayed, the late sixteenth and early seventeenth centuries may be considered an era of remarkable progress and fulfilment for the reformed church's work in the Highlands.

Both before and after 1560, the church's organisation in the Highlands conformed, in all essentials, to the patterns which prevailed elsewhere in Scotland; and, so far as geographical and linguistic factors permitted, integration, not separation, remained a salient feature of the ecclesiastical structure. Nonetheless, the somewhat surprising claim has been advanced that 'the very remoteness of the highland dioceses inevitably made contact with the papacy somewhat infrequent'.[6] Yet, remoteness, depending on perspective, is surely a relative matter: the differences in distance between St Andrews and Rome, and between Dornoch or Lismore and Rome are comparatively slender and, one suspects, largely insignificant. Indeed, the comparative wealth of highland entries in supplications to Rome suggests contact and involvement, not separation and remoteness.[7] The church in the Highlands, in structure and worship, was an integral part of the universal or, at any rate, western church, and, as such, shared its strengths and shortcomings. Besides, many of the higher clergy in highland dioceses were lowlanders, cosmopolitan figures,

[5] W. C. Mackenzie, *A Short History of the Scottish Highlands and Isles* (Paisley, 1906), 123.

[6] I. B. Cowan, 'The Medieval Church in the Highlands', *The Middle Ages in the Highlands*, ed. L. Maclean (Inverness, 1981), 91–100, at 91.

[7] See *Calendar of Scottish Supplications to Rome, 1418–1422*, edd. E. R. Lindsay and A. I. Cameron (Edinburgh, 1934); *Calendar of Scottish Supplications to Rome, 1423–28*, ed. A. I. Dunlop (Edinburgh, 1956); *Calendar of Scottish Supplications to Rome, 1428–1432*, edd. A. I. Dunlop and I. B. Cowan (Edinburgh, 1970); *Calendar of Scottish Supplications to Rome, 1433–1447*, edd. A. I. Dunlop and D. MacLauchlan (Glasgow, 1983); *Calendar of Papal Letters to Scotland of Clement VII of Avignon, 1378–1394*, ed. C. Burns (Edinburgh, 1976); *Calendar of Papal Letters to Scotland of Benedict XIII of Avignon, 1394–1419*, ed. F. McGurk (Edinburgh, 1976).

who, all but invariably, had been educated at a university in the Lowlands or on the continent, and some, moreover, were frequently employed in royal service, all of which facilitated contact and communication between the Highlands and the church elsewhere. Even the continued interest in Latin learning fostered by the learned orders in Gaelic society – clergy, medical men, bards and scribes – served to promote links with the educated world.[8] Again, the essentially Latin services of the pre-Reformation church were presumably neither more nor less intelligible to highlanders than they were to many lowlanders. In the Highlands, as elsewhere, the parish priest's formidable task was the care of the souls of the living and departed: the spiritual welfare of the whole community, visible and invisible; and by administering five of the seven sacraments and by assisting his parishioners in the rites of passage from baptism to burial, the priest was seen to be entrusted with delivering men from the powers of evil by reconciling them to God. Only confirmed unbelievers or habitual absentees could remain untouched by the church's claims and incantations.

But if the church transcended the geographical, linguistic and social divisions of the country, the political centre of gravity, for long enough, had been located in the Lowlands where the crown displayed a readiness to integrate aspects of highland life more fully with prevailing patterns in the rest of Scotland. This it sought to do by inculcating lowland values and culture. The policy was by no means a novel one; but it reached a fresh intensity in the early seventeenth century.

Though identifiable geographically with the mountainous centre and west of the country, the highland region linguistically also covered adjacent lower-lying areas and the western isles, where Gaelic speech predominated – a region which, in the sixteenth century, encompassed roughly half the land-mass of Scotland, and, as John Major observed, half the people of Scotland were Gaelic in language and culture.[9] The Gaidhealtachd was confined to no mere 'Celtic fringe' but then stretched over the western half of the country from Kintyre, Lennox, Menteith, Strathearn and Strathardle onward through part of Mar and Moray, almost all of Ross, Sutherland in its entirety, and the western portion of Caithness. The ecclesiastical structure, however, did not adequately or, at any rate, equitably reflect these considerations.

[8] D. S. Thomson, 'Gaelic Learned Orders and Literati in Medieval Scotland', *Scottish Studies*, xii (1968), 57–78.

[9] J. Major, *A History of Greater Britain* (Edinburgh, 1892), 50.

Despite the existence of early religious foundations in the Celtic church from Kingarth to Applecross, the late medieval church could boast hardly any monastic houses in the heartland of the Highlands: by the sixteenth century, all that existed were the decayed Cistercian abbey of Saddell in Kintyre, the small Valliscaulian priory at Ardchattan in Argyll and the even smaller houses of Augustinian canons at Strathfillan in Perthshire and at Fearn (depicted as ruinous and neglected in 1541) in Easter Ross. Beauly (in origin Valliscaulian) was no more than a dependency of Cistercian Kinloss situated in the north-east coastal plain, and Inchmahome and Inchaffray were both small Augustinian priories in Perthshire. Nor had the islands fared any better, for only Iona and Oronsay could lay claim to religious houses. If it is thus a little difficult to resist the conclusion that the monastic revivals of the middle ages had left the Highlands largely untouched, it is also evident that the work of the friars, associated as they were with the towns, did not extend to the Highlands proper, except for a Dominican house in the essentially lowland outpost of Inverness, two friaries in lowland Elgin and a Carmelite friary at Kingussie. Yet again, the fifteenth-century renewal detectable in the fashion for endowing collegiate kirks had no consequences for the Highlands beyond the three isolated examples of Tain, Innerpeffray and Kilmun; and hospitals, too, with the shadowy medieval exceptions of Killearnan in Ross, Helmsdale in Sutherland and St Magnus in Caithness, were conspicuous by their absence throughout the Gaidhealtachd. This being so, ecclesiastical ministrations were traditionally dependent on the services which the diocesan and parochial structure might supply. But, here again, deficiencies were evident.

The seven predominantly-highland dioceses of Caithness, Ross, Moray, Dunkeld, Dunblane, Argyll and the Isles, stretching over half of Scotland and comprising over half the country's thirteen dioceses, were administered not from the rural heartland of the Highlands, with its conspicuous absence of townlife, but from the relative safety of cathedral cities situated, for the most part, on the edge of the Highlands, in decidedly frontier territory, where the values and customs of the Lowlands intermingled with the Gaelic culture of the hinterland. The series of cathedral cities from Dunblane and Dunkeld to Elgin, Fortrose and Dornoch almost served to delineate the highland boundary; and the wholly Gaelic dioceses of Argyll and the Isles which lacked these focal points, based as they were on the insular cathedrals of Lismore and Iona, proved even harder to administer effectively, especially when, all too often, the bishops preferred residence in Dunoon or Rothesay, or, better still, in Glasgow itself. There was, no doubt, good reason for bishops to secure safe quarters: after all, the crown itself had reminded the pope in 1538 how some church buildings in Argyll, 'very frequently exposed to the rude treatment of the people', were apt to become ruinous; and conditions were even worse in parts of the Hebrides where, it was earlier revealed, the inhabitants of some islands were devoid not just of baptism and the other sacraments, but even of the very Gospel itself.[10] Archdeacon Munro, it is true, had toured the Hebrides in 1549 but, apart from listing the existence of four-dozen or so parish kirks, his account had nothing at all to say about the religious life of the islanders or about the priests who ministered to them.[11] Others, however, had recognised the urgency of reinvigorating episcopal super-vision through the appointment of suffragans, especially in the Isles and Highlands,[12] but the advice, it seems, went unheeded and nothing effective was done. Even the dearth of Christian symbolism on gravestones in the area has been considered a commentary on the difficulties which organised religion faced in parts of the Highlands.[13]

The fundamental problem, however, went deeper than any arising merely from personal shortcomings, in so far as a serious imbalance had existed for long enough in the proportion of parishes assigned to highland and lowland areas. In the moun-tainous terrain of the north-west, the parish structure, though long complete, remained much weaker and less developed than the cohesive and compact system operating in the south. After all, in an age when half the population still lived in the lands north of the Tay, the parishes of the Gaidhealtachd, numbering around 180, formed little more than a fifth of the country's parishes; yet these same highland parishes covered fully half the land-mass of Scotland; and this being so, in comparison to their lowland counterparts, they could not be other than inordinately large and exceedingly difficult to serve, with all the attendant problems which so wild and mountainous a territory was apt to harbour.

This, then, was the legacy which the protestant reformers inherited in and after 1560; and in so far as they were intent on taking over the parish churches for protestant service, the

[10] *Letters of James V*, ed. D. Hay (Edinburgh, 1954), 345–6; 162.

[11] *Monro's Western Isles of Scotland and Genealogies of the Clans, 1549*, ed. R. W. Munro (Edinburgh, 1961), 46–88.

[12] *Calendar of State Papers relating to Scotland and Mary, Queen of Scots* [*CSP Scot.*], ed. J. Bain *et al.*, 13 vols. (Edinburgh, 1898–1970), i, no. 285.

[13] G. Donaldson, *All the Queen's Men* (London, 1983), 24.

reformers held out little prospect for overcoming this outstanding problem. Instead of remodelling parochial boundaries, the
immediate emphasis was on repairing kirks and securing reformed
service for the existing parish system.[14] The Reformation, of
course, was nowhere effected overnight. This was true of the
Highlands, as elsewhere in Scotland where the political outcome
of the religious revolt was secured through English intervention
in 1560. In parts of the west Highlands and Islands, however, a
pro-English tradition had earlier been fostered with effect, in so
far as numerous chiefs had shown a readiness in 1545 to fall in
with Henry VIII's schemes, designed to encourage dissension in
Scotland, by mounting a rebellion in the west promoted by the
Earl of Lennox with English funds and forces in favour of
Donald Dubh, claimant to the lordship of the Isles.[15] In all of
this, religion ostensibly was not a factor; but Henry's anti-papal
policies (whose Scottish dimension centred on removing Cardinal
Beaton from power and thereby French influence in Scotland)
were undoubtedly understood and appreciated by some Highlanders.

In his flattering letter to Henry VIII, whom he acknowledged
as 'Defender of the Christen Faithe, and in erth next unto God,
of the Churche of England and Irland supreme hed', the highland
cleric and adventurer, John Eldar, was prepared not merely to
urge the political case for an Anglo-Scottish union, with Henry
as 'superiour and kynge', but to denounce the 'proud papisticall
buschops' of Scotland, 'the pestiferous Cardinall', Beaton, 'the
father of mischief', along with 'Beelzebub's flesmongers, the
abbotes and all ther adherentes' who deserved to be 'quyte
expulsed and drywyne away'. As one who had been born in
Caithness and educated in Skye and Lewis before studying for
twelve years in St Andrews, Aberdeen and Glasgow, Eldar, for
Henry's benefit, drew a pointed contrast between the behaviour
of contemporary churchmen and the primitive form of Christianity once preached in Scotland by 'Sanctus Columba, a Pict
and a busshep who in prechinge of Goddis worde syncerly in
Eyrish, in followinge of the holy apostlis in godlie imitacion,
doctryne and povertie, excellid then our proude Romische
Cardinall and his bussheps now adaises in Scotlande'. Not
content with all of this, Eldar impressed on the English king how
'ther is no people . . . in no region in Europe, so perturbed, so

[14] *The First Book of Discipline*, ed. J. K. Cameron (Edinburgh, 1972), 104ff,
202–3.
[15] D. Gregory, *The History of the Western Highlands and Isles of Scotland*
(London, 1881), 164–79.

molestide, so vexide, and so utterly opprest withe bussheps, monckes, Rome-rykers, and preistis . . . as they which inhabite the realme of Scotland'.[16]

Discounting the exaggerated language and extravagant claims, the opinions expressed, though belonging to one man, are unlikely to have been uniquely held; and Eldar evidently considered others shared his sentiments. At any rate, he enjoyed the patronage of the Earl of Lennox, even to the extent of becoming Lord Darnley's tutor, but with Mary Tudor's accession he was obliged to modify his beliefs. It may not be wholly fortuitous, however, that another highland cleric ready to associate himself, as a notary, with the insurrection in the west and later to record his attachment to the Reformation was John Carswell, notary public to the Isles, treasurer of Lismore, parson of Kilmartin and later reformed superintendent of Argyll.[17] Yet again, further north, Lennox's own brother, Robert Stewart, who, by favouring the rebellion in 1545 had lost his bishopric of Caithness but gained a canonry of Canterbury and then recovered his see, was one of three bishops who showed their active support for the Reformation by undertaking reformed service in their dioceses.[18]

Evidence of reforming beliefs, though sparse, can nonetheless prove illuminating: there was presumably sound purpose behind Cardinal Beaton's earlier action in empowering the bishop of Ross to proceed against heretics from his diocese; and, further west, the bishop in charge of the Isles for much of the 1540s had been trained at Lutheran Wittenberg, while his successor for much of the 1550s was accepted into the reformed ministry in Galloway.[19] In Breadalbane, more than a hint of anticlericalism can be traced in the satirical verses, commemorating Duncan MacGregor, in which the curate, vicar and parson, dean and bishop, prior, abbot and friars are each upbraided for their worldliness; the services of 'trew kirkmen' equipped to preach 'the trew worde of God' are sought; and the moral and religious

[16] *Collectanea de Rebus Albanicis*, ed. Iona Club (Edinburgh, 1833), 23–32.
[17] See above, 289ff.
[18] *The Scots Peerage*, ed. J. B. Paul, 9 vols. (Edinburgh, 1904–14), v. 355; R. Keith *An Historical Catalogue of the Scottish Bishops* (Edinburgh, 1824), 215–6; J. Dowden, *The Bishops of Scotland* (Glasgow, 1912), 249–50; see above, 309.
[19] *St Andrews Formulare, 1514–1546*, ed. G. Donaldson, 2 vols. (Edinburgh, 1944), ii, no. 416; J. Durkan, 'The Cultural Background in Sixteenth-Century Scotland', *Innes Review*, x (1959), 428; G. Donaldson, 'Alexander Gordon, Bishop of Galloway (1559–75) and his work in the reformed church', *Transactions of the Dumfriesshire and Galloway Natural History and Antiquarian Society*, xxiv (1947), 111–28.

mood of the poem ends by focusing attention on Christ's Passion:[20]

'*In manus tuas*, Lorde that deit on rude,
  Commendo spiritum meum with humilitie:
Redemisti me with thy pretious blude,
  Fra endles pane of hell to mak me frie:
Sen for my saik thou damned wes to die,
Grant me thy grace eftir this warldlie stryf
For to obtene the euirlasting lyf.'

Though familiar with Latin and at home in a Gaelic setting, the poet himself chose Scots as his medium of expression, designed to appeal to a courtly audience and readership; and it was, no doubt, for the entertainment of Colin Campbell of Glenorchy, whose family figured in the work and who, it seems, was responsible for MacGregor's death in 1552, that the poem was composed. The religious content of the poem might well be expected to win the laird's approval: his protestant inclinations, at any rate, were such that he had urged the Earl of Argyll in 1556 to retain the services of John Knox on hearing him preach in Castle Campbell; thereafter he threw in his lot with the lords of the Congregation at Perth in 1559; and by 1561 he had his chaplain at Finlarig castle installed as minister of Kenmore, for whose services 'in teching and preching synceirly the Word of God, and mynistering of the sacramentis to the glory of God and instructione of the pepill', he undertook to provide a stipend, manse and glebe.[21]

Financial support of this kind was by no means exceptional. In the small lowland parish of Monymusk, situated to the east of Gaelic-speaking Strathdon, the tacksman of the priory and parsonage on acquiring a lease for three years at Candlemas 1560 (February 1560/1) agreed to provide a 'preacheour' at Monymusk, and resident, qualified ministers at the other appropriated churches of Alford, Keig, Kindrocht and Leochel, 'to the contentment of the parrochenaris'. There, too, the expectation was that some of the Augustinian canons of the priory, as vicars pensionary, 'suld and aucht to furnes ministeris for serving of the cuir thairin or at the lest remane thameself for doing thairof'.[22] Similarly, in the predominantly Gaelic parishes of Logierait and Blairgowrie, the ministers by 1562 (and probably earlier) were in receipt of stipends paid by the protestant-inclined commendator

---

[20] *The Black Book of Taymouth*, ed. C. Innes (Edinburgh, 1855), 152–73.
[21] *The Works of John Knox*, ed. D. Laing, 6 vols. (Edinburgh, 1846–64), i, 253, 357; *CSP Scot.*, i. no. 480, p.220; W. Gillies, *In Famed Breadalbane* (Perth, 1938), 127, 261–3.
[22] National Library of Scotland [NLS], Adv. MS. 31.3.12, fos. 137v–8v.

of Scone to whose abbey the parishes belonged.[23] But, there again, the Catholic bishop of Ross was willing to finance a protestant preacher for his kirks of Nigg and Tarbert in Easter Ross.[24] Besides, if it were so (as was claimed in 1561) that stipends had been assigned to 'the ministeris in every kirk that is sustenit thair' by the protestant commendator of Arbroath (whose abbacy, in truth, was sustained by over three-dozen annexed parishes), then it would seem that the partly-Gaelic parishes of Kirriemuir and Kingoldrum were equipped with reformed service at an early date, an impression strengthened by the occurrence of a minister for the parishes in 1563.[25] In Inverness, however, where the parish also belonged to Arbroath, the town council itself had taken the initiative in countenancing the Reformation by arranging payment of the minister's stipend in January 1560/1.[26]

Elsewhere, despite scarcity of evidence, reformed activity can be traced in Dunkeld whose treasurer, in office since 1549, conformed by 1561 to serve in the reformed ministry as exhorter there.[27] The treasurer of Ross, whose length of service was no less, lost little time in becoming minister at Fortrose by 1561 and contributed stipends for ministers at the kirks of Urquhart and Logie-Wester.[28] At that stage, too, Dingwall and Kiltearn had the services of a minister; Alness possessed an exhorter and Cromarty a reader; while further north Thurso was also equipped with a minister by 1561.[29] Much of this early conformity, it seems, was the product of individual initiative, for as yet no concerted campaign for the north had been launched by the general assembly in the south. Again, it is true that early reforming activity for which evidence has survived tended to take place on the periphery of the Highlands, perhaps because of proximity to lowland influences, and perhaps also because of the improved prospects in these areas for the accurate recording and preserving of the evidence itself. Less clear, however, is the extent to which these early candidates for the reformed ministry could be said to possess a Gaelic background: certainly some had surnames (itself indicative of earlier lowland contact) which are

[23] Ibid., fo. 36v.
[24] Edinburgh University Library [EUL], MS. Dc.4.32, fo. 102v.
[25] NLS, Adv. MS. 31.3.12, fo. 80v; *The Accounts of the Collectors of Thirds of Benefices*, ed. G. Donaldson (Edinburgh, 1949), 232.
[26] *Records of Inverness*, edd. W. Mackay and H. C. Boyd, 2 vols. (Aberdeen, 1911–24), i, 50.
[27] *Thirds of Benefices*, 92.
[28] Ibid., 91; EUL, MS. Dc.4.32, fo. 115r.
[29] EUL, MS. Dc.4.32, fo. 113r-v, 115r; *Thirds of Benefices*, 92, 151.

most apt to be associated with highland areas; few, however, were identified by a patronymic; and nomenclature, in any event, is an indifferent guide. John Robertson, treasurer of Ross, seems to have possessed or, at any rate, preferred a lowland back- ground, for ultimately he retired to Linlithgow where he died in May 1597, bequeathing his scattered library at Fortrose and Linlithgow to his kinsman, James Robertson, the subdean of Ross.[30] Although Gaelic was the language customarily spoken in the parishes of Urquhart and Logie-Wester, which formed the treasurer's prebend, there was no requirement before 1560 for Robertson himself, resident as he was at Fortrose cathedral, to have any knowledge of languages other than Scots and Latin, but his very willingness after the Reformation to serve the parish of Urquhart as minister (so described in 1565) may suggest a competence in communicating with his Gaelic parishioners. Elsewhere, from the evidence of their names alone, it is more than a guess that William Ross Thomassone, exhorter at Logie-Easter in Ross, and Alexander Patrie Grahamsoun, exhorter at Canisbay in Caithness, were the products of a Gaelic setting.[31] The kirk in those early years was certainly short of staff, and Gaelic-speaking staff at that, but it is not self-evident that the supply of Gaelic-speaking entrants was markedly lower than the level of recruitment to the ministry as a whole.

In Caithness, Bishop Robert Stewart's conformity and readiness to serve in the new kirk acted as a stimulus to the recruitment of staff in his diocese. At the Reformation, the bishop himself was already resident in his diocese where he witnessed a charter at Dornoch in August 1560 and another at Scrabster in February 1560/1.[32] Although some of his associates who occur as witnesses to these charters – notably the dean, chancellor, archdeacon and precentor of Caithness and the parsons of Canisbay and Olrig – do not appear to have followed the bishop's example by entering the new ministry, it is nonetheless a testimony of reformed activity in the diocese, promoted by the bishop and others, that within a decade Caithness's two-dozen parishes were equipped with a staff of twenty, recruited mainly at the level of reader.[33] In the neighbouring dioceses of Ross and Moray, where no reforming bishop came forward to act as leader, protestant influences were undoubtedly at work well before the general

[30] SRO, CC8/8/35, Edinburgh Testaments, fos. 31r-32r.
[31] *Register of Ministers, Exhorters and Readers, and of their Stipends, after the period of the Reformation* (Maitland Club, Edinburgh, 1830), 51, 53; *Thirds of Benefices*, 209.
[32] SRO, GD96, Mey Papers, nos. 79, 81; cf. no. 115.
[33] *Register of Stipends*, 53-4.

assembly's belated selection in 1563 of Donald Munro, the former archdeacon of the Isles, as commissioner for Ross, and of Robert Pont, from Fife, for Moray (where a family link may be detected in James Pont, monk of Kinloss, presumably a kinsman).[34] The fruits of their efforts, however, were amply evident a decade later with the recruitment of thirty-four staff to serve thirty-five parishes in Ross (with eight more readers required) and fifty-two readers and twenty-six ministers for Moray's seventy-three kirks (with vacancies for two more ministers and eight readers).[35] A similar pattern emerged in Dunkeld and Dunblane where neither bishop was induced to join the ranks of the reformers and so, again, reliance was placed on the reforming work of commissioners or of a neighbouring superintendent. The outcome of this activity was that practically all the parishes of these two dioceses were equipped with reformed personnel by the late 1560s.[36]

Further west, Argyll could claim the services of its own superintendent, John Carswell, who, with the patronage of successive Earls of Argyll, championed the Gaelic and protestant causes by publishing his *Foirm na n-Urrnuidheadh*, a version of the Book of Common Order for use in public worship, so much so that by 1574 every parish in Lorne, central Argyll and Cowall had a resident reader or minister.[37] Carswell's pioneering work in Gaelic had no immediate successor until 1631 when the synod of Argyll succeeded in publishing a Gaelic translation of Calvin's *Catechism*, followed by a translation of the *Shorter Catechism* in 1653. Although Irish translations of parts of the Bible appeared in the early seventeenth century, it was not until 1767 that the first edition of the New Testament in Gaelic was forthcoming, and only in 1801 was the complete Bible finally made available in Scottish Gaelic, all of which merely emphasises the outstanding novelty of Carswell's enterprise in 1567.

Within a remarkably short interval, despite many obstacles and setbacks, the kirk had established at least a presence in most highland parishes on the mainland. Much of the spadework had thus been accomplished with some effect in those early years, but it remained to be seen whether this initial impact could be sustained and consolidated in territory often hard to traverse and

[34] *The Booke of the Universall Kirk: Acts and Proceedings of the General Assemblies of the Kirk of Scotland* [*BUK*], ed. T. Thomson, 4 vols. (Edinburgh, 1839–45), i, 40; G. Ferrerio, *Historia Abbatum de Kynlos*, ed. A. W. Leith (Edinburgh, 1839), 80.

[35] *Miscellany of the Wodrow Society*, ed. D. Laing (Edinburgh, 1854), 334–41.

[36] See above, 326–9.

[37] See above, 330–2.

sometimes hostile to inhabit, for wild terrain was apt to breed wild men. For much of the time, however, the kirk increasingly could count on support from such highland families as the Munroes of Foulis, the Rosses of Balnagown, the Mackenzies of Kintail, the Macintoshes of Dunachton, the Frasers and, of course, the Campbells; but it also had its opponents among clans whose inclinations lay with Catholicism or, at least, with an innate conservatism, notably some of the Gordons and cadets of Huntly's house, as well as the Chisholms of Strathglass, the MacDonalds of Keppoch, Glengarry and Clanranald.

Regardless of religious attachment, no clan chief could ignore the rôle of the kirk, for chiefs and gentry, like their lowland counterparts, were already recipients of ecclesiastical resources at every level, in the form of feus, leases or pensions, finances won at the expense of the reformed ministry. At the Reformation, the Earls of Caithness and Sutherland, who had acquired most of the property of the bishopric of Caithness, remained conservative in religion, though Sutherland was said to have been well-pleased with the proceedings of the Reformation parliament, and Caithness did nothing to prevent one of his sons from entering the reformed ministry.[38] Moreover, Caithness's wife, Elizabeth Graham, was evidently a woman of independent mind: not only had she renounced her consent to a contract between her husband and Bishop Robert Stewart in 1557, because she had been forced to agree through fear, but she entertained her own thoughts on religion and had the reader of Wick witness her testament in October 1572.[39]

The Grants of Freuchie, who had an interest in the abbacy of Kinloss and other kirk rents, conformed to protestantism and profited from service to the crown. The fifth laird, born in 1568, received a protestant upbringing from his tutor who was later minister at Kirkwall; he lent his support to a bond in defence of kirk and king in 1590, employed the reader at Cromdale to witness his father's testament in 1584, was later a royal commissioner to the synod of Moray in 1607 and a member of the general assembly in 1610. Grant was also responsible in 1618 for paying a stipend of 520 merks to the minister of the linked

---

[38] *Origines Parochiales Scotiae*, ed. C. Innes, 2 vols. (Edinburgh, 1851–5), ii, 610ff; *Registrum Magni Sigilli Regum Scotorum [RMS]*, ed. J. M. Thomson *et al.* 11 vols. (Edinburgh, 1882–1914), iv, no. 2782; W. Fraser, *The Sutherland Book*, 3 vols. (Edinburgh, 1892), i, 112–3; 116; iii, 116–24; *Fasti Ecclesiae Scoticanae*, ed. H. Scott, 9 vols. (Edinburgh, 1915–61), vii, 97; SRO, GD96, Mey Papers, no. 171; *The Scots Peerage*, ed. J. B. Paul, 9 vols. (Edinburgh, 1904–14), ii, 338; vii, 339.

[39] SRO, GD96, Mey Papers, nos. 69, 162.

charge of Cromdale and Inverallan, though two years earlier he had been severely rebuked by the archbishop of St Andrews for 'abstractinge the rents of the kirk' in Strathspey, at the expense of ministers' stipends, a sin which, in the archbishop's eyes, was 'equal to that of murtheringe soulls'.[40]

Throughout the Highlands, chiefs and clan gentry alike could also count on the parochial teinds from benefices in their territory which they had acquired as tacksmen: Munro of Dalbuthcartie,[41] the Rosses of Balnagown and Logie,[42] Ogilvie of Airlie[43] and Gordon of Auchindoun[44] were typical beneficiaries of parochial finance in the north, as were MacDonald of Sleat[45] and the captain of Clanranald in the Isles.[46] Nor was it long before clans appreciated that service to the crown and kirk was profitable and defiance, ultimately, unprofitable. New links were gradually forged; and co-operation through the creation of formal bonds between chiefs,[47] and between chiefs, crown and kirk became commonplace. Thus, the crown's commission to numerous highland and northern lairds in 1590 for punishing 'adversaries of the trew religioun' proceeded on an understanding that the recipients were well-affected in religion. Indeed, the inclusion of Hebridean chiefs like MacDonald of Dunivaig and the Glens, Maclean of Duart, Macdonald of Sleat and Macleod of Harris as commissioners for the Isles rather suggests that the earlier work of successive bishops of the Isles had met with some success. All this accompanied a subscription to a 'general band' for defence of the kirk and king.[48]

Over wide areas of the Highlands much potential goodwill towards the kirk was there to be harnessed, and even where it was not, a Catholic like Huntly recognised his obligations to the kirk. Whatever the accuracy of a report in 1588 that he had dispossessed several ministers and readers at churches in his control, Huntly as a Catholic patron discharged his duty by presenting protestant ministers to benefices in his patronage. In

[40] W. Fraser, *The Chiefs of Grant*, 3 vols. (Edinburgh, 1883), i, 132, 163, 181–2, 205; ii, 41, 56, 422–3; iii, 286–92.

[41] SRO, GD274/1, Stuart and Stuart, Cairns and Co. W.S., Collection.

[42] SRO, GD199/27, Ross of Pitcalnie Muniments; SRO, GD274/1, Stuart and Stuart, Cairns and Co. W.S., Collection.

[43] SRO, GD16/47/29, Airlie Muniments.

[44] SRO, GD44, Gordon Castle Muniments, Sec. 8, 14 July 1572.

[45] SRO, RH4/90, Clan Donald Lands Trust, nos. 2, 14, 16; 19/2, 11.

[46] SRO, GD201/3/1, Clanranald Papers.

[47] E.g. SRO, RH4/90/19/2, Clan Donald Lands Trust, 30 May 1587; SRO, GD71/4, Monro of Allan Muniments; *Mackintosh Muniments, 1442–1820*, ed. H. Paton (Edinburgh, 1903), no. 89; *The Chiefs of Grant*, i, 162.

[48] *BUK*, ii, 750–9; *Register of the Privy Council of Scotland [RPC]*, ed. J. H. Burton et al., 1st ser. 14 vols. (Edinburgh, 1877–98), iv. 787–89.

1580, he had suffered a rebuff when the bishop of Moray had thwarted his efforts to install an unsuitable kinsman as minister of Rhynie and Essie; and so in 1589 he dutifully presented a minister to the kirk of Glass, and again in 1618 (by which time he had become a protestant), and he was also expected to assist in restoring the kirk of Kingussie in 1623.[49] Similarly, the captain of Clanranald, though sympathetic to the work of the Irish Franciscan missionaries[50] in the 1620s, was nonetheless prepared to make arrangements in 1630 with MacDonald of Morar for furnishing the elements of bread and wine for the celebration of reformed communion at certain churches in his territories.[51]

The provision by 1574 of 223 readers and ministers for 215 parishes in the largely Gaelic-speaking dioceses of Caithness, Ross, Moray, Dunkeld and Dunblane[52] was undoubtedly a creditable achievement which coincided with a reorganisation of the kirk's finances, begun by the crown in 1573, and which called for a redistribution of ministers and readers by placing one minister in charge of three or four adjacent parishes, each served by a resident reader. The scheme was not without its critics in the church and one who went so far as to denounce the device as 'develish' was evidently impressed by the argument that ecclesiastical funds ought not to be readily diverted for the crown's own use through economies on the numbers of ministers but ought instead to be directed towards providing each parish with a resident, adequately-paid and qualified minister.[53] Not every parish, it is true, could attract or afford the full-time services of a minister, and so the scheme had the merit of providing every parish with the prospect of, at least, the service of a reader, supervised and supplemented by a neighbouring minister, until such time as additional finance and recruitment to the ministry were secured.

All this had particular implications for highland parishes, whose very size made the arrangements harder to administer. In Caithness, twenty-two parishes, with funds assigned for resident readers, were either paired together or placed in groups of three under the supervision of eight ministers and one commissioner for the whole diocese. Only Assynt, perhaps because of its size and remoteness, remained unattached, served only by a reader,

---

[49] *BUK*, ii, 717; SRO, GD44, Gordon Castle Muniments, Sec. 15; SRO, CH2/271/1, Synod of Moray Records, 1.
[50] *Franciscan Mission to Scotland*, 62, 66.
[51] SRO, GD201/3/2, Clanranald Papers.
[52] *Wodrow Miscellany*, 396.
[53] D. Calderwood, *The History of the Kirk of Scotland*, ed. T. Thomson, 8 vols. (Edinburgh, 1842–9), iii, 314–26 at 318.

whose office, though shortly to be filled, was vacant in 1574. Five years later, the position was much the same, with nine ministers and thirteen readers on record: in the interval, one minister had been gained but three readers had been lost; and it was expressly noted now there was then 'na reidare at Ra'.[54] Plainly, there was still much to be accomplished.

By 1585, the parish ministry in the diocese had expanded to twelve but this, it seems, was achieved only at the expense of readers whose numbers fell to seven; and although the diocese still had its commissioner, Dornoch itself temporarily lacked a minister with only the service of a reader. By then, however, fewer parishes were paired; no minister was placed in charge of more than two parishes; both Wick and Thurso had a resident minister *and* reader, while Olrig, Creich, Rogart and Kildonnan could boast ministers of their own. Yet such improvements were not always sustained. The recorded ministry declined to nine in 1586, fortified only by the work of four readers and the commissioner himself. Even in 1599, the ministry stood at twelve, with additional support from two readers (at Wick and Nigg) and two commissioners who then appeared on record. By 1601, however, the ministers at work increased to fifteen but the only reader retained was the reader at Olrig – and that depite the presence of a full-time, resident minister in the parish. At that date, too, the diocese could claim the restoration – though not the presence or services – of a bishop in the person of the non-resident George Gladstanes from St Andrews, elected in 1600, whose only service as titular bishop consisted in representing the ecclesiastical estate in parliament. For doing so little, he nonetheless drew a handsome stipend of £847 – money which might more appropriately have been spent on raising the generally depressed level of stipends in a hard-pressed diocese.[55]

In 1585, for example, most salaries in Caithness remained at the level assigned in 1574. Only four ministers in the diocese had a stipend above £100 and the salary of the reader at Kilmalie had not risen above £16. Many ministers, therefore suffered a drop in real earnings, especially those whose stipends were valued in cash and not in kind. The minister of Wick's salary, calculated not in victual, with its cushioning effect, but in silver at a time when inflation and increased corn prices further reduced the purchasing power of stipends, was set at £80 in 1574, £133 in 1579 and 1585,

---

[54] *Wodrow Miscellany*, 332–4; SRO, E47/2 (1579), Register of Assignations of Stipends, fos. 5r-6r.

[55] SRO, E47/3 (1585), fos. 5r-6r; E47/3 (1586), fos. 5r-6r; E47/8 (1601), fo. 4r-v.

and £140 in 1599, a figure well below the level of an adequate minimum stipend in the south; and although his status was altered to 'reader' in 1599, seemingly a clerical error, he was again recognised as minister in 1601.[56]

Despite the poor stipends on offer, unattractive even to those who sought no more than a modest competence, new recruits were still to be found. By 1607, the diocese's two-dozen parishes had a complement of twenty ministers (half of whom were graduates), and a solitary reader. Four vacancies for ministers still existed; two ministers had the oversight of three parishes; sixteen parishes were paired; and eleven more were equipped with their own ministers. The gradual expansion of the ministry in Caithness is not to be attributed, however, to any intervention by Bishop Gladstanes, who seems never to have visited the diocese; indeed, his assumption of diocesan duties occurred only after his promotion to the archbishopric of St Andrews in 1604; so he was able to remain in St Andrews, freed of any encumbrance in the north. By then, however, responsibility for the northern diocese had passed to Alexander Forbes, another lowlander. But a revival in the fortunes of episcopacy was not reflected in the diocese, where the size of the ministry had fallen in 1614 to just thirteen ministers (ten of whom were graduates) placed in charge of twenty specified parishes. Nine parishes had their separate ministers; three ministers were assigned joint charges; one minister was placed in charge of three churches; Farr and Durness were temporarily without a minister; and the office of reader was wholly eclipsed within the diocese.[57]

The promotion of a graduate ministry in the parishes had certainly made strides since the days when the ministry of the diocese had only one graduate in 1574. But there were drawbacks, too, in these developments, not least the shortage of manpower in the parishes, which had earlier been overcome through the employment of readers and which, with their elimination, could only be countered through a judicious deployment of the eldership. Even the transition from the earlier scheme for financing stipends primarily from the thirds of benefices to the subsequent methods of assigning stipends from local teinds (or tithes) in consultation with the tacksmen (or leaseholders) who had acquired the teinds may also have had a dislocating effect in providing stipends, for while it was the task of commissioners from 1606, whom parliament had appointed,

---

[56] Ibid.
[57] SRO, E47/9 (1607), fo. 4r-v; E47/10 (1614), fo. 50r-v; D.E.R. Watt, *Fasti Ecclesiae Scoticanae Medii Aevi ad annum 1638* (Edinburgh, 1969), 61.

to fix stipends, much still depended on the disposition and goodwill of the tacksmen in possession of the teinds. At Dunnet, responsibility for paying the minister's stipend lay with the Earl of Caithness, who provided a salary in 1615 of 200 merks in silver and 40 bolls of victual for the minister, who had also the benefit of manse and glebe.[58] Somewhat later, the assistance of Lord Reay was sought in 1638 in creating a new parish in the diocese 'for the better edifying of the people' by detaching portions from the parishes of Farr and Ardurness to form another parish centred on the kirk at Kirkiboll, whose minister was assigned a manse, glebe and stipend of 500 merks financed from the two other parishes.[59]

In neighbouring Ross, sustained recruitment to the ministry was rather more encouraging. There, by 1574, a staff of nine ministers and twenty-five readers served thirty-five parishes, with eight vacancies for readers mainly in central and eastern districts and at Gairloch in the west. Five years later in 1579, the diocese had gained six more ministers and retained its complement of readers, enabling all but two vacancies (at Gairloch and Lemlair) to be filled. Lochbroom, Applecross, Kincardine and Kilchrist had each a full-time, resident minister, though Lochalsh and Lochcarron had to share the services of a reader. Some parishes remained detached; but two dozen, each with a resident reader, were either paired or grouped in units of three under a supervising minister. Avoch on the Black Isle was exceptional, however, in having the benefit of a full-time minister *and* reader. In ensuing years, the ministry of the diocese showed signs of steady expansion, though at the expense of the temporary reader's office, which went into decline. By 1585, twenty-one ministers and eleven readers were at work, again supervised by a commissioner, for the only protestant bishop provided to the see before 1600 was Alexander Hepburn, who remained in office only from 1574 till 1578. Most parishes were paired; six stayed separate, with their own full-time staff; and four smaller parishes were grouped together under the supervision merely of a minister and reader. Lochalsh and Lochcarron continued under the united charge of one minister, presumably because together they were much the same size as the adjacent parish of Applecross or, again, Kintail, both of which were supplied with a resident minister, and certainly much smaller than Lochbroom, with its minister, or Contin, equipped only with a reader, which

[58] SRO, E47/10 (1615), fo. 49r.
[59] SRO, GD84/29/3, Reay Papers.

left Gairloch the only parish still lacking service of any kind. The recruitment of graduates also rose steadily from five in 1574 to twenty-two Masters of Arts in 1614. Again, all this was achieved despite the highly unsatisfactory level of stipends.[60]

The poverty-stricken minister of Kincardine had to make do with a frugal stipend of £33 in 1585; but worse was in store at Cullicudden and Alness whose minister was expected to survive on a miserable pittance of £10 with five chalders of barley, a manse and glebe; and the only financial reward on offer to the graduate minister of the combined parishes of Lochalsh and Lochcarron was the exceedingly slender sum of £18. This, too, was the income of the minister of Kintail (who was not a graduate), and it was merely a few shillings more than the stipend assigned to his colleague, the non-graduate minister of the equally wild and mountainous parish of Applecross. Plainly, many stipends were hopelessly inadequate; there was also a glaring disparity in levels. At the higher end of the scale, the minister of Tain and Edderton, who held the subdeanery of Ross, could look forward to what, by comparison, must have seemed the princely sum of £200 (far surpassing the commissioner's salary of 100 merks), though, in truth, the figure was modest enough by standards in the south. Indeed, the generally-depressed levels of stipends in the diocese may be summed up in the observation that (like Caithness) only four ministers in Ross could boast of salaries of £100 or more.[61]

If the financial recompense for ministers was bleak, the position of readers was dire; and only outside employment as notaries or schoolmasters enabled them to obtain an income capable of sustaining their existence. The highest-paid reader in the diocese was to be found at Tain where his salary of £20 in 1585 surpassed that of some ministers, but the stipends of the readers at Urray and Kiltarlity stood at just £8 or so, the reader at Chanonry £6, at Cromarty £5 (with over a chalder of barley) and at Logie-Easter the reader's stipend of merely £4 (forthcoming from a third of the vicarage) was so pitiful that £10 was added 'be the new providit persoun' of the benefice. Whatever attracted men to the reformed ministry, it was not the lure of financial reward; and the real surprise is not that every parish was not immediately filled but that recruitment to the ministry was sustained in a period when stipends in the area not only remained

---

[60] *Wodrow Miscellany*, 334–6; SRO, E47/2 (1579), fos. 7r-9r; E47/3 (1585), fos. 7r-9r; E47/10 (1614), fo. 42r-43v.
[61] SRO, E47/3 (1585), fos. 7r-9r.

disappointingly low but suffered a decline in purchasing power during years of inflation and higher prices.[62]

Despite the problems, progress was sustained, with two further ministers added by 1586. Although most entries in the register of assignations of stipends, by that date, ceased to be arranged on a diocesan basis until the practice was resumed by 1614, it can be calculated from the entries which, for Ross, appear to be listed on a presbyterial basis under Tain and Ardmeanach that twenty-two ministers and a reader were in service in 1599, with an additional reader on record in 1601. Less satisfactory, however, were the disappearance of a minister for Applecross and the futile attempt to link the parishes of Applecross, Gairloch, Lemlair and Dingwall, stretching from coast to coast, under the charge of a single minister, a practice still operating in 1607 but abandoned by 1614, when Gairloch (with its kirk at Kinlochewe) and Applecross shared the services of a minister. By that date, too, twenty-five ministers and one reader were at work in a diocese which was then considered to consist of thirty-five specified churches. All in all, the figures remained much the same as those in 1585, except that the reader's office had suffered a marked decline almost to the point of extinction.[63]

In the wealthier diocese of Moray, with its fertile and productive lowland plains, as well as the more rugged highland terrain to the interior, financial support for the ministry was not noticeably at variance with patterns elsewhere in the north. Only four ministers in 1585 had a stipend above £100 (at Inverness, Spynie, Kirkmichael and the linked charge of Alves and Lhanbryde), and the only salary above £200 was at Alves and Lhanbryde whose minister received the comparatively handsome stipend of £293. By contrast, all that the minister of Urquhart could command was the paltry figure of £8 and four chalders of victual; the minister at Birnie fared much the same with £10 and two chalders of barley; and, again, the minister of Laggan or of Abernethy or of Advie and Cromdale, each with a stipend of £26, was badly off compared with the reader at Elgin, whose reward for his labours was a salary of £56, at a point when the readers at Inverallan, Knockando and at Conveth and Comar could claim no more than 20 merks, and the reader at Kinedward and Essil was essentially in the same category with a stipend of £14.[64]

[62] Ibid.
[63] SRO, E47/3 (1586), fos. 7r-9v; E47/8 (1599), fos. 6r-7v; E47/8 (1601), fos. 5r-6v; E47/9 (1607), fo. 6v; E47/10 (1614), fos. 42r-43v.
[64] SRO, E47/3 (1585), fos. 10r-11v.

With the scale of stipends generally so impoverished, a decided drain on resources in the diocese was the continued existence of Bishop George Douglas, an adventurer from pre-Reformation days, who, with his election in 1573, had difficulty in satisfying the general assembly of his qualifications for the job, but his lavish reward of £2,000 in cash as well as victual was not matched by his performance in the diocese, where the presence of a commissioner was considered necessary to do the bishop's work for a slender salary of 100 merks in 1585.[65] Episcopacy, it seemed, was an expensive luxury, especially if contrasted with the cheaper and more effective method of oversight by commissioners whose adoption the church, on the whole, had preferred since the 1560s.

Dunkeld also had a bishop of sorts who, in return for a stipend in 1585 of £1,182 plus victual, did agree to act for a spell as commissioner for the diocese. There thirty parishes in the central portion of the fragmented diocese were served in 1585 by ten ministers and sixteen readers: Ardeonaig had then lost its minister; and despite the inclusion of their names in the register, it was belatedly recorded that the reader at Rannoch had been 'thre yeir syne deid' and his colleague at Blair Atholl, it was said, had been 'deid four yeir syne', and no successors as yet appointed. By 1586, Strathfillan and Killin were without a minister and, if accurate, the records then show a fall in staffing to nine ministers and thirteen readers in charge of thirty churches. Yet again, only four ministers had stipends over £100 and at the foot of the scale the reader of Logieallochie was expected to survive on a miserable £3 15s 4d. By 1599, Dunkeld was still poorly equipped with eleven ministers and four readers for thirty named parishes; and by 1607 twenty-five parishes on record were served by thirteen ministers and two readers. In 1614, however, the seventy parishes of the whole diocese could command a staff of forty-six ministers and three readers, of whom thirty-nine were graduates. Most parishes had a resident minister, five were temporarily vacant and twenty-six were placed in small groups with linked charges. Least satisfactory was the grouping of Blair Atholl, Lude, Strowan and Kilmaveonaig under the charge of one minister, while committing to another minister so extensive a territory as that covered by the parishes of Inchaiden, Strathfillan, Killin and Ardeonaig. Here the voice of the kirk was at its weakest.[66]

[65] *BUK*, i, 288, 295, 300–1, 303, 308, 315, 317, 321, 323; SRO, E47/3 (1585), fos. 10r, 11v.

[66] SRO, E47/3 (1585), fos. 21v-22v; E47/3 (1586), fos. 25r-26r; E47/8 (1599), fos. 22v-23v; E47/9 (1607), fos. 24v-25r; E47/10 (1614), fos. 31r-34v.

Further south in Dunblane, whose bishop showed little interest in the diocese beyond receiving his stipend, a commissioner was active in the area: by 1585 diocesan boundaries had been superseded for certain purposes; and for recording stipends, sixteen parishes had been assigned to a smaller administrative unit centred on Dunblane, served by seven ministers and seven readers. By 1614, however, readers had been eclipsed, and under the supervision of a new bishop thirty-seven parishes in the diocese could claim the services of twenty-four ministers, twenty-two of whom were Masters of Arts.[67]

Argyll, said to be mainly protestant soon after the Reformation,[68] was one of only five areas of the country to benefit from the services of a reformed superintendent. There the activities of superintendent John Carswell extended from such conventional pursuits as conducting visitations and granting collation to benefices to his outstanding enterprise in publishing a Gaelic adaptation of the Book of Common Order for use in protestant worship. That a minister was active soon after the Reformation at Inishail, for example, whose insular church was strategically placed towards the northern end of Loch Awe, is indicated in the Earl of Argyll's grant of property to Carswell in January 1562/3, whose terms expressly reserved a manse and garden to the minister of Inishail.[69] It is probable, too, that one of the witnesses to this charter, Patrick Graham, parson of Kilmore, entered reformed service, as he was later to be found associating himself with procedures for ecclesiastical appointments.

In legal matters, Carswell could count on the assistance of Gavin Hamilton, who had probably served his apprenticeship under Carswell, himself a trained notary, and who, at the age of 22, was admitted notary by the lords of council in 1570. Hamilton's duties, as the superintendent's 'servitour', led him to record Carswell's instructions in June 1572 for granting a recruit to the ministry, Donald McVicar, institution to the parsonage of Kilmolew, to which, as Argyll's presentee, he had received collation in May 1570. Also preserved is the text of a letter to 'his brother in Christ' Neil McCallum, parson of Lochawe, and to all other professors of the true Christian faith and members of the church, in which Carswell duly affirmed McVicar's undertaking to serve by ministering and exhorting in the kirk; mention, too,

---

[67] *Stirling Presbytery Records, 1581–1587*, ed. J. Kirk (Edinburgh, 1981), xiii-xv, xxii-xxiv; *Visitation of the Diocese of Dunblane and other churches, 1586–1589*, ed. J. Kirk (Edinburgh, 1984), viiff; SRO, E47/3 (1585), fo. 23r-v; E47/10 (1614), fos. 52r-53r.

[68] *The Hamilton Papers*, ed. J. Bain, 2 vols. (Edinburgh, 1890–2), ii, p.749.

[69] *RMS*, iv, no. 1592; Inverary Castle, Argyll Inventory, vi, 6.

is made of other ministers and exhorters in the diocese; and a commission was issued to McCallum for granting the entrant institution. Among the witnesses were Patrick Graham, parson of Kilmore, Neil McCallum, parson of Lochawe, and Donald Carswell, parson of Kilmartin, and there is more than a hint that all three were then understood to be serving in the reformed ministry. Similarly, a witness to another charter in August 1572, John White, was explicitly identified as minister of Lochgoilhead, and clearly was established in office by that date.[70]

Then, with John Carswell's death in 1572 and the eclipse of the superintendent's office in the area, it fell to the conforming but hitherto inactive James Hamilton as bishop of Argyll, from his far-removed residence at Monkland, to issue a commission, again to Neil McCallum, parson of Lochawe, granting Donald Carswell institution to the vicarage of Inishail, in the knowledge that the presentee had been commended for collation by the ministers of the Word and by the Earl of Argyll, as patron. Indeed, supporting testimony of the reformers' success in the area is forthcoming in the report, in 1574, that every parish in Lorne, central Argyll and Cowal had the services of ministers and readers, with stipends provided.[71]

The crown had also a rôle to play in Argyll, as elsewhere, by presenting suitably-qualified candidates to certain benefices at the king's disposal: Kilblane in Kintyre in 1580,[72] Kilmacochar-mick in Knapdale in 1587 and 1591, and Kilmodan in Glassery in 1595 were all duly filled by the crown's presentees.[73] By the early seventeenth century, forty-four parishes in the diocese had the service of no fewer than thirty-two ministers (though without the assistance of readers).[74] Some parishes, however, were amalgamated under the services of one minister. In 1617, Kilcolmkill was united with Kilblane; Kilkerran, Kirkmichael and Kilchusland were also combined, despite petitions for their separation in 1621;[75] and in 1618 the large and mountainous parish of Glenorchy was joined with Inishail. A lack of adequate finance rather than a shortage of staff was the underlying reason; but such a solution was plainly a retrograde step, detrimental to

[70] SRO, GD112/5/10, Breadalbane Muniments, Protocol Book of Gavin Hamilton, 1569–1604, 1, 5–6; Argyll Inventory, vi, 180, cf. 186.

[71] SRO, GD112/5/10, Protocol Book of Gavin Hamilton, 10; CSP Scot., v, no. 28.

[72] Registrum Secreti Sigilli Regum Scotorum [RSS], ed. M. Livingstone et al. 8 vols. (Edinburgh, 1908–82), v, no. 2566.

[73] SRO, PS1/56, Register of the Privy Seal, fos. 71, 184; PS1/62, fo. 137v.

[74] Fasti, iv, 1–103, 126–39.

[75] Acts of the Parliaments of Scotland, edd. T. Thomson and C. Innes, 12 vols. (Edinburgh, 1814–75), iv, 605–9.

that essential feature in the church's life, the cure of souls, by placing one man in charge of an area which even two or three ministers would have found it hard to provide with effective pastoral care. Despite such shortcomings, however, the impression gained from the random surviving evidence, in the absence of any register of stipends for the area, is that a reformed ecclesiastical machinery operated with some effect in Argyll and that the area was at least as well served with reformed staff as many other parts of the country.

From 1639, with the presence of records for the synod of Argyll, a more detailed picture emerges of a church whose machinery conformed in all essentials to structures elsewhere. There, too, the eldership began to assume a new political importance as the Covenanting crisis deepened. Yet continuing efforts were made to ensure a supply of appropriately-qualified, Gaelic ministers; and preparations were under way for the provision of more schools and bursaries, and for the augmentation of ministers' stipends. 'Several kirks', it was reported in 1639, were 'not yet planted', but even in the notoriously-troubled area of Lochaber, Cameron of Lochiel and other heritors eagerly petitioned in 1642 for the appointment of a new minister for the kirks of Kilmonivaig and Kilmallie, since, as they claimed, not only were 'many souls ignorant of the Word of God throw the want of the preaching thereof', but the parishioners were 'forced to repair to other kirks long distant out of our own bounds to baptize infants and get lawfull mareages'. The ministrations of the kirk, far from being shunned, were anxiously sought by some. Thus, to assist parishioners from the mainland attend the kirk of Kilmaluag on the island of Lismore, Maclean of Kingairloch, in 1639, was urged to provide a ferry-boat for his tenants at Kingairloch in Ardnamurchan. By 1641, however, in the knowledge that 'all the people could not conveniently resort' to the kirk on Lismore, Campbell of Ardnamurchan had sought the services of the minister of Lismore *per vices* for his newly-erected kirk of Appin. Strenuous attempts were also made to reverse the trend towards the union of parishes: in 1642, the synod produced a comprehensive report for the division of parishes upon which it was expected the commission of parliament for the valuation of teinds and plantation of kirks would take decisive action.[76] Headway, it seems, was made; and firm foundations had been laid for the reformed ministry in Argyll, upon which it would have been possible to build had

[76] *Minutes of the Synod of Argyll, 1639–1651*, ed. D. C. Mactavish, 2 vols. (Edinburgh, 1943–4), 6, 42; 14, 26, 49–59.

progress not been arrested by the civil war with its accompanying dislocation and devastation.

If the growth of the ministry in Argyll can be traced, at least in outline, during James VI's long reign, what was happening in the Isles is far harder to discover. What is clear, however, is that the conventional claim which assigns the first recorded appointments of ministers in Hebridean parishes to 1609 and the Statutes of Iona[77] cannot be entertained. It is flatly contradicted by surviving documentary evidence, and its abandonment is, therefore, long overdue. For a start, a tradition of what might be described as a sympathetic understanding of protestantism was apparent not least in the careers of three pre-Reformation bishops of the Isles. In 1545, in his endeavours to become bishop, Roderick Maclean, trained at Lutheran Wittenberg, had enjoyed the support of Governor Arran, then inclined to protestantism, and he eventually secured papal provision in 1550; his successor, Alexander Gordon, bishop-elect of the Isles from 1554 to 1557 and better known as bishop of Galloway, conformed to protestantism at the Reformation; so, too, did his successor, John Campbell, bishop-elect of the Isles from 1557 till the Reformation, when he was then considered to be a 'good protestant'. Not only did the inclinations of these three bishops hold out little support for the forces of Catholicism, but, thereafter, as superintendent of Argyll, John Carswell undertook to visit the Isles, as his jurisdiction was understood to extend to the Hebrides.[78]

In 1564 not only did Carswell arrange 'to veseit sum kirkis' in the Isles but he granted Argyll's presentee collation to benefices in Harris and Skye, which the crown confirmed in 1567. His gift from Queen Mary of the bishopric of the Isles and the annexed abbacy of Iona in 1567 helped strengthen his authority in the area, and he committed himself to paying the stipends of ministers planted within the diocese.[79] What reformed staff he possessed in the diocese of the Isles is not disclosed, but it seems unlikely that Patrick MacMaster Martin, parson of Barvas in Lewis, was one of them, for despite his association with Carswell in a notarial instrument of 1566, Martin was then said to have acted as 'confessor', terminology hardly reformed.[80] But during

[77] *Irish Franciscan Mission*, vii; I. B. Cowan, *Scottish Reformation*, 169.

[78] Watt, *Fasti*, 205–6; *CSP Scot.*, i. p.471; J. K. Cameron, *The First Book of Discipline* (Edinburgh, 1972), 117; Argyll Inventory, vi, 67, 137.

[79] *Wodrow Society Miscellany*, 285–6; *RSS*, v, nos. 3246; 1885, 3373.

[80] *The Book of Dunvegan*, ed. R. C. MacLeod, 2 vols. (Aberdeen, 1838–9), i, 33–4.

the episcopate of John Campbell (who earlier had held the bishopric in 1557 and who entered the reformed ministry as a 'preacher of the Word of God'), reformed service did exist on Iona where Fingon Macmullen was minister in 1573.[81]

Bishop Campbell, it is true, repeatedly complained of expropriation of his revenues, especially by Macleans (who had tried to dispossess him in favour of their own candidate), and for a spell he had been forced 'to leif the cuntre'; but even with all his difficulties, it is inconceivable that he operated with only one minister committed to his jurisdiction. The bishop, plainly, was accustomed to working with his reformed staff: hence the provision in 1573 that any obedience should be rendered to the bishop 'and his ministeris and clergie that sall assemble with him for the time'. Besides, by concluding an agreement with Macleod of Lewis in 1573, Bishop Campbell was simply re-enacting the example set by his predecessor, John Carswell, whereby Macleod undertook to adhere to 'all guid ordinances, lawis and constitutionis and correctionis concerning the kirk, as the actis and constitutionis of the reformit Kirk of Scotland beris, and wes usit in the last bischoppis tyme'. Further financial contracts followed between the bishop and Hebridean and Highland chiefs; one, in 1580, obliged MacDonald of Dunivaig to 'pas with our forssis throw all the Ilis' to enable the bishop to collect his revenues; and he then reaffirmed an earlier contract with the bishop in 1579 'baith anent kirkis and landis within our said boundis'.[82]

Through the use of written and legally-binding arrangements of this kind, the bishop hoped the better to administer his farflung diocese; and there is evidence that he achieved a measure of success. It was presumably the bishop himself, as the assembly's commissioner, who was the recipient in 1580 of a royal presentation in favour of Hector MacAlister to the parsonage of Kilmorie in Arran and to the vicarage of Kilcalmonell in Kintyre, directed to the superintendent or commissioner in the Isles and Argyll.[83] Reformed staff are recorded at Rothesay from 1589 and at Kingarth on Bute in 1597, and, again, on the island of Seil (in Argyll diocese) by the 1600s.[84] Further presentations by the crown in the 1590s testify to the solicitude of king and kirk in securing ministers for Hebridean parishes. Colin Campbell, son

---

[81] *Origines Parochiales*, ii, 297.
[82] *RPC*, iii, 62, 124–5; 517; *Collectanea de Rebus Albanicis*, 13–19; 7, 8–13.
[83] *RSS*, vii, no. 2463.
[84] *Fasti*, iv, 34, 39; J. Bannerman, 'The MacLachlans of Kilbride and their Manuscripts', *Scottish Studies*, xxi (1977), 1–34 at 24. I am grateful to Dr Bannerman for drawing my attention to John MacLachlan, minister of Seil and Luing.

of Campbell of Kilberry, was presented to the whole benefice of
Gigha, with manse and glebe in 1592, and the presbytery or
commissioner was charged to examine his aptitude to serve in the
ministry; and that year, too, Alexander MacDougal was presented to Kildalton and Kilnachtan; but the presentation of the
king's 'lector', Daniel Chalmer, from the Lothians, to the
benefices of Kilchoman, Kilarrow and Kilchiaran on Islay does
not seem to have entailed any obligation that the recipient should
serve on Islay.[85] In addition, appointments continued to be made
to the archdeaconry of the Isles.[86] Nor was this all. By 1605 a
minister was active at Rodel in Harris, in the service of Macleod
of Harris;[87] another was present on Barra, where he was
murdered in 1609;[88] and at least two ministers were to be found
at work at Duirinish and Sleat by 1609.[89] And if ministers are to
be found in the Outer Hebrides from Barra to Harris, it is more
than a guess that further parishes in the Inner Hebrides possessed
reformed service by that date. Only in this light, presumably,
does the phraseology of the Statutes of Iona about 'ministeris
alswele plantit as to be plantit'[90] become readily intelligible.

The appointment of so many ministers over so wide an area,
itself a tribute to the kirk's commitment in the Highlands, was
attained only after a prolonged struggle to surmount a host of
problems. The generally-poor level of stipends on offer to
ministers in highland parishes was not readily remedied, despite
James VI's efforts in his later years to resolve the issue. But
although stipends for northern ministers remained depressed,
some assistance was forthcoming in localities through the work
of the commissions established to assign stipends. Improvements
were introduced as a consequence, In 1618, the Earl of
Dunfermline, as titular of the teinds and patron of Urquhart kirk
in Moray, agreed to pay the minister a stipend of 273 merks and
40 bolls of barley; and, as he was also patron and proprietor of
the teinds at Bellie, he undertook to ensure, with Huntly's
agreement as tacksman, that the minister's stipend there should
be set at 570 merks.[91] All this was a cautious step in the right
direction.

[85] SRO, PS1/64, fos. 139r; 136r; PS1/65, fo. 18r.
[86] Watt, Fasti, 211.
[87] Book of Dunvegan, i, 215.
[88] Highland Papers, ed. J. R. N. MacPhail, 4 vols. (Edinburgh, 1914–34), iv, 227.
[89] Book of Dunvegan, i, 39, 48; Fasti, vii, 168, 174.
[90] RPC, ix, 26–30.
[91] SRO, GD44, Gordon Castle Muniments, 23 January 1618.

At the same time, no far-reaching solution had been found for reducing the enormous size of most highland parishes: in some cases, the problem had merely been compounded by uniting parishes instead of dividing them. Here and there, however, local efforts had been made to overcome some of the worst features of this inherited system. In the diocese of Caithness, this took the form of the creation of a new parish in Strathnaver, which came into being in 1638.[92] In Moray, the synod, perceiving a 'g[ret] prejudice is arysing to the peple by the unioun of the kirkis', took fresh steps to secure additional ministers and stipends; and in Argyll, too, the synod continued its campaign in 1642 for a division of parishes, a complex issue which involved the rights of patrons and heritors, and needed the consent of parliament.[93]

More readily resolved was the problem of ministers' access to manses and glebes. During the 1600s, at least, as the register of stipends shows, most ministers in highland parishes had gained possession of their manses and glebes, an entitlement recognised by statute law as early as 1563, which enabled them to make residence at their churches. A stone-built manse, especially in the Highlands, was a much-prized acquisition – and not just by ministers. The outstandingly well-documented history of possessors of the manse pertaining to the precentor of Moray at Elgin illustrates the extent to which such a dwelling was coveted by laymen.[94] Where a manse was not available for a minister, the consequences could be serious: non-residence at the kirk usually ensued, if lodgings could not be found. The problem had been raised in the general assembly in 1575 when seven northern ministers had been censured for non-residence; and the commissioner of Caithness responded to a similar charge in 1587 by observing that he had neither manse nor glebe, despite all his efforts to resolve the issue by law.[95] Even where a manse was available, the occurrence of 'deadly feuds', which led to open warfare between kindreds, sometimes made it advisable for a minister to seek refuge away from his kirk. This was the excuse offered by one highland minister in 1575;[96] and another, who happened to be the Earl of Caithness's son, failed to take up residence at Rogart in Caithness, situated in the 'high parts' of Sutherland in the country of the Murrays, on account of a feud between the Sinclairs and Murrays; but, at least, he did provide

---

[92] SRO, GD84/29/3, Reay Papers.
[93] SRO, CH2/271/1, Synod of Moray Records, 3; *Synod of Argyll*, i, 49–59, cf. 27.
[94] SRO, GD94/14, 17, 23–34, 39–40, Lordship of Urquhart.
[95] *BUK*, i, 336, 342; ii, 692.
[96] Ibid., i, 342.

from the revenues of the chancellory of Caithness, which he possessed, the wherewithal to pay the stipends of a minister and reader at Rogart.[97]

In Inverness presbytery, all but two ministers were resident at their churches by 1623; and the two who were not excused themselves by their being 'impedit to mak residence at thair kirkis by the stormie winter'; while in the adjacent presbytery of Inveravon, the minister at Abernethy, with his newly-acquired glebe, was able to set about the task of building a manse, and soon was able to take up residence. Even with the attainment of a settled ministry, local problems still arose: the minister of Lismore, as late as 1639, was considered a non-resident 'seeing his wife resorts oft times to Sownairt'; the minister of Craignish in 1640 had to be reminded 'to make his residence continually both summer and winter at his kirk'; and in 1641 the synod of Argyll remedied the minister of Ardnamurchan's grievance that he lacked both manse and glebe.[98]

The programme for building and refurbishing parish kirks, so evident a feature of the early seventeenth century, is another sign of consolidation and confidence. In the early 1620s, under the synod of Moray's direction, churches were built or repaired at Kingussie, Kincardine, Urquhart and Glenmoriston, Ardclach and Edinkillie, and at Conveth and Kiltarlity whose 'old and ruinous foundatiounis' were to be restored despite the preference of the parishioners of Conveth for a 'mediat kirk' to be built at less expense to serve both parishes.[99]

Despite occasional scares, Catholic recusancy in the Highlands was not then considered to be an ineradicable problem. The Franciscan mission in the 1620s remained small, with only four of the eight missionaries persevering till 1637; their effect was limited; and, aware of the numerical strength of the ministry in the northern highlands, they concentrated efforts on the Hebrides and south-west Highlands, especially the Uists and Barra, Canna, Rum, Eigg and Muck, the Ross of Mull, Oronsay, Colonsay and Jura, and in Kintyre, Moidart and Glengarry on the mainland, though their glowing reports of the conversion of heretics (who, by definition, were presumably protestant) were greeted with some initial scepticism in Rome. Certainly, by 1639, the synod of Argyll, whose jurisdiction included the Hebrides, perceived no effective Roman Catholic opposition and relied on

[97] SRO, GD96/158, Mey Papers, 19 May 1575; cf. *Wodrow Miscellany*, 333 n. 3.
[98] SRO, CH2/271/1, Synod of Moray Records, 2–3, 5, 13, 18; *Synod of Argyll*, i, 4, 20, 26.
[99] SRO, CH2/271/1, Synod of Moray Records, 1, 6–7, 11, 13, 18.

the apprehension of priests and on the power of persuasion by local ministers to win over a few prominent Catholics in Dunoon, Inveraray and Skye. Nor did the problem loom large in the work of the synod of Moray during the 1620s; two parishioners of Inverness were suspected of Catholicism and the minister of Glass had dealt with two more cases in 1626; Inveravon presbytery took action against a doctor of medicine reputed 'ane papist and ane reasoner against sound religioun'; a family in Kingussie parish who 'did nevir resort to the kirk' were considered Catholic, as was another, also in Badenoch, where Jesuits had begun 'to draw all quhom thei might conqueise to thair pernicious wayes, boith of men and women'; and a list of priests detected within the diocese disclosed the presence of eight named missionaries: a secular priest, a Minorite friar, two Jesuits, a Capuchin friar 'commonly called the Archangell', and three others.[100] In truth, many decades were to ensue before sizable communities of Catholics were to be found in the Highlands.

The ministrations of the Jacobean kirk, by contrast, extended over much of the Highlands. By later standards, its services were, no doubt, woefully inadequate. Yet few areas were totally deserted, and each minister could expect support from his elders drawn from the various communities and settlements within the parish. Even before John Carswell had commended the work of the 'learned elders' in his *Foirm na n-Urrnuidheadh* of 1567, elders were active in Inverness by 1562; and much later the crown obliged several Hebridean chiefs in 1614 to give due obedience 'to thair ministeris and assistantis' and to punish offenders according to the discipline of the kirk. Only in 1642 did elders in Skye, at a visitation, voice the exceptional complaint that their minister treated them merely as 'cyphers, because he did all be himself without requyreing either there advyce or assistance'.[101]

While regular attendance at church by inhabitants from outlying regions was not – and never had been – expected, most clans (from whose ranks recruits to the ministry were often forthcoming) still looked to the kirk to perform the essential rites of passage, especially baptism and lawful marriage; and they complained when these services were not readily forthcoming. Nonetheless, communion services, held infrequently, were occasions when all parishioners were expected to give their attend-

---

[100] *Irish Franciscan Mission*, xii–xiii, and *passim; Synod of Argyll*, i, 60, 67; SRO, CH2/271/1, Synod of Moray Records, 6, 18, 24–26.
[101] See above, 303; *Records of Inverness*, edd. W. Mackay and H. C. Boyd, 2 vols. (Aberdeen, 1911–24), i, 93–5; *RPC*, x, 699; *Synod of Argyll*, i, 45.

ance. In 1623, the synod of Moray insisted that any non-communicants should be given adequate warning, in presence of two witnesses, twenty days before the next celebration, 'for taking away all pretence of excuis from them'; and in 1626 ministers were urged to keep full registers of all their parishioners. But, for failing to minister communion 'this yeir at all to his people', the minister of Kingussie in 1627 was instructed to notify the date of the next celebration 'unto his whole peple bot speciallie to gang to suche as he suspectis most within his boundis, taking with him two or three witnesses and to desyr them to communicat that so nain pretend ignorance'. All in all, with a single-minded determination, the kirk was adamant that everyone should be confronted by its presence in the parishes and should conform to its judgments.[102]

Occasional reports of disturbances at highland kirks merely highlight the exceptional and obscure the routine observance of the Sabbath by many highlanders. In 1617, several McMurchies complained to the council of how their womenfolk had been attacked, in their absence, by Mackay of Farr's retainers, while they themselves were worshipping on Sunday at the kirk of Coygach. In Moray, too, some troublemakers had lain in wait for a parishioner at Knockando kirk in 1619, 'quhair thay thocht he had bene for the tyme at the preitching'; and at Gartly in Strathbogie, some miscreants in 1620 had not only interrupted a service in the kirk, without respect for 'the Lordis hollie Sabbothe', but seized a parishioner, who was present 'for heiring that dayis sermone', and created 'a verie greit tumult . . . which was unseamlie to behold'. Again, the conscientious minister of Aboyne was violently attacked by a parishioner whom he visited in 1612 'for admonischeing him to resoirt more frequentlie to the said kirk nor formerlie he wes in use to do'; but, far from despairing, the minister took the case to the privy council, which fined the offender a hefty £80. Conformity with the requirements of the kirk and respect for the law were increasingly the standards inculcated in highland society.[103]

At the same time, the needs of that society were met wherever possible by ensuring that recruits to the ministry in Gaelic areas were themselves Gaelic-speakers. In 1623, 'becaus of his want of the Yrish toung', the synod of Caithness had translated one of its ministers from Creich (where he had served seven years) to Kilmalie (or Golspie) where some Scots was spoken; and his successor, Robert Monro of Creich, a son of Monro of Assynt,

---

[102] *Synod of Argyll*, i, 42; SRO, CH2/271/1, Synod of Moray Records, 2, 20, 28.
[103] *RPC*, xi, 4, 601; xii, 383; ix, 330.

was obviously the product of a thoroughly-Gaelic setting. In similar vein, the synod of Moray in 1624 found Patrick Dunbar unsuitable as minister of Dores 'and that only throughe want of the language'. The insuperable difficulties which could ensure when a minister untrained in Gaelic was let loose on a parish whose inhabitants had no knowledge of Scots were revealed in 1626 at a visitation of the kirks of Alvie and Laggan in Badenoch, whose incapacitated minister was said to be 'of verie gryt age, infirme in body and hes no thing of the Irishe language, quhilk be thair vulgar'; and he himself 'earnestlie craved to be disburdened of that charge quhairin he found himselff able to do no guid'. In belated recognition that 'no man in any measure can be able to serve baithe' parishes, the synod granted the minister a retire-ment pension and sought two qualified recruits capable of restoring the Gospel in Badenoch, 'quhilk lyeth destitut of the confort of the Word and sacramentis, for the most part, and altogidder without disciplin quhairby the grytest part lyethe in damnable atheisme'.[104]

The kirk may have had its spectacular failures, as well as its successes, but in attempting to right wrongs it relied on its system of administration and oversight, which had developed in somewhat erratic fashion in the decades after 1560. Weaknesses in the structure, therefore, could often lead to shortcomings in the parishes. Nor, in the early years, had the kirk been assisted in its task by the new breed of bishops who had assumed control of the dioceses in the 1570s but who had largely failed to supply the initiative and direction needed to succeed in the missionary enterprise upon which the kirk had embarked.

The appearance of protestant bishops twelve years after the Reformation, to whose appointment the general assembly had accorded its recognition, turned out to be a mixed blessing for the kirk. Instead of providing energetic leadership within their dioceses, as the commissioners who preceded them had sought to do, the new bishops, being the crown's nominees, too frequently appeared as careerists more intent on squandering episcopal revenues than as acting as effective pastors of pastors. All this looked very much like a recurrence of the old pre-Reformation abuse which the reformers had intended to eliminate. Yet the original purpose of the Convention of Leith, which inaugurated a reformed episcopate in 1572, had been to promote protestant ministers of repute and ability to those bishoprics, already

---

[104] *Fasti*, vii, 82; cf. SRO, GD128/36/9, Fraser-Mackintosh Collection (I owe this reference to Allan Macinnes); SRO, CH2/271/1, Synod of Moray Records, 7, 19, 24–5.

declared vacant by the crown's decision to forfeit the surviving
Roman Catholic bishops, who, up till that point, had succeeded
in retaining possession of their bishoprics regardless of the
Reformation.[105]

No action had then been deemed appropriate in Argyll, where
the conforming but idle James Hamilton had retained the
bishopric till his death in 1580, or, for that matter, in Caithness
where the aged Robert Stewart, who remained bishop but only in
name till his death in 1586, had retired to spend the last sixteen
years of his life in the comparative comfort of St Andrews priory,
where he was able to practise his archery and golf. In each of
these cases, the work of administering the diocese, in the absence
of a working bishop, had fallen either to a superintendent or,
more usually, to a commissioner appointed by the general
assembly. But with the deaths of Hamilton and Stewart, the way
was open for fresh appointments to be made. In Argyll, this took
the form of a succession of Campbells between 1580 and 1613,
followed by the appointment of Andrew Boyd, a lowlander and
Glasgow graduate, who had served as minister of Eaglesham and
who continued as bishop under the Caroline regime till his death
in 1636.[106] The promotion of two Campbells, father and son, as
bishops is no doubt a recognition of Clan Campbell's dominance
in the region and an indication of the crown's willingness to
support Argyll's kinsmen. But the appearance of Boyd as bishop
in 1613 reflects King James's subsequent determination to take
an independent line by promoting his own choice of candidates –
trusted servants whose primary allegiance lay with king and kirk.
Besides, it was no longer in the crown's interest to perpetuate the
unrivalled power of Argyll in the south-west Highlands.

At the same time, however, the bishop found that he could
make little headway in weaning the inhabitants of his diocese
'from their wonted savage behaviour', as he put it, without the
earl's presence and support. In 1615, Argyll himself was ready
not only to profess his protestantism but also, in the bishop's
words, to 'cause all obedience to be given to discipline, churches
to be buildit, and violent detineris of ministeris gleibis and
mansis thairof dispossessed; in all of which, as was required, he
did perform'. But, by 1618, Argyll's support was no longer
forthcoming, for the antics of the maverick 7th earl, who,
without the king's consent, had proceeded to the Spanish Nether-

[105] J. Kirk, *The Second Book of Discipline* (Edinburgh, 1980), 23ff.
[106] R. Keith, *An Historical Catalogue of the Scottish Bishops*, ed. M. Russel
(Edinburgh, 1824), 215–16, 289–91.

lands, there to proclaim his conversion to Catholicism, ended in his disgrace and conviction for treason.[107]

Further north, in Caithness, King James's attempts to secure a succession of bishops for his most northerly mainland diocese had run into difficulty. There the crown's nominee to fill the vacancy caused by Bishop Stewart's death was Robert Pont, the highly-respected provost of Trinity College, Edinburgh, who had earlier laboured so energetically over many years, despite his lack of Gaelic, as one of the assembly's commissioners in the north. But Pont himself was sympathetic to the presbyterian party in the church, and in submitting to the assembly's judgment was prepared to agree only to become minister at Dornoch, not bishop; and the assembly, in turn, bluntly informed King James that they understood that Pont, as minister, was already a bishop according to St Paul and eligible to serve the parish of Dornoch, and even to act as commissioner or visitor, but not as a diocesan bishop, which they condemned as unlawful.[108]

In reaching this verdict, the assembly, of course, had ample experience of the inept behaviour of earlier protestant bishops. In Dunkeld, for example, the forfeiture in 1571 of Robert Crichton, the last Catholic bishop, had enabled the appointment to take place of James Paton, whose family came from the parish of Muckhart and he himself had served as minister at Dollar. He was therefore unlikely to have any familiarity with Gaelic, the everyday language spoken in much of his diocese; but, in any event, his career as bishop was not a success, and five years after his appointment he was denounced as a dilapidator and deprived of office by the assembly.[109] In neighbouring Dunblane, Andrew Graham, who in 1573 had replaced the forfeited Catholic bishop, William Chisholm, likewise failed adequately to fulfil the duties expected of a bishop, not surprisingly perhaps, as he had no previous pastoral experience; and his antecedents as titular vicar of Wick (a device enabling him to have the revenues but not the work) served mainly as a prelude to his squandering episcopal patrimony on a lavish scale in Dunblane.[110]

[107] *Original Letters relating to the Ecclesiastical Affairs of Scotland*, ed. D. Laing, 2 vols. (Edinburgh, 1851), ii, 422–3; *Scots Peerage*, i, 346–9.

[108] *BUK*, ii, 696–7.

[109] Keith, *Bishops*, 96–7; Kirk, *Second Book of Discipline*, 21, 30, 32–4. It is not inappropriate that the only known, surviving letter by Bishop Paton concerns financial matters: SRO, GD38/2/1/1, Dalguise Muniments, 25 August 1575.

[110] Keith, *Bishops*, 180–1; Kirk, *Second Book of Discipline*, 30, 32, 34; *Stirling Presbytery Records*, xiii-xv, xxii-xxiv; *Visitation of the Diocese of Dunblane*, x-xi, xiv, xxiii-xxiv, xlii.

In Ross, where Alexander Hepburn, a former schoolmaster and minister, had replaced the Catholic John Leslie as bishop by 1574, the new bishop was immediately confronted with an old problem, familiar enough to some of his predecessors: there one of the Mackenzies of Kintail had again taken up residence in the steeple of the cathedral at Fortrose, which previously pertained to the chancellor of the cathedral and 'quhilk now is becum ane filthie sty and den of thevis', and a base 'not only to oppress the cuntrie with maisterfull reif, soirning and daylie oppressioun, bot alsua for suppressing of the Word of God quhilk wes ay prechit in the said kirk preceding his intery thairto'. But worse was to follow, for, as the bishop's widow later explained, Mackenzie had laid siege to the episcopal palace or castle and prevented the supply of 'meit and drink and all uther releif of cumpany or confort of nychbouris and freindis'; and as a result of 'sic inhumane and cruell dealing aganis him', the bishop 'fell seik and nevir recoverit quhill he depairtit this life'.[111] These were some of the hardships which a bishop in a highland diocese was liable, on occasion, to encounter and endure.

Hepburn's tenure of the see for four years was clearly too short to have much impact, but he was at least a respectable bishop, with the unusual distinction of having avoided incurring the assembly's censure. He was, perhaps, far too respectable for some of the people with whom he had to deal. Coming as he did from Angus, Hepburn, like so many of the bishops in highland dioceses, seems to have had no adequate knowledge of Gaelic, which may not exactly have assisted communication with people like Mackenzie of Kintail, who, rather significantly, achieved his objective of possessing the bishop's castle; and during the long episcopal vacancy which ensued on Hepburn's death, Mackenzie was even recognised by the privy council as the castle's legitimate holder;[112] so he gained his way in the end.

If resort to violence by a highland chief could secure the desired results, the outcome for two highland ministers who attempted to obtain their unpaid stipends by armed force was rather different. The minister of Urquhart in the diocese of Moray, who had not been paid his third in stipend from Pluscarden priory, took the law into his own hands, and with the assistance of others, 'bodin in feir of weir', forcibly removed the corn teinds owing to him, but was immediately prosecuted by the privy council for his unlawful action. And the minister of Dyke, who followed his clerical colleague's example and

[111] *RPC*, iii, 88–9, 90–1.
[112] Ibid., iv, 208.

'accompaneit with ane greit nowmer of armit men . . . tuke away certane drawn oxin, horse, meris' and the teind sheaves of the corn crop from the priory in lieu of his stipend, was constrained by the privy council in 1574 to return the victual on the understanding that the prior would promptly pay his stipend.[113] Higher standards were evidently expected from highland ministers than from highland chiefs like Mackenzie of Kintail.

By and large, the early protestant bishops had not been energetic overseers or valiant exponents of reformed religion, and so the assembly from 1576 had come to place reliance once more on commissioners or visitors, who, freed as they were from the political and financial pressure to which the bishops had so readily succumbed, were able to provide a measure of effective co-ordination and leadership within the system. With diocesan episcopacy effectively eclipsed, the assembly had pushed ahead with its plans for establishing presbyteries. But the adaptation of presbyteries to meet the particular features of highland geography and the peculiar circumstances of highland life, devoid as it very largely was of towns and centres of population, proved harder to achieve.

A scheme, however, was devised to establish two presbyteries in Caithness at Wick and Dornoch, three presbyteries in Moray at Forres, Elgin and Inverness, three more for Ross at Fortrose, Tain and Dingwall, and for Banff at Deer, Kildrummy and Banff itself, and three again for Dunkeld at Perth, Dunkeld and Crieff. The need to include this lowland element of towns and market centres as the meeting places for presbyteries was evidently considered essential for success. But such a plan, of course, took little account of the exceedingly large parishes in the Highlands, where the enormous distances involved made it impossible for many parish ministers even to consider travelling regularly to presbytery meetings held, as they were, in towns located on the edge of the Gaidhealtachd. Yet, by 1606, some twenty presbyteries were operating in parts of the north and, in some measure, in the west, including Argyll and the Isles.[114]

King James, however, perceived the highlanders and presbyterians as two menaces whose influence he was intent on undermining with renewed vigour after 1603 from the safe vantage of London. He had already advised his son, Prince Henry, to 'hate no man more than a proud puritan' and urged him to declare war on 'vain puritans' and 'proud papal bishops' alike. On the Highlands and Islands, James was no less dogmatic.

[113] Ibid., ii, 423–4.
[114] *BUK*, ii, 566, 569, 586–7, 627, 648–9, 669–75, 748; iii, 799–800, 1035–7.

The highlanders, he considered, 'are barbarous for the most part and yet mixed with some show of civility'; but the islanders, he affirmed, 'are utterly barbarians without any sort or show of civility'. For those Gaels who declined to be educated out of their culture, James had another remedy: 'the rooting out or transporting the barbarous and stubborn sort and planting civility in their rooms'. But these remarks were not merely the theorisings of a pedant. What he wrote in his little book, *Basilikon Doron*, came close to being put into practice when James and the privy council decided in 1607 that the Marquess of Huntly should be placed in control of the northern Hebrides (Skye and Lewis excepted), which Huntly agreed to undertake 'be extirpatioun of the barbarous people of the Yllis within a yeare'.[115] In the end, saner policies prevailed; and in securing more lasting achievements, James owed much to the statesmanship of his new bishops in the Highlands.

For James, bishops were essential for his success in church and state; and in his efforts to resuscitate episcopacy, the king hit first on the expedient of appointing 'parliamentary' bishops: in 1600 three ministers were promoted to the northern bishoprics of Caithness, Ross and Aberdeen, with power to vote in parliament but with no ecclesiastical duties as bishops to perform. But the way was open for James to have his bishops, and by 1606 diocesan episcopacy was effectively restored. To Caithness, James advanced Alexander Forbes from Angus, a graduate of St Andrews and apparently of Heidelberg, who also gained a seat on the privy council on account of the 'incivile and barbarous behaviour of the moste parte of oure subjects of Caithnes, Sutherland and Strathnaver'.[116] Another recruit from Angus, Patrick Lindsay, was promoted to Ross and to a seat on the council; and his kinsman, Alexander Lindsay, also from Angus, became bishop of Dunkeld, a justice of the peace for Perthshire and privy councillor. In Moray, Alexander Douglas, who had been minister at Elgin for twenty years, became bishop for another twenty years, and served as a justice of the peace, while Adam Bellenden, originally from Fife, left his ministry in Falkirk to become bishop of Dunblane in 1615.

In Argyll, Andrew Boyd, son of Lord Boyd and a Glasgow graduate with at least a taste for Hebrew if not for Gaelic, was active in his diocese, both as bishop and as a justice of the peace.

---

[115] *The Basilicon Doron of King James VI*, ed. J. Craigie, 2 vols. (Edinburgh, 1944–50), 70, 80–1; *RPC*, vii, 341–2, 360–2.
[116] *RPC*, ix, 237–8.

But the bishop's authority, considerable as it was, was evidently not sufficient in itself to prevent the captain of Clanranald from ejecting the new minister of Ardnamurchan. This he did by sending 'a young man in to the kirk in the middis of the preatching armed with a sword, a targe and a hagbuitt, and verrie rudlie with ane awfull and feirce countenance addrest him selff directlie to the minister', handing a letter from his chief ordering the minister to quit 'and nevir to be sene thair agane upoun the perrill of his lyffe'. But, in remitting the matter to the privy council in 1624, Bishop Boyd significantly remarked that such action by a chief in recent years was quite unheard of in the area.[117] Respect for the king's law, it would seem, could no longer be quite so readily disregarded.

Perhaps the most remarkable of these Jacobean bishops was Andrew Knox, bishop of the Isles. Knox, who belonged to the family of Ranfurly in Kilbarchan parish, had studied at Glasgow under the Melville regime, and had come to the king's attention when he was minister of Paisley for assistance in uncovering the Spanish 'blanks', signed by northern earls, which helped no doubt to secure his promotion to the Isles in 1605. It was entirely appropriate, too, that Knox's newly-designed episcopal seal should depict a bishop seated in an open boat, a book in his left hand and pointing with his right hand over the boat, for Knox was one of James's most indefatigable servants in advancing the king's cause in the Hebrides.[118]

In 1608, Stewart of Ochiltree and Bishop Knox had received a commission from James aimed at reducing the powers of the chiefs. Many of the unsuspecting Hebridean chiefs were lured on board the king's ship off Mull, ostensibly to hear a sermon by the bishop (in which language is not disclosed) but in reality they found themselves ensnared and were shipped off to prison in the Lowlands. But in 1609, Bishop Knox secured their release and, armed with a fresh commission, he embarked on a policy of conciliation. At Iona, nine of the leading chiefs in the Hebrides met the bishop and, in more trusting circumstances, accepted the Statutes of Iona, which *inter alia* obliged them to acknowledge the reformed faith and promote the work of the ministry within their domain. In particular, the chiefs agreed that 'the ministeris alswele plantit as to be plantit within the parrochynis of the saidis Illandis salbe reverentlie obeyit'; they also undertook to ensure

---

[117] Ibid., xiii, 427–8.
[118] J. Durkan and J. Kirk, *The University of Glasgow, 1451–1577* (Glasgow, 1977), 272, 375, 379, 381; J. B. Craven, *Records of the Dioceses of Argyll and the Isles* (Kirkwall, 1907), 36.

that ministers' stipends should be fully paid, that parish churches be repaired, the Sabbath observed and discipline exercised. The nine Hebridean chiefs who assented to this, and to other measures for upholding the king's law, consisted of MacDonald of Dunivaig on Islay, Maclean of Duart and Maclean of Lochbuie on Mull, MacDonald of Sleat and MacKinnon of Strathardle on Skye, Macleod of Harris, Maclean of Coll, the captain of Clanranald and MacQuarrie of Ulva, all of whom now found submission, rather than resistance, the easier path to follow.[119]

As well as religion, education was also promoted as a vehicle for advancing lowland values and culture in the Isles. All men of substance were to ensure that their eldest sons were educated in English in the Lowlands, a requirement which the Gaelic custom of fosterage might have rendered easier to apply. But there already was, of course, an established tradition for the sons of some highland lairds to seek an education in lowland schools. Farquhar Macrae, for example, was sent by his father, the constable of Eilean Donan castle, to Perth grammar school and then to Edinburgh University before returning to the Highlands as minister of Gairloch in 1608.[120]

Not only did continued efforts to enforce the Statutes of Iona meet with some success, but Thomas Knox, promoted in 1619 from his ministry on Tiree to the bishopric of the Isles after his father's election to the Irish bishopric of Raphoe, continued to apply his father's policies in the Isles. In 1622, MacDonald of Sleat, Macleod of Harris, MacKinnon of Strathardle and the Macleans of Coll and Lochbuie all appeared personally before the council in Edinburgh where they promised to repair their parish churches to the satisfaction of their bishop. Further pressure was exerted in 1623 when the Hebridean chiefs were called before the council once again to give an account not only of what they had done to repair their churches but also what steps they had taken to provide English schools in the diocese and to ensure that their ministers, with an elder from each church, attended meetings of the synod, and that the bishop and his officers had safe passage throughout the Isles.[121]

By 1626, the bishop evidently had used that assurance of secure passage through his diocese to good effect, for this was the year that he compiled a report of his visitation of the Isles. His scattered diocese stretched from Bute in the Firth of Clyde to Barra, the Uists and Lewis in the north. Bute was then served by

[119] *RPC*, ix, 24–30.
[120] *Fasti*, vii, 152.
[121] *RPC*, xiii, 20–1, 34, 256, 297, 308, 319, 322, 362, 744–5, 819.

three ministers, and Arran by two. One minister was placed in charge of Jura and Gigha; Colonsay had merely a reader. Mull possessed two ministers; so, too, did Islay, Coll and Tiree each had its minister. Muck, Eigg, Rum and Canna, however, lacked a resident minister and were served by a minister from Skye, which possessed three ministers and a reader. The Uists and Barra had one minister who resided on Barra and whom Knox described as 'ane verie auld man', which rather suggests he had ministered for a considerable time and was certainly no fresh recruit. Finally, Lewis was served by two ministers. The provision of ministers for the Isles, then, was less than ideal, but it was far from being wholly inadequate. Indeed, the very existence of nineteen ministers and two readers for the Isles is an indication of the kirk's resolution to discharge its responsibilities in this area and to fulfil its mission as a national church.[122]

In the absence, for the most part, of the records of ecclesiastical courts, it is not easy to gauge the state of reformed religion in the Highlands; but testimony of the care which James's later bishops took in overseeing their dioceses and of the impact of the kirk in local communities is forthcoming, not least, in the remarkable succession of ministers to a majority of parishes in the Highlands; and, all but invariably, these ministers, by the early seventeenth century, had been trained at a university in the Lowlands. At the same time, care was also taken, with few exceptions, to ensure that their command of Gaelic was appropriate for the parishes they intended to serve. King James might pontificate on the need to root out the supposed barbarism and incivility associated with Gaelic culture, but his bishops and ministers in the Highlands, more realistically, continued to use the Gaelic language as the medium of instruction in most highland parishes.

Yet the achievements won by the Jacobean church in this formative phase of the kirk's work in the Highlands were to be threatened in later years. An element of discontinuity and disruption ensued by the mid-seventeenth century, with the divisive wars of the Covenant, which had their repercussions for the Highlands, and with the renewed efforts of missionaries to reclaim parts of the west Highlands for Catholicism, all of which contrasted with the years of King James's peace when the firm foundations were laid for the presence of the reformed kirk in parishes throughout the Highlands.

[122] *Collectanea de rebus Albanicis*, 122–5.

Index